THE
Jane Austen
COMPANION

THE
Jane Austen
COMPANION

with
*A Dictionary of
Jane Austen's Life and Works*
by H. Abigail Bok

J. David Grey, Managing Editor
A. Walton Litz and Brian Southam,
Consulting Editors

Macmillan Publishing Company · New York

Readers interested in the Jane Austen Society may contact:

Jane Austen Society of North America
Post Office Box 252
Wayne, PA 19087

The Jane Austen Society
Ivalls, Bentworth
Alton, Hampshire
GU34 5JU
England

Copyright © 1986 by Macmillan Publishing Company,
a division of Macmillan, Inc.

All rights reserved. No part of this book may be reproduced or transmitted in any form or by any means, electronic or mechanical, including photocopying, recording or by any information storage and retrieval system, without permission in writing from the Publisher.

Macmillan Publishing Company
866 Third Avenue, New York, N.Y. 10022
Collier Macmillan Canada, Inc.

Library of Congress Cataloging-in-Publication Data

The Jane Austen companion.

Includes bibliographies and index.
1. Austen, Jane, 1775-1817—Criticism and interpretation.
I. Grey, J. David. II. Litz, A. Walton. III. Southam, B. C.
PR4037.J318   1986   823'.7   85-18314
ISBN 0-02-545540-0

Macmillan books are available at special discounts for bulk purchases for sales promotions, premiums, fund-raising, or educational use. For details, contact:

Special Sales Director
Macmillan Publishing Company
866 Third Avenue
New York, N.Y. 10022

10 9 8 7 6 5 4 3 2 1

Printed in the United States of America

CONTENTS

LIST OF ABBREVIATIONS	vii
Preface	ix
Acknowledgments	xi
Family Tree	xii
Amateur Theatricals at Steventon/*George Holbert Tucker*	1
Architecture/Buildings/*John Dixon Hunt*	5
Auction Sales/*David Gilson*	13
Jane Austen and Bath/*Anne-Marie Edwards*	16
Biographies/*Park Honan*	18
Characterization in Jane Austen/*John Bayley*	24
Chawton/*J. David Grey*	35
Children/*J. David Grey*	41
Chronology of Composition/*A. Walton Litz*	47
Chronology Within the Novels/*Jo Modert*	53
Jane Austen's Comedy/*Robert M. Polhemus*	60
Completions/*David Hopkinson*	72
Jane Austen and the Consumer Revolution/*Edward Copeland*	77
Criticism, 1814–70/*Joseph Duffy*	93
Criticism, 1870–1940/*Brian Southam*	102
Criticism, 1939–83/*A. Walton Litz*	110
Dancing, Balls, and Assemblies/*Joan Grigsby*	118
Dramatizations of the Novels/*Andrew Wright*	120
Dress and Fashion/*Penelope Byrde*	131
Editions and Publishing History/*David Gilson*	135
Education/*Juliet McMaster*	140
Jane Austen's Family/*George Holbert Tucker*	143
Jane Austen and Contemporary Feminism/*Margaret Kirkham*	154
Food and Drink/*Peggy Hickman*	160
Jane Austen's Novels: Form and Structure/*David Lodge*	165
Games/*Katrin Ristkok Burlin*	179
Gardens/*Marion Morrison*	184
Grandison/*Brian Southam*	187
History, Politics, and Religion/*Marilyn Butler*	190
Houses/*J. David Grey*	209
Illustrating Jane Austen/*Joan Hassall*	215

Illustrations for Jane Austen/*Maggie Hunt Cohn*	219
Improvements/*Alistair M. Duckworth*	223
Influence on Later Writers/*Norman Page*	228
Janeites and Anti-Janeites/*Brian Southam*	237
Juvenilia/*Brian Southam*	244
Lady Susan/*Ruth apRoberts*	256
Jane Austen's Language/*Norman Page*	261
Letters/Correspondence/*Jo Modert*	271
Life of Jane Austen/*J. David Grey*	279
Jane Austen in London/*Anne-Marie Edwards*	283
Love and Marriage/*Juliet McMaster*	286
Manners and Society/*Rachel Trickett*	297
Medicine/*David Waldron Smithers*	304
Military (Army and Navy)/*J. David Grey*	307
Music/*Patrick Piggott*	314
Nature/*Alistair M. Duckworth*	317
Obituaries/*David Gilson*	320
Persuasion: The Canceled Chapters/*Brian Southam*	322
Pets and Animals/*J. David Grey*	324
The Picturesque/*John Dixon Hunt*	326
"Plan of a Novel," "Opinions of *Mansfield Park*," and "Opinions of *Emma*"/*Mary Gaither Marshall*	331
Plot Summaries/*A. Walton Litz*	333
The Portraits/*Helen Denman*	342
Post/Mail/*Jo Modert*	345
Jane Austen's Reading/*Margaret Anne Doody*	347
Jane Austen and Romanticism/*Susan Morgan*	364
Sanditon/*Brian Southam*	369
The Sequels to Jane Austen's Novels/*Marilyn Sachs*	374
Servants/*Janet Todd*	377
Topography/*J. David Grey*	380
Travel and Transportation/*Lorraine Hanaway*	388
Verses/*David Gilson*	392
The Watsons/*David Hopkinson*	394
A Dictionary of Jane Austen's Life and Works/*H. Abigail Bok*	399
CONTRIBUTORS	494
INDEX	497

Abbreviations

SS	*Sense and Sensibility*, ed. R. W. Chapman, 3rd ed. (Oxford, 1933); by page number
PP	*Pride and Prejudice*, ed. R. W. Chapman, 3rd ed. (Oxford, 1932); by page number
MP	*Mansfield Park*, ed. R. W. Chapman, 3rd ed. (Oxford, 1934); by page number
E	*Emma*, ed. R. W. Chapman, 3rd ed. (Oxford, 1933); by page number
NA and P	*Northanger Abbey and Persuasion*, ed. R. W. Chapman, 3rd ed. (Oxford, 1933); by page number
Minor Works	*Minor Works*, ed. R. W. Chapman, rev. ed. by B. C. Southam (London, 1969)—contains the *juvenilia*, fragments, verses, prayers, and miscellany; by page number
CG	*Sir Charles Grandison*, ed. Brian Southam (Oxford, 1981); by page number
Letters	*Jane Austen's Letters*, ed. R. W. Chapman, 2nd ed. (London, 1952); by date of letter
Memoir	James Edward Austen-Leigh, *A Memoir of Jane Austen*, 2nd ed. (London, 1871); by page number
Life	Richard Arthur Austen-Leigh and William Austen-Leigh, *Jane Austen; Her Life and Letters* (London, 1913); by page number

Preface

Edmund Wilson once said that over the past century and a half "perhaps only two reputations have never been affected by the shifts of fashion: Shakespeare's and Jane Austen's. We still agree with Scott about Jane Austen, just as we agree with Ben Jonson about Shakespeare." One reason for this is that Jane Austen, like Shakespeare and Dickens, has always appealed to the widest possible audience of intelligent readers, and therefore her fiction has been peculiarly resistant to changing fashions or the extremes of specialized literary criticism. The best professional scholars writing about her work have kept a general audience in view, mindful that some of the most perceptive studies of Jane Austen have been produced by "amateurs." Richard Simpson, whose review of the 1870 *Memoir* is the finest piece of nineteenth-century criticism, was a composer, Shakespearean scholar, and writer on Roman Catholic issues; Reginald Farrer, whose 1917 anniversary essay anticipated in many ways the major trends in later criticism, was best known for his works on botany and English gardens. And in our own time the most impressive discoveries about Jane Austen's life and family background have been made by a retired journalist, George Tucker. Although academic study of Jane Austen has flourished in recent years (David Gilson's *Bibliography of Jane Austen* lists more studies for the period 1954–78 than for all the years between 1813 and 1954), some of the best writing continues to come from outside the academy, and we have kept this in mind in preparing the present volume. The list of contributors reflects the wide range of those who are deeply interested in Jane Austen: all speak with equal authority as lovers of her art.

Another quality that Jane Austen shares with Shakespeare and Dickens is the creation of a complete imaginative world, a world continuous with the real one in which she lived yet with a distinctive life of its own. Since her best readers have always wished to know as much as possible about both these worlds, and the relationships between them, we have aimed at an encyclopedic book that will be of value to both the specialist and the general reader. The individual essays, which appear in alphabetical order, cover a great variety of subjects: the life of Jane Austen and her family; the manners and literary tastes of her time; the composition of her fictions and their critical histories; the language and form of the novels; and many more. In selecting these topics we have tried to provide the reader with as many perspectives as possible on Jane Austen's worlds, and we have not shied away from subjects that may strike some readers as arcane or antiquarian. "Characterization" and "Servants," "Romanticism" and "Auction Sales," "Education" and "Gardens," are all topics that will be of intense interest to many readers. Nor have we tried to regularize the styles or approaches of the diverse contributors, except in matters of factual reference. This volume speaks with the many voices of Jane Austen's contemporary audience.

The conclusion to the book, "A Dictionary of Jane Austen's Life and Works", is a comprehensive guide to the places and people (both real and imaginary) and the literary allusions in Jane Austen's works, including the minor fiction and the letters. We wish to express our deep appreciation to H. Abigail Bok for her devoted work on this dictionary, which will be of great permanent value to all readers of Jane Austen, and for her careful editing of the essays. We would also like to thank Jacek Galazka, who first suggested the project, and Susanne Kirk, whose intelligent help at every stage in the preparation made this a better book.

J. David Grey
A. Walton Litz
Brian Southam

Acknowledgments

Some of the material found in David Gilson's essays has appeared previously in his *Bibliography of Jane Austen* published in 1982 by Oxford University Press.

Acknowledgment is gratefully made to Harvester Press for permission to use material published in Margaret Kirkham's *Jane Austen, Feminism and Fiction*, 1983.

AUSTEN

John Austen of Horsmonden, d. 1620
m. Joan Berry, d. 1604
↓
Francis Austen (5th son), d. 1688
↓
John Austen, d. 1705, m. Jane Atkins
↓
John Austen, d. 1704
m. Elizabeth Weller, by whom he had,
among other children:

- **Francis Austen (1698–1791)**
- **William Austen (1701–1737)** By his first wife William Austen was the father of:
  - m. (1) Rebecca Hampson w. William Walter M.D. by whom she had one son, William Hampson Walter, who was the father of Philadelphia, James, and Henry Walter → (2) Susannah Kelk (no issue)

- **Philadelphia Austen (1730–1792)**, m. Tysoe Saul Hancock
  - Elizabeth (Eliza) Hancock (1761–1813), m. (1) Jean Capotte, Comte de Feuillide
    - Hasting de Feuillide

- **Rev. George Austen (1731–1805)**, rector of Steventon and Deane, m. Cassandra Leigh (1737-1827)

- **and two other daughters**

Children of Rev. George Austen:

(1) Rev. James Austen (1765–1819), m. (1) Anne Mathew, by whom he had Jane Anna Elizabeth Austen, who m. Rev. Benjamin Lefroy and had issue (2) Mary Lloyd, by whom he had James Edward Austen (Austen Leigh after 1837) and Caroline Mary Craven Austen. James Edward Austen Leigh had issue

(2) George Austen (1766–1838), (mentally defective)

(3) Edward Austen (1767–1852) (Knight after 1812). He m. Elizabeth Bridges, by whom he had 11 children, including Fanny Catherine Austen (Knight after 1812), who m. Sir Edward Knatchbull

(4) Henry Thomas Austen (1771–1850). He m. (1) Eliza, Comtesse de Feuillide, his first cousin (no issue) (2) Eleanor Jackson (no issue)

(5) Cassandra Elizabeth Austen (1773–1845) never married

(6) Francis William Austen (1774–1865). He m. (1) Mary Gibson, by whom he had 6 sons and 5 daughters (2) Martha Lloyd (no issue)

(7) **Jane Austen** (1775–1817) never married

(8) Charles John Austen (1779–1852). He m. (1) Frances Palmer, by whom he had 4 daughters (2) Harriet Palmer, by whom he had 3 sons and one daughter

LEIGH

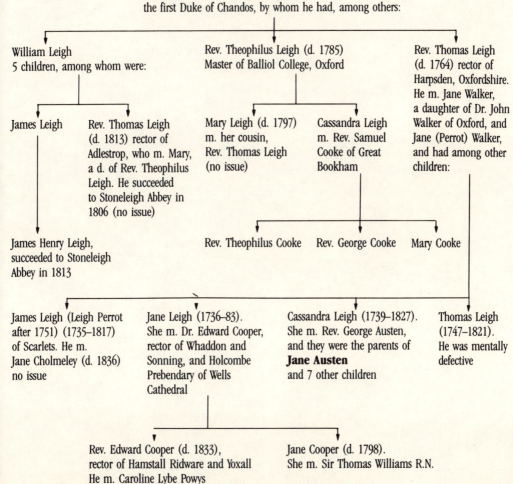

THE
Jane Austen
COMPANION

AMATEUR THEATRICALS AT STEVENTON

George Holbert Tucker

The rage for amateur theatricals that obsessed English society from the 1770s well into the nineteenth century—and which received a permanent literary memorial in *Mansfield Park*—reached Steventon in 1782, when Jane Austen was in her seventh year. Although at that time many members of the aristocracy erected scaled-down imitations of London playhouses in which amateur theatricals could be performed, most of those who felt the urge to act had to fall back on converting large rooms in their town or country houses into temporary theaters similar to the one planned for the theatricals at Mansfield Park that were terminated so dramatically by Sir Thomas Bertram's unexpected return from Antigua.

At Steventon, the dining parlor, presumably the largest ground-floor room of the rectory, was used as a temporary theater from 1782 to 1784. Tradition also says that the rector's barn was occasionally used as a theater, but that did not take place until the Christmas theatricals of 1787. There is evidence for the later date in an unpublished letter of that year in which a young half cousin of Jane Austen's stated: "My uncle's barn is fitting up quite like a theatre, & all the young folks are to take their part."

According to a manuscript volume of poems (now at Jane Austen's house at Chawton) by James Austen—Jane Austen's oldest brother, who wrote the prologues and epilogues for the Steventon theatricals—the first play known to have been performed there was acted in 1782. The play was *Matilda*, a tragedy by Dr. Thomas Francklin, a friend of Dr. Samuel Johnson's and a fashionable London preacher of the type admired by Henry Crawford in *Mansfield Park*. It was followed in 1784 by Richard Brinsley Sheridan's *The Rivals*, a much more ambitious undertaking than *Matilda*. It seems likely that neighbors of the Austens were recruited to augment the rectory family for the cast.

Two years later, on December 26–28, 1787, Susannah Centlivre's comedy *The Wonder! A Woman Keeps a Secret* was mounted; the principal motivator for the production was Jane Austen's sophisticated paternal cousin, Eliza, comtesse de Feuillide, then recently arrived from France. Eliza, who had taken part in amateur theatricals since she was a child and had also acted in private theatricals in France, was also a self-proclaimed flirt who lost no time in appraising the manly charms of her cousins James and Henry Austen, both of whom, according to family tradition, were captivated by her charms. As the precocious twelve-year-old Jane Austen was a perceptive spectator of the intrigues that accompanied the highly charged rehearsals of Mrs. Centlivre's comedy, it is reasonable to surmise that her observations at the time were drawn upon later as a basis for the theatrical episodes in *Mansfield Park*.

Susannah Centlivre's comedy was followed in January 1788 by the presentation of three other plays at Steventon. The first was David Garrick's adaptation of John Fletcher's comedy *The Chances*. It was followed shortly thereafter by another play, the title of which has not been preserved; it is merely described in the manuscript volume of James Austen's poems as "a private Theatrical Exhibition at Steventon 1788." Later, on March 22, 1788, the *Tragedy of Tom Thumb* was performed, either Henry Fielding's original burlesque or Kane O'Hara's later adaptation and condensation of it.

As far as is known, the last two plays presented at Steventon were *The Sultan, or A Peep Into the Seraglio* by Isaac Bickerstaffe and James Townley's farce *High Life Below Stairs*. No prologue or epilogue for the latter has been preserved among James Austen's surviving writings (although evidence exists for its performance), but the witty afterpiece he provided for Bickerstaffe's comedy (the plot of which has many similarities to the libretto of Mozart's *Abduction from the Seraglio*) is dated January 1790 and states it was "spoken by Miss Cooper as Roxalana." That Jane Cooper, Jane Austen's only female first cousin on her mother's side of the family, acted the part of Roxalana and that Townley's farce was also performed at the same time are facts confirmed by a letter written shortly thereafter by Eliza, comtesse de Feuillide, to a half cousin of the Austens' in which she said: "I suppose you have had frequent accounts from Steventon, & that they have informed you of their theatrical performances, *The Sultan & High Life Below Stairs*. Miss Cooper performed the part of Roxalana & Henry the Sultan."

Meanwhile, the amateur theatricals at Steventon rectory had inspired the young Jane Austen as the budding humorist of the family to try her hand at dramatic writing. This resulted in three short plays, "The Visit, a Comedy in 2 Acts"; "The Mystery, An Unfinished Comedy"; and "The First Act of a Comedy," all written between Jane's twelfth and eighteenth birthdays. "The Visit," the most interesting of the three, was dedicated to her eldest brother, James; the wording of the mock dedication is significant, as it either preserves the titles of two of her own *juvenilia* no longer in existence or two plays by James Austen that have not survived. After the preamble, the dedication reads: "The following Drama, which I humbly recommend to your Protection & Patronage, tho' inferior to those celebrated Comedies called 'The School for Jealousy' & 'The travelled Man', will I hope afford some amusement to so respectable a *Curate* as yourself; which was the end in veiw when it was first composed by your Humble Servant the Author" (*Vol. 1*, p. 49).

"The Visit," one of the wittiest of Jane Austen's *juvenilia*, is notable for its sprightly dialogue. "The Mystery" is more routine; its chief significance is that Jane undoubtedly drew her inspiration for its two whispering scenes from Sheridan's *The Critic*, then only recently produced in London, while "The First Act of a Comedy" is a brief but lively burlesque on a family en route to London.

Sometime between the Steventon performances of *The Sultan* and *High Life Below Stairs* and 1800, Jane Austen also presumably put the finishing touches on a short five-act play, a dramatization of some of the scenes from Samuel Richardson's *History of Sir Charles Grandison*, one of her favorite novels. Called *Sir Charles Grandison or the Happy Man*, the play, a free adaptation of episodes from Richardson's novel, is based on an attempt by the wicked Sir Hargrave Pollexfen to force a marriage on Harriet Byron, the heroine, who is rescued by Sir Charles Grandison and eventually becomes the latter's wife.

The play was long believed by the descendants of James Austen, in whose family the manuscript descended, to have been written down by Jane Austen from the dictation of James's daughter, Jane Anna Elizabeth Austen (later Mrs. Benjamin Lefroy), who was frequently at Steventon rectory from the time of her mother's death in May 1795 until her father's second marriage in January 1797. This tradition has recently been disputed by Brian Southam, who maintains in his introduction to *Jane Austen's 'Sir Charles Grandison'* (1980) that the earliest part of the manuscript was written by Jane Austen before her niece was born in 1793, while the rest of the play was completed no later than 1800, when the same niece was between six and seven years of age.

In dismissing the family tradition that Jane's niece was the author of the play, which he suggests was possibly written by Jane Austen for an intimate family theatrical, Southam says:

> It is quite possible that during Anna's later visits to Steventon, between 1796 and 1800, Jane Austen was working intermittently on "Grandison", revising and continuing the early pages, with the young niece at her elbow, offering suggestions and even being allowed, as a special privilege, to write on the manuscript itself—inserting a word or two here and there, changing a phrase, bringing a character on stage. That, almost certainly, was the extent of Anna's contribution; and if we grace it with the name of collaboration, that was the sum of it. (pp. 10–11)

The theatrical performances known to have taken place at Steventon rectory apparently ended with the performances of *The Sultan* and *High*

Life Below Stairs in 1790. There is a family tradition, however, that claims Henry Austen, Jane's favorite brother, and Eliza, comtesse de Feuillide, revived playacting at Steventon after the latter's husband was guillotined in Paris in February 1794 during the French Revolution, the outcome being Eliza became Henry's wife. This tradition is questionable, however, for the movements of both Henry Austen and the Comtesse after the latter's return to England (presumably during the early part of 1790) are well documented in *Austen Papers, 1704–1856* (edited by Richard A. Austen-Leigh and privately printed in 1942), and no mention of private theatricals, either at Steventon or elsewhere, occurs. Nor are there any surviving prologues or epilogues by James Austen or any other member of his family for the period to confirm the tradition that playacting went on at Steventon or any other place connected with the Austens during that time. There is also no mention of amateur theatricals of any description in any of Jane Austen's letters for 1796, the only year of the period in question for which correspondence is available.

In view of the masterful way in which Jane Austen handled the playacting episodes in *Mansfield Park*, it is apparent that those impressions she absorbed during the earlier well-documented period, when amateur theatricals were given at Steventon (1782–90), were retained in her memory, thereby constituting a mine of firsthand information that she drew upon later when she wrote *Mansfield Park*.

Bibliography

All of the facts in this account of the amateur theatricals at Steventon can be found, with substantial notes, in GEORGE HOLBERT TUCKER, *A Goodly Heritage: A History of Jane Austen's Family* (Manchester, England: 1983).

ARCHITECTURE/ BUILDINGS

John Dixon Hunt

Austen's characters inhabit or visit a variety of buildings: major houses or mansions, usually in the country; parsonages of all sorts and sizes; cottages; lodgings in London; and a number of fashionable resorts. They also see villages, country towns, and cities such as Bath. Her books describe largely the same range of architecture that she herself knew firsthand, such as Stoneleigh Abbey in Warwickshire, with its monumental west wing fifteen bays long and three and a half stories high, articulated by four massive pilasters, crowned by a balustrade and with the windows of the two principal floors enriched with pediments. Another large house Austen knew well is Godmersham Park in Kent, a plain house (ca. 1732), seven bays wide with lower bays connected by links on either side. We also know that she visited other mansions (Lord Portsmouth's Hurstbourne Park, Lord Dorchester's Greywall, and Lord Bolton's Hackwood among others) and attended a ball at Goodnestone in 1796. Her knowledge, then, was largely of early Georgian architecture. In addition, however, she had visited and lived in Bath, knew Clifton (a beautiful eighteenth-century development of Bristol), lived in Southampton, and knew firsthand several south-coast resorts. She mentions only one architect by name, Joseph Bonomi, whom Lord Courtland, Robert Ferrars's friend, had invited to submit plans—so awful, apparently, that Ferrars says he threw them into the fire (*SS*, p. 252). Bonomi had died in 1808 after spending the previous forty-one years in England. One living architect and landscape designer, Humphry Repton, is invoked disparagingly in *Mansfield Park* (pp. 53ff.). Austen also suggests by her comment that Mansfield Park deserves "to be in any collection of gentlemen's seats" (p. 48) that she was acquainted with illustrated volumes by Watts or Angus (see bibliography).

Austen's architectural opportunities, then, were considerable enough. But she strikingly avoids making use of buildings she had seen herself; further, what descriptions she does provide are rarely circumstantially detailed. Indeed, Nikolaus Pevsner states in a major article of 1968, "She is without exception vague, when it comes to describing buildings" (p. 404). The duke of Wellington, first president of the Jane Austen Society, was categorical that "Jane Austen cared nothing for the visual arts" (p. 185). A fellow novelist, Margaret Lane, delivering the annual address to the Austen Society in 1962, expressed disappointment that Austen's interiors were so meagerly described: "interior description is a thing Jane Austen disciplined herself to do without." Yet Lane retained a vivid impression of the insides of buildings in the novels and felt that they were "conjured up . . . out of thin air, and very nearly without the aid of description" (pp. 226–234).

"Very nearly without the aid of description" is surely the revealing phrase. For there are in the novels sufficient hints of interiors and exteriors for an architectural historian to flesh them out from his own knowledge: Mr. Woodhouse's Hartfield is "modern and well-built," with small but pretty grounds (*E*, p. 272); Randalls, where Mr. Weston and Miss Taylor remove upon marriage, has two living rooms on each side of a middle passage, with facing doors (*E*, p. 248); Barton Cottage, where the Dashwoods live, is similar, having been recently and "regularly" built, with two sitting rooms of sixteen square feet on either side of the passage, four bedrooms, and two garrets—presumably for the three servants (*SS*, pp. 26–29). These hints declare a familiar country architecture ("cottage") of the early nineteenth century; any greater precision of description would be redundant. Sometimes, it is true, the details seem rather random, as when Tilney's Woodston parsonage, more lavish than most, is described as "a new-built substantial stone house, with its semi-circular sweep and green gates" and having a "commodious, well-proportioned" dining parlor and stables (*NA*, pp. 212–14).

Perhaps Austen considered excessive architectural description too "enthusiastic": for Marianne in *Sense and Sensibility* "would have described every room [at Allenham] with equal delight" (she has just described the upper sitting room), if she had not been interrupted (p. 69). But more probably, as Virginia Woolf recognized, Austen "stimulates us to supply what is not there." Wickham's minute account of Pemberley (*PP*, p. 143) is not divulged to the reader, though this is presumably to allow us to see it through Elizabeth's eyes at a crucial point of the narrative (pp. 245ff.). Yet even then the exterior is simply "a handsome, stone building, standing well on rising ground"—which would go for most of the mansions illustrated by Angus and Watts, while the interior is just as vague. The dining parlor, for example, is "a large well-proportioned room, handsomely fitted up," and of the other rooms we learn only that from their windows the beauties of the park were seen from new angles (see under the essay "Picturesque" also). The questions therefore remain *What* does Austen wish us to supply for ourselves, and *why* are we thus left to our own resources?

A reader confronted with elaborate details of setting in a novel is doubtless obliged to attempt to see things after the author's fashion or to skip, whereas a reader able—however deliberately or unconsciously—to supply his own vision of place from authorial hints commits himself to an imaginative involvement with the work. Such a reader response probably contributes to the special enthusiasm of Austen's admirers: by investing his own understanding, a reader feels intimately part of her imaginative world. But the subtlety and scope of those authorial pointers and suggestions are nonetheless a prerequisite. Austen's practice may be codified in two ways: she will use highly charged details to indicate either the symbolic atmosphere of a building or room, or she will imply far less forthrightly what she expects readers to register from their own familiarities with architecture or furnishings. The latter technique especially is a sort of code, drawing on contemporary assumptions and commonplace recognitions that need no elaborate exposition but which the modern reader has to recover for a full understanding of the narrative.

Clear examples of this latter mode are Lady Catherine de Bourgh's chimneypiece at Rosings, which Mr. Collins, who also enthuses about the glazing, tells us cost £800 (*PP*, pp. 156 and 75); as Pevsner has shown (p. 408), this was exceptionally expensive by contemporary standards. Similarly, General Tilney has acquired a Rumford (*NA*, p. 162): an up-to-date kitchen range named after its inventor, it was entirely of a piece with the general's progressive estate—spacious and convenient new service rooms, a "village of hot-houses" and "luxuriant plantations" (pp. 177–78)—but ironically at odds with Catherine Morland's gothick expectations and her affectation for "no furniture of a more modern date than the fifteenth century" (p. 182). Blaise Castle, to which John Thorpe proposes an excursion (*NA*, p. 85), was a modern folly built by Thomas Farr in 1766 and contained neither "winding vaults" nor "long galleries"; furthermore, it was set in the grounds and gave its name to a neoclassical mansion by William Petty of the 1790s.

Architecture, buildings, and their furnishings function clearly as metonyms for moral and social qualities in Austen's novels. In *The Watsons*, the banker, Tomlinson, is registered by his brand-new house with its modish shrubbery and "sweep" of driveway, built at the end of town to gratify his ambition for a "country seat" (p. 322). By contrast, the furnishings of Sotherton—"solid mahogany, rich damask, marble, gilding and carving," in other words a William Kentish mid-eighteenth-century interior—and its rarely used James II chapel (*MP*, pp. 85 and 86) reveal a house uncared for and unconsidered by its owner until the bug for improvement infects him. Mansfield Park itself, "spacious," "commodious and well fitted up" and set in "a real park five miles round" (pp. 48 and 41), is barely described; but the dislocations of its interior spaces for the theatricals suggest a dwelling otherwise well adapted to social uses.

Donwell Abbey is more precisely delineated: its "respectable size and style," its rambling and irregular design, its "low and sheltered" situation, its "coolness and solitude," and its proper juxtaposition to its tenant farms signal its value as a place of tradition and growth (*E*, pp. 358–60). By contrast, Uppercross Cottage (*P*, p. 36) has a novel "viranda, French windows, and other prettinesses" and catches the traveler's eye, thereby suggesting the younger Musgroves' bent for appearances. Architectural hints employed in similarly unobtrusive but eloquent ways concern Mr. Collins's "rather small" parsonage (*PP*, p. 157) or Mr. Elton's "old and not very good house . . . much smartened up by the present proprietor," which is further placed by its location away from the main street and beyond "a few inferior dwellings" (*E*, p. 83). Details speak volumes: when Admiral Croft removes from Kellynch "some of the large looking-glasses," Anne deduces that the estate has in fact passed into "better hands" (*P*, pp. 125 and 127). Somewhat more elaborate details are given of Fanny Price's surroundings at Mansfield: her position upon arrival, as well as the attitudes of her hosts, are clearly identified by the allocation to her by Mrs. Norris and Sir Thomas of the "little white attic . . . not far from the girls, and close by the housemaids" (pp. 9–10). Her slow progress into maturity and acceptance by the Bertrams is further indicated by her colonization of the East Room with her plants, books, sketches, transparencies, and writing desk; formerly (and significantly for this *Bildungsroman*) the schoolroom, it is not warmed by a fire on Mrs. Norris's instructions (p. 151) until, after Sir Thomas's strategic visit, Fanny is allowed one every day (p. 322). Such cultural nuances in the disposition and use of rooms, which Mark Girouard has chronicled in his *Life in the English Country House*, are at the very basis of Austen's allusions to buildings.

Social space is a prominent theme in Austen. Her letters show her concern for these matters (see, especially, January 3, 1801), and the novels invest both animate and inanimate occupancy of living areas with sharp significance. Furniture can signal moral and social meanings, as when Frank Churchill presents Miss Fairfax with a "very elegant looking instrument—not a grand, but a large-sized square pianoforté" (*E*, pp. 214–15) or when Emma's introduction of a "large modern circular table" is the occasion for more of Churchill's games (pp. 347ff.). It is typical of Churchill, too, that he would assess the ballroom "capabilities" of the Crown Inn (197–98) or that Robert Ferrars would calculate the amenities of various rooms for the same purpose (*SS*, p. 252). But nowhere is space more telling than in Austen's presentation of lodgings, a central motif of *Persuasion* where the plot starts from the Elliots' removal from their old home. In lodgings, space has not been shaped by long residence of particular people: Mrs. Smith, crippled, a "widow, and poor" (p. 152), is confined to "a noisy parlour, and a dark bed-room behind" (p. 154). But that even lodgings may accommodate and express human qualities is made explicit in the account of Captain Harville's winter quarters at Lyme, with "its ingenious contrivances and nice arrangements . . . to turn the actual space to the best possible account, to supply the deficiencies of lodging-house furniture, and defend the windows and doors against the winter storms" (*P*, p. 98).

Architecture/Buildings

Fanny Price learns to appreciate the ample, well-adjusted social spaces of Mansfield Park when she is sent back to the family house in Portsmouth: here small, noisy, and messy rooms do not allow either privacy or regulated and distinct social activities; it lacks books (Mansfield Park has a library), while its narrow passage and stairs (p. 388) are emblematic of its lack of scope for the Price sisters' adequate development. Between the unloved and seemingly empty spaces of Sotherton and the cramped dwelling at Portsmouth, Mansfield Park suggests that it is perfectly suited to its occupants and their range of social activities. The same is true of its gardens, and it is clear that Austen's preferred garden designs (considered part of architecture) are those that are useful and hospitable to the various social needs of their users. Sotherton's gardens, aesthetically out-of-date, are too restricting, with their walls, palisades, wilderness, and iron gates, and they promote unacceptable social behavior as a means of circumventing those design deficiencies. At Portsmouth, if Fanny wishes to take a walk, she can go into the town. It is only at Mansfield Park that she and the other inhabitants are afforded a garden that is a satisfactory part of the whole domestic space. Once again the reader only gets hints—notably of the shrubbery, the growth of which (p. 208) is stressed and which aptly becomes the locale of Fanny's own maturation. A shrubbery that provided different walks (*PP*, p. 352) without becoming the wilderness of Sotherton, walks that with a gravel surface were usable in most weathers, and walks that allowed of some privacy without cutting off its strollers from the social world of the house are everywhere hinted at in Jane Austen. Jane Bennet and Bingley take to them, Emma is proposed to by Knightley in the shrubbery, and Anne Elliot and Frederick Wentworth retire to the gravel walk to make the "present hour a blessing indeed" (*P*, p. 240). Despite what Bradbrook (p. 67) terms Repton's reputation as a "notorious improver," the shrubbery and similarly useful areas near the house became a significant item in his garden designs. Austen obviously reserves her ironies for those garden architects who forget utility and social appropriateness. So Mr. Palmer is ensconced, morosely superior, in a Grecian temple, while the Dashwoods, to keep the "general good opinion of their surrounding acquaintance," indulge in so-called improvements: old walnut trees have to come down to make room for Mrs. John Dashwood's greenhouse, which thereupon becomes "a fine object from many parts of the park" (*SS*, pp. 3, 226, and 302). A hermitage in *Pride and Prejudice* (p. 352) is similarly the object of some irony.

Apart from individual buildings, Austen introduces larger architectural complexes into the novels: country towns, London, Bath, and some south-coast resorts, among them the brand-new Sanditon. Again, they perform as indexes of taste, social standing, and morality largely by hint and suggestion. The fullest description of some architectural complex is that of

Uppercross in Somerset, and it speaks volumes on the village's social fabric:

> A moderate-sized village, which a few years back had been completely in the old English style; containing only two houses superior in appearance to those of the yeomen and labourers,—the mansion of the 'squire, with its high walls, great gates, and old trees, substantial and unmodernized—and the compact, tight parsonage, enclosed in its own neat garden. (*P*, p. 36)

Larger are the two market towns of Meryton in *Pride and Prejudice* and Highbury in *Emma*, both of which have assembly rooms and shops that are used briefly to focus essential background; Ford's shop "that every body attends every day of their lives" (*E*, pp. 199–200) or the milliner's where the Bennet girls go in pursuit of the militia officers (*PP*, p. 28).

Neither streets, monuments, nor houses in London and Bath are described; but as Pevsner noted, "the choice of addresses is brilliantly made" (p. 412). The two plans he reproduces reveal that Austen locates her wealthy characters in Mayfair and just north of Oxford Street: Mrs. Jennings's house was off Portman Square, for example ("handsome and handsomely fitted up": *SS*, p. 160), but her late husband had traded in "a less elegant part of the town" (p. 153). Apart from some references to posh shops (*SS*, pp. 164, 199, and 220), there are a few other references to such buildings as the Drury Lane Theatre (*SS*, p. 330) or the Bedford Coffee House in Covent Garden's square (*W*, p. 356, and *NA*, p. 96). Bath figures even more prominently than London, and Austen's instinct for apt locations is equally sure. The Musgroves take an apartment at the White Hart (*P*, p. 216), the leading hotel. General Tilney is placed in Milsom Street (*NA*, p. 91), which Mrs. Allen knows is the best (p. 238). Sir Walter Elliot's titled relations, of whom he is so proud, live in the New Town, started properly only in 1788 (*P*, p. 149). Austen's letters show that she was alert to location, status, and cost of a variety of lodgings (*Letters*, January 3, 1801). Various prominent locations, such as the Royal Crescent and the Pump Room, are mentioned (*NA*, pp. 20, 26, and 97) but not described.

No resorts feature as centrally as Bath until Sanditon, although there are references to Southend (*E*, p. 101), Ramsgate (*MP*, p. 51), Lyme Regis, with its main street "almost hurrying into the water" (*P*, p. 95), Dawlish (*SS*, p. 360), Weymouth (*E*, p. 160), and Brighton, where Wickham seduces Lydia Bennet. But it is above all in *Sanditon* that Austen makes the most of her shrewd eye for the fashion in seaside resorts. Its leading promoter and speculator, Mr. Parker, has built himself Trafalgar House, "a light elegant Building, standing in a small Lawn with a very young plantation round it" and what is implied as a too-large Venetian window (*S*, p. 384). Parker puffs and praises the new town (pp. 368–69), but its rawness and incompletion—it has only one hotel, a library that doubles as a store for trinkets, and several milliners—are equally striking. The hotel has a "Billiard Room," there is one terrace "aspiring to be the Mall of the Place" (p. 384), and a Waterloo Crescent is planned (p. 380). All this has been radically transformed in a few years from "a quiet Village of no pretensions" (p. 371). Pretensions ("a tasteful little Cottage Ornèe, on a strip of Waste Ground," p. 377) have triumphed, together with the bathing machines, Prospect House, and Bellevue Cottage (p. 384). In this, Austen makes architecture play a large role, revealing a society in the process of total transformation. This intriguing fragment of a novel ends with a visit, like that to Sotherton in *Mansfield Park*, to Sanditon House (p. 426). Earlier we had heard that it was the "last Building of former Days in that line of the Parish" (p. 384), and Charlotte's first view of "Beauty & Respectability" and a handsome approach seem to confirm that. But its entrance gates and fence, curiously abutting on the road, suggest that the estate has been forced to accommodate itself, awkwardly, to the new dispensation. Right at the end of her career Austen seems to be focusing her moral and social vision through architectural imagery, as she had done in her earlier novels; it is still, however, suggestive and undetailed, leaving readers to amplify her hints from their own resources.

Bibliography

ANGUS, WILLIAM. *The Seats of the Nobility and Gentry, in Great Britain and Wales* (Islington, 1787; reprinted, New York, 1983).
BRADBROOK, FRANK W. *Jane Austen and Her Predecessors* (Cambridge, 1966).
DUCKWORTH, ALISTAIR M. *The Improvement of the Estate* (Baltimore and London, 1971).
GIROUARD, MARK. *Life in the English Country House* (New Haven and London, 1978).
GORNALL, F. G. "Marriage, Property & Romance in Jane Austen's Novels," *Hibbert Journal*, 65 (1967), 151–56 and 66 (1967), 24–29.
LANE, MARGARET. Untitled address in *Collected Reports of the Jane Austen Society, 1949–1965* (London, 1967), 226–34.
MINGAY, G. E. *English Landed Society in the Eighteenth Century* (London, 1963).
NEALE, JOHN P. *Views of the Seats of Noblemen and Gentlemen*, 6 vols. (London, 1818–23).
PEVSNER, NIKOLAUS. "The Architectural Setting of Jane Austen's Novels," *Journal of the Warburg and Courtauld Institutes*, 31 (1968), 404–22.
SCHNEIDER, M. LUCY. "The Little White Attic and the East Room: Their Function in *Mansfield Park*," *Modern Philology*, 63 (1965–66), 227–35.
SPRING, DAVID. "Aristocracy, Social Structure, and Religion in the Early Victorian Period," *Victorian Studies*, 6 (1962–63), 263–80.

WATTS, WILLIAM. *The Seats of the Nobility and Gentry, in a Collection of the Most Interesting and Picturesque Views* (Chelsea, 1779; reprinted, New York, 1983).

THE DUKE OF WELLINGTON. "Houses in Jane Austen's Novels," *Collected Papers of the Jane Austen Society, 1949–1965* (London, 1967), 185–88.

AUCTION SALES

David Gilson

Manuscripts

Of the minor works and *juvenilia, Volume the Second* was sold at Sotheby's in July 1977, £44,000, and *Volume the Third*, also at Sotheby's, in December 1976, £30,000. *Lady Susan* was sold in June 1893 by Puttick & Simpson, then at Sotheby's in December 1898, £22.10s., and finally, again at Sotheby's, in June 1933, from Lord Rosebery's library, £2,100. The first six leaves of *The Watsons* were sold at a Red Cross charity sale at Sotheby's, in April 1915, £55, while the remaining, larger portion appeared at Sotheby's in July 1978, £38,000. A continuation of *Sanditon* by Anna Lefroy was sold at Sotheby's in December 1977, £1,900. Jane Austen's *Three Prayers* appeared at Sotheby's in November 1927, £175. A dramatic adaptation of Samuel Richardson's *History of Sir Charles Grandison* was sold at Sotheby's in December 1977, £17,000 (in Jane Austen's hand, but her authorship is not proven). The only other literary manuscripts to have appeared at auction are verses: one version of the lines in memory of Mrs. Lefroy was sold at Sotheby's in April 1934, £24; another, also at Sotheby's, in May 1948, £26; one text of the lines on Mr. Gell and Miss Gill, formerly R. W. Chapman's, at Sotheby's, March 1979, £520; a manuscript containing "Verses to Rhyme with 'Rose,'" "On Sir Home Popham's Sentence," and "To Miss Bigg," at Sotheby's, October 1962, £500; "To Miss Bigg" (the text actually sent), at Sotheby's, July 1959, £240 (previously sold there in July 1917 with a scrap of an autograph letter, £17); one text of the "Lines on Maria Beckford," at Christie's, July 1983 (from Godmersham), £6,480 (previously sold at Sotheby's, December 1931, £50).

The autograph originals of surviving letters have appeared at auction on numerous occasions. Ten of those in Lord Brabourne's possession were offered at Sotheby's in May 1891 (when Letter 74 fetched £1.2s.); some of these probably reappeared in his posthumous sale at Puttick & Simpson in June 1893, when sixty-four letters were put up for sale in small lots, two or three at a time. Forty-one of these passed into the collection of Alfred Morrison and reappeared as one lot at Sotheby's, in December 1918, £260. Ten letters were in the Frederick Lovering sale at Sotheby's, in May 1948, sold individually at prices from £55 (Letter 79) to £120 (Letter 78), while £130 was paid for Letters 120, 126, and 126a together. Letters sold individually at other times include Letter 83, Anderson Galleries, New York, December 1909, $60; Letter 117, Sotheby's, July 1924, £38; Letter 74.1,

Sotheby's, April 1930, £1,000; Letter 127, Sotheby's, June 1975, £2,400; Letter 43, Sotheby's, June 1982, £10,000. Occasionally unpublished fragments of letters appear (last five lines and signature, Sotheby's, July 1967, £35; six lines on each side of a strip of paper, Sotheby's, October 1968, £65).

Early Editions and Translations

These always fetch higher prices when in original paper boards or wrappers; the prices of bound copies fluctuate according to binding, condition, provenance, presence or absence of half titles, and other factors. Cassandra Austen's set of first editions (possibly the novelist's own), complete except for *Sense and Sensibility*, was sold at Sotheby's, in July 1967, £2,200. Sample prices for first editions of *Sense and Sensibility* are:

January 1912, Anderson Auction Co., Robert Hoe's copy, bound, $172.50

July 1924, Sotheby's, Bernard Buchanan MacGeorge's copy, original boards, £152

February 1926, Sotheby's, Francis A. Skeet's copy, bound but preserving original spine labels, £122

January 1929, Anderson Galleries, Jerome Kern's copy, original boards, $3,600

April 1938, American Art Association, Cortlandt F. Bishop's copy, bound, $230

April 1941, Parke-Bernet, A. Edward Newton's copy, original boards, $950

April 1945, Parke-Bernet, Frank J. Hogan's copy, original boards, $340

June 1948, Sotheby's, W. Marchbank's copy, original boards, £150

May 1963, Parke-Bernet, Barton W. Currie's copy, original boards, $1,700 (resold in November 1974 from the William E. Stockhausen collection, $5,500)

July 1968, Sotheby's, Viscount Norwich's copy, bound, £160

October 1974, Sotheby's, bound, £400

July 1976, Sotheby's, R. W. Chapman's copy, bound, poor condition, £140

October 1976, Sotheby Parke Bernet, Katharine de Berkeley Parsons' copy, bound, $700

July 1978, Christie's, S. Kensington, earl of Stair's copy, original boards, £4,800

February 1981, Christie's, New York, Marjorie Wiggin Prescott's copy, original boards, $13,000

June 1983, Christie's (at Godmersham), Elsie Tritton's copy, bound, £1,404

Auction Sales

Early American editions appear very rarely at auction. The 1816 Philadelphia *Emma* was in the Frank J. Hogan sale at Parke-Bernet in April 1945 for $160, whereas *Elizabeth Bennet*, Philadelphia 1832, has ranged from 1s. (June 1915, Sotheby's) to £14 (January 1964, Sotheby's) and $130 (September 1974, Freeman, Philadelphia). The 1832 *Persuasion* was sold at Parke-Bernet in December 1951 for $15, the 1833 *Northanger Abbey* at Sotheby's in June 1915 for 1s., and the 1833 *Sense and Sensibility* at Sotheby's in January 1964 for £13, and Christie's in February 1934 for £3.

Early French translations are even rarer. The Empress Marie-Louise's handsomely bound copy of *Raison et Sensibilité*, 1815, brought £10.10s. at Sotheby's in June 1933, while a copy in wrappers of *La Nouvelle Emma*, 1816, was in a sale at the American Art Association-Anderson Galleries in November 1938 for $7.

Miscellaneous

Six titles from Jane Austen's library were sold by auction at Bexhill in 1932, probably very cheaply, since the bookseller C. Howes subsequently offered Ariosto's *Orlando Furioso* in English, 1783, 15s., Goldsmith's *History of the Earth*, 1774, 6gns., Hume's *History of England*, 1759–62, £5.10s., and Thomson's *Works*, 1773, 5gns. Of other such books sold separately, volume 6 of an eight-volume edition of *The Spectator*, 1774, was sold at Hodgson's in 1926 for £11; Bage's *Hermsprong*, 1796, Bang's Galleries, New York, 1900, $18.75; Berquin's *L'Ami des Enfans*, 1782–83, American Art Association, 1923, $320, and *A Companion to the Altar*, ca. 1793, Sotheby's, 1927, 100gns.

Of material other than books, the original portrait drawing of Jane Austen by her sister Cassandra fetched £130 at Sotheby's in May 1948.

JANE AUSTEN AND BATH

Anne-Marie Edwards

Jane Austen portrays Bath, that most elegant of English Georgian cities, through the eyes of a wide range of characters. Like Catherine Morland in *Northanger Abbey* (published in 1817–18, although the first draft was written at Steventon when Jane was in her early twenties), she probably approached Bath for the first time at the age of nineteen "all eager delight" (p. 19). Like her, she enjoyed being caught up in the whirl of fashionable activities that each day in this fascinating city brought her. As Catherine exclaims to Henry Tilney: "here are a variety of amusements, a variety of things to be seen and done. . . . Oh! who can ever be tired of Bath?" (pp. 78–79).

A vivid picture of other elements in Bath society is given in *Northanger Abbey*. Among the finest are the loving but foolish Mrs. Allen, who must comment on all she sees and "had no doubt in the world of its being a very fine day, if the clouds would only go off, and the sun keep out" (p. 82), and the shallow flirt Isabella Thorpe, well placed in Edgar's Buildings at the top of fashionable Milsom Street to watch for handsome young men—when not immersed in one of her "horrid" romances.

But a rather different view of Bath emerges from the pages of *Persuasion* (also published in 1817–18). Jane Austen had been a resident of Bath for five years (1801–06), and during that time her father had died, her mother had been very ill, and rumor has it that a young man, met on holiday, whom her sister Cassandra thought Jane might have married, had also died. Bath itself was changing. Although still popular with invalids, it was no longer the glittering magnet to the wealthy and fashionable it had been during the eighteenth century. They were being tempted away to fast-growing seaside resorts like Brighton. It was becoming more a place to retire to than elope from. The more sedate heroine of *Persuasion*, Anne Elliot, finds "the white glare" of Bath (p. 33) exhausting. But Jane never underrates the attraction of the city. Anne's friend, the sensible Lady Russell, returns to Bath with delight:

> driving through the long course of streets from the Old Bridge to Camden-place, amidst the dash of other carriages, the heavy rumble of carts and drays, the bawling of newsmen, muffin-men and milkmen, and the ceaseless clink of pattens, she made no complaint. No, these were noises which belonged to the winter pleasures; her spirits rose under their influence. (p. 135)

Today Bath is still the city of Jane Austen. As you walk the narrow streets that link arms around its beautiful medieval abbey or climb the hill slopes to the north through the magnificent squares and terraces and crescents built of honey-colored limestone in Jane's footsteps and those of her characters, you would not feel surprised to meet Anne Elliot on Captain Wentworth's arm as he tells her of a love time could not diminish. Stand on the crest of Beechen Hill to the south, from where the autumn leaves fall to drift over the city, and you may yet overhear Henry Tilney instructing Catherine Morland on the art of the picturesque.

Bibliography

EDWARDS, ANNE-MARIE. *In the Steps of Jane Austen* (London, 1979).
FREEMAN, JEAN. *Jane Austen in Bath* (Alton, 1969).

BIOGRAPHIES

Park Honan

This discussion focuses on the two major works by the Austen-Leighs, the *Memoir* (1870; revised 1871) and the *Life* (1913), and on Elizabeth Jenkins's *Jane Austen* and Lord David Cecil's *Portrait of Jane Austen*, but mention will be made of other helpful biographical works, too.

A Memoir of Jane Austen by her nephew James Edward Austen-Leigh was published on December 16, 1869; the second edition (1871) is fuller, with the first printed texts of *Lady Susan*, *The Watsons*, the canceled chapter of *Persuasion*, and extracts from *Sanditon*. The author was James Austen's son, born in Deane on November 17, 1798. As he came to know his aunt well between 1806 and 1817, knew Steventon, and visited her at Southampton and at Chawton, his descriptions of locales and of her own appearance, inclinations, and habits are very valuable. He was vicar of Bray in Berkshire when, between March 30 and September 1869, he wrote the book, aided by few letters (none dating before 1800) but by his sister Caroline, his half sister Anna Lefroy, and a good memory. His sinuous style, intelligent family piety, feeling for place, Coleridgean belief in inexplicable "genius," and conviction that his aunt was a proper and happy Christian woman permeate his *Memoir*. "Her own family were so much, and the rest of the world so little" (p. 11), he writes while concentrating on her indulgent parents and cheerful home and the personalities of her sister and brothers, among whom James (his father) had "a large share in directing her reading and forming her taste" (p. 12); he treats her early writings, friendship with Mrs. Lefroy, her "person, character and taste" (p. 82), habits of composition, concern for success and anonymity, the slow growth of her fame, and her last illness, resignation, humility, and death. He is not always consistent, as when he says that Cassandra had "the colder and calmer disposition" (p. 15) and then insists that Jane's own disposition "was remarkably calm and even" (p. 196), or when he says inaccurately that Jane "never touched upon politics, law, or medicine" (p. 14) and then, in an aside, admits that she held "strong political opinions" as a girl (p. 83). He is vague on her male friends but suggestive on her dancing, needlework, housework, and three stages of her artistic development. He views her letters as trivial: "the materials may be thought inferior to the execution," he says tactfully (p. 57). But he is alert, revealing, charming, and important in recollecting the aunt that he, Caroline, and Anna really knew, as when he reveals how Aunt Jane entertained them all by telling them secret details or "particulars" about her fictional people in the lives they led outside her novels (p. 148). "We learned that Miss Steele never succeeded in catching the Doctor" (pp. 148–149), he reports about what Aunt Jane, in the Chawton years, said about *Sense and Sensibility, Pride and Prejudice, Mansfield Park*, and *Emma*,

> that Kitty Bennet was satisfactorily married to a clergyman near Pemberley, while Mary obtained nothing higher than one of her uncle Philip's clerks, and was content to be considered a star in the society of Meriton; that the "considerable sum" given by Mrs. Norris to William Price was one pound; that Mr. Woodhouse survived his daughter's marriage, and kept her and Mr. Knightley from settling at Donwell, about two years; and that the letters placed by Frank Churchill before Jane Fairfax, which she swept away unread, contained the word "pardon." (*Memoir*, chap. 10)

And he adds, as if to caution naive critics who think she simply put people she knew into her work, that "Her own relations never recognised any individual in her characters" (p. 147). With Miss Jenkins's *Jane Austen: A Biography* and Mary Lascelles's splendid *Jane Austen and Her Art*, the *Memoir* is one of the three most elegantly written and delightful works on Jane Austen that we have.

In 1913 James Edward's son William Austen-Leigh published with his nephew and junior by twenty-nine years, Richard Arthur Austen-Leigh, another essential work, *Jane Austen: Her Life and Letters, a Family Record*. Richard Arthur later kept a private "Annotated Copy" of this work (for over three decades) in which he jotted marginal additions. The *Life* is definitive, and despite a few errors not corrected in the second edition (also of 1913), such as "Holk" for Kelk (p. 4), *Northanger Abbey* "written in 1797 and 1798" for Cassandra's surely more accurate "written about the years 98 & 99" (p. 96), and "1879" for 1883 (p. 173), it is an accurate, staid, reliable, and at times vivid and suggestive work written in the emerging twentieth-century manner of scholarly lives. It corrects the *Memoir* in showing that Jane Austen went into society and with "characteristic aloofness" loved it, in pointing to the "emotional and romantic" side of her experience, and above all, in giving a new wealth of reliable details. Drawing on many letters and family documents, the authors give a good account of the Austen and Leigh ancestry ("1600–1764"), of Warren Hastings and the Hancocks, the life itself and the novels, and the last illness. If the *Memoir* portrays Jane Austen as an ordinary woman, oddly gifted with "genius" and living in near isolation, the *Life* shows sources of her inspiration in people she knew. Both give us Austen-Leigh versions of her character and perhaps err in making small use of Anna Lefroy's statements about variations in her temper and hostility to her at

Godmersham or of Catherine Hubback's remark about a delay in resolving the Harris Bigg-Wither proposal, for example, and neither makes full use of Fanny Lefroy's manuscript "Family History" or of Eliza de Feuillide's holograph letters (which R. A. Austen-Leigh freely edits and truncates in his *Austen Papers, 1704–1856*, published in 1942).

Not seeking far into family manuscript material but assessing with fine tact and insight what she saw, Elizabeth Jenkins in *Jane Austen* writes the best of the modern biographies on the subject. Scanty on family background, she offers a detailed and convincing portrait of Jane Austen in her Georgian and regency settings, with intelligent insights into her family and friends, in a narrative finely alert to persons. Miss Jenkins expertly writes a factual story with continuity, so that all of its details seem functional, important, and interesting; she is artful and exact in her treatment of locales, clothes, architecture, and the outward impressions the Austens and their acquaintances made on each other. She delves with a novelist's intuition into Jane Austen's development and finds her a person of "unchildlike combination of emotion and detachment" (p. 33) who with "tearing high spirits" writes her juvenile works and in her personality rather tritely "an exhilaration glittering with wit and joy" (pp. 30–31) and a "temper that needed no control" (p. 46). As her older sister, "Cassandra was an ideal being. She was very intelligent . . . and completely tranquil," Miss Jenkins imagines (pp. 45–46). If Jane and Cassandra are sometimes guessed at and slightly idealized, the narrative compensates with less fanciful comments on cousin Eliza, on Jane Austen's romances, on Fanny Burney's novels, on James Austen and Mary Lloyd, and on the background of Jane Austen's England with its "mania for sensibility" and its flirtations with the gothic. Manners are attended to expertly; we see Jane Austen's daily life, dress, habits, without losing sight of her growth as an artist. Sometimes the feelings of a twentieth-century novelist are attributed to the subject, and the intellectual and political aspects of the times are scanted in favor of Miss Jenkins's emphasis on other cultural features of Jane Austen's England; but this book is assured, graphic, and masterly in weaving in as much of the Georgian context as it does.

Lord David Cecil's *Portrait of Jane Austen*, though not deeply researched, offers a mild and affectionate portrait of the novelist with due attention to her milieux and her "pleasing and reassuring region, with its green smiling landscape" (p. 10). Lord David's style is a great charm, and it is as untroubled as his Jane Austen, who "was at ease in the world she was born into" (p. 10). One feels that the restrained good sense of the biographer saves him from pressing evidence too hard and that if he says too little he is seldom wholly wrong. Scrupulously keeping his distance, always urbane, sometimes insightful, Lord David suggests a woman of unfailing good sense, perhaps a person (as critics of *A Portrait* have said) who could have charmed her family but who could not have written Jane Austen's novels. Lacking here is a probing assessment of her ideas, contradictions, or motivations; but the discriminating estimate of Jane Austen as a comic artist and the cautious and reasonable tone of this donnish and good-tempered book recommend it. *A Portrait* is marred by an unusual number of minor errors (Francis Austen did not go to sea "as an officer" at fourteen, for example, p. 32) but the genteel and cultivated voice of the biographer corresponds to much in the outward temper of the Austens' lives. Rather less convincing is Joan Rees's *Jane Austen: Woman and Writer*, even though it is more accurate in detail; here a shallow portrait has been made out of the novelist's letters. More intelligent is Jane Aiken Hodge's *Double Life of Jane Austen*, which is based on the logical thesis that Jane Austen in private life was a more conventional figure than the woman who, with so much intelligence and art, managed to write the novels. Hodge's book has valuable remarks on Jane Austen and her publishers. Less can be said for Constance Pilgrim's chatty *Dear Jane* or for John Halperin's thinly researched *Life of Jane Austen* (1984), which has many factual errors.

A real advance in the study of the Austens is made in George H. Tucker's brief, fresh, and accurate *Goodly Heritage: A History of Jane Austen's Family*, which makes use, as other studies do, of valuable short works by the Austens or their descendants. Of first importance among these are Henry Austen's "Biographical Notice" of his sister (1818; slightly expanded as "Memoir of Miss Austen," 1832); Caroline Austen's *My Aunt Jane Austen: A Memoir*, which gives belated recognition to the loyal sister who actually wrote part of James Edward's *Memoir* of 1870; and Mary Augusta Austen-Leigh's *Personal Aspects of Jane Austen*. After Jane Austen's death, her favorite nieces quarreled (when Anna failed to sympathize with Fanny's dismay in Kent over the elopement of her brother Edward Knight with Mary Dorothea Knatchbull, the eldest daughter of Fanny's husband Lord Knatchbull by his previous marriage); and Anna's side of the family in turn became suspicious of Francis Austen's daughter, the novelist Mrs. Catherine Hubback; in consequence, Austen-Leighs became anxious to present *their* version of Jane Austen's life and character to the world, while distrusting or neglecting some family evidence about her personality, life at Godmersham, and other relevant matters. Hence, the few publications of descendants of the Austens of Steventon who are not Austen-Leighs have a special value. Frank and Charles Austen, who became admirals, are illuminated in J. H. Hubback and E. C. Hubback's *Jane Austen's Sailor Brothers*, and Catherine Hubback is the focus of "Niece of Miss Austen" (still in typescript) by David and Diana Hopkinson (née Hubback). Good works with biographical data include Constance Hill's *Jane Austen: Her Homes & Her Friends*, Brian Southam's study of her mental development in *Jane Austen's Literary Manuscripts*, and short studies of the author in her locales such as Emma Austen-Leigh's *Jane Austen and Lyme Regis*, R. A. Austen-Leigh's *Jane Austen and Southampton*, Winifred Watson's *Jane Austen in London*, Jean Freeman's *Jane Austen in Bath*, and Anne-Marie Edwards's *In the Steps of Jane Austen*, an intelligent biographical guide for the able walker. The best chronology of her life, keyed to his edition of her *Letters*, is contained in R. W. Chapman's *Jane Austen: Facts and Problems*, a work of notable caution and accuracy, though it confuses Mrs. Bellas (née Louisa Lefroy) with her elder sister Fanny Lefroy (1820–85), from whom it quotes, on pages 64–65). Marghanita Laski's *Jane Austen and Her World* is an intelligent, well-illustrated "coffee-table" life; and Brian Wilks's *Jane Austen* has pictorial value. Park Honan is working on a detailed life of Jane Austen, and others have in progress biographical works relating to the novelist or her family in feminist and other perspectives. In biography, of course, the last word is never said.

Bibliography

AUSTEN, CAROLINE M. C. *My Aunt Jane Austen: A Memoir* (Alton, 1952).
AUSTEN, HENRY. "Biographical Notice" in *Northanger Abbey and Persuasion* (London, 1818, rev. 1832).
AUSTEN-LEIGH, EMMA. *Jane Austen and Lyme Regis* (London, 1946).
AUSTEN-LEIGH, MARY AUGUSTA. *Personal Aspects of Jane Austen* (London, 1920).
AUSTEN-LEIGH, RICHARD ARTHUR. *Jane Austen and Southampton* (London, 1949).
AUSTEN-LEIGH, WILLIAM, AND RICHARD ARTHUR AUSTEN-LEIGH. *Jane Austen: Her Life and Letters, a Family Record* (London, 1913).
CECIL, LORD DAVID. *A Portrait of Jane Austen* (London, 1978).
CHAPMAN, R. W. *Jane Austen: Facts and Problems* (Oxford, 1948).
EDWARDS, ANNE-MARIE. *In the Steps of Jane Austen* (London, 1979).
FREEMAN, JEAN. *Jane Austen in Bath* (Alton, 1969).
HILL, CONSTANCE. *Jane Austen: Her Homes & Her Friends* (London and New York, 1902).
HODGE, JANE AIKEN. *The Double Life of Jane Austen* (London, 1972).
HUBBACK, JOHN H. AND EDITH C. *Jane Austen's Sailor Brothers* (London and New York, 1906).
JENKINS, ELIZABETH. *Jane Austen: A Biography* (London, 1938).
LASCELLES, MARY. *Jane Austen and Her Art* (London, 1939).
LASKI, MARGHANITA. *Jane Austen and Her World* (London and New York, 1969).
REES, JOAN. *Jane Austen: Woman and Writer* (London and New York, 1976).
SOUTHAM, B. C. *Jane Austen's Literary Manuscripts* (London, 1964).

Biographies

TUCKER, GEORGE HOLBERT. *A Goodly Heritage: A History of Jane Austen's Family* (Manchester, Eng., 1983).
WATSON, WINIFRED. *Jane Austen in London* (Alton, 1960).
WILKS, BRIAN. *Jane Austen* (London, 1978).

CHARACTERIZATION IN JANE AUSTEN

John Bayley

Tolstoy always maintained that a novelist must write about the things most important to him, which should also—and for that reason—be the things most important to everyone else. Birth, death, love, marriage, faith and belief, how a man should live: it was as natural for him to be as absorbed by such matters in his art as in his living and thinking. And Tolstoy is only a particularly emphatic example of what the nineteenth century, its great classic period, came to take for granted where the novel was concerned.

There is a natural logic about this, because the novel, an art form that had not previously been taken seriously, came in the course of the century to seem the natural vehicle for discussion and ventilation of what most mattered in life. For Dickens such seriousness was everything, and yet Dickens was writing for a wide popular audience that had to be kept interested in installments from week to week. Seriousness, in his sense, was quite compatible both with popularity and with sensationalism. But for Jane Austen things were rather different. Seriousness for her was a matter of literary propriety, of grafting the received morality of eighteenth-century literature—sermons, poems, and essays—onto the novel form. Her originality as a novelist had nothing to do with this kind of seriousness.

And this seems to be the key to the way in which she creates her characters. However much alive they may be or become, she is not deeply and seriously involved with them in the sense in which Tolstoy or George Eliot were; in the way that even Dickens was when he absorbed himself in the fortunes of Little Nell or Oliver Twist, Pip or David Copperfield. It is often said or implied not only by thoughtful readers such as Richard Simpson in the latter part of the nineteenth century but by such critics as Mary Lascelles and C. S. Lewis in our own time that Jane Austen is earnest in revealing the development of her heroines, as if, like Dickens's Pip, they were intimate studies in the growth of self-knowledge.

Henry James has often been cited for his unexpected obtuseness in referring to her lack of pondered idea, leaving us no more conscious of her process than of "the brown thrush who sings his song." In fact, this image of spontaneity is by no means infelicitous, suggesting it does the high spirits with which Jane Austen sees her characters, understanding them by not inquiring too closely and not making a show of establishing the grounds of inquiry. However "deeply studied and elaborately justified," George Eliot's characters are not, for Henry James, "seen in the irresponsible plastic way." James touches here on the crux of the matter. Jane Austen does not study her characters but enjoys them. And she enjoys them in two ways.

In the first place, they are people who excite humor. It is surely essential, even now, to state that she values her characters above all for their humorous potential. Humor in her case, of course, means a great deal more than being funny, displaying comic characters who make us smile. Although she scarcely could have been aware of it consciously herself, humor for Jane Austen and her art is the ground of existence. By being ludicrous, we survive and endure: the virtuous possibilities of human existence are for her all involved in the sense of absurdity. Since her work has been so widely admired and her stature as a novelist so fully accepted, we have had eloquent essays about her moral vision and weighty analyses of her perception of social and personal values. These can be very illuminating, particularly when done by such thoughtful critics as Lionel Trilling or Denis Donoghue, for much matter for the intelligence and the intellect follows from her peculiar genius for the absurd. Yet such studies have the grave drawback of assuming that Jane Austen was herself intellectually original, incisive, even profound. This she was not, and never attempted to be.

It is true that she plays into the hands of the modern critic by taking what might be called an "interest in ideas" and assuming, with an innate modesty, that the novel should be a vehicle for moral and social demonstration and improvement. That was a tradition she took for granted. She leaned most heavily here, perhaps, on Samuel Richardson, her great progenitor. But just as Richardson himself had concealed, however unconsciously, the true impetus and the real fascination of his writings—their grasp of sex and power and of the reader's avid response to these matters —and concealed them in the proper conventions of literary and moral culture, so Jane Austen, with an equal lack of hypocrisy or intention, enlisted under the same moral and literary tradition.

She worked its method conscientiously, for her genius was quite compatible with it, though also quite separate. And of course she *was* serious, in her own way. She took her art very seriously indeed, labored at it, sought eagerly for others' opinions about it. But this kind of seriousness is very different from that attributed to her by her modern critics. She was not a morally imaginative explorer; she went along with what other people thought. Her seriousness as a novelist is intimately connected with her own secret, life-giving pleasure in the absurdity of human existence.

Naturally, "absurdity" does not have here its modern existentialist sense. The comic is for Jane Austen the saving grace of life, the comfort of it, the irradiation of the sympathetic and the human. "I am comical, therefore I exist" might be the Cartesian formula underlying her sense of her personages and of her own self, too, her self as artist. This basic perception of her being seems to me so obvious as to be something taken for granted; and yet it is, surprisingly, ignored or even denied by many of Jane Austen's most important and most intelligent critics. They talk of her wit, her irony, the sharpness of her eye and ear, and the keen edge of her pen, but they are apt to pass over the fact that not only is she humorous, but also her successful characters embody that humor and achieve their reality by means of it.

The liveliest are both comic themselves and keenly aware of comedy, although this awareness is never conscious or superior. Indeed, one of the secrets of Jane Austen's art is to deprive humor of the superiority of those who are continually aware of it. As with Falstaff, her sense of humor is the reason why the same sense is in others. It makes her modest rather than exclusive. We would not value her art so highly or find her characters so attractive if she deliberately set out to substitute her own style of comic vision for the traditional modes of the novel. It is because she is so obedient to the idea of precept and moral demonstration that her art reveals its real independence of them.

This point was intuited by Thomas H. Lister in his anonymous review of Harriet Martineau's novel *Deerbrook (Edinburgh Review*, 1839) in which he compared the two artists. "Miss Austin [sic] is like one who plays by ear, while Miss Martineau understands the science. Miss Austin has the air of being led to right conclusions by an intuitive tact—Miss Martineau unfolds her knowledge of the principles on which her correct judgment is founded" (Southam, p. 121). There could hardly be a deadlier though more inadvertent disclosure of the difference between a major artist and a very minor one. Miss Martineau does indeed "unfold her principles"; she sets them, and herself, busily before us on every page. Jane Austen conceals herself and her interests and convictions behind the perfect conventionality of principles and morals that lend her novels their appropriate weight but none of the creative magic.

A clear example is her first wholly successful heroine, Catherine Morland in *Northanger Abbey*. Her two earliest heroines, Elinor and Marianne in *Sense and Sensibility*, are constructed from principles that invade their speech and behavior to such an extent that the second never achieves the true status of a Jane Austen character, and the first only precariously. The story enlivens them in its onward movement, and so do their mother and the John Dashwoods, but they remain derivative of Jane Austen's models and lack that potential for and of the absurd that is the clue to the success of her main characters, heroines included. Catherine Morland is the prototype of all her heroines, and she probably arrived almost by accident, however much she may owe to Fanny Burney's Evelina and other ingenues of the eighteenth century. The vitality of Catherine derives from her combination of instinctive sense, taste, and humanity in all detailed social contexts—Emma Watson of the fragment *The Watsons* has the same kind of spontaneity—and her extreme and engaging silliness in relation to art and life in general. The imagination that informs the novel seems unawares to have seen and developed the link between silliness and goodness. Catherine's illusions form a natural incongruity with her equally unreflecting goodness. Jane Austen has hit upon the way to portray a virtuous heroine without the slightest symptom of priggishness and without any of the lack of naturalness caused by adherence to "principle." Marianne and even Elinor Dashwood are cardboard figures beside Catherine Morland.

Indeed, so potentially successful is Catherine that Elizabeth Bennet develops from her, and Emma brings her promise to full and perfect fruition. The most interesting thing about Emma as a character is the way in which Jane Austen sets her vitality against the almost overpowering commonplaceness of her daily living, in the past and in the future. This is Jane Austen at her most "natural," that is to say, the point at which her art is most effectively in harmony with what she knew and experienced in life. The consciousness of her heroines dominates the fools (who are never allowed to get out of hand) because it knows and accepts how much it depends itself on triviality. The difference between Emma and Elizabeth, on the one hand, and Mr. Collins, Lady Catherine de Bourgh, the Eltons, and Mr. Woodhouse, on the other, is that whereas the latter are entirely absorbed in the trivial, which they exemplify, Elizabeth and Emma transcend it by their very awareness of its life-giving essentiality.

The use Jane Austen makes of the process can be seen in its first schematic form in some of the rather laborious conversations in *Sense and Sensibility* between Elinor and her brother John Dashwood. His anxiety to appear poor in order not to have to help his sisters is set forth in Jane Austen's most artfully ludicrous vein; but Elinor becomes the stock figure in a satiric exercise, the figure whose sense and discernment act as the gauge and scale of folly. This stereotyping is the more marked because Jane Austen's ear for absurdity is already unerring, and she knows just how to exaggerate it to the right pitch, as when Dashwood deplores the fact that his father left his household linen and china to his mother and sisters: "Far be it from me to repine at his doing so; he had an undoubted right to dispose of his own property as he chose" (p. 225).

The insipid orotundity of those phrases places John Dashwood fairly in the tradition of English comic satire. "Far be it from me" is a locution perfect in its character and context, but so it would be, too, for a Dickens character like Mr. Chadband. The tendency is for the figure of comic satire to become the main, indeed the true, center of animation in the novel, leaving little interest to the rational characters who act as a foil to him and a gauge of his absurdity. This is so usual a result of comic method, as it is handed down from Smollett to Dickens and beyond, that it becomes almost an acceptable and expected tradition, allying the novel to the stage of comedy. It was instinctive for Jane Austen to use it at first, but it was another and surer instinct of her genius to transform it, as she did, into a wholly different method of uniting the characters and discourse of a fiction into a harmony that discards the oppositional method of satire and with it the open demonstration of moral principles. In her mature fiction Jane Austen has discarded both the cipher figure who stands for principle and the figure of folly or vacuity who engrosses the vitality of the story by displaying these satirized characteristics.

We can catch the contexts of transition now and again in *Sense and Sensibility*, the novel that, by being the first she worked on, reveals most about the nature of things to come. Elinor Dashwood's sister Marianne, the "sensibility" figure of the novel, can only be convinced of the way things are by "better knowledge of mankind" (p. 261). This is bald enough, but it is emphasized by Jane Austen's inability to detach Marianne from her function as the representative of sensibility other than by manipulating her arbitrarily into such "knowledge" and by demonstrating in Dr. Johnson's vein how she acquires it. She and Elinor converse like two exemplary ladies in a *Rambler* essay, and in these conversations Elinor herself, as representative of "sense," becomes as wholly formal and artificial in her function as her sister. But when Elinor is faced with one of the absurd figures of the fiction, she begins to come alive, and Jane Austen achieves this by relating her, in a subtle way, to the world of comic triviality. Instead of acting as the rational foil to Robert Ferrars's tales of how he persuaded his grand friends to follow his advice, she capitulates to his world of absurdity with a compliance that is in itself quietly comic. "Elinor agreed to it all, for she did not think he deserved the compliment of rational opposition" (p. 252).

At once Elinor herself becomes human, with a full humanity lacking in the caricatures like Robert but present in her because of her reaction to him. The notion of rationality itself becomes comic because of Elinor's drolly resigned inability to exercise it. The moment looks forward to Emma's exchanges with her father in which the spirit of comic truth and comic redemption descends equally on both of them by virtue of the fact that they belong together without the need for argument or comprehension. After an exchange about marriage, and the respect due to brides, Mr. Woodhouse becomes a little agitated and says to his daughter, "My dear, you do not understand me." What follows has the logic of real comedy. "Emma had done. Her father was growing nervous, and could not understand *her*" (p. 280).

In terms of Jane Austen's art of characterization, the exchange is a crucial one. Not only do the "caricatures" not understand the "characters," but the incomprehension is now admitted to be mutual. No longer do reader, author, and primary character unite in forming the scale of reason against which the John Dashwoods, Mr. Collinses, and Miss Bateses perform their amusing and predictable antics. The world is no longer divided, along the lines of conventional comedy, into those who provide the mockery and those who have the superiority of enjoying it.

This, perhaps, is the real significance of the famous episode with Miss Bates on Box Hill, where Emma treats her openly with the kind of mockery that author, reader, and heroine have always been apt implicitly to share. The result is the diminution of Emma's own high spirits; she feels wretchedly dull and depressed, and book and reader suffer with her. It is a signal instance of the way in which the withdrawal of the comic spirit, which is the inspiration and animation of her characters, reveals the vulnerability of those who assume they direct it. They must be mockable themselves if they are the cause of mockery's being enjoyed in relation to others.

The mature heroines are therefore, like the dyer's hand in Shakespeare's sonnet, subdued to what they have to work in and with, the trivialities and diversions and preoccupations that make up the world in which they can exist as creatures of Jane Austen's art. Sometimes these conditions almost parody themselves as part of the humor extracted by that art from the small repetitive business of living. There is a whole perspective of comedy in the remark that Emma makes to Harriet Smith about the way of life she may expect to be enjoying if she still remains a spinster at fifty. "Woman's usual occupations of eye and hand and mind will be open to me then, as they are now. . . . If I draw less, I shall read more; if I give up music, I shall take to carpet work" (p. 85).

There is a comic contrast (the word ironic, too often used in Jane Austen's context, is seldom suited to it) between this vision and the actual pleasure we are obtaining in the society of Emma. "Woman's usual occupations of eye and hand and mind" are transformed by the text and then abruptly brought into contact with the world outside it. Emma's merry presentation of herself as a spinster at fifty not only reveals the actual anxieties and hopes she must be entertaining about herself in relation to a woman's possible destinies but also brings before the reader a kind of continuous Emma, outside time, untroubled by what its necessities may bring to a woman but which the text itself cannot share.

The reading and the "carpet work" imply a cheerful acceptance of life as it has to be lived in this world. The riches of the novel are themselves gently mocked by reference to the repetitive monotonies that lie behind them. Most implicit in the comedy, however, is the feeling that this Emma at fifty would be still our Emma, still able to take part in a novel that the author could produce and she as heroine play in. Such a novel would be, it slyly assures us, the literary equivalent of carpet work and the like, an occupation for eye and mind with which we are thoroughly familiar, comfortable, and at home. If Emma, on the other hand, were to marry like Elizabeth Bennet, the novel would have nothing to say about her; her status as heroine would have gone irretrievably, together with the eye and mind that have been creating themselves for us in the novel's world.

All this and more lies behind Emma's playful words, words that reveal with the most realistic clarity Jane Austen's outlook and methods as a mature artist. It could be said that her problem is to bring the "carpet work" of her comedy—with all its truth of small daily events and absurdities—as close as possible to the larger events that lie outside it: work and business, birth, death, and marriage. Our sense of these things must not contrast with the comedy and be revealed as the mere artificial mechanism of plot and story but must be enhanced by the comedy and acquire from it its own background reality. This would be another way of saying that in Jane Austen's mature art there is no distinction between character and caricature but that the fools who are laughed at, and the persons of sense and sensibility who laugh at them with us, are united—as we ourselves are—in a common absorption in the banalities of existence.

In *Emma* the process is seen at its most artful, an art that wholly dissolves the distinction that D. W. Harding made in his essay "Character and Caricature in Jane Austen." No novel gets more enjoyment out of the submission of all parties to the long littleness of life; and we may remember that Emma's contemplation of her future in carpet work at the age of fifty recalls the chief pastime of the widowed Mrs. Jennings in *Sense and Sensibility*. No doubt the Bateses, too, mother and daughter, are redoubtable practitioners of the craft. Jane Austen's finest achievement is to make us in love in art with what might appear most wearisome, tedious, and petty in living, with what we have to do every day and prefer to forget.

The key to her characters, therefore, is their immersion for art's sake in the tedium of existence. Where most novelists have to heighten the feeling of living in the interests of their art, Jane Austen deliberately lowers it and, by doing so, gives its quotidian dullness an unexampled vitality. Her lively sense of the ridiculous makes all kinds of tedium amusing, and we smile at the thought of the conversation at Cleveland (*SS*) "which a long morning of the same continued rain had reduced very low" (p. 304). Not the extravagances but the deprivations of being are the deepest spring of her comedy, and she realized this in the ways an artist does. When she remarked to her sister that *Pride and Prejudice* wanted light and shade, had too much brilliancy about it, she professed the intention of writing on more serious topics, questions of "ordination" and of "principles" (*Letters*, January 29, 1813). What actually takes place is the installation of dullness in the place of honor, the foreground of the next novel. From this solid posture it makes everything else in *Mansfield Park* as real and solid. The humdrum comfort of the sofa encompasses both Fanny Price and Lady Bertram, and when Fanny goes to her mother in Portsmouth, the humdrum takes a more virulently comic form, which helps to give a touching kind of truth and vitality to Fanny herself. Mansfield Park, that abode of insipid and sleepy decorum, seems to her a romantic paradise compared to the sordid facts of life in a Portsmouth tenement. Such touches thoroughly humanize Fanny, and in just the same way that the forlorn situation of Anne, in *Persuasion*, rests upon a comic rather than a tragic basis. The heart of Anne's situation is to be compelled to share a small sofa with the large Mrs. Musgrove and listen to her lamentations. Her deprived and isolated state appears all the more poignantly in the background from the fact that it is foregrounded in comic tedium.

In *Mansfield Park* there are penalties to be paid for the inspired move into monotony as a comic principle. Its funniest manifestation in the novel is the appearance of Sir Thomas Bertram, blandly uncomprehending, in the drawing room at Mansfield where all the excitement of the theatricals is going forward. Victorian connoisseurs of Jane Austen used to deplore the fact that those rehearsals, with all their possibilities of a comic *scène à faire*, were so abruptly cut off. Modern critics, less robust and more anxious to demonstrate Jane Austen's fine moral discriminations, are eloquent on the significance of her disapproval of the acting and performing ego. The real reason is surely that anticlimax is for her much more full of comic potential than any number of big scenes. She brings the theater business to a hilarious close by confronting it with all the natural dullness of restored Mansfield routine.

The penalty, however, is that the characters who represent rebellion against that routine cannot share in its life-giving powers, the reality conferred by the comic principle of humdrum monotony. Leaving aside the hopeless case of Willoughby in *Sense and Sensibility*, even the much more subtle and comprehensive picture of the Crawfords in *Mansfield Park* suffers from the inability of her art to draw them inside its charmed circle of comic boredom. Jane Austen's eye for the ridiculous is happy with them in the theatrical connection, but her mature vision can find no compromise between enjoying the Crawfords as adding to the gaiety of life and dismissing them to the fate of caricatures for their bad principles and shocking want of decency. By being as interesting as they are, the Crawfords show how genuine, and in a sense how honest, are Jane Austen's limitations where character is concerned. She will not "explore" a character, and if she suggests ambivalence—as in the case of the Crawfords—she is quick to sacrifice them to plot and to fall back on simplistic commentary. "Let other pens than mine dwell on guilt and misery..." (p. 461). It is not just a formula for winding up the fiction, however; it is entirely true to Jane Austen's own wishes and preferences. Other pens than hers must equally dwell on passion and consummation. She dismisses her heroines equally along with her wrongdoers, without a peep into their future or a suggestion that they possess one. Comedy abandons them, but the leave-taking is itself part of the comic mode.

In *Sense and Sensibility*, in fact, it is only at the end that comedy comes into its own. As she prepares to take leave and is no longer weighed down by the responsibilities of demonstrating the behavior of the sensible and the sensitive girl, the author's eyes begin to sparkle. Elinor, along with her mother, has by now been fully humanized by the intimacy of humor, but we can see the precise moment at which she, too, is abandoned to humor of a different sort, the objective and no longer intimate flourish of high spirits. Elinor's meeting with Edward Ferrars produces "a most promising state of embarrassment" (p. 288), and when the plot has arranged matters and he can declare his feelings, embarrassment is still the best indication of the author's kindness, the understanding of them that writing her novel has produced. "When Elinor had ceased to rejoice in the dryness of the season, a very awful pause took place" (p. 359).

This is the same kindness with which Jane Austen regards Catherine Morland, after Henry Tilney has come to propose, but it is the kindness of leave-taking. The marriages of Elinor and Marianne take second place, in the winding up of the novel, to comedy's pleasure in the vigor and cunning with which Lucy Steele, now Mrs. Robert Ferrars, gets herself back into the good graces of her mother-in-law and establishes herself as indispensable in that sphere of watchful imbecility and competitive conceit of which she is the type and paramount.

There is no need for Jane Austen to have to pass judgment on Lucy, as she has to do on the Crawfords, and the ending of *Sense and Sensibility*, in its spontaneous high spirits, is more natural to her art than the adjustments that have to be made at the end of *Mansfield Park*. So misleading is D. W. Harding's concept of "regulated hatred" as informing the comedy of her work that it would be truer to see her natural high spirits, so abundant at the end of *Sense and Sensibility* and *Northanger Abbey*, having to be regulated by the more sober conceptions she undertook in *Mansfield Park* and *Persuasion* and being freely indulged again, at the end of her writing life, in the composition of *Sanditon*.

Emma, the heroine "whom nobody but myself will like" (*Memoir*, p. 157), of course fits most harmoniously the play of these high spirits and their natural pleasure in limitation. Significantly, it is the only novel in which Jane Austen can remain with her heroine, rejoicing in the swaddled humor of her situation, with her invalid father, the husband who will be a second sort of father, the house and village from which she will never move. Here is limitation enough to satisfy even Jane Austen's art and enough implicit absurdity to feed it forever. For its intelligence and high spirits require their opposites to work on, and Emma in her situation is the symbol and social paradigm of that work in progress. By opposing Emma's high spirit and intelligence to the utter banality of her life, Jane Austen reveals the heart of her own formula and the way in which humor is for her characterization not only the medium of the moral life but of the romantic life, as well. Without it, neither affection nor "principles" can be made convincing in fictional terms.

Reality itself depends on it. When he deplores Jane Austen's refusal to draw more upon the other kinds of life she knew, to introduce her heroines into more varied and worldly social scenes and more extended opportunities, Angus Wilson takes for granted that fiction has always the duty and the need to bring everything in, to expand to the limits of observation. Jane Austen no doubt knew, felt, and saw more than she wrote about, but this gives a special compression and quality to what she *did* write about. Into banality itself she can put a kick like the strongest drink: she never coyly compounds, as Mrs. Gaskell and other women writers were to do, for insipidity and coziness of manner by implying that cozy and homely subjects required them. There is nothing in the least homely about any of her characters.

Her plots, of which the leading characters form a part, give them an extraordinary sense of *potential*. It matters not that nothing but the most ordinary married state awaits them; for the duration of the novel they enjoy as much vividness and variety of consciousness as if they were taking part in a Shakespeare play. Potentiality is closely tied to limitation; nor would it be misleading to claim that for Jane Austen both are aspects of the romantic life, the life that relates to reverie, speculation, and daydream. The principal fascination of all her heroines is the gap between the play of their consciousness and the conditions under which they live. In *Jane Austen: A Study of Her Artistic Development*, A. Walton Litz quotes from the eighteenth-century philosopher Shaftesbury an extremely significant sentence, on which Jane Austen's eye may have rested more than once. "The natural free spirits of ingenious men, if imprisoned and controlled, will find out other ways of motion to relieve themselves in their constraint." Her characters exemplify the link between such an observation and the romantic sensibilities of her own time. She made her own kind of use of them, and a unique one.

Philip Larkin has noted a similar quality—the quality of "innocent irony"—in the work of a novelist whose unpretentious but altogether outstanding art has contrived to make the best possible use of Jane Austen's—Barbara Pym. In her novels, too, the heroines live in a world of comic limitation and potential wonder, whereas other fictional heroines of our time appear to have drained all experience—sensory and intellectual, sexual or marital—to the dregs before the novels in which they figure are well under way.

Bibliography

DONOGHUE, DENIS. "A View of *Mansfield Park*," in B. C. Southam, ed., *Critical Essays on Jane Austen* (London, 1968), 39–59.

HARDING, D. W. "Regulated Hatred: An Aspect of the Work of Jane Austen," *Scrutiny*, 8 (1939–40), 346–62.

———. "Character and Caricature in Jane Austen," in B. C. Southam, ed., *Critical Essays on Jane Austen* (London, 1968), 83–105.

JAMES, HENRY. "The Lesson of Balzac" (1905), in Leon Edel, ed., *The House of Fiction* (London, 1957), 60–85.

LASCELLES, MARY. *Jane Austen and Her Art* (London, 1939).

LEWIS, C. S. "A Note on Jane Austen," *Essays in Criticism*, 4 (1954), 359–71.

LISTER, THOMAS H. Review of Harriet Martineau's *Deerbrook* (1839), excerpted in B. C. Southam, ed., *Jane Austen: The Critical Heritage* (London and New York, 1968), 121.

LITZ, A. WALTON. *Jane Austen: A Study of Her Artistic Development* (London and New York, 1965).

SIMPSON, RICHARD. Review of the *Memoir*, reprinted in B. C. Southam, ed., *Jane Austen: The Critical Heritage* (London and New York, 1968), 241–65.

TRILLING, LIONEL. "In Mansfield Park," in his *The Opposing Self* (London and New York, 1955), 206–30.

———. "*Emma* and the Legend of Jane Austen," in his *Beyond Culture* (London and New York, 1965), 31–55.

CHAWTON

J. David Grey

In Saxon times, under Edward the Confessor, Chawton—"Celtone" in the Domesday Book and later "Chauton"—was owned by Oda de Wincestre. Since the reign of William the Conqueror, only two successions of families have held the property, each for four and a half centuries. The first line bore the names of de Port (later St. John), Poynings, Bonville, and West (the De La Warrs). In 1524 William Knight, the first of the other line, rented the property. His grandson purchased the land, Manor and Advowson, and built the present house in about 1585. This is the Great House as it is seen today, only a few minor additions having been made in the eighteenth century. No traces remain of any pre-sixteenth-century buildings, although there was probably a hall on the site as far back as 1224. The Knights, successively, became Lewkenors, Martins, Mays, Brodnaxes, and finally Knights again before Edward Austen, Jane's brother, was adopted by his second cousin around 1790. He inherited the estates of Godmersham (Kent) and Chawton on the latter's death and assumed the name Knight himself on the death of his cousin's widow in 1812.

Edward's own wife had died in 1808. Perhaps to have his mother and sisters close by or perhaps because their quarters in Southampton, which they shared with the Francis Austens, were undoubtedly cramped, he offered them the option of homes either near his estate in Kent (at Wye) or at Chawton, where he occasionally stayed. Mrs. Austen, Cassandra, and Jane had visited Chawton Manor in September 1807, so they were familiar with the neighborhood. Their former residence was at Steventon, seventeen miles away, which may have influenced their choice to remain in Hampshire. In a letter to Cassandra (October 24, 1808) Jane Austen wrote: "everything you say about [Chawton] in the letter now before me will, I am sure, as soon as I am able to read it to her, make my mother consider the plan with more and more pleasure." In the opinion of her nephew, "during the temporary residence of the party at Bath and Southampton she was only a sojourner in a strange land; but here [at Chawton] she found a real home amongst her own people" (*Memoir*, 2nd ed., p. 79). Cassandra looked over the "cottage" in February 1809, and the move was accomplished in July of that year. The three Austen women were joined by Martha Lloyd, who became Francis Austen's second wife in 1828. Three weeks after the move, Jane expressed her feelings, in verse, to her brother Francis (July 26, 1809):

> As for ourselves, we're very well;
> As unaffected prose will tell.—
> Cassandra's pen will paint our state,
> The many comforts that await
> Our Chawton home, how much we find
> Already in it, to our mind;
> And how convinced, that when complete
> It will all other Houses beat
> That ever have been made or mended,
> With rooms concise, or rooms distended.
> You'll find us very snug next year,
> Perhaps with Charles & Fanny near,
> For now it often does delight us
> To fancy them just over-right us.

Charles was Jane's second seagoing brother, and "over-right" would place him at Chawton Manor; indeed, he did stay there, but not until 1811.

The village of Chawton is located on the north chalk downs about a mile south of Alton and fifty miles from London. It is near the source of the Wey in an area that is loosely referred to by The Knight chroniclers (in *Chawton Manor & Its Owners*) as the valley of the Thames. In medieval times the Pilgrim's Way passed through Chawton and Alton, and the district "was known to have been for a very long period of time the resort of robbers" (Austen-Leigh and Knight, p. 14). In Langland's poem *Piers Plowman*, Peace is described as being robbed on his way to Winchester Fair:

> Ye, through the pass of Aultone
> Poverte myght passe
> Withouten peril of robbynge,
> For where poverte may pass,
> Peace followeth after. (p. 15)

With the exception of a lower crime rate, little has changed in the village over the centuries. The recent construction of a motor bypass has probably rendered it even quieter than it was in the days of Jane Austen. (Her niece, Caroline Austen, in 1867 was already calling it "tranquillized.") Her house is situated at the *Y* juncture of the Portsmouth and Winchester/London roads where, across the way and in the crux of the *Y*, there was a good-sized pond until it was drained for sanitary reasons early in this century. The constant noise from private vehicles and horses, day and night, was punctuated periodically by the clamor surrounding the passing of six daily coaches. There were two from Winchester, morning and evening, the evening coach drawn by six horses, and one from Portsmouth at noon.

The number of habitations listed in the Domesday Book had not, by

1753, significantly increased. The names they bear today were surely familiar to Jane Austen, and the simplicity of them gives evidence to their antiquity: Malt House Cottages, Elm Cottage, Clinkers, Prowtings Farm, Pond Farm, Old and New Park Farms, and the like.

Jane Austen's house, according to R. W. Chapman (p. vii), would in her day be more logically dubbed the "Small House." It was built during the reign of William III (early Georgian, say some authorities) as a posting inn and alehouse and served as such until Edward Knight's bailiff and steward inhabited it:

> The front door opened on the road. . . . A good-sized entrance and two parlours, called dining and drawing room, made up the length of the house, all intended originally to look on the road, but the large drawing-room window was blocked up [to shut out the noise from the traffic] and turned into a bookcase . . . and another was opened at the side which gave to view only turf and trees. A high wooden fence shut out the road (to Winchester) all the length of the little domain, and trees were planted inside to form a shrubbery walk which, carried round the enclosure, gave a very sufficient space for exercise. . . . There was a pleasant irregular mixture of hedgerow and grass and gravel walk, and long grass for mowing, and Orchard. . . . There was besides, a good kitchen garden; large and many out buildings, not much occupied. . . . Everything indoors and out, was well kept, the house was well furnished, and it was altogether a comfortable ladylike establishment. . . . The house was quite as good as the generality of Parsonage Houses then were, and much in the same style, the ceilings low and roughly finished, some bedrooms very small, none very large.

This description was written by Caroline and appears in Mary Augusta Austen-Leigh's *Personal Aspects of Jane Austen* (pp. 139–41). What sort of kitchen garden it was is left to the imagination, but at least there is an answer to Jane's query of October 24, 1808: "Is there a kitchen garden?" And she was relieved to learn there were actually six bedrooms—"just what we wanted to be assured of. [Henry] speaks also of Garrets for store-places" (November 20, 1808).

Her life at Chawton was routine. "At 9 o'clock she made breakfast—*that* was *her* part of the household work—The tea and sugar stores were under *her* charge—*and* the wine—Aunt Cassandra did all the rest" (Caroline Austen, p. 7). She practiced the piano in the morning, one suspects to gather her thoughts. Shopping was done in Alton, a short walk and later a donkey-cart ride, down Mounter's Lane. There were walks to Chawton Park, "a noble wood," and visits to her niece Anna, now Mrs. Ben Lefroy, at Wyards Farm. "They had no carriage, and their visitings did not extend far—there were a few families living in the village—but no great intimacy was kept up with any of them—they were upon *friendly* but rather *distant* terms, with all" (ibid., pp. 7–8). "It was a very quiet life," writes Miss Lefroy, "according to our ideas, but they were great readers, and besides the housekeeping our aunts occupied themselves in working for the poor and in teaching some boy or girl to read or write" (quoted in Hill, pp. 177–78).

Both sisters apparently kept a watchful eye on the Great House and its tenants (for five years, the Middletons) for Edward. Jane Austen reports to Cassandra, then on one of her frequent and long visits to Godmersham, on the completion of its chimneys and seems to disapprove of Mr. Tilson's grief that the trees in Chawton Park "should not be turned into money" (June 6, 1811). To Francis Austen she commends Edward for his plans to make a new garden: he "is very well & enjoys himself as thoroughly as any Hampshire born Austen can desire. Chawton is not thrown away upon him" (July 3, 1813). Writing herself from Godmersham, she tells Cassandra that Edward "is very much obliged to you for your attention to everything" (October 11, 1813), in this case the construction of a new "Coin," and "wants to be expressly told that all the Round Tower &c. is entirely down, & the door from the Best room stopt up" (October 14, 1813).

One of the most pleasant periods at Chawton was the occasion of the Knights' five-month stay at the Great House while their home in Kent was being painted. Edward brought his entire family. Jane Austen writes: "The pleasure to us of having them here is so great, that if we were not the best creatures in the World we should not deserve it.—We go on in the most comfortable way, very frequently dining together, & always meeting in some part of every day" (July 3, 1813). She certainly welcomed the chance to spend so much time with her favorite niece and confidante, Fanny, who was then approaching the age of twenty.

In the summer of 1813 Jane Austen was putting the finishing touches on *Mansfield Park*; *Sense and Sensibility* had sold out its first edition that year, and *Pride and Prejudice* had been published in January. She was at her peak. It is most significant that all six novels emanated from the house at Chawton. The first three were revised and the remaining composed there in surroundings that she must have felt most conducive to expressing her talents. Sudden warnings from a creaking door that promoted an effort to secrete hurriedly the sheets of paper on which she was inscribing literary history—this was the milieu that suited her genius. "My Aunt's life at Chawton, as far as I ever knew, was an easy and pleasant one—it had very little variety in it, and I am not aware of any particular trials, till her own health began to fail—" (Caroline Austen, p. 11).

Jane Austen left Chawton for the last time in May 1817. Her mother and sister passed the rest of their lives in the cottage and are buried in the churchyard of St. Nicholas. After Cassandra's death in 1845 it was divided into three tenements. Her nephew wrote: "The public generally take some interest in the residence of a popular writer . . . but I cannot recommend any admirer of Jane Austen to undertake a pilgrimage to this spot. The building indeed still stands, but divested of everything which gave it character" (*Memoir*, 1st ed., p. 105).

An American visitor in 1893 states that "one end [of the cottage] is devoted to the use of a laborers' club. What was once the Austen drawing-room, where 'Emma' and 'Persuasion' were written, is now a reading room, furnished with rough chairs and tables; and one or two laborers were going in and out as I entered the room" (Adams, p. 604). After World War II an appeal was raised that drew £1,500 from both sides of the Atlantic. T. Edward Carpenter bought the house for £3,000 in 1948 and presented it to the Jane Austen Society in memory of his son, who was killed in action in 1944. The funds raised earlier were used to refurbish the interior, and it was formally opened to the public on July 23, 1949. The society's Annual General Meeting is held on the grounds of Chawton Manor every July on the Saturday nearest to the date of her death, July 18.

Edward Austen Knight's eldest son took up residence at the Great House in 1826 and lived there until his death in 1879, Godmersham having been sold in 1874. In 1951 the houses in the village, which then still belonged to the Chawton estate, were auctioned off, most of the buyers being sitting tenants. The prices fetched were low, in the vicinity of £150: "One man paid more for the television set in his cottage than for the cottage itself."

Bibliography

ADAMS, OSCAR FAY. "In the Footsteps of Jane Austen," *The New England Magazine*, n.s. 8 (1893), 594–608.
ANONYMOUS. "Chawton House, Hants, the Seat of Mr. M. G. Knight," *Country Life*, 13 (1903), 874–81.
———. "Jane Austen and Chawton," *Times Literary Supplement* (29 July 1949), 489.
AUSTEN, CAROLINE. *My Aunt Jane Austen* (Alton, 1952).
AUSTEN-LEIGH, MARY AUGUSTA. *Personal Aspects of Jane Austen* (London, 1920).
AUSTEN-LEIGH, WILLIAM AND KNIGHT, MONTAGU GEORGE. *Chawton Manor and Its Owners* (London, 1911).
CARPENTER, THOMAS EDWARD. *The Story of Jane Austen's Home* (Chawton, 1954). This has been revised and reissued, in 1983, by the then curator, John Coates, as *Jane Austen's Chawton Home*.
CHAPMAN, R. W. *Jane Austen: Facts and Problems* (Oxford, 1948).
HILL, CONSTANCE. *Jane Austen: Her Homes & Her Friends* (New York and London, 1902).

Jane Austen

Hussey, Christopher. "Chawton House, Hampshire," *Country Life*, 97 (1945), 200–203, 244–47.

Jane Austen Society. "Jane Austen and Jane Austen's Home," *Collected Reports of the Jane Austen Society, 1949–1965* (London, 1967), 1–12. (Cf. also: "Chawton in 1753" by Barbara Carpenter Turner, pp. 11–13.)

CHILDREN

J. David Grey

"A family of ten children will be always called a fine family, where there are heads and arms and legs enough for the number" (*Northanger Abbey*, p. 13).

In England in the eighteenth century children were not considered members of the adult world either in real life or in fiction. The period during which Jane Austen was writing was a transitional one in respects other than those exemplified in the development of her unique prose style. Social behavior was in the process of change, and so was the attitude of society toward the acceptability of a position for children within its precincts. An eighteenth-century child, for instance, would never have attended a ball.

Jane Austen gives significance to children in both her major and minor works. In 1920 her great-niece, Mary Augusta Austen-Leigh, wrote:

> [Her children] provide motives for action and conversation on the part of their elders, and are even allowed on one occasion to take a small share in the carrying on of the plot . . . If we try to imagine Jane Austen's novels deprived of their children, we shall see that in some cases they could hardly be carried on at all, while in every instance that sense of simple truthfulness, of warmth, and of life which they now possess would be greatly lessened or altogether wanting. (pp. 115–16)

Appearances of children in *Sense and Sensibility* are intrinsic to the plot. Four-year-old Henry Dashwood is in fact the unconscious villain of the piece:

> in occasional visits with his father and mother [John and Fanny Dashwood] at Norland [to their uncle Dashwood, he] had so far gained on the affections of his [great] uncle, by such attractions as are by no means unusual in children of two or three years old; an imperfect articulation, an earnest desire of having his own way, many cunning tricks, and a great deal of noise. (*Sense and Sensibility*, p. 4)

Little Harry eventually provides a convenient excuse for retiring his step-grandmother and young aunts to Barton. The Middletons, cousins at Barton Park, have four children, and Jane Austen shows no compunction toward displaying them in her typical innovative manner. Sir John and

Lady Middleton bring their eldest, John, to welcome their distant cousins to Barton Cottage: "On every formal visit a child ought to be of the party, by way of provision for discourse" (*Sense and Sensibility*, p. 31). The visit is returned the next day, and "Lady Middleton seemed to be roused to enjoyment only by the entrance of her four noisy children after dinner, who pulled her about, tore her clothes, and put an end to every kind of discourse except what related to themselves" (p. 34). Deference to their obstreperousness, allied with the customary discussion of the boys' relative heights, is later used to underscore the sycophancy of the Steele sisters. It is this doting attendance on the children that gives Elinor and Marianne the clue to the shallowness of their behavior.

Mrs. Jennings's second daughter, Charlotte Palmer, gives birth to a boy. When Mr. Donavan is summoned to treat his "red gum," that apothecary informs Mrs. Jennings of the engagement that has existed between Edward Ferrars and Lucy Steele "above this twelvemonth." Elinor is no longer bound to her secret, and the wheels are thus set in motion to drive the novel toward its conclusion. Jane Austen has used an infant to further her plot.

Although children are inconsequential to the plotting of *Pride and Prejudice*, the parenting of them is not. It is no mystery how the same set of parents can produce two pairs of sisters such as Jane and Elizabeth and Kitty and Lydia. No mystery, that is, to any family with five daughters: influence on the elder is soon replaced by indulgence of the younger, and the indifference of a father helps along the selfish concern of a nonthinking mother.

Charlotte Lucas's younger sister, Maria, is a teenager, perhaps the same age as the shadowy Margaret Dashwood. Her younger brother echoes the self-importance of their father, Sir William Lucas, that the latter has adopted since his presentation at court. The boy expostulates: "If I were as rich as Mr. Darcy, I should not care how proud I was. I would keep a pack of foxhounds, and drink a bottle of wine every day" (*PP*, p. 20).

One of the most likable couples in Jane Austen's works is the Gardiners, some portion of which admiration she achieves through the occasional appearances of their children. They have two girls, six and eight years old, and two younger boys, always together in a lively troop. They are full of "eagerness for their cousin's [Jane Bennet's] appearance" (p. 152) in Gracechurch Street but are well trained enough on the occasion not to intrude downstairs. When the Gardiners and Elizabeth travel north to Derbyshire, they are left to the care of Jane, "who was the general favorite, and whose steady sense and sweetness of temper exactly adapted her for attending to them in every way—teaching them, playing with them and loving them" (p. 239). There is no doubt, therefore, about the temperament of the future Bingley generation. The reader also senses the relief experienced by the enervated threesome returning from the North to have the little Gardiners, attracted by the sight of a chaise . . . standing on the steps [of Longbourn], as they entered the paddock; and when the carriage drove up to the door, the joyful surprise that lighted up their faces, and displayed itself over their whole bodies, in a variety of capers and frisks, was the first pleasing earnest of their welcome.

Elizabeth jumped out; and, after giving each of them an hasty kiss, hurried into the vestibule. (p. 286)

This pleasant interlude is welcomed by both the participants and the reader, as Jane Austen well understood. Earlier in the novel she observed, speaking of Darcy, "that they who are good-natured when children, are good-natured when they grow up" (p. 249).

Emma's five nieces and nephews, much closer in inspiration to the Gardiners than the Middletons, are the most ingratiating in the novels. They are well behaved, and their character must mirror that of some of Jane Austen's own twenty-four nieces and nephews. Her sense of this fivesome's intrinsic worth is obvious in her choice of names for them: Henry is the namesake of his grandfather and the eldest; John and Isabella are named after their parents; and George and baby Emma, after their aunt and uncle on either side. Emma Woodhouse's affection for them finds evidence in the pride with which she displays her very own portraits of them to Harriet Smith. The two boys' insistence on verbatim reports of Miss Smith's encounter with gypsies reminds us of Caroline Austen's account of the entertainment she derived from her famous aunt's storytelling expertise.

It is ironic that Harry Dashwood's "good" fortune is represented as precocious avarice, whereas Emma's six-year-old nephew, Henry, suffers much the same fate through her marriage to Mr. Knightley. Earlier in the book Emma is appalled to think that Knightley might marry Jane Fairfax, thereby removing the inheritance from the little boy. The inconsistency of Emma's thought processes is evident, also, when her retraction from marriage making is weakened. She receives the news that her former companion, Mrs. Weston, has given birth to a daughter: she immediately anticipates a future liaison between the baby and one of her own nephews. All the children in *Emma* are pampered, just as the heroine herself was as a child. Spoiled as they are, none are as intrusive as the Middletons'. The children in *Emma* provide the necessary vehicle for revelatory discourse, but in absentia.

In *Mansfield Park* the counterpoint to the ease and comfort available to the Middleton and Knightley children, in the country and in the city, is found at the Prices' in seaside Portsmouth. A tipsy father has a careless, slovenly wife who mismanages both a household and its servants. (But the haphazard parenting of Sir Thomas and Lady Bertram at the park has even more disastrous results. Thus, Jane Austen underscores the relative insignificance of wealth in rearing children.) Besides Fanny and William there are seven other Price children. John and Richard, about sixteen and seventeen, are both away from home, one in London, the other at sea. Susan, the backbone of the Price household, is the most like Fanny and finally becomes her successor at the Bertram mansion. Sam, eleven, squabbles, thumps, and escapes from the house at the slightest pretext. Tom, nine, and Charles, eight, are "rosy-faced boys, ragged and dirty" noisemakers who chase around "tumbling about and hallooing," (pp. 381–82) "quite untameable by any means of address" (p. 391). Betsey, five, is spoiled and "thoroughly without a single recommendation" (p. 385). Not a prepossessing group, they have received too much attention from critics as representative of Jane Austen's attitude toward children.

The Morlands in *Northanger Abbey* have ten offspring. By the time she meets her brother James in Bath, Catherine has long outgrown that tomboyish stage that is probably based on Jane Austen's own early years at Steventon. Three others, Sarah, George, and Harriet, are "at the door, to welcome her with affectionate eagerness" (p. 233) when she returns to Fullerton at the end of the novel. The younger females of the Morland family have been exposed, assuredly, to "Fordyce's Sermons," as was Catherine, and are as presentable and well-mannered as any whose childhood was spent in the company of *Adelaide and Theodore*, to which Anna Weston was to be subjected, and have parents who are sincerely concerned with their children's education.

In *Persuasion*, Anne Elliot's two nephews, Charles and Walter Musgrove, play prominent parts in two scenes. To their mother they are noisy and unmanageable, but her opinion is suspect. Her husband tells Anne that he could "manage them very well, if it were not for Mary's interference" (p. 44). The boys' grandmother, accused by Mary of indulging them with sweets and everything else, confides to their Aunt Anne: "They are quite different creatures with you!" (ibid.). She confesses to overfeeding them as an expediency that obviates the necessity for correction. Charles, Jr., conveniently falls, injures his back, and dislocates his collarbone, thereby giving his aunt the much-desired excuse for avoiding a meeting with Captain Wentworth. Two-year-old Walter is not so obliging. Disobedient, he climbs on Anne's back and refuses to move after repeated admonitions. On this occasion, Wentworth is present:

But not a bit did Walter stir.
   In another moment, however, she found herself in the state of being released from him; some one was taking him from her, though he had bent down her head so much, that his little sturdy hands were unfastened from around her neck, and he was resolutely borne away, before she knew that Captain Wentworth had done it.

> Her sensations on the discovery made her perfectly speechless. She could not even thank him. (p. 80)

There ensues the mutual reawakening of the feelings shared by the two eight years before, accomplished through a plot mechanism that involves children.

The senior Musgroves appear to be about as detached as parents can be. Aside from Charles, Henrietta, and Louisa, they have "numerous" other children, not yet grown up. Jane Austen obviously approves of them, but one wonders how different from the Price household theirs would be without money. There is an amusing glimpse of them all, including the Harville clan, at Uppercross during the Christmas season:

> On one side was a table, occupied by some chattering girls, cutting up silk and gold paper; and on the other were tressels and trays, bending under the weight of brawn and cold pies, where riotous boys were holding high revel; the whole completed by a roaring Christmas fire, which seemed determined to be heard, in spite of all the noise of others. (p. 134)

Jane Austen gave Charles Blake, a ten-year-old in *The Watsons*, the most important role she ever bestowed on a child. Emma Watson attends her first ball in the neighborhood of Stanton, a ball also attended by a party from Osborne Castle. Miss Osborne has previously engaged Charles for the first two dances but inconsiderately jilts him in favor of a more promising partner. Emma overhears and "did not think, or reflect;—she felt & acted—. 'I shall be very happy to dance with you Sir, if you like it'" (pp. 330–31). Charles is overjoyed, his mother ecstatic, and his uncle, Mr. Howard (according to Austen family rumor), is eventually to have Emma's hand despite Lord Osborne's rivalry. This is one of the many instances in which Jane Austen invites the reader to judge her characters by their attitude toward children. Mrs. Gardiner, for instance, needs no further recommendation after she concludes her lengthy, revelatory letter to her niece with "The children have been wanting me this half hour. Your's, very sincerely" (*PP*, p. 325). No one, least of all Elizabeth Bennet, could be more aware of her worth both as a parent and as an aunt.

It must be noted, finally, that several of the major characters appear briefly as children in the beginnings of their stories or have some scenes from their childhood revealed either by themselves or by others. This occurs in the cases of Darcy, Wickham, Fanny Price, Julia and Maria Bertram, Emma, Frank Churchill, Catherine Morland, and Anne Elliot. For a discussion of the relationships of adult characters, as children of their parents, the reader is referred to Jane Nardin's work cited in the bibliography. Then there are others, many others, who would be considered children by today's standards at the ages at which they appear in the novels, for instance, Kitty and Lydia Bennet. David Grylls sums up Jane Austen's attitudes toward, and treatment of, children nicely: "She reveals in her fiction little belief in the wisdom or innocence of children and what she prizes most in young people is obedience and respect" (p. 130).

Bibliography

AUERBACH, NINA. "Artists and Mothers: A False Alliance," *Women & Literature*, 6 (1978), 3–15.

AUSTEN-LEIGH, MARY AUGUSTA. *Personal Aspects of Jane Austen* (London, 1920).

CLARK, E. V. "Some Aspects of Jane Austen," *Contemporary Review*, 183 (1953), 236–40.

GRYLLS, DAVID S. *Guardians and Angels: Parents and Children in Nineteenth-century Literature* (London and Boston, 1978), 112–32.

NARDIN, JANE. "Children and Their Families in Jane Austen's Novels," in Janet Todd, ed., *Jane Austen: New Perspectives,* Women & Literature, n.s. 3 (New York and London, 1983), 73–87.

CHRONOLOGY OF COMPOSITION

A. Walton Litz

Although the chronology of Jane Austen's work after 1811 is known in some detail, there is a good deal of controversy as to the course of her earlier writing. The table below outlines my own view of the sequence of her artistic career; it is followed by a series of brief discussions justifying the dates. In general, I accept the traditional opinion that Jane Austen's artistic career divides into two periods, which are separated by the disruptive years of residence in Bath and Southampton (1801–1809).

I. STEVENTON, 1775–1801

ca. 1788–93	*Juvenilia*
1794 or 1795	*Lady Susan* (without the conclusion)
ca. 1795	*Elinor and Marianne*, the earliest version of *Sense and Sensibility*, cast in epistolary form
October 1796– August 1797	Composition of *First Impressions*, original of *Pride and Prejudice*
November 1797	*Sense and Sensibility* begun "in its present form"
1798–99	Drafting of *Northanger Abbey* (then called *Susan*, later *Catherine*)

II. BATH AND SOUTHAMPTON, 1801–09

1803	*Susan* prepared and offered for publication
1803–1804	*The Watsons* (unfinished)
ca. 1805	Fair copy of *Lady Susan* (and possibly composition of the conclusion)

III. CHAWTON, 1809–17

1809	Reawakening of interest: inquiries to the publisher concerning *Susan*, later *Northanger Abbey* (which had been sold to Crosby and Co. in 1803 but never published); scattered revisions in the *juvenilia*; possibly a retouching of *Susan*

1809–11	*Sense and Sensibility* revised and prepared for publication
November 1811	Publication of *Sense and Sensibility*
ca. 1812	Radical revision of *Pride and Prejudice*, based on the almanacs of 1811–12
February 1811–summer 1813	Composition of *Mansfield Park*
January 1813	Publication of *Pride and Prejudice*
May 1814	Publication of *Mansfield Park*
January 1814– March 1815	Composition of *Emma*
ca. 1815	*Plan of a Novel*
December 1815– January 1816	Publication of *Emma*
August 1815– August 1816	Drafting of *Persuasion*
1816	"Advertisement" to *Catherine* (later *Northanger Abbey*)
January–March 1817	Work on the fragment *Sanditon*
December 1817– January 1818	Posthumous publication of *Northanger Abbey* and *Persuasion*

Juvenilia

The dates in the *juvenilia* (those assigned to the pieces by Jane Austen or ascertainable on the basis of the dedications) range from 1790 to 1793. Probably most of the pieces were written before Jane Austen was seventeen, and she may have begun writing as early as the age of eleven; her niece Caroline remembered that Aunt Jane once advised her to cease writing until she was sixteen, and Caroline was less than twelve when this advice was given (*Memoir*, pp. 47–48). Many of the *juvenilia* must have been written well before their dedication dates. In general, the pieces of *Volume the First* can be dated before those in the second and third volumes. The authors of the *Life* believed that *Volume the Third* marked a "second stage in her literary education: when she was hesitating between burlesque and immature story-telling" (p. 57). The volumes of *juvenilia* were a "collected edition, not the original manuscripts" (R. W. Chapman's preface to the *juvenilia* in the Oxford edition of the *Minor Works*), and they were treasured by the family. Evidence that Jane Austen's interest in the *juvenilia* persisted long after she had turned to other works may be found in the circumstance that a letter in *Evelyn* (*Volume the Third*) is dated "Augst 19th 1809," while in a revision of "Catharine," Hannah More's *Cœlebs* (first published in 1809) was substituted for a reference to Bishop Secker on the catechism. Presumably, these late retouchings were connected with the general revival of Jane Austen's literary activity in 1809.

Lady Susan

This work survives in a fair copy made no earlier than 1805 (as witnessed by the watermarks). The authors of the *Life* believed that *Lady Susan* was written around 1794 (p. 80), which seems quite likely. In spite of the work's complex irony and the skillful management of the epistolary form, I feel that *Lady Susan* is closely related to the more mature pieces in the *juvenilia* (especially "Catharine," "The Three Sisters," and "A Collection of Letters"). That *Elinor and Marianne* was Jane Austen's last known use of the epistolary structure suggests a similar date for *Lady Susan*. The hasty conclusion to the work opens with a hit at the novel-in-letters, and Mary Lascelles is probably right in her supposition that the conclusion "was added at some time nearer to the date of the fair copy, when Jane Austen had lost patience with the device of the novel-in-letters" (pp. 13–14).

Northanger Abbey

We know from Cassandra Austen's Memorandum that "Northanger Abbey was written about the years 98 & 99." (The authors of the *Life* altered these dates to 1797–98, and subsequent critics repeated the error; B. C. Southam was the first to notice this discrepancy [see his note in *TLS*, October 12, 1962].) In the "Advertisement" to *Northanger Abbey*, written in 1816, Jane Austen speaks of the novel as "finished in the year 1803, and intended for immediate publication." In the spring of 1803 the manuscript, then called *Susan*, was sold to Crosby and Co. for ten pounds (see the *Life*, pp. 229–33, where the identity of *Susan* and *Northanger Abbey* is established). But it never appeared, and in 1809 an inquiry revealed that the publisher was willing to return the manuscript "for the same as we paid for it" (*Letters*, April 8, 1809). We know from this inquiry that Jane Austen possessed "another copy" of the novel, which makes retouching at any time after 1803 a possibility.

After the publication of *Emma* in December 1815 the manuscript of *Northanger Abbey* was purchased from the publisher and its title altered to *Catherine* (possibly, as R. W. Chapman suggests, because a novel called *Susan* had appeared in 1809 [Introductory Note to *Works*, vol. 5]). In 1816 Jane Austen wrote the "Advertisement," but in March 1817 she informed Fanny Knight that "Miss Catherine is put upon the Shelve for the present, and I do not know that she will ever come out" (*Letters*, March 13, 1817). The novel was not published until after her death.

There is no reason to believe that *Northanger Abbey* underwent extensive reworking after 1803. Jane Austen's own statement that the novel was "finished" in 1803, combined with the lack of topical references after that date (in her other revisions topical references tend to creep in), leads me to believe that *Northanger Abbey* as a whole is the earliest representative of her mature art. In this I agree with the authors of the *Life*, who say that *Northanger Abbey* offers "the best example of what she could produce at the age of three- or four-and-twenty" (p. 96).

Sense and Sensibility

Cassandra Austen, in her Memorandum on the composition of her sister's novels, says that *Sense and Sensibility* was begun in November 1797 but that "something of the same story and characters had been written earlier and called Elinor & Marianne" (facsimile, *Minor Works*, facing p. 242). Of the first version of *Sense and Sensibility* we know nothing beyond the few details given in the *Life* (p. 80)—that it was cast in the epistolary form and written around 1795. The author of the *Memoir* tells us that *Sense and Sensibility* was "begun, in its present form," immediately after the completion of the first version of *Pride and Prejudice* (*First Impressions*) in November 1797 (p. 49). But certain details in the final text, such as the references to Walter Scott, point to another revision before publication, and the author of the *Memoir* says elsewhere that the first year of Jane Austen's residence at Chawton (i.e., 1809–10) was "devoted to revising and preparing for the press" *Sense and Sensibility* and *Pride and Prejudice* (p. 101). The revisions immediately before publication must have been more than cursory; it is hard to believe that chapter 2, for example, was written in 1797–98.

The Watsons

The manuscript of this fragment is a first draft with revisions, and the watermarks show that it could not have been composed before 1803. It seems probable that the composition did not stretch too far beyond this date; as R. W. Chapman has pointed out, paper was costly and likely to be used soon after purchase (pp. 49–50). However, Chapman's argument is not decisive—parts of *Sanditon* (1817) bear an 1812 watermark—and I would lay more emphasis on the failure of Crosby and Co. to publish *Susan*. This failure must have been evident to Jane Austen by the end of 1804 and probably had a great deal to do with her decision to break off work on *The Watsons*. Another disruptive event was the death of her father in January 1805; Fanny Catherine Lefroy, a granddaughter of James Austen, once stated that "somewhere in 1804 she [Jane Austen] began 'The Watsons,' but her father died early in 1805, and it was never finished" (p. 277).

Pride and Prejudice

According to Cassandra's Memorandum, *Pride and Prejudice* (then called *First Impressions*) was begun in October 1796 and finished in August 1797. It was later published with "alterations and contractions." On November 1, 1797 Jane Austen's father wrote to Cadell, the publisher, offering for publication at the author's expense "a manuscript novel, comprising 3 volumes, about the length of Miss Burney's *Evelina*," but this offer was declined (*Life*, pp. 96–98). The final version of *Pride and Prejudice* is actually quite a bit shorter than *Evelina*, pointing to a general revision prior to publication. On January 29, 1813 Jane Austen wrote to Cassandra: "I have lop't and crop't so successfully . . . that I imagine it must be rather shorter than S. & S. altogether." It is impossible to tell whether Jane Austen "lop't and crop't" *First Impressions* or—as R. W. Chapman has suggested (*Works*, vol. 2, p. xiii)—an intermediate 1811 version; but in any case the late revisions were radical ones. R. W. Chapman and Sir Frank MacKinnon have demonstrated that Jane Austen used the calendar of 1811–12 in plotting the novel (see the Appendix to *Works*, vol. 2), and Chapman is surely right when he says that "so intricate a chronological scheme cannot have been patched on to an existing work without extensive revision."

Mansfield Park

Jane Austen recorded in a fragmentary memorandum on the dates of her own novels (facsimile in *Plan of a Novel*, ed. R. W. Chapman [Oxford, 1926]) that *Mansfield Park* was begun "somewhere about Feb^{ry} 1811" and finished "soon after June 1813."

JANE AUSTEN

Emma

According to Jane Austen's own memorandum, *Emma* was begun on January 21, 1814 and completed on March 29, 1815.

Persuasion

The novel was begun on August 8, 1815 and finished on August 6, 1816 (Jane Austen's memorandum). The manuscript of the canceled chapter 10 and the original chapter 11 (now 12) bears the date *"Finis. July 18. 1816."*—presumably, the period from July 18 to August 6 was devoted to the rewriting of chapter 10. Although in a letter of March 13, 1817 Jane Austen speaks of *Persuasion* as ready for publication, we may assume that the entire manuscript would have undergone a general retouching if she had lived. It seems to have been Jane Austen's habit to allow a manuscript to rest for some time before undertaking the final revision.

Bibliography

CHAPMAN, R. W. *Jane Austen: Facts and Problems* (Oxford, 1948).
LASCELLES, MARY. *Jane Austen and Her Art* (London, 1939).
LEFROY, FANNY CATHERINE. "Is It Just?" and "A Bundle of Letters," *Temple Bar*, 67 (February 1883), 270–88.
LITZ, A. WALTON. *Jane Austen: A Study of Her Artistic Development* (New York and London, 1965).
SOUTHAM, B. C. *Jane Austen's Literary Manuscripts* (London, 1964).

CHRONOLOGY WITHIN THE NOVELS

Jo Modert

Days, weeks, months, and seasons roll by in an Austen novel as surely as the earth orbits the sun. Just how or when Jane Austen perfected this chronological device—the basis for comedy since classical times (see Langer, pp. 326–50)—remains a mystery. We know she admired Richardson's epistolary novels, which incorporated calendar dates, and that *Elinor and Marianne* and possibly *First Impressions* were originally cast in epistolary form (see "Chronology of Composition"). We can only say with certainty, however, that by the time Jane Austen wrote *The Watsons*, probably around 1804, she had developed the system inherent in the novels.

The only major studies of interior dating were made in the 1920s when R. W. Chapman and Sir Frank MacKinnon devised chronologies to verify the tradition that Jane Austen had used almanacs and to prove that the novels were based on specific or ideal calendars. "We do not suppose," Dr. Chapman wrote, "that Miss Austen used an almanac for any purpose except that of convenience, or that she conceived the events of the story as necessarily belonging to an actual year" (*MP*, p. 554).

Mary Lascelles, the only scholar to examine the chronologies collectively in order to trace Jane Austen's growing artistry, accepted the Chapman-MacKinnon conclusions without question (pp. 171–73, 185–94). Other scholars have examined individual novels to question the Chapman-MacKinnon chronologies in determining dates of composition; only those relevant to interior dating are included here. This survey will emend several Chapman-MacKinnon chronologies and will indicate that the use of calendars added pattern and meaning to Jane Austen's novels.

First, it will be useful to describe some almanacs of Jane Austen's time that I suspect Dr. Chapman and Sir Frank MacKinnon never saw. *Rider's "British Merlin"* and *The Royal Kalendar*, published by the Company of Stationers (which held a virtual monopoly), are almost identical, both to each other and from year to year. Others varied considerably in form but contained the same general information.

Each verso gives a specific month with six vertical columns listing month-day; week-day; "Feasts and Fasts" of the Anglican church (the *Book of Common Prayer* itself is in part a calendar); the time the sun rises and sets; moon age; and weather predictions. The facing recto gives that month's quarters of the moon, agricultural and health tips, general information, and useful tables.

The previously mentioned column which gives Feast and Fast days includes Old-Style (O.S.) holidays, which may need explanation. When the Julian (O.S.) calendar was converted to the New-Style Gregorian (N.S.) in 1752, eleven days between September 2 and September 14 were omitted. As holiday customs often depended on seasonal phenomena, Old-Style festivities were celebrated well into the nineteenth century. For instance, thanks to Dr. Chapman's inquiries, we know that Jane Austen celebrated Old Michaelmas on October 11, 1813 (*Letters*, p. 346n.; Chapman, p. 258).

Before examining chronologies within individual novels, it should be stressed that Dr. Chapman's enthusiasm for Jane Austen's precision was somewhat overstated: calendar errors, discrepancies, and ambiguities are evident in every published novel. A. Walton Litz's observation that in *Mansfield Park*, "a close examination of the dates . . . makes it evident that Dr. Chapman has stated only one of several possibilities" (p. 221) also obtains in most other cases.

The Watsons, Jane Austen's incomplete novel, is the first example we have of a "complete" date (i.e., the month-day plus week-day) by which a year can be determined through use of a perpetual calendar. It begins on "Tuesday Octr ye 13th" (p. 314). As October 13 fell on Tuesday only in 1801 and 1807 during this period, the date helps confirm that Jane Austen wrote *The Watsons* around 1804.

Sense and Sensibility begins "early in September" (p. 28), takes Elinor and Marianne Dashwood to London after Christmas, to the Palmers' estate for the Easter holidays, and ends with Elinor's wedding and move to Delaford by Michaelmas (p. 374), thus coming full circle within a year. It lacks any complete date and is the only novel without a Chapman-MacKinnon chronology. "The only internal indication of date," wrote Dr. Chapman, "seems to be the mention . . . of Scott as a popular poet. . . . [This] would not have been possible in 1798" (*SS*, p. xiv).

Patricia Craddock has suggested a dating method based on the Easter sequence, by which the most likely interior years would be 1794–95, 1797–98, 1800–1801, or 1805–1806. Her theory assumes that the Palmer party leaves London very early in April (*SS*, p. 301) in order to arrive before Easter Sunday. However, the Palmers' earlier plans were to "remove to Cleveland about the end of March, for the Easter holidays" (p. 279); possibly, some cause for delay was omitted in the revised version. Thus, a late March Easter cannot be ruled out: I like especially the possibility of Easter March 31, 1793, as the 1792–93 calendars would agree with the earliest assumed composition of *Elinor and Marianne*.

Pride and Prejudice, like *Sense and Sensibility*, begins in September with the hunting season, takes Jane Bennet to London after Christmas,

Elizabeth to the Collinses over Easter, on a northern tour during the summer, and back to Longbourn, where the novel concludes in the fall. It contains three "complete" dates. Monday November 18 (pp. 61 and 63) and Tuesday November 27 (pp. 86 and 262) agree with the calendars for 1799, 1805, and 1811. But Mr. Gardiner's letter, dated "Monday, August 2" (p. 302) does not agree with the identical calendars for 1800 and 1806 or with that of 1812, a leap year.

This discrepancy was first noted in 1910 (see T. G. Aravamuthan et al.). Dr. Chapman and Sir Frank MacKinnon concluded that Jane Austen used the 1811–12 calendars when revising *First Impressions* and that "Monday, August 2" was an error for Monday August 17 (*PP*, p. 405). Despite some dissent, most scholars agree.

Northanger Abbey occurs mostly during eleven weeks (p. 231), beginning early in the year when Catherine Morland visits Bath. After seven weeks (p. 154) she visits the Tilneys and returns home four weeks later (p. 220). The novel rapidly culminates with her marriage to Henry Tilney "within a twelvemonth from the first day of their meeting" (p. 252).

No "complete" date is given; February (p. 63), March (p. 177) and April (p. 216) are named. Dr. Chapman and Sir Frank MacKinnon differed, the former devising an "ideal" calendar by assuming the first Sunday in Bath was the first of February in a nonleap year (*NA*, Chronology, pp. 297–301). Sir Frank assumed the year was 1798, with the first Sunday as February 4. By his reckoning, Catherine's first Monday at Northanger Abbey, when "at four o'clock, the sun was now two hours above the horizon" (p. 193), would be March 26 in 1798. Dr. Chapman noted Sir Frank's chronology might be a week late: "On March 19 sunset at Greenwich is at 6 hrs. 9 minutes" (p. 299).

A check of contemporary almanacs proves that the spring equinox is indeed the way to date *Northanger Abbey*—but only if one knows which almanac Jane Austen used. *Rider's "British Merlin"* and *The Royal Kalendar* for March 1813 and 1814 list March 19 as "Equal Day and Night" with sunrise and sunset at "6–0–6," which confirms Sir Frank's theory, since March 19 fell on Monday only in 1798. However, Moore's *Vox Stellarum* (one of the oldest and most popular almanacs) for March 1797 and 1798 gives March 18 as "6–0–6" with "6–1, 5–59" for 1799 (Monday March 18 occurred in 1793 and 1799), whereas *The Gentleman's Diary* for 1798 lists Tuesday March 20 as "Equal day and night." (Monday March 20 occurred in 1797.) In any case, Catherine's visit to Bath must begin during the last week of January and end on Sunday (pp. 229 and 233) after the third full week in April.

Mansfield Park opens with the marriage of Miss Maria Ward to Sir Thomas Bertram "About thirty years ago" (p. 3). The main plot begins twenty-six or more years later in July when Fanny Price is eighteen (p. 40), ends in May the next year, and extends several more years to include Fanny's marriage and an implicit hint of parenthood. Thus, the novel comes full circle within the thirty-year span of a generation.

Sir Thomas's ball, Thursday December 22 (pp. 253 and 256), supplies the one "complete" date, applicable to 1796, 1803, 1808, or 1814. Dr. Chapman and Sir Frank MacKinnon agreed that 1808–1809 was intended (pp. 554–57) but admitted problems with Easter April 2, 1809, which is said to be "particularly late this year" (p. 430). Because April 2 falls within Fanny's intended stay at Portsmouth, it is completely unacceptable as the Easter of the novel; and they could only conclude that Jane Austen had allowed herself a "license" (p. 554).

Novelist Vladimir Nabokov, persuaded by Edmund Wilson to include *Mansfield Park* in his Cornell University lectures (Simon Karlinsky, ed., pp. 17–18, 236, 238, 241, 246, 253, 254n., 272, and 273n.), devised his own chronology, which agrees in most respects with Dr. Chapman's. (See facsimiles of annotated p. 3 of *MP* and chronology, pp. 8 and 61, in Fredson Bower, ed., introduction, pp. 1–7, "Mansfield Park (1814)," pp. 8–61.) Nabokov ignored the Easter dilemma and the opening "About," dated the beginning as 1781 with the "main action 1808" (ibid., p. 8), and used the chronology to establish internal relationships, though not without some errors. His chronology correctly dates the weddings of the two other Ward sisters as six years after Lady Bertram's (ibid., p. 61; *MP*, p. 3), but the text has all three occurring in 1781 (ibid., p. 13). Though little noted, Nabokov's lecture is a landmark in Austen studies, as he is the first to recognize that Jane Austen's use of chronology is intrinsic to her composition and not merely an indication of her "artistry."

Two alternatives to the Chapman-MacKinnon (and Nabokov) chronology were proposed in 1961. Bernard Ledgwick argued for the calendars of 1809–10 in which the Easter date would be April 22, treating the December date as the only "clue" inconsistent with his thesis. Meanwhile, A. Walton Litz posited a much earlier first draft, based on the calendars of 1796 (when December 22 also fell on Thursday) and 1797, when Easter came on April 16.

None of these conjectures is entirely satisfactory, though the Easter April 16, proposed by Litz, fits most neatly into the novel's sequences. At least one other possibility should be considered. From January 20, 1813, almost two years after Jane Austen began *Mansfield Park*, until that summer, a number of inquiries and comments on the novel appear in her letters, including her "complete change of subject—ordination" remark (*Letters*, January 24, 1813, and notes for pp. 292, 294; January 29, 1813, and note for p. 298; February 16, 1813, and note (addenda) for p. 504; September 25, 1813). During this time, the specific date of Thursday December 22 might have been added for some reason not now known to an original version based on the 1809–10 calendars.

Emma begins late in September with a wedding and comes full circle a year later with three more. There being no complete date, Dr. Chapman concluded it takes place in "the present" (*E*, p. 498). By correcting two Chapman readings, *Emma* can be shown to follow the 1813–14 calendars with main events occurring on holy/holidays, both New- and Old-Style. There may be a hidden calendar game for the reader in *Emma* as chapter 9, which deals with riddles, contains allusions to Michaelmas (p. 75), Christmas (p. 79), Valentine's Day (p. 70; see verses of "Kitty, a fair frozen maid," pp. 489–90), Easter (p. 79), and May Day/Midsummer Eve (p. 75).

Emma's Christmas holiday sequence establishes the 1813 calendar. Sunday comes after Christmas and before the John Knightleys' departure (p. 138), which Dr. Chapman took to be December 28, based on Emma's remark that "Mr. John Knightley must be in town again on the 28th" (p. 79). Detailed descriptions, however, of the Knightleys' entourage of five children, nurserymaids, two carriages, with a midway change (pp. 91–92), indicate that they must leave on the twenty-seventh for him to attend to business the next day. Only the 1813 (and 1802) calendar has this sequence: Friday, Christmas Eve; Saturday, Christmas; Sunday, December 26; Monday, December 27.

Appropriately, the next day, when Emma extols the naive Harriet, is December 28, Innocents' Day. On Wednesday, January 26, 1814, Emma hears of Mr. Elton's engagement (p. 176). He returns the first week of February (p. 181), stays about a week, and leaves the same day Frank Churchill arrives (pp. 186 and 190) on a Wednesday (p. 221), making it February 9. After two more days, Frank goes to London on Saturday (pp. 190, 196, and 205). Jane's pianoforte arrives on Monday, which is thus February 14 (pp. 214–15). This concealed Valentine date explains why both Emma and Mrs. Weston at the Coles' party on Tuesday the fifteenth surmise the gift is from a lover (pp. 217–18, 226). Frank leaves the following Tuesday (p. 266), which is February 22, Shrove Tuesday, after almost confessing to Emma. This holy period/holiday also explains the Eltons' hurried nuptials, as no marriages were performed during the Lenten season, which begins the next day.

Emma's dinner for the Eltons is on a "cold sleety April" Thursday (pp. 303 and 308). Subsequent events mark this as the second week in April; thus, her dinner is on the fourteenth, Easter Thursday. Events between the Crown Inn ball and the first of June (p. 343) show it occurs during the second week in May. No weekday is given, but I suggest Thursday the twelfth (Old May Day Eve) with Harriet's encounter with the gypsies on Old May Day—Friday the thirteenth.

The Midsummer holiday sequence confirms the 1814 calendar. The Donwell Abbey party is "almost Midsummer" (p. 357) with Box Hill the next day. That evening Frank returns to Richmond (p. 383); Mrs.

Churchill dies thirty-six hours later on June 26 (pp. 387 and 440). Thus, Donwell Abbey was June 23, Midsummer Eve—and also Harriet's birthday (p. 30)—with Box Hill on Midsummer. "About ten days after Mrs. Churchill's decease" (p. 392), Frank returns, which we learn later is Monday (p. 436). Dr. Chapman counted ten days from June 26, making Frank's disclosure fall on Wednesday July 6 in 1814 (p. 497). By definition, however, "about" means "almost" or "nearly." By counting June 26 and the Monday as full days, Frank's return is nine days later, on Monday July 4. Tuesday July 5, the day of the cold July storm, is then Old Midsummer Eve, with Wednesday July 6, the day of Mr. Knightley's proposal, Old Midsummer.

Persuasion, the only Austen novel with an explicit year, begins during the summer of 1814 (p. 8). The Elliots leave Kellynch in September, with the Crofts taking possession at Michaelmas (pp. 33, 48, and 206). Anne spends Christmas with Lady Russell; soon after, they go to Bath where the novel ends in late February or early March. (Easter fell on March 26 in 1815.)

The introductory history has a calendar error: Lady Elliot's death in 1800 is inconsistent with the thirteen-year time lapse (*P*, p. 302). As Dr. Chapman notes, there is another discrepancy: "Writing on 'February 1st' [Mary] refers to Louisa's return 'to-morrow' [163], which the postscript shows to be Tuesday. But Feb. 1 was not a Monday in 1815, but a Wednesday" (p. 304). It should be noted, however, that "Tuesday" might be a printer's error for "Thursday," which would be correct.

"The English migrate as regularly as rooks," Robert Southey noted in *Letters from England* (p. 164), a book read by Jane Austen (*Letters*, October 1, 1808). By moving her characters in accord with established calendar patterns, Jane Austen imbued her novels with the natural rhythm of life itself; and the chronologies within her novels merit far more attention than has been given them thus far.

Bibliography

ANDREWS, P. B. S. "The Date of *Pride and Prejudice*," *Notes and Queries*, 213 (1968), 338–42.

ARAVAMUTHAN, T. G. "'Pride and Prejudice': Calendar Mistake," *Notes and Queries*, 11th ser. 2 (1910), 147. Answers by Edward Bensley, ibid., 434, and "St. Swithin," ibid., 477.

CAPP, BERNARD. *English Almanacs: 1500–1800* (Ithaca, N.Y., 1979).

CHAPMAN, R. W. "Michaelmas Goose," *Notes and Queries*, 180 (1941), 258.

CRADDOCK, PATRICIA. "The Almanac of 'Sense and Sensibility,'" *Notes and Queries* (June 1979), 222–26.

EMDEN, C. S. "'Northanger Abbey' Re-dated?" *Notes and Queries*, 195 (1950), 407–10.

FLEISHMAN, AVROM. *A Reading of "Mansfield Park": An Essay in Critical Synthesis* (Minneapolis, Minn., 1967; paperback reprint, Baltimore, Md., 1970).

HARVEY, SIR PAUL, ed. Appendix III, "The Calendar," in *Oxford Companion to English Literature*, rev. ed. by D. Eagle (Oxford, 1932; 4th ed. 1967), 932–61.

LANGER, SUSANNE K. *Feeling and Form: A Theory of Art* (New York, 1953).

LASCELLES, MARY. *Jane Austen and Her Art* (London, 1939; Oxford paperback ed., 1963; reprinted, 1968).

LEDGWICK, BERNARD. "The 'Strange Business in America,'" *Collected Reports of the Jane Austen Society, 1949–1965* (London, 1967), 197–203.

LITZ, A. WALTON. "The Chronology of *Mansfield Park*," *Notes and Queries*, 208 (1961), 221–22.

MANSELL, JR., DARREL. "The Date of Jane Austen's Revision of *Northanger Abbey*," *English Language Notes*, 7 (1969–70), 40–41.

NABOKOV, VLADIMIR. *The Nabokov-Wilson Letters: 1940–1971*, Simon Karlinsky, ed. (New York, 1979).

———. *Vladimir Nabokov: Lectures on Literature*, Fredson Bowers, ed. (New York, 1980).

NASH, RALPH. "The Time Scheme for *Pride and Prejudice*," *English Language Notes*, 4 (1966–67), 194–98.

SOUTHEY, ROBERT. *Letters from England: by Don Manuel Alvarez Espriella. Translated from the Spanish*, 3 vols. (London, 1807; reprinted, London, ed. Jack Simmons, 1951).

JANE AUSTEN'S COMEDY

Robert M. Polhemus

I want to discuss the nature and some of the implications of Jane Austen's comedy and comic vision. By "comedy" I mean what Dr. Johnson meant: "a representation of human life as may excite mirth" (*The Rambler*, no. 225); and by "comic vision" I mean Austen's particular insight and sense of the world that allowed her to find or "excite" mirth, to justify life, and to imagine the means of its benevolent regeneration in the future.

For Austen the full potential of personality, society, and literature should include a radiant sense of humor, and nothing seems more important or original about her than her comedy. She was, after all, the first woman to write great comic novels in the English language, a fact that has great historical as well as literary significance. She led the way in making comic fiction a chief means of exploring the individualization of women's lives and the revolution in the relation of the sexes that was well under way at the beginning of the nineteenth century. Her comic sense was indispensable to her in finding and showing the possibilities of goodness and value in life—in justifying the ways of God to woman.

A comic imagination could mean joy and freedom, transforming the oppressiveness of everyday life to pleasure; but she also felt it could be an irresponsible license. She strove in her fiction for a union of comic and moral imagination. This struggle to fuse comic perception and ethical sensibility distinguishes and gives tension to her art. Sometimes her comic sense and the conventional moral code that she consciously upheld come into conflict. Whoever reads her fiction and letters with any care can sense at times a pull between her urge to be funny and her will to support moral orthodoxy. To appreciate the drama and achievement of Austen, we need to realize how deep was her passion for both reverence and ridicule. She wanted a comedy of union, and her comic imagination reveals both the harmonies and the telling contradictions of her mind and vision as she tries to reconcile her satirical bias with her sense of the good. It is the daring, fresh, problematic, and dangerous quality of that comic imagination—its moral vulnerability and its freedom—that makes Austen live and count for so many readers. In her work, comedy is not only mode, method, and entertainment; it is also one of her crucial subjects.

Jane Austen's Comedy

1

Says Elizabeth Bennet in *Pride and Prejudice*, "I dearly love a laugh.... Follies and nonsense, whims and inconsistencies *do* divert me, I own, and I laugh at them whenever I can" (*PP*, p. 57). Austen was disposed, through comic license, to ridicule. The inadequacies and constraints of her society could not help but stir rebellious impulses—deflected and sublimated though they might be—in such a woman of genius and relative leisure, and her comedy was a way of both expressing and controlling her critical spirit. To reconcile her intelligence to the world and preserve orthodox allegiances, she developed a transfiguring comic imagination. She could use it defensively to mock whatever was insufficient or threatening in a woman's life and joyously as a mode of hope. Comic vision in Austen often unites with the world to broaden and change the terms of life.

Her critical and energetic spirit shows her art to be much more radical (though not in a narrow political sense) than it is often thought to be. We can see a significant union of feminine independence, commitment to comedy, and implied criticism of the man's world in which she dwelled developing in her correspondence with J. S. Clarke, domestic chaplain to the prince regent. He had asked her "to delineate in some future Work the Habits of Life and Character and enthusiasm of a Clergyman," and she answered: "I am quite honoured by your thinking me capable of drawing such a clergyman as you gave the sketch of in your note.... But I assure you I am *not*. The comic part of the character I might be equal to, but not the good, the enthusiastic, the literary" (*Letters*, November 16, 1815 [from Rev. Clarke]; December 11, 1815).

Why not? Her self-deprecating reasons carry the ironic undertone of an indictment of a system that kept her in comparative ignorance:

> Such a man's conversation must at times be on subjects of science and philosophy, of which I know nothing; or at least be occasionally abundant in quotations and allusions which a woman who, like me, knows only her own mother tongue, and has read very little in that, would be totally without the power of giving. (ibid.)

When Clarke again asked that she write about "an English clergyman" and suggested that she dedicate "to Prince Leopold: any historical romance, illustrative of the history of the august House of Coburg" (March 27, 1816), she replied: "I could not sit seriously down to write a serious romance under any other motive than to save my life; and if it were indispensable for me to keep it up and never relax into laughing at myself or other people, I am sure I should be hung before I had finished the first chapter" (*Letters*, April 1, 1816).

If we substitute "woman" for "man" in the following excerpt from

Shaftesbury's essay "The Freedom of Wit and Humour" (1709), we can understand, partly at least, how and why Austen's ingenious comic sense was generated:

> The natural free spirits of ingenious man, if imprisoned or controlled, will find out other ways of motion to relieve themselves in their constraint; and whether it be in burlesque, mimicry or buffoonery, they will be glad at any rate to vent themselves, and be revenged on their constrainers.... 'Tis the persecuting spirit has raised the bantering one.

Out of the muffled but pervasive persecuting spirit of society as she sometimes felt it came, for example, the satirical comedy of banal Bath life, boorish beaux, and bad books in *Northanger Abbey*; of ill-behaved children and romantic nonsense in *Sense and Sensibility*; of fatuous toadying and domestic idiocy in *Pride and Prejudice*; of officious, tyrannizing relatives in *Mansfield Park*; of cloying, dull provinciality in *Emma*; of patriarchal vanity in *Persuasion*; of salesmanship and the monotonous din of self-serving speech in *Sanditon*; in short, the satire in all the novels of the boring mindlessness to which an intelligent woman could be held subject.

2

The comic motive that Thomas Hobbes identified in his notorious explanation of laughter moves Austen and animates her work. "*Sudden Glory*, is the passion which maketh those *Grimaces* called LAUGHTER; and is caused either by some sudden act of their own, that pleaseth them; or by the apprehension of some deformed thing in another, in comparison whereof they suddenly applaud themselves" (*Leviathan*, 1651). In *Emma*, the heroine responds to some outrageous vulgarity by thinking, "Much beyond my hopes" (*E*, p. 279). Austen's comic fancy can stand reality on its head: the mind can make comedy of gracelessness and an amusement park out of constricting space. The fancy of humor, by which what is bad can be converted into a source of delight and what is wrong can fill one with pleasure at one's own superiority, is, for Austen, one of "the best blessings of existence" (*E*, p. 5).

But for her ridicule also can be frighteningly disruptive and threaten moral order, tradition, and the will to reverence. "I hope," says Elizabeth Bennet, "I never ridicule what is wise or good" (*PP*, p. 57). That wish bespeaks a deeply felt source of fear and anxiety for Austen. With a psyche that contained impulses both to conserve and to subvert, she knew that comic genius could serve divided intentions. Austen's comic imagination, better probably than that of any other woman who had ever written before, was her own most distinctive gift and the one talent it would have been death for her to hide. Nevertheless, the novels *Mansfield Park* and *Emma* and the characters Mary Crawford and Emma Woodhouse also show clearly that comic imagination was for her a Frankenstein that needed control. She felt and imagined in her fiction the power of comedy in some such way as many have felt and do feel the power of scientific knowledge: something liberating, inseparable from progress, but scary and potentially destructive, too.

Consider a famous joke in *Mansfield Park* that Austen condemns. Mary Crawford, when her aunt dies, can no longer live with her uncle: "Admiral Crawford was a man of vicious conduct, who chose, instead of retaining his niece, to bring his mistress under his roof" (*MP*, p. 41). To Edmund Bertram's question "You have a large acquaintance in the navy . . . ?" Mary replies, "Certainly, my home at my uncle's brought me acquainted with a circle of admirals. Of *Rears* and *Vices*, I saw enough" (*MP*, p. 60). Edmund later criticizes the impropriety of this remark, and Austen explicitly makes it an early instance of Mary's slack moral sense. It is hard to miss, however, the satirical flash, success, and justice of Mary's comic strategy here and Austen's surreptitious delight in it. Whatever she professes, she is of two minds about witty ridicule. After all, she invented "Rears and Vices" and obviously lavished her genius in creating all the other sardonic wit and humor that crowd her pages.

Austen renders the elective, self-esteeming powers of the comic, but she also claims for it more socially positive and responsible functions. She wanted to use comedy as a means of reconciling herself to traditional faith and conventional society by releasing doubts and resentments harmlessly. Poised between the decorous rationalization of eighteenth-century society and religion and the restless energy and ambition of nineteenth-century individualism, she was striving for a form and a creation that would preserve the best of the past, including Christian ethics, but would allow for the change and development her expanding feminine soul craved.

"A mind lively and at ease, can do with seeing nothing, and can see nothing that does not answer" (*E*, p. 233), she says of Emma in a crucial sentence. It is comic understanding that creates such a mind and infuses nothingness with worth and gaiety. The comic union Austen seeks is the marriage of comedy itself with the world; the ability to see what is ridiculous and to devise happy and moral endings on earth becomes a very basis for her faith. But it is an uneasy faith.

3

Briefly, the typical components of Austen's comedy are the comic heroine; the animating powers of mind amid triviality, stupidity, and actual or potential immorality; a clear set of values; the use of speech and conversation for satirical and witty effects; a distinctive and habitual irony; and the movement toward rational love and fitting union.

Her comedy depends on her comic heroines, and the wittiest and most famous of these are Elizabeth Bennet and Emma Woodhouse—characters whose largeness and consequence match the greatest comic figures in all literature. If these two did not exist, it is fair to say that neither would Austen's reputation as a comic genius. Each is a comic heroine in three different ways: as central figure of the romantic plot ending in marriage; as a possessor of a fine and irrepressible sense of humor very much like her author's; and as a subject of comic irony—Emma especially is often laughable and ridiculous. Like their creator, they assert their individuality through comedy, and they use their humor—even when, as in Emma's case, it sometimes goes awry—to try to distinguish themselves from the mediocrity, triviality, and male pride that can swallow up women's lives.

Austen, in two key passages from *Pride and Prejudice* and *Emma*, ascribes the same attribute to her heroines: liveliness of mind. It is a lively mind that gives each her sense of humor and her starring role in the comic vision of her novel. Elizabeth, near the end, asks Darcy why he ever fell in love with her: "Did you admire me for my impertinence?" He replies, "For the liveliness of your mind, I did" (*PP*, p. 380). The words I have already quoted describing Emma, "A mind lively and at ease, can do with seeing nothing, and can see nothing that does not answer," epitomize the pattern and workings of her mind and the novel's whole comedy: out of trying, boring circumstances, she uses her imagination to please herself, correct her fancy with actual perception, come to understand her privilege and good luck, and become happier and more responsible. Of course, to complete the comic vision the lively-minded comic heroines must find love, vulnerability, and proper union with another. Love and marriage for them signify the control of egoism and misperception and the regenerative merging of the self with the ongoing community. But as Darcy and Knightley both testify, it is their comic gifts—wit, spontaneity, and imagination—that make them so fascinating and lovable.

One other specific example shows how Austen identifies a lively mind and a capacity for comedy, but it reveals also how problematic a comic sense could be for her. In *Mansfield Park*, the antiheroine Mary Crawford mocks wittily and with wicked irreverence certain religious practices, and the pious Edmund Bertram, close to falling in love with her, reprimands her: "Your lively mind can hardly be serious even on serious subjects" (*MP*, p. 87). However fine or flawed we may judge *Mansfield Park* to be, it is atypical of Austen's social comedies; the woman with the liveliest mind and best sense of humor in the story is judged harshly and fails. The author does not integrate Mary's wit and adventurous mind into an overall comic vision, as she does with the morally flawed Emma and the prejudiced and proud Elizabeth.

Though less given to comedy than those two, the heroines of *Sense and Sensibility* and *Persuasion*, Elinor Dashwood and Anne Elliot, also have ironic comic imaginations and lively minds. We get close to the heart of Austen's comic vision when we see how her novels render the comic richness of lively minds and their dialectical interplay with the world.

4

Austen's values are utilitarian, secular, intellectual, moral, and material. She is continually evaluating her characters and their behavior, and the world she creates is a hierarchy in which status depends on uniting intelligence, morality, a sense of humor, wealth, social standing, health, and physical attractiveness: people rank according to how great a sum of these parts they possess *in toto*. She does not pretend that a rich, full life is possible if one does not have both enough money and a benevolent, intelligent mind. She defines morality pragmatically: ultimately, what causes worthwhile people pain is immoral; what brings them joy is moral. No great novelist is freer of canting idealism. Want is bad; plenty is good. Happiness depends on having a lively, candid perception of things and an imagination that can play over reality and find attainable aims that will help achieve connection and harmony between the self and the world.

Historically, Austen's comedy is about and for an ambitious middle-class audience, expanding in numbers, power, and riches. Material and moral values are complementary, not antithetical. We have folly and error, but the main burden of social and class guilt is missing. Novels like *Emma* and *Pride and Prejudice* have the optimistic tone of a buoyant individualism in which personal success, comprehending intellectual, ethical, and physical well-being, can be a praiseworthy and possible goal.

5

Speech in Austen defines character, reflects quality of mind, and does much to create her comic mood. She makes conversation the means and opportunity for her intelligent figures to touch and move one another, often, in the process, displaying their wit and sense of the laughable. Proper speech in some way brings about change for the better, and wit—which discovers unsuspected connections, generates new awareness, and lets loose hostilities in civilized fashion—can lead to moral and mental progress. Wit, therefore, though it can be misused, is usually a positive virtue and an indicator of potential merit.

The talk of the unintelligent, however, reveals their ridiculousness—the humor, in the old-fashioned sense of the word, of one-track minds that cannot properly connect. They betray their trivial obsessions and their ignorance of both themselves and others. Expression should inform, join, please, alter, and clarify minds.

Monologue in Austen often signals folly and limitation. Miss Bates in *Emma* talks and talks, but Emma can mimic and sum her up in a single phrase: "So very kind and obliging!" (*E*, p. 225). Silly talk stagnates and is, quite literally, of no consequence except that it shows the obstacles that keep people apart and provides wry pleasure to the wise. See, for example, John Thorpe's retarded rattling in *Northanger Abbey*, Marianne's romantic simpering in *Sense and Sensibility*, Collins's fatuous verbiage in *Pride and Prejudice*, Mrs. Norris's monologues of miserliness, Mr. Woodhouse's hypochondriacal dithering in *Emma*, and Sir Walter Elliot's snobbish twaddle in *Persuasion*.

Austen seems to revel in composing foolish speeches, and they show something essential about her comic imagination. "You divert me against my conscience," says Mrs. Weston laughingly to Emma, who is mimicking Miss Bates (*E*, p. 225). But, of course, Austen, in composing Miss Bates's talk, is doing exactly the same kind of thing as Emma and mocking the intellectual limitations of her world. Austen uses the eccentricities of her foolish characters, as these emerge in their speech, to flatter her readers; the subliminal message they reiterate is "You are not like this. You are superior; you are one of the elect." The comic artist can take the banal speech of others and make an audience feel just what Emma feels when she makes a game out of the banalities of her world: "she knew she had no reason to complain and was amused enough" (*E*, p. 233). As for the best speakers, like Elizabeth, Darcy, Emma, Knightley, Anne Elliot, and Wentworth, the function of their language is usually to open up, in one way or another, the comic possibilities for happiness in the future.

6

Austen is justly famous as an ironist, and irony depends on its audience to detect and complete meanings extending beyond the literal sense of the language. Austen's habitual irony distances her from appearances and behavior in her society, but it unites her with her readers by drawing us into a conspiracy of intellect. Whoever does not perceive it becomes its target. Irony is her mind's bridge between what is and what may be or ought to be, and at times it spans and supports alternative interpretations of reality, none of which she is ready to discard. It emphasizes her willingness to question social surface and conventional assumptions, and it stresses her moral pragmatism, together with her belief in the tentative nature of perception. It mocks the presumptions and pretensions of others by accepting them at face value in order to make clear their foolishness. It protects by performing a nearly miraculous psychological reversal, turning incongruous misfunctioning and the inconsistencies of the world into a positive source of delight for the mind. This verbal irony liberates by suggesting different options in assessing life and different strategies for coping with it. Austen's ironic prose suggests and suspends several meanings, and it demands participation and ingenuity on the part of the audience.

Here, from *Emma*, is one typical example of her irony:

> It may be possible to do without dancing entirely. Instances have been known of young people passing many, many months successively, without being at any ball of any description, and no material injury accrue either to body or mind;—but when a beginning is made—when the felicities of rapid motion have once been, though slightly, felt—it must be a very heavy set that does not ask for more.
> (*E*, p. 247)

At first this appears to be just a piece of rather obvious irony directed against the tendency of young people and others to make much of little. Of course it is "possible to do without dancing." But on second thought there is a deeper irony. Humanity may be able to do without dances, but we can't be very sure, since the race seems seldom to have tried. Dancing is as permanent and as old as warfare. And that precise, yet generalizing, elegant, typically Austenian phrase "the felicities of rapid motion" extends the irony further. All dances are essentially mating dances, and the end, as well as the means, of dancing is the felicity of rapid motion. Through such prose and such manifold strands of irony Austen brings home the importances of the "little things" she writes about and of the whole tenor of women's belittled lives. A conventional ironist might find balls trivial, much ado about nothing, but the ironist of genius may discover that dancing is even more significant than anxious dancers can imagine and that just as a dance may be much more important to a particular woman than a Napoleonic war, so might the fact of dancing be just as significant to the human race as the face of battle.

Austen's irony sometimes exposes the folly and blindness of social habit. Of course, as a mode of life it can be misused, as Mr. Bennet, Mary Crawford, Mr. Palmer in *Sense and Sensibility*, and even Emma show. However, in general for Austen, it can also create a kind of uncertainty principle, with a liberating effect. It implies that the mind is free to proceed hypothetically in its practical search for understanding and gratification as long as it recognizes its own fallibility and the inherent confusion between seeming and being; it must retain its flexibility toward the future. For Austen, life itself is the principal ironist, the meanings of which can and do change with the passing of time and the flux of perception.

7

Austen makes marriage the aim and end of her fiction, and perhaps that fact has been taken too much for granted. To believe in the goodness and central importance of marriage is to have faith in the goodness of this world. Marriage, promising generation and new life, has often been to comedy what death is to tragedy: the fundamental human experience that supports, in the thoughts and feelings it arouses, the validity of the mode. Marriage has been the traditional point of fusion between personal and social life. It is the most private kind of relationship, and yet it is the outstanding evidence that proves one's obligation to the community and one's need of its sanction. Marriage institutionalizes sex and the means of regenerating the race. It has been a comic compromise between self-gratification and social responsibility. In it, biology, psychology, theology, anthropology, and economics are wed. Austen also offers a good marriage as the hope of intimacy and a potential remedy for the incompleteness of personality in an individualistic age. That people long for it to work that way explains why, in the face of much evidence to the contrary, it is the conventional happy ending of so much fiction of the past two hundred years.

She, however, takes more care than most comic writers do in matching the qualities of her romantic leads and in showing exactly the kind of union that ends her plot. For example, Catherine Morland needs Henry Tilney's intelligence and humor; Darcy needs Elizabeth's lively mind, and she needs his responsible love; and Emma, of course, needs to learn to love, but so does Knightley. It is not enough to be right, proper, and truly moral; one must also be capable of loving another person. "I could not think about you so much without doating on you, faults and all," says Knightley to Emma, "and by dint of fancying so many errors, have been in love with you ever since you were thirteen at least" (*E*, p. 462). From the point of view of moral orthodoxy, that might be suspect, but surely there is nothing more appealing about this character than his love for Emma. The unspoken ideology behind Austen's comedy is that the community must love and cherish the individual—the comic creature the single human being is—or the culture will be sterile. In Austen's fiction, comic concern for one individual woman includes comic concern for the society. Her comedy of union turns out to be the witty celebration of potent individualism embracing the world.

8

That world needs laughter and a woman's laughing mind. Elizabeth Bennet, near the end of *Pride and Prejudice*, in the full bloom of her love, nevertheless thinks this of Darcy: "She remembered that he had yet to learn to be laught at, and it was rather too early to begin" (*PP*, p. 371). In her happy ending, Austen insists on Elizabeth making Darcy finally "the object of open pleasantry" (*PP*, p. 388). And the happy ending of *Emma* makes indispensable comic energy. When all's well for Emma, we get this:

> She was in dancing, singing, exclaiming spirits; and till she had moved about, and talked to herself, and laughed and reflected, she could be fit for nothing rational.... Serious she was, very serious in her thankfulness, and in her resolutions; and yet there was no preventing a laugh, sometimes in the very midst of them. She must laugh at such a close! (*E*, p. 475)

There is a marvelous, almost manic, liveliness about Emma's inner experience, and Austen wants to revel in the exuberance of consciousness. (Hence, just as she does when describing Anne Elliot in *Persuasion* in her happy time of love, Austen uses those performing-art metaphors "dancing, singing, exclaiming" for the emotions.) What stands out here is that at a point of seriousness Emma's comic sense bursts out. That laugh, the imperative of laughter ("she must laugh") at a time when we have just been witnessing, in her meditations, the flowering of her education in moral responsibility, represents the triumph and the power of humor in Austen's imagination and art. The will to find comic delight in the surprise and resiliency of human behavior unites with the comic heroine's ultimate seriousness. High seriousness must not prevent a laugh, and laughter must not exclude moral seriousness.

For me one of Botticelli's finest paintings, *Venus and Mars*, symbolizes nicely the essence of Jane Austen's comedy. Stupid-looking Mars lies sprawled, gaping in sleep, his weapons of war and his armor scattered carelessly beside him. His crude force has been tamed by the beautiful, robed, dominant female figure resting opposite him. This Venus is wide awake, her intelligent-looking, intent, lovely, slightly disdainful and dissatisfied face gazing knowingly into the distance. Comic imps, sporting, laughing, looking back at her, like children of her thoughts under her direction, play with Mars's weapons, crawl in his armor, and jestingly prepare to sound in his ear the battle-announcing conch. They parody and make silly the antics and trappings of raw, barbarous power and cavort in mockery of violence and dull mental torpor. The picture fuses elegant love, feminine power, and a pointed, ironic sense of the ridiculous in order to control and satirize brutishness and to honor civilized life. So does Austen's comic spirit.

Bibliography

BABB, HOWARD S. *Jane Austen's Novels: The Fabric of Dialogue* (Columbus, Ohio, 1962).
BRADBROOK, FRANK W. *Jane Austen and Her Predecessors* (Cambridge, England, 1966).
BROWN, JULIA PREWITT. *Jane Austen's Novels: Social Change and Literary Form* (Cambridge, Mass., 1979).
BUTLER, MARILYN. *Jane Austen and the War of Ideas* (Oxford, 1975).
COOPER, ANTHONY ASHLEY, THIRD EARL OF SHAFTESBURY. *Sensus Communis: An Essay on the Freedom of Wit and Humour* (London, 1709).
HALPERIN, JOHN, ed. *Jane Austen: Bicentenary Essays* (Cambridge, England and New York, 1975).
HARDING, D. W. "Regulated Hatred: An Aspect of the Work of Jane Austen," *Scrutiny*, 8 (1939–40), 346–62.
HARDY, BARBARA. *A Reading of Jane Austen* (London, 1975).
HOBBES, THOMAS. *Leviathan* (London, 1651).
JOHNSON, SAMUEL. *The Rambler*, no. 125 (London, 28 May 1751).
KROEBER, KARL. *Styles in Fictional Structure: The Art of Jane Austen, Charlotte Brontë and George Eliot* (Princeton, N.J., 1971).
LASCELLES, MARY. *Jane Austen and Her Art* (Oxford, 1939).
LEAVIS, Q. D. "A Critical Theory of Jane Austen's Writings," *Scrutiny*, 10 (1941–42), 61–75.
LERNER, LAURENCE. *The Truthtellers: Jane Austen, George Eliot, D. H. Lawrence* (New York and London, 1967).
LIDDELL, ROBERT. *The Novels of Jane Austen* (London, 1963).
LITZ, A. WALTON. *Jane Austen: A Study of Her Artistic Development* (London and New York, 1965).
LODGE, DAVID, ed. *Jane Austen: "Emma"—a Casebook* (London, 1968).
MORGAN, SUSAN. *In the Meantime: Character and Perception in Jane Austen's Fiction* (Chicago, Ill., 1980).
MUDRICK, MARVIN. *Jane Austen: Irony as Defense and Discovery* (Princeton, N.J. and London, 1952).
PARIS, BERNARD J. *Character and Conflict in Jane Austen's Novels: A Psychological Approach* (Detroit, 1977).
POLHEMUS, ROBERT M. *Comic Faith: The Great Tradition from Austen to Joyce* (Chicago, Ill., 1980).
SOUTHAM, B. C., ed. *Critical Essays on Jane Austen* (London and New York, 1968).
———, ed. *Jane Austen: The Critical Heritage* (London and New York, 1968).
———. *Jane Austen's Literary Manuscripts* (London, 1964).
TAVE, STUART M. *Some Words of Jane Austen* (Chicago and London, 1973).
WATT, IAN. *Jane Austen: A Collection of Critical Essays* (Englewood Cliffs, N.J., 1963).

WIESENFARTH, JOSEPH. *The Errand of Form: An Assay of Jane Austen's Art* (New York, 1967).
WILSON, EDMUND. "A Long Talk About Jane Austen," in *Classics and Commercials* (New York, 1950), 196–203.
WRIGHT, ANDREW H. *Jane Austen's Novels: A Study in Structure* (London and New York, 1953).

COMPLETIONS

David Hopkinson

Her own death stilled Jane Austen's pen in 1817, as, I believe, her father's death had done in January 1805. Thus we have been left with two incomplete novels that she had certainly intended to finish and, if possible, to publish. *The Watsons* is the earlier and *Sanditon* the later of loved but prematurely abandoned progeny. The sterner of Jane Austen's critics have puzzled themselves over these fragments, particularly over *Sanditon*; but countless readers have accepted them as truly representative of a genius as ineffably entertaining as in the completed novels.

Efforts to furnish the fragments with appropriate conclusions were at first confined to members of the Austen family. In the twentieth century, however, other authors have thrown their hats into the ring. In England the first completion was published in 1850 and the most recent in 1983. The circumstances leading to the 1850 publication are of some interest and little known. Its author, Catherine Hubback, was the daughter of Jane Austen's brother Adm. Sir Francis Austen; she married a successful barrister in 1842 and had three sons. Unhappily, her husband suffered a mental breakdown that incapacitated him for life. Mrs. Hubback and her young family then lived with her father, and she embarked on a career as a novelist, basing her first book on her aunt's fragment, in which the relatively humble Watson family contrasted with the titled, landowning aristocracy represented by the Osbornes. The manuscript had been left to another niece, Anna Lefroy, but Catherine Hubback was thoroughly familiar with its contents because she had been brought up by her stepmother, who was the old family friend Martha Lloyd. Cassandra, Jane Austen's only sister, was a frequent visitor in their household. Thus, Catherine Hubback derived her ideas of the characters and the plot of Jane Austen's unfinished work from the two women who had been closest to her aunt Jane and completely in her confidence. It is certain that Jane had discussed her story with them and had revealed her intentions for the development and conclusion of the story, probably begun in 1804.

Catherine Hubback worked from her memory of Jane Austen's abortive effort, and the family's recollections of what had been intended, to produce her first novel, *The Younger Sister*. Its opening pages contain turns of phrase and indeed whole speeches that are almost identical with those contained in her aunt's manuscript. Catherine Hubback was well soaked in the language of Jane Austen's novels; moreover, in general outlook and in temperament there were affinities between aunt and niece. As long as she sticks with the characters sketched in by Jane, her novel has a vigorous thrust to it; spirited dialogue is within her power; but the pace slows down as the plot expands. To satisfy the demands of the market, she was required to produce a three-volume work, but it appears that having virtually completed the retelling of the story, as she had heard it from Cassandra and Martha Lloyd, she was not yet at the halfway mark. For the original story was clearly to center on one particular member of the Watson family, Emma, who charms us from its opening scene. There is something in her of Elizabeth Bennet, Elinor Dashwood, and though she is younger, Anne Elliot, too. Catherine Hubback found Emma Watson in the society of Osborne Castle, where she was valued for her good taste, forbearance, and firmness of character by Lord Osborne, his mother, and the young clergyman at the parsonage. All these and others appreciate her qualities, so that it becomes clear that she is to make an impact on their lives. To expand the plot, however, Catherine Hubback found it necessary to remove her heroine to the pretentious, philistine society of her elder brother's family, where Emma's distinctiveness goes unrecognized. To people the second half of her novel, she invents pasteboard characters of no interest to a reader appreciative of Jane Austen. Stylistically, too, the novel deteriorates sadly, for instance, when the villain advances on Emma with the words "No—you need not shrink from me—I am not so mad as to do you harm; you are safe under the protection of the laws. I would not risk my freedom for all the girls in Surrey." Rescued from his insulting attentions by her younger brother, Emma is "on the verge of a fit of hysterics," a condition totally uncharacteristic of Jane Austen's mature heroines.

If one niece errs on the side of excessive length, the other, Anna Lefroy, sells us short. Her attempted continuation of *Sanditon*, published for the first time in 1983, was probably written in the 1830s. It breaks off incomplete and hardly advances the story at all. Anna possessed a certain literary talent but was without the creativity, the confidence, and the motivation of Catherine Hubback, a more robust personality. Her effort to reproduce her aunt's style is no more successful than her cousin's. In Jane Austen's manner she endeavors to present figures in a landscape and to regulate speeches and movements so that new aspects of each character are revealed or old ones reemphasized. In this some success is achieved. We learn a little more about Lady Denham, her late husband's nephew and his sister, and particularly her companion, the mysterious Clara Brereton, but the Lefroy continuation peters out before any significant development of plot has taken place. In this respect it is a disappointment, the more so because James Edward Austen-Leigh had made an allusion in his *Memoir* of Jane Austen to what Cassandra might have told her nieces about the development of this story, as he had done in the case of *The Watsons*.

Until her death at her brother Frank's house in 1845, the *Sanditon* manuscript was in Cassandra's possession. At that time it was apparently copied by Catherine Hubback, who must therefore have regarded *The Watsons* as the easier fragment to expand into a novel of her own. There is no evidence that she intended any such use of the *Sanditon* manuscript. Anna Lefroy, however, thought otherwise, and a somewhat surprising letter she wrote to James Edward Austen-Leigh in 1862 seems to suggest that disappointment over her failure to complete the task she had begun still rankled.

> I agree with you that the MS as it stands is very inferior to the published works and *perhaps* by no corrections could it be worked up to an equality with any other 12 opening chapters; for *that* I think the fairest sort of comparison. If publishing the MS can only gratify curiosity at the expense of the authoress's claim of course under ordinary circumstances it ought not to be attempted—but then comes the question of how entirely to prevent it. The copy, which was taken, not given, is now at the mercy of Mrs. Hubback. And she will be pretty sure to make use of it as soon as she thinks she safely may.

In fact, by 1862 Catherine Hubback had stopped writing.

Between 1922 and 1932 three continuations were published; one, disarmingly entitled *Somehow Lengthened*, was subtitled *A Development of Sanditon*. This "development" goes a long way and in an unexpected direction. Alice Cobbett, its author, chose to exploit her local knowledge of the south coast of Sussex and the town of Hastings. She was also well-read in Byron biography and able to base one of her principal new characters on Lady Bessborough, the mistress of Lord Granville Leveson-Gower, whose letters had recently been published. With such help she created an exciting romance to include smuggling, rape, a duel, and good works among the very poor as new features. The story soon leaves Sanditon, and the Parkers are quietly dropped. It is just consistent with Jane Austen's characterization that Sir Edward Denham should play a nefarious part in the smuggling business, as well as attempting an abduction, but only at the very end does he appear as the laughingstock that he was intended to be. *Somehow Lengthened* is amusing and full of vitality but only just admissible as a Jane Austen completion.

Miss L. Oulton's novel *The Watsons* (1923) is a very short one, with an undated preface appearing over the signature J. E. Austen-Leigh. It turns out to be an extract from the first edition of the *Memoir*, written over fifty years previously. No mention is made of Austen-Leigh's outline of Jane Austen's intentions as transmitted to Cassandra, but Miss Oulton develops the plot in the familiar way. Mr. Watson dies. Lord Osborne proposes marriage to Emma, but it is Mr. Howard whom she loves. It is Lady Osborne and not her daughter, as R. W. Chapman later proposed, who seeks to marry Mr. Howard. Miss Osborne becomes a jealous, arrogant figure, not the real friend to Emma that in *The Younger Sister* she proves herself to be. As a writer, Miss Oulton hardly possesses the Austen touch, as can be seen when she ends a chapter thus: "How little did [Mr. Howard] realize that his idle words were as a naked sword in her breast."

Mrs. Edith Brown wrote a completion in partnership with her husband, Francis. As Catherine Hubback's granddaughter and the part author of *Jane Austen's Sailor Brothers*, she naturally avoided lapses like Miss Oulton's. She had *The Younger Sister* to guide her, and she began by following that text closely. But the main problem—that of disentangling the essence of the original story from the ponderous elaboration of plot and the multiplicity of characters with which Mrs. Hubback had burdened it—remained unsolved. Her book is curiously halfhearted and as attenuated as Miss Oulton's; in both, the length of the continuation is little greater than that of the original fragment.

The next to appear as *The Watsons* was a continuation by John Coates (London 1958 and later New York). Here there is the vigor and confidence lacking in earlier efforts. It is a shock at the start to find Jane Austen corrected and rewritten. Mr. Coates defends this decision because he half wishes to turn her characters into new ones, better suited to the story he intends to tell; but even so, it seems hardly excusable to alter Austen's crisp "Emma did not think, or reflect;—she felt & acted" (p. 330) into "On a sudden impulse and without pausing to reflect on the possible consequence of her action, Emily offered herself. . . ." But such limp prose is uncharacteristic. The story moves at a brisk pace, and among the original characters the author has his successes, particularly Lord Osborne and Penelope Watson, who seems to take over the central role from Emma—somewhat to our relief, for in Mr. Coates's hands Emma becomes unbearably priggish. The author, in defense of his innovations, makes the point that the people Jane Austen has sketched out in her opening scenes tend to look too much like existing Austen characters. His own seem not to run that risk.

Two completions were published in the 1970s with greater initial success in England than their predecessors. *Sanditon*, by Jane Austen "and Another Lady" was first published in America; but *The Watsons*, completed by another anonymous, and this time male, writer has not appeared there. *Sanditon* is the bolder of these two ventures. The author takes her stance on the assumption that however different the scene and the mood of Jane Austen's last novel, the plot was inevitably bound to conform with the general pattern discernible in all her published work. Where others have hesitated about the events to come, this author moves boldly in. Charlotte Heywood is the heroine; Sidney Parker, not a counterfeit like Henry Crawford but a genuine hero with an extraordinary propensity for manipulating the lives of others. A second young man must necessarily be provided for Clara Brereton, here treated as the Jane Fairfax of the story. An elopement has to take place, and an abduction is attempted. All ends happily in the true spirit of comedy, with Sir Edward Denham's total humiliation hilariously presented.

The most recent completion was a companion piece to the above—*The Watsons* once again. Like Edith Brown, the author based his work on *The Younger Sister*. Although he eliminates almost all of Mrs. Hubback's new characters, he invents none of his own, making it his aim to get as near as he can to a retelling of the straightforward story that Cassandra, after reading the incomplete manuscript to her niece, must have gone on to tell. To achieve some echo of the Austen manner, its author shortens and sharpens Mrs. Hubback's sentences and dispenses with her moralizing passages. He confines the action to the four settings that Jane had introduced or indicated. There the characters walk and drive or travel between locations—the castle, the two parsonages, the lawyer brother's small town house—by carriage, post chaise, or gig. The story unfolds gently, with no extraneous dramatic effects attempted.

Both of these books received, as compared with their predecessors, a warm reception from English critics, and they met in Britain with such success that the public's affection for Jane Austen's work was once again emphatically displayed.

Bibliography

Completions
AUSTEN, JANE AND ANOTHER. *The Watsons* (London, 1977).
——— AND ANOTHER LADY. *Sanditon*. (Boston and London, 1975).
———, EDITH BROWN, AND FRANCIS BROWN. *The Watsons* (London, 1928).
——— AND JOHN COATES. *The Watsons* (London, 1958; reprint ed., Westport, Conn., 1973, and New York, 1977).
——— AND ALICE COBBETT. *Somehow Lengthened* (London, 1932).
——— AND MRS. HUBBACK. *The Younger Sister*, 3 vols. (London, 1850).
——— AND ANNA A. LEFROY. *Sanditon: A Continuation* (Chicago, 1983).
——— AND L. OULTON. *The Watsons* (London, 1923).
Studies
CHAPMAN, R. W. *Jane Austen: Facts and Problems* (Oxford, 1948).
HUBBACK, JOHN H. AND EDITH C. HUBBACK. *Jane Austen's Sailor Brothers* (London and New York, 1906).

JANE AUSTEN AND THE CONSUMER REVOLUTION

Edward Copeland

The industrial revolution and the French Revolution may lie at the far horizons of Jane Austen's novels, but the consumer revolution, the extraordinary explosion of economic energy that took place in Great Britain during her lifetime, most certainly does not. Recent studies, especially the distinguished works of Alistair Duckworth and Marilyn Butler, emphasize the significance of landed wealth in Austen's novels. The estate, however, since it lies solely in the hands of men, cannot provide her heroines with an active, managing role in the new economy. In contrast, consumer spending, its dangers and rewards, can. For good and for ill this activity lay within the power of all women, and as contemporary women's fiction, cookbooks, women's magazines, and tracts on domestic economy insist, responsible consumer spending had suddenly become one of the first female virtues.

Austen approaches the consumer economy with two closely related but separate concerns: the demands of her class and the responsibilities of her sex. David Spring's recent essay "Interpreters of Jane Austen's World" usefully defines Austen's own class as the "pseudo-gentry," the nonlanded professionals of the rural elite she writes about, who were, writes Spring, "gentry of a sort, primarily because they sought strenuously to be taken for gentry" (p. 60). These included, writes Spring, "first and foremost the Anglican clergy; second, other professions like the law—preferably barristers rather than solicitors—and the fighting services; and last, the rentiers recently or long retired from business" (p. 59). The intense interest displayed by this class in "positional goods" and annual income is part and parcel of their striving for station. Heiresses' fortunes in Austen's novels are regularly read in terms of yearly spendable income based on their investment in government funds: in *Pride and Prejudice*, in the 4 percent funds; in the other novels, in the 5 percent funds. As Mr. Collins tells Elizabeth, "I am well aware . . . that one thousand pounds in the 4 per cents. which will not be yours till after your mother's decease, is all that you may ever be entitled to" (*PP*, p. 106). Even land-based wealth in Austen's novels is reported in terms of yearly income: Colonel Brandon, for example, has £2,000 per annum; Mr. Bennet, £2,000; Mr. Darcy, £10,000; Mr. Crawford, £4,000.

Women, however, are in a paradoxical situation in such an economy: they are important consumers, but they have no means of generating income. The question of finding a responsible role for women in these circumstances is central in Austen's works from "Love and Freindship" to *Sanditon*. As David Spring suggests, Jane Austen's novels celebrate the rise of the pseudo-gentry but, even more, they address the fate of women in that society (pp. 63 and 68). For Austen and for her contemporaries woman's fate was intimately bound up in her adjustments to the consumer revolution.

According to the authors of *The Birth of a Consumer Society*, Neil McKendrick, John Brewer, and J. H. Plumb, the signs of a profound change in the economy were obvious to even the most casual observer of English life. Consumer goods, which formerly people might have hoped to acquire by inheritance, were now within the reach of anyone with ready cash. "The children of farmers, artificers, all come into the world as gentry," Clara Reeve complains in *Plans of Education* (1792, p. 61). The sudden and rapid inflation caused by the French wars, over 100 percent in the 1790s, together with new government taxes were distressing to all, but especially to people on fixed incomes: "Every article of consumption is nearly doubled, nay, trebled, within the last twenty years!" claims Mary Ann Hanway in her novel *Falconbridge Abbey* (1809); "Of the luxuries of life we do not speak. . . . There are imposts that cannot be evaded by the man of small fortune that deprive him of every decent, every accustomed comfort" (vol. 1, pp. 72–73). In fact, the cost of the necessities of life rose at a greater rate during the period than consumer luxuries, according to John Burnett's study *A History of the Cost of Living* (p. 137). Anyone who could cover the cost of subsistence with his income and had something left over could spend it for heretofore prohibitively priced material possessions. A character in Mary Meeke's novel *Conscience* (1814) announces in outrage, "now every petty clerk sports boots, pantaloons, jackets, and bang-up great-coats; and spends more in clothes in one year than he earns in two" (vol. 1, pp. 280–81).

The rush for capital, both for consumer spending and for investing, affected all classes, from artisans to aristocrats. With banking practices primitive and corporate arrangements nonexistent, any man with ready capital, even with small amounts, was in an enviable position to profit in the new economy. The contemporary economist John Trusler in his work *The Master's Last, Best Gift, to His Apprentice* (London, 1812) cautions a young tradesman not to marry until he can find a woman with a fortune of at least one thousand pounds. Among the aristocrats, Lord Sefton, in 1791, instructed his heir "not to look at less than 60,000" (quoted in Thompson, p. 19). Elizabeth Bennet jokingly confronts this economic fact of life when she asks Colonel Fitzwilliam, "And pray, what is the usual price of an Earl's younger son? Unless the elder brother is very sickly, I suppose you would not ask above fifty thousand pounds" (*PP*, pp. 183–84). No man, or so it seemed to contemporaries, could afford to marry without money. "In the present age," writes Jane Marshall in *A Series of Letters* (1788), "people in a middle station, with perhaps a genteel income but a small capital, wish ardently to have their daughters disposed of in marriage." The chances, however, are likely, she concludes, that the girl will be left "to live on the scanty interest of a few hundreds, which in her parents' lifetime would scarcely defray the expence of her chair-hire" (vol. 1, pp. 113–14).

In this time of rising prices, opening markets, competition for capital, and rampant spending, heroines became both prey and victim. Contemporary women novelists looked about and found, quite simply, horrors. In Fanny Burney's *Cecilia* (1782), the heroine loses her fortune and runs mad in the streets; in *Camilla* (1796), the heroine runs mad again, this time after discovering that her father has been imprisoned for her debts. The heroine of *The Wanderer* (1814), reduced to earn her own bread, was, writes Burney, "a being who had been cast upon herself; a female Robinson Crusoe, as unaided and unprotected, though in the midst of the world, as that imaginary hero in his uninhabited island" (vol. 5, pp. 394–95). Emily St. Aubin, in Mrs. Radcliffe's *Mysteries of Udolpho* (1794), does not escape the clutches of the villainous Montoni until she receives an independent income from her late aunt's will. In Maria Edgeworth's *Castle Rackrent* (1800) and in *Belinda* (1801), the spending of money is associated with madness, disease, and death. Jane Austen also found horrors—John and Fanny Dashwood, to name only two—but the tone she strikes, the attitude toward money, that she presents in her novels, issues from a profoundly different conception of her task as a novelist. Rather than project her inner fears onto the stage in the costumes of melodrama, she addresses her society in its own terms—its own economic terms. Austen is unique, I think, among contemporary women novelists in meeting the new economy with positive enthusiasm, even admiration, for the power of the economic metaphor to describe contemporary life.

She meticulously attaches the economies of her novels to the contemporary economy. The incomes of her characters, for example, are never really private. Although John Dashwood slyly avoids telling his sister Elinor his precise income, she learns all she needs to know, as does the reader, from the economic subtext Jane Austen provides. The trip to London for the season, for example, affirms incomes of from £4,000 to £5,000 per annum and upward (Thompson, pp. 25–26). Bingley, Darcy, Henry Crawford, and Mr. Rushworth make the trip. Sir Thomas Bertram spends the season in town until indolence inclines Lady Bertram to stay home. Sir Walter Elliot and Elizabeth go until they can no longer afford to, their loss of the London season indicating the precise extent of their financial difficulties. The John Dashwoods, by contrast, celebrate their rise to fortune by making the trip for the first time—Mrs. Ferrars, with her "noble spirit," giving Fanny an extra £200 to help with unexpected expenses (*SS*, pp. 224–25).

Carriages perform the same service in indicating the income of a private gentleman. John Trusler in *The Economist* (1774) suggests that a gentleman can keep a carriage on an income of £800. Samuel Adams and Sarah Adams in *The Complete Servant* (1825) recommend it only for incomes between £1,000 and £1,500 per annum. In *Northanger Abbey*, Henry Tilney, whose income is not provided in cash figures, drives a curricle of his own, thus confirming his father's assertion that he is not "ill provided for" (p. 176) in his church living. The income from Mr. Knightley's estate that he allows himself for personal expenses is suggested with some precision by the fact that he does not use his carriage except on rare occasions (*E*, p. 213). When Mr. Perry, the apothecary in Highbury, is rumored to be setting up his carriage, his income and his social pretensions become the focus of village interest. Mr. Weston, who has recently bought a small estate and set up his own carriage, is cautious in accepting the story: "just what will happen, I have no doubt, some time or other; only a little premature" (*E*, p. 345). Robert Ferrars takes a carriage on the £1,000 per annum that his mother gives him; Mrs. Dashwood sensibly relinquishes her carriage when her income falls to only £500 (*SS*, pp. 26 and 354). After Anne Elliot's marriage to Captain Wentworth, she is seen driving a "very pretty landaulette" (*P*, p. 250)—Wentworth's £25,000 fortune invested in the 5 percent government funds will yield £1,250 per annum.

Servants supply the public evidence for the lower ranges of incomes in Austen's novels. These, significantly, are women's incomes. In *Persuasion*, Mrs. Smith has no servant; in *Emma*, Miss Bates has one; in *Mansfield Park*, Mrs. Price has two; in *Sense and Sensibility*, Mrs. Dashwood has three; and in the same novel Mrs. Jennings imagines four servants on the same income for Lucy Steele and Edward Ferrars, but she probably takes into account the garden and the savings on rent at the Delaford parsonage.

At this lower scale, the number of servants, or their lack, speaks volumes. Mrs. Smith, who is "unable even to afford herself the comfort of a servant," possesses the lowest income of a genteel character in the novels. The lowest taxable—that is, marginally respectable—income in Austen's time was £50 per annum. Of this sum, James Luckcock writes in his *Hints for Practical Economy* (1834), "It would appear a very ungracious task to attempt to exhibit a lower scale" (p. 9). He does not suggest the possibility of its supporting a servant. A tract entitled "Considerations of the expedience of raising, at this time of dearth the wages of . . . clerks in public office" (1767) describes the life of a single man living on this sum:

I have driven him to the dirtiest and meanest parts of town to seek for a cheap lodging; I have cloathed him in the plainest and coarsest manner; I have scarcely allowed him to be clean enough for the place of his stated appearance ... and yet, with all this economy and penury the wretch, at the year's end, has no more than twelve shillings and ninepence to lay by for sickness and old age. (quoted by George, pp. 77–78)

It closely suggests Mrs. Smith's predicament: "a noisy parlour, and a dark bed-room behind"; her anxiety over medical expenses—"the absolute necessity of having a regular nurse, and finances at that moment particularly unfit to meet any extraordinary expense" (p. 154); and a bad part of town—"Westgate-buildings must have been rather surprised by the appearance of a carriage drawn up near its pavement!" exclaims Sir Walter Elliot (pp. 157–58). Isabella Thorpe's sentimental hypocrisy in *Northanger Abbey* is never clearer than in her assertion to Catherine Morland that if her "union" with James Morland "could take place now upon only fifty pounds a year, I should not have a wish unsatisfied" (p. 136).

The first income to merit having a servant attached is £100 per annum. Samuel and Sarah Adams recommend one servant to the possessor of this income: "*A Widow* or other *unmarried Lady*, may keep a *Young Maid Servant*, at a low salary; say from 5 to 10 Guineas a year" (p. 5). This fits Miss Bates, even in her unmarried state, except that she has her mother to support, as well. Her one servant, Patty, cleans, cooks, and answers the door. Any additional expense on an income at the one-servant level arrives as a shock: "Oh!" cries Miss Bates upon hearing that the chimney needs sweeping, "Patty do not come with your bad news to me" (*E*, p. 236). A potential medical fee for Jane Fairfax's cough requires courage: "The expense shall not be thought of," Miss Bates claims bravely (p. 162). Apples from Mr. Knightley and pork from Mr. Woodhouse are luxuries indeed, as any contemporary would know.

Mrs. Price's two servants in *Mansfield Park* are a similarly public statement of income. The Adamses suggest that on an income of £300 per annum Mrs. Price could have her two servants (p. 5); Luckcock claims that it would take £400 per annum (p. 14); Trusler says that precisely £370 16s. a year would be necessary (*Economist*, p. 5). Since Mr. Price's income as a half-pay naval officer, according to Colquhoun's tables of 1803, would be about £45 per annum, inadequate for such a show, the contemporary reader would look to the fortune Mrs. Price brought to the marriage, which must have been equal to Lady Bertram's, £7,000. This amount invested in 5 percent government funds would return the Price family the necessary £350, which together with Mr. Price's half pay would support their style of life, such as it is. This is a moderate income, which, as Fanny must admit, her Aunt Norris could have managed much more respectably.

Finally, Mrs. Dashwood goes to Barton Cottage in *Sense and Sensibility* on £500 per annum, taking two maids and a man. This meets the Adamses' recommendations with only minor alterations in the staff. When the Austens retire to Bath in 1801, Jane writes Cassandra, "We plan having a steady Cook, & a young giddy Housemaid, with a sedate, middle aged Man, who is to undertake the double office of Husband to the former & sweetheart to the latter.—No Children of course to be allowed on either side" (*Letters*, January 3, 1801). This, in wages at least, is what the Adamses would recommend for the £500–600 per annum income of the Austen family (p. 5).

All of Jane Austen's novels share these three basic signposts of income —the London season, the carriage, and servants. The early novels, however—*Northanger Abbey, Sense and Sensibility*, and *Pride and Prejudice* —differ in important ways from the mature works of *Mansfield Park, Emma,* and *Persuasion*. In the first group, dramatic shifts of fortune, from high to low and from low to high, characterize the economic patterns; great wealth exercises power in grand and unanswerable gestures; heroes and heroines bridge huge gaps in fortune by sweetness and candor, unlooked-for good fortune, or shining intelligence. The more hard-grained economic facts of life among the gentry and the pseudo-gentry, such as we discover in the later novels, simply do not appear in the early ones: the real disadvantages of a low income experienced by Miss Bates, Mrs. Price, and Mrs. Smith; the Eltons' officious vulgarity; the economic decisions that plague Maria Bertram and Mary Crawford; Charles and Mary Musgrove's tiresome financial mismanagement. At the same time, the economic forces that do move the action of the early novels give pause. They are mysterious, threatening, and sometimes personally malevolent.

The economic world of *Northanger Abbey* would appear at first glance to be the exception. The novel's plentiful display of consumer goods of Bath in the 1790s possesses a gaiety and "harmless delight" no more threatening than Mrs. Allen's pleasure in "being fine." Hats, cravats, muslins, coquelicot ribbons, even "parties of ladies . . . in quest of pastry, millinery, or . . . young men" (p. 44) are treated with a measure of tolerance and good humor. General Tilney's improvements at the Abbey, though they reflect his vanity and his excessive love of money, also keep out the rain, make rooms cozy, and present an attractive table. Isabella Thorpe's unstable principles are matched by the confusion of hats, turbans, and broken hearts in the letter she writes Catherine, but "such a strain of shallow artifice could not impose even upon Catherine" (p. 218). When John Thorpe calls Catherine's brother James a "fool" for not keeping a horse and gig of his own, Catherine's answer is prompt and sound: "No, he is not . . . for I am sure he could not afford it" (p. 89). And though Thorpe's greedy boorishness displays itself in his overweening interest in the fine points of used carriages, consumer luxuries carry with them no intrinsic associations of either social unrest or moral failings, as they often do in the works of Austen's contemporaries. It takes only a "very short trial" to convince Catherine that Henry Tilney's curricle is "the prettiest equipage in the world.... And then his hat sat so well, and the innumerable capes of his great coat looked so becomingly important!" (pp. 156–57). The potentially disturbing spirit represented in General Tilney is countered by Mr. Morland's generous gift to James of a £400-per-annum living and by the comfortable church living possessed by Henry Tilney. There is a moment, however, when a genuine chill of economic danger descends on two characters. Significantly, it is a small sum—a woman's sum. Eleanor Tilney suddenly remembers to ask Catherine as they wait for the coach that will take her away from the abbey if she has "money enough for the expenses of her journey." Catherine finds she does not, and Eleanor lends her five pounds—but "the distress in which she must have been thereby involved filling the minds of both, scarcely another word was said by either during the time of their remaining together" (p. 229). This is real fear instantly verifiable by every reader.

The economic world of *Sense and Sensibility* reflects a far more sober, even frightened response to the predicament of women in a remorselessly money-oriented society. Here we find an economy of sudden loss, unpredictable gain, arbitrary power, economic treachery, and mean-spirited, grasping people in all ranks. The greed of the John Dashwoods and the ruthless ambitions of old Mrs. Ferrars make mockery of the family itself. The novel, in fact, opens with an act of familial ingratitude: Henry Dashwood's uncle secures the major part of his fortune for the benefit of the John Dashwoods' four-year-old son, thereby completely discounting "all the value," writes Austen, "of all the attention which, for years, he had received from his niece and her daughters" (p. 4). "He meant not to be unkind however," she adds, "and, as a mark of his affection for the three girls, he left them a thousand pounds a-piece." That is, each of the Dashwood girls is left with a potential income of only £50 per annum. Anne Plumptre in her novel *The History of Myself and My Friend* (1813) meets this sum more directly than does Austen's quiet irony: "to the daughters he nobly bequeathed a thousand pounds each," she writes of a father who leaves all the rest of his large estate to the eldest son, "after having given them ideas, from the style of living in his house, which ought not to have been given to any young ladies unless they were to have an annual income of nearly that amount." "Poor things!" a sympathetic older woman cries. "And what are they all to do now?" (vol. 1, pp. 4–5).

In *Sense and Sensibility* the wicked, the stupid, and the selfish are rewarded financially, exercise power without control, and are by their own lights successful without check. The series of financial acts that direct the plot are themselves negative assertions of economic tyranny: the ungrateful uncle disinherits his nieces; Fanny and John Dashwood refuse to help the Dashwood women in their straitened circumstances; Mrs. Ferrars will not settle an income on Edward; Mrs. Allen drops Willoughby from her will; Willoughby abandons Marianne; Lucy Steele refuses to return the money she borrows from her sister. Even Willoughby's seduction of Miss Williams shocks everyone not so much for its sexual treachery but for the fact that he leaves her destitute. Mrs. Jennings and Sir John Middleton are kind, but they cannot right the economic wrongs suffered by the protagonists. Colonel Brandon, with his £2,000 per annum, is generous, but his gift to Edward of the living of Delaford at £200 per annum is not adequate to compensate for what he has lost. In fact, typical of the economic action of this novel, Colonel Brandon's gift is as arbitrary and unexpected as any of Mrs. Ferrars's mercurial decisions, and as John Dashwood notes, not nearly as natural as her motherly revenge (pp. 294-95). Finally, Mrs. Ferrars's gift, which enables Edward and Elinor to marry at the end of the novel, is as surprising as anything else she has done and is certainly "more than was expected by Edward and Elinor" (p. 374).

The abstract quality of material possessions in *Sense and Sensibility* results, I think, from the frightening power that money seems to have in this novel. The gaps in income are enormous: Marianne Dashwood can bring £1,000 to a marriage, or £50 per annum; Miss Grey brings £50,000 or £2,500 per annum. Robert Ferrars has £1,000 per annum; Edward has only one-tenth that amount. Fine prints, music, and books of poetry for Marianne and Elinor remain in Edward's imagination (p. 92); the gift of Willoughby's horse is refused with only a mild ruffle of spirits—we never see it; the earrings that John Dashwood considers for his sisters never make it out of the shop in Sackville Street (p. 226). Edward's ring with the lock of Lucy Steele's hair and Lucy's miniature of Edward have more power as emblems of oppression than they have as objects of costume, much in the same way that Robert Ferrars's toothpick case is a token of his own "natural, sterling insignificance" (p. 221). Mrs. Jennings's "finest old Constantia wine" stays in our minds, I think, because it is small, intimate, and offers comfort in this novel's strangely inhuman world of things.

Although greatly different in spirit, *Pride and Prejudice* shares with *Sense and Sensibility* an economic world that operates on much the same set of principles. Large incomes dwarf the smaller ones; great sums of money arrive from nowhere; the potential loss of Longbourn by entail—a fall from fortune without remedy—echoes the Dashwood women's predicament; and consumer goods are more present in the minds of greedy, ambitious characters than they are in experience. Mr. Collins, for example, knows the price of a chimneypiece at Rosings (£800), and the cost of the glazing (pp. 75 and 161); he boasts that Lady Catherine has "several" carriages (p. 157); he insists that Elizabeth admire every article of furniture in his humble abode "from the sideboard to the fender," but the demand is accumulative, not specific. For the economic fools in *Pride and Prejudice*, display is all that counts: "What pin-money, what jewels, what carriages you will have!" cries Mrs. Bennet in an ecstasy of consumer delight: "Jane's is nothing to it—nothing at all" (p. 378).

Austen's language of money and possessions, however, is richer in *Pride and Prejudice* by dint of the better-furnished minds of its protagonists. The piano that Darcy buys for his sister, though we never see or hear it, the fresh fittings he has prepared for her favorite room, together with the "beautiful pyramids of grapes, nectarines, and peaches" (p. 268) he supplies his guests, weigh more heavily in the imagination than all the glazing at Rosings because it appears that there is someone at Pemberley to appreciate the piano, the furnishings, and the fruit for the pleasure they can give, to invest them with the human values that material possessions can bear in Austen's novels—a topic handled so well by Barbara Hardy in her book *A Reading of Jane Austen*.

The potential of the economic metaphor to chart the most intimate feelings of her characters, a source of great and insistent power in *Mansfield Park*, enters Austen's novels as early as *Pride and Prejudice*. Jokingly, Elizabeth tells Jane that she dates her love for Darcy "from my first seeing his beautiful grounds at Pemberley" (p. 373), her self-conscious awareness of the irony of her rise to riches removing the sting. But the consumer metaphor that lies open here for laughter becomes a significant expression of Elizabeth's free mind, her ability to choose, a power that in *Sense and Sensibility* is precisely what is missing. As Elizabeth ruefully reviews her feelings after the news of Lydia's elopement, Austen sets her thoughts about Darcy in terms almost subconscious of consumer choice: "She began now to comprehend that he was exactly the man, who, in disposition and talents, would most suit her. His understanding and temper, though unlike her own, would have answered all her wishes." Her mind then moves to another, related economic metaphor, "partnership," which later in *Persuasion* becomes a central value in the marriage plot: "It was an union," she thinks, "that must have been to the advantage of both" (p. 312).

In Austen's last three novels, *Mansfield Park*, *Emma*, and *Persuasion*, she shifts her focus from the business of getting or marrying money to the more complex task in her novels of spending it. A spokesman for the author in Hannah More's *Cœlebs in Search of a Wife* (1809) characterizes the combined moral and economic action of *Mansfield Park* to perfection: "there is no surer test both of integrity and judgment, than a well proportioned expenditure" (vol. 2, p. 172). Fanny Price, the heroine, is herself introduced into the novel as an "expense." Sir Thomas Bertram and Mrs.

Norris debate the wisdom of it in the early pages of the novel, and not until the final pages is the question resolved. When Sir Thomas Bertram consents to the marriage of Fanny and his son Edmund, he does so not only in the same terms of the initial debate but with specific memories of that event as well: "the high sense of having realised a great acquisition in the promise of Fanny for a daughter, formed just such a contrast with his early opinion on the subject when the poor little girl's coming had been first agitated. . . . His liberality had a rich repayment" (p. 472). The question of a "well-proportioned" expenditure brackets the action of a novel in which nearly all the characters are tested in some way by their notion of a proper expense.

Lady Bertram has no notion of expense at all; she asks Sir Thomas. Mrs. Norris bustles about with her economies, but in the great project of the theater she is so busy saving "half-a-crown here and there to the absent Sir Thomas" (p. 163) that she misses the impropriety of the overall expense, not to mention the subversion of all Sir Thomas's domestic values. The third sister, Fanny's mother, presides over an ill-managed house in Portsmouth, "wishing to be an economist, without contrivance or regularity" (p. 389).

Domestic economy and moral economy hold true in their relationship for the younger generation, as well. Mary Crawford, with an irony that reflects on her own faulty principles, suggests that Maria Bertram has paid a high price in taking Mr. Rushworth for a husband: "she will open one of the best houses in Wimpole Street. . . . and certainly she will then feel—to use a vulgar phrase—that she has got her penny-worth for her penny" (p. 394). For Edmund's sake, Fanny worries about Mary's notions of a proper expenditure: "A house in town!—*that* she thought must be impossible. Yet there was no saying what Miss Crawford might not ask" (p. 417). In Fanny's most despairing moment, Edmund's future with Mary opens before her in terms of economic catastrophe: "He is blinded, and nothing will open his eyes, nothing can, after having had truths before him so long in vain.—He will marry her, and be poor and miserable" (p. 424). A house in town, as Austen's readers would recognize instantly, would be a disastrous venture on £1,700 per annum—Mary bringing £1,000 per annum from her £20,000 fortune and Edmund contributing £700 per annum from his Thornton Lacey living.

Objects of consumer display are also measured by Hannah More's "sure test" of judgment. Fanny's first thought when Mary Crawford offers her a gold necklace to wear with her amber cross is that "the gift was too valuable" (p. 258). She looks in Mary's collection for the "least valuable" but is subtly pressured into taking one more expensive than the one she prefers and, to her horror, the very one that is the least appropriate of all. An act of supposed kindness turns into a sorry shopping trip, with Mary as the cunning vendor and Fanny the unsuspecting buyer. Mary displays her charms before Edmund Bertram in the same way. She poses herself in Mrs. Grant's parlor in the mode of the fashion plates of the *Lady's Magazine* or of *La Belle Assemblée*: "A young woman, pretty, lively, with a harp as elegant as herself; and both placed near a window, cut down to the ground, and opening on a little lawn, surrounded by shrubs in the rich foliage of summer, was enough to catch any man's heart" (p. 65). Fanny surrounds herself with material goods as well, and the books she buys "from the first hour of her commanding a shilling" (p. 151) make a picture for us, and for Edmund, in the old schoolroom. But no visitor is expected; the design to "catch any man's heart" is absent.

Shopping, however, is not itself a reprehensible activity in Austen's novels. The metaphor tells against Mary Crawford, but it tells for Fanny Price. Jane Austen announces the transfer of Edmund's feelings from Mary to Fanny in much the spirit of an unexpectedly successful shopping expedition: "Scarcely had he done regretting Mary Crawford, and observing to Fanny how impossible it was that he should ever meet with such another woman," writes Austen, "before it began to strike him whether a very different kind of woman might not do just as well—or a great deal better" (p. 470). In effect, Mary is placed back on the shelf to wait in London for "her beauty, and her 20,000*l*." to attract "idle heir apparents" (p. 469), while Fanny is taken home to Mansfield Park by Edmund as a richly appreciated "acquisition."

If *Mansfield Park* looks inward for tests of integrity and judgment, *Emma* turns outward to all ranks and types of the gentry and pseudo-gentry for the social test. Incomes and spending in *Emma* are an open book for all Highbury to read, to interpret, and to misinterpret. In *Mansfield Park*, Fanny Price's amber cross from her brother William, with its gold chain from Edmund, is a token of affection intensely private; in *Emma*, Jane Fairfax's counterpart gift, a Broadwood piano, is large, public, and subject to the speculation of the entire village. The plot of *Emma* begins on a wave of consumer acquisitions. We learn that Miss Taylor has married Mr. Weston and now has a carriage of her own; that Mr. Weston has retired from trade and has bought a small estate; that Mr. Elton "has fitted up his house so comfortably that it would be a shame to have him single any longer" (p. 13). It is a society in movement, with every step marked by significant positional goods. The Coles are on the way up: they have a new dining room, more servants, a new pianoforte, and more "expenses of every sort" (pp. 207 and 215). Mrs. Perry talks of Mr. Perry's setting up his carriage (p. 344); Mr. and Mrs. Elton parade with unremitting vulgarity their new joint income in a new carriage, more servants than they can remember names, and, of course, Mrs. Elton's lace and pearls. In contrast, Miss Bates, Mrs. Bates, and Jane Fairfax are on the way down: "ours is rather a dark staircase," Miss Bates warns (p. 239).

Consumer luxuries lead the imaginations of Highbury about like will-o'-the-wisps. Mr. Perry's potential carriage gives interesting speculations to Mrs. Perry, Mrs. and Miss Bates, the Coles, and Jane Fairfax before reaching Frank Churchill and then surfacing again in Frank's public blunder on the grounds of Hartfield. Jane Fairfax's new pianoforte stimulates Emma to imaginative excesses that come back to haunt her. The appearance of Mr. Knightley's carriage at the Coles' dinner party with Jane Fairfax and Miss Bates turns Mrs. Weston's mind toward matrimony. Too much of Mr. Weston's "good wine" literally leads Mr. Elton's mind astray. Emma's drawing of Harriet Smith, the "precious deposit" that Mr. Elton takes to London for a frame, misleads, too —Harriet, Emma, and Mr. Elton. The picture, in fact, is a deliberately falsified advertisement of Harriet's charms with eyebrows, eyelashes, and height more elegant than she actually possesses.

The only right way of dealing with the confusion is found in Mr. Knightley's praise of Robert Martin's financial accounting: "He always speaks to the purpose; open, straight forward, and very well judging" (p. 59). Emma and Mr. Knightley must speak this language together before the novel can close. Money is one of the few subjects that Austen gives them that, when Emma is not being deliberately perverse, they can consider in the same terms, though not always at the same time. "Mr. Elton," says Mr. Knightley bluntly, "knows the value of a good income as well as anybody.... I have heard him speak with great animation of a large family of young ladies that his sisters are intimate with, who have all twenty thousand pounds apiece" (p. 66). When Emma's eyes are opened, she speaks with equal plainness: "He only wanted to aggrandize and enrich himself; and if Miss Woodhouse of Hartfield, the heiress of thirty thousand pounds, were not quite so easily obtained as he had fancied, he would soon try for Miss Somebody else with twenty, or with ten" (p. 135). Emma's first response to Frank Churchill's trip to London for a haircut is little different from Mr. Knightley's. "It did not accord with the rationality of plan," she thinks, "the moderation in expense, or even the unselfish warmth of heart which she had believed herself to discern in him yesterday" (p. 205). Mr. Knightley is heard to mutter, "Hum! just the trifling, silly fellow I took him for" (p. 206). And finally, it is plain talk about economics that furnishes the denouement of the novel at Box Hill, when Mr. Knightley rebukes Emma for insulting Miss Bates:

> Were she a woman of fortune, I would leave every harmless absurdity to take its chance. . . . but, Emma, consider how far this is from being the case. She is poor; she has sunk from the comforts she was born to; and, if she live to old age, must probably sink more. Her situation should secure your compassion. It was badly done, indeed! (p. 375)

"Comforts" mark Miss Bates's fall, and they also mark the distance Emma has strayed from kindness, compassion, and from the social responsibilities of her rank. "Never had she felt so agitated, mortified, grieved, at any circumstance in her life. She was most forcibly struck. The truth of his representation there was no denying" (p. 376). It is fitting that in this insistently "comforts"-oriented novel Mrs. Elton should have the last word on the union of Emma and Mr. Knightley: "Very little white satin, very few lace veils; a most pitiful business!—Selina would stare when she heard of it" (p. 484).

In *Persuasion*, Austen focuses on women's role as managers of the family budget. It was a topic that had become more and more frequent in novels, in tracts on women's education, and in practical household guides. Good sense with money becomes the distinguishing characteristic of heroines in the novels of Hannah More, Margaret Cullen, Mary Brunton, Susan Ferrier, and many others. "A discreet woman . . . adjusts her expenses to her revenues," writes More in *Cœlebs*: "She will live within her income be it large or small; if large, she will not be luxurious, if small she will not be mean" (vol. 2, p. 172). Jane West in her *Letters to a Young Lady* (1806) recommends to women the study of arithmetic: they "should understand the value of commodities, be able to calculate expenses, and to tell what a specific income will afford" (vol. 3, pp. 259–60). Mrs. Maria Eliza Rundell's famous *New System of Domestic Cookery* (1806, 4th ed. 1818) claims that "many families have owed their prosperity full as much to the propriety of female management, as to the knowledge and activity of the father" (p. xxix).

In *Persuasion*, the late Lady Elliot, Anne Elliot, Lady Russell, Mrs. Croft, even Mrs. Smith, show abilities in this line. While Anne's mother had lived, "there had been method, moderation, and economy, which had just kept him within his income; but with her had died all such right-mindedness, and from that period he had been constantly exceeding it" (p. 9). Lady Russell's "exact calculations" and "plans of economy" to prevent Sir Walter from having to leave Kellynch Hall are rejected out of hand: "What! Every comfort of life knocked off!" (p. 13). Anne's proposals are not even heard: "She considered it as an act of indispensable duty to clear away the claims of creditors, with all the expedition which the most comprehensive retrenchments could secure, and saw no dignity in any thing short of it" (pp. 12–13). When the family must finally leave, it is Anne who responsibly makes a "duplicate of the catalogue" of the books and pictures of Kellynch.

By contrast, Mrs. Croft is her husband's partner in economic decisions. The admiral and his wife meet Mr. Shepherd to discuss renting Kellynch Hall: "And a very well-spoken, genteel, shrewd lady, she seemed to be," Mr. Shepherd reports to Sir Walter: "asked more questions about the house, and terms, and taxes, than the admiral himself, and seemed more conversant with business" (p. 22). This is the kind of marriage that Anne implicitly finds with Captain Wentworth. As the two lovers talk together at Sir Walter's and Elizabeth's evening party, Captain Wentworth asks Anne's opinion on a hypothetical economic decision: "Tell me," says Wentworth, "if, when I returned to England in the year eight, with a few thousand pounds, and was posted into the Laconia, if I had then written to you, would you have answered my letter? would you, in short, have renewed the engagement then?' 'Would I!' was all her answer; but the accent was decisive enough" (p. 247).

The new economy provides Austen with a metaphor that embraces morals, ethics, social responsibility, and even love. Implicit in its language is choice in all the great affairs of life. In the early novels, the heroines possess values that simply outshine the harsh conditions of economic worlds that are arbitrary and unanswerable in their operations. In the later novels, women take more control of their fates through active engagement with the economy. In *Mansfield Park*, Fanny's personal integrity defeats Mr. Crawford's fortune, but Maria Bertram falls willing victim to Mr. Rushworth's £14,000 per annum. Mary Crawford's faulty principles are seen simultaneously as moral and economic. Emma must learn to act on the "straight forward" and "well judging" principles, economic, social, and moral, that Mr. Knightley admires in Mr. Martin in order to take on her role as mistress of Donwell Abbey. Anne Elliot joins Captain Wentworth in a marriage conceived in the metaphor of a partnership, its economic potential not the least of its charms.

Women find their place in Austen's novels within the family economic unit, but in a far different manner than that of the later "angel in the house." Austen's women are not sequestered from the world, since their frame of reference is the same as that of the larger world, the language of the burgeoning new consumer economy in which carriages, horses, servants, and pianofortes are crucial signals in a feverishly competitive society. Her niece, Fanny Knight, remembered Aunt Jane in later years as being "not so *refined*, as she ought to have been from her talent. . . . They were not rich and the people around with whom they chiefly mixed, were not at all high bred, or in short anything more than *mediocre* and *they* of course tho' superior in *mental powers* and *cultivation* were on the same level as far as *refinement* goes" (quoted by Greene, p. 1027). There could hardly exist better testimony to Jane Austen's tough-minded relationship to her own class and its values. She took its values, its daily language, and its "*mediocre*" tone and turned them into art.

Bibliography

ADBURGHAM, ALISON. *Shopping in Style: London from the Restoration to Edwardian Elegance* (London, 1979).
ALEXANDER, DAVID. *Retailing in England During the Industrial Revolution* (London, 1970).
ASHTON, T. S. *An Economic History of England: The 18th Century* (London, 1955).
AUSTEN-LEIGH, EMMA. *Jane Austen and Steventon* (London, 1937).
———. *Jane Austen and Bath* (London, 1939).
BANFIELD, ANN. "The Influence of Place: Jane Austen and the Novel of Social Consciousness," in David Monaghan, ed., *Jane Austen in a Social Context* (London, 1981), 28–48.
BRIGGS, ASA. *The Age of Improvement, 1783–1867* (London and New York, 1959).
BURNETT, JOHN. *A History of the Cost of Living* (Harmondsworth, 1969).
BUTLER, MARILYN. *Jane Austen and the War of Ideas* (Oxford, 1975).
COCKSHUT, A. O. J. *Man and Woman: A Study of Love and the Novel, 1740–1940* (London, 1977).
Collected Reports of the Jane Austen Society, 1949–1965 (London, 1967).
COPELAND, EDWARD. "What's a Competence? Jane Austen, Her Sister Novelists, and the 5%'s," *Modern Language Studies*, 9, no. 3 (1979), 161–68.
COURT, W. H. B. *A Concise Economic History of Britain from 1750 to Recent Times* (Cambridge, England, 1954).
DAICHES, DAVID. "Jane Austen, Karl Marx, and the Aristocratic Dance," *American Scholar*, 17 (1947–48), 289–96.
DEANE, PHYLLIS AND W. A. COLE. *British Economic Growth, 1688–1959*, 2d ed. (London, 1967).
DUCKWORTH, ALISTAIR M. *The Improvement of the Estate* (London, 1971).
———. "'Spillikins, Paper Ships, Riddles, Conundrums and Cards': Games in Jane Austen's Life and Fiction," in John Halperin, ed., *Jane Austen: Bicentenary Essays* (Cambridge, England, 1975), 279–97.
EVERSLEY, D. E. C. "The Home Market and Economic Growth in England, 1750–80," in E. L. Jones and E. E. Mingay, eds., *Land, Labour and Population in the Industrial Revolution* (London, 1967).
FLEISHMAN, AVROM. "*Mansfield Park* in Its Time," *Nineteenth-century Fiction*, 22 (1967–68), 1–18.
GEORGE, MARY D. *English Social Life in the Eighteenth Century* (London and New York, 1923).
GILBOY, ELIZABETH WATERMAN. "Demand as a Factor in the Industrial Revolution," in Ronald M. Hartwell, ed., *The Causes of the Industrial Revolution in England* (London, 1967), 121–38.
GORER, GEOFFREY. "Poor Honey: Some Notes on Jane Austen and Her Mother," *London Magazine*, 4, no. 8 (1957), 35–48.
GREENE, D. J. "Jane Austen and the Peerage," *PMLA*, 68 (1953), 1017–31.

HARDY, BARBARA. *A Reading of Jane Austen* (London, 1975).
———. "Properties and Possessions in Jane Austen's Novels," in Juliet McMaster, ed., *Jane Austen's Achievement* (London, 1976), 79–105.
KENT, CHRISTOPHER. "'Real Solemn History' and Social History," in David Monaghan, ed., *Jane Austen in a Social Context* (London, 1981), 86–104.
LOVELL, TERRY. "Jane Austen and Gentry Society," in Francis Barker, ed., *Literature, Society, and the Sociology of Literature* (Colchester, England, 1977), 118–32.
MARSHALL, DOROTHY. *English People in the Eighteenth Century* (London and New York, 1956).
MCKENDRICK, NEIL, WITH JOHN BREWER AND J. H. PLUMB. *The Birth of a Consumer Society* (London, 1982).
MINGAY, G. E. *English Landed Society in the Eighteenth Century* (London, 1963).
MONAGHAN, DAVID. *Jane Austen: Structure and Social Vision* (London, 1980).
———. "Jane Austen and the Position of Women," in his *Jane Austen in a Social Context* (London, 1981), 105–21.
NARDIN, JANE. "Jane Austen and the Problem of Leisure," in David Monaghan, ed., *Jane Austen in a Social Context* (London, 1981), 122–42.
O'MALLEY, IDA BEATRICE. *Women in Subjection: A Study of the Lives of Englishwomen Before 1832* (London, 1933).
PERKIN, HAROLD. *The Origins of Modern English Society 1780–1880* (1969).
RAGG, LAURA MARIA. *Jane Austen in Bath* (London, 1938).
RICHARDS, ERIC. "Women in the British Economy Since About 1700," *History*, 59 (1974), 337–57.
SOUTHAM, B. C. "*Sanditon*: The Seventh Novel," in Juliet McMaster, ed., *Jane Austen's Achievement* (London, 1976), 1–26.
SPRING, DAVID. "Interpreters of Jane Austen's Social World: Literary Critics and Historians," in Janet Todd, ed., *Jane Austen: New Perspectives* (New York and London, 1983).
THOMPSON, FRANCIS M. L. *English Landed Society in the Nineteenth Century* (London and Toronto, 1963).
THOMPSON, JAMES. "Jane Austen's Clothing: Things, Property, and Materialism in Her Novels," *Studies in Eighteenth-century Culture*, 13 (1984), 217–31.
WILLIAMS, RAYMOND. *The Country and the City* (London and New York, 1973).

CRITICISM, 1814–70

Joseph Duffy

In a generally unfavorable *Edinburgh Review* notice of Fanny Burney's *Wanderer*, William Hazlitt emphasized as the merit of fiction its truthfulness to life. The four great eighteenth-century novelists—Fielding, Richardson, Smollett, and Sterne—were Hazlitt's touchstones for fiction. Except when novels indulged in "violently satirical" and "violently sentimental" effects, Hazlitt claimed that readers of fiction were given "the closest imitation of men and manners" and were admitted "to examine the very web and texture of society.... If the style of poetry has 'something more divine in it,'" Hazlitt states, "this fiction savours more of humanity" (p. 320).

An 1823 contribution to Jane Austen criticism in the *Retrospective Review* provides information about the contemporary status of Jane Austen's work and echoes, as well, Hazlitt's view of fiction as a record of real life. The *Review* observed a change in the novel—a "revolution"—from the imaginative and often fantastic delineation of emotion and incident to a more ordinary representation of men and women as they engaged in "reasonable" thought, feeling, and action. For the reviewer, Fanny Burney and Jane Austen, "each the favourite of her generation," are types of "the opposite tastes of two successive ages" (p. 107; unless otherwise noted, all citations are from Southam). Fanny Burney's works, though "monuments of genius," could no longer be read with the same pleasure as eighteenth-century readers had derived from them. Instead, Jane Austen represented the taste of the new century: "Without any wish to surprise us into attention, by strangeness of incident, or complication of adventure ... the stream of her Tale flows on in an easy, natural, but spring tide" (p. 109).

We may observe in this review and in Hazlitt's statement the predication of the most powerful line marked out by the English novel—the representation of character and incident in a familiar context. The concept of the novel as history, unformulated here except in the most ingenuous terms, anticipates the prevailing notion of realism as the mainstream tradition of the English novel. Jane Austen may or may not be, as F. R. Leavis once so imperiously claimed in *The Great Tradition*, "the inaugurator of the great tradition of the English novel" (p. 7). Certainly she is one of the earliest and most distinguished of English realists. Critical reaction to her work has varied according to the demands of a particular critic or to the novelistic concerns of the period during which the critic wrote. Now, that fiction appears difficult and complex, whereas once it was considered simple and unpremeditated. Her place in the realistic tradition, however, seems a matter of universal agreement. Again and again, it was her realism, divested of ulterior aims, shorn of pseudoartistic appurtenances and idiosyncrasies, that caught the attention and stimulated the criticism of readers throughout the century.

By the time she was sixteen, Jane Austen was a practiced and prolific, if not an accomplished, writer of tales; the three volumes of her surviving *juvenilia* are dated between 1790 and 1793. By 1797 she had written *First Impressions*, the first, epistolary version of *Pride and Prejudice*; and by 1803 *Susan*, which became *Northanger Abbey*, was ready for publication. Then there were a number of years of negligible literary activity for Jane Austen. At last, in October or November 1811, her "sucking child" (*Letters*, April 25, 1811), *Sense and Sensibility*, was published.

Although the popular and critical response to *Sense and Sensibility* was by no means overwhelming, it was lively enough to have been gratifying to the novelist. By July 1813 she could report to her brother Francis that the first edition was sold out and had netted her £140 in addition to the return of the copyright. The criticism of the novel was discreet but encouraging enough to stimulate further efforts at publication. Calling it a "genteel, well-written novel," the *Critical Review* added that it was "one amongst the few" that could claim "this fair praise" (p. 35). Although the reviewer admitted that the work might seem "trifling" to those readers "insatiable" for novelty, he approved the writing, the naturally drawn characters, and the probable incidents, as well as "the excellent lesson" and "the useful moral" of the novel (ibid.). The editors of the *British Critic* apologized for the allotment of only a single page for its review, for they had thought so "favourably" of *Sense and Sensibility* that they had reluctantly, on account of the multiplicity of publications they were faced with, declined to offer a review among their principal articles. From a reading of the novel, "female friends" among their readers might learn "many sober and salutary maxims for the conduct of life, exemplified in a very pleasing and entertaining narrative" (p. 40).

Both reviews perform a perfunctory and not untypical job of contemporary criticism. In each case, the reviewer followed a set pattern of responses in which certain items—naturalness, probability, style—were checked without attempt at analysis. Moreover, both publications adhered to a routine general attitude toward fiction—one comes to regard it as the ceremonious performance of a ritual—condescending tolerance toward an inferior genre and watchfulness over the moral lesson of the work, especially on behalf of the "female friends" whose presumed sensibilities came to cast a long shadow over the English novel during the century.

Although *Pride and Prejudice* and *Mansfield Park* were discussed among the reading public, the critics generally ignored these novels; and it was not until the publication of *Emma* that the *Quarterly Review* was inclined to notice her work in a long and respectful notice by Sir Walter Scott. Here Scott manifested a special interest in the new group of novels of which *Emma* was an example—novels of ordinary life. The problem this new fiction faced was that mere resemblance to life was not sufficient: an élan in the portrayal was required to compensate for the want of excitement, which, in other novels, was provided for by striking incident and highly charged sentiment. Jane Austen's success in *Emma* was notable and unique, Scott felt; and he summed up her achievement in an image that has been echoed in later criticism and that is close to the author's own candid description of her writing as done on a "little bit (two Inches wide) of Ivory on which I work with so fine a Brush" (*Letters*, December 16, 1816):

> The author's knowledge of the world, and the peculiar tact with which she presents characters that the reader cannot fail to recognize, reminds us something of the merits of the Flemish school of painting. The subjects are not often elegant, and certainly never grand; but they are finished up to nature, and with a precision which delights the reader. (p. 67)

In another *Quarterly Review* article, a late review of the posthumously published *Northanger Abbey* and *Persuasion*, Richard Whately discussed Jane Austen in a style that was at first wrongly identified as Scott's. Surveying the rise in prestige of fiction among readers of all classes, Whately announced that it was no longer unusual for novels to be discussed "by some of the ablest scholars and soundest reasoners of the present day" (p. 87). This new respectability of fiction was to be accounted for, Whately maintained, by the higher quality of the novels themselves rather than by a change in public taste. Whately found novels of everyday life practically more useful because they instructed readers far more than romantic novels, even though the latter might be superior in artistic quality. Whately assigned Jane Austen's work to the front rank of this new fiction, which guided the readers' judgment by injecting them into vicariously experienced situations: "On the whole, Miss Austin's [sic] works may safely be recommended, not only as among the most unexceptionable of their class, but as combining, in an eminent degree, instruction with amusement, though without the direct effort at the former, of which we have complained, as sometimes defeating its object" (p. 105).

The ambiguousness of Whately's approach to the binding of art with instruction is significant and provocative: he becomes engaged rather treacherously in a matter that throughout the century stimulated abundant and formidable discussion. More fortunate than the work of some other "classic" novelists—Fielding before her and Charlotte Brontë, George Eliot, and Hardy after her—Jane Austen's novels were usually regarded as morally innocuous even when they were dismissed as negligible. But she did not entirely escape censure, as appears conspicuously in later criticism of her seeming indifference in religious matters. While Whately admired her "essential" merit of being "evidently" a Christian writer, sixteen years later Newman complained about the "vileness" of her parsons and charged that he had "not a dream of the high Catholic ἦθοσ" (p. 117).

The reviews of the posthumously published novels marked the peak of Jane Austen's critical reputation during her lifetime and immediately afterward. Read as a unit, the reviews establish clearly and in some detail the grounds for her evident success. In addition, they help to locate her work in the perspective of the fiction of the period. The exhaustion of the earlier sentimental and romantic schools seems amply to be confirmed here as a literary fact. The realistic novel of manners, the history of which extends back into the eighteenth century, filled the vacancy caused by this absence of interest. Variants of such fiction were the provincial novels and the novels of fashionable life. Furthermore, new novelistic concerns provided Scott with a method of achieving his enormously popular compromise in fiction that coalesced romance, sentiment, and fidelity to nature. The novel of ordinary life gave the reader the satisfaction of seeing lives like his own fixed in the plastic and apparently immortal shape of fiction (reading such novels induced a type of comfortable self-apotheosis); historical novels such as Scott's appealed in credible, comprehensible, and yet splendid terms to the reader's consciousness of history—at a time when that consciousness was enlarged by the English triumph over Napoleon. In his essay on Trollope, James distinguished "two kinds of taste in the appreciation of imaginative literature: the taste for emotions of surprise and the taste for emotions of recognition" (pp. 259–60). Scott gratified the former of these tastes and Jane Austen the latter. And in the process both types of fiction contributed to the reader's feeling of self-importance.

But the rise in the prestige of fiction occurred at a time when the novel was entering upon one of its least interesting periods, which lasted from the middle 1820s to the end of the 1830s. The parents of nineteenth-century fiction, as George Saintsbury called Scott and Jane Austen, fostered an unburnished brood. Scott was followed by scores of mediocre imitators of the historical novel, and the novel of ordinary life deteriorated into the insipidity of the fashionable or "silver-spoon" novel, which was often no more than a fatuous excuse for backstairs society gossip. To what extent the novels of Jane Austen maintained their popularity during this period cannot be accurately determined. We know that she was read because there are references to her work in private papers, in magazines, and in at least one novel. At the same time, an unsigned review by Thomas H. Lister of Mrs. Catherine Gore's *Women as They Are* in the *Edinburgh Review* complained in 1830 that in an "age of literary quackery" Jane Austen had not "received her reward," because she was "too natural" for her readers: "It seemed to them as if there could be very little merit in making characters act and talk so exactly like the people whom they saw around them every day" (p. 113).

We may speculate that interest in Jane Austen's fiction had early begun to take on a specialized aura. The Bentley Collected Edition of the novels published in five volumes in 1833 is evidence of the existence of an active body of readers. But the late issuance of a collected edition also signifies a limited reader response. Jane Austen's readers may have been devoted, but they were not numerous enough to bring about a notable increase in publication of her fiction until the last third of the century. By that time most of her contemporaries had ceased to interest the reading public, and even Walter Scott had passed his zenith as a popular novelist.

Time was required to provide the objective distance for perceiving the permanence of Jane Austen's art: to bring about the effacement of ephemeral contemporaries and to project new writers whose work would provide a fruitful basis for comparison. This process of assessing Jane Austen's merits and adjusting her literary position was begun in the years between the first and second Reform Bills. During this period, especially in the 1830s and 1840s, the conditions for hospitality toward fiction such as Jane Austen's would seem to have been generally absent from English life; the concern over contemporary problems, the love of the idealized and the sentimentalized, and the desire for instruction were all compelling forces away from her kind of artistic attainment. The advent of the great Victorians—Dickens, Thackeray, Charlotte Brontë, Mrs. Gaskell, George Eliot, and Trollope—would alone have provided prodigious competition. But beyond these were the lesser novelists whose productions were devoured by the public and discussed by the critics: such purveyors of moral uplift, social reform, or historical information as Charlotte Yonge, Harriet Martineau, G. P. R. James, and Edward Bulwer-Lytton; novelists of the supernatural and terrifying like Wilkie Collins and Sheridan Le Fanu; and celebrants of the audaciously immoral like George Lawrence.

After the *Quarterly Review* notice of *Northanger Abbey* and *Persuasion* in 1821, thirty-one years elapsed before an article entirely devoted to Jane Austen's work appeared. During the early posthumous years the novels were old enough to be neglected; later they were too recent to be revived. Among the critics and writers of the period 1833–67, three attitudes toward Jane Austen's fiction may be discerned. One group of readers thought her work was of inconsequential value because of the limitations of treatment or of material. Others recognized the novelist's skill but because of its seemingly minor range excluded her fiction from the category of significant art. Finally, some readers were so impressed by the perfection of the novels that they felt their artistic merit alone called for recognition.

In Charlotte Brontë's reaction to Jane Austen, whom she first read in 1849 and 1850, we have a clear explanation of Jane Austen's appeal for certain readers. She read Jane Austen under the influence of George Henry Lewes, who expected her to profit from the example of her predecessor. Lewes, however, encountered an intractable pupil in Charlotte Brontë. Instead of taking the author of *Emma* as an artistic mentor, which the earlier novelist could not be for her, Charlotte Brontë approached her as an artistic and sexual adversary.

Introduced to the merely "shrewd and observant" Jane Austen through *Pride and Prejudice*, Charlotte Brontë felt uneasy and confined because of the symmetry of the fictive life. Two years later she found in *Emma* "a Chinese fidelity, a miniature delicacy in the painting," but she also noted an absolute want of passion: "the Passions are perfectly unknown to her. ... Jane Austen was a complete and most sensible lady, but a very incomplete, and rather insensible (*not senseless*) woman" (p. 128). A comparison of these comments with the reservations expressed by even conventionally favorable critics of Jane Austen would show a difference in degree but not in the kind of response. Emotional power implied something massive to these Victorians. When Elizabeth Barrett Browning complained in 1855 that Jane Austen's characters wanted "souls," she was obviously referring to that same absence of visible passion and storm of which Charlotte Brontë wrote: powerful emotion was authenticated by an egregious display of sound and color in the writing.

The first full-length article since Whately's review of *Northanger Abbey* and *Persuasion* observed that the novelist had not "even yet . . . reaped her rightful share of public homage" (p. 135). To explain this neglect, the *New Monthly* writer made in 1852 what is probably one of the earliest attempts to explain the existence of an "art novel," a form of fiction that could be appreciated only by a select group. "Too natural" for the superficial, Jane Austen appealed rather to readers "of more refined taste and critical acumen" and left these special readers dissatisfied with "the labored unrealities" of most other domestic novelists (p. 136). The distinction attempted here indicates a lowered ability among the reading public to understand even the various kinds of available fiction, for once special skills are postulated for reading fiction, acknowledgment has been made of the deterioration of the simple capacity for comprehending the English language. Although the condition described in the present essay was not as serious as it later became, the preparation for a "highbrow" response to fiction is there. One of the main lines of Jane Austen criticism throughout the century is that not everyone can appreciate her writing. This unsatisfactory state of affairs encourages cultism on the one hand and unreasonable antagonism on the other. But its existence cannot be denied. In proportion to the growth of the reading public, Jane Austen's fiction was not read by larger numbers of people but with growing enthusiasm by smaller groups—and with increasingly complex endorsement by critics.

As the most thoughtful of these critics, George Henry Lewes's comments on fiction require special consideration. Writing in *Fraser's Magazine* in 1847, Lewes outlines three categories of novel readers: the enthusiasts who indiscriminately read and "adore" all novels; the scoffers who pretend to despise fiction and yet are well acquainted with circulating libraries; and the moderate group, among whom he included himself, who are "somewhat fastidious" but whose "enjoyment is keen and hearty." Lewes believed that "novel-writing, or novel-reading, so far from being frivolous or injurious, is really a fine thing, and the novel rises to the first rank of literature" (Lewes, p. 686). And in a statement that shocked Charlotte Brontë, Lewes said that he would "rather have written *Pride and Prejudice*, or *Tom Jones*, than any of the Waverley novels" (ibid., p. 687). Again, in 1852, writing on "The Lady Novelists" in the *Westminster Review*, Lewes paid tribute to Jane Austen's genius: "First and foremost let Jane Austen be named, the greatest artist that has ever written, using the term to signify the most perfect mastery over the means to her end" (p. 140). Despite this encomium, Lewes was crucially aware of the narrow appeal of this great art: "Only cultivated minds fairly appreciate the exquisite art of Miss Austen." Readers who required "strong lights and shadows" found her "tame and uninteresting" (p. 141).

Lewes's article, "The Novels of Jane Austen," which appeared in *Blackwood's Magazine* in 1859, was the most important single item published between the 1821 *Edinburgh Review* piece and an essay in the *North British Review* in 1870. Its relevance lies not only in its literary analysis but also in its discussion of Jane Austen's status as a novelist. Lewes called it "a demonstrated fact" that Jane Austen's fiction was "very extensively read" and observed that without ever having been popular these novels had survived the work of more widely read contemporary authors—Maria Edgeworth, for example.

In Lewes's view the work of other novelists had more interest than Jane Austen's fiction, but the interest was often disproportionate to artistic quality; these novelists possessed more inventive talent or had the power of stirring the emotions of their readers. But Jane Austen surpassed all other artists except Sophocles and Molière in that quality the neglect of which accounted for the most defective art—"the economy of art . . . the easy adaption of means to ends, with no aid from extraneous or superfluous elements" (p. 152). George Eliot, whose *Scenes from Clerical Life* had been published the previous year, was judged inferior to Jane Austen in economy of art "but equal in truthfulness, dramatic ventriloquism, and humour, and greatly superior in culture, reach of mind, and depth of emotional sensibility" (p. 156).

Jane Austen lacked "depth and massiveness"; consequently, her work could never appeal to "the great public" but must always be the limited fare of a "cultivated" group. Moreover, Lewes observed, there were few attractions of "general vigour and culture" in Jane Austen's work, and he concludes with a repeated acknowledgment of the limits of her art—this time in terms that remind the modern reader that Victorian requirements of a purposeful art were fundamental to the most enlightened as well as to the most intolerant criticism of the period:

> The delight derived from her pictures arises from our sympathy with ordinary characters, our relish of humour, and our intellectual pleasure in art for art's sake. . . . Her fame, as we think, must endure. Such art as hers can never grow old, never be superseded. But, after all, miniatures are not frescoes, and her works are miniatures. Her place is among the Immortals; but the pedestal is erected in a quiet niche of the great temple. (p. 166)

"Art for art's sake," still an alien term in England, was to become within a few years the rallying slogan for an extreme aesthetic approach to art. Its somewhat apologetic use by Lewes to describe the appeal of Jane Austen's fiction is interesting, since it reflects his ultimate and strong uneasiness with an art that appeared to him autotelic. As the representative of the best in fiction criticism between the two Reform Bills, Lewes nevertheless conforms to the prevailing sentiment on behalf of what might be called artistic utilitarianism.

In the critical evaluation of Jane Austen's work, some writers who supported the novel of purpose were able to discover a prevailing moral lesson in her fiction. But her main claim on the attention of the critics was the unapproachable realism with which she described incident and character. The esteem in which she was held depended on the value that a particular critic attached to realistic representation. Lewes, as we have seen, constantly remarked on this quality as her primary achievement. In 1860 W. F. Pollock viewed Jane Austen as a renovator who had returned the craft of fiction to its true province:

> To Miss Austen all subsequent novelists have been infinitely indebted. She led the way in the return to nature; she again described individuals instead of classes or nationalities; she re-indicated and worked the inexhaustible mines of wealth for the writer of fiction which everywhere lie beneath the surface of ordinary life. (p. 174)

Jane Austen's fiction was predominantly external to the social and cultural atmosphere of the early and middle Victorian period. Her eighteenth-century good sense did not make a ready appeal to bourgeois gravity—the compression of life's immensity into an earnest and busy routine of duties and obligations—or to bourgeois sentimentality—the reduction of life's calamities to simplistic emotional terms. Her novels, it is clear, were not in harmony with Victorian desires for fiction: they did not provide solace to the distressed, emotional stimulus to the jaded, or information to the inquisitive. This externality provided a test for the critic, since he was forced, then, either to impose standards on Jane Austen's fiction that did not apply or to accept the novels, within limits, at their own value. The remarkable fact is that Jane Austen did rise at this time to a position of literary prominence: the articles and references in reviews, limited as they are, give visible proof of the growing impact of Jane Austen's fiction on a segment of the reading public. Without revealing the entire process, they indicate—by the end of the 1860s—a fait accompli: the establishment of a reputation during a period that was earlier described as potentially inhospitable to her art and which, in fact, permitted almost all of her contemporaries except Scott to languish at last in the oblivion of unread novelists. By assuring Jane Austen a place, however minor, among the "Immortals" of art, the critics and readers of the period through the middle 1860s prepared the way for the extraordinary varieties of critical concern among subsequent generations.

Bibliography

HAZLITT, WILLIAM. Review of Fanny Burney's *The Wanderer*, *Edinburgh Review*, 24 (1815), 320.

JAMES, HENRY. "Anthony Trollope," in Leon Edel, ed., *Henry James: The Future of the Novel* (New York, 1956), 259–60.

LEAVIS, F. R. *The Great Tradition* (London, 1948).

LEWES, GEORGE HENRY. "Recent Novels: French and English," *Fraser's Magazine*, 36 (1847), 686–95.

SOUTHAM, B. C., ed. *Jane Austen: The Critical Heritage* (London and New York, 1968).

CRITICISM, 1870–1940

Brian Southam

The seventy years from 1870 to 1940 saw the emergence of Jane Austen as a popular author, the most widely read and loved of all the classic novelists of English literature. At its most extreme, the Jane Austen following was a cult of devotees (see "Janeites and Anti-Janeites," below) who regarded the writer and her characters as intimate friends. From this there developed a considerable Janeite literature. Yet the period also saw the growth of a truly critical approach to "the art of the novel," stemming largely from the prefaces and essays of Henry James and culminating in *Jane Austen and Her Art* by Mary Lascelles, a study that achieves a proper balance of historical scholarship, subtle and rigorous critical method, and an abundant affection for the writer.

From the time of Bentley's edition in 1833, the novels were continuously in print, and Jane Austen was recognized as a distinctive writer commanding an enthusiastic following. But it was a private rather than a public reputation, sustained within families and literary circles, and the body of formal, published criticism down to 1870 is small. What changed the situation overnight was the publication of the *Memoir* in 1870. A writer previously shadowy and little known was at once invested with an attractive personal identity and a formidable literary reputation. The *Memoir* provided its reviewers with the opportunity to draw the attention of the public at large to a writer long neglected. The *Memoir* itself made a considerable critical contribution, since two of its chapters recorded the body of commendation that had accumulated since her death. This critical anthology, added to the notable review-essays by R. H. Hutton, Richard Simpson, and Mrs. Oliphant (reprinted in Southam, 1968), should have set Jane Austen criticism on an informed and productive course.

But the Jane Austen revival took a different turn—to popularization at once snobbish and sentimental. The snobbishness derived from the celebration of the novels as fit only for readers of cultivation and taste, encouraged by Austen-Leigh's anecdote about Mr. Cheney, an acquaintance who "had established it in his own mind, as a new test of ability, whether people *could* or *could not* appreciate Miss Austen's merits" (p. 136). The *Memoir* was also responsible for rendering "dear Aunt Jane" to Victorian taste. This sentimentalized vision found many takers. There was need for reading that would not offend the Victorian domestic proprieties, for stories that could be read aloud *en famille*. As such was Jane Austen commended. The love children, the adulteries and the elopements, the Willoughbys and the Crawfords, were passed over. In 1870, Trollope produced such a certification, assuring his audience that the novels were "full of excellent teaching, and free from an idea or word that can pollute.... Throughout all her works, and they are not many, a sweet lesson of homely household womanly virtue is ever being taught" (pp. 104–105).

In such a climate of adulation, there was no place for the Jane Austen drawn by Simpson and Mrs. Oliphant; and by reviewers of the expanded *Memoir* of 1871 (which included some of the minor works) who concentrated on a writer of artistry and power. Simpson drew an analytical portrait of the writer's mind, her intelligence, her essentially critical genius. Equally unappealing to popular taste was Mrs. Oliphant's Jane Austen—a discomforting artist, armed with a "fine vein of feminine cynicism," "full of subtle power, keenness, finesse, and self-restraint," blessed with an "exquisite sense" of the "ridiculous," "a fine stinging yet soft-voiced contempt," whose novels are "so calm and cold and keen" (Southam, 1968, p. 216). This was certainly not a writer the public could take to its heart. The taste of the hour was for a lovable Jane, and the essayists and journalists ready to pander to this need duly churned out the "pleasant twaddle"—as Henry James called it—the "sentimentalized vision" that occupied the scene for the next thirty or forty years. James was himself to play a part in the encouragement, an anticritical stance, setting his authoritative seal upon the idea that Jane Austen, in her artless and unconscious perfection, stood inviolably beyond the critical embrace. "Instinctive and charming," he described her in 1902; and he advised his readers to look elsewhere "for signal examples of what composition, distribution, arrangement can do, of how they intensify the life of a work of art" (p. 206).

Nonetheless, there continues, through these thirty years or so, a thin line of sound and perceptive writing, still in touch with true critical standards amidst the outpouring of "pleasant twaddle." This is to be seen in the Jane Austen entry by Leslie Stephen in the 1885 *Dictionary of National Biography*, an orthodox account derived from the consensus of "the best critics." Stephen registers his distaste at the promotion of Jane Austen, the "fanaticism" of her admirers. His Jane Austen is truly a writer, fully conscious of "the precise limits of her power" and subtle in "the unequalled fineness of her literary tact" (p. 260). Mrs. Humphry Ward, writing in the same year, lamented the absence of "a more peremptory critical standard than any we possess in England" and proceeded to exercise precisely such a "standard" upon Jane Austen, observing the novelist's "great deficiencies," terming her a classic "small" and "thin," yet identifying the force of her "concentration ... an exquisite power of choice and discrimination" (p. 84). Mrs. Ward would have been less scathing if she had seen the Harvard Prize dissertation, *Jane Austen's Novels*, by George Pellew, published in Boston in 1883. Pellew opposed the current view of Jane Austen "as a singular and inexplicable phenomenon, without connection with the past" (p. 5) and argued that the job of the "modern critic" was to be a "historian," not an impressionist. When James read the essay, he reflected the mood of the time in remarking at the application of "scientific criticism" to his "delightful Jane." A few years later, Howells was to comment, with accuracy, that Pellew's essay was "one of the first steps in the direction of the new criticism—the criticism which studies, classifies and registers" (1892, p. vii). Howells was also to stand with Leslie Stephen and Mrs. Oliphant in deploring the loss of critical standards. Writing in *Harper's Magazine* in 1889 on the "formlessness" of English fiction, he asked, "How, for instance, could people who had once known the simple variety, the refined perfection of Miss Austen, enjoy anything less refined and less perfect?" (p. 32). His *Harper's* essays were assembled and reshaped in *Criticism and Fiction*, published in 1891. Here Jane Austen stands supreme: "Jane Austen was the first and last of the English novelists to treat material with entire truthfulness. Because she did this she remains the most artistic of the English novelists" (p. 38).

This was a resounding claim, duly challenged. The most fruitful objection is found in Agnes Repplier's *Atlantic Monthly* article of 1890. Tongue in cheek, she questioned the exclusiveness of Howells's regard for the novelist's "truthfulness," fearful that this would lead to a new shibboleth as silly and offensive as Austen-Leigh's Cheney test.

In 1890 appeared the *Life of Jane Austen* by Goldwin Smith, a sober and well-written life-and-letters, standing, after Pellew, as the second study of Jane Austen to attempt a responsible critical and scholarly approach. The two earlier life-and-letters volumes—*Jane Austen and Her Works* by Sarah Tytler in 1880 and *Jane Austen* by S. F. Malden in 1889—were both firmly in the "twaddle" tradition. Smith, however, belonged to the no-nonsense school of criticism and was quick to say so: "Criticism is becoming an art of saying fine things, and there are really no fine things to say about Jane Austen. There is no hidden meaning in her; no philosophy beneath the surface for profound scrutiny to bring to light; nothing calling in any way for elaborate interpretation" (p. 185). This opinion caught the mood of the hour: a Jane Austen for Everyman. For over the next ten years came a notable Jane Austen boom by way of fancy and illustrated editions, calculated to catch the taste of the 1890s for elaboration and fine bookwork. Thus, the promotion of Jane Austen, as James put it, "so amenable to pretty reproduction in every variety of what is called tasteful, and in what seemingly proves to be saleable form" (1905, p. 63). Nonetheless, the publishing boom of the 1890s had a positive critical outcome. These new editions carried introductions, and while some of them are in the twaddle tradition, others were good. George Saintsbury's preface to Hugh Thomson's illustrated edition of *Pride and Prejudice* of 1894 opens in full Janeite style, announcing that it is written by a Janeite for fellow devotees. But this posture is soon dropped. It leads on to a placing of Jane Austen first within the history of the English novel and then in the open territory of literature, English and European. Joseph Jacobs, introducing *Emma* in 1896, opens with a well-documented account of the novel's composition and publication, discusses the reviews of Scott and Whately, quotes Goldwin Smith to disagree with him, draws attention to the place of *Emma* in the second group of novels, and makes detailed critical observations that are fresh and intelligent.

This more scholarly and methodical approach is also reflected in the textbook histories of fiction and prose. Notable among these are Sir Walter Raleigh's *English Novel* (1894); *English Prose; Selections* (1893–96), edited by Henry Craik; *Modern English Literature* (1897) by Edmund Gosse; and *The Development of the English Novel* (1899), by Wilbur L. Cross. These works are not to be despised. Raleigh, for example, was ready to reexamine the comparison with Shakespeare, finding in both writers "the sameness of artistic impersonality, of serene abstraction from life" (p. 262), and ready also to oppose the concept of the perfect but limited artist, claiming, "The world of pathos and passion is present in her work by implication" (p. 203). Craik rejects the image of "gentle Jane," asking the reader to consider the pressure of experience that stands behind her characters (the "years of provocation under the torture of some domestic Mrs. Norris") and inviting the reader to register the "sarcasm" and "cynicism" deployed upon the characters at the end of *Sense and Sensibility*.

The other consequence of the 1890s boom was to inspire both Howells and Agnes Repplier with the confidence that there was a large popular audience for their particular style of magazine journalism. Thus encouraged, Agnes Repplier was to supply her readers with a wealth of informal commentary; not formal criticism in our modern sense but unmistakably the fruit of a searching critical intelligence. To take a single example: she observes the way in which the novelist "reveals to us with merciless distinctness the secret springs that move a human heart" through merely "the casual conversation, the little leisurely, veracious gossip." She also commented on the state of Jane Austen criticism, objecting to the "bellicose enthusiasm" of "a little school of critics" who "endeavoured to exalt these half-dozen admirable novels by denying them competitors, by reducing all English fiction to one common denominator—*Emma*" (p. 514). No names are given, but Howells must certainly have been among the culprits. On his part, Howells commenced in 1900, in the June issue of *Harper's Bazar*, a remarkable series of essays, treating the heroines of fiction, from Fanny Burney's onward, on the grounds that "a novel is great or not, as its women are important or unimportant." The following year, the series was published in book form under the title *Heroines of Fiction*. Here we see the most accomplished of literary journalism, addressed to a wide audience and rich with critical insight. On *Emma*, for example: "so far as the novel can suggest that repose which is the ideal of art 'Emma' suggests it, in an action of unsurpassed unity, consequence, and simplicity" (p. 68). Or on *Persuasion*: "imagined with as great novelty and daring as 'Pride and Prejudice'" (p. 50). Or that Emma Woodhouse is possibly "the most boldly imagined" of the heroines, "for it took supreme courage to portray a girl, meant to win and keep the reader's fancy, with the characteristics frankly ascribed" [to her]. Or that Emma "is charming in the very degree of her feminine complexity."

Thus, while there was an increasing student readership, there was as yet no sense that the discussion of Jane Austen was a specialized academic topic. The critical debate was of public interest. Objectors to Howells's "divine" Jane Austen and supporters of his focus upon women could have their say in the pages of the magazine *Nineteenth Century*. Similarly, when in 1910 A. C. Bradley addressed the English Association, he claimed to speak as one of the "faithful" and declared of Elizabeth Bennet, "I was meant to fall in love with her and I do" (1911, p. 7). And this is the essay that came to replace Scott and Whately as the prime document for the serious study of Jane Austen. The importance of its scholarly method and critical thinking is confirmed by Miss Lascelles's acknowledgment in 1939 that "quotations from Bradley's essay might well head most parts" of her book (p. v).

In 1913 came the definitive family biography, the *Life and Letters*. Howells took this as an occasion to reflect on "a certain chill, creeping paralysis of respectability" coming to envelop her, the critics "sobered, not to say awed, in the presence of her fame" (1913, p. 959). This was fair comment. But the chorus of praise was not universal or unlively and unoriginal. There was, for example, the youthful feminist rejection by Rebecca West, charging Jane Austen with a lack of imaginative "virility." Reviewing the *Life*, Virginia Woolf discerned the "curious atmosphere of symbolism" about the gate scene in *Mansfield Park*. Yet she sided with Rebecca West in suggesting, "It is where the power of the man has to be conveyed that her novels are always at their weakest" (p. 189). Howells also lamented the absence of criticism enlivened "with the bursts of naturalness and even light-heartedness" (1913). He was soon to be answered. In 1917 there appeared in the *Quarterly Review* precisely what Howells was seeking—a brilliant, amusing, yet expert essay, a masterpiece of Jane Austen criticism, by Reginald Farrer, epitomizing the amateur tradition, since he was no academic, not even a journalist, but a world authority on alpine flowers!

Avowedly addressing unacademic enthusiasts, Farrer's hidden agenda is to dispose systematically of the myths and fallacies that had grown up around Jane Austen, to renew contact with sound criticism and reveal the "genuine" writer—"radiant and remorseless," "dispassionate yet pitiless," with her "quiet but destructive merriment," "the steely quality, the incurable rigour of her judgement." The received Jane Austen is replaced by a great and "conscious" novelist, a writer of "intense concentration," whose heroines are in the possession of "minds," whose characters are "unfolded through love." The writer's art is defined in terms of "technical problems," "technical mastery," "technical triumphs." His account of the "problem" of *Emma* reminds us of the modern rhetoric of fiction. The "radical dishonesty" and the "sheer bad art" of *Mansfield Park* remind us of Mrs. Leavis and Marvin Mudrick. Elsewhere, his comments recall Richard Simpson, Mrs. Kavanagh, and Mrs. Oliphant—the nineteenth-century tradition of intelligent and unsentimental criticism—for so long lost sight of, now recovered and extended.

Farrer was delivering a centenary tribute. Others came notably from writers—from G. K. Chesterton, George Moore, Frank Swinnerton, and Howells again in an introduction to *Pride and Prejudice* in 1918. These professional views were bolstered in 1921 by a continuation of the Jamesian approach in *The Craft of Fiction* by Percy Lubbock. This approach was soon to be supported in the bibliographically detailed editions of the novels and minor works by R. W. Chapman, the first scholarly presentation of any of the great English novelists.

Inevitably, these editions reawakened the debates of the 1890s. Was she "a classic of very sound security . . . her books not only contemplated but loved," as the *TLS* asserted (November 1, 1923, p. 725)? Or "a sedulously overpraised writer . . . a piece of literary cant," as George Sampson declared in the *Bookman* for January 1924 (pp. 191–93)? Certainly her fellow novelists took Jane Austen seriously, as we can see in the various reviews and essays of Virginia Woolf, J. B. Priestley, Edith Wharton, Rebecca West, E. M. Forster, and Edwin Muir.

In 1926, Herbert Read was to describe it as a "sophisticated rage for Jane Austen." D. H. Lawrence saw "the mean Jane Austen," a novelist of "personality" rather than character (p. 58). And the grand attack was delivered by the Oxford professor H. W. Garrod in a "Depreciation" read to the Royal Society of Literature in 1928; to be answered, in "A Reply," by R. W. Chapman, a year later. Meanwhile, scholarship was beginning to proceed along its own paths. In 1927 came Michael Sadleir's pioneering investigation into the gothic novels referred to in *Northanger Abbey* (*Edinburgh Review*, 246, pp. 91–106); and in 1929 the first full *Bibliography*, by Geoffrey Keynes. Gradually, in all this scholarly and critical activity of the 1920s, we see a separation of paths, a widening gap between the various groups. Critic was beginning to speak unto critic, and scholar to scholar, leaving the ordinary reader without a Farrer or a Howells.

It is also important to understand the impoverished nature of the critical heritage of the 1920s and 1930s. The historical narrative suggests a continuous living stream, a tradition of criticism constantly increased and enriched by the accumulating wisdom of the past. But this was not the case. Whereas A. C. Bradley was remembered and deferred to as an authority with the dignity of academic standing, the unqualified, untenured, and unacademic were not. From the 1870s Richard Simpson and Mrs. Oliphant were forgotten or ignored; similarly, Howells and Farrer. The same was to happen to Rebecca West. In 1932 she contributed a preface to a forgotten edition of *Northanger Abbey* presenting Jane Austen as a writer of "quite conscious ... feminism" and the novel itself as a critique of "the institutions of society regarding women, ... the fruit of strong feeling and audacious thought." The novelist as a critic of society, the novel as "disconcerting," were ideas entirely new. But their impact at the time was nil.

Three years later, Lord David Cecil delivered the Leslie Stephen Lecture at Cambridge, a remarkable performance, successfully combining the roles of Janeite, Howellsian popularist, and thoroughgoing critic, equipped with "rules," "laws," and the method of analysis to define her as "one of the supreme novelists of the world" for the "universal significance" conveyed in the characters and the author's view of life. But the space of a lecture could no more than sketch these issues, and it is fitting that the period should end with *Jane Austen and Her Art* by Mary Lascelles in 1939—a full-scale analysis that owes much to the essays of James and yet defies him in seeking to exemplify and investigate the artistry that he described as "instinctive and charming." Miss Lascelles explains the origins of the book in the fact that "the professed critics"—she names A. C. Bradley, Saintsbury, Raleigh, John Bailey, and Chapman—all worked on a scale "so small that the reader does not see how they have reached their conclusions until he has patiently found his own way to them" (p. v). Miss Lascelles's understanding that Jane Austen required examination on a large scale, that her "art" was amenable to methodical analysis, and that there was an audience for close and subtle discussion—all this signifies the furthest point to which the criticism of Jane Austen was brought at the end of this middle period. The day of the "amateur" essayist addressing "the common reader" was now past. Henceforth, criticism was seen to be a serious activity, the preserve of academics addressing the academic community.

Bibliography

BRADLEY, A. C. "Jane Austen: A Lecture," *Essays and Studies by Members of the English Association*, 2 (1911), 7–36.
CRAIK, HENRY, ed. *English Prose; Selections*, 5 vols. (London and New York, 1893–96).
FARRER, REGINALD. "Jane Austen, *ob*. July 18, 1817," *Quarterly Review*, 228 (1917), 1–30.
HOWELLS, WILLIAM DEAN. *Criticism and Fiction* (New York and London, 1891).
———. Preface to *The Poems of George Pellew* (Boston, 1892).
———. *Heroines of Fiction* (New York and London, 1901).
———. ["On the Immortality of Jane Austen,"] *Harper's Magazine*, 127 (1913), 958–61.
JAMES, HENRY. "The Lesson of Balzac," in his *The Question of Our Speech; The Lesson of Balzac: Two Lectures* (Boston, 1905).
———. "Gustave Flaubert" [1902], in Leon Edel, ed., *The House of Fiction* (New York, 1957), 206–207.
LASCELLES, MARY. *Jane Austen and Her Art* (Oxford, 1939).
LAWRENCE, D. H. *À propos of Lady Chatterley's Lover* (London, 1930), 58.
MALDEN, S. F. *Jane Austen* (London, 1889).
PELLEW, GEORGE. *Jane Austen's Novels* (Boston, 1883).
RALEIGH, SIR WALTER, ed. *The English Novel* (New York and London, 1894).
READ, HERBERT. *Reason and Romanticism* (London, 1926), 182–85.
REPPLIER, AGNES. "Literary Shibboleths," *Atlantic Monthly* (May, 1890).
———. "Conversation in Novels," in her *Essays in Miniature* (New York, 1892).
———. "Jane Austen," *Critic*, 37 (1900), 514–15.
SAMPSON, GEORGE. Review of the Chapman editions, *Bookman*, 65 (1924), 191–93.
SMITH, GOLDWIN. *Life of Jane Austen* (London, 1890).
SOUTHAM, B. C., ed. *Jane Austen: The Critical Heritage* (London and New York, 1968); the second ed., 2 vols.: *1812–1870* and *1870–1939*, is forthcoming in 1985.
STEPHEN, LESLIE. ["Jane Austen,"] *Dictionary of National Biography*, II (London, 1885), 259–60.
TROLLOPE, ANTHONY. "On English Prose Fiction as a Rational Amusement" [1870], in his *Four Lectures*, Morris L. Parrish, ed. (London, 1938), 89–139.
TYTLER, SARAH [PSEUD. OF HENRIETTA KEDDIE]. *Jane Austen and Her Works* (London, 1880).
WARD, MRS. HUMPHRY. Review of Lord Brabourne's edition of the letters, *Macmillan's Magazine*, 51 (1884), 84–91.
WEST, REBECCA. Preface to *Northanger Abbey* (London, 1932), v–xi.
WOOLF, VIRGINIA. Review of the *Life, Times Literary Supplement* (May 8, 1913), 189–90.

CRITICISM, 1939–83

A. Walton Litz

Writing a brief survey of recent criticism and scholarship on Jane Austen is like writing a pocket-size guidebook to a continent: all one can hope to do is indicate the major landmarks and general contours. In his *Bibliography of Jane Austen* David Gilson lists more studies for the years 1954–78 than for all the years between 1813 and 1954, and the flood of publications shows no sign of abating. Those interested in exploring the full range of recent criticism should consult Gilson's *Bibliography* and the *Annotated Bibliography of Jane Austen Studies, 1952–1972* compiled by Barry Roth and Joel Weinsheimer. (Professor Roth is preparing a companion volume for the years 1972–82.) This survey is concerned with trends and tendencies rather than the contents of individual works and does not pretend to cover all the important or interesting studies.

The history of Jane Austen criticism divides neatly into three phases. In the first phase, stretching from the earliest reviews to the 1870 *Memoir*, most of the important questions raised by modern critics were at least touched upon. (The crucial essays and reviews from this period are reprinted in *Jane Austen: The Critical Heritage*, edited by B. C. Southam.) Walter Scott, in his anonymous review of *Emma* (1815), firmly identified the genre of Jane Austen. In contrast to the romance or the sentimental novel of *la belle nature*, Jane Austen's fiction needs no apology; like the Flemish school of painting, it displays "the art of copying from nature as she really exists in the common walks of life, and presenting to the reader, instead of the splendid scenes of an imaginary world, a correct and striking representation of that which is daily taking place around him" (Southam, p. 63). In short, whereas "the author of novels was, in former times, expected to tread pretty much in the limits between the concentric circles of probability and possibility" (p. 61), Jane Austen has rejected the "land of fiction" in favor of a precise rendering of "characters and incidents introduced more immediately from the current of ordinary life than was permitted by the former rules of the novel" (p. 59). This theme was developed further by Richard Whately in his 1821 review of the posthumous *Northanger Abbey* and *Persuasion*, where he deliberately builds on Scott's earlier notice and proposes an elaborate Aristotelian rationale for the new novel of domestic realism.

The arguments of Scott and Whately, which also lie behind the early appreciations by G. H. Lewes, were refined and extended by the Shakespearean scholar Richard Simpson in his marvelous study of 1870, a review of the recently published *Memoir* that develops into a full critical assessment of Jane Austen's fictional world. Published anonymously in the *North British Review*, Simpson's article lay in obscurity until the 1950s, when it was rediscovered and the proper attribution made. There is a certain rightness, as well as a certain irony, in the timing of this discovery, since Simpson anticipated many of the central concerns of Jane Austen criticism during the 1940s and 1950s. He recognizes the critical faculty, the power of wit and irony, as the secret of her art. He clearly traces the links between novels, documenting the growth in "general intention" from *Sense and Sensibility* to *Persuasion*. He is candid in acknowledging the narrowness of Jane Austen's subjects, the unfurnished quality of her world, but—like Lewes—he finds the novels redeemed by her incomparable "art of telling."

If Austen studies had gone the way indicated by Simpson's review, Henry James would have had no occasion to lament the lack of "the critical spirit." But instead they went the way of the *Memoir*, new and tantalizing facts about her life producing a long series of uncritical appreciations. There are exceptions, of course, such as A. C. Bradley's essay of 1911 (the last of the nineteenth-century "Shakespearean" appreciations) and Reginald Farrer's anniversary essay of 1917, which anticipates in many ways the "subversive" and ironic readings of later critics. But in general the work of 1870–1939 is a falling off from the standard set by Simpson's essay. This second phase of genteel appreciations and antiquarian interest culminated in R. W. Chapman's edition of the novels (1923), a monument to Janeite curiosity that nonetheless provided in its elaborate apparatus the necessary foundation for a more exacting period of critical activity.

There are many reasons for Jane Austen's central place in modern criticism of the novel. As David Lodge points out in *Language of Fiction* (1966), taking his cue from Percy Lubbock, "novels are such vast and complicated structures, and our experience of them is so extended in time, that it is impossible for the human mind to conceive of a novel as a whole without blurring or forgetting the parts through the accumulation of which this totality has been conveyed" (p. 78). Criticism of fiction is constantly vexed by a conflict between the analysis of local effects and the charting of larger "architectural" designs. We may be laboring under an illusion when we speak of comprehending a lyric poem "in an instant of time," but the illusion is a fruitful one for practical criticism. In the looser form of the novel, however, the methods of the New Criticism—developed from a study of the lyric poem—encounter grave difficulties. Hence, the popularity of Jane Austen's novels as a testing ground for the Jamesian poetic of the novel and for the application of New Critical methods to the analysis of imagery and language: within the range of English novelists, Jane Austen presents the most compact and manageable works, in which dense local passages can be scrutinized without losing sight of the larger designs of plot and action. Mary Lascelles's *Jane Austen and Her Art* (1939), although marked by the charm and reticence of the best old-fashioned "appreciation," is essentially an attempt to apply the Jamesian poetic, as mediated through the more systematic critical studies of Percy Lubbock and Joseph Warren Beach. And Miss Lascelles's elegant study was followed by a large number of analytic works, in which the New Critical values of irony, wit, and the effaced narrator were asserted. It was really not until the appearance of Ian Watt's influential *Rise of the Novel* (1957), which concludes with Jane Austen, that critics began serious study of her place in the early traditions of English prose fiction.

At the same time as the novels were subjected to this scrupulous "close reading," aimed at the discovery of fashionable aesthetic values, another group of critics (often using the same methods) sought to prove Jane Austen's "moral significance" by uncovering the social and ethical bases of her irony. Following the example of Reginald Farrer, who had presented Jane Austen as a severe and ironic critic of society, D. W. Harding developed the "subversive" theme in his extremely influential 1940 essay "Regulated Hatred," in which Harding claims that Jane Austen is "a literary classic of the society which attitudes like hers, held widely enough, would undermine" (p. 347). Her values are precisely the opposite of those held by her admirers; her caustic irony subtly undermines the assumptions of the society she portrays. Jane Austen emerges from this examination as the archetypal modern figure, isolated and self-protective, using her verbal and dramatic ironies to preserve her personal integrity. It is this view that allows F. R. Leavis to find an uneasy place for Jane Austen in his Great Tradition of the English novel and that inspired the most controversial critical study of the 1950s: Marvin Mudrick's *Jane Austen: Irony as Defense and Discovery* (1952). Mudrick's work has the chief virtue of a narrowly conceived but highly intelligent critical enterprise—a cutting edge. Although most readers today find it schematic and overstated, Mudrick's book brings into focus one important and undeniable aspect of Jane Austen's artistic personality. It remains a precise point of reference in the landscape of Jane Austen studies.

In their emphasis on irony and dramatic structure, in their aggressively antihistorical bias, the "subversive" critics and the more austere technicians of the New Criticism found a common ground. By the end of the 1950s the general tendency in Austen criticism was clear-cut: the novels are best viewed as autonomous worlds, to be understood through the exploration of inner harmonies in style and structure. *Emma* is the masterpiece, because it successfully embodies the Jamesian poetic for the novel; the author of *Emma* is a "modern" writer, her heroine a direct ancestor of Flaubert's Madame Bovary. *Mansfield Park* is atypical, an apostasy on Jane Austen's part, since in it she abandons the indirections of irony in favor of direct moralizing.

Surveying the critical scene in 1963, Ian Watt summarized the achievements of the past twenty years in a passage that both did justice to that period and anticipated the course of much later criticism.

> In general, the criticism of Jane Austen in the last two decades is incomparably the richest and most illuminating that has appeared; but in demonstrating how the restrictions of her subject matter are the basis for a major literary achievement, recent criticism has perhaps failed to give the nature of Jane Austen's social and moral assumptions an equally exacting analysis. It is surely mistaken to assume that the affirmative elements in her morality and her humor are not as real as the subversive ironies which occasionally accompany them; or even to assume that awareness and insight, so often, and rightly, ascribed either to Jane Austen as narrator or to her major characters, are self-sufficient virtues: for how one sees is surely not more important than what one makes a point of seeing, or not seeing. (p. 13)

Many of the most significant recent studies of Jane Austen have indeed emphasized *what* one sees rather than *how* one sees, attempting to reconstruct the literary and social environment in which the novels were written; and inevitably the center of this enterprise has been *Mansfield Park*. Those critics of the 1940s and 1950s who established Jane Austen as a master of irony and narrative control naturally found *Mansfield Park*, with its debilitated heroine and curious uncertainties of tone and viewpoint, the most uncongenial of the novels; but often they went beyond rational criticism to attack *Mansfield Park* as if it were an affront to their personal artistic and ethical values. Hovering in the background was the Leavisite notion that criticism can only proceed by blood sacrifice, the exaltation of one author or work demanding the death of another. Therefore it is not surprising that when *Mansfield Park* finally received sympathetic attention, the critical claims were as extravagant and unyielding as the previous attacks.

The first step toward rehabilitation was Lionel Trilling's brilliant essay in *The Opposing Self* (1955), where the restraint and personal submission of *Mansfield Park* are seen as the necessary complements or countertruths to all that is "light, and bright, and sparkling" (*Letters*, February 4, 1813) in Jane Austen's other works. With its emphasis on rest rather than motion, on social cohesion rather than individual freedom, *Mansfield Park* represents for Trilling one side of Jane Austen's divided mind; it embodies a longing for "classical" stability and repose that is an essential part of her imagination. In *Mansfield Park* Jane Austen presents and then exorcises the "modern personality."

Trilling's subtle argument is so persuasive because he does not gloss over the ambiguities and contradictions of the novel but tries to explain them as products of a special historical and personal situation. In Trilling's view, Jane Austen clearly understands the demands of "personality" and modern individualism, while at the same time she has an elegiac regard for vanishing forms of social behavior. Aware that any effort to make a traditional writer "our contemporary" runs the risk of grotesque distortion, Trilling is determined to place *Mansfield Park* in a broad historical context. Unfortunately, the essay does not supply enough detailed evidence to support each step in the argument, and those later critics who have tried to flesh out Trilling's argument with more detailed historical evidence have been so heavy-handed that one returns to Trilling's essay with a feeling of liberation.

The problem with many of the recent attempts to "place" Jane Austen in a historical context, as Brian Southam observed in one of the best commentaries on modern studies of Jane Austen (1971), is that the only history most of her critics know is *literary* history. Her novels are filled with literary references, but many of them are either trivial or misleading, and conventional source studies such as Frank W. Bradbrook's *Jane Austen and Her Predecessors* (1966) show how little vital background is uncovered by an investigation of these allusions. More success has been achieved by those critics who see the literary references as part of a general cultural environment and who try to relate the historical background to the structure and verbal texture of the novels. Notable among these studies is Alistair M. Duckworth's *Improvement of the Estate* (1971), which takes the "estate" as a symbol for all inherited structures—manners, religion, language—and contends that it must be cherished and "improved" without the disruptions of radical change. Like Trilling, Duckworth finds Jane Austen poised between two worlds, that of the eighteenth-century "providential" novel and that of the modern "contingent" novel, always seeking a compromise that will embody her personal desire for restrained social reformation. *Mansfield Park* is her nearest approach to this ideal and therefore "fundamental to Jane Austen's thought."

This view, while attractive, tends to overschematize the novels, and at times Duckworth's argument resembles that of less talented historical critics who, in their attempts to restore Jane Austen to the cultural and literary life of her time, have succeeded only in locating her in an abstract history of ideas. It seems fair to say that scholarship of the 1960s and early 1970s overstressed Jane Austen's affinities with the eighteenth century, and in more recent works—such as Marilyn Butler's *Jane Austen and the War of Ideas* (1975), Susan Morgan's *In the Meantime* (1980), and Jan Fergus's *Jane Austen and the Didactic Novel* (1983)—we find a greater subtlety and sophistication in the handling of the political, literary, and educational backgrounds.

But if too many critics have made Jane Austen a prisoner of the history of ideas, with its mechanical choices between sense and sensibility, "classic" and "romantic," I would agree with B. C. Southam (in the 1971 review just mentioned) that the dogmatic "rhetoricians of fiction" neglected the historical reality of the novels in their search for formal patterns.

> The tendency, in all this, has been to regard the novels as autonomous verbal structures, closed systems, which provide, each within itself, the terms for its understanding. Jane Austen's concern is seen to be with human nature and human values and these matters are timeless. In taking her own society for the stage and setting for the novels it is said that she was merely turning to the material to hand; that she was concerned not with the face and form of the Regency world but with its inhabitants; and that the foreground identity that we call the comedy-of-manners is simply the costume of the age, beneath which stand the essential and unchanging facts of personality and character and human experience, facts that we can grasp and penetrate in Jane Austen by dint of our own native intelligence and sensibility. (p. 57)

Formal analysis of Jane Austen's novels in the 1940s, 1950s, and early 1960s tended to shy away from cultural history, partly out of a fear of Janeite antiquarianism. Fear of being a Janeite has been almost as debilitating as the illness itself. But in the 1960s and 1970s a number of critics with a sense of history have illuminated her fiction through a discriminating study of her language. Unlike the environment of the historical novel, which is given in overt and massive detail, the environment of a Jane Austen novel is established indirectly through the nuances of dialogue and narrative description, and therefore the best criticism will always be that which focuses on the details of her style and narrative method.

The potentialities of such study are demonstrated in David Lodge's *Language of Fiction* (1966), Norman Page's *Language of Jane Austen* (1972), Stuart M. Tave's *Some Words of Jane Austen* (1973), and Barbara Hardy's *Reading of Jane Austen* (1975). Lodge shows how in *Mansfield Park* Jane Austen uses a "vocabulary of discrimination" to control the reader's evaluation of the action. Tave, in his gracefully written study, explores not only those terms that are the counters of the history of ideas—"sensibility," "imagination"—but others such as "amiable" and "exertion" that are the more personal signals of Jane Austen's mature style. Page, working from a background in linguistics and the rhetoric of fiction, analyzes the minute shifts in style that establish the individual tones of the novels (each slightly different from its companions). And Hardy, a master of close reading, shows how Jane Austen moved far beyond earlier novelists to create a "flexible medium" that firmly controls both her characters and her readers. In these studies we find modern criticism of Jane Austen at its best.

Turning to the areas of textual and biographical scholarship, the first major event took place in 1954 with the publication in one volume of the minor works, containing the *juvenilia, Lady Susan, The Watsons, Sanditon,* "Plan of a Novel," Opinions of *Mansfield Park* and *Emma,* verses, and prayers (volume 6 in the Oxford edition of *The Works of Jane Austen,* edited by R. W. Chapman). In 1969 the volume was reprinted with revisions and corrections made by B. C. Southam, whose study of *Jane Austen's Literary Manuscripts* (1964) established the chronology of her literary career and cast new light on both the nature of the minor works and their relationship to the six novels. The publication of David Gilson's *Bibliography of Jane Austen* in 1982 was another turning point in Jane Austen scholarship: in addition to full bibliographical descriptions of the original and later editions, it provides copious information on translations, dramatizations, continuations, and completions and lists in chronological order biographical and critical items from 1813 through 1978.

The appearance in 1948 of R. W. Chapman's *Jane Austen: Facts and Problems*, a by-product of his work in editing the letters and the Oxford edition of the novels, led most critics and scholars to assume that little of importance remained to be discovered about Jane Austen's life. Elizabeth Jenkins's biography of 1938 had been based mainly on Chapman's editions, and later biographical studies—such as Marghanita Laski's useful *Jane Austen and Her World* (1969)—drew on the same fixed body of information, although Miss Laski brought to her work a rich understanding of regency England. But this easy assumption was shattered in 1983 by the publication of George Tucker's *A Goodly Heritage*, a history of the Austen family containing a great deal of new and revealing information that is not only fascinating in itself but crucial to an understanding of Jane Austen's development as an artist. It seems safe to predict that new and much better informed biographies will soon be written based on the kind of original and imaginative research that produced *A Goodly Heritage.*

The bicentennial of Jane Austen's birth in 1975 was the occasion for many celebrations and conferences and for at least five collections of essays.* Scanning these collections, one does not find the call for "revaluation" that is usually a part of such ritual occasions. The question addressed by the critics was not that of placing Jane Austen in some

---

* *Jane Austen Today*, Joel Weinsheimer, ed. (Athens, Ga., 1975); *Jane Austen's Achievement*, Juliet McMaster, ed. (London, 1976); *Jane Austen: Bicentenary Essays*, John Halperin, ed. (Cambridge, England, 1975); and two special numbers of journals: *Nineteenth-century Fiction* (Dec. 1975) and *Studies in the Novel* (Spring 1975).

hierarchy of literary or social values but of trying once again to explain her accepted excellences. But in spite of this common ground, the essays reflect in their varieties of approach and emphasis the whole range of modern criticism, from textual and biographical study to structuralist analysis. One notable aspect of these collections is the number of essays devoted to the roles of women in Jane Austen's fiction or to her own position as a woman writer. Some of the best criticism of Jane Austen in the 1970s and early 1980s has been written from a feminist perspective, or at least from the perspective of one intelligent woman writing about another supremely intelligent woman. Patricia Spacks's *Female Imagination* (1976), Nina Auerbach's *Communities of Women* (1978), Juliet McMaster's *Jane Austen on Love* (1978), Julia Prewitt Brown's *Jane Austen's Novels: Social Change and Literary Form* (1979)—these works and many others have taught new ways of looking at Jane Austen and indicate an important direction for future criticism.

One final thing to note about the bicentennial collections is that the essays, like most studies of Jane Austen, are marked by moderation and good sense. Jane Austen's fiction has always been resistant to critical fashions and the extremes of critical theory. Just as in the past the novels provided barren ground for the work of doctrinaire Marxist, formalist, and archetypal critics, so at present they have resisted the more heavy-handed practitioners of structuralism and deconstruction. When, in the heyday of archetypal criticism, Douglas Bush wrote his amusing parody "Mrs. Bennet and the Dark Gods" (*Sewanee Review*, 1956), his target was not archetypal critics of Jane Austen but the method in general; and he chose Jane Austen because dogmatic explication always seems most absurd when applied to her novels. The best criticism of Jane Austen has always been, and will remain, a reflection of her art—sensible, disciplined, and above all lucid.

Bibliography

GILSON, DAVID. *A Bibliography of Jane Austen* (Oxford, 1982).
HARDING, D. W. "Regulated Hatred: An Aspect of the Work of Jane Austen," *Scrutiny*, 8 (1939–40), 346–62.
LODGE, DAVID. *Language of Fiction* (London and New York, 1966), esp. 94–113.
ROTH, BARRY AND JOEL C. WEINSHEIMER. *An Annotated Bibliography of Jane Austen Studies, 1952–1972* (Charlottesville, Va., 1973).
SOUTHAM, B. C. "General Tilney's Hot-houses," *Ariel*, 2 (1971), 52–62.
———, ed. *Jane Austen: The Critical Heritage* (London and New York, 1968).
WATT, IAN. Introduction to *Jane Austen: A Collection of Critical Essays* (Englewood Cliffs, N.J., 1963), 1–14.

DANCING, BALLS, AND ASSEMBLIES

Joan Grigsby

Dancing, whether in assemblies, in private balls, or even for impromptu evening entertainment, sparkles through the pages of Jane Austen's six finished novels like candles on a Christmas tree. It provided an equally important background to her own youth.

In the first of her extant letters, written to her sister Cassandra (January 9, 1796), Jane Austen describes at some length "an exceeding good ball" that she had enjoyed the night before. She was just twenty-one. The same year saw the first drafts of *First Impressions* (published as *Pride and Prejudice*, 1813) and *Elinor and Marianne* (later *Sense and Sensibility*, 1811). In the second chapter of *Pride and Prejudice* the Bennet girls are discussing the forthcoming assembly at the nearby town of Meryton, which is described and relived in the following pages. Every ball or private dance in the novels may be divided into three parts: the preparation and discussions leading up to the event, the ball itself, and the subsequent "heightenings of imagination and all the laughs of playfulness which are so essential to the shade of a departed ball" (*MP*, p. 284). This pattern is particularly noticeable in *Emma* in which the preparation for the ball at the Crown Inn, its changes in proposed venue, its postponements, and its final accomplishment provide one of the outstanding themes in the novel.

Two other outstanding balls that play a significant part in the fate of the heroines are the one at Netherfield in *Pride and Prejudice* and that given by Sir Thomas Bertram at Mansfield Park for his niece Fanny and her brother William. At Netherfield everything goes wrong for Elizabeth and her sister Jane Bennet, owing to the appalling behavior of their mother and sisters. For Fanny, by contrast, everything goes right from the start. Fanny, the true Cinderella of the story, suddenly (to her own modest confusion) becomes the belle of the ball. We have some way to go yet before all is resolved, but the reader begins to suspect that the slipper is to fit Cinderella. Again a ball has produced a turning point in the story.

In *Sense and Sensibility* we are invited to no big balls or assemblies, but a great deal of impromptu dancing goes on in the evening at Barton Park; and in *Persuasion* there is informal dancing at the Great House at Uppercross, for which the piano is played by our heroine, Anne Elliot. In *Northanger Abbey* we have the larger, more formal balls in the Upper and Lower Rooms at Bath and are entertained by a long and mocking dissertation from Henry Tilney on the country dance as an emblem of marriage.

Country dances, which were enjoyed by Jane herself and by her heroines, took different forms. "Longways for as many as will" was the most popular, the men facing the women and moving up and down the set (similar to the Virginia reel), but there were square dances for eight couples and round dances for "as many as will." All took up a good deal of room; hence, Frank Churchill's careful planning of space in Randalls (*Emma*). The cotillion, mentioned in *Northanger Abbey*, would have been a modified version of a French peasant dance in which the women wore a variety of under-petticoats. It required slightly shorter skirts than was customary, and the top skirts would have been looped up.

The only other dance that is mentioned by name is the Boulanger (*Letters*, September 5, 1796; *PP*, p. 13). Like the country dances, it was "longways for as many as will." All these dances required a great deal of energy and were largely the prerogative of the younger members of the party, their elders attending balls and assemblies as chaperones or whist players.

When the Austen family lived in Southampton (1806–09), Jane determined to "go to as many Balls as possible" (*Letters*, December 9, 1808), but by now in her thirties, she probably considered herself an onlooker. In the same letter she describes an assembly in honor of the queen's birthday and shows some surprise that she was asked to dance. Once established at Chawton Cottage in 1809, her interest in dancing centered around her nieces, James's daughter Anna in particular. Some of the music of the country dances that she played for their amusement may be seen at the Jane Austen House at Chawton today. Commenting on Anna's first ball at a house where she herself danced as a girl, Jane says in a letter to Cassandra, "The Manydown ball was a smaller thing than I expected, but it seems to have made Anna very happy. At *her* age it would not have done for me" (January 10, 1809).

Few of the houses where the young Jane Austen danced exist today, although the descendants of their owners may still be found in Hampshire. The site of the Angel Inn at Basingstoke, where the Austens attended the monthly assemblies, is now occupied by a bank, and Manydown House, where they spent the night, no longer exists. The Dolphin Hotel in Southampton is still standing, but the room where she attended the queen's birthday assembly is no longer recognizable.

DRAMATIZATIONS OF THE NOVELS

Andrew Wright

About adaptations of Jane Austen of various kinds—translations, simplifications, abridgments, continuations, as well as dramatizations—it can be said that most attempts to render her works fall short, for the most part very short indeed. As might be guessed in advance, there is the all too easily demonstrable fact that no one writes Jane Austen as well as Jane Austen. Any tinkering means a change for the worse. Should one then leave Jane Austen completely alone? Possibly, but there are counterarguments of some weight, principally the argument that dramatization can make her novels more widely known.

While I have examined all the published adaptations of Jane Austen that I have been able to locate, and a large number of unpublished versions as well, I have not been able to achieve the record of the indefatigable and peripatetic David Gilson, whose *Bibliography of Jane Austen* is a cornucopia of blessings that admirers of Jane Austen have only begun to count. Gilson, however, has not discussed the dramatizations, though he has made the draconian judgment that they "read uniformly badly" (Gilson, p. 405). Nor can the present essay lay claim to presenting a survey of all or most of what has been done. On the contrary, it seems preferable to consider the problems and challenges that face the adapter of Jane Austen's novels: they remain stubbornly similar from novel to novel and from year to year. Therefore, I have confined myself to representative dramatizations of *Pride and Prejudice*, with special, though not exclusive, attention to three places in the novel, differing in mode of presentation by Jane Austen: chapter 1 entire; the letter of Mr. Collins to Mr. Bennet in chapter 13; and the conversation between Elizabeth and Lady Catherine in chapter 56 (chapter 14 of the third volume).

The strength of the first of the dramatic adaptations of *Pride and Prejudice*, that of Mary K. M. MacKaye (1906), lies in its faithfulness at many points to the actual words of Jane Austen; but of course no play can begin to encompass all that is in the novel. In the MacKaye *Pride and Prejudice* there are three rather than five daughters, Mary and Kitty having

---

Parts of this chapter have been published in "Jane Austen Adapted," *Nineteenth-century Fiction*, 30 (1975–76), 421–53, © 1975 by the Regents of the University of California, and incorporated here by permission of the Regents.

been jettisoned (as in the later Helen Jerome version); Mr. Collins is at Longbourn at the beginning of the play, ready for the courtships, which he launches into promptly; and—among many other simplifications—it is Lady Catherine who informs Elizabeth of Darcy's role in arranging the marriage between Lydia and Wickham ("It was a patched-up business at the expense of *my nephew*"), whereas in Jane Austen, Lady Catherine is, of course, ignorant of his role ("a patched-up business, at the expence of your father and uncles'" p. 357): afterward Elizabeth thinks with great discomfort of Lady Catherine's possible representations to Darcy of "the evils attached to a connection with her" (p. 360). Darcy is Fitzgerald Darcy of Pendleton, Derbyshire; later, however, he is said to be of Pemberley. Mrs. Bennet speaks with more extravagantly ungrammatical force than in Jane Austen; of Mr. Collins she says: "He certainly does seem to have all the luck in the world. Here he has just got this good living from that grand Lady Catherine de Bourg [sic]."

The *Pride and Prejudice* of Eileen and J. C. Squire, produced as early as 1922 but not published until seven years later, is notable chiefly for the splendid cast that was brought together "in aid of the Bedford College extension and endowment fund hall of residence appeal," including Dame May Whitty as Mrs. Bennet and Ellen Terry (in a nonspeaking part) as Mrs. Long. The play begins with Lydia bursting into the morning room at Longbourn full of hope (shared by Kitty) of going to Brighton, in pursuit of the militia. But Mr. and Mrs. Bennet do then appear in an abridged version of the chapter 1 conversation, staying remarkably close to Jane Austen. The initiatory letter from Mr. Collins is produced by Mr. Bennet but not read. However, Mr. Collins himself utters some of the words of the letter when he appears; the transference is effective. Elizabeth reports to Jane what she overheard Darcy say at the ball: "She is tolerably pretty . . . but I cannot be tempted to dance"—an unfortunate alternative to Jane Austen's dialogue. Rather distressingly, the Squires do innovate freely; there is, for instance, a conversation between Caroline Bingley and her brother about Jane Bennet in which Caroline imputes to Jane a duplicity that is absent in Jane Austen: Jane Bennet is said to be "playing a most deep game with you; while nominally engaged to Collins, she is boldly angling for the better catch, and no doubt would throw off the former should the latter bite." Pemberley is relocated in Sussex, and Mr. and Mrs. Bennet (accompanied by Kitty and Mary) go to have a look at it. As for Darcy, he goes to Brighton to *unmask* Wickham, "to show him up as the villain he is," because of a desire to win Elizabeth's good opinion. Lady Catherine's interview with Elizabeth is in many respects faithful to the original; when it is not, there is cause for regret. Darcy comes in before the end of the exchange, at which Lady Catherine says, "(*Fuming at him*) So you are actually here, calling upon her at this moment." Her ladyship even argues with her nephew: "Come, Fitzwilliam, this cannot be! Think for one moment. Think of this girl's relations, her connections; and then her manner! So obdurate, and self-willed, so cool and assured, so unwilling to listen to a word of advice or ruling from one who would be placed by your action in the relationship of her aunt. What sort of niece will she be to me if you persist in your resolve to make her so?"

The well-known Helen Jerome dramatization of *Pride and Prejudice* had respectable runs in both New York and London in 1935 and 1936, respectively. Later, this version became the basis for the screenplay by Aldous Huxley and Jane Murfin (1940), produced by Metro-Goldwyn-Mayer; and the musical *First Impressions*, which had a run in New York in 1959, claims kinship with Helen Jerome's version. Throughout her *Pride and Prejudice*, Helen Jerome paints with broader strokes than does Jane Austen. There are three daughters: Jane, Elizabeth, and Lydia. Elizabeth, on first meeting Darcy, says, "Lady Lucas was telling us of your estate at Pemberley"—the approach direct; an Irish maid is introduced at the Gardiners' ("'Tis wild she is about the tay party, ma'am. Do you like the way I've lad it?"); Colonel Fitzwilliam refers to his cousin Darcy as a "sobersides." Fortunately, the New York and London productions appear to have been so well acted as to minimize these limitations; but a number of reviewers complained that Mrs. Bennet, Mr. Collins, and Lady Catherine jarred because they were presented as mainly farcical. Taken as a whole, the play has a backward-looking aspect, an Edwardian flavor, rather as if it had been written by Galsworthy than by Jane Austen.

In Jane Austen, Mr. Bennet says of Bingley's coming to Netherfield Park and Mrs. Bennet's hope that he may marry one of their daughters: "Is that his design in settling here?" Mrs. Bennet: "Design! nonsense, how can you talk so!" (p. 4). Helen Jerome causes her to say: "Design! Nonsense—don't be so stupid!" A moment or two later, Mr. Bennet refuses to promise to call at Netherfield Park, saying: "It's more than I engage for, I assure you." Helen Jerome's revision: "Oh, come now, that is going rather far—you know my habits." There is also Mr. Bennet's response to his wife's complaint about the suffering she must undergo on account of her poor nerves. "Ah!" says Mrs. Bennet in Jane Austen, "you do not know what I suffer." To which her husband replies, "But I hope you will get over it, and live to see many young men of four thousand a year come into the neighbourhood" (p. 5). Helen Jerome's Mr. Bennet replies: "That's right, my dear, have a nice little cry, it always seems to help your nerves. I think I'll go out and get some air—my horse needs exercising. I'll be back in half an hour—for tea."

Mr. Collins's letter about coming to Longbourn is not read aloud. Mr. Bennet says, merely: "In his letter he hinted—only hinted, mind you, that he wishes to look over our daughters, with the object of choosing one for a wife so that he can partly atone for the guilt of inheriting the estate." This is fair enough as a report, but it is a pity to miss the direct expression of his conceit and sycophancy.

In the exchange between Lady Catherine and Elizabeth there is some business in the Jerome version that is absent from, and indeed unthinkable in, Jane Austen. Lady Catherine at Longbourn examines a table, according to a stage direction, "tapping it with her lorgnette to see if it is genuine." Elizabeth, observing her, says, "The piece is quite genuine." And though much Jane Austen remains in this scene, much also is omitted, and much is altered. For instance, when Jane Austen's Lady Catherine tells Elizabeth, "Mr. Darcy is engaged to *my daughter*. Now what have you to say?" Elizabeth replies, "Only this; that if he is so, you can have no reason to suppose that he will make an offer to me." But Helen Jerome's Elizabeth says, "Only that if this is true, why are you worrying? How could he make an offer to me? Or has he a case of bigamy in view? (*smiles*) It is still a crime in England, you know." Subsequently, when Jane Austen's Lady Catherine tells Elizabeth, "I have not been in the habit of brooking disappointment," Elizabeth responds as follows: "*That* will make your ladyship's situation at present more pitiable; but it will have no effect on *me*" (p. 356). The Jerome response: "That is unfortunate. It is rather late in life for your ladyship to be receiving your first taste of it."

Another stage version of *Pride and Prejudice*, by A. A. Milne, was written at approximately the same time as Helen Jerome's. It is called *Miss Elizabeth Bennet*, and it was published in 1936. In the introduction, Milne says:

> On the day it was finished I read that a dramatized version of *Pride and Prejudice* was about to be produced on the New York stage.... Should one hurry to get the play on [in London] with any cast that was available? In the end the risk was taken; arrangements were made for the early autumn; the Elizabeth I had always wanted began to let her hair grow; the management, the theatre, the producer, all were there ... and at that moment the American version arrived in London.

Actually, Helen Jerome was—and perhaps still is—Australian.

The Milne version is superior to that of Helen Jerome—more thoughtful and more faithful; whether it is as actable, I cannot say. And it is entirely understandable that two or more persons should be engaged in the same enterprise at the same time, in ignorance of the fact that the other was similarly occupied. What is less easy to understand is that neither Helen Jerome nor Milne appears to have been acquainted with the other dramatizations. Even more surprising is that Aldous Huxley and Jane Murfin based the film adaptation on the Jerome rather than the Milne play.

In the introduction to *Miss Elizabeth Bennet*, Milne sets out a number of rules by which he says the writer should be guided in adapting Jane Austen for the stage. "In the case of those passages which are a household word to the faithful, he should either use the exact dialogue or omit the passage altogether. He should be very reluctant to 'improve,' however dramatically necessary this may seem." Not that Milne refuses to invent. Indeed, he lays down the following as one of his rules: "The play must be written throughout as the dramatist would naturally write it, not as Miss Austen would have written it. That is to say, he must never ask himself, 'Would Jane Austen have made So-and-so say this?' but 'Would So-and-so have said it?'" He confesses to trying to make Darcy more attractive to modern audiences than he is in the original and Bingley more articulate—more verbally lively—than he is in the novel.

In any event, the play by Milne is much more a work of its decade than its author perhaps realized. Just as the musical *First Impressions* (1959) reeks of Lerner and Loewe, so *Miss Elizabeth Bennet* savors of Noel Coward. To be sure, there are a number of novelties in *Miss Elizabeth Bennet* that have nothing to do with Noel Coward. Aunt Norris is imported from *Mansfield Park*—not quite in person but as the aunt referred to by Lydia. ("My aunt Norris says that *I* shall be married first, because I have the liveliest disposition.") Bingley speaks of "My Lord Chatham" as if he were still alive. Mrs. Bennet says, "La, Mr. Darcy, how you do take me up." But there is about the Milne version altogether an absence of reticence, and there is a stylized rendering of the ordinary, together with a patina of the fantastic, that mark the writing of *Miss Elizabeth Bennet* as belonging halfway in time between *Private Lives* and *Blithe Spirit*. Thus, the opening scene of the play is more elaborate than Jane Austen's first chapter, all five daughters being present as the news about the letting of Netherfield is made known. Mrs. Bennet tells her husband that "a handsome man of large fortune . . . came down in a chaise and four." So far, so faithful. But Milne has Mr. Bennet reply, "In a chaise and four they are particularly handsome." And, a little later, Mrs. Bennet angrily says to her husband, "How you can want to see Charlotte Lucas queening it at Netherfield Park is more than I can understand."

In the first proposal scene, Darcy says, "In vain have I struggled. It will not do. My feelings will not be repressed. You must allow me to tell you how ardently I admire and love you" (p. 189). So Jane Austen. Milne makes the declaration into the following: "It is no use! I struggle and struggle in vain. You have caught me! I cannot escape!" Elizabeth: "Mr. Darcy!" Darcy: "I cannot do without the light in your eyes, the sound of your voice; they go with me everywhere. In vain, in vain have I struggled to escape them. I love you." It is impossible not to detect here the sort of dialogue that would have gone better between Gertrude Lawrence and Noel Coward himself than between the characters in Jane Austen's novel.

Later, in the conversation between Lady Catherine and Elizabeth, the former asks, as Jane Austen has it, "Is this your gratitude for my attentions to you last spring? Is nothing due to me on that score?" (p. 355). To this Elizabeth makes no immediate response; but in the Milne play there is the following exchange: "Is this your gratitude for my attentions to you last spring?" Elizabeth: "Your ladyship puts a higher value upon a dinner than I do. If I had known that your invitations carried with them a perpetual right of interference they would not have been accepted."

The scenario, by Aldous Huxley and Jane Murfin, for the 1940 film of *Pride and Prejudice* is professedly based on Helen Jerome; but it departs very frequently from the earlier version and from Jane Austen, as well. The action begins with a scene in the Meryton village draper's shop to which Mrs. Bennet and her two eldest daughters have gone to look for some materials for dresses for the assembly ball. A clatter of carriages in the village street interrupts the conversation; and these carriages contain the new tenants of Netherfield Park. Lady Lucas also makes her appearance here; and the dialogue presents the two mothers as equally ambitious to entrap one or both as husbands for their daughters. There is a good deal of non-Austenian business, including a Punch-and-Judy show, giving Lydia the opportunity to flirt with Wickham and Kitty (she and Mary are both in evidence in this version) the opportunity to flirt with Denny; there is also a carriage race between Mrs. Bennet and Lady Lucas, each of whom is determined to make arrangements for hospitality for the newcomers by having her husband call on Bingley before the other. None of this is in Helen Jerome; the following remarkable exchange is also unique in Huxley-Murfin:

> Mr. Bennet (*patiently*). Mrs. Bennet, for the thousandth time, this estate was entailed when I inherited it. It must by law go to a male heir—a male heir, Mrs. Bennet—and as you possibly remember, we have no son.
> Mrs. Bennet. All the more reason why you should take some responsibility about getting husbands for them. But *you* escape into your unintelligible books and leave all that to me.
> Mr. Bennet. Yes, what *is* to become of the wretched creatures? Perhaps we should have drowned them at birth!

The scene at the ball in which Darcy does not deign to dance with Elizabeth contains the following variation on Jane Austen: "Oh, she's tolerable enough ... but not impressively handsome. And I'm in no humor tonight to give consequence to provincial young ladies with a lively wit."

Besides the race between Lady Lucas and Mrs. Bennet and other novelties at the beginning of the scenario, there are other large-scale innovations. A stage direction indicates that the action of this *Pride and Prejudice* takes place between 1820 and 1825, well after the death of the author of the novel. Jane is the second daughter (though inadvertently introduced by Mrs. Bennet to Mr. Collins as "my eldest daughter"). There are also an archery scene, a recitation by Darcy of "She Walks in Beauty Like the Night," and—most egregious of all—a Lady Catherine with a heart of gold beneath the bluster. She is also depicted as having the power of the purse over Darcy; and so in her scene with Elizabeth she is able to threaten her antagonist as follows: "Are you aware that, as the trustee of my sister's estate, I can strip Mr. Darcy of every shilling he has?" Actually, this Lady Catherine very much likes being stood up to—it is refreshing after so much sycophancy—and in a subsequent scene with Darcy gives the union her blessing. If the Jerome adaptation looks backward to Galsworthy and the Milne belongs to the fashion set by Noel Coward, the Huxley-Murfin *Pride and Prejudice* may be regarded as a kind of Hollywood apotheosis, representing the best and worst of that dark and bright heyday, a period piece indeed. The published biographies of Huxley do not provide evidence of his degree of resistance to some of the more outrageous departures from Jane Austen; but the file copy of the scenario contains tantalizing hints of Hunt Stromberg's determination to reinterpret *Pride and Prejudice* in accordance with a conception of the novel that differs radically from that of the author and—at least by inference—from that of Huxley himself. The brilliance of the film remains undimmed, however: Laurence Olivier's Darcy and Greer Garson's Elizabeth are unforgettable.

No sampling of Jane Austen adaptations would be properly representative without a consideration of *Pride and Prejudice* set to music. On March 19, 1959, *First Impressions*, by Abe Burrows, made its appearance in New York, and though it did not set the Hudson River on fire, it had a run of eighty-four performances. The music was written by Robert Goldman, Glenn Paxton, and George Weiss. Judging from the Columbia record of songs from the play, there was drastic miscasting. Polly Bergen's sophistication, her characterization of Elizabeth as a knowing urbanite, was the most disastrous aspect of the production altogether. Even Hermione Gingold, for all her experience and versatility, failed as Mrs. Bennet. If, as was suggested by Brooks Atkinson at the time, *First Impressions* represents an attempt to repeat the success of *My Fair Lady*, Hermione Gingold was the intended counterpart of Stanley Holloway in the other musical. The play as a whole is nonetheless a sad decline from Helen Jerome (with whom it claims allegiance), not to mention Jane Austen. When Lady Catherine comes to Longbourn for her interview with Elizabeth, she is made to say to Mr. Bennet, "You appear to be a gentleman." To which he replies: "A fallen gentleman, Your Ladyship. I was forced to abandon my class because I had no stomach for rudeness." And Mrs. Bennet, of all people, says: "You must excuse us all, Lady Catherine. We've had a very trying week." The play ends with Darcy agreeing that his intended mother-in-law dwell in his house in London, upon which Mrs. Bennet congratulates herself, and Elizabeth sings a reprise of the romantic song "Love Will Find Out the Way," for all the world like a chanteuse in the Rainbow Room.

A more faithful—or less unfaithful—musical version of *Pride and Prejudice* was issued in Johannesburg in 1964. Although Mark Eldon, the author of the musical's book, takes many liberties, he preserves much of the spirit of the original by presenting with the minimum of alteration certain central scenes, including the discussion of Mr. and Mrs. Bennet in the first chapter. Thus, Mr. Bennet is made to say, in response to his wife's "Oh! single, my dear, to be sure! A single man of large fortune; four or five thousand a year" the following: "You have lost no time in gathering all the essential information"—a remark perhaps called for in the interest of dramatic emphasis and certainly not out of character. Mary and Kitty are omitted from this version; and there are some remarkable, but not discordant, innovations, such as a scene in the foyer of a theater to which Mrs. Gardiner has taken Elizabeth and Jane to see a performance of Mrs. Siddons and John Kemble in *Macbeth*. There the party encounters, between the acts, the Bingley entourage, including Darcy himself; it seems an effective piece of mime. The music, which is included in the published version, is simple and tuneful, utterly lacking in the Lerner and Loewe-style metropolitanism of the music for *First Impressions*. For this reason, the music of the South African adaptation is less dated, belonging as it does to the longer line of English music-hall composition. It is less easy to make a judgment about the lyrics, the titles of which stand out perhaps more starkly in the pages of a book than in their theatrical context. Jane sings a song, after meeting Bingley, called "It Takes Two to Fall in Love." Mr. Collins and Lydia sing, "Whom Shall I Ask to Marry Me?" Elizabeth sings, "Should I Dance with You, Should I?" and Darcy, "You Should Dance with Me, You Should."

Certain conclusions emerge from the study of the many adaptations for dramatic performance of Jane Austen's novels. The first is that no version escapes its time or place. English, American, Australian, and South African renderings all bear the marks of their origins. Second, the internal circumstances of the countries in which the adaptations make their appearance are inevitably reflected. Thus, the many BBC performances demonstrate the advantage of a radio and television network that is able to present plays and readings without having to make them pay; American radio and television versions are outsize—or undersized—in various ways, not all of them having to do with commercial interruption. And the film script of *Pride and Prejudice*, although it bears the name of Aldous Huxley, is a Hollywood product through and through. Finally, as has been remarked from time to time already, the closer the rendering for the stage of the words of Jane Austen, the better: this is perhaps the most important lesson for the would-be adapter, a lesson that has been taken to heart in the most recent dramatizations on the BBC, all of which represent a much more satisfying level of accomplishment than earlier versions.

Published Dramatizations of Jane Austen's Works

Entries are arranged chronologically under the following headings and in the following order: *Sense and Sensibility*, *Pride and Prejudice*, *Mansfield Park*, *Emma*, and "Love and Freindship." Arrangements of scenes from Jane Austen's novels, whether published or not, are omitted from the present list. Likewise omitted are all unpublished dramatizations of the novels, a number of which are of great interest; for the period up to 1975 such adaptations are included in my "Jane Austen Adapted." The bulk of these were performed on the BBC and can be examined at the BBC Written Archives Centre, Reading, Berkshire; the script of the film version of *Pride and Prejudice* is on deposit at the UCLA Research Library, Los Angeles. For cast lists, production details, and other adaptations of Jane Austen's works (abridgments, simplifications, continuations, sequels) up to 1975, see my "Jane Austen Adapted." See also the excellent listing of published dramatizations through 1978 in Gilson's *Bibliography of Jane Austen*.

Sense and Sensibility

KENDALL, JANE [*pseud.* of Anne Louise Coulter Martens]. *Sense and Sensibility* (Chicago, 1948).

ANTONY, JONQUIL. *Sense and Sensibility: A Play in Three Acts* (London, 1949).

BLAKESLEY, MILDRED LENORÉ. *The Dashwoods: A Play in Three Acts* (New York, 1974).

Pride and Prejudice

MACKAYE, MARY K. M. *Pride and Prejudice: A Play Founded on Jane Austen's Novel* (New York, 1906).

MACNAMARA, MARGARET. *Elizabeth Refuses: A Miniature Comedy from Jane Austen's "Pride and Prejudice"* (London and Boston, 1926).

SQUIRE, EILEEN H. A. AND J. C. SQUIRE. *Pride and Prejudice: A Play in Four Acts* (London, 1929).

JOHNSON-JONES, ANNE. *Pride and Prejudice: A Play in Four Acts* (London, 1930).

JEROME, HELEN. *Pride and Prejudice: A Sentimental Comedy in Three Acts* (Garden City, N.Y., 1935).

MACNAMARA, MARGARET. *I Have Five Daughters: A Morning-Room Comedy in Three Acts* (London, 1936).

MILNE, A. A. *Miss Elizabeth Bennet: A Play* (London, 1936).

PHELPS, PAULINE. *Pride and Prejudice: A Comedy* (Sioux City, Iowa, 1941).

KENDALL, JANE [*pseud.* of Anne Louise Coulter Martens]. *Pride and Prejudice, Adapted from Jane Austen's Novel* (Chicago, 1942).

KENNETT, JOHN. *Pride and Prejudice: A Play* (London and Glasgow, 1955).

BURROWS, ABE. *First Impressions: A Musical Comedy* (New York, 1962).

ELDON, MARK. *Pride and Prejudice: A Musical Comedy in Two Acts* (Johannesburg, 1964).

COX, CONSTANCE. *Pride and Prejudice: A Play* (London, 1972).

DUFFIELD, BRAINERD. *Jane Austen's Pride and Prejudice* (Elgin, Ill., 1972).

Mansfield Park

COX, CONSTANCE. *Mansfield Park: A Comedy in Three Acts* (Bakewell, Derbys., 1977).

Emma

BODEEN, DEWITT. *Romances by Emma: A Comedy of Humors and Manners in Three Acts* (New York, 1938).

MACKAYE, MARION M. *Emma: A Play* (New York, 1941).

LINDSAY, JOHN AND RONALD RUSSELL. *Emma: A Play in Three Acts* (London, 1943).

GLENNON, GORDON. *Emma: A Play* (London, 1945).

Northanger Abbey

HOLME, THEA. *Northanger Abbey: A Play in Three Acts* (London, 1950).

Cox, Constance. *Northanger Abbey: A Comedy in Three Acts* (London, 1950).

"Love and Freindship"

Wigginton, May Wood. *Love and Freindship: Play in Five Acts* (New York and London, 1925).

Bibliography

Gilson, David. *A Bibliography of Jane Austen* (Oxford, 1982).
Wright, Andrew. "Jane Austen Adapted," *Nineteenth-century Fiction*, 30 (1975–76), 421–53.

DRESS AND FASHION

Penelope Byrde

Although Jane Austen never describes the dress of her heroes and heroines in any detail and firmly states in one novel that "Dress is at all times a frivolous distinction, and excessive solicitude about it often destroys its own aim" (*NA*, p. 73), her letters reveal a natural, lively, and informed interest in the subject of fashion. She reports the latest developments in London or Bath, discusses her shopping expeditions, and details the cut, construction, and decoration of her clothes.

The length and frequency of such descriptions have led some critics to accuse her of triviality, but it should be remembered that this was common practice among letter writers of the period. News of changing styles or advice on points of etiquette (such as the correct wear for mourning) were more often relayed by word of mouth or letter than by newspapers or the fashion magazines, which were only just being produced on a regular basis. Relatives or friends in London and the larger towns were expected to supply information and carry out commissions for clothes as a regular duty; thus, the first part of Mrs. Gardiner's business on her arrival to stay with the Bennets "was to distribute her presents and describe the newest fashions" (*PP*, p. 139). Clothes were also discussed in detail because so few items could be bought ready-made. Garments were produced individually by hand, paper patterns were not yet in common use, and the dressmaker relied on the customer for directions as to the intended style and decoration. Decisions were reached after consultation with family and friends, though not always with ease. "I cannot determine what to do about my new gown," Jane Austen wrote in 1798. "I wish such things were to be bought ready-made. I have some hopes of meeting Martha at the christening at Deane next Tuesday, and shall see what she can do for me. I want to have something suggested which will give me no trouble of thought or direction" (*Letters*, December 24, 1798). Sometimes the new and fashionable clothes of neighbors could be copied, and existing garments were used as patterns in themselves—Harriet Smith talked of her "pattern gown" (*E*, p. 235).

Clothes requiring skill in cutting or fitting were professionally made, and Jane Austen mentions several dressmakers by name, but most women were able to make their own undergarments, alter gowns, and vary trimmings. Both Elizabeth and Lydia Bennet trimmed their own bonnets

(*PP*, pp. 6, 219), and Jane Austen (herself a skilled needlewoman) did her own alterations; one lilac sarcenet (silk) gown she was determined to trim with "black sattin ribbon with a proper perl edge; & now I am trying to draw it up into kind of roses, instead of putting it in plain double plaits" (*Letters*, March 5, 1814).

There are many references to dress fabrics that were bought in lengths (called "a gown") of between seven and ten yards (e.g., *Letters*, January 25, 1801; April 18, 1811). During the last quarter of the eighteenth century light, thin cottons and linens in white or pale colors began to replace the stiffer and more richly colored and patterned silks. This coincided with a change in the style of dress from rather formal gowns with rigidly boned bodices and hoop-petticoated skirts to simple, clinging, high-waisted and shiftlike dresses inspired by the draperies of ancient Greek and Roman statues. Muslin (a general term for finely woven cotton) was at the height of popularity and came in many varieties of texture and pattern, as Jane Austen enumerates in *Northanger Abbey*. Catherine Morland "lay awake ten minutes on Wednesday night debating between her spotted and her tamboured muslin," although the author warned ladies of how little the heart of man "is biassed by the texture of their muslin, and how unsusceptible of peculiar tenderness towards the spotted, the sprigged, the mull or the jackonet." Henry Tilney's discussion of muslin with Mrs. Allen is one of the comic scenes of this novel (*NA*, pp. 28 and 73–74).

Unlike silk, muslin washed well, and the fashion for white gowns could be indulged. White was considered the most elegant and refined color, especially for evening dresses. Fanny Price, afraid of appearing overdressed for a dinner party, was assured by her cousin Edmund that "a woman can never be too fine while she is all in white. . . . I see no finery about you; nothing but what is perfectly proper" (*MP*, p. 222). Those who could afford to wore white all the time, as did the elegant Eleanor Tilney (*NA*, p. 91), but when circumstances did not warrant it, this was thought to be pretentious (see *Letters*, May 21, 1801); and Mrs. Norris approved of a housekeeper who "turned away two housemaids for wearing white gowns" (*MP*, p. 106). For more practical daytime wear colored gowns were common: Jane Austen talks of her own pink, brown, and yellow dresses (*Letters*, January 25, 1801), and Isabella Thorpe took to wearing nothing but purple in order to please James Morland (*NA*, p. 218).

For warmth out-of-doors the spencer (a short-waisted, long-sleeved jacket) and the pelisse (a coat cut on similar lines but full-length), made of silk, velvet, or woolen cloth, were both fashionable. Shawls and cloaks of light wool, silk, muslin, gauze, or lace were worn indoors, but most coveted were the fine wool shawls imported from the East; Lady Bertram was anxious to have at least two when her nephew in the navy returned from the East Indies (*MP*, p. 305).

Caps, hats, and bonnets were important accessories to dress. Caps were worn indoors by all married women and those unmarried once past their first youth. Jane Austen adopted caps at an early age (twenty-three), but she liked them. "They save me a world of torment as to hair-dressing, which at present gives me no trouble beyond washing and brushing" (*Letters*, December 1, 1798). For evening wear, caps would be elaborately trimmed with ribbon, lace, feathers, or flowers. Hats and bonnets could also be decorated, and in 1799 she describes a particular fashion for trimming hats with artificial flowers and fruit that she was happy to follow, although she found it absurd (*Letters*, June 2 and 11, 1799). A veil of net or lace could be attached to the hat or bonnet brim for added formality; Mrs. Elton was scornful of the "very few lace veils" apparently worn at Emma's wedding (*E*, p. 484). Parasols also protected the complexion from the sun (*S*, p. 381).

On their feet women wore flat pumps in the house but stouter ankle boots for walking—Emma broke off the lace of her half boot when out with Harriet and Mr. Elton so that she could tactfully fall behind (*E*, p. 89). Servants and countrywomen still wore pattens (wooden overshoes raised on an iron frame) in wet or muddy weather, and Anne Elliot found the "ceaseless clink of pattens" among the trying noises of Bath (*P*, p. 135).

Women's underwear is mentioned in the letters. Jane Austen buys linen shifts (a basic undergarment) and silk stockings, for which she seems to have had a weakness (*Letters*, November 25, 1798; October 25, 1800). Corsets were also worn, and in 1813 she learned from "Mrs. Tickars's young lady, to my high amusement, that the stays now are not made to force the bosom up at all; *that* was a very unbecoming, unnatural fashion. I was really glad to hear that they are not to be so much off the shoulders as they were" (*Letters*, September 15, 1813).

The small number of references to male dress probably reflects her lack of interest in the subject, although she noted the added attraction that a military or naval uniform could give a man (*PP*, p. 29); William Price in his lieutenant's uniform was clearly "looking and moving all the taller, firmer, and more graceful for it" (*MP*, p. 384). The fashionable hat, caped greatcoat, and riding boots also had their appeal, and Henry Tilney evidently wore his with style in spite of being a clergyman (*NA*, pp. 157 and 210); but as Mary Crawford remarked of another cleric, "Luckily there is no distinction of dress now-a-days to tell tales" (*MP*, p. 416). Linen shirts and cravats—which required no tailoring—could be made at home, and Jane Austen, Fanny Price, and Catherine Morland were all kept busy sewing for their brothers (*Letters*, September 1, 1796; *MP*, p. 390; *NA*, p. 240). Another accessory to be mentioned are gloves, and Frank Churchill looked at "the sleek, well-tied parcels of 'Men's Beavers' and 'York Tan'" when he visited Ford's shop with Emma (*E*, p. 200).

Jane Austen is quick to make fun of both male and female vanity (Sir Walter Elliot in *Persuasion*, Robert Ferrars in *Sense and Sensibility*, Mrs. Elton in *Emma*) but her highest praise is always for "elegance" in dress and manners (*E*, p. 270; *NA*, pp. 55–56). Like Emma and Mr. Knightley, who had "no taste for finery or parade" (*E*, p. 484), it seems likely that her other heroes and heroines all dressed and behaved with perfect propriety.

Bibliography

BUCK, ANNE. "The Costume of Jane Austen and Her Characters," in *The So-called Age of Elegance: Costume 1785–1820*, Proceedings of the Fourth Annual Conference of the Costume Society, 1970 (London, 1970), 36–45.

BYRDE, PENELOPE. *A Frivolous Distinction: Fashion and Needlework in the Works of Jane Austen* (Bath, England, 1979).

EDITIONS AND PUBLISHING HISTORY

David Gilson

Sense and Sensibility was first advertised by its publisher, Thomas Egerton of Whitehall, London, on October 30, 1811, and was published anonymously at about that date, price 15s. for the three small volumes printed in large type, bound in paper-covered boards of two colors with a printed paper spine label. It was published "for the Author," Jane Austen retaining the copyright and paying expenses but taking receipts, subject to payment of 10 percent commission to the publisher for handling the book. Publication is assumed to have been partly financed by the novelist's brother Henry, with whom she was staying in London when she wrote to her sister in April 1811 of correcting proofs of her novel. About 750 or 1,000 copies were printed, and by July 1813 all of these had been sold, with a profit to Jane Austen of £140. The publisher advised a second edition, which was issued in October 1813, with the price increased to 18s.; the size of this second edition is not known.

With the second novel to be published, *Pride and Prejudice*, the copyright was sold outright to Thomas Egerton for £110 in November 1812; the novel was first advertised on January 28, 1813 (the author having received her first copy on the previous day) and published—anonymously again—at 18s. for three volumes in an edition possibly of 1,500 copies, which presumably sold fairly quickly, since Egerton issued a second edition later the same year, probably in October, again at 18s., and also a third edition in 1817. With this third edition (of which, as with the second edition, the size is not known), the text was rearranged for publication in two volumes; price, 12s.

Jane Austen's letters show that her brother Henry was reading what must have been proofs of *Mansfield Park* in March 1814; she hoped this third novel would come out in April, but the first advertisement appeared on May 9, 1814, and the novel was published then by Thomas Egerton, again anonymously, in an edition possibly of 1,250 copies, with the novelist again retaining the copyright. The price was again 18s. for the three volumes. By November 1814 all copies were sold, but although the question of a second edition was discussed with Egerton in that month, Jane Austen changed her publisher, and the second edition of *Mansfield Park* was ultimately brought out by John Murray in February 1816—750 copies were printed—and sold again at 18s. for three volumes. Sales were not brisk, and progressive price reductions were made; in January 1820, 498 copies were still on hand, and these were remaindered at 2s. 6d.

The manuscript of *Emma* seems to have been submitted to John Murray in the late summer or early autumn of 1815; it was read for Murray by William Gifford (editor of the *Quarterly Review*), who reported favorably on it on September 29, 1815. John Murray offered £450 for the copyright, plus the copyrights of *Mansfield Park* and *Sense and Sensibility*, but the final arrangement seems to have been as before publication at Jane Austen's expense, with profits to her after payment of 10 percent commission to the publisher and the copyright remaining her property. Again she was staying in London with Henry when she received proofs in November 1815. The first advertisement was on December 2, but publication, again anonymous, was not until December 23, with title pages dated 1816. The novel was dedicated to the prince regent; a copy was specially bound in red morocco gilt at a cost of 24s. and sent to the regent at Carlton House on or before December 21. Two thousand copies were printed and sold at £1 1s. for the three volumes. By October 1816, 1,248 copies had been sold, with a profit to Jane Austen of just over £221, but John Murray set his initial loss on the second edition of *Mansfield Park* against this, and the first payment for *Emma*, made as late as February 1817, was only of £38 18s. By 1820, 539 copies were still in stock, and these were remaindered at 2s.

The manuscript of *Northanger Abbey* (then called *Susan*) was sold in 1803 for £10 to the publishers Richard Crosby & Son of London, who went so far as to announce it for publication but for some reason failed to bring it out. Jane Austen wrote to Crosby under a pseudonym in April 1809 to ask why publication had not taken place, saying she had another copy of the manuscript if the first had been lost; Crosby replied that no date had been stipulated for publication and that the manuscript could be returned for the price paid for it. After the publication in 1809 of an anonymous novel entitled *Susan*, Jane Austen seems to have changed her own title and her heroine's name to *Catherine*, but no other action was taken until 1816 when, after the publication of *Emma*, the manuscript of *Catherine* was bought back by Henry Austen; however, it was not published until after Jane Austen's death, in company with *Persuasion*, with the title again changed (presumably by Henry) to *Northanger Abbey*.

Jane Austen wrote to her niece Fanny Knight on March 13, 1817 that she had an unnamed novel (in fact *Persuasion*) ready for publication "which may perhaps appear about a twelvemonth hence. It is short, about the length of Catherine." The two novels did not, in fact, appear until late in December 1817, dated 1818, in a set of four volumes, sold at 24s., with the author's identity revealed in Henry Austen's "Biographical Notice" of his sister. The first advertisement was on December 17, 1817; John Murray printed 1,750 copies, with copyright retained by the Austen family. Initial sales were rapid, with only 321 copies remaining at the end of 1818; the total profits, which the author did not live to receive, were £515 17s. 7d.

An American edition of *Emma*, apparently unknown to Jane Austen, was published by Mathew Carey of Philadelphia in 1816. The circumstances, even the size, of the edition are unknown, and at present only three copies have been traced. Then, in 1832 and 1833, Carey & Lea of Philadelphia issued all six novels, each in two volumes (*Pride and Prejudice*, renamed *Elizabeth Bennet; Persuasion* and *Mansfield Park* in 1832; *Northanger Abbey, Sense and Sensibility*, and *Emma* in 1833), in editions of 750 copies for the first title and 1,250 copies each for the remaining five. The texts were reissued by the same firm, now Carey, Lea & Blanchard, in 1838, the first American collected edition, two volumes in one large volume of small print in double columns, and again as separate titles, each in one volume, in 1845, still in double columns, the publisher's name now being Carey and Hart.

Meanwhile, in December 1832, the London publisher Richard Bentley issued *Sense and Sensibility*, dated 1833, as no. 23 in his Standard Novels series, in one neat volume, cloth bound with paper spine labels, in small but clear type, with engraved frontispieces and engraved vignette title pages, which sold at 6s. apiece; the remaining novels appeared in the same series in 1833 (*Northanger Abbey* and *Persuasion* together). These were the first illustrated editions of Jane Austen published in England. Bentley's separate issues were reissued in October 1833 as a set of numbered volumes in a different cloth binding, to form the first English collected edition. The separate Standard Novels issues and the collected edition were reprinted at various dates and in different styles of binding until 1866; in 1870 a reset edition for separate sale was published by Bentley in a larger format, retaining the 1833 frontispieces, in dark green blind-stamped cloth, many times reprinted. This text setting was used also for the Steventon Edition of 1882, a collected edition printed on handmade paper in brown ink with border rules, still with the 1833 frontispieces; 375 sets only.

But from the 1840s, or in some cases even before, when the copyrights lapsed, other publishers were in competition with Bentley on both sides of the Atlantic. *Sense and Sensibility* and *Pride and Prejudice* were issued in London by H. G. Clarke in 1844, *Mansfield Park* by Simms and M'Intyre in Belfast in 1846, *Pride and Prejudice* in Boston, Massachusetts, by Wilkins, Carter & Co. in 1848, and *Sense and Sensibility* in London by George Routledge in 1849. Bunce & Brother of New York issued *Pride and Prejudice* in 1855 and *Sense and Sensibility* in 1856; the firm was taken over by Derby & Jackson of New York, who brought out all the novels in 1857, the same plates being used for a reissue by Ticknor and Fields of Boston, Massachusetts in 1863–64. In 1864 Bernhard Tauchnitz of Leipzig issued *Sense and Sensibility* for the Continental market, subsequently including all the novels in his paperback Collection of British Authors. In 1870 all six novels were brought out in London by Chapman and Hall, reprinted from the plates of the 1833 Bentley editions, and while all the novels continued to be available in cheap series from George Routledge in London in the 1870s and 1880s and in New York in 1880–81 from George Munro, the Bentley plates were used yet again in London in 1881 by Ward, Lock and Co. Collected editions appeared in 1892, in London from J. M. Dent, ten volumes, illustrated, the first to contain editorial matter (by R. Brimley Johnson), and in Boston from Roberts Brothers, twelve volumes, also illustrated, lacking editorial matter but including also *Lady Susan, The Watsons*, and the majority of the letters from the Brabourne edition of 1884. The 1890s also saw the appearance, chiefly from George Allen and Macmillan, of editions profusely illustrated from line drawings by Hugh Thomson, the Brock brothers, and Chris Hammond. More collected editions came out, the Dent edition being reissued in 1898 with new, colored illustrations by the Brocks, and in the same year a ten-volume set from another London publisher, Grant Richards, later reissued by John Grant of Edinburgh with two further volumes containing letters, *Lady Susan*, and *The Watsons*. From the turn of the century separate editions proliferate, especially in inexpensive series from firms such as Cassell, Nelson, Blackie, Collins, and others. The Dent texts were reissued in 1906 in the Everyman's Library series (still available), and from 1907 also in Dent's Series of English Idylls, with fresh illustrations in delicate color halftones by the Brock brothers, many times reprinted. There were more collected sets: the Hampshire Edition, London: R. Brimley Johnson, 1902, six volumes; the Old Manor House Edition, New York: Frank S. Holby, 1906, ten volumes (many times reissued under different names); a ten-volume set from Chatto & Windus, London, 1908–1909; the Adelphi Edition, London: Martin Secker, 1923, ten volumes—all superseded by the publication in 1923 by the Clarendon Press, Oxford, of R. W. Chapman's standard edition in five volumes, first in large format, later reprinted (and still in print) in smaller size, with the addition in 1954 of a sixth volume containing the minor works. Notable among later separate issues are those in Oxford University Press's World's Classics series, without editorial matter but with introductions by distinguished writers. Illustrated editions include those from the American Limited Editions Club (from *Pride and Prejudice*, 1940, onward), the English Folio Society, with wood engravings by Joan Hassall (from *Pride and Prejudice*, 1957, onward), and on another level the Macdonald Illustrated Classics series with color plates by Philip Gough, 1948–61. The various special editions (abridged for schools, foreign students, and so on) can only be mentioned, as well as the immediate post-World War II flood of reissues from many publishers and the numerous paperback series (of which the best are the Riverside Edition published by Houghton Mifflin of Boston (from *Pride and Prejudice*, 1956, onward) and the Penguin English Library (from *Persuasion*, 1965, onward). The latest edition, with fresh editorial matter of consequence, is that in the Oxford English Novels series, 1970–71.

EDUCATION

Juliet McMaster

"I think I may boast myself to be, with all possible vanity," Jane Austen wrote to a literary admirer, "the most unlearned and uninformed female who ever dared to be an authoress" (*Letters*, December 11, 1815). She exaggerated, of course. Her own formal education had been quite as extensive as that of most women of her day and class. She was taught first by her father, who took in other pupils besides his children, and then sent to boarding schools in Oxford, Southampton, and Reading until she was eleven. Subsequently, she seems to have taught herself, like the Bennet girls in *Pride and Prejudice*: "such of us as wished to learn, never wanted the means. We were always encouraged to read, and had all the masters that were necessary" (*PP*, p. 165). Reading, and learning the proper response to what was read, were a large part of the content of her self-education, as her novels testify. She was well-read in Shakespeare and in eighteenth-century literature, her favorite authors being Richardson and Johnson.

Formal education in her novels usually takes place offstage. The young Morlands in *Northanger Abbey* are taught at home by their mother, and only the boys go to school. But we hear of schools, some more fashionable than others, for girls, too. There are elegant establishments "where young ladies for enormous pay might be screwed out of health and into vanity," but Jane Austen seems to prefer Mrs. Goddard's "real, honest, old-fashioned Boarding-school" in *Emma*, "where a reasonable quantity of accomplishments were sold at a reasonable price, and where girls might . . . scramble themselves into a little education, without any danger of coming back prodigies" (*E*, pp. 21–22). The more pretentious training provided in the seminaries, or by governesses in richer homes like Mansfield Park, she suggests may be only a matter of rote learning of miscellaneous facts. The Bertram girls despise Fanny for lacking their ability "to repeat the chronological order of the kings of England . . . and of the Roman emperors as low as Severus; besides a great deal of the Heathen Mythology, and all the Metals, Semi-Metals, Planets, and distinguished philosophers" (*MP*, pp. 18–19).

"Accomplishments," which took the form of some degree of skill in music, the visual arts, and the modern languages, were usually considered part of a girl's education and had their social importance. The warmhearted Bingley in *Pride and Prejudice* is impressed that all young ladies seem able to "paint tables, cover skreens and net purses," but his more exacting sister Caroline expects of the accomplished woman that she should "have a thorough knowledge of music, singing, drawing, dancing, and the modern languages" (*PP*, p. 39). There is some prominence given to these pursuits in the novels: Elinor and Emma draw, Marianne and Jane Fairfax play the piano and Mary Crawford the harp, Elizabeth sings and plays, and Anne plays and is expert in Italian. But accomplishments, like other things, can be overdone, and Mary Bennet, who has "worked hard for... accomplishments" (*PP*, p. 25), bores her audience by her plodding display of them.

Jane Austen glances at education as a profession for women in her treatment of governesses. To be a governess is virtually the only career open to a girl of gentle birth and education, but it is regarded as a dreadful fate by Jane Fairfax in *Emma*, who speaks of the employment agencies for governesses as "Offices for the sale—not quite of human flesh—but of human intellect" (*E*, p. 300).

Education for boys in the novels is more elaborate than that for girls and usually proceeds from a private tutor to public school and university. Jane Austen sometimes shows a wistful regret that women are debarred from these privileges. "Men have had every advantage of us in telling their own story," says Anne Elliot. "Education has been theirs in so much higher a degree; the pen has been in their hands" (*P*, p. 234). But Jane Austen's view of the exclusively male enclaves of higher education is not always respectful. Edward Ferrars, brought up to be a gentleman of leisure, confides, "I was therefore entered at Oxford and have been properly idle ever since" (*SS*, p. 103).

For Jane Austen education involves much more than the mere gathering of information. Like John Locke, she considered that a system of education should address the whole person and be a moral as well as an intellectual training. Moral education, in fact, becomes a major issue in many of her novels. The Bertram girls, so informed on the Roman emperors, are "entirely deficient in the less common acquirements of self-knowledge, generosity, and humility," and their father must learn that he has made a "direful mistake in his plan of education" because "they had never been properly taught to govern their inclinations and tempers" (*MP*, pp. 19 and 463). Similarly, Darcy learns to regret that his moral education was only partial: "As a child I was taught what was *right*, but I was not taught to correct my temper" (*PP*, p. 369). He has to learn that from Elizabeth.

There are many mentors in the novels who help to provide the moral education for the main character that may have been lacking during upbringing. Tilney, Edmund Bertram, and Mr. Knightley all help to form the principles of the heroines, whom they come to love in the process. Darcy and Wentworth have as much to learn from the heroines as to teach them. But the exchange of knowledge about right conduct is often seen as a strong basis for love.

Largely considered, education is a major theme in all the novels. Catherine, Marianne, Elizabeth, Emma, and Wentworth all go through a process of learning that involves the acquisition of self-knowledge and the ability to judge and regulate their behavior. Minor characters, too, like Mr. Bennet and Sir Thomas Bertram, must learn. Jane Austen always valued intelligence, good sense, and developed taste. But in her novels the learning that matters most, the moral education, comes as much from the precepts and examples of the surrounding characters, and from experience, as from the schoolroom and the textbook.

Bibliography

CRAIK, W. A. *Jane Austen in Her Time* (London and New York, 1969).
DEVLIN, D. D. *Jane Austen and Education* (London and New York, 1975).
LASKI, MARGHANITA. *Jane Austen and Her World* (London and New York, 1969).
SIMPSON, RICHARD. Review of the *Memoir* in *North British Review*, 52 (April 1870) 129–52.
TRILLING, LIONEL. *Sincerity and Authenticity* (London and Cambridge, Mass., 1972).

JANE AUSTEN'S FAMILY

George Holbert Tucker

On her paternal side Jane Austen was descended from six generations of Kentish landowners who had gradually achieved eminence by way of the broadcloth trade. The Leighs, her mother's family, were more aristocratic. Not only was their social position higher than the Austens; their distinguished pedigree extended backward to Hamon de Legh, lord of the moiety of High Legh in Cheshire at the time of Henry II.

Jane Austen's earliest-known paternal ancestor was John Austen of Horsmonden, Kent (ca. 1560–1620), who married Joan Berry in 1584. They were the parents of eight sons and one daughter, one of the younger sons, Francis Austen (1600–87), being Jane Austen's third great-grandfather. Unlike his father, who had been content to remain a prosperous farmer, Francis Austen became a clothier, that is, a fabricator of woolen cloth, for which Kent had been famous since the time of Edward III. Prosperity enabled Francis Austen to purchase the still-existing Tudor manor houses of Grovehurst and Broadford near Horsmonden that were subsequently owned by generations of his family. When he died, these were inherited by his only son, John Austen of Grovehurst (1629–1705), who married Jane Atkins. They were the parents of John Austen of Broadford (d. 1704), Jane Austen's paternal great-grandfather, who married Elizabeth Weller of Tonbridge, Kent. One of their younger sons, William Austen (1701–37), a surgeon, was Jane Austen's paternal grandfather. His wife, born Rebecca Hampson (1696–1732), was descended from Henry Hampson, who lived at Brodwell in Oxfordshire during the reign of Henry VIII. She and William Austen were the parents of three daughters and one son, only two of whom are important in Jane Austen's story. The first was Philadelphia Austen (1730–92), and the second was George Austen (1731–1805), Jane Austen's father.

Philadelphia was sent out to India in 1752, presumably to seek a husband, a common practice for dowerless spinsters in the England of that time. She married Tysoe Saul Hancock, a surgeon in the employ of the East India Company and a man twenty years older than herself. They were supposedly the parents of one child, Elizabeth Hancock, born in Calcutta in 1761. Contemporary gossip suggests that Warren Hastings, later governor of Bengal and an intimate friend of the Hancocks', may have been the father of Philadelphia's child. After Hancock's death in Calcutta in 1775, his wife and daughter, who were already in England, removed to the Continent where Elizabeth (who meanwhile had altered her given name to Eliza) married her first husband, Jean Gabriel Capotte, comte de Feuillide, a captain of dragoons in the Queen's Guard, in 1781. They had only one child, Hastings de Feuillide (1786–1801), who was never healthy.

The comtesse was frequently at Steventon during the early period of Jane Austen's life, and as "a clever woman, and highly accomplished, after the French rather than the English mode," she is reputed to have helped Jane perfect her knowledge of French, introduced her to Italian, encouraged her musical abilities, and familiarized her with at least some of the fashionable French literature of the period. In gratitude, the fifteen-year-old Jane Austen dedicated "Love and Freindship," the best of her *juvenilia*, to her worldly cousin in June 1790.

The comtesse was also in England when her husband was guillotined in 1794 during the French Revolution. After enjoying the role of a flirtatious widow for three years, she married her first cousin, Henry Thomas Austen, Jane Austen's favorite brother, in 1797, after which the couple settled in London.

George Austen, Jane Austen's father, was born in Tonbridge in 1731. He became a scholar at Tonbridge School when he was ten and remained there until 1747, at which time he went to St. John's College, Oxford. He was awarded his bachelor of arts degree in 1751, and was made a master of arts in 1754. The same year he was ordained a deacon in Oxford, while in 1755 he was ordained a priest of the Established Church. In 1760 he was awarded his bachelor of divinity degree, and during the academic year of 1759–60 he served as junior proctor of Oxford University, his good looks gaining him the name of "the handsome Proctor." In 1761 he was presented with the living of Steventon in Hampshire by Thomas Knight I of Godmersham, Kent, his second cousin by marriage, but he did not take up his duties there until after his own marriage in 1764.

Twelve years after being instituted to Steventon he also became rector of the adjoining parish of Deane, the living having been purchased for him "for this time only" by his father's elder brother, Francis Austen, a wealthy solicitor of Sevenoaks, Kent. From then on he combined his clerical duties with those of farming and instructing private pupils. In 1801 he appointed his eldest son James as his deputy at Steventon and retired to Bath with his wife and two daughters, Cassandra and Jane Austen. He died there in January 1805, and his memory was long cherished because of his gentleness, his strong attachment to his family, his scholarship, and his faithful performance of clerical duties. His real distinction, however, was his early and appreciative perception of Jane Austen's literary gifts.

Jane Austen's mother, born Cassandra Leigh, was a younger daughter of the Reverend Thomas Leigh (1696–1764), rector of Harpsden, Oxfordshire, and Jane Walker (1704–68), a daughter of Dr. John Walker's, an Oxford physician. His wife, Jane Perrot (d. 1709), was a member of an ancient Pembrokeshire family. Jane Austen's mother was also a niece of Dr. Theophilus Leigh (1693–1785), master of Balliol College, Oxford for more than half a century, and also vice-chancellor of Oxford University. He and Mrs. Austen's father were in turn descended from Sir Thomas Leigh (1498–1571), lord mayor of London at the time of the accession of Queen Elizabeth I, who knighted him during his mayoralty.

Besides his eldest son, Rowland Leigh of Longborough and Adlestrop, Gloucestershire, from whom Jane Austen was descended, Sir Thomas Leigh was also the father of two other sons and two daughters. The descendants of these included William Pitt the Elder, the first earl of Chatham; his son, William Pitt the Younger, who was prime minister of Great Britain for much of Jane Austen's lifetime; William Lamb, second viscount Melbourne, Queen Victoria's first prime minister, and John Churchill, the first duke of Marlborough, from whom Sir Winston Churchill (1874–1965) was descended.

Born in 1739, Jane Austen's mother was a younger sister of James Leigh (Leigh Perrot after 1751; 1735–1817), and Jane Leigh (1736–83), who married Dr. Edward Cooper, a well-to-do Anglican clergyman who was also Holcombe prebendary of Wells Cathedral. James Leigh Perrot married Jane Cholmeley, a formidable woman, who was tried and acquitted of stealing a card of white lace in Bath in 1799. This childless couple were always referred to as "my Uncle" and "my Aunt" in Jane Austen's letters. The Coopers were the parents of a son and a daughter, Jane Austen's only first cousins on her maternal side. They were the Reverend Edward Cooper (1770–1833), a well-known Evangelical preacher whose sermons Jane Austen did not like; and Jane Cooper (b. 1771), later Lady Williams, a school companion of Jane Austen's, who was killed in a carriage accident on the Isle of Wight in 1798.

Jane Austen was the seventh of the eight Hampshire-born Austens, as she once playfully referred to her sister and herself and her six brothers. The first was James Austen (1765–1819), who became a clergyman like his father and who succeeded him at Steventon. It was James Austen who is credited by family tradition with having had a large share in directing the early reading and forming the taste of his talented younger sister. Characterized by his mother as possessing "Classical Knowledge, Literary Taste and the power of Elegant Composition," James's surviving writings, particularly his introspective but biographically revealing poems, show him to have been a deeply religious man, a lover of natural scenery, and a person of wide reading. It was also he who wrote the prologues and epilogues for the amateur theatricals that were an important part of the social life at Steventon rectory from 1782 to 1790, a period embracing Jane Austen's seventh to her fifteenth years. He also founded and wrote at Oxford the greater number of a weekly periodical called *The Loiterer*, one of the many imitations of *The Spectator* and *The Rambler*. These essays were later issued in two volumes after the paper ceased publication in 1790.

James Austen married twice. His first wife was Anne Mathew, a daughter of Gen. Edward Mathew, a former governor of Grenada and commander-in-chief in the British West Indies, and Lady Jane Mathew, a daughter of Peregrine Bertie, second duke of Ancaster. Their only child, Jane Anna Elizabeth Austen (1793–1872), later Mrs. Benjamin Lefroy, was the "Anna" of Jane Austen's letters. She was also one of the principal contributors to the *Memoir of Jane Austen*, written by her half brother, the Reverend James Edward Austen-Leigh, first published in 1870. She also wrote children's books, including *The Winter's Tale: To which is Added Little Bertram's Dream* (1841) and *Springtide* (1842). Anna owned the manuscript of *Sanditon*, the novel on which Jane Austen was working at the time of her death, to which she added a continuation of her own. She was the mother of one son and six daughters and has many living descendants.

James Austen's second wife was Mary Lloyd, whom Jane Austen had liked when she was a girl but who grew up to be a fidgety, cheeseparing woman, as the many unfavorable references to her in Jane's letters amply reveal. By her he had a son and a daughter. The son, James Edward Austen (Austen-Leigh after 1837; 1798–1874), was a great favorite of his aunt Jane's, and it was he who wrote the *Memoir of Jane Austen* (1870), the book on which all subsequent biographies of his aunt have been based. He was the father of eight sons and two daughters and has many living descendants. The daughter, Caroline Mary Craven Austen (1805–80), a particular favorite of Jane Austen's, was also an important contributor to her brother's memoir of their aunt. Her reminiscences, incorporated in *My Aunt Jane Austen*, the most detailed firsthand account of the Chawton period—with the exception of Jane's surviving letters—that has come down to us from a person who knew and loved her, is one of the seminal biographical works concerning her famous aunt.

George Austen (b. 1766), the second child of the Reverend George and Cassandra Austen, was the unfortunate member of the family. Although he lived to the age of seventy-two, dying one year after Queen Victoria ascended the throne, the family was so reticent that very little is known about him. No mention is made of him in Jane Austen's surviving letters or in the *Memoir*, but a grandson of the author of the latter has stated that George "grew up weak in intellect, and did not die till 1838." That George (who was always cared for away from home by persons paid for that purpose) may have been deaf among other things is indicated by Jane Austen's mentioning in a letter that she was able to communicate with persons so afflicted by means of sign language.

Edward Austen (Knight after 1812; 1767–1852) was the third Hampshire-born Austen. He was the most fortunate of all the family as far as worldly wealth was concerned. Having early attracted the attention of his father's childless third cousin, Thomas Knight II of Godmersham, Kent, he was frequently invited to visit him and his wife there during his childhood. This relationship finally resulted in his being adopted by the Knights. When his adoptive father died in 1794, he left his estates in Kent and Hampshire to his widow for life, after which they were to be inherited by Edward, who, in the meantime, had been sent on the Grand Tour by his adoptive parents instead of continuing his education at Oxford. By 1797, Mrs. Knight realized she was unequal to the task of managing the estates left her by her husband, so she turned over Godmersham and Chawton Manor in Hampshire to Edward and retired to Canterbury on an annual income of £2,000. Edward then became the squire of Godmersham, one of the most beautiful estates in East Kent, where Jane Austen visited him frequently from then on.

Edward, who finally changed his surname to Knight after the death of his adoptive mother in 1812, was characterized by his own mother as a practical man of business whose clear head, active mind, and sound judgment were tempered by a good disposition. He also made a good marriage with Elizabeth Bridges, a daughter of Sir Brook Bridges of Goodnestone Park, Kent, and they were the parents of eleven children, many of whom have living descendants today.

The most important of these, as far as Jane Austen is concerned, was the eldest, Fanny Catherine Austen (Knight after 1812; 1793–1882), whom Jane Austen regarded as "almost another sister." But Fanny's later snobbishly critical remarks concerning her famous aunt (contained in a private letter to a sister) clearly reveal that Jane Austen's Georgian forthrightness had become offensive to her Victorian proprieties, and the unjust indictment she wrote concerning the aunt who had valued her above all of her other nieces remains as an inexcusable case of ingratitude.

In 1820 Fanny became the second wife of Sir Edward Knatchbull of Provender, Kent, and it was to her that Cassandra Austen, Jane's elder sister, left the original manuscript of *Lady Susan*, as well as the greater part of those of Jane's letters she saved when she destroyed most of her sister's intimate correspondence a few years before her own death. To Fanny's credit, she saved this precious legacy, and the letters were edited and published after her own death by her son, the first Lord Brabourne.

Henry Thomas Austen (1771–1850), Jane Austen's favorite brother, was allegedly the brightest of all of the Hampshire-born Austens, but his mercurial temperament also resulted in his being the least stable member of an otherwise satisfactory family. Tall and physically attractive, he was remembered in the family for his conversational powers and his eager and sanguine disposition, which, in the words of his niece, Anna Lefroy, adapted itself "to all circumstances, even the most adverse," serving "to create a perpetual sunshine." Other members of the family, however—particularly those who lost heavily when the bank in which he was a partner became insolvent in 1816—had reason to feel resentful at his "almost exasperating buoyancy and sanguineness of temperament and high animal spirits which no misfortunes could depress and no failures damp."

Henry's parents had hoped that he, like his elder brother James, would become a clergyman, but these plans were thwarted by his worldly cousin Eliza, comtesse de Feuillide (whom he married in 1797), who, like Mary Crawford in *Mansfield Park*, had little regard for the cloth as a gentlemanly profession. Instead, after having completed his education at St. John's College, Oxford, Henry became captain, paymaster, and adjutant of the Oxford militia. Later, he set up as a banker and army agent in London. By far the most sophisticated member of his family as far as the arts were concerned, Henry's residence in London was greatly beneficial to Jane Austen, who visited him frequently there, during which times he introduced her to the current artistic, musical, and theatrical attractions of the London of the period. Henry's residence in the capital also benefited Jane in a literary way, for it was he who handled the business transactions involving her novels from the time of the publication of *Sense and Sensibility* in 1811 until *Emma* came out in 1815. Henry's serious illness in the latter year, at which time he was nursed by Jane Austen and was treated by one of the prince regent's physicians, who apprised the prince of her presence in London, also resulted in her being invited to Carlton House, the prince's London residence, where she was shown over the library and other state rooms by the Reverend James Stanier Clarke, the prince's librarian. The visit resulted in her dedicating *Emma* to the prince, who, according to Clarke, was a great admirer of Jane Austen's novels.

Meanwhile, Henry Austen had been appointed receiver general for taxes for Oxfordshire, while the banks in London and Alton in which he was a partner prospered because of the inflationary economy created by the war with France. After Waterloo, however, a severe economic depression brought ruin to many British speculators, and in March 1816, Henry Austen's banks became two of the hundreds of victims of the postwar depression that followed Napoleon's final downfall.

Optimistic as ever, Henry characteristically exchanged the role of a bankrupt banker for that of an Anglican clergyman and was ordained early in 1817. He subsequently served as curate at Chawton, rector of Steventon, domestic chaplain to the British minister in Berlin, curate of Farnham, Surrey, and perpetual curate of Bentley, a village on the road from Farnham to Alton. He also published a series of *Lectures Upon Some Important Passages in the Book of Genesis* (1820) and two sermons (1826 and 1829), copies of which are in the British Library. Henry's first wife, the former Eliza, comtesse de Feuillide, having died in 1813, he remarried in 1820, his second wife being Eleanor Jackson, who survived him. There were no children by either marriage.

Henry, who was remembered in the family as "an earnest preacher of the evangelical school," also supervised the publication of *Northanger Abbey* and *Persuasion* after Jane Austen's death in 1817. For these he wrote a biographical notice of his sister, a seminal work, as it contains many intimate details concerning Jane Austen both as a woman and as a writer. He resigned his Farnham curacy in 1826 and his curacy at Bentley in 1839, after which he is said to have lived for a time in France. He died in 1850 in Tonbridge Wells, Kent, and was buried in Woodbury Park Cemetery there, where his tombstone may still be seen.

Cassandra Elizabeth Austen (1773–1845), the fifth of the Hampshire-born Austens and the elder of the two daughters of the Reverend George Austen, was unquestionably the most important person in Jane Austen's life. As their niece Anna Lefroy expressed it: "They were everything to each other. They seemed to lead a life to themselves within the general family shared only by each other. I will not say their true, but their *full* feelings were known only to themselves. They alone fully understood what each had suffered and felt and thought."

Cassandra, who was almost three years older than Jane, was, according to the *Memoir*: "always prudent and well judging, but with less outward demonstration of feeling and less sunniness of temper than Jane possessed" (p. 150). It was also remarked that "Cassandra had the *merit* of having her temper always under command but that Jane had the *happiness* of a temper that never required to be commanded" (p. 225).

Altogether, Cassandra and Jane had only about five years of formal schooling, first at a private school in Oxford that later moved to Southampton and still later at the Abbey School at Reading, where they were pupils until 1787, when Cassandra was fourteen and Jane eleven. According to family tradition, however, their regular schooling was supplemented at home by their scholarly father, their clever mother, and their two elder brothers, James and Henry Austen, who were both Oxford men. Their return to Steventon from Reading in 1787 also coincided with Jane Austen's first literary efforts. At this time, Cassandra was her younger sister's first critical audience of one, and her encouragement no doubt prompted Jane to write down her burlesques of the then-popular sentimental novels in the three surviving notebooks that Cassandra fortunately preserved, although she later destroyed many of her sister's other papers.

Cassandra, who was the more regularly pretty of the two sisters, became engaged in 1795 to the Reverend Thomas Fowle, a former pupil of her father's, but after his death of yellow fever in St. Domingo in 1797, she evidently never entertained the idea of marriage again. This was posterity's gain. Having always inspired a feeling of deference in Jane as a kind elder sister, Cassandra became even more protective after the tragic termination of her engagement, and this reassurance provided Jane with the necessary security in which her genius came to fruition. As Cassandra also spent a great deal of time with her brother Edward after his marriage in 1791, there was a frequent exchange of letters between Jane and herself. Unfortunately, none of Cassandra's letters to her sister has survived. But those of Jane's that are still available constitute one of the few contemporary sources concerning her movements from 1796, the year the letters begin, until 1817, the year of her death. The letters are revealing as far as the intimate relationship between the two sisters is concerned, for although Jane loved her father and respected her mother as a parent, she was much closer to Cassandra; as she grew older she was increasingly dependent on her, becoming restless when they were separated for any length of time.

The years between 1809 and 1817, when the two sisters lived with their mother at Chawton, were the most productive of Jane Austen's life. Between those dates *Sense and Sensibility, Pride and Prejudice, Mansfield Park,* and *Emma* were published. In 1816, however, Jane Austen became ill of what is now presumed to have been Addison's disease, and although Cassandra accompanied her to Cheltenham for a hoped-for cure, it was ineffective. Early in 1817, Jane Austen made her will, leaving most of her small property to her sister, and at the end of May of the same year the two sisters went to Winchester, where Jane hoped to receive better medical treatment. But this was ineffective, and Jane Austen died on July 18, 1817, after which Cassandra wrote to her niece Fanny Knight: "I *have* lost a treasure, such a Sister, such a friend as never can have been surpassed,—she was the sun of my life, the gilder of every pleasure, the soother of every sorrow, I had not a thought concealed from her, & it is as if I had lost a part of myself" (*Letters*, Appendix 1, pp. 513–14).

After Jane Austen's burial in Winchester Cathedral, Cassandra returned to Chawton, where she nursed her aged mother until the latter's death in 1827. She continued to live on at Chawton until her own death, which occurred in 1845 when she was away on a visit to her brother Francis's home near Portsmouth. Her body was brought back to Chawton for burial in the village churchyard.

Cassandra outlived Jane Austen by twenty-eight years, but the intimacy that had existed between herself and her younger sister never faded. Once when a great-niece was staying at Chawton long after Jane's death, she was "greatly struck and impressed" by the way Cassandra spoke of her sister: "there was such an accent of *living* love in her voice."

Francis William Austen (b. 1774), the sixth of the Hampshire-born

Austens and the elder of Jane Austen's sailor brothers, also outlived all of his sisters and brothers, dying greatly honored at the age of ninety-one as Sir Francis Austen, Queen Victoria's admiral of the fleet. Francis was the first member of his family to become a member of the Royal Navy and entered the Royal Naval Academy at Portsmouth in 1786, a few days before his twelfth birthday. Although Henry was Jane Austen's favorite brother because of their shared gaiety of temperament, Francis also stood high in his sister's estimation for his quiet humor, his pride in her literary accomplishments, his neatness (a characteristic they both shared), and his brotherly affection.

After leaving the Royal Naval Academy, Francis served aboard the king's ships as a midshipman and lieutenant in the East Indies. After his return to England in 1793, he was intimately connected with the naval operations of the long war with France until Napoleon's exile to St. Helena in 1815. A deeply religious man and singular for being "*the* officer who knelt in church," he was also a strict disciplinarian "without ever uttering an oath or permitting one in his presence." But Francis was no authoritarian prude, for beneath his official exterior he was a warmhearted man, a considerate son and brother, and a devoted husband and father who reveled in the comforts of home and family when he was ashore. He was also famous for his manual skills and was never happier than when he was creating sturdy toys for his children or fashioning nets to protect his cherries and currants from predatory birds at Portsdown Lodge, his home ashore near Portsmouth. This manual dexterity, he believed, was an inspiration to Jane Austen when she was writing *Persuasion*, for he later stated: "I do not know whether in the character of Capt. Wentworth the authoress meant in any degree to delineate that of her Brother; perhaps she might—but I rather think parts of Capt. Harville's were drawn from myself—At least some of his domestic habits, tastes and occupations bear a strong resemblance to mine."

Unfortunately for Francis, his ship, with others, was dispatched by Lord Nelson from Cadiz to Gibraltar for water and supplies, which made him miss the Battle of Trafalgar in 1805, but his previous and subsequent naval duties brought him into intimate contact with the enemy. As he and Jane Austen are known to have exchanged letters frequently when he was at sea, she was therefore well acquainted with firsthand information concerning the naval aspects of the war between Great Britain and France. That she used only those portions of this information in her writings germane to her purpose is indicative of her artistic integrity.

Francis Austen's first wife was Mary Gibson of Ramsgate, whom he married in 1806. They were the parents of six sons and five daughters, many of whom have descendants now living. After his first wife's death in 1823, he married Martha Lloyd, an intimate friend of Jane Austen's. There were no children by his second marriage.

Francis became a rear-admiral in 1830, was made a knight commander of the Bath carrying the title Sir Francis Austen in 1837, vice-admiral in 1838, and full admiral in 1848. In 1862 he became rear-admiral and vice-admiral of the United Kingdom. Three years later he was promoted to admiral of the fleet. He died in 1865 and is buried at Wymering, near Portsmouth.

Jane Austen (1775–1817), the seventh of the Hampshire-born Austens, was followed by Charles John Austen (1779–1852), the last of the children of the Reverend George and Cassandra Austen and the younger of the two Austen naval brothers. Playfully referred to by Jane and Cassandra as "our own particular little brother," a phrase they adapted from a description of a character in Fanny Burney's *Camilla*, Charles was particularly beloved by his family for his manly charm and affability. In July 1791, when he was twelve, he followed his brother Francis to the Royal Naval Academy at Portsmouth, where he remained until 1794. He then became a midshipman under Capt. Thomas Williams (later Sir Thomas Williams), who had married Charles's first cousin, Jane Cooper. For the next ten years Charles was actively engaged in European waters in the war with France. When his ships were in port, however, he was frequently at Steventon, where he took particular delight in accompanying his sister Jane to balls and assemblies. In a letter of November 20, 1800, he is described as having "danced the whole Evening, & today is no more tired than a gentleman ought to be."

Unlike his brother Francis, who was reserved, Charles was impetuous by nature. During his activities in the Mediterranean between 1797 and 1802, he assisted in making prizes of several privateers. From 1804 until 1811, Charles served on the North American Station, during which time he married Frances Fitzwilliam Palmer, a daughter of a former attorney general of Bermuda. When she died in England in 1812, after she had borne him four daughters, he married her sister Harriet, by whom he had three sons and a daughter. Some of these children married and have descendants living today.

In Charles's letters from at sea, Jane Austen had still another source of information concerning what was happening in the European tumult that had followed the French Revolution, but unfortunately none of the letters from either of her naval brothers has been preserved. Charles's naval career, however, was equally as exciting as that of his older brother Francis. After Napoleon's escape from Elba in 1815, Charles served in the Mediterranean until his vessel was driven ashore by a hurricane on the coast of Asia Minor. Fortunately, the disaster was later proved to have been caused by the ignorance of Greek pilots, for Charles was fully acquitted of all blame by a court-martial held in 1816. He did not go to sea again until 1826, when he was dispatched to the West Indies, where he was principally engaged in the suppression of the slave trade. While there, he was presented with a naval sword by Simon Bolivar.

In 1838, after having been a captain for nearly thirty years, Charles was dispatched to the Mediterranean, where he participated in the joint French and English campaign against Mehemet Ali, viceroy of Egypt. For his share in this campaign Charles was made a companion of the Bath in 1840 and in 1846 was promoted to rear-admiral. In 1850, he was made commander-in-chief of the East India and China Station with headquarters at Trincomalee. Two years later he contracted cholera during a naval expedition against Burma; and although he partially recovered, he resumed his command too quickly, suffered a relapse, and died shortly afterward. At that time one of his officers wrote: "Our good Admiral won the hearts of all by his gentleness and kindness while he was struggling with disease, and endeavoring to do his duty as Commander-in-chief of the British naval forces in these waters. His death was a great grief to the whole fleet. I know I cried bitterly when I found he was dead."

Bibliography

All of the facts in this account of Jane Austen's family can be found, with substantiating notes, in: George Holbert Tucker, *A Goodly Heritage: A History of Jane Austen's Family* (Manchester, England, 1983). Also useful is Richard Arthur Austen-Leigh's *Austen Papers, 1704–1856* (London, 1942).

JANE AUSTEN AND CONTEMPORARY FEMINISM

Margaret Kirkham

Jane Austen grew up and became a novelist in the 1790s, when feminist/antifeminist controversy was strong and when the novel itself was of particular importance to the debate. Since the publication of *Pamela* in 1740–41, questions of feminist concern, such as the moral status and education of women and the right basis of marriage and authority within the family, had formed an important part of the ethical subject matter of fiction, but by the end of the century women themselves had found a public voice as novelists. After the 1770s and 1780s, when Mary Wollstonecraft's *Mary* (1788) and Fanny Burney's *Evelina* (1778) appeared, the novel was at least as important as the treatise, conduct book, or educational work in defining women's attitudes toward the rights and duties of their own sex.

While it would be misleading to speak of a well-defined school of eighteenth-century feminist thought in England, it is possible to see some development of ideas and practical concern, going back to Mary Astell's feminist treatises written between 1694 and 1705, continuing in the lives, letters, and other writings of the learned ladies associated with the bluestocking salons, and emerging in a more controversial way in fictional and theoretical works by women at the end of the century.

Eighteenth-century feminism begins with questions about the moral and spiritual status of woman with which, from the beginning, improvement in female education was associated as the main practical concern. By the end of the century, philanthropy, often of an educational kind, had also become important. Ray Strachey speaks of Mrs. Trimmer and Hannah More as founders of the women's movement, though it would have shocked them to know it. Hannah More, despite her conservative sympathies, adopted a "revolutionary role" by "marking out a new sphere for the young women of the middle classes," from which "their revolt against their own narrow and futile lives followed" (Strachey, p. 13). Women novelists, even where, unlike Jane Austen, they showed no understanding of feminist

---

* Acknowledgment should be made to Harvester Press for permission to make use of material first used in *Jane Austen, Feminism and Fiction*, 1983.

moral argument, fulfilled a similar role simply by becoming published authors.

But Austen does show a clear and consistent commitment to the rational principles on which women of the Enlightenment based their case. The essential belief was that women, not having been denied powers of reason by providence (no matter what was denied them by poets, rhapsodists, Rousseau, and Dr. Fordyce), must learn morals in the same way as men and must therefore be taught to think. As Janet Todd (*A Wollstonecraft Anthology*, p. 10), points out, Mary Wollstonecraft, by the time she wrote *A Vindication of the Rights of Woman*, saw the "revolutionary implication" of teaching women to think and made it apparent. Mary Astell perhaps did not, but the central feminist position on morals and education could be held by "a true daughter of the Church of England," like Astell, or by the less orthodox. Wollstonecraft represents the heroine of *Mary* as having read "Butler's Analogy and some other authors," thus having become "a Christian from conviction." In *Vindication* she could still make use of an ethical system acquired from Bishop Butler, and Dr. Price at Newington, for in both, revealed religion was seen as confirming what a rational being might learn solely from secular experience and reflection upon it, God having designed the world and human nature with this in mind. Wollstonecraft's anger is reserved for the failure of moralists to apply such a system, regardless of gender: "For though moralists have agreed that *man* is prepared by various circumstances for a future state, they constantly concur in advising *woman* only to provide for the present" (*Vindication*, p. 118).

The feminist claim that women had the same moral nature and capacity as men and should be educated accordingly always carried a long-term political implication, but the demand for constitutional rights, even at the time of the French Revolution, when it became explicit in Condorcet, Olympe de Gouges, and Wollstonecraft, was not in the forefront of English feminist writings. By 1794 Condorcet was dead in a prison cell and de Gouges at the guillotine. Englishwomen might well feel that improvement in the status and education of their sex was not one of the benefits to be had of the Revolution. Wollstonecraft makes it clear in the Dedicatory Letter to Talleyrand, which forms a preface to *Vindication*, that she is pessimistic about women in France, for she sees the influence of Rousseau as hostile to their improvement. In a recent study, *Histoire du féminisme français*, Albistur and Armogathe attribute the early suppression of feminism in revolutionary France to the influence of Rousseau. Marat, Robespierre, and other *"ardents patriotes"* had been convinced of the natural inferiority of women by him (p. 236).

Enlightenment feminism is sometimes spoken of as though it had no English roots and as though those who supported the Revolution were, in general, feminists. Such beliefs do not bear scrutiny, for feminism cut across other political, national, and religious interests, and it is worth remembering, when considering Mary Wollstonecraft's ideas in relation to the Austen novels, that *Vindication* draws on an English feminist tradition in which women of orthodox religion, not associated with revolutionary politics, have their place, as Wollstonecraft acknowledges in her respectful treatment of Hester Chapone (p. 206).

Arnold Kettle, in his 1951 essay on *Emma*, saw Jane Austen's "highly critical concern over the fate of women in her society" as a "positive vibration," and it has since become common to notice a degree of feminist concern in Austen but not to associate it with the central "moral interest" that Leavis, in 1948, saw as "the principle of organization and the principle of development" in all her work, nor to connect Austen's criticism of romantic writers with Wollstonecraft's attack on Rousseau and his followers. The republication of Wollstonecraft's writings, with those of others (see, e.g., the Garland facsimile collection edited by Gina Luria, *The Feminist Controversy in England, 1788–1810*), has made it easier to place Austen, as moralist, in the context of rational feminism. Some elements in the novels, attributed to Evangelical influence, now need reassessment in the light of feminist strictness about morals; and Austen's antiromanticism, sometimes seen as a mark of her isolation from contemporary literary and intellectual engagement, also needs reconsideration. Burke has often been brought in to elucidate Austen's "conservatism," but it is now clear that Wollstonecraft and the ethical attitudes of Enlightenment feminists must be brought in, as well.

In France, Germaine de Staël became the major woman novelist and literary historian of the postrevolutionary era. She had supported the Revolution, but she was not a feminist. G. E. Gwyn says she "abandoned the cause of women in general" in favor of the "woman of genius," whose exceptional gifts of sensibility and imagination exempted her from the restrictions generally placed on women. In England, Jane Austen declined to concern herself with the *femme de génie*, concentrating, like Wollstonecraft, on ordinary women of the middle class, whose lives are unexceptional, though her heroines have more than their share of intelligence. Austen follows *Vindication* in the belief that "women . . . may have different duties to fulfil; but they are *human* duties," to be regulated in accordance with rational principle. Wollstonecraft, having read a "eulogium on Rousseau" by Mme. de Staël, expressed distaste and classed her among the "Writers Who Have Rendered Women Objects of Pity, Bordering on Contempt" (chap. 5).

Jane Austen made an obscure joke about *Corinne* and refused to meet its author, Mme. de Staël. The "myth of Corinne" took a powerful hold on the imagination of some later English women (Moers), but Austen shows no interest in "performing heroinism" except as the subject of satire. De Staël thought one of the Austen novels, probably *Pride and Prejudice*, "*vulgaire*" (Southam, p. 116), and it is clear that from "Love and Freindship" to *Sanditon*, Austen mocks the literature of sensibility from which the "performing heroine" is born. In *Persuasion*, Sophia Croft is drawn in contrast to the "ideal wife" of *Émile*, the "Sophie" who represents Rousseau's restricted view of female nature, described by Wollstonecraft as "a fanciful kind of *half* being—one of Rousseau's wild chimeras" (*Vindication*, p. 124).

Jane Austen was ready to publish her first novel in the year that Mary Wollstonecraft died. Had Cadell accepted *First Impressions*, it would have come out in 1798, when Godwin's *Memoirs* provoked a storm of hostile criticism against Wollstonecraft and her ideas. Between 1798 and 1803 her reputation was destroyed and her ideas made unspeakable (see Todd and Tomalin). The Reverend Richard Polwhele, in *The Unsex'd Females*, divided literary women into feminist goats and modest sheep, between whom there could be no connection. He thought it a sign of the corruption of the age that women's work should be considered on its merits, like men's, and saw "the sparkle of confident intelligence" as, in itself, a mark of immodesty in a female author. If Jane Austen's three novels of the 1790s had been published when they were first written, her confident mockery of Rousseauist assumptions might not have escaped hostile notice. As it was, *First Impressions* was rejected and *Susan* rather mysteriously withdrawn by a publisher who had bought and advertised it in 1803. *Sense and Sensibility* came out belatedly at the author's own expense in 1811, when the controversy had died down, silence on her work having replaced abuse of Wollstonecraft's personal character.

Among early reviewers, Scott shows an uneasy awareness of Austen's feminist morals, while Whately reveals a more sympathetic understanding (see Southam, items 8 and 16, and Kirkham, pp. 162–63), but neither discusses it overtly, perhaps because it could not be discussed without resurrecting discreditable scandal and misunderstanding. By the mid-nineteenth century, no one thought of connecting Austen and Wollstonecraft as feminist moralists, and in the mid-twentieth, "the enduring problem of Jane Austen criticism" was defined as "scale versus stature; the slightness of the matter and the authority of the manner" (Watt, p. 12). As more has become known about Wollstonecraft as "female philosopher" and about the rational feminism of her time, it has become easier to place the Austen novels in a context of feminist ideas, where the "enduring problem" can be seen in a new light.

In 1968 Gilbert Ryle noted that the title of *Sense and Sensibility* was to be taken seriously, as indicating a philosophical interest in "Thought and Feeling, Judgement and Emotion," and that the Austen novels generally show "a deep interest in some perfectly general, even theoretical questions about human nature." Considered in the context of Enlightenment feminism, this "perfectly general" interest may be seen to have a particular application. Trilling, in 1957, spoke of Emma Woodhouse as having "a moral life, as a man has a moral life . . . quite as a matter of course, as a given quality of her nature." It is because the Austen heroines, not only Emma, are shown as representatives of "human" rather than "feminine" nature, learning morals as rational beings were intended to learn them, that we may speak of her as a feminist moralist, connected with Wollstonecraft in opposing the antifeminist view most powerfully expressed in *Émile*.

Bibliography

ALBISTUR, MAÏTÉ AND DANIEL ARMOGATHE. *Histoire du feminisme français du moyen âge à nos jours* (Paris, 1977).
ASTELL, MARY. *A Serious Proposal to the Ladies* (London, 1694).
———. *The Christian Religion, as Profess'd by a Daughter of the Church of England* (London, 1705).
———. *Reflections Upon Marriage* (London, 1706).
AUERBACH, NINA. "Jane Austen and Romantic Imprisonments," in David Monaghan, ed., *Jane Austen in a Social Context* (London, 1981).
BROWN, LLOYD W. "Jane Austen and the Feminist Tradition," *Nineteenth-century Fiction*, 28 (1973–74), 321–38.
BUTLER, JOSEPH. *Analogy of Religion* (London, 1736).
CONDORCET, ANTOINE CARITAT, MARQUI DE. *Lettres d'un bourgeois de New-Haven* (Paris, 1787).
———. "Sur l'admission des femmes au droit de cité," *Journal de la Société 1789*, 5 (1790).
FORDYCE, JAMES. *Sermons to Young Women*, 6th ed. (London, 1766).
GODWIN, WILLIAM. *Memoirs of the Author of A Vindication of the Rights of Woman*, 2nd ed. (London, 1798).
GOUGES, OLYMPE DE. *Déclaration des droits de la femme et de la citoyenne* (Paris, 1791).
GWYN, G. E. *Madame de Staël et la révolution française* (no loc., 1969).
JIMACK, P. D. "The Paradox of Sophie and Julie: Contemporary Responses to Rousseau's Ideal Wife and Ideal Mother," in Eva Jacobs et al., eds., *Women and Society in Eighteenth-century France* (London, 1979).
KETTLE, ARNOLD. "Jane Austen: *Emma*," in his *An Introduction to the English Novel*, 2 vols. (London, 1957).
KINAIRD, JOAN. "Mary Astell, Inspired by Ideas," in Dale Spender, ed., *Feminist Theorists* (London, 1983).
KIRKHAM, MARGARET. *Jane Austen, Feminism and Fiction* (London, 1982).
LEAVIS, F. R. *The Great Tradition* (London, 1948).

LURIA, GINA, ed. *The Feminist Controversy in England 1788–1810* (New York, 1974).
MOERS, ELLEN. *Literary Women* (London, 1978).
OKIN, SUSAN MOLLER. *Women in Western Political Thought* (London, 1980).
POLWHELE, RICHARD. *The Unsex'd Females* (London, 1798).
PRICE, RICHARD. *A Review of the Principal Questions in Morals* (London, 1758).
ROUSSEAU, JEAN-JACQUES. *Émile* (Paris, 1762).
RYLE, GILBERT. "Jane Austen and the Moralists," in B. C. Southam, ed., *Critical Essays on Jane Austen* (London and New York, 1968).
SOUTHAM, B. C., ed. *Jane Austen: The Critical Heritage* (London and New York, 1968).
STAËL, GERMAINE DE. *Corinne* (Paris, 1807).
STRACHEY, RAY (Pseud. of Mrs. Rachel Conn Strachey). *"The Cause": A Short History of the Women's Movement in Great Britain* (London, 1928).
TOMALIN, CLAIRE. *The Life and Death of Mary Wollstonecraft* (New York, 1974).
TODD, JANET, ed. *A Wollstonecraft Anthology* (Bloomington, Ind., 1977).
TRILLING, LIONEL. "*Emma* and the Legend of Jane Austen," in David Lodge, ed., *Jane Austen: "Emma," a Casebook* (London, 1968).
WATT, IAN. Introduction to his *Jane Austen: A Collection of Critical Essays* (Englewood Cliffs, N.J., 1963).
WOLLSTONECRAFT, MARY. *Mary, a Fiction* (London, 1788).
———. *A Vindication of the Rights of Woman* (1792), ed. by Miriam B. Kramnick (Harmondsworth, 1975).
———. *Maria, or The Wrongs of Woman* (London, 1798).

FOOD AND DRINK

Peggy Hickman

On November 17, 1798 Jane Austen wrote to her sister Cassandra, "My mother desires me to tell you that I am a very good housekeeper, which I have no reluctance in doing, because I really think it my peculiar excellence, and for this reason—I always take care to provide such things as please my own appetite, which I consider as the chief merit in housekeeping." That year, Mrs. Austen, who was often unwell, handed over such duties to her elder daughter, in whose absence Jane proved a willing substitute. Carrying the keys of the wine cellar and closet made her feel grand, she said; she ordered the meals, and "our dinner was very good and the chicken boiled perfectly tender" (October 27, 1798).

Both girls had been taught by their capable mother to cook and supervise maids in the stillroom and dairy. The first twenty-five years of Jane's life were spent at Steventon. Almost everything consumed there by George Austen's large family was homegrown. With the help of a bailiff he farmed his glebe lands and produced wheat for bread making; pigs for succulent pork, hams, and brawn; sheep for mutton (said to be "the finest that was ever ate," December 1, 1798); and five Alderney cows for milk, butter, and cheese. In Mrs. Austen's poultry yard all manner of fowls were reared. The orchard and vegetable garden were productive. Beehives produced honey (from which mead was made), and ample game and fish were available from nearby Hampshire woods and streams. So the Austens, though by no means prosperous, lived simply and well.

It was natural that coming from such a background, Jane grew up to appreciate wholesome food, and like many intelligent women of her time —and indeed of our own—she took an abiding interest in its preparation. She wrote long letters recording daily happenings to her beloved sister Cassandra when they were parted by visits, and in these there are many references to meals enjoyed and new ideas for cookery; for as she said (January 3, 1801), "I have now attained the true art of letter-writing, which we are always told, is to express on paper exactly what one would say to the same person by word of mouth."

In "Love and Freindship," written when she was fourteen, clearly her ideas concerning the importance of food and drink to successful family life were already formed. Edward, one of the characters, dismisses the value of "Victuals and Drink" with contempt; to which his sister replies that she knows of none other "so efficacious" (p. 83)—a view apparently held by the young author.

While Mrs. Austen's large family of six boys and two girls was young, she can have had little time for normal entertaining, but once her good-looking brood was grown up, she might have said, like Mrs. Bennet in *Pride and Prejudice,* "as to not meeting with many people in this neighbourhood, I believe there are few neighbourhoods larger. I know we dine with four and twenty families" (p. 43). The young Austens attended dinners, assemblies, and all the grandest balls held in the district. Through these occasions, and visits to wealthy relations—Uncle James Perrot in Bath, the Leighs of Stoneleigh Abbey, and the well-established brothers, Edward at Godmersham and Henry in London—Jane gained insight into the way of life of leisured classes, which is depicted so delightfully in her novels. However, although she enjoyed sophisticated cookery, her appetite for simple things was retained. Thus, after a nursery meal at Steventon with a little niece (January 14, 1796) she wrote that "Caroline, Anna, and I have just been devouring some cold souse, and it would be difficult to say which enjoyed it most." (Souse, made from wheat flour boiled with herbs, was eaten with brawn made from pigs' ears and feet.) After the arrival of an unexpected guest (December 1, 1798) she said: "I was not ashamed at asking him to sit down to table, for we had some pease-soup, a sparerib, and a pudding"; and, many years later (October 17, 1815), she said, "I am very glad the new cook begins so well. Good apple pies are a considerable part of our domestic happiness." Yet both sisters welcomed unfamiliar delicacies. Some meals taken during long coach trips were specially good. After a dinner at Devizes she wrote (May 17, 1799): "amongst other things we had asparagus and a lobster, which made me wish for you."

While staying with Edward at Godmersham and Henry in London, Jane liked to pick up ideas for "experimental housekeeping." She tried out a ragout of veal and resolved next time an oxcheek was cooked to put little dumplings into it "that I may fancy myself at Godmersham" (November 7, 1798). Henry kept a French cook, and Jane wrote to Cassandra, who was with him (January 25, 1801): "You will have a turkey from Steventon . . . and pray note down how many full courses of exquisite dishes M. Halavant converts it into."

Following her father's retirement the family lived in Bath from 1801 to 1806. Until then they had not needed to buy anything except tea, coffee, spices, citrus fruits, and sugar. Now, without home produce, it became necessary to study prices. Jane noted that meat was "8$d.$ per pound, butter 12$d.$, cheese 9½$d.$," and fish "exorbitant" (May 5, 1801).

After her husband's death Mrs. Austen decided to move with Jane and Cassandra in order to be near her elder sailor son Frank. They found a house, with a small garden, in Castle Square, Southampton. There they were joined by Jane's staunch friend Martha Lloyd (who years later became the second wife of Adm. Sir Francis Austen). Martha shared Jane's interest in cookery and had for years compiled household recipes in a handwritten book. These were of particular interest, since they were contributed by Mrs. Austen and many mutual friends and relations. Martha's book now belongs to the Jane Austen Memorial Trust. Many extracts from it were reproduced in *Jane Austen Household Book, with Martha Lloyd's Recipes.*

In a letter to Cassandra (December 27, 1808) Jane described an evening party she and Martha had given. It had lasted rather too long owing to delay on the part of chairmen in collecting their guests, "but the tray had an admirable success. The widgeon and the preserved ginger were as delicious as one could wish." The black butter, however, had not been boiled enough, and they had finished it later in "unpretending privacy." (Black butter, a popular conserve in the Channel Islands, was made from apple pulp pounded up with butter.)

Mr. Bingley promised a ball at Netherfield "as soon as Nicholls had made white soup enough" (*PP*, p. 55). Martha included no recipe for this, but two well-known cookery books of the period did (Mrs. Fraser's, 1801, and Mrs. Randall's, 1816). White soup was made from the gravy of any meat, with the yolks of four eggs pounded fine, two ounces of ground almonds, and some cream. It was the custom to serve hot soup strengthened with negus at balls. This was warming and pleasantly intoxicating—which perhaps accounts for Miss Bates' delighted exclamations during the ball at the Crown (*E*, p. 330): "Soup too! Bless me! I should not be helped so soon, but it smells most excellent," and for Fanny Price's feelings (*MP*, p. 281), when "feverish with hopes and fears, soup and negus, sore-footed and fatigued" she crept upstairs after the ball.

French wine was kept for visitors to Steventon; but Jane and Cassandra enjoyed mead and homemade currant and orange wine. She wrote from Godmersham to Cassandra (June 30, 1808), "The Orange Wine will want our Care soon.—But in the meantime for Elegance & Ease & Luxury.... I shall eat Ice & drink French wine, & be above vulgar Economy," and (October 26, 1813) "I find time in the midst of Port & Madeira to think of the 14 Bottles of Mead very often."

She lived in an age when there was much heavy drinking, but in all her major novels except *Sense and Sensibility* there is no hint of this. Mrs. Norris at her niece's wedding only took "a supernumerary glass or two" (*MP*, p. 203). There is a delightful account of Mr. Elton's proposal to Emma, who thought he "had been drinking too much of Mr. Weston's good wine" (*E*, p. 129), but only enough to "elevate his spirits, and not at all to confuse his intellects" (p. 30).

From the late eighteenth century the times at which meals were eaten slowly changed. People engaged in all kinds of activities before a late breakfast at ten o'clock. Most of them were then ready for something substantial—though Jane Austen only mentions tea with rolls and butter for hers. "This was a favourite meal with Mrs. Jennings, it lasted a considerable time" (*SS*, p. 181); and after Henry Crawford and William had left Mansfield Park, Fanny noticed the remains of theirs: "cold pork bones and mustard" and "broken egg-shells" (p. 282). General Tilney in *Northanger Abbey* drank chocolate for his, and Catherine's mother hoped she had not been "spoiled," while in his home, by the French bread there. In 1806 Mrs. Austen described a splendid breakfast at Stoneleigh Abbey: "Chocolate, Coffee, Tea, Plumb Cake, Pound Cake, Hot Rolls, Cold Rolls, Bread, butter and dry toast for me."

Dinner was gradually shifting to a later hour. Jane Austen wrote from Steventon to Godmersham on December 18, 1798: "We dine now at half after Three, & have done dinner I suppose before you begin.... I am afraid you will despise us," but by December 9, 1808 she was saying, "we never dine now before five." Dinner at Godmersham and in fashionable circles was at six-thirty.

As the gap between breakfast and dinner lengthened, people felt the need of sustenance at midday, so cold meats, pies, and jellies were usually laid out on dining-room sideboards, and slowly "luncheon" was mentioned—at first as something rather special.

Picnics were popular, and several appear in the novels. Sir John Middleton "was a blessing to all the juvenile part of the neighbourhood, for in summer he was for ever forming parties to eat cold ham and chicken out of doors" (*SS*, pp. 32–33).

Dinner was an elaborate meal. Mrs. Bennet, though she kept a good table, decided against asking Mr. Bingley and Mr. Darcy to an impromptu meal because "any thing less than two courses, could [not] be good enough for a man, on whom she had such anxious designs, or satisfy the appetite and pride of one who had ten thousand a-year" (*PP*, p. 338). Each course had a "removal" or two and numerous side dishes. Mrs. Bennet was overjoyed by the dinner eventually given to her future sons-in-law. We do not know what side dishes she provided, but "The venison was roasted to a turn.... The soup was fifty times better than what we had at the Lucas's last week; and even Mr. Darcy acknowledged, that the partridges were remarkably well done; and I suppose he has two or three French cooks at least" (p. 342).

Cards, music, and conversation followed dinner; then came supper. Fanny, trapped in conversation with Henry Crawford, welcomed the arrival of Baddeley, the butler at Mansfield Park, heralding a solemn procession bearing tea and "the tray."

The weaknesses and foibles of some characters in the novels become clear from their likes and dislikes of food. Dr. Grant, for instance, "was very fond of eating, and would have a good dinner every day; and Mrs.

Grant, instead of contriving to gratify him at little expense, gave her cook as high wages as they did at Mansfield Park" (p. 31). Mrs. Norris disapproved of his "enormous great wide table," with five sitting around it but enough food for ten (pp. 220–21). This gross overfeeding "brought on apoplexy and death, by three great institutionary dinners in one week" (*MP*, p. 469).

But Mr. Woodhouse in *Emma* was a fastidious eater anxious for his own and his guests' digestions. He had touching faith in his cook and said, "Serle understands boiling an egg better than any body" (p. 24). She could even be trusted with pork, "very thoroughly boiled" (for no stomach, he said, could stand roast pork, p. 172). Poor old Mrs. Bates was disappointed when "there was a delicate fricassee of sweetbread and some asparagus brought in at first, and good Mr. Woodhouse, not thinking the asparagus quite boiled enough, sent it all out again" (p. 329). But he did allow her to eat a baked apple.

Although Jane Austen enjoyed food and drink, she was never greedy and mocked those who were. For instance, in her letters she tells us scarcely anything about Mr. Robert Mascall except that "he eats a great deal of Butter" (October 11, 1813)—a comment that speaks volumes.

After his wife's death, Edward Knight decided to spend more time on his second estate at Chawton in Hampshire. He offered his mother a cottage near his own house, and in 1809 she moved there with her daughters and Martha Lloyd. Jane Austen found it delightful to be in their own part of Hampshire again. The cottage was charming, with plenty of space for fruit, flowers and vegetables, and poultry. It gave her great pleasure, too, to see more of Edward and his family, for Jane Austen was essentially a family person—fond of her nephews and nieces and devoted to her sister and brothers.

On November 6, 1813 she wrote from Godmersham to Cassandra: "By the bye, as I must leave off being young, I find many Douceurs in being a sort of Chaperon for I am put on the Sofa near the Fire & can drink as much wine as I like." It is pleasant to think of her like this, at ease but bright-eyed and observant, watching the younger generation, whom she loved so well.

Bibliography

CECIL, LORD DAVID. *A Portrait of Jane Austen* (London, 1978).
HICKMAN, PEGGY. *A Jane Austen Household Book, with Martha Lloyd's Recipes* (Newton Abbot, 1977).
JENKINS, ELIZABETH. *Jane Austen: A Biography* (London, 1938).

JANE AUSTEN'S NOVELS: FORM AND STRUCTURE

David Lodge

Each of Jane Austen's novels has its own distinctive identity, but they also have a strong family resemblance, one to another. Since it is impossible in the space available to do justice to the specific form of each novel, I shall try to bring out what they have in common in this respect. It is essentially a question of genre: what *kind* of fiction did Jane Austen write? The short answer is that she fused together the sentimental novel and the comedy of manners with an unprecedented quality of realism.

By the "sentimental novel," in this context, I mean the didactic, heroine-centered love story of which the prototype was Samuel Richardson's *Pamela; or Virtue Rewarded* (1740–41) and which survives today in the popular women's fiction generally known as "romance." This latter designation is somewhat ironic, since Samuel Richardson prided himself on writing a kind of prose fiction that eschewed the characteristic devices and implausibilities of traditional romance and would be morally improving precisely because it was "true to life." The eponymous heroine of *Pamela* is a young maidservant in a great house who, at the death of her mistress, is subjected to the sexual advances of the latter's son and heir, Mr. B——. Although she admires her master, the principled Pamela resists all his efforts to seduce her with such spirit and steadfastness that his lust is converted into love and he eventually makes her his wife. The story, which Richardson claimed was based on an actual case, is told entirely in the form of letters and journal entries, mostly written by the heroine; and it initiated a long line of sentimental epistolary novels, among them the first version of *Sense and Sensibility*, called *Elinor and Marianne*. Richardson's epistolary technique became obsolete with the development (in which Jane Austen played a crucial part) of more subtle and flexible methods of representing a character's thoughts and feelings in literary narrative. The basic structure of *Pamela* as a love story has, however, had a remarkably long life and proved adaptable to many literary purposes, high and low. Though invented by a male author, it is an essentially feminine kind of fiction, usually written by women, centered on a heroine rather than a hero and directed particularly at a female audience. It arose at a time when women were beginning to assert their right to choose their partners in marriage but were restricted by social convention to a very passive role in the courtship process. The "happy ending" of the didactic love story rewards the heroine, who copes with various emotional, social, economic, and ethical obstacles to union with the man she loves without losing her integrity. If there were no obstacles, of course, there would be no story.

Structurally, then, the love story consists of the delayed fulfillment of a desire. The delay puts the heroine under stress and thus generates the "sentiment"—that is, the representation of feelings, anxieties, and moral choices that is the real source of interest and value in the sentimental novel. In *Pamela*, the cause of delay is very simple: Mr. B—— wants extramarital sex, but Pamela wants love and marriage, and eventually she wins. This plot was too explicitly sexual, and perhaps too democratic in its implications (Pamela is promoted from the bottom to the top of the class system by sticking to her principles), for Richardson's more genteel, mainly female successors in the sentimental novel tradition, such as Fanny Burney, Maria Edgeworth, and Jane Austen. The heroine, though often inferior to the hero in social status and fortune, is not as remote in class terms as Pamela was from Mr. B—— before her marriage. The hero is not morally compromised by having designs on the heroine's purity, and illicit sexuality is displaced onto other characters—a seducer whose designs are frustrated by the hero, for instance, or a seductress or "fallen woman" who throws into relief the heroine's moral integrity. The necessary delay in the union of hero and heroine then has to be contrived by other means. For example, the lovers get off on the wrong foot, and one or both take some time to recognize the true nature of their feelings; they are alienated by misunderstandings, by other characters' intrigues, by apparently insurmountable obstacles to do with fortune, family prejudice, and the like. In many of these novels (e.g., Fanny Burney's *Evelina* [1778] and Maria Edgeworth's *Belinda* [1801]), some of the romance motifs that Richardson had rigorously excluded from his *Pamela* begin to seep back into the sentimental novel as a way of resolving the plot in a flurry of wills, confessions, discoveries of long-lost daughters/sons/parents, and so on. Jane Austen did not use such devices; indeed, she pointedly abstained from them. But all her novels have the basic structure of the didactic love story that derived from Richardson, albeit with much variation, modification, displacement, and even inversion of its basic components.

Of all Jane Austen's works, perhaps *Pride and Prejudice* cleaves most closely to the paradigm of the classic love story. Here the delay of the lovers' union is caused by their mutually unfavorable "first impressions" (the original title of the novel). Darcy offends Elizabeth by his arrogance, by his interference in the promising relationship between Mr. Bingley and her sister Jane, and by his alleged ill-treatment of Wickham. She refuses his first, totally unexpected proposal of marriage, thus demonstrating her integrity as well as her impulsiveness, because the match is a tempting one in material terms. When, for a number of reasons, her feelings toward

Darcy change, she is rewarded with a second chance to accept him. Elizabeth rejects the cynical *realpolitik* of the marriage market as expounded and practiced by Charlotte Lucas; she also survives unscathed the temptations of the erotically attractive but immoral male, represented by Wickham. Wickham demonstrates his dangerous power on Elizabeth's younger sister, Lydia, and Darcy's moral rescue operation in this crisis precipitates his union with the grateful and admiring Elizabeth—a good example of the displacement of the Richardsonian seduction plot onto secondary characters. Something similar happens at the end of *Mansfield Park*, where the adultery of Henry Crawford with Maria Bertram and Mary Crawford's failure to condemn it "justify" Fanny's earlier refusal of Crawford and precipitate her union with Edmund. The peripeteia (the surprising but satisfying reversal of expectation) in Jane Austen's plots very frequently takes the form of sexual misbehavior, or something like it (such as Lucy Steele's marriage to Robert Ferrars in *Sense and Sensibility*).

The classic love story consists of a delay not only of the heroine's desire but also of the reader's desire—to know the answer to the basic question raised by the narrative: will the heroine get the man she wants? There are three principal sources of interest in narrative: suspense, mystery, and irony. Suspense raises the question What will happen? Mystery raises the question Why did it happen? When the reader knows the answer to the questions but the characters do not, irony is generated. Thus, all rereadings of novels tend to create an effect of irony, but this is especially true of Jane Austen's novels, which are permeated with irony, rhetorical as well as dramatic, and which can sustain an infinite number of readings. On first reading they tend, like most love stories, to engage the reader's interest through suspense rather than mystery. *Emma* is an exception, since it is full of enigmas (—why is Mr. Elton so keen to attend the Westons' dinner party when Harriet is ill?—Who sent the piano to Jane Fairfax?—What are Frank Churchill's real feelings about Emma?). This follows from the fact that Emma does not fall in love until the book is almost over; therefore, the question Will she get the man she wants? cannot provide the main source of narrative interest. In *Pride and Prejudice*, too, though to a lesser extent, the heroine's knowledge of her own heart is delayed, and enigmas, mainly to do with Wickham and Darcy, supply narrative interest, together with the suspense plot concerning Bingley's intention toward Elizabeth's sister Jane. In the other novels Jane Austen makes relatively little use of mystery as a means of engaging the reader's interest, and in *Northanger Abbey* she mocked Mrs. Radcliffe's rather mechanical reliance on this device in *The Mysteries of Udolpho* (1794).

In *Northanger Abbey*, Jane Austen played a delightful (and risky) double game with both the conventions of the sentimental novel and the conventions of traditional romance that were beginning to reinvade it through the contemporary cult of the gothic—a process in which Mrs. Radcliffe played a crucial role. At first sight, Jane Austen seems to be simply justifying the former at the expense of the latter. The famous conclusion to chapter 5, in which the narrator defends the novel as a form "in which the greatest powers of the mind are displayed, in which the most thorough knowledge of human nature, the happiest delineation of its varieties, the liveliest effusions of wit and humour are conveyed to the world in the best chosen language" (*NA*, p. 38), explicitly cites titles by Fanny Burney and Maria Edgeworth. Catherine's naive addiction to the gothic novel retards the happy consummation of her love for Henry Tilney—first, by leading her into uncritical friendship with Isabella Thorpe and her brother John, whose intrigues constantly threaten her happiness, and second, by tempting Catherine into a ludicrous suspicion, during her stay at Northanger Abbey, of General Tilney's having murdered his wife, thus herself temporarily forfeiting Henry's good opinion.

But as several commentators have observed, Catherine's opinion of the general is not totally unwarranted, since he shows himself to be a thoroughly nasty man. Furthermore, the conventions of the more realistic sentimental novel are themselves subjected to ironic undermining—none more devastating than the passage in which the narrator tells us that Henry Tilney's affection for Catherine "originated in nothing better than gratitude, or, in other words, that a persuasion of her partiality for him had been the only cause of giving her a serious thought" (*NA*, p. 243); and none more witty than the narrator's admission that the anxiety of Henry and Catherine about the general's opposition to their marriage "can hardly extend, I fear, to the bosom of my readers, who will see in the tell-tale compression of the pages before them, that we are all hastening together to perfect felicity" (*NA*, p. 250). It seems that there is no great "virtue" in this heroine, and the narration of her "reward" is almost contemptuously offhand, making the reader feel guilty of the pleasure he takes in it and sending him back, perhaps, to reread that highly equivocal defense of the novel as a genre in chapter 5.

Of all Jane Austen's novels, *Northanger Abbey* is the only one that lends itself to a modern deconstructive reading, for it does seem to deny the reader any sure ground for interpretation and discrimination and to make explicit the impossibility of getting the world into a book. The other novels take the paradigm of the didactic love story more seriously, invest it with deeper significance, and center it on heroines of more worth than Catherine Morland—but without sacrificing comedy and humor.

Comedy is not easily combined with the sentimental novel. *Pamela* is only unintentionally funny, a weakness Henry Fielding riotously exploited in *Shamela* (1741) and *Joseph Andrews* (1742). His own most sentimental novel, *Amelia* (1751), is his least amusing. In Richardson's *Clarissa*

(1747–48) and in Rousseau's *La Nouvelle Héloïse* (1761), the sentimental pursuit of personal authenticity leads to tragedy, or at least pathos, to gestures of renunciation and loss, in which neither Jane Austen nor her heroines are interested. Emma's happiness—her eventual marriage to Knightley—entails disappointment for Harriet Smith, whose misplaced hopes of marrying him were unintentionally encouraged by Emma herself. Emma is sorry for Harriet, but not extravagantly so:

> For as to any of that heroism of sentiment which might have prompted her to entreat [Knightley] to transfer his affection from herself to Harriet, as infinitely the most worthy of the two—or even the more simple sublimity of resolving to refuse him at once and for ever, without vouchsafing any motive, because he could not marry them both, Emma had it not. (p. 431)

Both Fanny Burney and Maria Edgeworth leavened the sentimental novel with comedy, and Jane Austen undoubtedly learned from them; but their comedy is, compared with hers, more in the nature of "comic relief" from the main story and often takes a rather robust, farcical form reminiscent of the comic fiction of Fielding, Sterne, and Smollett, which itself derived ultimately from Rabelais, Cervantes, and the picaresque tradition. Jane Austen's comedy seems more theatrical in its origins, reminding us faintly of Congreve, Molière, and even Shakespeare.

One of the most venerable distinctions in general poetics is that drawn by Plato in Book III of *The Republic*, between diegesis (description of actions by an authorial narrator) and mimesis (representation of action through the imitated speech of characters). Drama is pure mimesis, in this sense, but the epic, and the novel which formally derives from it, combine diegesis and mimesis. Among the classic novelists, Jane Austen tends toward a dominantly mimetic method. Her stories are unfolded in a series of scenes, with a minimum of authorial description, and her skill in revealing character through speech is justly celebrated. Many passages from the earlier novels (e.g., the discussion between Mr. and Mrs. John Dashwood in chapter 3 of *Sense and Sensibility*, and the dialogues between Mr. and Mrs. Bennet in *Pride and Prejudice*) could be performed as written (and have been, on radio, television, and film). Action, in Jane Austen's novels, is social interaction of people in pairs, in groups, in social situations such as parties, dinners, balls, courtesy calls, walks, and excursions—situations that lend themselves naturally to "scenic" presentation and emphasize "manners." This is one reason why the comedy in Jane Austen does not seem tacked on to the love story but permeates it. This is true even of *Mansfield Park*, the most earnest of the novels and often disliked on that account. The comings and goings in the "wilderness" at Sotherton (rather reminiscent of Shakespeare's Forest of Arden), for instance, and the whole saga of the theatricals are exquisitely comic in a highly dramatic way, culminating in the wonderfully funny moment when the astonished Sir Thomas Bertram, unexpectedly returned home from the West Indies, interrupts Mr. Yates rehearsing his part in *Lovers' Vows*:

> He stept to the door ... and opening it, found himself on the stage of a theatre, and opposed to a ranting young man, who appeared likely to knock him down backwards. At the very moment of Yates perceiving Sir Thomas, and giving perhaps the very best start he had ever given in the whole course of his rehearsals, Tom Bertram entered at the other end of the room; and never had he found greater difficulty in keeping his countenance. His father's looks of solemnity and amazement on this his first appearance on any stage, and the gradual metamorphosis of the impassioned Baron Wildenhaim into the well-bred and easy Mr. Yates, making his bow and apology to Sir Thomas Bertram, was such an exhibition, such a piece of true acting as he would not have lost on any account. It would be the last—in all probability the last scene on that stage; but he was sure there could not be a finer. (pp. 182–83)

Here Jane Austen very characteristically turns the conventions of a falsifying kind of art inside out in order to reinforce the truthfulness of her own representation of experience. The encounter between Mr. Yates and Sir Thomas takes place on the interface between life and art and is equally disconcerting to both parties on that account. Sir Thomas walks unintentionally onto a stage for the first time in his life and becomes willy-nilly an actor in a scene, just as Yates is startled by the reality of the encounter out of the artificial rant and exaggerated gesture of melodrama into a genuine "start" from which he recovers by a piece of "true" social acting. The touch of genius in the passage is, however, the introduction of Tom Bertram as a kind of audience for this piece of real-life theater. It is through his eyes that we see and relish the ironies of the spectacle—and to recognize that fact is to recognize that, scenic as it is, Jane Austen's fiction is an achievement of narrative, not dramatic art. This kind of focalizing of the action through an individual viewpoint is peculiar to written narrative and is one of the constituents of fictional "realism."

The realism of Jane Austen's novels, the illusion of life that they create, has always been one of the chief attractions of her work to many generations of readers, from Sir Walter Scott's tribute, in his journal of 1826, to "the exquisite touch, which renders ordinary commonplace things and characters interesting, from the truth of the description and the sentiment," to Arnold Kettle's declaration, in 1951, that "*Emma* is as convincing as our own lives, and has the same sort of concreteness"

(Kettle's essay is reprinted in Watt, p. 113). More recently, realism as a literary effect has fallen into disfavor. Poststructuralist criticism, especially that which derives from the work of Roland Barthes, has identified the "classic realist text" as an instrument of ideology, a genre founded on bad faith, on the pretense that bourgeois culture is "natural," using the dominance of the authorial voice over all the other discourses in the text to limit meaning in the interests of control, repression, and privilege. To engage fully with this argument as it applies to Jane Austen is beyond the scope of this essay. It is certain that she took for granted the existence of class-society (though she did not see it as fixed or static), that she subscribed to the Christian-humanist notion of the autonomy and responsibility of the individual self, and that her novels unequivocally endorse certain values and reject others. If these are grounds for condemnation, then she stands condemned—though it seems a perverse and anachronistic judgment. Jane Austen's admirers have, however, often seemed handicapped in defending and celebrating her art by the poverty of their critical tools for analyzing it. Without a metalanguage (a language for talking about an object language—in this case the language of literary realism), criticism is apt to find itself reduced to mere paraphrase, retelling Jane Austen's stories in language that is of the same kind as hers but inferior in eloquence, precision, and wit. Part of the problem is that realism is a literary effect that works by disguising its own conventionality. Some of the concepts and methods of structuralist and formalist criticism may help us to see through that disguise and understand how Jane Austen constructs a fictional world "as convincing as our own lives."

For example, Roland Barthes's analysis of the classic realist text in *S/Z* as a "braiding" of multiple codes of signification—some having to do with the raising and resolution of narrative questions, some contributing to the creation of character, others imparting through devices of connotation the underlying themes and values of the story—all bound together in a kind of aesthetic "solidarity," so that any segment of the text can be shown to be communicating several messages simultaneously: this would seem to be highly relevant to Jane Austen's fiction, in which every detail, every nuance of gesture and conversation, is charged with significance. One must make the reservation, however, that the codes of connotation in Jane Austen operate under much stricter constraints and offer the critic much less opportunity for exegetical display than Balzac (the subject of *S/Z*). Another way of putting this is to say that Jane Austen's novels exhibit in a very pure form the dominance of metonymy over metaphor that Roman Jakobson argued is characteristic of realism as a literary mode (Jakobson; Lodge 1977). Metonymy is a trope that works by manipulating relationships of contiguity (as opposed to metaphor, which manipulates relationships of similarity). "Metonymic" discourse thus emphasizes sequence and causality, and Jane Austen's novels illustrate this bias very well. Her novels have a seamless quality, one episode leading logically and naturally to the next. She is particularly artful in the way she introduces, or reintroduces, one character to fill the space left in the story by another. Thus, in *Emma*, when the enigma of Mr. Elton's equivocal behavior toward Emma and Harriet is solved to their mutual embarrassment and mortification and he departs Highbury in a huff, the advent of Jane Fairfax and Frank Churchill, heralded many pages previously, provides a new focus of attention; and when Churchill, in turn, leaves the scene of Highbury, back comes Mr. Elton with Mrs. Elton (whom he has very plausibly married on the rebound from Emma). The reader of Jane Austen never feels, as he so often does with classic fiction, that the action has been patently contrived, new characters invented, new settings provided, to satisfy the exigencies of the plot and theme or simply to preserve the momentum of the text. Motivation of character conforms scrupulously to a code of psychological causality. In reading sentimental fiction by Jane Austen's contemporaries, one's credulity is frequently strained by the ability of hero and heroine to misunderstand each other (Fanny Burney's *Camilla* of 1796 is a particularly flagrant example of a novel kept going, for some nine hundred pages, virtually by this means alone); but the mistakes and misjudgments of Jane Austen's characters satisfy the modern reader's most stringent standards of plausibility.

Metaphor and metaphorical symbolism are used very sparingly by Jane Austen, and under strict constraints. Mark Schorer showed how, in *Emma*, buried or "dead" metaphors drawn from the language of commerce and property imply a scale of values that contrasts ironically, and almost subliminally, with the emotional and moral issues to which they are applied, and I have written elsewhere about the extraordinarily subtle and delicate way in which the pathetic fallacy is used in the same novel to mark the transition of the heroine from despair to joy (Lodge 1971). Even in *Persuasion*, by general consent the most "poetic" or "romantic" of the novels, the seasonal symbolism that attaches to the heroine's progress from an autumnal mood of resignation to a joyful "second spring of youth and beauty" (*P*, p. 124) arises metonymically out of the actual seasonal span of the main action; and the metaphor of "bloom" that articulates this theme most insistently (Anne is said to have lost her bloom at the beginning of the novel but to have recovered it by the end) is so conventional as scarcely to be perceived as a figurative expression.

One of the most fruitful concepts in modern narrative theory has been the Russian formalist distinction between fabula (the story as it would have been enacted in real time and space) and *sjuzet* (the story as it is represented in the text). In the case of fiction (as distinct from historiography), the fabula is not a prior reality but an extrapolation from the *sjuzet*, to be used as a tool of comparison. By observing how the narrative text selects, manipulates, and "deforms" the raw material of the fabula, we can uncover the formal choices that realistic illusion tends to disguise and relate those choices to the thematic and affective properties of the text. These choices crucially concern the handling of time, and what in Anglo-American criticism is loosely called "point of view" (loosely, because it concerns not merely the perspective from which the action is seen but also the voice in which it is narrated).

Gérard Genette has identified three categories of time in which there may be more or less disparity between fabula and *sjuzet*: order, duration, and frequency. Jane Austen's narratives rarely deviate from chronological order. If there is a retrospective account of some event antecedent to the main action or a delayed explanation of some event in the main action, either it is incorporated into the time span of the main action in the form of a letter (e.g., Darcy's letter to Elizabeth explaining his involvement with Wickham, *PP*, pp. 196–203) or in dialogue (e.g., Willoughby's apologetic confession to Elinor, *SS*, pp. 319–29), or it is briefly summarized in a nonscenic way by the authorial narrator (e.g., the account of Anne Elliot's former relationship with Wentworth at the beginning of chapter 4 of *Persuasion*. In other words, there is a minimal disturbance of chronological order in Jane Austen's novels. We don't encounter in them the effect of flashback, in which the temporal progress of the main action is suspended and for a while effaced by the scenic presentation of an earlier event; nor do we encounter anything like a "flashforward"—a proleptic glimpse of what is to come. The former effect is characteristic of fiction in which reality is seen as highly subjective—*Tristram Shandy*, for example, or the modern stream-of-consciousness novel; the latter effect is one in which the author as omniscient maker and manipulator of the fiction is apt to show his hand. By eschewing both these effects, Jane Austen strengthens the correspondence between her fictional world and the public, "commonsense" notion of time as a plane on which we all move, from a known past toward an unknown future, according to a logic of causality that becomes intelligible only in retrospect.

By "duration," Genette means the relationship between the time putatively occupied by the action of the fabula and the "reading time" it is accorded in the text. The main action of Jane Austen's novels never occupies more than a year, and usually rather less. *Emma*, for instance, begins with Mrs. Weston's marriage in the autumn and ends with the heroine's marriage the following autumn. *Persuasion* begins in autumn and ends the following spring. *Mansfield Park* stands out from the other novels in having a longish prelude describing Fanny's background and how she was adopted as a young child by the Bertram family, but the main action properly begins with the arrival of the Crawfords at *Mansfield Park* "in the month of July, and Fanny had just reached her eighteenth year" (*MP*, p. 40). It ends the following summer. Why is there this consistency in the time span of Jane Austen's novels? Perhaps six months is about the shortest time in which to portray plausibly the development of a meaningful relationship between hero and heroine, particularly if it entails a revolution in feeling, as in Elizabeth Bennet's attitude to Darcy, Edmund Bertram's to Mary Crawford and Fanny, Wentworth's to Anne Elliot; and anything longer than twelve months would draw attention to ellipses in the temporal continuity of the narrative and slacken its grip on the reader.

The tempo of a fictional narrative can seem faster than reality (e.g., the thriller) or slower (the stream-of-consciousness novel) or to move at about the same pace. Jane Austen's novels seem to have the tempo of life itself, yet their stories occupy several months, and the reading of them takes only a few hours. The illusion is achieved by the highly selective and dominantly scenic presentation of experience. Jane Austen notoriously—it is one of the chief causes of critical controversy about her—left out a great deal from her novels: physical love, the work men do, historical events, "local color." Her novels are concerned with the personal and social relations of young middle-class women confined to a very limited field of activity. The plot, which is concerned ultimately with the choice of a husband, is furthered in a series of social encounters or "scenes" that, because of the amount of direct speech in them, create the effect of more or less neutral duration, neither noticeably slower or faster than the tempo of "reality"; and because of the habitual, repetitive quality of these scenes, we are scarcely aware of the intervals between them.

Consider, for example, the events in the second volume of *Emma* (chapters 19–36 in most modern editions): Emma and Harriet visit the Bateses and hear of Jane Fairfax's impending arrival; they visit again and meet Jane; Knightley calls at Hartfield, and so does Miss Bates, with news of Mr. Elton's marriage; Harriet visits the Martins; Frank Churchill arrives and visits Hartfield and walks in the village with Emma; all the principal characters meet at the Coles's dinner party; Emma, Harriet, Mrs. Weston, and Frank Churchill call on the Bateses; discussions take place at Randalls and the Crown Inn about the proposed ball; Frank Churchill, summoned by his aunt, calls at Hartfield to say good-bye; Emma meets Mrs. Elton and gives a dinner party in her honor. Two or three months have passed, yet we have no sense of the acceleration of the normal tempo of life.

By "frequency," Genette refers to the ratio between the number of times an event occurs in the fabula and the number of times it is narrated in the *sjuzet*. As we might expect, Jane Austen generally follows the historical, "commonsense" norm of one-to-one. She does, however, use summary (narrating once what happened several times) in linking passages and to express with sometimes disconcerting candor the tedium and repetitiveness of the social round to which her heroines are confined—for example, "that kind of intimacy must be submitted to, which consists of sitting an hour or two together in the same room almost every day" (*SS*, p. 124). Jane Austen seldom repeats the narrative presentation of a single event, unless we count Emma's reflections on the Elton-Harriet debacle (*E*, pp. 134–39) or Edmund's and Fanny's inquests on the behavior of Mary Crawford (*MP*, pp. 63–64). She never presents successive accounts of the same event as experienced by two or more characters, in the manner of Richardson. This brings us to the topic of "point of view."

The great advantage of Richardson's epistolary technique—and the reason it enjoyed such a vogue—was that it short-circuited the simple alternation of diegesis and mimesis, author's voice and characters' voices, in traditional narrative by making the characters tell their own story virtually as it happened. The gain in immediacy and realistic illusion was enormous, but the technique had certain disadvantages, which, we may speculate, caused Jane Austen to abandon it after some early experiments. The machinery of correspondence was clumsy, uneconomical, and likely to strain credulity, while the elimination of the authorial voice from the text deprived it of an important channel of meaning. The nineteenth-century novel developed a new and more flexible combination of author's voice and characters' voices than the simple alternation of the two one finds in traditional epic narration, from Homer to Fielding and Scott—a discourse that fused, or interwove, them, especially through the stylistic device known as "free indirect speech." This technique, which Jane Austen was the first English novelist to use extensively, consists of reporting the thoughts of a character in language that approximates more or less closely to their own idiolect and deleting the introductory tags, such as "he thought," "she wondered," "he said to himself," and the like, that grammar would normally require in a well-formed sentence. For instance, after Mr. Elton's unwelcome declaration to Emma, the next chapter begins: "The hair was curled, and the maid sent away, and Emma sat down to think and be miserable.—It was a wretched business, indeed!—Such an overthrow of every thing she had been wishing for! —Such a development of every thing most unwelcome!—Such a blow for Harriet! That was the worst of all" (*E*, p. 134). Free indirect style, which enters this passage at the second sentence, allows the novelist to give the reader intimate access to a character's thoughts without totally surrendering control of the discourse to that character (as in the epistolary novel). The passage continues in a more summary and syntactically complex style, in which the narrator's judicial authority is perceptible, though Emma's consciousness remains focal:

> Every part of it brought pain and humiliation, of some sort or other; but, compared with the evil to Harriet, all was light; and she would gladly have submitted to feel yet more mistaken—more in error—more disgraced by mis-judgment, than she actually was, could the effects of her blunders have been confined to herself. (ibid.)

Free indirect style, combined with presentation of the action from the spatiotemporal perspective of an individual character (the usual meaning of "point of view" in literary criticism) allows the novelist to vary, from sentence to sentence, the distance between the narrator's discourse and the character's discourse, between the character's values and the "implied author's" values, and so to control and direct the reader's affective and interpretive responses to the unfolding story. Thus, for instance, we identify, and identify with, Elinor rather than Marianne as the heroine of *Sense and Sensibility* because we see much more of the action from Elinor's perspective, because we have much more access to her private thoughts, and because there is much greater consonance between the narrator's language and the language of Elinor's consciousness. Marianne's unhappiness at Willoughby's desertion is consistently ironized, implicitly judged as self-indulgent, by an authorial rhetoric of oxymoron: "this nourishment of grief was every day applied. She spent whole hours at the pianoforté alternately singing and crying" (p. 83); "in such moments of precious, of invaluable misery, she rejoiced in tears of agony to be at Cleveland" (p. 303). Compare Elinor, confronted with apparent proof of Lucy Steele's engagement to Edward Ferrars: "for a few moments, she was almost overcome—her heart sunk within her, and she could hardly stand; but exertion was indispensably necessary, and she struggled so resolutely against the oppression of her feelings, that her success was speedy, and for the time complete" (p. 134).

There is considerable variation between the novels in the amount of switching from one character's perspective to another's and in the degree to which the narrator explicitly invokes her authority and omniscience. In *Pride and Prejudice*, for instance, such effects are frequent. Although Elizabeth is the dominant center of interest, and consciousness, the narrative frequently moves away from her perspective. Here is a characteristic shift:

> Occupied in observing Mr. Bingley's attentions to her sister, Elizabeth was far from suspecting that she was herself becoming an object of some interest in the eyes of his friend. Mr. Darcy had at first scarcely allowed her to be pretty. . . . But no sooner had he made it clear to himself and his friends that she had hardly a good feature in her face, than he began to find it was rendered uncommonly intelligent by the beautiful expression of her dark eyes. (*PP*, p. 23)

It is important to the effect of the novel that the reader should know this and Elizabeth should not. A little later in the same scene, Elizabeth is "eagerly succeeded" at the piano by her sister Mary.

> Mary had neither genius nor taste; and though vanity had given her application, it had given her likewise a pedantic air and conceited manner, which would have injured a higher degree of excellence than she had reached. Elizabeth, easy and unaffected, had been listened to with much more pleasure, though not playing half so well. (*PP*, p. 25)

This brutally frank comparison of the sisters comes to us straight from the authorial narrator, and Elizabeth is not compromised, here or elsewhere, by any suspicion of vanity or disloyalty to her mostly tiresome family. Throughout the novel the reader is put in a privileged position of knowing more than any of the characters know individually.

Emma follows an antithetical method. It is not quite true to say, as F. R. Leavis did, that "everything is presented through Emma's dramatised consciousness" (p. 19n.). There are two important scenes in which Emma is not present and therefore, axiomatically, cannot provide the point of view. The first of these is chapter 5 of volume 1, a dialogue between Mr. Knightley and Mrs. Weston about Emma that remains wholly "objective" until the last paragraph, which gives us a hint of Mrs. Weston's private hopes of a match between Emma and Frank Churchill. In the fifth chapter of volume 3, there is a shift of point of view to Knightley, when he begins to suspect Frank Churchill of "some double dealing in his pursuit of Emma" (p. 343) and "of some inclination to trifle with Jane Fairfax." (In the following chapter Mrs. Elton plans her strawberry-picking expedition when Emma is absent, but this scene is less important hermeneutically.) There are also some very clear authorial comments about Emma's character at the outset of the novel that should put the reader on his guard against identifying too readily with her attitudes and opinions: for example, "The real evils indeed of Emma's situation were the power of having rather too much her own way, and a disposition to think a little too well of herself" (p. 5). But with these reservations it is true that the action of the novel is narrated wholly from Emma's perspective, so that the reader is obliged, on first reading at least, to share her limited knowledge and perhaps her mistakes and surprises. There is, to my knowledge, no precedent for such a novel before *Emma*—that is, a novel in which the authorial narrator mediates virtually all the action through the consciousness of an unreliable focalizing character. The effect is not only a wonderful multiplication of ironies and reversals but also an intensification of what Henry James called the sense of felt life—a more intimate relationship between fictional discourse and the processes of human consciousness. And not until Henry

James himself, perhaps, was there a novelist in the English language who equaled the skill and subtlety with which Jane Austen carried out this difficult technical feat. To make that comparison inevitably recalls the astonishing perversity of James's own observation that "Jane Austen was instinctive and charming.... For signal examples of what composition, distribution, arrangement can do, of how they intensify the life of a work of art, we have to go elsewhere" (p. 207). He never said an untruer word.

Bibliography

BARTHES, ROLAND. *S/Z* (Paris, 1970; English translation by Richard Miller, New York, 1975).

GENETTE, GÉRARD. *Narrative Discourse*, J. E. Lewin, trans. (Oxford, 1980).

JAKOBSON, ROMAN. "Two Aspects of Language and Two Aspects of Aphasic Disturbances," in Jakobson and Morris Halle, *Fundamentals of Language* (The Hague, 1956).

JAMES, HENRY. *The House of Fiction*, Leon Edel, ed. (London, 1957).

KETTLE, ARNOLD. *An Introduction to the English Novel*, vol. I (1951).

LEAVIS, F. R. *The Great Tradition* (London, 1948).

LODGE, DAVID. *The Modes of Modern Writing* (London, 1977).

———. Introduction to *Emma*, James Kinsley and David Lodge, eds. (London and New York, 1971).

SCHORER, MARK. "The Humiliation of Emma Woodhouse," *Literary Review*, 2 (1959); reprinted in Watt.

WATT, IAN P., ed. *Jane Austen: A Collection of Critical Essays* (Englewood Cliffs, N.J., 1963).

GAMES

Katrin Ristkok Burlin

"Real civilization cannot exist in the absence of a certain play-element, for civilization presupposes limitation and mastery of the self, the ability not to confuse its own tendencies with the ultimate and highest goal, but to understand that it is enclosed within certain bounds freely accepted" (Johan Huizinga, p. 211). Jane Austen's novels employ not only the game motif but also game structures. More important, the play of mind, the playfulness that is the defining characteristic of her letters, testifies to her belief in the essentially creative nature of play. Huizinga's distinctions between "true play" ("its aim is in itself, and its familiar spirit is happy inspiration," p. 211) and "false play" ("used consciously or unconsciously to cover up some social . . . design," p. 205) apply to Austen and her characters. She always plays true; they generally play false. While her attitude toward play, especially to its social and cultural significance, varies as her artistic vision matures and her society itself changes, playfulness remains a permanent characteristic of her creative mind. For a different, because largely negative, reading of the game motif in Austen's fiction the reader should see Alistair Duckworth's "'Spillikins, Paper Ships, Riddles, Conundrums, and Cards.'" Those interested in the intricacies of individual games should consult *Goren's Hoyle Encyclopedia of Games*.

"Till the heroine grows up, the fun must be imperfect" (*Letters*, September 9, 1814). Austen in the novels is impatient with most children's games. Little boys indulge in meaningless noise and riots; girls waste expensive stuff in making fashionable trinkets. She values play that develops children's skills and dexterity and approves of their physical activities. But children who play like adults, exploiting social inferiors to entertain themselves (the Bertram sisters in *MP*, the little Musgrove girls in *P*), are condemned as harshly as adults who play childishly (Frank Churchill, Jane, and Emma in *E*). The clearest examples of false play are the double games adults play under cover of child's play. True play with children is sufficiently rare to signal real moral worth. The only children's games Austen allows adults to play blamelessly are the genuinely merry ones—the "evening games" at Abbey-Mill Farm (*E*, p. 28) and the "charming game of play with a litter of puppies" (*NA*, p. 214).

A single disapproving allusion condemns as noisy the game of "consequences" in *Sense and Sensibility*, but billiards, with its valuable clue to the psychology and habits of men, draws a whole catalog of references. Players range from the obsessed and fastidious to the casual and undemanding, while game jargon enables Austen to write confidently in the language of men. All but two of her novels (*NA* and *P*) are rich in allusion to specific card games, the dominant game in Austen's fiction: commerce (*NA* and *PP*); cassino (*W*, *SS*, and *PP*); whist (*W*, *SS*, *PP*, *MP*, and *E*); vingt-un (*W* and *PP*); loo and lottery tickets (*PP*); quadrille and backgammon (*PP* and *E*); speculation and cribbage (*W* and *MP*); and piquet (*SS*, *PP*, and *E*).

She chose her games shrewdly for their thematic, ethical, and structural values. Her expertise in the vocabulary, ideal number and placement of players, procedures and strategies, the proportion of skill to chance, and the aesthetics and ends of individual card games enabled her, through the game motif, to type her characters, discriminate between the interests and habits of different sexes and generations, dramatize group dynamics, and explore the sources of class movement.

Since in the early novels "everyday social life" was "a kind of round-game in which everyone joined in together" (Girouard, p. 238) card play offered Austen at the same time a valuable thematic and structural resource for these works. As she makes explicit in *The Watsons*, the formal social circle still rules, forbidding people from moving freely or grouping naturally by interest or inclination. She made numerically precise use of specific games to organize her characters into single or doubled card tables, thereby conferring a different significance on the "outsiders" (her own term for nonplayers; *PP*: lottery tickets and whist, quadrille and cassino, loo and an outsider; *SS*: a card table of cassino and a worktable; *MP*: whist and speculation). "Separate tables" structure both the dialogue at individual tables and the frequently highly charged dialogue between tables. Players not only eavesdrop on each other but, when one game breaks up, become observers of the other. Games may superficially unify society, but they also prevent intimacy and privacy. To indicate the displacement of games in *Mansfield Park*, Austen limits its card-table scenes but develops them fully for maximum moral resonance.

Because of their predominantly literary focus, the juvenile works and *Northanger Abbey* make minor use of the card-playing milieu. *Northanger Abbey* uses "commerce," a card game in which exchange or barter is the chief feature, to expose the commercial core of Isabella Thorpe's artificial sensibility. *The Watsons*, her first predominantly social satire, is also the first to penetrate the inner structure of her card-playing society to mock the snobbery of fashions in round games and the social configurations they were designed to enliven.

Although games in *Sense and Sensibility* bore the intelligent and irritate the sensitive, they serve an important unifying function for ordinary society. Play can be avoided only through ruse (Elinor) or rudeness (Marianne). Not to play is to be a "blank in the circle." Most of this society clings to play as a refuge from the impoverished real world, attempting to find consolation in noise (Sir John Middleton and Mrs. Jennings), if not in genuine merriment, or in the elegance of the game world (Lady Middleton). Play in *Pride and Prejudice*, in which the heroine's civilizing playfulness regenerates the saturnine hero, has less social than spiritual significance. Thus, card play is cheerful as well as dull, and a really bad player is a flawed human being. Working with nine different kinds of card game, Austen also makes the game motif function as an efficient satiric device. Card games identify every level of skill, intelligence, social class, and financial condition. In Wickham we have even a "gamester," a throwback to the literary satire of the *juvenilia*.

Two orders of mind, the secular-playful (Mary) and the spiritual-serious (Edmund), conflict in *Mansfield Park*, as Austen pits sermons against cards. Mary and Edmund move in autonomous, mutually resistant worlds, he in the ethical world, where questions of right and wrong are central and "the contemplation of the ultimate," which frees "the human mind . . . from the magic circle of play," a regular and public duty (Huizinga, p. 212). Mary moves in the amoral world of games (ibid.), thinking herself as dutiful to its absolute rules of order as Edmund is to his.

At the card table, she is more willful than playful. While they are playing speculation, she makes a metaphor of the game to aim a worldly sermon on right-minded ambition at Edmund. Meanwhile, her secret, internal speculations concern a future in which her secular spirit would govern his by making a kind of game of his sacred profession. But when the conversation between the card tables establishes that Edmund will do nothing to change the fundamental seriousness of his world, she is made angrily conscious of the "time-bound" nature of games (Huizinga, p. 203). A different order, unfriendly to the game world, has taken over: "All the agreeable of *her* speculation was over for that hour" (*MP*, p. 248). As Huizinga argues, "when the combat has ethical value it ceases to be play" (p. 210). Clever Mary understands this: "It was time to have done with cards if sermons prevailed."

When the characters once again gather at a round table, they play with language. Word games—charades, conundrums, anagrams, enigmas, riddles, acrostics, and other puzzles—dominate card games. What does not get played out in *Mansfield Park*, the creative value of play, becomes the subject of *Emma*, a novel rich in the game motif. Indeed, *Emma* is itself a word game, anagrammatic in theme (the matching of verbal characters to signify the matchmaking of human characters) and plot structure (the rearrangements of a set number of characters and Characters to effect meanings). Games and art begin to touch as Austen explores her medium, language. To answer the conundrum "What two letters of the alphabet express perfection?" with "$M + A$," the syllabic construction of the name

"Emma," is to point not only to the character Emma, but metonymically to the larger verbal construct, *Emma*, the novel itself. Thus Austen engages with the central question of aesthetics concerning perfection in art, here specifically in literary art. That she should frame the question playfully as a conundrum suggests her belief in the creative relationship of play and art. The box of children's "alphabets" with which her characters play at anagrams potentially contains *Emma*. Their activity as they order the letters into words might reflect their author's creative play.

But as they are played in this novel, word games permit the player a greater degree of control than card games ruled by chance. As skill becomes a greater factor, ulterior ends threaten to rob play of its disinterestedness (Huizinga, p. 9). Detection of the element of false play is vital. Violating the rules of the anagrams game in their calculating play with "proper nouns" (like Emma in her matchmaking), Austen's characters do play false. They manipulate the "alphabets" not to form and exchange mutually comprehensible words, but to communicate covertly, to break the circle of understanding. Pure play would actually support the "continuity of a public and 'open' syntax of morals and manners" Duckworth sees as vital to the preservation of culture (Duckworth, 1971, p. 165). For games are highly schematic, with fixed rules that demand general and absolute adherence.

The ordering power Huizinga cites as making play aesthetically attractive, its offer of a "temporary, a limited perfection," is what draws Emma to games. But she persists in conflating play with work and the lower forms of art. The charade she extorts from Mr. Elton to use in her matchmaking, written by him in the spirit of commercial speculation, is the product not of play but of "ectotelic art, skilled work" (Ducasse, p. 80). Under Emma's editorship, pure play—Harriet's riddle book—is falsified. Was Austen using Emma's games to study the potential dangers of her own word games?

Certainly *Persuasion* proves no more playful than *Mansfield Park*. Although specific card games are no longer prominent, card play itself has not disappeared. Games still have sufficient social resonance for Captain Wentworth to read in Anne's fidelity in disliking cards a statement of general fidelity to larger values. The status of card play at the end of *Persuasion*, symbolized by the lovers' happy indifference, expresses a change in Austen's attitude to social games. Gathered in sympathetic activity at the White Hart Inn, true friends dispense with games. Only the Sir Walters and Lady Dalrymples, living by the values of the *Baronetage*, still cling to the old games for the sake of their precise structures and rules. Theirs is a pantomime of good society, a kind of dumb play. All around them society is changing, re-forming into more plastic groups. The game element declines as society abandons the unifying social circle and round game (Girouard) and heads for the open sea. Adventures and ventures, commercial and spiritual, displace the games of the play world. As Huizinga says, "Civilization . . . is no longer played" (p. 206).

Bibliography

ANDERSON, DOUGLAS. *All About Cribbage* (New York, 1971).
DUCASSE, C. J. "Creative Art, Work, and Play," in Vincent Tomas, ed., *Creativity in the Arts* (Englewood Cliffs, N.J., 1964), 71–83.
DUCKWORTH, ALISTAIR M. *The Improvement of the Estate* (Baltimore and London, 1971).
———. "'Spillikins, Paper Ships, Riddles, Conundrums, and Cards': Games in Jane Austen's Life and Fiction," in John Halperin, ed., *Jane Austen: Bicentenary Essays* (Cambridge, England, 1975), 279–97.
GIROUARD, MARK. *Life in the English Country House* (New Haven, Conn. and London, 1978).
GOREN, CHARLES H. *Goren's Hoyle Encyclopedia of Games* (New York, 1961).
HUIZINGA, JOHAN. *Homo Ludens: A Study of the Play-element in Culture* (Boston, © 1950, 1955).

GARDENS

Marion Morrison

"We hear that we are envied our House by many people, and that the Garden is the best in the Town." Jane Austen, in a letter to her sister (February 20, 1807), sounds rather pleased about it. But it must be a sobering thought for keen gardeners who are also friends of Jane Austen's that the only gentleman in her novels who digs his garden himself is the insufferable Mr. Collins. Other gentlemen own gardens that are both ornamental and productive, but they also own gardeners. It is Mr. Collins himself who gets on with it. Picture him at his humble abode, bent over the soil behind his laurel hedge; he is digging for victory, as well he may, in 1812, with the French wars going on and prices rising. But although Jane Austen laughs at Mr. Collins, perhaps for once she is looking at him with unexpressed tolerance as he digs away in his sloping plot.

She certainly enjoyed her own gardens and those of her well-connected friends. She was a country girl, her life not all tea and backgammon in the drawing room or flirtation at the local balls. "Matters concerning the garden" were important (*Letters*, April 21, 1805), and she was so familiar with the seasonal work involved that her novels and letters are full of details to interest gardeners among her readers today, be they botanists, ambitious architects, or just enterprising cooks.

One does not, of course, think immediately of Jane Austen as writing about gardens at all. People were her main concern. But on closer inspection, one observes that the people she created have fine houses and the houses have fine gardens, superb back cloths for the stage on which she brings her groups together. She was an observant critic of the changing scene around great country houses as Humphry Repton and other more ruthless "improvers" moved in. In her novels, the elegant gardens, "improved" or not, bring her characters to life, and although they are only lightly sketched, the reader immediately fills in the picture.

We watch the country gentlemen and their visitors surveying happily their groves and coppices, their lime walk, their stretch of water, their ha-ha, their prospects and vistas, dovecotes, stewponds, and succession houses. Mr. Bennet escapes to the little copse at Longbourn; Mr. Woodhouse, warmly wrapped, walks in the shrubbery at Hartfield; Colonel Brandon, in his flannel waistcoat, is ensconced in the yew arbor at Delaford; the Musgrove children play on the lawn at Uppercross. Familiar "props" appear again and again: the plantation, the summer house or arbor or bower (sometimes damp), the gravel walk, the sweep, the paddock, and above all, the shrubbery.

Lawns were still a problem, with lawn mowers not yet invented. The shrubbery, with its dry gravel path, was ideal for "taking a turn," especially in winter, when lanes were muddy. It was a haven of privacy for Jane Bennet and Bingley, a retreat for poor Fanny Price. Typically, Jane Austen leaves us to imagine *which* shrubs grew there, though she had her favorites, among them syringa (she may mean philadelphus, as lilac, too, is mentioned). The most memorable shrubbery scene occurs in *Emma*. The rain is over, the clouds are breaking up, Emma's spirits are rising, and right on cue Mr. Knightley appears and makes his tender proposal at last. Off they walk, around the shrubbery. . . .

Mrs. Elton, the expert, declares emphatically, "Surry is the garden of England" (*E*, p. 273), but Jane Austen finds beautiful gardens in several counties, and while revealing her own taste, she writes coolly, without sentiment. Only once is a flower—a rose—presented as a gift (*Evelyn*, p. 184). Surely Farmer Robert Martin brought posies for Harriet to make a cowslip ball? Were there no hothouse lilies for Elizabeth at Pemberley? No China roses from Donwell for old Mrs. Bates instead of more cooking apples? We are not told. Mary Musgrove makes a perfunctory flower arrangement, and Catherine Morland recalls admiring some hyacinths in Bath, declaring, however: "I am naturally indifferent about flowers" (*NA*, p. 174). Fanny Price is not indifferent. It is the earliest spring flowers that she loves, in the "warmest divisions" of Lady Bertram's garden (*MP*, p. 432).

Jane Austen herself is by no means indifferent, behind her formidable facade of irony. "The Garden is quite a Love," she wrote from her brother Henry's house in London (August, 1814). And in Canterbury she bought a "sprig" of flowers—"for my old age," this inscrutable spinster of thirty-eight wrote to Cassandra, perhaps ruefully. Her letters contain repeated allusions to sowing and planting and to the exchange of seeds and roots. Mignonette, auricula, columbine, Sweet William—old favorites are cherished; but Jane the gardener is a realist, aware of groundsel, thistles, and nettles, noticing a dung cart. Houseplants are there: is it not a relief to know that Fanny Price can keep geraniums in her cold East Room? The temperature cannot be more than a few degrees below freezing! But Jane Austen always likes to make us laugh, and among her gardening enthusiasts is greedy Mrs. Norris, clutching her specimen of heath from Sotherton, revealed predictably as the keen collector of loot from other people's gardens.

Jane Austen has a totally realistic attitude toward the kitchen garden, with its variety of herbs and vegetables, as the sisters were of necessity much involved at Chawton in the cultivation and preserving of "garden-stuff" both for the table and for the essential medicaments of the day. Mrs. Austen dug up the potatoes, Cassandra had charge of the beehives, and

Jane picked the currants. "I have lop't and crop't," she wrote to Cassandra (January 13, 1813), not, indeed, referring to seasonal pruning, but to her meticulous revision of the early script of *Pride and Prejudice*. The gardening terms sprang easily to her mind. And gardeners are one class of servant whom Miss Austen found interesting enough *not* to ignore, especially the Scot Mackenzie, with whom Anne Elliot had considerable conversational difficulties.

GRANDISON

Brian Southam

According to the family biographies, from Henry Austen onward, Samuel Richardson's *History of Sir Charles Grandison*, an epistolary novel published in 1753 and 1754, was Jane Austen's favorite work of her favorite novelist. Her intimate knowledge of *Grandison* and its profound influence on her own writing is attested to in her letters and the six novels. Yet her admiration of *Grandison* was not unqualified. While she learned much from Richardson's dialogue and representation of social and family life, she was also amused by his mannerisms of style and absurdities of opinion; and there are a number of Grandisonian jokes in the *juvenilia*.

The most important piece is a lively dramatic skit entitled (as it is on the manuscript) *Sir Charles Grandison or The happy Man, a Comedy in 6 acts*, finished about 1800. Strangely, the manuscript seems never to have come to the notice of R. W. Chapman and thus finds no place in his edition of the *Minor Works*. Possibly he accepted the family tradition that the play was actually the work of a favorite niece, Anna Lefroy (eldest daughter of James Austen), and that Jane Austen merely wrote it out to the girl's dictation. But the nature of the work itself and the chronology of its composition put Anna's authorship out of the question. At most, her contribution may have been a line or two or an idea here and there; Jane Austen, understanding the young girl's pride and pleasure, would have allowed her to claim the play as her own, a childish exaggeration that would have fooled no one at the time.

The style of the play's title page and opening pages enables us to date this section alongside the other literary and dramatic jokes of the early 1790s, somewhat before Anna's birth in April 1793. It proved to be a false start that Jane Austen did not continue, putting the manuscript to one side until about 1799/1800, when she took it up to provide the Steventon household with a performable play. This was a revival of the tradition of family dramatics she had herself enjoyed in her childhood, which was now to be continued for the next generation. The last pages of the manuscript are written hastily, and it may well have been at this stage that Anna came along with her suggestions. There are one or two words scribbled in a childish hand; these could have been her actual contributions to the manuscript.

But there can have been little more to their collaboration, for the play itself is a sophisticated literary joke, an "abridgment" that parallels Jane Austen's *History of England*, a mock reabridgment of Goldsmith's

Abridgement of his own full-scale *History of England*. Similarly, schoolroom abridgments of *Grandison* abounded. And just as Jane Austen's *History* is potted but unbowdlerized, so is her *Grandison*. One part of the joke was the reduction of the mammoth novel into a minuscule play (five brief acts rather than seven volumes), the abbreviation of an epic work of fiction into a domestic comedy. The other part of the joke was to perform this shrinkage without any concessions to the sensibilities and innocence of the schoolroom readership. Far from avoiding them, Jane Austen takes the scenes at Paddington—where the threat of rape hangs heavy on the air—as the center of her comic melodrama and reserves for them her best lines. Far from shunning the strain of erotic titillation in Richardson, she laughs it off the stage. Are we to suppose this the work of a child of seven?

The subtitle, "The happy Man," is in itself an important allusive joke, since it is the key phrase in *Grandison*, referring to the hero in his happy state of marriage-in-prospect, the marriage ceremony, and married life. But the "happy" in this and other phrases attached to Grandison and other characters echoes and re-echoes insistently and flatly throughout the novel's seven volumes. The wholesome message is rammed home, reminding us that Richardson designed *Grandison* as a conduct book, a didactic entertainment, from which young and old could learn an instructive and enjoyable lesson. Jane Austen does not question the spirit of this message. Nonetheless, she mimics its less than subtle delivery. In a household where *Grandison* was a "family" book, Jane Austen's choice of such a subtitle was a clear signal of the satire to come.

Within the play itself, the quality of the literary burlesque varies considerably. In part, this unevenness arises from the fact that the play was not written all of a piece. More important, it was written for the family—for their performance, for their entertainment—so a multitude of small parts were necessary. The walk-on characters appear and disappear, unattached either to the play or to Richardson. Equally, lines of dialogue exist merely to give characters something to say. The opening scene—with Mrs. Reeves and the milliner chatting about dresses—is wholly of Jane Austen's devising and has no direct source in the novel. But no doubt the audience would have been amused to see items of family and local history worked into the play—diluting the literary satire but adding immensely to the immediate entertainment.

So in reading Austen's *Grandison* today we have to keep in mind that its humor is not on a level with the timeless, universal comedy of the six novels. Much of its reference is particular and private to family and neighborhood jokes that we can only guess at. Nonetheless, literary historians will value her *Grandison* as part of Jane Austen's response to Richardson. Her appreciation of his achievement was a fine mixture of admiration and irreverence; and her eye for absurdity was focused as sharply on him as on any other of her literary idols.

It should be said that some reviewers of Southam's edition entered reservations about Jane Austen's part in the writing of the play. As yet, however, no objection to this attribution has been raised by anyone who has studied the actual manuscript materials.

Bibliography

SOUTHAM, BRIAN C., ed. *Jane Austen's "Sir Charles Grandison"* (Oxford, 1980).

HISTORY, POLITICS, AND RELIGION

Marilyn Butler

Most readers have not thought that Jane Austen's novels had any politics or that their history needed explaining. Her life and circumstances could belong to a private woman in any period since her own. She was born in 1775, five years after Wordsworth, four or five years after Scott. She lived mostly in two Hampshire villages, more than half her life in her father's rectory. Her books were published anonymously, and she knew no other writers. She died, unmarried, at forty-one. Do we need to know more? Does even this simple outline tell us anything about the novels that the characters and settings could not tell for themselves?

The critical orthodoxy that treats individual works of art as both coherent and self-sufficient seems perfectly adapted to Austen's novels. Her uniquely high critical standing among novelists—she is the one writer apart from Shakespeare, Edmund Wilson wrote in 1950, who seems impervious to shifts in fashion—derives from this artistic self-sufficiency, which ensures that she can be studied by the same formal, exclusive literary conventions as a polished poet like Keats. A partial exception has admittedly been made for the purely literary background with which much Austen criticism has been preoccupied since the 1930s, throughout the era of the New Critics: the novels have been placed in their genre, the "women's novel" in the Richardson-Burney tradition, and in an "Augustan" intellectual milieu, shared with Johnson and Cowper, Bishop Butler, and (more speculatively) Shaftesbury. Studies of the intellectual background have generally observed the principle that ideas, in the sense of issues that divide society, filter into imaginative works, if at all, only through the medium of another book.

The belief that in this sense, but in no other, "background" matters is not one we need regard as binding. It seems arbitrary to insist that a writer, a social animal like the rest of us, takes in ideas from books while remaining impervious both to ideas derived from experience and to the general cultural ambience. The literary concept of the source of one book in another book denies the work done in other disciplines on the way we acquire our general opinions, ideology, or world view. Political scientists do not nowadays attribute our political beliefs to some inner debate prompted by a book or a speech or the guidance of a parent, teacher, or friend. Social ideas and socialization are inseparable; our theories relate to our perceptions of ourselves as members of a limited group within a larger one, society. This makes our politics intuitive, not analytical; interested, but not narrowly self-interested—for we idealize our group and consider that the community will benefit if we prevail. An account of Austen's politics that relied too heavily on the conclusions of the political scientist, anthropologist, or social historian would be unduly reverential to generalities, over the specific evidence available in her individual case; but to glean her opinions from her writings without attention to her circumstances is equally unsatisfactory. She thought, and changed her thinking, along with certain groups in society, who were living, as it happens, through a time of national crisis: the gentry, and also gentry hangers-on in southern England; the Church of England, and that church's Evangelical movement. She was also a novelist, and a woman novelist, when sharp ideological pressures were being felt by writers. A full reading of the novels recognizes their rich life in time and place.

The Novel and Politics

A stylized genre like the eighteenth-century novel of manners constitutes a kind of language: minute transformations in a stereotyped scene, character, or situation convey to the experienced reader nuances that the uninitiated do not pick up. Such nuances at the time included the political, for it is anachronistic to view the eighteenth-century novel as untendentious and nonideological. Especially in the half century after 1740, a period of much-enhanced activity in European publishing, general literature, or "belles lettres," aimed directly or obliquely to convey opinions, and these opinions tended to be unfriendly toward the status quo. Even the more trenchant critics of the anciens régimes, like the *philosophes* in France and the *Sturm und Drang* writers in Germany, fell far short of advocating the immediate overthrow of existing society; the cultured classes, who were also the politicized classes, nevertheless gave their leisure and their money to works that steadily conveyed some alienation from government and from the power structure. As examples, more fully detailed in my books *Jane Austen and the War of Ideas* and *Romantics, Rebels and Reactionaries*, the cult of Sensibility opposed a highly sentient, naturally virtuous individual to a formal, greedy, or corrupt world; the cult of primitivism reacted against "advanced society" and proposed that a simpler, less hierarchical social structure would promote more freedom, virtue, and happiness.

Novels could not be as boldly polemical as those favorite forums for literary iconoclasm, the Pindaric ode and the long didactic poem. Novels were known to circulate widely among a popular audience, especially among women, who were thought particularly likely to follow their grandmother Eve down the path of temptation. So conservative moralists like Samuel Johnson put pressure on novelists (redoubling it if the novelist was a woman) to maintain the proprieties in ideas, language, and conduct and thereby helped to ensure that the genre played a part in giving women an increasingly narrow and stereotyped self-image.

Yet in spite of the moralists and in spite of women writers' eagerness to win their approval, the novel in the half century after 1740 managed in some respects to be libertarian, too. It usually gave a flattering representation of the consciousness of its heroine, who was almost invariably sensitive and discriminating. It dignified her domestic life and the main concern of her existence, the choice of a marriage partner. Older literary forms required their readers to know a wider world or to know other books, perhaps in learned languages; novels democratized reading and did away with the advantage poetry gave to the upper classes and the male sex. Most novelists also canvassed for a humane understanding of marriage, which they represented as a relationship based on affection rather than a financial transaction and a decision to be taken by the young people rather than by their parents. Rousseau in *Julie, ou la Nouvelle Héloïse* (1760) went much further by portraying his heroine's sexual passions as intrinsically noble, even though the man she loved was not the man she had married. Many libertarian end-of-the-century plays and novels followed Rousseau's lead by urging that the fulfillment of passion should take precedence over the conventions governing marriage. In Kotzebue's *Lovers' Vows*, the play to be acted in *Mansfield Park*, one heroine expresses herself by bearing an illegitimate child, another by boldly proposing to her tutor.

Any eighteenth- or early-nineteenth-century novel centered on a heroine displays some of the feminist traits inherent in the form, the more so if it is written by a woman. Here the previously inarticulate are speaking, and the underprivileged command a central role. The genre, by being woman centered and domestic, cannot help challenging the male point of view that takes priority in epic and in tragedy. Julia Prewitt Brown and Gilbert and Gubar eloquently make the case for the radicalism of Austen's work, defining radicalism in universal and abstract terms. But it is overgeneralizing to suggest that an individual novelist is feminist because her book possesses attributes possessed by most novels of the same period, especially novels by women. Too many arguments in favor of Austen's alleged feminism pick out features common to the form instead of identifying those areas where the variants are intellectually significant and where the option chosen by Austen signaled an ideological message to her contemporaries.

Austen began to write in the mid-1790s, at a point when the arts were moving into a period of conservatism. The most obvious reason for this was the French Revolution, a movement with enormous intellectual élan that quickly exported subversion and republicanism to neighboring countries. The Low Countries, Switzerland, the Rhineland, Italy, and Spain quickly fell to the French; Britain, Prussia, Austria, and Russia resisted, and armed themselves spiritually to resist, with ideas dubbed already at the time as a "counterrevolution." Quite apart from fear of the French and what they currently stood for, there were forces working for conservatism in both British and German society. Steadily increasing prosperity swelled the numbers of leisured classes, bringing within them more of the urban bourgeoisie and younger branches of gentry families like the Austens, who in other times might have sunk. These people were naturally suspicious of the values of the established upper classes—fashionable, frivolous, mannered, "French." Guarding the homelands against innovation and keeping the propertied in the saddle entailed dispensing with much of the culture of the previous era, including sensibility and primitivism in its more political forms. The very concept of art as a carrier of "Opinion," so universal in the Enlightenment, passed quickly out of fashion. Even Shelley, most insistently radical of poets, was soon declaring, "Didactic poetry is my abhorrence." It became more reputable and serious to portray man alone, or communing with God or Nature, not man in society.

The novel in Austen's lifetime took a different aesthetic route from poetry, though equally in the direction of political conservatism or quietism. As novels were written by women and other amateurs, to claim that the form existed to express the writer's inner life or personal aspirations would have been undesirable. On the contrary, it was often stressed that most novels had been too indulgent to women's dreams and aspirations. The fashion of focusing on a protagonist's inner life gave place to a concern with the conditions of external life; fantasy and the gothic, to a more closely documented treatment of history and society, notably Scott's. The best critics of the novel of Austen's heyday—Jeffrey, Croker, Ward, Foster, Scott himself—agreed that the significant modern technical innovation in the novel was a minute realism, fidelity to the facts as they were.

Novelists of all ideological complexions are severe in the 1790s on sensibility, romance, and sexuality. Two of the most liberal, Wollstonecraft and Edgeworth, had Dissenter and middle-class connections, and they participate in the movement of taste away from aristocratic aesthetic values that is as much a class as a political phenomenon. This does not mean that their views cannot be distinguished from those of a conservative such as Austen. When they criticize Rousseau, the heroine they concentrate on is not the expressive Julie but the passive Sophie, heroine of *Émile* (1762), who is uninstructed and pretty, woman formed for man's enjoyment. Wollstonecraft and Edgeworth dislike the feminine woman and want girls to receive the same education as boys. They criticize the role conventionally given to romance in women's lives and the inequality of marriage: Wollstonecraft protests against husbands' legal and economic rights (*Maria*, 1798); Edgeworth urges that women should be trained to support themselves (*Madame de Fleury*, 1809) or urges (passim) that gentry marriage should be an equal working partnership in managing estates and educating children. Above all, both declare their liberalism by refusing to accept the postrevolutionary dictum "the little-missy phrase," as one Edgeworth woman character sarcastically puts it, "that ladies have nothing to do with politics" (*Helen*, vol. 2, p. 233).

On this last point, the conservative Austen was luckier with posterity than her rivals. Their campaigning soon looked unfashionably didactic, while her ladylike avoidance of "themes" has always been received as proof of her artistry. Austen's approach to ideas is so discreet that she seldom allows her male characters, and virtually never her female characters, to discuss general issues. A concept like Sensibility is mocked, not argued with, for the characters who profess it (the protagonists in "Love and Freindship," Margaret Watson in *W*, Fanny Dashwood and Lucy Steele in *SS*) do not really believe in individualism or feeling, but pretend they do, to mask some selfish calculation. Like most writers reacting against Sensibility, Austen plays down romantic love and prefers family obligations, affection between brothers and sisters (*W* and *MP*) and the care of an ailing parent (*W* and *E*). In fact, she goes out of her way to represent marriage "sensibly," as a gentlewoman's means of securing her future. Austen is uncommon in making us aware of the incomes of her women characters before and after marriage; though sometimes she encourages us to deplore female materialism (Lucy Steele, Charlotte Lucas, Maria Bertram), she also allows us to rejoice that all her heroines, most notably the iconoclast Elizabeth Bennet, end up much better off; they accomplish the genteel woman's objective of marrying well. When Elinor and Marianne argue over income (*SS*, p. 91), they are arguing not over a principle but over the minimal sum needed to live in comfort. While Austen is certainly not here denying the importance of affection, her shift of emphasis toward the dynastic considerations that operated in life for her class must have been read as conservatism. Finally, marriage is the only career Austen shows women following, though teaching is mentioned. Her women characters' passivity on this subject contrasts with the protests made by Charlotte Smith in prefaces to her novels and with Burney's study in *The Wanderer* (1814) of the hardships and humiliations imposed on a woman who tries to earn her own living.

Contemporary critics seemed clear about Austen's ideological position;

it was the conservatives who were first to praise her. Whately, a future Anglican archbishop, preferred her to Edgeworth because she was Christian. John Ward, a Tory M.P. and future foreign secretary, also preferred her to Edgeworth because she left out the latter's ideas, which he unfairly typified as "chemistry, mechanics, or political economy" and called "vile, cold-hearted trash in a novel." Scott seized on a significant ideological point when he claimed that Elizabeth married Darcy because she perceived that it would be good to be mistress of Pemberley.

By deploying her genre as she did, Austen kept women within the domestic sphere, from which feminists and liberals wished to release them. And yet (to many modern readers, it is a crucial caveat) she succeeds in rendering the plight of women, within these confines, more tellingly than anyone else. Her letters suggest alienation and misanthropy, especially as she passed through her years of dwindling chances of marriage, from her mid-twenties to her mid-thirties. Among the finished novels, *Sense and Sensibility*, with its comic and unpleasant opening between John and Fanny Dashwood, its disaffected portrait of life in town and country, best reflects this mood. It is even more remarkably caught in *The Watsons*, a painful exploration of the plight of aging, impoverished spinsters exposed to repeated snubs and ridicule in their increasingly desperate search for husbands. The watermarked paper shows that the earliest date at which Austen could have written this was 1803, when she was twenty-seven—the same age as Elizabeth Watson, whose sour first observations on courtship set the mood. When the odious Robert Watson comments to Emma on the imprudent remarriage of her loved aunt, it is hard to believe Austen felt anything but revulsion against his transactional attitudes toward all women:

> "A pretty peice of work your Aunt Turner has made of it!—By Heaven! A woman should never be trusted with money. I always said she ought to have settled something on you, as soon as her Husband died." "But that would have been trusting *me* with money, replied Emma, & *I* am a woman too.—" "It might have been secured to your future use, without your having any power over it now.—What a blow it must have been upon you!—To find yourself, instead of heiress of 8 or 9000 £, sent back a weight upon your family, without a sixpence.—I hope the old woman will smart for it." (pp. 351–52)

Scenes like this can be cited as evidence of Austen's deep sympathy with her sex; and postromantic criticism is generally more alert to such renderings of experience than to the presence (or significant absence) of ideas. If we are reading for the latter, as Austen's first readers must have done, we will weigh such a scene against the refusal to generalize, even in the letters, about any social issue, including the lot of women; and indeed the failure to leave a scene as blunt as this one in any novel she prepared for publication.

The Austens: A Tory Family

The Austens are described as Tory by Jane Austen's niece Caroline, but the meaning of the term is nowadays not quite clear, because it was changing in Austen's lifetime. Early in the eighteenth century a Tory signified the kind of conservative who adhered to the exiled Stuarts; in religion, a High Churchman or Catholic; in Parliament (though the classic Tory stayed on his country estate), a member of the Opposition to the triumphant Whigs. Some of Austen's ancestors, her mother's family the Leighs, had been noted Royalists in the Civil War, and it may be that Austen does not write wholly in jest when, in her jocular adolescent "History of England," she lavishly praises the most glamorous figures of the Stuart dynasty, Mary Queen of Scots and Bonnie Prince Charlie. In the middle of the eighteenth century, Westminster politics became less ideological and less organized on party lines; governments were made up of Whig factions, and those representatives of the shires who remained aloof were not called Tories but "independent country gentlemen." At the beginning of the 1790s, the prime minister, Pitt, the Opposition leader, Fox, and the parliamentary orator Burke were all notionally Whigs, but the polarizing of opinion brought about by the war with revolutionary France made the concept of "party" as an ideological grouping meaningful once more. Pitt declared war in 1793 for old-fashioned reasons: France, much the greatest European state, looked aggressive and expansionist. It was Burke, at first apparently hysterically, who saw even the bourgeois French Revolution of 1789, still more the popular Revolution of 1792, as fundamental challenges to traditional aristocratic society and to the ownership of property everywhere. Burke advocated an ideological crusade against France, war to the death with the principle of revolution.

Within the 1790s, the decade when Austen grew up, naturally loyalist and socially conservative middle- and upper-class opinion adhered behind Pitt and the war effort and increasingly this meant taking on many of Burke's ideas. A host of conservative publicists, some of the most effective of whom were churchmen, gave the war a convincing rationale by representing it as the defense of religion, the family, and the gentry way of life. The upper and middle orders were given a coherent if idealized self-image, which has been the basis of British Toryism ever since: a personal ideal compounded of independence, honor, decency, patriotism, public service, chivalry to women, and civility to inferiors. Although Austen is famous for not debating the French Revolution or the consequent war as issues, the war years, 1793–1815, account for almost all her adult life, and her novels give telling evidence of the changes worked by that war in the consciousness of her class.

The gentry or landowning class had enjoyed great power, prestige, and prosperity in the eighteenth century, on terms somewhat different from the aristocracies that governed other countries of Europe. In Britain, power went with the ownership of land, and a strict system of primogeniture kept large estates together. Aristocracy and gentility were not legally defined states, as in France and Germany, and the younger sons and all daughters had to act positively to maintain their social position either by entering a profession or by making an advantageous marriage, or both. The Austens were certainly gentry in the sense that they had "good" family connections on both sides. George Austen, Jane's father, was related to owners of large tracts of land in Kent and Hampshire; her mother, Cassandra, née Leigh, had a wealthy brother, James, who later took the name of Leigh Perrot, and a cousin, Thomas Leigh, who inherited the great house of Stoneleigh Abbey, Warwickshire. But neither George nor Cassandra inherited money, so that they and their eight children grew up in the knowledge that they had their way to make.

The Austen line affords a good example of the relative openness of the British class system. Austens had been Kentish gentry for generations, their income deriving from land and from the broadcloth industry. They fell on hard times early in the eighteenth century, but the family fortunes were remade by a younger son, Francis Austen (Jane Austen's great-uncle), who became a solicitor at Sevenoaks, Kent, initially with a capital of £800 and a bundle of quill pens, and made a fortune by the two classic routes, through his profession and through two remarkably wealthy marriages. Francis Austen paid for his nephew George Austen to attend Tonbridge School, after which George won a scholarship to St. John's College, Oxford, and in 1761 was presented with the living of Steventon in Hampshire by a Kentish second cousin, Thomas Knight I of Godmersham Park. Twelve years later Francis Austen bought George the living of the neighboring parish of Deane, which was then worth £110 a year. Even with Steventon's income of £100, with tithes, living-in pupils, and what could be made by farming the glebe lands, the annual sum George Austen owed to his kinsmen never exceeded £600, and, like Mr. Bennet's income in *Pride and Prejudice*, it could not be handed on automatically to his children.

The careers of Jane Austen's brothers are instructive. James, born 1765, became his father's curate at Deane in 1793 and took over the parish of Steventon in 1801. George, born 1766, may have been mentally retarded and always had to be supported by the family. Edward, born 1767, was thus the obvious choice for adoption by the childless Thomas Knight II, of Godmersham Park, Kent; his widowed adoptive mother, Mrs. Knight, turned over the estates in Kent and Hampshire to Edward in 1797, and in 1812, on her death, he changed his name to Knight. None of the remaining children had prospects by inheritance. Henry, born 1771, was the right age for a wartime career and became successively a soldier in the militia, a banker and army supplier, a bankrupt, and (after the war) a clergyman. Frank, born 1774, and Charles, born 1779, the two youngest sons, were already destined for the navy, but the war meant additional opportunities, and each rose to the rank of admiral.

These careers of the Austen brothers are precisely the careers of younger male characters in the novels: landowners (Brandon, Darcy, Knightley), clergymen (Ferrars, Tilney, Edmund Bertram), and officers in the navy (William Price, Wentworth). They are only a few of the careers open to gentlemen, and the considerations that would have gone into choosing them are interesting to contemplate. In 1808 Maria Edgeworth wrote with her father a work called *Professional Education,* following it with her novel *Patronage* (1814). Both books advocated careers in which promotion was by merit rather than by influence and patronage: law and medicine were open and competitive; the church and the armed services were not. Edgeworth's own brothers accordingly went into law, medicine, the less socially acceptable engineering, and Indian administration. The contrast throws into relief the situation and attitude of the Austens. Much less well off than the Edgeworths (R. L. Edgeworth's income as an Irish landed proprietor ranged from £2,000 to £4,000), they did enjoy, through their family contacts on both sides, access to useful patronage. The qualities admired in male characters in Austen's novels include vigor and effectiveness, the qualities of those who rise by talent; the qualities reprobated are laziness, dullness, and frivolity, especially in high places. Austen is no friend to the idle rich, and she does not love a lord. It is insufficiently exact, then, to align her with the landed gentry; her values resemble those of her younger professional brothers, the sailors, who had to advance by two means—gentility, meaning the right personal characteristics as well as the right influential backing, and "merit," or competence. It is important that Austen felt and thought with these professionals (and indeed as a writer herself joined yet another profession) rather than with the older brothers, who fitted the classic gentry mold, the clergyman and landed proprietor.

Austen gives many readers the impression that she describes immemorial English village life, centered on the great house and rectory, but this is not so. In the only novel in which the great house and rectory are important, *Mansfield Park,* the village community does not appear. In fact, Austen never experienced this "normal" rural situation in her own life. At Steventon, in her girlhood the major landowner, Thomas Knight II, was an absentee; when her brother Edward took over in 1797, he continued to live in Kent, and his large houses at Steventon and Chawton were let to tenants. This meant that the rector's family was of consequence around Steventon, as representatives of the landowner, but it also confined their circle to the clergy of adjoining parishes and the owners or tenants of half a dozen substantial houses within reach. "Three or four families in a country village," Austen's favorite topic, sounds like a clever artistic contrivance, but in a sparse countryside the families it was not demeaning to visit were similarly limited. When she stayed at her brother Edward's home in Kent, by contrast, she moved between the great houses of his wealthy neighbors —but as an outsider, the spinster and aunt living, after her father's death in 1805, on a personal spending allowance of £20 a year. Her niece Fanny Knight, afterward Lady Knatchbull, did not remember her as a social equal:

> They [Cassandra and Jane] were not rich & the people around with whom they chiefly mixed, were not at all high bred, or in short anything more than *mediocre* & *they* of course tho' superior in Mental Powers & *cultivation* were on the same level as far as *refinement* goes—but . . . Aunt Jane was too clever not to put aside all possible signs of "common-ness" (if such an expression is allowable) & teach herself to be more refined, at least in intercourse with people in general. . . . If it had not been for Papa's marriage . . . they would have been . . . very much below par as to good Society and its ways. ("Aunt Jane," *Cornhill Magazine*, 163 [1947–49], pp. 72–73)

Austen's life divides into three phases: the first twenty-five years in the rectory at Steventon; the next nine, in various lodgings at Bath and in a household shared with Frank at Southampton; the last eight, in a small house owned by Edward at Chawton, where the final versions of all the novels were written. The letters and novels suggest that her life was not uniformly happy in these locations. The middle period was personally the bleakest, but for more general reasons, too, her perspective darkened, and her last years are less sanguine than her youth. At Steventon she was actively in search of a husband; she records the visits and the assemblies at nearby Basingstoke attended for that purpose and takes note of the marriageable men. Her father's decision to move to Bath at the end of 1800 may have been intended to improve his daughters' chances of marriage, but in Bath he and they lost the advantage they had enjoyed at Steventon, of kinship with the landowner. At Bath they became neighbors of Mrs. Austen's brother, James Leigh Perrot, and his wife, about whom Austen's letters are not warm; perhaps the couple resembled the Viscountess Dalrymple and her daughter Miss Carteret (*P*), for whose acquaintance the Elliots pay too high a price. Austen's letters from Bath suggest a growing distaste for social gatherings—"Another stupid party last night . . . I cannot anyhow continue to find people agreable" (*Letters*, May 12, 1801), and an episode at Southampton frankly suggests that the problem was being poor when others were rich: "whether [Mrs Lance] boasts any offspring besides a grand pianoforte did not appear.... They will not come often, I dare say. They live in a handsome style and are rich, and she seemed to like to be rich, and we gave her to understand that we were far from being so; she will soon feel therefore that we are not worth her acquaintance" (*Letters*, January 7, 1807).

Austen returned to Hampshire in 1809 a much more experienced social observer than when she had left it. She had stayed at Bath, Devon coastal resorts, the naval town of Southampton, and Godmersham and other Kentish mansions. But she had also learned a new perspective on this gentry society from the sibling she grew closer to after 1800, the sailor Frank. She saw Frank in 1805 in Kent, for he was in charge of coastal defenses there at a time when Napoleon was believed to be about to invade. There is a disparaging remark in one of her letters of that summer that the Kentish gentry were fretful because the troop movements of that anxious summer might disturb the game (*Letters*, August 30, 1805; the episode is explored in Warren Roberts, pp. 80–88). In 1807–1809, while she lived at Southampton, she saw naval activity at close quarters; up to this time, it was sailors rather than soldiers who had done almost all the fighting on the British side and won all the victories. It seems a fair speculation that the more sharply focused and critical portrait of the gentry she gives in her last three novels, *Mansfield Park, Emma*, and *Persuasion*, the only three begun at Chawton, was fostered by the alternative way of life and more combative, energetic values she met during her exile from the countryside.

Chawton is physically unlike barren, upland Steventon. It is prettier, more fertile and prosperous looking, and at that time was much busier, since it was at the fork of two main roads, from London to Gosport and to Winchester. Mrs. Austen and her daughters were soon on friendly terms with Edward Knight's tenants at Chawton House—who oddly enough were called Middleton, like the family in the great house near the Dashwoods in *Sense and Sensibility*, the novel that Austen now revised (1811). The Austens were soon calling frequently at other genteel households within walking distance, one naval officer retired on half pay, the clergymen of Chawton and neighboring parishes, other clergy widows and daughters like themselves; Jane also walked about exchanging library books of the flourishing Book Society or walked (in her last years, drove a donkey cart) a little over a mile into the nearby town of Alton. From Alton it was possible to take a coach to London and get there in the day; Winchester, where Edward's sons were at school, was also within reach. This accessibility of Chawton must have helped to bring in its heterogeneous society, unlike Steventon's, its rentiers and retired gentlefolk with no link with the land. Chawton society, as Oliver MacDonagh has pointed out, resembles the almost suburban world of *Emma* rather than the traditional nuclear village grouped around the great house and rectory.

Highbury in *Emma* is a community in a transitional phase: though it has a full complement of small-town occupations (squire, parson, lawyer, apothecary, draper, innkeeper, baker, schoolmistress, smith, parish clerk, ostler, steward, servants), it continues to observe social hierarchy with great nicety, and the place is small enough for everyone to feel bound to be civil to everyone else. At only sixteen miles from London, Highbury no longer feels quite like country; but then Hampshire has a border with suburbanizing Surrey not far from Chawton, and as Austen's letters suggest and other observers from about 1810 confirm, real-life counterparts of the Coleses, Westons, and Bateses were now moving into its prettier, more accessible villages.

Austen was accurately recording social change, but only some of it. When Arthur Young visited Hampshire in 1767, he observed a prosperous county, with wages at the national average and laborers' housing good. There were enough light industries in the towns, and weaving in the cottages, for laborers' families to make up for the drop in farm wages in winter. During Austen's lifetime, these light industries failed; her nephew, James Edward Austen-Leigh, born in 1798 at Steventon, could only just remember weaving in the cottages there, for it was superseded by the factories setting up nearer to supplies of coal. As the price of corn rose under wartime conditions, more Hampshire common land was enclosed; the rich became very rich, but there was less work for the poor, and many of the fittest went to the towns, often to the booming dockyards of Portsmouth and Southampton or to the new seaside resorts. With peace in 1815, prices fetched by corn fell again, bringing distress to landlords, farmers, and laborers alike. According to the returns sent back to the Board of Agriculture in 1816, the year of *Emma*, many Hampshire rents had fallen by 25–33 percent, and many farms were deserted, while laborers were wandering about in search of work. (See the *Victoria County History: Hampshire*, vol. 5, pp. 502–504.)

Austen would not have failed to observe the lot of the poor, toward whom she always gave charitably. She could not have failed to, because the destitute were supported by local taxes, a parish rate levied on the better off. Many Hampshire farmers now saved money by laying off their laborers after the harvest, so that the rest of the community, their neighbors, had to support the laborers' families through the winter. This kind of economic selfishness by sections of the community brought into focus a postwar phenomenon, conscious class hostility, and bore hard on those just above the poor, such as widows and daughters on small fixed incomes. In fact, the Austens as a whole family felt the postwar financial insecurity. The failure of the Alton bank, in which Henry was a partner, brought down his London firm in 1816. Even their wealthy brother Edward suffered damage, as Henry's guarantor; and Edward had his own trouble, a rival claimant to the Chawton estate, which brought in two-thirds of his income. The case eventually had to be settled out of court for £15,000, roughly the equivalent of half a million dollars in today's currency.

Austen's social world, which her biographers often represent as enviably stable, was in flux: fortunes being made elsewhere, new families moving in, resorts booming, while the estates, farms, and remoter inland villages decayed. Her letters do not record this condition: they display none of that zeal for documentation so common at the time. Her novels say nothing of the plight of the Hampshire farmer and laborer, which her contemporary Cobbett protests so eloquently about, nothing of the impact of enclosure on landscape that so grieved Clare in Northamptonshire. Perhaps the feminine taboo against comment and generalization kept her from discussing the lives of classes other than her own. Yet her novels, especially the last two and *Sanditon*, closely and brilliantly record economic and social change in southern English village life and the implications for received manners and attitudes of the gentry. More in *Persuasion* and *Sanditon* even than in *Emma*, social mobility is enacted by restless characters; the consumer boom appears in the reckless profusion of objects in the Musgrove parlor at Uppercross, the blue shoes and nankin boots in the shoemaker's window at Sanditon. The last group of novels do generalize, in that they depict southern England, turning successively to the counties bordering Hampshire: Surrey in *Emma*, Dorset in *Persuasion*, Sussex in *Sanditon*. The Parkers and Denhams of *Sanditon* are the ultimate, most trenchant examples of that kind of social observation that first appeared with the Bertrams and Rushworths of *Mansfield Park* and is extended with the Elliots and Musgroves of *Persuasion*: these are the representative gentry of the postwar era, coldly and even satirically viewed. How is such outspokenness compatible with the acceptance of feminine limitation that is so marked a feature of the earlier novels and of the letters? The answer is most readily found in that sphere in which a general change can be observed among the Austens, the sphere of religion.

Austen's Religion: Anglicans and Evangelicals

Austen's was a clergy family even more decidedly than it was a gentry family. Her father and two of her brothers were clergymen, as were her mother's father and grandfather and several cousins. Her sister Cassandra was engaged to a clergyman, and it was believed in the family that Jane fell in love with one. The eighteenth-century church was a prime choice of career for a wellborn younger son, since landed families had livings to bestow or could buy them. This situation is so standard that in her three novels begun in the 1790s Austen represents clergymen in almost wholly matter-of-fact career terms. The decision of Edward Ferrars in *Sense and Sensibility* to enter the church is made against his family's wishes, and perhaps the reader infers that Edward feels a strong sense of religious vocation, but this is not said. When Colonel Brandon presents him with a living, he reacts not by visiting his new parishioners but by worrying because he can now afford to get married, which unhappily means marrying Lucy Steele. Even after his marriage to Elinor, it is not his clerical duties that we hear about but the couple's home building as they choose their wallpaper and plant the shrubbery. Henry Tilney of *Northanger Abbey* is introduced in even more secular guise, as a fashionable man-about-Bath and nonresident in the parish his father has given him. Catherine's father, the Reverend Richard Morland, possesses two good livings. Nonresidency and pluralism came under sustained attack as clerical abuses about the turn of the century, but in the 1790s Austen cannot have perceived them as delicate issues.

What she does suggest throughout her work is that Church of England clergymen are better when they are born gentlemen. Her clerics divide into attractive ones, who are invariably the social equals of the squire, and unattractive ones, who are socially inferior. Ferrars, Tilney, and Edmund Bertram, like Catherine Morland's brother James, obtain their livings through the patronage of a father or other family connection; Mr. Collins and Mr. Elton, having got theirs through more awkward maneuvering, have more difficulty afterward in maintaining their dignity. Taken out of context, the satirical vignette of Lady Catherine de Bourgh and her toady Mr. Collins might appear to satirize the close link between state and church, for it resembles many contemporary squibs against the Establishment. But when all Austen's clergymen are considered together, they suggest that she took as axiomatic the interdependence of great house and rectory and wanted the social status of the church side of the alliance kept up.

In eighteenth-century terms, the Reverend George Austen was a virtuous, even exemplary, clergyman. But styles were changing before he retired, and both his mild pluralism, as rector of adjoining parishes, and his zest for reading comedy and watching his children act plays could have been questioned in the first decade of the next century. By then, his eldest son, James, who began his clerical career in the early 1790s as a rector or curate of four small parishes, and did not reside in three of them, was turning down the offer of a second living in addition to Steventon, apparently as a matter of principle. The sailor Frank, whose patron Admiral Gambier was a noted Evangelical, attracted attention with his piety: an observer at Ramsgate noticed him as "the officer who knelt in church" (Hubback and Hubback, p. 114). In 1805 and 1806 Frank went on two voyages to the West Indies, during which he called at Antigua and formed a hostile view of the treatment of slaves there. Meanwhile, Cassandra was reading works intended for women by the Evangelicals Thomas Gisborne and Hannah More and recommending them to Jane. Their brother Henry at last in 1816 reverted to his earlier idea of taking orders, to become "an earnest preacher of the evangelical school" (*Life*, p. 333). Austen's brothers and sister were part of the movement that did so much to change the tone of genteel life in the early nineteenth century.

Jane Austen's own letters in her last decade exhibit a new willingness to speak directly of religion and some remorse for the sprightliness and even malice she had freely allowed herself in the 1790s. She also composed prayers that illustrate the Evangelical habit of self-scrutiny: "Teach us to understand the sinfulness of our own hearts.... Incline us oh God! to think humbly of ourselves, to be severe only in the examination of our own conduct, to consider our fellow-creatures with kindness" (*Prayers*, pp. 453 and 456). In 1814 Fanny Knight, the eldest daughter of opulent Godmersham Park, that niece who afterward remembered her aunt Jane as dowdy, sought Austen's advice about a proposal of marriage. Fanny was evidently inclined to view the young man, John Pemberton Plumtre, as comically unfashionable because he was Evangelical. Austen's reply, most gently and tactfully worded, may have helped create the suspicion that she was "below par," for it defends Plumtre's style as well as his principles: "I am by no means convinced that we ought not all to be Evangelicals" (*Letters*, November 18, 1814).

It is easy for moderns to confuse Evangelicals with eighteenth-century Methodists or with the lower-middle-class Low Church party in the Victorian era; as Fanny Knight shows, some contemporaries did dislike them for snobbish reasons. Another view of their social position in Austen's day is given by Spring, Garside, Monaghan, and Roberts, whose relevant writings are listed in the bibliography. During the war against France and against "revolution principles," pressure for a renewed commitment to religious and moral principle was not so much petit bourgeois as characteristic of members of the gentry, especially of those sections of the gentry that were, like the younger Austens, merging with the new professional classes. William Wilberforce, the campaigner against slavery, was a Tory landed gentleman; Zachary Macaulay, a wealthy London merchant, whose *Christian Observer* demonstrated the cultivated, intellectual tastes of the best-known group of Evangelical activists, the so-called Clapham Sect. What energized these lobbyists and gave them a sense of common cause was the wartime need for leadership, duty, setting a good example to inferiors, without which the hierarchical society in which these social conservatives believed could not survive the challenge from outside and from below. "Reform or ruin," a rallying cry of Wilberforce's from the 1790s, was adopted by the propertied classes sufficiently generally to signal the beginning of that seriousness that we think of as Victorian.

The shift in contemporary religious sensibility plays an important part in the evolution of the three last and best Austen novels. *Pride and Prejudice*, best of the earlier group, remains intellectually unformed and inconsistent. Not only Lydia but the author seems to find Mr. Collins absurd when he proposes to read sermons to the Bennet daughters; again, this is a detail that suggests unawareness rather than hostility to an Evangelical campaign. And yet there are hints elsewhere in *Pride and Prejudice* that Austen aligned herself with criticisms of the higher aristocracy, notably the Whig grandees, who in the eighteenth century competed in the display of their wealth as well as their taste. Lady Catherine's haughtiness crudely caricatures the idea of aristocracy. Her nephew Fitzwilliam Darcy conveys more subtly Austen's reservations about the higher reaches of her class. The name Fitzwilliam links him to one leading Whig family, and his estate, Pemberley, with another, for to us it strongly evokes Chatsworth, the Derbyshire home of the fabulously wealthy and fashionable duke of Devonshire. But if Pemberley suggests Chatsworth because of its location and in the external impression of house and grounds, once Elizabeth views the inside, it is not, pointedly, Chatsworth at all. The fifth duke of Devonshire had pillaged Europe to assemble one of the world's great art collections. Pemberley is the ideal gentleman's house conceived by an austerer taste, where the paintings are portraits of ancestors and prestige is measured by the approval of tenants—and even more significantly, of Elizabeth's lawyer uncle, Mr. Gardiner, a professional man from a family of gentry.

Here criticism of aristocracy and profligacy is not yet connected with religion. The first novel to show overt Evangelical influence, indeed the one thoroughgoing Evangelical novel Austen wrote, is *Mansfield Park*. As already suggested, this novel, begun in 1813, betrays the personal influence of her sailor brother Frank, who, to judge by her letters, represents her final ideal image of masculinity: she writes, for example, of the "thinking, clear, considerate" style of his letters and of his cheerful, useful domestic activities, and she loyally seconds his claims for promotion (*Letters*, March 5, 1814; February 20, 1807; December 24, 1798). It must have been her involvement in Frank's activities that led her in 1813 to read Pasley's *Essay on the Military Policy and Institutions of the British Empire* (1810), an uncharacteristic book for her, about how the nation could use its unique spirit and skill to fight off the French even if the national shield, the navy, failed. *Mansfield Park* resembles a novelist's and civilian's meditation from

Pasley's starting point, an imaginative defense of the nation against enemies without and within. It is concerned not so much with the spiritual redemption as with the moral rearming of the gentry.

Mansfield Park sketches the gentry of the end-of-war period unflatteringly: the Bertrams; some friends of their elder daughter and elder son, Rushworth and Yates; the rector, Dr. Grant, who would not be there but for Tom's extravagance; and Mrs. Grant's brother and sister, the fashionable Crawfords. It is thus the eldest children, the two with the best hopes of becoming landowners, who let in feckless strangers carrying a moral infection that gains ground during their father's absence. The younger son, the would-be clergyman Edmund, upholds the new Evangelical professionalism and seriousness; with his father's approval, he means to reside in his parish—despite Henry Crawford's offer to rent his rectory and Mary Crawford's campaign to deter him from being a clergyman at all.

Fleishman argues that Austen cannot be considered an Evangelical because the details of Edmund's ordination do not fit current Evangelical precept. This is to miss the underlying goal of the movement, a broad change of feeling rather than specific reforms. The novel unmistakably refers to a range of issues that the contemporary reader would identify as Evangelical, though Austen refrains from directly advocating them: nonresidence; family worship; private self-examination (Fanny's use of the schoolroom) rather than worldly knowledge and accomplishments (her cousins'); slavery, which Sir Thomas tries to discuss on his return from Antigua, though only Fanny is interested; and amateur acting, which Evangelicals disliked both because rehearsing encouraged familiarity and because so many current plays were unsuitable.

On all these topics, Fanny thinks rightly, though by making her a child in the first half of the book, Austen avoids any need for her to preach. Fanny emerges from a naval family at Portsmouth, and she is the means of introducing to Mansfield her sailor brother William, whose energetic pursuit of his ill-rewarded civic-minded career reflects tellingly on the idleness of the Bertrams and Crawfords. Critics have surely dwelt too much on Fanny's awareness of the discomforts of the household at Portsmouth, when she returns there, and on her preference for life at Mansfield. Portsmouth has bred into Fanny and William self-reliance, religion, brotherly and sisterly affection, and the work ethic. Not the drunken Lieutenant Price or the slatternly Mrs. Price but (despite both of them) the profession of seafaring equips the Price children to save Mansfield Park.

For her sailor characters, Austen draws on her own brothers. Charles in 1801 sent her a topaz cross, like William's amber one in *Mansfield Park*, while Frank's attributes and career are divided between Wentworth, Harville, and Benwick, the sailors in *Persuasion*. More importantly, the sailors in *Persuasion* again stand for energy, feeling, patriotism, a better alternative than what is available on land, against the snobbery and selfishness of the Elliots, the moral chaos and incompetence of the Musgroves, the cold calculation and vulgarity of William Walter Elliot and Mrs. Clay. Feeling is not just an amiable personal characteristic. The Crofts and Wentworth, the landless weather-beaten professionals Sir Walter Elliot despises, have just saved the country by winning what Austen certainly regarded as a Christian war. Britain had, "in spite of much Evil," a claim to the protection of heaven against a less godly power (such as America in 1814), for Britain, "a Religious Nation," was improving in religion (*Letters,* September 2, 1814). Without losing her faith in leadership and religion, the two ideals of her order, Austen had now separated them from the landowners and clergy and given them to sailors.

Modern readers, who expect literature to be primarily concerned with private experience, also think of religion as a private affair. Because Austen's novels become religiously more explicit, critics have claimed that she becomes "inner-directed" in the nineteenth-century, or romantic, manner. Expressing it in such terms ignores the national significance and the public aims of the wartime religious reform movement spearheaded by the Evangelicals. Austen's last three novels are profounder than the first three not because they express an inward religious intensity but because they are caught up in a national mood of self-assessment and regeneration. This most retired and reticent of novelists both observes movements of history and participates in them.

Bibliography

BROWN, JULIA PREWITT. *Jane Austen's Novels: Social Change and Literary Form* (Cambridge, Mass., 1979).
BUTLER, MARILYN. *Maria Edgeworth: A Literary Biography* (Oxford, 1972).
———. *Jane Austen and the War of Ideas* (Oxford, 1975).
———. *Romantics, Rebels and Reactionaries: English Literature and Its Background, 1760–1830* (Oxford, 1981 and New York, 1982).
———, ed. *Burke, Paine, Godwin and the Revolution Controversy* (Cambridge, England, 1984).
DUCKWORTH, ALISTAIR M. *The Improvement of the Estate* (Baltimore and London, 1971).
EDGEWORTH, MARIA. *Helen*, 3 vols. (London, 1834).
FLEISHMAN, AVROM. *A Reading of "Mansfield Park"* (Minneapolis, Minn., 1967).
GARSIDE, PETER AND ELIZABETH MCDONALD. "Evangelicalism and *Mansfield Park*," *Trivium*, 10 (1975), 34–50.
GILBERT, SANDRA M. AND SUSAN GUBAR. *The Madwoman in the Attic* (New Haven and London, 1981).

HODGE, JANE AIKEN. *The Double Life of Jane Austen* (London, 1972).
HOPKINSON, DAVID. "The Naval Career of Jane Austen's Brother," *History Today*, 26 (1976), 576–83.
HUBBACK, JOHN H. AND EDITH C. HUBBACK. *Jane Austen's Sailor Brothers* (London and New York, 1906).
MACDONAGH, OLIVER. "Highbury and Chawton: Social Convergence in *Emma*," *Historical Studies* [Melbourne], 18 (1978–79), 37–51.
MONAGHAN, DAVID. *Jane Austen: Structure and Social Vision* (London, 1980).
———, ed. *Jane Austen in a Social Context* (London, 1981).
———. "*Mansfield Park* and Evangelicalism: A Reassessment," *Nineteenth-century Fiction*, 33 (1978–79), 215–30.
ROBERTS, WARREN. *Jane Austen and the French Revolution* (London, 1979).
SHELLEY, PERCY BYSSHE. Preface to *Prometheus Unbound* (London, 1820).
SMITHERS, DAVID WALDRON. *Jane Austen in Kent* (Westerham, Kent, 1982).
SOUTHAM, B. C. "*Sanditon*: The Seventh Novel," in Juliet McMaster, ed., *Jane Austen's Achievement* (London, 1976).
SPRING, DAVID. "Aristocracy, Social Structure, and Religion in the Early Victorian Period," *Victorian Studies*, 6 (1962–63), 263–80.
TUCKER, GEORGE HOLBERT. *A Goodly Heritage: A History of Jane Austen's Family* (Manchester, 1983).
Victoria County History: Hampshire and the Isle of Wight, H. Arthur Doubleday, ed., 6 vols. (London, 1900–1912).

HOUSES

J. David Grey

As in her descriptions of terrain, weather, costume, physiognomy, and so forth, Jane Austen leaves most of the details concerning her houses to the reader's imagination. Through the gift of her genius, however, her unique style somehow evokes the setting, architecture, even furnishings, of the houses in her novels so perfectly that as abodes they are only slightly less "real" than her characters. Each is a dwelling as different from any other as the social position, temperament, and aspirations (or lack of them) of its occupants demand. More importantly, each has a varying degree of emotional significance to its inhabitants.

Jane Austen touchingly recounts the pangs of separation that Marianne Dashwood suffers the evening before her enforced departure from "Dear, dear Norland" Park in Sussex: "when shall I cease to regret you!—when learn to feel a home elsewhere!—Oh! happy house" (*SS*, p. 27). She and her mother and sisters move to Barton Cottage in Devonshire, and Jane Austen gives an unusually detailed description of the cottage to serve as contrast to the vacated Norland:

> As a house, Barton Cottage, though small, was comfortable and compact; but as a cottage it was defective, for the building was regular, the roof was tiled, the window shutters were not painted green, nor were the walls covered with honeysuckles. A narrow passage led directly through the house into the garden behind. On each side of the entrance was a sitting room, about sixteen feet square; and beyond them were the offices and the stairs. Four bed-rooms and two garrets formed the rest of the house. (p. 28)

The cottage is furnished in a style that pleases Mrs. Dashwood, but she immediately sets about planning such improvements as widening the staircase, enlarging one of the two parlors, and adding a new dining room "in the spring, if I have plenty of money" (p. 29). Books, a pianoforte, and Elinor's drawings are quickly put in place "to form themselves a home" (p. 30). The regularities of the building, its tile roof and nongreen shutters, plus its lack of vine encrustation, however, do "not satisfy Marianne Dashwood's enthusiasm for tumble-down cottages. . . . her taste for the picturesque was . . . not long to be tried by a residence so ineligible, as she was mistress of Delaford within a year of becoming acquainted with its master" (*Architect*, p. 293). Appealing to Marianne's sensibility, Willoughby later objects to any consideration of altering such a "dear cottage. . . . Not a stone must be added to its walls, not an inch to its size, if my feelings are regarded" (p. 72).

The Middletons' Barton Park, half a mile away, is "large and handsome" (p. 32) and Mrs. Jennings's town house in London "handsome and handsomely fitted up" (p. 160). Delaford, in Dorsetshire, is a "nice old fashioned place, full of comforts and conveniences" (p. 196), just the right habitation for the reclusive and sedentary Colonel Brandon and, according to Gerald Wellesley, duke of Wellington, "a typical South country manor house of the Wren period" (p. 525). There is a dovecote, a stewpond, a canal, fruit orchards, and some excellent timber in Delaford Hanger. This typifies Barbara Hardy's "sympathetic habitat," one that persists throughout Jane Austen's novels: "She invented the suitably malleable material which made the house the right kind of shell for its occupant" (p. 137). Edward Ferrars and Elinor Dashwood, when themselves a happily married couple at Delaford, finally occupy what is undoubtedly the largest parsonage in the novels—it has five sitting rooms and possible sleeping facilities for fifteen! The landscaping at the Palmers' Cleveland, in Somersetshire, is given special attention. Fir, mountain ash, Lombardy poplars, and open shrubbery surround a gravel road that leads to the "spacious, modern-built house, situated on a sloping lawn" (p. 302).

"The houses in *Pride and Prejudice* are nearly all taken for granted by the author because they are taken for granted by the characters" (Hardy, p. 152). Neither Longbourn (according to Wellington, ca. 1770, p. 525) nor Netherfield receives any detailed treatment of its interior or surrounding grounds. The former had "decent looking rooms" in it according to Lady Catherine de Bourgh, that arbiter of taste (p. 353). Her own Rosings Park in Kent is another vague "handsome modern building, well situated on rising ground" (p. 156). One expects the entrance hall and the fabulously priced (£800) fireplace, which Wellington states could only have been commissioned by the great chimneypiece maker Carter, among whose clients were the Adams brothers. He concludes, therefore, that Rosings was built "almost certainly from the designs of Robert Adams" (p. 525). Mr. Collins is careful to point out Rosings' elaborate frontal fenestration in order to emphasize the expensive taste of the de Bourghs. Mrs. Phillips is mollified to learn that her single Meryton drawing room is the same size as Rosings' small summer breakfast parlor. Mr. Collins's Hunsford Parsonage lies just across the lane from the park. His own library, the dining parlor, and the drawing room (with its sideboard and fender) were "backwards," that is, they faced the lane. His wife, the former Charlotte Lucas, preferred a back sitting room, a situation that would be less apt to invite her husband's presence.

Pemberley looms large in the canon of Jane Austen's houses. With £10,000 a year, Darcy could have an establishment that would be almost ducal. After progressing half a mile past the entrance lodge, the Gardiners and Elizabeth Bennet arrive "at the top of a considerable eminence" from which Pemberley is visible across the valley. Once again we discover "a large, handsome, stone building, standing well on rising ground," but this house is "backed by a ridge of high woody hills" and fronted by "a stream of some natural importance" (p. 245). The housekeeper conducts the party through the large, lofty, well-proportioned ground-floor rooms, suitably furnished (Wellington: Chippendale or later) "to the position of their proprietor . . . neither gaudy nor uselessly fine; with less of splendor, and more real elegance, than . . . Rosings" (p. 246). Upstairs, they pass through Georgiana Darcy's elegant and light sitting room, some "principal bedrooms" (p. 250), and the imposing picture gallery. (This gallery leads Wellington to believe that Pemberley is either Elizabethan or Jacobean.) Returning from a saunter around the grounds—not the full ten-mile circuit, naturally:

> they were shewn through the hall into the saloon, whose northern aspect rendered it delightful for the summer. Its windows opening to the ground, admitted a most refreshing view of the high woody hills behind the house, and of the beautiful oaks and Spanish chesnuts which were scattered over the immediate lawn. (p. 267)

Indeed, "to be mistress of Pemberley might be something!" (p. 245).

If everything is right about Pemberley, all is definitely wrong about the houses in *Mansfield Park*. This is a novel, after all, about improvements, literal and figurative, architectural and individual. The grounds at Mansfield Park are half the size of Pemberley's. The former is "spacious," "modern-built" and "well placed," "wanting only to be completely new furnished," in Mary Crawford's opinion (p. 48). There is the usual complement of rooms, to which is added Fanny Price's unheated accommodations in the attic story. These were, at least, lighted by dormers. For Wellington, the billiard room was significant: "The erection of the stage for the theatricals damaged the plasterwork, which was therefore in high relief. Very likely it was the work of the Italian plasterers Atari or Bugatti, who decorated the houses of Gibbs and his contemporaries" (p. 525). He concludes that Mansfield was Palladian, dating about 1740. Mrs. Norris has purposely chosen to remove herself from the parsonage after her husband's demise, to the small White House, "being only just large enough to receive herself and her servants, and allow a spare room for a friend" (p. 28). Thornton Lacey, "a solid walled, roomy, mansion-like looking house" (p. 243) is Edmund Bertram's impending living, and Henry Crawford (who has his own estate at Everingham, Norfolk), thoroughly imbued with Humphry Repton's ideas and the current craze for improvement, has some rather radical changes to suggest for it. The farmyard must be eliminated and the house itself "turned" to face the east. A new garden should be planted on the south side and "something done with the stream" (p. 242).

But it is Sotherton Court, a "capital freehold mansion, and ancient manorial residence, . . . with all its rights of Court-Leet and Court-Baron" (p. 82), that everyone except its owner Mr. Rushworth considers in dire need of renovation. Maria Bertram deplores the condition of the cottages in the village and would silence the church bells. The parsonage, almshouses, and a steward's house all precede the lodge gates, a mile from the house, with its 700 acres. "The house was built in Elizabeth's time, and is a large, regular, brick building—heavy, but respectable looking, and has many good rooms. It is ill placed. It stands in one of the lowest spots of the park; in that respect, unfavourable for improvement" (p. 56). The rooms are "all lofty, and many large, and amply furnished in the taste of fifty years back, with shining floors, solid mahogany, rich damask, marble, gilding and carving, each handsome in its way" (p. 84). After a visit to the private chapel, "a mere, spacious, oblong room, fitted up for the purpose of devotion" (p. 85), in which even Fanny is disappointed, the gathering moves outdoors: "The lawn, bounded on each side by a high wall, contained beyond the first planted ærea, a bowling green, and beyond the bowling-green a long terrace walk, backed by iron palissades, and commanding a view over them into the tops of the trees of the wilderness immediately adjoining" (p. 90). With £2,000 more a year than Mr. Darcy, there would have been great hopes for the Rushworths' future enjoyment at Sotherton and in their London town house on Wimpole Street, had Maria not incurred her own permanent banishment from the scene.

There is absolutely no hope for improving the thin-walled Price household in Portsmouth. Fanny mistakes her parents' downstairs parlor for a passage room, and

> there was nothing to raise her spirits in the confined and scantily-furnished chamber that she was to share with Susan. The smallness of the rooms above and below indeed, and the narrowness of the passage and staircase, struck her beyond her imagination. She soon learnt to think with respect of her own little attic at Mansfield Park, in *that* house reckoned too small for anybody's comfort. (p. 387)

Jane Austen pays least attention to the houses in *Emma*. Hartfield, only a "notch in the Donwell Abbey estate" (p. 136), has "small, but neat and pretty" grounds and is "modern and well-built" (p. 272) but is otherwise only identifiable by Augusta Elton's ebullient comparison of it with Maple Grove. According to Emma Woodhouse, George Knightley's Donwell Abbey, larger than Hartfield, is "rambling and irregular, with many comfortable and one or two handsome rooms.—It was just what it ought to be, and it looked what it was" (p. 358). Its future mistress approves of its style, size, and situation and, apparently, the lack of improving influence that neither "fashion nor extravagance" had spoiled. Randalls is large enough to have two rooms thrown across to accommodate a ball, but if that were done, Mrs. Weston would be "in distress about the supper" (p. 248). The Eltons, despite both their pretensions, are relegated to an "old and not very good house, almost as close to the road as it could be. It had no advantage of situation; but had been very much smartened up by the present proprietor" (p. 83). Miss Nash, along with the rest of us, is invited to admire its yellow curtains and hope for the best in the future.

There are two Northanger abbeys—the real one and one that exists in Catherine Morland's fantasy world, channeled through the vivid imagination of Henry Tilney. (The latter's embroidery can be found on pp. 157–60.) Catherine's fancy is bolstered when she learns that Northanger had once been a "richly endowed convent," acquired by the Tilneys after the Dissolution, and that much of the ancient edifice had been incorporated into the modern dwelling. Her initial approach to the abbey was too rapid for more than a glimpse of the exterior. Passing through the porch and the hall, Catherine was astonished by "the profusion and elegance of modern taste" (p. 162). "The prettiest English China" adorns the fireplace, a rather small one of recent design. Nikolaus Pevsner says that this is actually a kitchen range, first designed by Sir Benjamin Thompson, "Count Rumford," for a nobleman in Munich in 1789. If nothing else, General Tilney is au courant. The window arches of the abbey are pointed, but the mullion and tracery have been replaced with large, clear panes—there is no stained glass, not even dirt or cobwebs. The absence of such gothic appurtenances was very distressing to Catherine. Further to her disappointment, there was no tapestry in her own room, only wallpaper, no velvet, only carpeting. The "noble" dining room, though, was "fitted up in a style of luxury and expense which was almost lost on [her] unpractised eye" (pp. 165–66). An account of Catherine's tour of the abbey may be found on pages 182–84 of the novel.

The Elliots' Kellynch Hall in Somerset is left completely to the imagination except for a reference to the excessive number of looking glasses with which it is endowed. The senior Musgroves' Great House at Uppercross has "high walls, great gates, and old trees" (p. 36). The Musgrove children throw the "old-fashioned square parlour, with a small carpet and shining floor" into a state of confusion with their "grand piano forte and a harp, flower-stands and little tables placed in every direction" (p. 40). Wellington claims that "Uppercross was obviously a William and Mary or Queen Anne house" (p. 524).

Anne Elliot is at first astonished by the small size of the Harvilles' accommodations near the Cobb in Lyme Regis. The surprise soon turns to admiration for Captain Harville's "ingenious contrivances and nice arrangements" (p. 98), which render the cottage homey and homely. The display of curious and valuable objects that he has accumulated worldwide lend her something "more, or less, than gratification."

Naturally, Sir Walter rents the best house in Camden Place in Bath. The superiority of his drawing rooms there rendered his and his daughter's acquaintance "exceedingly sought after" (p. 137): Anne marvels

> as Elizabeth threw open the folding-doors, and walked with exultation from one drawing-room to the other, boasting of their space, at the possibility of that woman, who had been mistress of Kellynch Hall, finding extent to be proud of between two walls, perhaps thirty feet asunder. (p. 138)

"Anne Elliot is alone among Miss Austen's heroines in marrying a man who has no settled home. . . . Anne marries a sailor and her future must all be imagined" (*Architect*, p. 294).

All of Jane Austen's houses are homes. Their loss, either potential or real homelessness, is crucial to the lives of many key characters. The Dashwoods are uprooted from the east to the west of England. The inevitable removal from Longbourn is a constant source of fear to the Bennets. Fanny Price is sent from home, and she and Edmund must eventually settle for far less than what was given them at Mansfield. Jane Fairfax is on the brink of anonymity as a governess. Sir Walter's extravagances force the belt-tightening removal from Kellynch to Bath. As homes, the houses in Jane Austen can be either inviting or cold. The happy few have a Pemberley or Donwell Abbey in which they will spend their lives in happiness and security.

Bibliography

ANONYMOUS. "Jane Austen's Country Houses," *Architect*, 101 (1919), 293–94.
HARDY, BARBARA. *A Reading of Jane Austen* (London, 1975).
PEVSNER, SIR NIKOLAUS. "The Architectural Setting of Jane Austen's Novels," *Journal of the Warburg and Courtauld Institutes*, 31 (1968), 404–22.
WELLESLEY, LORD GERALD (LATER 7TH DUKE OF WELLINGTON). "Houses in Jane Austen's Novels" (1926); reprinted in *Collected Reports of the Jane Austen Society, 1949–1965* (London, 1967), 185–88.

ILLUSTRATING JANE AUSTEN

Joan Hassall

There are two types of pictures with which one can illustrate a book, setting aside decorative additions that are not necessarily connected with its subject. There is the "comment," usually in the form of a headpiece or tailpiece, where the artist makes his extension of the text; and there is the more direct representation of incident, people, and places as dictated by the author. Both of these have their own special joys and hazards. I am aware that my best work is on a small scale, which is why I have tended to prefer the first category, but when one is asked to illustrate such beloved books as those of Jane Austen, all caution flies to the winds. How can an artist do justice to such writing? He or she can only give a "sort of idea" of the people and places of which every reader will have formed his own images.

I have often been asked how I choose which episodes to depict, and the answer has surprised the questioner. Let us take for example *Persuasion*, for which I was to do thirteen wood engravings in the text and a frontispiece. There is a temptation to choose one's favorite incidents, with the result that all the pictures might fall close together in one part of the book. That would not do at all! An illustrated book must not be like an ill-mixed cake with all the fruit in one place. My method of choosing was simple. I put thirteen paper markers into the book at regular intervals and then looked to see what event near the markers would inspire me. The books are so packed with incident that I was never at a loss. With the frontispiece, one's choice was more free. The only compulsory factor was that the subject should make a good upright design.

The next stage was to do very rough compositions, deciding whether they should be upright or landscape, and these were sent to the publisher, who could then proceed with making up his pages of type, leaving appropriate gaps for the blocks. When possible, the longways or landscape shape looks better on a page with type. Finally, there was the assembling of the references needed, and this sometimes necessitated journeys to Bath, Lyme Regis, and so on. The accident to Louisa Musgrove becomes much more intelligible when one sees the unprotected steps on the Cobb.

The subject of fashion is delightful and of paramount importance. Should one use the mode of the time in which the book was written or of when it was published? I have chosen the former. One must be cautious when using fashion plates, and a moment's consideration of the drawings that appear in the press of our own day and the relation they bear to the humans who look at them will exemplify this. How many of us are over seven feet high with impossibly slender legs and figures to match! Fashion plates of the past told the same pleasing lies, nor must we forget that the lady's own stuffs would be made up by the village dressmaker or the great house's sewing maid, who did their best to copy them. I am old enough to remember one of the last of the sewing ladies, who used to come in by the day to a room made over for her use. I am afraid she was very poor. Her productions were singularly shapeless and not much like the model, which was often a dress belonging to a better-off cousin. Rich ladies would go to a fashion house where many underpaid girls would stitch by hand and in wonderfully short time produce a passable imitation of the latest fashion, the final fit being achieved with pins in the girl's own bedroom by the lady's maid. She would be equally necessary for the undressing, and one does wonder how Fanny Price managed to dress herself for her first ball without a maid, even though Lady Bertram sent Dawson to her, too late to be of any use. For these reasons I find it more useful to look at portraits, conversation pieces, and children's books for ideas. One must not forget that elderly ladies would remain attached to the fashions of their prime, and in those days, when dresses were built to last, economy caused the wearer to cling to a garment. I like to preserve these niceties in my illustrations. Before the later Victorian period artists and writers seem to have been oblivious of preceding styles and were quite content for their characters to appear in contemporary costume, with a few embellishments to denote royalty or a foreigner. Emily Brontë in *Wuthering Heights* gives a definite date, 1778, having just described her heroine as wearing a fine tartan silk dress over white trousers, a typical early Victorian costume for a child. I am aware that these refinements will go unnoticed, but the characters in Jane Austen's books are so real to me that I find myself pondering over different aspects of their lives. As with the clothes, so also with the surroundings. I am sure Mr. Woodhouse would have furnished his house for his bride, and therefore Emma would have grown up in the interiors of a generation earlier, and the same could be said of Northanger Abbey and Pemberley, though of the latter we are told that a pretty sitting room, lately fitted up with greater elegance and lightness than the apartments below, had just been completed to give pleasure to Miss Darcy.

There is another aspect to be considered, of illustration in general and theatrical productions, which is that the designer is unable to escape the influence of his own period. Faces and figures change over the years, but one of the most unyielding personal features is the hair style. If one thinks back to the lavish theater productions and paintings of the Victorian and Edwardian eras, one will recall statuesque ladies with wasp waists and bouffant hair attired in carefully researched dresses. The same applies to the cinema epics in which no expense has been spared on the costumes but the stars still cling to their modern hairdos. I am sure that my own work will display the same trends to future generations, but I am too close to my own era to see it.

I have looked with interest at the work of earlier artists in the collection of illustrated editions of Jane Austen in the British Library. In 1875 a very pretty version of *Mansfield Park* was produced by Groombridge, with four-color wood engravings in shades of lavender and gray, but when I turned the pages, there was Henry Crawford in a huge bushy black beard, addressing Fanny in flounces! Another edition of 1892 had generalized pictures, not illustrations of incidents, such as *Alone* or *Elinor drawing*. Hugh Thomson's lovely drawings must be known to most people, as they have often been reprinted since the beginning of the century. In 1898 a version came out illustrated by an artist who cannot have read the books attentively or else was badly affected by the "own period" trouble mentioned above, because Harriet Smith is shown as a tall, mannish woman with a determined chin!

And now we return full circle to the question of the illustrator's attempting to portray the characters in a well-loved book. Sometimes an author is fairly explicit, but Jane Austen does not give us a great deal of help. We are left to imagine what we like of Mr. Knightley and most of the men, but she does tell us that Marianne Dashwood had a clear brown skin, as also had Mary Crawford; it was evidently a quality she admired. To my mind, Marianne was like the portraits of Emma Hamilton by Romney, but I have often wondered what Miss Austen meant by saying that Elinor's figure was more "correct." The most one can hope to achieve is a pleasing presence in a suitable setting. I can truthfully assert that all places, landscapes, clothes, and furnishings are founded on references and that the figures inspired by photos, prints, and drawings are as flexible as a hard medium like wood engraving can allow. The second issue of the Folio Society books had additional pictures on scraper board, which gave greater freedom. I entirely reengraved the frontispiece to *Sense and Sensibility* because in the first version Elinor was not worthy of my conception of her. This was hard on the publisher, I know, as I was already past the deadline, but it seemed to me to be inevitable, and it had to be done. The decorative chapter-heading bands were formed from motifs taken from contemporary cotton prints, of which I once had a good collection. They are now in the Museum of Costume in Scotland and came into my possession in an interesting way. During World War II I was teaching art in Edinburgh, and there, in a sale of work for a good cause I saw a tea cozy made from patches of stuff that I recognized as being late eighteenth-century and regency prints. The lady who had brought it to the sale said her mother had made it from the patchwork bag of her great-grandmother, her own mother being then ninety years of age. She asked me to her house to meet the old lady, who was so good as to allow me to rummage in the precious bag and to keep any that I liked, as they were all destined to be made into bags and knickknacks. In this way I formed a collection of beautiful designs from about 1750 to 1840. This aged lady, who lived to be nearly one hundred, declared that her grandfather had been out with the 1745 rebellion! The design for the paper used on the boards of the binding came from the same source. In each case I engraved the design on wood, took a number of prints, and pasted them together to make a repeat pattern.

An illustrator cannot make too many studies before proceeding with a design. To do things "out of one's head" simply means that after a while that head will start repeating itself and rely on clichés, mannerisms, and types. To do so is to do less than one's best work.

ILLUSTRATIONS FOR JANE AUSTEN

Maggie Hunt Cohn

Jane Austen's first illustrator was her sister Cassandra. In her teens, Jane Austen wrote a "History of England"; it was dedicated to her sister, and for it Cassandra drew miniatures of thirteen of its famous personages. These reveal her witty eye, sense of character, and keen interest in fashion, although she clothed these distant historical figures in styles contemporary to herself. Henry VIII is red-capped, moustachioed, roguish; Henry VI is portrayed in dark clerical-type garb; Elizabeth is pointedly old, ugly, overdecorated with plumes and flowers, while lovely Mary, "Q of Skotts," is romantically swathed in a white shawl. Twelve of these portraits are reproduced in *Love and Freindship and Other Early Works*; Richard III is omitted.

None of the later illustrators could be as unselfconscious. It is not easy to do justice to such writing. In fact, most editions of the novels have been issued without pictures. At most, there is an illustration on the frontispiece, often a version of the only authentic portrait, also done by Cassandra. But admirers of beautiful books have wanted illustrations, and editors have done their best to oblige. One solution is to use materials contemporary to the novels: art, portraits, architecture, fashion, carriages, and the like. R. W. Chapman's editions opt for this method.

There are, however, seven or eight artists at least who have brought Jane Austen's scenes to visual artistic life in pictures for all six novels. Many, besides, illustrated individual novels, usually *Pride and Prejudice*. Richard Bentley's Standard Novels of the 1830s can claim to be the first complete works with illustrations—though with only a single picture in each novel. One "Pickering" did the originals; William Greatbatch engraved them. Tiny reprints in David Gilson's *Bibliography* show a gothic romantic gloom and wasp-waisted heroines. In the 1890s, when the novels gained a new popularity, three illustrated editions appeared: William C. Cooke's in 1892, with ornaments by F. C. Tilney; Hugh Thomson's in 1894; and Charles Edmund Brock and Henry M. Brock's in 1898. In 1908 A. Wallis Mills illustrated Jane Austen for St. Martin's Illustrated Library of Standard authors.

In 1934 Maximilien Vox provided watercolors for one complete set that were reproduced in four-color halftone. This set never became popular, and reprints of this edition replaced them with plates after Charles E.

Brock's old favorites. Warren Chappell, ten years later, quite lavishly and with a humorous style illustrated a complete set. His media were pen-and-ink and wash for full pages, gauffage and pen and ink for insets. Between 1957 and 1962 Joan Hassall illustrated the Folio Society's edition. Hassall also illustrated Brontë books, and her woodcuts are especially suited to the grim rigors of Yorkshire moors and to Jane Austen's darker mood in *Mansfield Park*.

The work of Hugh Thomson and of Charles E. Brock have proved the most popular. Each has his admirers. Hugh Thomson was commissioned to illustrate profusely, a unique assignment among the illustrators—first, *Pride and Prejudice* and then the other five. There are 160 black-and-white illustrations in *Pride and Prejudice* alone! Besides his full-page illustrations, the text is broken by quick little glimpses of the characters in action, and the initial letters are "illuminated," not with gold or color but with a playful mind that lights up the theme of each chapter. Two examples: "Mister" is the first word of the chapter on Mr. Collins's learning that Elizabeth truly is refusing him. In the *M* Cupid falls, overthrown. The word "Elizabeth" begins the chapter on Darcy's first proposal. The *E*'s middle horizontal forms a desk for Elizabeth, and the top horizontal swirls around in imitation of her thoughts.

Thanks to a memoir by friends, we know something personal of Thomson. When he received the assignment to do *Pride and Prejudice*, he at first "doubted its suitability for illustration." Growing up in an Irish farming community, he learned drawing by sketching farm animals and flowers at the kitchen table, surrounded by brothers and sisters. Later, he was apprenticed to a linen manufacturer in Ulster. A presentation scroll that he illuminated with rich detail from nature brought him a transfer to a printer. Then came more schooling, London recognition, a very successful set of illustrations for *The Vicar of Wakefield*, and finally Jane Austen. Once he accepted, he found the novels' spirit. His comic sense creates countless memorable moments. Mr. Collins steals over from Longbourn to Lucas Lodge to propose to Charlotte; Lydia dreams of "tenderly flirting with at least six officers at once." His gentlemen are gallant; their coaches and horses, dapper. His heroines? Some people would not recognize Elizabeth in the round-faced young lady he draws. His heroines do not suggest charm, and one wonders if he really did like the ladies very much. Certainly his ladies did not attract the young Sheila Kaye-Smith, who says of Thomson's illustrations: "Unless a character was notoriously middle-aged and unattractive the general run of faces was entirely without expression. [They are] old-fashioned tailors' and dressmakers' dummies" (p. 2). But generally his work was popular; 25,000 copies sold by 1907; he continued to receive remuneration for years since he had contracted to do the set for £500 plus a royalty of 7 pence a copy after the sale of 10,000. Many more recent editions have used at least some of his drawings.

Charles E. Brock's eye for these ladies and gentlemen was fonder. His people are far more capable of tender feelings than Thomson's. An example: the heart catches as Mr. Woodhouse leans forward with nervous intentness when Emma gently tells him she will marry Mr. Knightley. Though allowed far fewer pictures than Thomson, Brock had a different advantage: glossy enamel pages in six-color lithography. He draws with a subtly varied line, then colors the shapes with pale pastels. This is an old-fashioned technique, but Brock's drawings reproduce well in black and white and have been much used since.

I speak primarily of Charles Brock. Originally, he did *Sense and Sensibility, Emma*, and *Persuasion*: his brother, Henry M. Brock, also an eminent illustrator, did *Pride and Prejudice, Mansfield Park*, and *Northanger Abbey*; but Charles's were so much more successful that he was later commissioned to redo Henry's volumes.

The artist's own decade suffuses the perception of others, and it can be difficult to render a period's style faithfully. This is nowhere better seen than in William Cooke's drawings. His Elizabeth is a "Gibson Girl," a personality that seems to fit her. Since the 1890s, illustrators of the complete novels seem very much guided by concern for historical accuracy. For them, no jaunty disregard of era in the fashion of the romantically costumed *Pride and Prejudice* movie with Laurence Olivier. Jane Austen in print has seemed to require the stage props of her own lifetime.

Hugh Thomson and the Brocks both had a keen interest in historical accuracy. Henry Brock was an illustrator of period furniture pieces. Hugh Thomson had done a book on fashionable horse-drawn vehicles.

This discussion has been of the illustrated complete works. It cannot attempt the study of all Jane Austen illustrations. It must, however, mention the charming stamps issued by the British post office to commemorate, in 1975, the bicentenary of Jane Austen's birth. These were drawn by Barbara Brown. The Scott catalog number is G.B., pp. 754–57. And it must use two different illustrated editions of *Pride and Prejudice* as examples of the last aspect of illustration it will treat, *the art medium used*. The influence of the medium has already been touched on in Brock's and Hassall's work. Medium already foreshadows result. A watercolorist like Edgard Cirlin, whose charming illustrated *Pride and Prejudice* can be found in many public libraries, will usually evoke emotion, affection, a romantic feeling. But what of airbrush, used by Vera Willoughby in her *Pride and Prejudice*? The unexpected technique and its sensitive use (Willoughby exudes sensuality) evoke that character reevaluation that Janeites thrive on. This is a far cry from Cassandra's drawing. Yet such fresh use of modern technology suggests that perhaps some computer artist with a "mouse" may in the future bring us new illuminations of Jane Austen's spirit in art.

Bibliography

Complete editions (arranged chronologically)
The Novels of Jane Austen, R. Brimley Johnson, ed., with illustrations by William C. Cooke and ornaments by F. C. Tilney, 10 vols. (London, 1892).
[Jane Austen's Novels,] illustrated by Hugh Thomson, 5 vols. (New York and London, 1894–97).
The Novels of Jane Austen, illustrated by Charles E. Brock and Henry M. Brock, 10 vols. (London, 1898; Pride and Prejudice originally appeared in 1895).
The Novels of Jane Austen, illustrated by A. Wallis Mills, 10 vols. (London, 1908–10).
The Novels of Jane Austen, R. W. Chapman, ed., 5 vols. (Oxford, 1923; rev. ed., 1965).
The Works of Jane Austen, illustrated by Maximilien Vox, 7 vols. (London, 1933–38); in 1945 these editions were reprinted with Charles E. Brock's illustrations.
The Complete Novels of Jane Austen, introduction by Amy Loveman, illustrated by Warren Chappell, 6 vols. (New York, 1950).
[Jane Austen's Novels,] illustrated by Joan Hassall, 6 vols. (London, 1957–62): the Folio Society.

Individual works
Love & Freindship, and Other Early Works, preface by G. K. Chesterton (London, 1922).
Pride and Prejudice, illustrated by Vera Willoughby (London, 1929).
Pride and Prejudice, illustrated by Helen Sewell (New York, 1940): Limited Editions Club.
Pride and Prejudice, illustrated by Edgard Cirlin (Cleveland and New York, 1946).
Sense and Sensibility, illustrated by Helen Sewell (New York, 1957): Limited Editions Club.

Studies
GILSON, DAVID. A Bibliography of Jane Austen (Oxford and New York, 1982).
JERROLD, WALTER and MARION HARRY SPIELMANN. Hugh Thomson, His Art, His Letters, His Humour and His Charm (London, 1931).
KAYE-SMITH, SHEILA and G. B. STERN. Speaking of Jane Austen (New York and London, 1944).

IMPROVEMENTS

Alistair M. Duckworth

Jane Austen was no enemy to tasteful improvements and, in a modest way, was something of an improver herself at her homes in Southampton and Chawton, where she delighted in the progress of the flowers and shrubs, especially syringas. The estates she knew well, such as Godmersham and Goodnestone in Kent, were improved estates, as one may see in Watts's views of them (reproduced in R. W. Chapman's edition of the *Letters*). She knew of Humphry Repton's improvements at Adlestrop, also, where her mother's cousin, the Reverend Thomas Leigh, was rector; and when she visited Stoneleigh Abbey with Dr. Leigh in August 1806, shortly after his inheritance, she may have heard him speak of his plans to have Repton improve Stoneleigh. Repton appears by name, however, in a dubious context in *Mansfield Park*, and this raises problems for interpretation, since as John Dixon Hunt has argued, Repton's philosophy of "sensible" improvement seems to accord with that of Jane Austen. Her novels often view improvements as a civilized activity. After their marriage Edward and Elinor "superintend the progress of the Parsonage; . . . chuse papers, project shrubberies, and invent a sweep" (*SS*, p. 374), and Henry Tilney, Darcy, and Edmund Bertram are, or will be, the improvers of their properties. Darcy's Pemberley is, of course, a model of understated improvement, with a winding approach and stream whose natural flow has been "swelled into greater, but without any artificial appearance" (*PP*, p. 245). Elizabeth Bennet is impressed: "She had never seen a place for which nature had done more, or where natural beauty had been so little counteracted by an awkward taste" (ibid.). Darcy has evidently followed Pope's advice "to consult the genius of the place in all," or it may be that he has remembered Richardson's descriptions of the tasteful improvements at Grandison Hall, where "Sir Charles pretends not to level hills or to force and distort nature" (*Sir Charles Grandison*, 1753-54, vol. 3, letter 23).

Friend as she was to tastefully improved houses and grounds, Jane Austen was also, however, the inheritor of a long tradition of distrust regarding architectural and landscape improvements, and this tradition may to some extent explain her negative use of Repton. In *Absalom and Achitophel* (1681), for example, Dryden argues: "To change foundations, cast the Frame anew, / Is work for Rebels who base Ends pursue"; and a century later, in *Reflections on the Revolution in France* (1790), Burke repeatedly views England and its constitution as a house or estate endangered by the false "improvements" of its extravagant and fashion-seeking heirs. Between Dryden and Burke, Pope's "Epistle to Burlington" (1731) authoritatively distinguished between those improvements that, observing the virtues of "sense" and "use," were the proper goal of the landowner and those that, pursuing ostentation and costing extravagant sums, were the marks of false taste and vicious pride. In *The Deserted Village* (1770), Goldsmith castigated "the man of wealth and pride" whose landscape improvements resulted in the misery and eviction of the poor; and in Book III of *The Task* (1785), Jane Austen's favorite poet, Cowper, named improvements "the idol of the age." Cowper had Capability Brown in mind in his criticism, and by the 1790s the characteristic features of Brown's style—winding rivers, smooth lawns with interspersed clumps of trees, circuit walks—were being viewed with increasing disapproval from connoisseurs taught by Gilpin to appreciate the wilder beauties of Wales and the Lake District. Although Jane Austen was no enthusiast for the shaggy naturalism advocated by Richard Payne Knight in *The Landscape* (1794), she is likely to have read his attacks on Brownian improvements with interest and may, like Knight, Uvedale Price, and others, have unfairly associated Brown's work—or perhaps his notoriety—with that of Repton, his successor. Like Scott, at any rate, she distrusted "capability-men," and like Wordsworth found features to deplore in "the modern system of gardening."

In *Mansfield Park*, the rich and empty-headed Rushworth considers his old-fashioned house, Sotherton, to be a "prison" that "wants improvement . . . beyond any thing" (*MP*, p. 53). His sentiments are endorsed by his fiancée, Maria Bertram, who suggests that Repton would be his "best friend," and by the officious Mrs. Norris, who claims that given the means, she would be "always planting and improving." Henry Crawford, a "capital improver" (p. 244), is asked for his advice. Only Edmund and Fanny oppose improvements. Edmund admits the need of "modern dress" at Sotherton but opposes the employment of a professional improver; Fanny, remembering Cowper's sentiments, deplores Rushworth's intentions to cut down an avenue. The opposition recurs in the debate between Edmund and Crawford over the improvement of Thornton Lacey. Though only a parsonage, Thornton Lacey resembles Knightley's Donwell Abbey and Colonel Brandon's Delaford in having escaped the attentions of the eighteenth-century improvers. The unimproved condition of these estates—their "old neglect of prospect" (*E*, p. 358), their abundance of timber, the proximity of house to farm, church, or village—does not signify their cultural atrophy but, on the contrary, their value as neighborhoods that have evolved naturally and harmoniously, without any helping or improving hand. In this perspective, Crawford's plans at Thornton Lacey to clear away the farmyard, screen the blacksmith's shop, reorient the house, and so on, imply a threat to an organic social world. Edmund recognizes that "there is now a spirit of improvement abroad" (p. 339), but Crawford's plans at Thornton Lacey, like his plans for an improved style of sermon delivery (p. 341) or his sister's response to the news that prayers had been discontinued at Sotherton ("Every generation has its improvements"), reveal a brittle irreverence and a culpable disregard of an inherited culture.

Improvements are suspect elsewhere in the novels. If Mrs. Dashwood's plans for the improvement of Barton Cottage (*SS*, pp. 29–30) merely reveal the folly of an extravagant woman, her daughter Marianne's wish to give Allenham "modern furniture" exposes her selfish desire to replace traditional ways with "modern manners" (p. 69). Much more suspect are the improvements of her half brother, John Dashwood, who has enclosed Norland common, engrossed a neighboring farm, and to Elinor's dismay, cut down old walnut trees behind the house to make way for a greenhouse and flower garden for his wife (pp. 225–26).

The John Dashwoods are perhaps the most viciously materialistic of Jane Austen's characters, and in associating them with improvements, she is criticizing members of the gentry in whom social and moral obligations have been subordinated to greed, the wish for power, and the love of display. In *Pride and Prejudice*, Lady Catherine de Bourgh adds arrogance and vulgarity to materialism, as her estate, Rosings, gaudy opposite of elegant Pemberley, reveals. Northanger Abbey is another center of power and show, its modernity resulting from General Tilney's improvements. Part of Jane Austen's intention is to deflate Catherine Morland's "gothic" anticipations. To her dismay, Catherine encounters modern furniture, a smoke-free Rumford fireplace, and a breakfast room with a set of Staffordshire china; the kitchen is medieval, but even here the general's "improving hand" has introduced the most up-to-date appliances (p. 183). In the grounds are a huge kitchen garden with countless walls and "a village of hot-houses" (p. 178). Such detailed descriptions serve purposes beyond the deflation of the heroine. As Brian Southam has argued, General Tilney may be a portrait of the inventor Count Rumford; he is also Pope's Timon brought up-to-date; there is something manic and Brobdingnagian about his improvements, and in his preoccupation with the new, as in his aggressive pursuit of a financially rewarding marriage for his son, he reveals the true source of his tyranny to be not gothic but a very modern form of selfish ambition.

In *Persuasion* Jane Austen continues the improvements theme, but with a different emphasis. Anne Elliot can only approve the changes initiated by Admiral Croft at Kellynch Hall (they are a correction of her father's vanity), and while she does not approve of the modernization evident at Uppercross, her disapproval is tentative in comparison with Jane Austen's earlier defense of the old. The great house at Uppercross, with its walls, gates, old trees, and nearby parsonage, exists in contrast to Uppercross Cottage, "with its viranda, French windows, and other prettinesses" (*P*, p. 36). The "veranda" is later described as "black, dripping, and comfortless" (p. 123), but Jane Austen seems less concerned to criticize the modern in *Persuasion* despite her exposure of selfishness in the younger generation. The elder Musgroves are "in the old English style," while their children have "more modern minds and manners." Yet, like their houses, the Musgroves are "in a state of alteration, perhaps of improvement" (p. 40).

In *Sanditon* improvements take the form of the transformation of an old village into a seaside resort for valetudinarians. The contrast between the old and the new is given focus in the contrast of Mr. Parker's two houses: on the one hand, the house of his ancestors, "rich in . . . Garden, Orchard & Meadows" (but like Donwell Abbey unfashionably low and sheltered); on the other, Trafalgar House, lacking kitchen garden and shade trees and built near a cliff "on the most elevated spot on the Down" (*S*, pp. 379 and 384). The location of the new house suggests the precariousness of Mr. Parker's speculative ventures. Yet the tone of Jane Austen's last fragment is not one of gloom. So widespread are the transformations of Regency England, so rapid their rate, that satire, even amusement, may have seemed preferable to moral criticism as a fictional response. Charlotte Heywood is the most detached of Jane Austen's heroines, and her attitude toward the modern may represent something of her author's resilience in the winter of 1817: "A little higher up, the Modern began; & in crossing the Down, a Prospect House, a Bellevue Cottage, & a Denham Place were to be looked at by Charlotte with the calmness of amused Curiosity" (p. 384).

Bibliography

BATEY, MAVIS. "Jane Austen at Stoneleigh Abbey," *Country Life*, 160 (1976), 1974–75.

DUCKWORTH, ALISTAIR M. *The Improvement of the Estate* (Baltimore and London, 1971).

HUNT, JOHN DIXON. "Sense and Sensibility in the Landscape Designs of Humphry Repton," *Studies in Burke and His Time*, 19 (1978), 3–28.

MALINS, EDWARD. *English Landscaping and Literature: 1660–1840* (London, 1966).

PRICE, UVEDALE. *Three Essays on the Picturesque* (London, 1810).

SCOTT, SIR WALTER. Review of Sir Henry Steuert's *The Planter's Guide*, *Quarterly Review*, 37 (1828), 303–44.

SOUTHAM, B. C. "*Sanditon*: The Seventh Novel," in Juliet McMaster, ed., *Jane Austen's Achievement* (London, 1976), 1–26.

IMPROVEMENTS

WORDSWORTH, WILLIAM. Letter to Sir George Beaumont, October, 17 1805; reprinted in William A. Knight, ed., *Memorials of Coleorton*, 2 vols. (Edinburgh and Boston, 1887).

INFLUENCE ON LATER WRITERS

Norman Page

As Ian Watt has shown in the final chapter of *The Rise of the Novel,* Jane Austen succeeded in creating a form of fiction that combined two different elements in the eighteenth-century novel: "she was able to combine into a harmonious unity the advantages both of realism of presentation and realism of assessment, of the internal and of the external approaches to character" (p. 297). At the same time, her work owes something, especially in its dialogue, to the Restoration and eighteenth-century comedy of manners; and what Virginia Woolf, speaking of Congreve, refers to as a "genius for phrase-making" is a quality very evident in some of Jane Austen's most memorable passages. When, for instance, Elizabeth Bennet in *Pride and Prejudice* puts Lady Catherine firmly in her place—

> "Upon my word," said her Ladyship, "you give your opinion very decidedly for so young a person.—Pray, what is your age?"
> "With three younger sisters grown up," replied Elizabeth smiling, "your Ladyship can hardly expect me to own it." (pp. 165–66)

—the witty elegance of her retort stands in a tradition that runs from Congreve and Sheridan to Wilde and Shaw. This "epigrammatism" (to use the term that Jane Austen herself applies to the style of *PP*) is also to be found in passages of authorial or narratorial comment, such as the famous openings of chapter 1.I of *Pride and Prejudice* and 3.XVII of *Mansfield Park.* Less ostentatious and pretentious than Fielding's introductory chapters to the eighteen books of *Tom Jones,* these brisk and ironic generalizations have their counterpart in the work of such morally engaged later novelists as George Eliot, Trollope, and E. M. Forster. This blend of dramatic action and stagelike dialogue, psychological realism, social comedy, and moral and ethical conviction constitutes the inheritance that Jane Austen bequeathed to her successors in the English novel.

Whereas her contemporary Scott opened up the novel to large-scale historical and epic themes, it was her distinctive achievement to reveal the possibilities of a fiction restricted in its range of subject matter as well as its range of social life but unrestricted in the seriousness and, if necessary, unconventionality of its moral judgments. In an interesting comparison of the two novelists in his *Introduction to the English Novel,* Arnold Kettle notes that she does not aspire to Scott's "breadth of reference" or his "broader worldliness": "she deals ... with men not Man." However, I think it may be necessary here to make a distinction between her explicit and her actual "breadth of reference." Her ultimate theme is nothing less than the Johnsonian question of how to live, and she is no less committed than D. H. Lawrence to exploring the nature of good and bad relationships between the sexes. Whereas Scott's medium was the panoramic and densely populated novel that offered a comprehensive picture of society and a sense of historical change, hers was the comedy and drama of ordinary, mainly middle-class provincial life. Her dialogue is less sharply contrasted but more finely differentiated than his; her scenes exploit the drama of private, not public, existence.

Scott is an important influence on Dickens, and his conception of the novel as epic, reinforced by the model of Shakespearean tragedy, leaves its mark on such nineteenth-century novels as *Wuthering Heights* and *The Return of the Native*. As a romantic in a sense that Jane Austen was not (or was only to a very limited extent) and as a European figure, which she was not at all, he is, with his contemporary Byron, also related to such later continental novelists as Balzac, Stendhal, and Tolstoy. Jane Austen's literary descendants, by contrast, conceived of the novel in different terms. Her domestic realism, her critical and ironic stance, her moral seriousness, conveyed with little overt moralizing and indeed, characteristically, through the medium of comedy and satire, and the prominence of her heroines (representing a convinced but unassertive feminism), all gave rise to a vigorous and significant tradition that is exemplified in the work of such major novelists as George Eliot, Elizabeth Gaskell, Henry James, and E. M. Forster.

Literary "influence" is a slippery concept, easy to assert in general terms, less readily demonstrable in detail, and in any case not necessarily manifested in particulars but potent rather at an earlier stage of a book's existence and as a determinant of such features as genre, plot, characterization, and tone. Jane Austen's presence can be felt in later fiction both locally and more pervasively. When Forster, for instance, begins chapter 6 of *Howards End* (1910) with the words "We are not concerned with the very poor. They are unthinkable, and only to be approached by the statistician or the poet," he seems to be echoing, and relying on his reader to recognize, the opening of chapter 3.XVII of *Mansfield Park*: "Let other pens dwell on guilt and misery. I quit such odious subjects as soon as I can" (p. 461). And when Barbara Pym has the heroine of her *Few Green Leaves* (1980) named Emma by her mother, who admires Jane Austen, we are clearly being invited to make such connections as seem appropriate between the two novels and the different (though in some respects also similar) worlds they evoke. Although these are small matters, they are perhaps symptomatic of larger debts; and we may feel reasonably confident that the claim of "influence" is not a foolish one, since it is supported by other evidence—for example, by Forster's acknowledgment in his critical essays and elsewhere of his admiration for Jane Austen and by other elements in Barbara Pym's novel and in her work as a whole.

The other kind of influence I have mentioned is less easy to point to in a text but, because of its greater pervasiveness, of more significance. Her use, for instance, of country house or village as a social microcosm or paradigm is paralleled in such later novels as *Cranford, The Portrait of a Lady*, and *Brideshead Revisited*; and her choice as protagonist of the young woman standing on the threshold of life anticipates Dorothea Brooke, Isabel Archer, and many later heroines. This essay can do no more than briefly examine a few case studies of her influence—an influence that, though not often recognized critically in the Victorian and Edwardian periods, was a positive creative force in the novel in England.

There are substantial and obvious differences between Jane Austen and George Eliot: the former described herself to the Reverend James Stanier Clarke as "the most unlearned and uninformed female who ever dared to be an authoress" (*Letters*, December 11, 1815), and George Eliot was very nearly the most learned and best informed—so impressively so, indeed, that few readers recognized her work as a woman's. George Eliot took a male pseudonym, whereas Jane Austen had been content to describe herself on the title page of *Sense and Sensibility* as "A Lady." George Eliot went on to write the kind of novel that Jane Austen was neither able nor eager to write (*Romola*, for instance, represents the kind of historical undertaking that she firmly declined to attempt); but if we look at the point at which she started, in *Scenes of Clerical Life* (1858), its world is not at all remote from that of Jane Austen. Even chronologically, the distance is not as great as it appears: the stories were written in the 1850s, but the first of them is set "five-and-twenty years ago," or less than a generation after Jane Austen's most creative period, and the other two stories are set even earlier. Provincial, parochial, domestic, they follow Jane Austen's example in finding significance in the events of everyday life, and their mode is scrupulously realistic. As George Eliot told her editor, Blackwood, in terms that Jane Austen would not have used but would surely have been prepared to endorse, "Art must be either real and concrete, or ideal and eclectic. Both are good and true in their way, but my stories are of the former kind." After Blackwood had read the opening portions of her next book, *Adam Bede* (1859), in manuscript, he praised it as "most lifelike and real." Even in her later work she often reverts to a mode of ironic commentary, and to a use of dialogue in which her characters unwittingly betray their own weaknesses, that recall Jane Austen; and there are sometimes closer parallels. When we are told that Dorothea Brooke in

Middlemarch (1871–72) is "certainly very naive with all her alleged cleverness," we can hardly help reflecting that Emma Woodhouse, another unmarried girl from the same social class, is first described as "clever" in the opening sentence of *Emma* and then, in the rest of the book, is shown to be "naive." Even in Eliot's last novel, *Daniel Deronda* (1876), another heroine, Gwendolen Harleth, inhabits at the outset a world of social ambition, eligible bachelors, scheming mothers, "matrimonial prospects," and poor relations that is, considering the two generations of change that separate them, strikingly similar to the world of Jane Austen.

There is evidence in George Eliot's letters that she and George Henry Lewes read and reread Jane Austen's novels with enjoyment; and it is noteworthy that Lewes was one of the early champions of Jane Austen's work—from 1845 onward, long before George Eliot's career as a writer of fiction was launched, he repeatedly and unorthodoxly praised Austen in his critical essays and reviews. Lewes was in the event one of the most important of Jane Austen's Victorian critics, and his high estimate of her must have been based on reading and discussion in much of which it is highly likely that George Eliot fully shared.

From about 1860, comparisons between Jane Austen and George Eliot became commonplace in reviews of the latter's work. In that year the *Saturday Review* noted (April 14) that she had "a minuteness of painting and a certain archness of style that are quite after the manner of Miss Austen." The same reviewer added that, like Jane Austen, she possessed "the art of taking the reader into her confidence.... She joins us in laughing at her characters." He found her "little inferior" to her predecessor in this respect. One of the most perceptive of Victorian reviewers, E. S. Dallas, opened his review of *Felix Holt* in *The Times* (June 26, 1866) by declaring: "Hitherto Miss Austen has had the honour of the first place among our lady novelists, but a greater than she has now arisen." He proceeded to discriminate at length between the two novelists. More grudgingly, W. H. Mallock in 1879 found George Eliot "less than Miss Austen in art," noting with regret, "She might have been a second Miss Austen."

One of George Eliot's most important early critics was Henry James, and in James's own practice as a novelist we can trace the influence of what may be called the Austen-Eliot tradition. His awareness of Jane Austen was not solely mediated through George Eliot, however, for his criticism also contains frequent references to the earlier writer, from an unsigned review published when he was only twenty-two to his very late essay "The New Novel." In his preface to *The Princess Casamassima* (1886) she is included in a list of writers who are "the fine painters of life," and in a famous passage in his late essay "The Lesson of Balzac" she is described as "one of the shelved and safe, for all time." (The latter essay registers the wide appreciation that had come to be accorded to her work by the turn of the century, though James also suggests that she may be in danger of being overestimated.) His own early fiction presents the kind of social world that I have already suggested is present in *Daniel Deronda* as an inheritance from Jane Austen: James's eligible bachelors may be Americans in Europe, his poor relations Europeans in America, and his heiresses and fortune hunters may inhabit Boston rather than the home counties, but in spite of the international theme the situations and motivations in the serious game of marriage and money are often similar. *The Portrait of a Lady* (1881) seems to stand in a direct line from *Emma* and *Middlemarch* or *Daniel Deronda*: the preface to James's novel defines the problem that faced him as that of endowing "the mere slim shade of an intelligent but presumptuous girl . . . with the high attributes of a Subject," and that is surely a respect in which Emma Woodhouse, Fanny Price, Dorothea Brooke, Gwendolen Harleth, and Isabel Archer are all sisters. Technically, too, James's narrative method in, say, *The Ambassadors* (1903) may be said to take up from where Jane Austen left off in *Emma* the attempt to present experience through the consciousness of one of the characters. *Emma* is an extraordinary technical tour de force, and in narrative method James is surely Jane Austen's lawful heir (a point perceptively made by Kipling, another writer with an absorbing interest in narrative method, in his story "The Janeites").

James's criticism also makes a number of references to Trollope, most notably in a long essay published in 1883, shortly after Trollope's death. Although, like George Eliot, Trollope colonized fictional territory that Jane Austen declined to enter, his debt to her was considerable and was recognized very early. Donald Smalley has noted in his *Anthony Trollope: The Critical Heritage* that "in evaluating Trollope's work critics of his time so often compared it to the work of Jane Austen." He adds, however, that her name was often invoked in order to make a point about Trollope's limitations: "Both Trollope and Austen could, it was felt, present the surface of society with remarkable deftness; but both stopped short of the depth of vision or the high seriousness that were essential to art of a more elevated sort." Still, it remains significant that the parallel occurred so readily to Victorian reviewers. Discussing *The Small House at Allington* on May 14, 1864, the *Saturday Review* suggested that Trollope was capable of doing "what Miss Austen did, only that he does it in the modern style, with far more detail and far more analysis of character, although, perhaps, with less of lightness of touch and gentle pervading wit." In its obituary assessment, *The Times* (December 7, 1882) saw the similarity as a very close one: in spite of the gap in time, the anonymous obituarist argued, "his world is the heir of Miss Austen's. There is nobody with whom Mr. Collins may be better compared than with Mr. Crawley; and Anne Elliot,

Catherine Morland, Emma, and the delightful Elizabeth Bennet herself are conceived in substantially the same mood... as Mary Thorne, Lucy Robarts, or Lady Lufton." A week later, the distinguished critic R. H. Hutton also used a comparison between the two novelists as a basis for defining Trollope's art, though his emphasis fell more heavily on Trollope's wider social and geographical range. A later critic, Michael Sadleir, in his *Trollope: A Commentary* (1927), describes Jane Austen as "the writer nearest to him as a novelist of manners."

Trollope himself made no secret of his warm admiration for Jane Austen: his *Autobiography* (1883) states that, as a young man, he made up his mind that "*Pride and Prejudice* was the best novel in the language," and he later planned to include a discussion of that novel in the history of English fiction that he quickly abandoned. It may well have been the prominence and brilliance of the dialogue in *Pride and Prejudice* that won his admiration and inspired his emulation: in the comments on fictional dialogue near the end of chapter 12 of his *Autobiography*, the ideal that he sketches in general terms ("the ordinary talk of ordinary people") is close to Jane Austen's own practice. In his novels Trollope shows the same interest in varieties of speech that are subtly individualized without being exuberantly eccentric in the manner of Dickens; and his middle-class heroines in particular, who are often pert, irreverent, and witty without going beyond the bounds of taste and decorum, have much in common with Jane Austen's. In *Framley Parsonage* (1861), for instance, Lucy Robarts resembles Elizabeth Bennet, just as her rival for Lord Lufton, Griselda Grantly, is like one of Jane Austen's own satirical portraits. Trollope's women characters in general seem to owe much to Jane Austen; and when Nora Rowley in *He Knew He Was Right* (1868–69) reflects that "the lot of a woman... was wretched, unfortunate, almost degrading. For a woman such as herself there was no path open to her energy, other than that of getting a husband," it may strike us as a somewhat blunter version of the truth acknowledged by Charlotte in *Pride and Prejudice* and others of Jane Austen's unmarried women—though hardly blunter than Jane Fairfax's bitter observations in *Emma* on the trade in governesses.

Trollope's slightly older contemporary Elizabeth Gaskell is chiefly associated with the social problem novel and with regional fiction; but in *Cranford* (1853) and at the end of her career in *Wives and Daughters* (1866) she depicts the manners of English provincial society in a way that invites comparison with Jane Austen. Both books depict small towns based on Knutsford in Cheshire, where she grew up; and both look back from the mid-Victorian period to an earlier generation—"those days before railways," as she puts it in the opening chapter of *Wives and Daughters*. Peter Keating has argued that it is a mistake to regard "period charm" (as expressed, for instance, in the well-known illustrations by Hugh

Thomson) as the main quality of *Cranford*, and that the novel is concerned with the "Condition of England" question. Nevertheless, the retrospective and nostalgic element is undeniably present, as it is in so much Victorian fiction (including George Eliot's) that is at the same time deeply involved with contemporary issues; and for Mrs. Gaskell Jane Austen represents that vanished—but not so very distant and vividly recalled—world and also serves as a model for the kind of storytelling that finds its material in the everyday events of family and neighborly relationships.

Among early twentieth-century novelists, E. M. Forster displays more clearly than anyone else the persistence of the Austen tradition. As Lord David Cecil has said in his *Poets and Story-tellers*, Forster "brilliantly continues that delicate comedy tradition that descends through the English domestic novel from Jane Austen onwards." But that is only half the story, and the same critic adds that Forster is "as much a didactic writer as George Eliot herself. . . . When he sets out to draw the world, it is its moral aspects that strike him most forcibly. The categories in which he ranges people are primarily moral, the pattern he imposes on experience is the pattern of his moral vision." We need not stop at George Eliot in tracing the ancestry of these commitments in the novel, for the same words can be applied with at least equal force to Jane Austen.

Once again there is direct evidence of Forster's knowledge and admiration of Jane Austen's work. His recently published letters reveal that he read her as an undergraduate and cared enough about her to spend some prize money on a set of her books. An essay of 1924 opens with the declaration "I am a Jane Austenite"; but long before this time he had shown, most obviously in his early "Italian" novels, that the novel of sharply critical domestic comedy and social observation was still viable in the Edwardian period. Like Jane Austen, he is a relentless moralist, enunciating with great conviction the true as distinct from the conventional bases of conduct; and like her he continually stresses the importance to individual integrity and happiness of independent moral choice, uninfluenced by—and even, if necessary, in defiance of—the expectations of one's social class.

In *E. M. Forster: The Perils of Humanism*, Frederick C. Crews has said that the moral of *A Room with a View* (1908) is "throw away your etiquette book and listen to your heart," and this may be said to be also the moral of, for instance, *Mansfield Park*, most notably in Fanny's rejection of Crawford in the face of Sir Thomas's stern displeasure and accusation of ingratitude. Nor does Elizabeth Bennet have much time for etiquette books. Forster himself said of his own *Where Angels Fear to Tread* (1905) that "the object of the book is the improvement of Philip"; and that noun "improvement," with its firm confidence in moral betterment through self-awareness and self-criticism, looks back from the threshold of the modern period to the moral climate of Jane Austen's world. Once again, it will not do to exaggerate the extent of Forster's indebtedness: there is clearly much in his fiction that has no counterpart in hers, and it would be very odd if things were otherwise. A novel such as *Where Angels Fear to Tread*, beginning with social comedy but turning into drama and even melodrama, and contrasting English middle-class narrowness with Mediterranean freedom and spontaneity, shows both what he derived from her and what has other roots. But the debt remains no small one.

Much recent British fiction would hardly have been different if the modernists had never written; and one way of putting this is to say that the nineteenth-century tradition of Austen, Eliot, Trollope, Gaskell, and the earlier James is still a force to be reckoned with. Barbara Pym's *A Few Green Leaves* was cited earlier in this essay as a novel in which the influence of Jane Austen is very close to the surface. It opens with an English village, its rectory and its great house, and its middle-class inhabitants—a late-twentieth-century version of Highbury, it seems. Quite quickly, it is true, this untroubled world is shown to lack reality: the great house is empty, the past is self-consciously preserved by a few local historians and bookish folk who are unworldly if not actually eccentric, and the church is out of touch with a society now preoccupied with cars and television and supermarkets. Nevertheless, the wit and irony, especially in the dialogue, are very much in Jane Austen's vein. It may be said that Jane Austen's novels hover behind those of Barbara Pym as shadowy but felt presences, the falling off from the vanished world being part of the modern writer's point. Her novels, too, are love stories, though the cheerful concluding peal of wedding bells is rarely heard, and they make extensive use of the kind of formal or semiformal occasion—the sherry party or church bazaar or supper visit—that has its equivalent in Jane Austen's work.

A concluding observation may draw attention to the power of Jane Austen's example as a woman writer. She is the first major writer of her sex in English, and the gradual recognition of her during the nineteenth and early twentieth centuries as in a class far above that of the Fanny Burneys and Maria Edgeworths can hardly have failed to act as a stimulus to other women writers. If George Eliot, Virginia Woolf, and others went on greatly to enlarge the frontiers of the novel, Jane Austen had shown them first that it was possible for a woman to do so.

Bibliography

CECIL, LORD DAVID. *Poets and Story-tellers* (London, 1949).

CREWS, FREDERICK C. *E. M. Forster: The Perils of Humanism* (Princeton, N.J., 1962).
FORSTER, E. M. "Jane Austen," in his *Abinger Harvest* (London, 1936).
———. *Selected Letters*, Mary Lago and P. N. Furbank, eds., vol. 1: *1879–1920* (Cambridge, Mass., 1983).
KETTLE, ARNOLD. *An Introduction to the English Novel*, vol. 1 (London, 1951).
PAGE, NORMAN. "The Great Tradition Revisited," in Juliet McMaster, ed., *The Achievement of Jane Austen* (London, 1976), 44–63.
SMALLEY, DONALD A., ed. *Trollope: The Critical Heritage* (London and New York, 1969).
TROLLOPE, ANTHONY. *An Autobiography* (Edinburgh and London, 1883).
WATT, IAN P. *The Rise of the Novel* (Berkeley, Calif. and London, 1957).

JANEITES AND ANTI-JANEITES

Brian Southam

The division of Jane Austen's readership into two opposing camps—the Janeite devotees and the anti-Janeites—is an amusing controversy, long antiquated and now forty or fifty years dead. Its beginnings can be seen in Jane Austen's contemporary readership. With Scott the leading novelist of the day, amidst the outpouring of "trash" fiction (Jane Austen's own term for it), her writing was caviar for the discriminating few, and those who admired her tended to admire her to extremes. This remained true in the next generation, into the age of Dickens.

Writing to one of his sisters in 1831, the historian Macaulay records a dinner party at which "everybody praised Miss Austen to the skies. Mackintosh said that the true test of the Austenian was Emma. 'Everybody likes Mansfield Park. But only the true believers—the select—appreciate Emma'" (p. 72). Macaulay harnessed this private admiration to a public campaign. Reviewing "The Diary and Letters of Mme D'Arblay" in 1843, he faced his readers with a sudden and unexpected association between Jane Austen and Shakespeare, as the writer to "have approached nearest to the manner of the great master" (Southam, 1968, p. 122) in the portrayal of character. Four years later, Jane Austen's second champion, G. H. Lewes, took up this stunning claim, announcing in *Frazer's Magazine* (in the middle of reviewing a batch of French and English novels) that she and Fielding were "the greatest novelists in our language" and instructing his reader to mark the "greatness" and "marvellous dramatic power" of Jane Austen, an artist no less than a "*prose* Shakespeare" (ibid., pp. 124–25).

It was this overwhelming claim that provoked Charlotte Brontë's classic statement of the anti-Janeite case, first in a letter to Lewes, challenging the claim, and then in her correspondence with W. S. Williams, her publisher's reader. In essence, she found a mind without a heart, a writer "only shrewd and observant" and lacking in poetry. "Can there," she asked, "be a great artist without poetry?" (ibid., p. 127). These questionings, however, remained private. In public, Lewes continued to conduct the Austen campaign undeterred: "the greatest artist that has ever written, using the term to signify the most perfect mastery over means to her end," he declared in the *Westminster Review* in 1852 (ibid., p. 140).

But in 1859, Lewes introduced a new note: that for all her greatness, Jane Austen was a writer appealing only to the "cultivated reader . . . to the small circle of cultivated minds" (ibid., p. 160). This qualification was realistic. Yet it reappeared equivocally in the *Englishwoman's Domestic Magazine* in 1866. We are informed, significantly, that she is a writer not for the public at large but for "minds of the highest culture" (ibid., p. 208). In the *Memoir*, published four years later, is gathered the chorus of praise that had sounded from the time of Scott onward. It is capped with Austen-Leigh's reference to a Mr. Cheney, "one of the ablest men of my acquaintance," who said "in that kind of jest which has much earnest in it, that he had established it in his own mind, as a new test of ability, whether people *could* or *could not* appreciate Miss Austen's merits" (p. 136).

In these last quotations are signs of the least attractive aspect of the Janeite cult, its claim to exclusivity and superiority—the Janeites grouped within the pale, the rest of the world standing ignorantly and obtusely without. This acrid whiff of snobbery could not escape reviewers of the *Memoir*, notably the novelist Mrs. Margaret Oliphant, who regarded Jane Austen as a great writer and saw that a popularization had been achieved (referring to the campaigning of Lewes and Macaulay) "by dint of persistency and iteration" that had awakened "a half-real half-fictitious universality of applause" (Southam, 1968, p. 225).

However, these comments did nothing to stem the flood. From the time of the *Memoir* onward, there was an increasing volume of appreciative "twaddle" (as Henry James was to call it), epitomized by the long review-essay that Anne Thackeray contributed to the *Cornhill Magazine* in 1871. Warmly addressed to "all those who love her name and her work" (p. 158), the piece is heavy with rhapsodic apostrophe and gaspings of delight: "Dear books! bright, sparkling with wit and animation, in which homely heroines charm, the dull hours fly, and the very bores are enchanting." So transported, Miss Thackeray alights upon the *Memoir*: "For the first time we seem to hear the echo of the voice, and to see the picture of the unknown friend who has charmed us for so long—charmed away dull hours, created neighbours and companions for us in lonely places, and made harmless mirth." This piece was twice reprinted in collections of her literary essays, in 1874 and again in 1883. By the time of the second collection, Miss Thackeray notes in the preface that Jane Austen had become "a dear household name," and the essay was revised accordingly, not with a sharpening of the critical edge but with an apostrophe even more fanciful, affectionate, and tearful. The changes in Miss Thackeray's essay mark a corresponding shift in public taste. Sentimental enthusings, not sober criticism, were the order of the day. Janeite idealization created a Jane Austen who never was. Reviewers and essayists celebrated her "perfection," a "perfection" placing her beyond the reach of criticism. The devotion was notably extreme and acknowledged to be so. In 1884, we read in the *Saturday Review* of "her worshippers" (November 15, 1884, p. 637) and in the *Dictionary of National Biography* (1885) Leslie Stephen wrote of the "fanaticism" of her "innumerable readers" (p. ii.260).

Mrs. Malden closed her *Jane Austen* (1889) with a notable reflection on the novelist's divided readership:

> Those who do appreciate her novels will think no praise too high for them, while those who do not, will marvel at the infatuation of her admirers; for no one ever cares moderately for Jane Austen's works: her readers either award them unbounded praise or find them insufferably dull. (p. 210)

The *Academy* reviewer was less neutral. Commending Mrs. Malden's *Jane Austen* contemptuously to the "Austenites," he announced that what "the external world" wanted was not idolatry but serious criticism. In this heated atmosphere, there came an important analysis in the *Spectator* by the Shakespearean scholar R. H. Hutton, who classified the reading public into those "few" who "love" the novels; that "very considerable number of remarkably able men" over whom "Miss Austen wields no spell at all"; and the "anti-Austenites" (p. 403). For the next twenty years, it was the Austenites who held sway, their enthusiasm fed by the succession of illustrated editions that poured out in the 1890s and early 1900s. Some of these were in the hands of professional Janeites, such as the editor Augustine Birrell, whom the American critic Agnes Repplier guyed mercilessly:

> He dwells rapturously over certain well-loved pages of *Pride and Prejudice* and *Mansfield Park*, and then deliberately adds, "When an admirer of Jane Austen reads these familiar passages, the smile of satisfaction, betraying the deep inward peace they never fail to beget, widens, like 'a circle in the water,' as he remembers (and he is always careful to remember) how his dearest friend, who has been so successful in life, can no more read Jane Austen than he can the Moabitish Stone."

In the decade up to 1900, the Austenites were rapidly growing in numbers, and the novelist William Dean Howells—himself a most affectionate admirer—observed it to be "a constantly, almost rapidly, increasing cult, as it must be called, for the readers of Jane Austen are hardly ever less than her adorers: she is a passion and a creed, if not quite a religion" (p. i.41).

In 1900, the Earl of Iddesleigh proposed to readers of the *Nineteenth Century* that it would be "a very delightful thing if a magazine could be started which should be devoted entirely to Miss Austen.... We are never tired of talking about her; should we ever grow weary of reading or writing about her?" (p. 811).

Lest this should seem to be the preserve of cranks and the besotted, it is worth recalling that George Saintsbury—in his preface to the 1894 edition of *Pride and Prejudice*, lavishly and overprettily illustrated by Hugh Thomson—announced himself as ready to write for "the sect—fairly large and yet unusually choice—of Austenians or Janeites" (p. ix) and confessed himself ready to marry Elizabeth Bennet. A. C. Bradley declared of this same heroine, in 1910, "I was meant to fall in love with her and I do" (1911, p. 7).

A few years earlier, in 1905, Henry James had provided the most astute analysis of the origins of Janeitism and its recent florescence. He viewed it as an instance of "a beguiled infatuation, a sentimentalized vision" and blamed "the stiff breeze of the commercial." It was not the "critical spirit" he accused:

> Responsible, rather, is the body of publishers, editors, illustrators, producers of the pleasant twaddle of magazines; who have found their "dear", our dear, everybody's dear, Jane so infinitely to their material purpose, so amenable to pretty reproduction in every variety of what is called tasteful, and in what seemingly proves to be salable, form. (p. 116)

At this time, the voice of un-Europeanized, un-Jamesian America found its most extreme and violent expression in the anti-Janeite animosity of Mark Twain, who claimed to feel nothing less than an "animal repugnance" for her writing. A Bowery barkeeper was how Twain saw himself, blundering into the tight social decorum of her "Presbyterian" world. Doubtless he would have applauded the equally extreme anti-Janeitism of D. H. Lawrence: "this old maid" was in his view "thoroughly unpleasant, English in the bad, mean, snobbish sense of the word" (p. 58), as he wrote in 1930.

Janeitism reappeared at the time of the *Life and Letters* in 1913; and again, in 1917, at the centenary of the novelist's death. Addressing the Royal Society of Literature that year, Montague Summers delivered a Janeite "Appreciation," theologically worded, announcing: "To-day the world is divided between the elect and the profane—those who admire Jane Austen, and those (one shudders to speak the phrase)—who do not" (p. 8). In the pages of the *Yale Review*, Wilbur Cross ministered to the flame: in 1922, reviewing *Love and Freindship*, he was delighted to find its author "none the less 'divine'" (p. 413); and three years later, reviewing *Sanditon*, he was again able to celebrate "the cult of 'the divine Jane'" (p. 387). Meanwhile, in England, a patriotic dimension was added to the cult in Kipling's short story "The Janeites" (1924), followed by "Jane's Marriage" (1926), a poem telling of her reunion, in Paradise, with Captain Wentworth and concluding with a rousing poetic toast "unto England's Jane!" Hardly surprising that Arnold Bennet, writing in his *Evening Standard* column in July 1927, should regard Jane Austen as "dangerous ground": "The reputation of Jane Austen is surrounded by cohorts of defenders who are ready to do murder for their sacred cause. They are nearly all fanatics. They will not listen. If anybody 'went for' Jane, anything might happen to him." Virginia Woolf had issued a similar warning three years earlier: "Anybody who has had the temerity to write about Jane Austen is aware ... that there are twenty-five elderly gentlemen living in the neighbourhood of London who resent any slight upon her genius as if it were an insult offered to the chastity of their Aunts." However, it was not the season for slights, and there was little need for these elderly gentlemen to rouse themselves. The establishment line, as we follow it in *The Transactions of the Royal Society of Literature*, continued avidly Janeite. At a meeting of the R. S. L. on February 23, 1927, the Shakespearean scholar Dr. Caroline Spurgeon read a fulsome eulogy endorsing the association of Jane Austen's name with that of Shakespeare and enlarging upon why "she is so characteristically English." Dr. Spurgeon also found for Jane Austen a new category: "more than a classic; she is also one of a little company —few, but very fit—whose work is of the nature of a 'miracle'" (p. 82). When, later that year, the address was published in the annual volume of transactions, the volume editor, Margaret Woods—who admitted in her preface to being of "the Tribe of Jane"—expressed her confidence that "all good Janeites will welcome Dr. Caroline Spurgeon's appreciation" and went on to rejoice at "the multitude and ardour of her adorers!" (pp. xi–xii).

Historically, this date marks the high point of Janeitism in the twentieth century; and it immediately provoked a full-scale anti-Janeite retort, a "Depreciation" delivered to the R. S. L. in May 1928 by H. W. Garrod, professor of poetry at Oxford, which was followed, in turn, by a "Reply" from Dr. R. W. Chapman, given to a meeting of the R. S. L. in November 1929.

The comic melodrama of those years is something that could never be repeated. There have been some notable exchanges. But in the past half century, with the rise of modern academic criticism, it has seemed naive and amateur to label oneself—as earlier critics were unashamed to do—as belonging to one side or the other. This is a loss to the comedy of criticism, a pity that never again shall we read a passage to match E. M. Forster's review of the Oxford edition of the novels in 1923:

> I am a Jane Austenite, and therefore slightly imbecile about Jane Austen. My fatuous expression, and airs of personal immunity—how ill they set on the face, say, of a Stevensonian! But Jane Austen is so different. She is my favourite author! I read and re-read, the mouth open and the mind closed. Shut up in measureless content, I greet her by the name of most kind hostess, while criticism slumbers. The Jane Austenite possesses little of the brightness he ascribes so freely to his idol. Like all regular churchgoers, he scarcely notices what is being said. (p. 514)

A new self-consciousness was abroad, at least among serious critics—and increasingly so amongst ordinary readers, too, as Agnes Repplier commented in 1931: "Jane is not for all markets, and this circumstance lends a secret and unworthy zest to her faithful followers. They do not want to share their pleasure with their neighbours. It is too intimate and too individual" (p. 51). The notable exceptions were Sheila Kaye-Smith and G. B. Stern, with *Talking of Jane Austen* (1943) and *More Talk of Jane Austen* (1950), volumes written by "true Janeites" for their fellows. Delightful as they are, these extended tributes lack the genius of a Forster, his sense of theater, of ungarrulous absurdity, in which realm alone can Janeites and anti-Janeites flourish for our enlightenment and delight.

Bibliography

ANONYMOUS. *Saturday Review*, 58 (1884), 637–38.
BENNET, ARNOLD. *Evening Standard* (July, 1927).
BRADLEY, A. C. "Jane Austen: A Lecture," *Essays and Studies by Members of the English Association*, 2 (1911), 7–36.
CROSS, WILBUR. Review of *Love and Freindship*, *Yale Review*, 12 (1922–23), 410–13.
———. Review of *Sanditon*, *Yale Review*, 15 (1925–26), 386–89.
FORSTER, E. M. Review of the Chapman editions, *Nation and Athenaeum*, 34 (1923–24), 512–14; reprinted in his *Abinger Harvest* (London and New York, 1936).
HOWELLS, WILLIAM DEAN. "Heroines of Fiction," *Harper's Magazine* (1900).
HUTTON, R. H. "The Charm of Miss Austen," *Spectator*, 64 (1890), 403–404.
IDDESLEIGH, WALTER STAFFORD, 2ND EARL OF. "A Chat About Jane Austen's Novels," *Nineteenth Century*, 47 (1900), 811–20.
JAMES, HENRY. "The Lesson of Balzac," *Atlantic Monthly*, 96 (1905), 166–80.
LAWRENCE, D. H. *À Propos of Lady Chatterley's Lover* (London, 1930).
MACAULAY, THOMAS BABINGTON, BARON. Letter to Hannah M. Macaulay, August 1831, published in George Otto Trevelyan, *The Life and Letters of Lord Macaulay* (London, 1876), vol. 1, p. 240.
———. Letter July 18, 1831, published in Thomas Pinney, ed., *The Letters of Macaulay* (London, 1974), vol. 2, p. 72.
MALDEN, S. F. *Jane Austen* (London, 1889).
REPPLIER, AGNES. Review of R. B. Johnson's biography, *Commonweal*, 14 (1931), 51–52.
SAINTSBURY, GEORGE. Preface to *Pride and Prejudice* (London, 1894), ix–xxiii; reprinted in his *Prefaces and Essays* (London, 1933), 194–209.
SOUTHAM, B. C., ed. *Jane Austen: The Critical Heritage* (London and New York, 1968); the second ed., 2 vols.: *1812–1870* and *1870–1939*, is forthcoming in 1985.

Spurgeon, Dr. Caroline F. E. "Jane Austen," in Margaret Woods, ed., *Essays by Divers Hands, Being the Transactions of the Royal Society of Literature of the United Kingdom*, n.s. 7 (1927), 81–104.
Stephen, Leslie. ["Jane Austen,"] *Dictionary of National Biography* (1885), vol. 2, 259–60.
Summers, Montague. "Jane Austen: An Appreciation," *Transactions of the Royal Society of Literature*, 36 (1918), 1–33.
Thackeray, Anna Isabella. Review of the *Memoir, Cornhill Magazine*, 24 (1871), 158–74.
Woolf, Virginia. "Jane Austen at Sixty," *New Republic*, 37 (1924), 261.

JUVENILIA

Brian Southam

Of Jane Austen's very earliest childhood writing we know nothing. But in three notebooks—*Volume the First, Volume the Second,* and *Volume the Third,* as they were mock-grandiosely inscribed by Jane Austen herself—has come down to us a virtually complete collection of her writing between about 1787 (the year she was twelve) and the middle of 1793. Not the original manuscripts, these are later transcriptions, preserving a permanent record of this miscellaneous early material, twenty-nine pieces in all, amounting to about ninety thousand words. There was a need to make these copies, since many of the individual pieces are dedicated to members of the family and the originals are likely to have been dispersed as presents. Moreover, there was an active tradition of family reading among the Austens, and when her turn came around, Jane would want to read from one of her *Volumes*. This was a tradition kept alive for the next generation, too, for her nephews and nieces. Doubtless Aunt Jane was frequently called upon to entertain them, and on at least one occasion, in 1809, she took the trouble to update a joke by replacing the title of an old book with that of a current one. Sometimes, even, there was participation. Her niece Anna Austen added a continuation to "Evelyn," a story that her aunt had written in 1792, the year before Anna's birth.

In his "Biographical Notice" of 1817, Henry Austen made no reference to this early writing. The 1870 *Memoir* was more forthcoming, speaking of "copybooks extant" and, in particular, of "an old copybook containing several tales, some of which seem to have been composed while she was quite a girl," stories "of a slight and flimsy texture." The copybook may have been *Volume the First*, although it is not certain which of the notebooks Austen-Leigh had seen. He gave no extracts, arguing that "it would be as unfair to expose this preliminary process to the world, as it would to display all that goes on behind the curtain of the theater before it is drawn up." However, this scruple did not stand long. In the 1871 second edition of the *Memoir*, he included much of the later manuscript material and printed "The Mystery," a little dramatic skit, from *Volume the First*. In fact, Austen-Leigh had wanted to include some of the *juvenilia* in the first edition, a plan opposed in some quarters of the family. Not only was it felt "unfair" to publish this "nonsense" (even if it was "clever nonsense"); it was also felt to be an intrusion. Family pieces, written for the family, should remain within it, unpublished.

The *Life and Letters* (1913) expanded upon the *Memoir*, providing a description of *Volume the Third* and printing some items from *Volume the First*. Eventually, the notebooks were published in full: *Volume the Second* (under the title *Love and Freindship*) in 1922; *Volume the First* in 1933; and *Volume the Third* in 1951. With the full body of writing in view, it became evident that there was yet a further element in the family's reluctance to publish this material. For the young Jane Austen was ready to joke about deformity, injury, death, drunkenness, childbearing and illegitimacy —subjects familiar in eighteenth-century literature but out of step with the Victorian sense of proprieties and quite out of character with the image of "gentle" Jane presented in the *Memoir*, the *Life*, and the other testimonials and recollections emanating from the family itself.

Today, however, we suffer under no such disadvantages. With the *juvenilia* before us, alongside the six novels, we are able to see Jane Austen whole—to mark out the precise stages of her literary development, the flowering, as it were, of a precocious genius; to observe her essentially critical response to eighteenth-century literature; and to see how she gradually abandoned this shrewd burlesque marksmanship, turning instead to the refinement of her own writing technique. It was an apprenticeship in transcribing scenes and characters from life around her, the prelude of trial and experiment that lay behind the accomplishment of the six novels.

The contents of the three *Volumes* are not ordered chronologically. Some of the earliest and last pieces are found in *Volume the First*, and it looks as if Jane Austen entered fresh material into whichever of the three notebooks was most conveniently to hand. Accordingly, the following chronology has been compiled:

1787–90	"Frederic & Elfrida," "Jack & Alice," "Edgar & Emma," "Henry and Eliza," "Mr. Harley," "Sir William Mountague," "Mr. Clifford," "The Beautifull Cassandra," "Amelia Webster," "The Visit," "The Mystery" (all *Vol. 1*)
June 1790	"Love and Freindship" (*Vol. 2*)
November 1791	"The History of England," "Collection of Letters" (both *Vol. 2*)
1792	"Lesley Castle" (*Vol. 2*), "The Three Sisters" (*Vol. 1*), "Evelyn" (*Vol. 3*)
August 1792	"Catharine" (*Vol. 3*)
1793	"Scraps" (*Vol. 2*)
June 1793	"Detached pieces" (*Vol. 1*), "Ode to Pity" (*Vol. 1*)

In some cases, Jane Austen recorded the dates of composition. In some, we are able to date items by reference to outside events. For example, "Jack & Alice" and "The Adventures of Mr. Harley" (both *Vol. 1*) are dedicated to her brother Francis: "Midshipman on board his Majesty's Ship the Perseverance" (pp. 12 and 40), in which he served from 1788 to November 1791. In this and other cases in which exact dates are not given, the items have been ordered on the evidence of style.

Within this chronology of the individual items are three distinct groups: the earliest *juvenilia*, written between 1787 and 1790; the two important burlesques, "Love and Freindship" and "The History of England"; and finally the works of 1792–93, in which burlesque is intermingled with the first experiments in realistic social comedy and more flexible narrative forms.

1787–90

The earliest pieces display an intriguing mixture of elements. On the one hand, there is the naturally high-spirited fun of childhood, knockabout farce, fanciful extravagance, solemn nonsense, and elaborate wordplay. Yet there is also sophisticated humor, a knowing and knowledgeable pinpointing of the false values and absurd conventions of sentimental fiction. The characteristic devices of the popular novel are set in ridiculous procession: the ubiquitous confidantes, the recital of life stories, catastrophes abounding, interpolated songs and verses, rhapsodic prose, the egocentric heroines. Then there are the weaknesses of rank bad writing—clumsy plots, action beyond the bounds of probability, a defiance of the simple verities of time and place, and every variety of inconsequence and digression.

The most distinctive feature of Jane Austen's burlesque method is in the manipulation of style. In these lines from "Jack & Alice" she mimics the inflated rhetoric, the rhythms and cliché diction of sentimental fiction: "Thus fell the amiable & lovely Lucy whose Life had been marked by no crime, and stained by no blemish but her imprudent departure from her Aunts, & whose death was sincerely lamented by every one who knew her" (p. 28). Exploiting the reader's familiarity with this stylistic norm, Jane Austen opens "Frederic & Elfrida" with phrasing neat and precise, a foil to the absurdity of the subject matter:

> The Uncle of Elfrida was the Father of Frederic; in other words, they were first cousins by the Father's side.
> Being both born in one day & both brought up at one school, it was not wonderfull that they should look on each other with some-

thing more than bare politeness. They loved with mutual sincerity but were both determined not to transgress the rules of Propriety by owning their attachment, either to the object beloved, or to any one else. (p. 4)

The most amusing effects are gained when Jane Austen exploits the disparity between the broad farcical comedy of the action and the studied formality of the sentimental language and behavior of the characters. In "Frederic & Elfrida" Charlotte is sitting with her aunt when she receives the old gentleman's proposal:

Scarcely were they seated as usual, in the most affectionate manner in one chair, than the Door suddenly opened & an aged gentleman with a sallow face & old pink Coat, partly by intention & partly thro' weakness was at the feet of the lovely Charlotte, declaring his attachment to her & beseeching her pity in the most moving manner.

Not being able to resolve to make any one miserable, she consented to become his wife; where upon the Gentleman left the room & all was quiet. (p. 8)

The comic effect is markedly theatrical. In the same way Lady Williams's account of her education ("Jack & Alice") begins in conventional terms and ends in the manner of a stage farce:

"Miss Dickins was an excellent Governess. She instructed me in the Paths of Virtue; under her tuition I daily became more amiable, & might perhaps by this time have nearly attained perfection, had not my worthy Preceptoress been torn from my arms, e'er I had attained my seventeenth year. I never shall forget her last words. 'My dear Kitty she said, Good night t'ye.' I never saw her afterwards" continued Lady Williams wiping her eyes, "She eloped with the Butler the same night." (p. 17)

In these sudden descents of language and action her audience would be reminded that Fielding, Smollett, Sterne, and the popular dramatists provided similar comic melodrama to ridicule the idealization of impulsive love and elopement.

But the clearest hint of Jane Austen's future power is not related directly to her methods of burlesque. It is glimpsed, rather, in an occasional succinct aphorism or finely turned comment, as in the description of Lady Williams—"a widow with a handsome Jointure & the remains of a very handsome face" (p. 13); and in Lady Williams's advice to Alice—"Preserve yourself from a first Love & you need not fear a second" (p. 16); or in the words of Mr. Johnson—"I expect nothing more in my wife than my wife will find in me—Perfection" (p. 26).

In seeking to explain the young girl's mastery of these styles of burlesque, we have no need to invoke the forces of "precocious genius." Genius, yes. But no precocity was involved, since her home life at this time was the perfect breeding ground for literary talent of a witty and critical bent. At Steventon Rectory, reading and writing were amusing and exciting activities, shared with the family, and not only through reading. In summer and winter, relatives and neighbors were recruited for amateur theatricals, which included performances of *The School for Scandal*, *The Rivals*, Garrick's *High Life Above Stairs*, and Townley's *High Life Below Stairs*. These and other plays, including *The Critic*, mocked sentimentalism as sharply as did Jane Austen herself; and from her brothers she must have been familiar with the serious moral arguments leveled against sentimental fiction. James and Henry edited an Oxford periodical, *The Loiterer*, that ran for sixty numbers between January 1789 and March 1790. Here we find material very close to Jane Austen's own burlesques; and in such an atmosphere of high spirits and serious literary and moral discussion Jane Austen's critical gifts flourished.

Family reading also played an important part. Under the guidance of her father and brothers, she was well-read in the mainstream of English literature from Shakespeare onward, including the eighteenth-century novelists up to Fanny Burney. She was also well acquainted with minor fiction, "The mere Trash of the common Circulating Library," she was to call it in *Sanditon* (p. 403). The young girl borrowed freely for her comic situations and characters; and her assurance of style—in the turn of phrase, the rhythm and structure of sentences, the design of paragraphs, and the handling of dialogue—can be traced back to the models of classical English prose.

1790–91

In this middle period come "Love and Freindship" and "The History of England," works on a larger scale than anything attempted hitherto and more sophisticated in their literary humor. The playful nonsense and allusive humor are still there, to amuse the children, as well as references to family affairs. But the entertainment is not wholly dependent on burlesque. In the brisk and sustained comedy of "Love and Freindship," the heroine's point of view is maintained throughout the letters. Controlling a variety of material, it gives the work an overall unity and form.

Jane Austen uses Laura as the mouthpiece for sentimental doctrine. Against this sounds the voice of common sense. When Edward, her husband, makes a declaration of sentimental "Manliness" in a refusal to accept his father's authority, Sir Edward coolly replies, "Where Edward in the name of wonder . . . did you pick up this unmeaning Gibberish? You have been studying Novels I suspect" (p. 81). In the course of the story, stealing—like parasitism, hypocrisy, and illegitimacy—is an occasion for the sentimentalist's self-glorification, an insistence on the individual's contemptuous superiority to mundane laws and conventions. But real life breaks in. The sentimentalists suffer rejection and imprisonment. They come to learn that prudence can be more profitable than the extravagance of their code. Sophia, indulging her sensibility, faints so long and so often in the dew that she succumbs to a fatal chill. From her deathbed she warns Laura to "beware of fainting-fits" (p. 102), advice that Laura (unsentimentally) follows and so survives.

At the end of her story, Laura writes of her retirement to a romantic highland village, where, in the style of the truly lachrymose heroine, she is able to "indulge in a melancholy solitude" her "unceasing Lamentations" (p. 109). But this indulgence is only possible because she has accepted an annuity from her father-in-law, whom she earlier cast in the role of a tyrannical villain. The sentimentalist is ready to compromise with reality if only to avoid its dangers and accept its gifts.

Jane Austen exhibits and ridicules sentimentalism in a comedy of exuberant burlesque. At the same time, there is a more serious theme in the questioning of motive; and it is here that the burlesque shades into a satire on affectation. In *Sense and Sensibility*, this theme is fully realized in the contrast between Marianne Dashwood's genuine temperamental sensibility and the Steele sisters, whose display of feeling is opportunistic. But in "Love and Freindship" the comedy is swift and hard. It is literary pretension that is on show, not the force of emotion in real people.

Jane Austen's other purpose was to show how the epistolary novel could be mangled and mishandled. Richardson's success with the letter form had demonstrated how well it was suited to the intense study of consciousness, the revelation of states of mind and feeling. But because of its simplicity as a narrative vehicle, by the 1780s and 1790s it had become the most popular device for all kinds of fiction, with a series of letters "in continuation" or "from the same to the same," interrupting the story as little as possible and merely using the letter to replace the division by chapters. The burlesque distortion in "Love and Freindship" is in the arbitrary opening and closing of Laura's correspondence, breaking the story in the midst of action as no conventional chapter divisions would do.

Ridicule is also at the heart of "The History of England"—announced as a work "by a partial, prejudiced, & ignorant Historian" to contain "very few Dates" (p. 138). Jane Austen's target was popular historical writing; and *Shamela* (1741), a skit on Richardson's *Pamela* (1740), may also be alluded to. In Goldsmith's *History of England* (1764) the description of Anne Boleyn is in the manner of any hack novelist: "Her features were regular, mild and attractive, her stature elegant, though below the middle size, while her wit and vivacity exceeded even her other allurements." In the hands of the popular historians, all too often fact reads like fiction. Jane Austen adds to the joke, not only imitating their style but heading each section with a miniature painted by Cassandra, sometimes making this portrait the point of the joke—excepting the "unfortunate" Edward V, who "lived so little a while that no body had time to draw his picture" (p. 140) while the portrait of Edward IV is produced as firm historical evidence! "This Monarch was famous only for his Beauty & his Courage, of which the Picture we have here given of him, & his undaunted Behaviour in marrying one Woman while he was engaged to another, are sufficient proofs" (p. 140).

Specifically, the "History" is aimed at Goldsmith's *History*, countering his anti-Stuart bias; more particularly, Jane Austen's potted entries poke fun at the *Abridgement* to Goldsmith published in 1774. Another target was the considerable branch of historical fiction devoted to embroidery on the life of Mary Stuart.

The manner of popular historical writing is taken to an extravagant conclusion. The historians treated the figures of the past as if their characters and feelings were fully known. Accordingly, Jane Austen writes of sovereigns and great men with an air of careless familiarity, as if they were figures of her own time. Richard III is "a very respectable Man" (p. 141); Charles I an "amiable Monarch" (p. 148); the Catholics "did not behave like Gentlemen to the protestants" (p. 147); "and even Sir Henry Percy tho' certainly the best bred Man of the party, had none of that general politeness which is so universally pleasing" (ibid.). These judgments belong to the drawing room. In the same way, historical events are treated as the occurrences of everyday life. Joan of Arc "made such a *row* among the English" (p. 140); Richard III "made a great fuss about getting the Crown" (p. 141); and in the reign of Henry IV "the Prince of Wales came and took away the crown" (p. 139). As a foil to this slangy colloquialism, in writing of Mary Stewart, Jane Austen adopts an elevated mock-formal style with rhetorical appeals to the reader, in striking contrast to the rest of the work, where in general the tone is jaunty, the manner inconsequential, with a purely verbal appearance of cause and effect, such as we find in the entry for Henry IV:

> Henry the 4th ascended the throne of England much to his own satisfaction in the year 1399, after having prevailed on his cousin & predecessor Richard the 2d, to resign it to him, & to retire for the rest of his Life to Pomfret Castle, where he happened to be murdered. It is to be supposed that Henry was married, since he had certainly four sons, but it is not in my power to inform the Reader who was his Wife. Be this as it may . . . (p. 139)

This extract is a parody of Goldsmith's worst manner, with its clumsiness and jingling prose. The passage is also significant for the air of casual indifference with which it treats material of human substance and historical importance, subject matter thereby trivialized. This point brings us to the heart of Jane Austen's criticism—that popularized history is as false to the nature of reality as the picture of life given in the sentimental novel, and perhaps more seriously false, for it purports to be dealing with the facts of great men and great events.

1792–93

Following the assurance and burlesque artistry of "Love and Freindship" and the "History," the last of the *juvenilia* read rather disappointingly. For now Jane Austen was beginning to attempt the portrayal of character and the realistic rendering of scenes from domestic life and polite society. In place of burlesque melodrama, she takes the problems of conduct and judgment that could face a girl in her day-to-day relationships, especially in the testing situations of love and marriage. She sets out to try her hand at a range of character types: the timorous simpleton, the witty and perceptive young woman, the well-bred fool, the anxious chaperone, the doting mother, the sentimental heroine, the high-spirited young man, the rich suitor, and the mature confidante and her opposite, the older woman, impertinent and bullying. Whether in burlesque or realistic pieces these figures are exhibited in hard, critical comedy that searches affectation and display, revealing the ignorance, pride, folly, malice, calculation, or self-interest that so often underlie the parade of manners. Only Miss Grenville (in "Letter the fourth," p. 160) and Eloisa Lutterell and Mrs. Marlow (in "Lesley Castle") are treated with sympathy. Jane Austen was sketching the surface of personality, noting the particular idiosyncrasy or accent of silliness that distinguishes one fool from another, the little tricks of speech and behavior through which the qualities of a person's breeding, education, and social position could be read.

There is considerable experiment in style in the "Collection of five letters" (pp. 150–170), moving from sentimental eloquence to natural dialogue. Letter three is furthest in the direction of realism, an early attempt at the clash between a girl of spirit and a patronizing and censorious older woman, an evident anticipation of the encounters between Elizabeth Bennet and Lady Catherine de Bourgh.

In "Lesley Castle" we find a similar experimentation across a range of styles, covering the story of Lady Lesley's marriage and its effect on her husband's grown-up daughters. Although as a whole the piece lacks unity, with an uneasy movement between burlesque and realism, there are some significant effects—for example, in the contrast between the rhetorical manner of popular fiction and the artificiality of society slang and gush:

> I have a thousand excuses to beg for having so long delayed thanking you my dear Peggy for your agreable Letter, which beleive me I should not have deferred doing, had not every moment of my time during the last five weeks been so fully employed in the necessary arrangements for my sisters Wedding, as to allow me no time to devote either to you or myself. (p. 112)

This is Charlotte as a butt. But when Jane Austen uses her as a commentator, the style changes completely, becoming aphoristic, cold in tone, and penetrating. She sees through Lady Lesley, who "plays, sings & Dances, but has no taste for either, and excells in none, tho' she says she is passionately fond of all" (pp. 119–20). She strips the pretense off the "violent partiality," which settled into

> a downright Freindship, and ended in an established correspondence. She is probably by this time as tired of me, as I am of her; but as she is too polite and I am too civil to say so, our letters are still as frequent and affectionate as ever, and our Attachment as firm and sincere as when it first commenced. (p. 120)

The shapeliness of expression, the severity and the caustic tone, are exactly what we find in the early letters of Jane Austen.

Letters eight and nine stand outside the mood of comedy and burlesque. Eloisa's heartbroken appeal for sympathy and Mrs. Marlowe's kindly reply might be taken from Richardson's *Familiar Letters* (1741), models to guide correspondents in dealing with such situations; and Richardson could not have bettered Jane Austen's handling of the delicate issues raised here.

Probably, she intended that these two letters should serve as a foil to the varieties of pretense and insincerity illustrated in the rest of the correspondence. The contrast is simply made. The letters provide an easy way of treating, separately, the serious and comic areas. This separation is convenient. Yet it weakens the structure of the work as a whole and reveals that Jane Austen's prose was not yet sufficiently flexible and receptive to contain comedy and pathos in close proximity.

"The Three Sisters" is a notable advance. With its firm design and neatly turned plot, it reads like a short episode from a full-scale novel. Free from passages of narrative and reported speech, the direct conversation gives a dramatic effect just right for social comedy; and the subject—marriage for a position of security—effectively brings out the tension between expediency and idealism.

The situation and characters are presented through the letters of the two strongly contrasted girls, Mary and her youngest sister, Georgiana. The elder girl is a fool, dazzled and confused by the prospect of marriage. Her opening letter begins on a note of naive delight and continues in a confusion of hopes and fears. Georgiana writes clearly and wittily. Whereas Mary, Marianne-like, calls Mr. Watts "quite an old Man, about two & thirty" (p. 58), Georgiana speaks sardonically, in practical commendation: "He is not more than two & thirty; a very proper age for a Man to marry at; He is rather plain to be sure, but then what is Beauty in a Man; if he has but a genteel figure & a sensible looking Face it is quite sufficient" (p. 61). The attitudes of the two sisters are further revealed in Georgiana's account of the dialogue and events that take place on Mr. Watts's visit to settle the marriage terms. This vivid scene is followed by another little comedy, the spectacle of Mary's "triumph," the visit she pays to the Dutton girls, before whom she preens herself in newly gained social consequence. The direction of Jane Austen's art is clearly marked in these passages. Her aim is to show how character is formed and defined in the events of ordinary life and how speech and behavior are determined by a complex of personal and social considerations. But this material required a less restrictive form, and in "Catharine or the Bower," the most important of the early works, there is much freer treatment of these issues in direct narrative.

It is in "Catharine" that we catch the unmistakable note of an original writer. Hitherto, Jane Austen's principal models for describing characters and society seem to have been Richardson and, more immediately, Fanny Burney. But now she begins to discover her own method for describing domestic life, her own way of moving the story along quietly and in the tempo of a country neighborhood, where the most exciting events are the arrival of visitors and a ball. The narrative is conducted with economy and concentration, and the principal episodes are developed with due regard to their place within the structure of the plot. All this is a far cry from the crowded agitation of Fanny Burney's melodramatic adventure stories. What we see in "Catharine" is a path that leads to the measured social comedy of *Northanger Abbey*. The treatment of the two heroines has much the same relationship, Catharine seeming in many respects a sketch for Catherine Morland. At the story's opening and close, Catharine is gently mocked as a sentimental figure, whereas in contact with Camilla Stanley she is drawn as a lively young woman of keen intelligence and wit; while, yet again, in many of her dealings with Edward Stanley, she is rendered as an ingenue of foolish simplicity, a treatment crude in comparison with the candid simplicity and trust that Catherine Morland displays toward Henry Tilney.

Jane Austen left "Catharine" unfinished, perhaps because she realized the weakness in her drawing of the heroine. She may also have been dissatisfied with the style of the narrative, which is very far from the ideal manner of social comedy, "light, and bright, and sparkling," with "the playfulness and epigrammatism of the general style," to use her own description of *Pride and Prejudice* (*Letters*, February 4, 1813). Much of the dialogue, which occupies nearly half of the work, is crisply handled, the individual mannerisms nicely differentiated. Outside the areas of speech, however, the prose often lapses into an elegant and formal periodic manner, satisfying and polished after its fashion but somehow distanced and anonymous, precluding the shifts of tone and emphasis, the expressive control essential to the play of irony and satire. This heaviness in the writing is particularly noticeable in the account of Cecilia Wynne's Indian marriage. Jane Austen's Aunt Philadelphia had been subjected to the same experience. We know from Jane Austen's letters and other works how strongly she felt about marriage without love. Yet the force of what must have been a personal emotion is not communicated. Her attitudes seem to have been muffled or displaced by an irrelevant concern for stylishness.

G. K. Chesterton described "Love and Freindship" as something "to laugh over again and again as one laughs over the great burlesques of Peacock or Max Beerbohm." In the same spirit, every reader will find nuggets of timeless comedy throughout the *juvenilia*.

The student of the oeuvre will glimpse again and again foreshadowings of the great novelist, vestiges of scenes and characters that appear later, fully realized in the mature writing. And anyone who reads the *juvenilia* solidly from beginning to end, through the frequent hilarity and the occasional longueurs, cannot fail to appreciate Jane Austen's feat in inventing (to quote George Moore) "the formula whereby domestic life may be described" (p. 34). To quote Moore again, in Jane Austen, we watch the transformation of the shapeless "wash-tub" of the eighteenth-century novel into her own elegant and proportioned "vase." Above all, the *juvenilia* assert the essential truth that Jane Austen "began" (as Richard Simpson wrote in 1870) "by being an ironical critic. . . . This critical spirit lies at the foundation of her artistic faculty" (Southam, p. 242). Mary Lascelles draws our attention to the other, historical aspect of Jane Austen's satire, which can be understood without a continual reference to specific targets, for she "very seldom aims merely at this or that wretched novel or novelist. It is her way to strike through a particular novel or type of novel, to the false conventions that govern it, and through these conventions to the false taste (in writer and reader alike) that have allowed them to come into being" (quoted in Litz, p. 18). Jane Austen's youthful critique, then, is of a culture itself, not just its literary expression.

Bibliography

AUSTEN, JANE. *Volume the First*, R. W. Chapman, ed. (Oxford, 1933).
——. *Volume the Second*, B. C. Southam, ed. (Oxford, 1963); published first as *Love & Freindship*, G. K. Chesterton, ed. (London, 1923).
——. *Volume the Third*, R. W. Chapman, ed. (Oxford, 1951).
Jane Austen's Literary Manuscripts, B. C. Southam, ed. (London, 1964), chaps. 1 and 2.
LITZ, A. WALTON. *Jane Austen: A Study of Her Artistic Development* (London and New York, 1965), chap. 1.
MOORE, GEORGE. *Avowals* (London, 1919), 33–41, 60–61.
SOUTHAM, B. C., ed. *Jane Austen: The Critical Heritage* (London and New York, 1968).

LADY SUSAN

Ruth apRoberts

Lady Susan is the longest of Jane Austen's minor works, and remarkable in various ways: it is her only extant epistolary narrative, it is her only work to center on an immoral character, and of all the varied and lively jeux d'esprit of the *juvenilia* and fragments, *Lady Susan* is the only highly finished piece of art.

It poses certain editorial and critical problems, being first printed by James Edward Austen-Leigh in the *Memoir* of 1871 from what was apparently a fair copy, of which some of the paper is watermarked 1805. The watermark and the high artistic finish would suggest a date about 1805; but family tradition and study of the early writings—we know there was an early epistolary form of *Sense and Sensibility* and might assume therefore an epistolary phase—has inclined critical opinion to an earlier date, 1793–94, with the brisk three-page "Conclusion" quite likely a later addition. The subject invites speculation on a real-life original, and it is hard to resist the idea that Jane Austen's cousin Eliza de Feuillide is the origin of Lady Susan the antiheroine (Tucker, pp. 134–42). Eliza was beautiful, brilliant, spoiled, selfish, in love with dissipation and flirtation, given in fact to flirting with Jane Austen's favorite brother Henry, her junior by ten years, quite probably persuading him against taking Holy Orders. (The relationship suggests also the Mary Crawford-Edmund Bertram flirtation in *Mansfield Park*.) She brought the air of France and the beau monde to the Austen household and lived for a time in London while her husband was in France, becoming, she herself said, the "greatest rake imaginable" (Tucker, p. 47). Eliza's husband was guillotined in 1794, and this horrendous event hardly slowed down her social life. She was eventually to marry Henry Austen, in 1797. Someone may yet argue for a later date for *Lady Susan* on the basis of its relationship to the Eliza-Henry affair, presuming the author wanted to pillory the femme fatale who had victimized her brother. In *Lady Susan*, however, the good brother in question, Reginald de Courcy, after being much dazzled and manipulated, sees the heroine's true colors in time and escapes her toils.

The context of *Lady Susan* is better understood, anyway, as literary-traditional than as biographical: the female rake was a well-known type in eighteenth-century literature. Fielding's Lady Booby in *Joseph Andrews* is a notable example, and we can look even further back to Lady Wishfort in Congreve's *Way of the World*. There is a kind of code of "honour" (p. 256) that one follows in the pursuit of pleasure; proprieties are observed in everything but actual morality. Lady Susan is adept in this witty mode. And then the epistolary novel itself was a standard eighteenth-century genre, established by Richardson and practiced widely by writers as varied as Smollett, Fanny Burney, and Goethe. It is not surprising that so literary a writer as Jane Austen should try her hand at it, as we know she did in the early version of *Sense and Sensibility*. In *Lady Susan* she exploits the form in a positively virtuoso manner, as though she would only give up the genre after having exhausted its possibilities. The central virtuosity of *Lady Susan* consists in the heroine condemning herself in her own words while she is bent on self-vindication. The character Lady Susan may seem to anticipate Thackeray's Becky Sharp, but the mode of the novel anticipates the first-person self-revelation of Thackeray's *Barry Lyndon*, another feat of virtuoso irony. In *Lady Susan*, at the same time, the series of letters by various hands drive the narrative forward unfalteringly to its dramatic denouement. Finally, however, to tie up the few remaining loose ends, Jane Austen turns away from the epistolary form, with a laugh that mocks the artifice itself: "Conclusion: This Correspondence, by a meeting between some of the Parties & a separation between the others, could not, to the great detriment of the Post office Revenue, be continued longer" (p. 311).

The first letter is all sweetness and good manners, as Lady Susan professes "Duty and affection" in accepting her late husband's brother Charles Vernon's invitation to join him and his wife in the country after bravely giving up her dear daughter to "one of the best Private Schools in Town" (p. 244). But in the second letter Lady Susan addresses her particular friend Mrs. Johnson, and we discover that she is obliged to leave her friends the Manwarings, because though only four months a widow she has been having an affair with Mr. Manwaring, and Mrs. Manwaring is unaccountably jealous; and she has flirted with the wealthy but dull Sir James Martin to detach him from Miss Manwaring and ally him to her daughter Frederica; and the dear Frederica is a hopeless simpleton, to be humbled and brought to heel at school; and Lady Susan plans, moreover, to bilk the school of their fees. Hereafter, Jane Austen in her ironic tour de force plays one side against the other: Lady Susan as she appears to the Vernons against Lady Susan as she reveals herself to her friend Mrs. Johnson.

There are forty-one letters in all, the largest in bulk being the eleven from Mrs. Vernon to her mother Lady de Courcy. Mrs. Vernon is the closest thing in the book to the later type of Austenian narrator. She is in a position to observe most of the action and therefore has the most to tell, and she supplies a clear-sighted moral center, not insensible to the hypocrite's charm but convinced by intuition as well as report that Lady Susan belongs to "a very bad set" (p. 297); she appreciates Frederica's virtues and acts to promote her interests against her mother's. These letters are balanced by the eleven self-revealing letters of Lady Susan to Mrs.

Johnson, and we see a little of Lady Susan at her hypocritical work in letters to Reginald. The daughter Frederica shows her good heart in her one pathetic epistolary appeal to Reginald, and the elder de Courcys write parental letters. Reginald himself writes at first to his sister that he is curious to see this Lady Susan who has such a bad reputation, but then in her company he is fascinated and persuaded that she is innocent and injured. This relationship Lady Susan has undertaken as a sort of challenge: "There is exquisite pleasure in subduing an insolent spirit, in making a person pre-determined to dislike, acknowledge one's superiority" (p. 254). She is in time, she reports, "gay and triumphant" and is not sure whether to punish him "by dismissing him . . . or by marrying & teizing him forever" (p. 293). She puts him off, ostensibly in her letter to him, for reasons of prudence and delicacy but actually because of her continuing sexual interest in Manwaring, and she comes to London needing "a little Dissipation for a ten weeks' penance" (p. 294) in the country. Mrs. Johnson has five letters that are masterpieces of the witty rakish idiom: her husband—who we can gather is a man of principle, for he has forbidden Lady Susan his house—is to go to Bath, "where if the waters are favourable to his constitution & my wishes, he will be laid up with the gout many weeks" (pp. 295–96). The poor man, however, is prevented from going by having to be nursed in a severe attack at home, and "it all falls upon me—& he bears pain with such patience that I have not the common excuse for losing my temper" (p. 298). This inconvenience hampers Mrs. Johnson and Lady Susan in the pursuit of their pleasures. When the scene shifts to London, the exchanges between Lady Susan and Mrs. Johnson become hurried notes, in a sort of epistolary stichomythia, arranging for an assignation. The London scenes remind us of the notoriously lax regency style and suggest a still-older style, that of the Restoration, while the plot takes on some of the elegance and neatness of the Restoration stage: Lady Susan is at last undone by the timely appearance to Reginald of the avenging jealous fury of Mrs. Manwaring. Our female rake is punished where it hurts most: loving wit and living by it, she is reduced to marrying the notoriously slow-witted Sir James Martin. The good-hearted Frederica will at last win the prize by her virtues: the intelligent, wealthy, titled, and good Reginald de Courcy.

Lady Susan displays a kind of hubris in an interesting passage to Mrs. Johnson in which she declares she feels equal to talking herself out of any difficulty: "If I am vain of anything, it is of my eloquence. Consideration & Esteem as surely follow command of Language, as Admiration waits on Beauty. And here [at the Vernons] I have opportunity enough for the exercise of my Talent, as the cheif of my time is spent in Conversation" (p. 268)—clearly, she would prefer the more-than-conversational satisfactions of her liaison with Manwaring. But the moral also is clear: Lady Susan's wonderful eloquence fails her at last when the truth is forced on Reginald. "Facts are such horrid things!" (p. 303) laments Mrs. Johnson in condolence. At first, Lady Susan is confident again that she can talk her way out once more—"Depend upon it, I can make my own story good with Reginald" (p. 303); but she fails, convicted at last by "facts," by actions.

The emphasis suggests the characteristic moral stance of Jane Austen, even here in this little novel that explores the psychology of evil—attractive, witty, intelligent evil. The morality that is to be the fulcrum of all her works is perfectly evident; what is remarkable in *Lady Susan* is the perspective. Eloquence, command of language, which after all were things the young Jane Austen could have been quite as vain of as Lady Susan was, can be absolutely meretricious, as this elegant exercise in novel writing shows. It is an exercise, a virtuoso piece, in that the difficulties of the epistolary form are deliberately and knowingly undertaken and worked out. The brisk three-page conclusion in third-person narration is sometimes read as an admission of failure, but in fact the main epistolary story achieves a virtual completeness, and the conclusion is as dry, stylish, and controlled as the whole thing.

The critical history of *Lady Susan* has been decidedly odd: the closest analyses of it have been developed to serve perverse ends. Q. D. Leavis, while she makes many acute incidental comments, promotes a theory of rewriting: *Mansfield Park* is essentially *Lady Susan* rewritten; but with a little reflection we find that the concept self-destructs. Marvin Mudrick, whose analysis is elaborate and valid at various points, nevertheless takes the heroine to be tragic, a victim of society, and this view is made to support his odd misreading of *Mansfield Park* (pp. 127–40) as a failure of artistic irony. B. C. Southam has answered Leavis's arguments, and A. Walton Litz has sorted the wheat from the critical chaff in both Leavis and Mudrick, while he himself presents the most just treatment of *Lady Susan* to date (pp. 39–57). Through the years, the verdicts have varied all the way from "failure" to "masterpiece," and it remains a curious, impressive, and challenging little work. It adds, finally, to our sense of Jane Austen's deliberate art; in this early phase we see her borrow, parody, or reject the various available traditions of literary narrative, to select and establish her own particular mode. *Lady Susan* is characteristic of her novels, too. She presents a microcosmic society with its various tensions; she engineers a well-rounded little plot; she practices the revelation of characters by their own idioms, here, especially, a self-condemnation; but above all here, as in the novels to come, she delights with her educative, informing, liberating laughter.

Bibliography

LEAVIS, Q. D. "A Critical Theory of Jane Austen's Writings, II," *Scrutiny*, 10 (1941–1942), 272–94.

LITZ, A. WALTON. *Jane Austen: A Study of Her Artistic Development* (New York and Oxford, 1965), esp. 39–57.

MUDRICK, MARVIN. *Jane Austen: Irony as Defense and Discovery* (Princeton and London, 1952).

SOUTHAM, B. C. "Mrs. Leavis and Miss Austen: The 'Critical Theory' Reconsidered," *Nineteenth-century Fiction*, 17 (1962–63), 21–32.

TUCKER, GEORGE HOLBERT. *A Goodly Heritage: A History of Jane Austen's Family* (Manchester, England, 1983).

JANE AUSTEN'S LANGUAGE

Norman Page

Traditional attitudes toward Jane Austen's language have been a particular instance of prevailing attitudes toward her work—that is to say, there was for a long time a widespread failure to recognize the range and variety, the originality and innovativeness, of her art. The wit, elegance, and precision of her style were often praised, but it was often felt that she operated, linguistically as in other respects, within narrow limits—in that "carefully fenced, highly cultivated garden, with neat borders" that was the world of her novels as perceived by Charlotte Brontë, who found in her a "Chinese fidelity" but a total absence of "poetry" (reprinted in Southam, pp. 126–28). Austen's nineteenth-century and early-twentieth-century critics, indeed, have remarkably little to say concerning her language and style; and when Macaulay compares her to Shakespeare (an encomium echoed by George Henry Lewes), it turns out that what he has in mind is less her gift for striking out an unforgettable phrase than her powers of delineating character.

In her admirable study *Jane Austen and Her Art*, Mary Lascelles has pointed out that Jane Austen's verbal effects are often "modelled ... in very low relief" (p. 94), and it is true that we must not look in her work for the kind of full-blown rhetoric that is found in Dickens or in Charlotte Brontë herself. Nonetheless, the variety and the contrasts are there, and some of her most telling effects are derived from minor modulations of style, slight departures from the norm that she has carefully created. Moreover, in her later novels, especially in *Emma* and *Persuasion*, there are some notable stylistic experiments that are hard to parallel in the nineteenth-century novel and that look forward to Henry James and Virginia Woolf.

A few quotations will help to illustrate this range and variety and to dispel (if it needs dispelling) the notion that Jane Austen's style exhibits a golden uniformity. She can execute, for her own purposes, a skillful imitation of the style of the eighteenth-century periodical essayists whom she had read, either seriously—"The indignities of stupidity, and the disappointments of selfish passion, can excite little pity" (*Mansfield Park*, p. 464)—or ironically, as in the famous opening sentence of *Pride and Prejudice*; but she can also, daringly and delightedly, throw overboard all notions of linguistic decorum and allow Elizabeth Bennet to exclaim, in the very accents of Shakespeare's Rosalind, "And is this all? . . . I expected at least that the pigs were got into the garden, and here is nothing but Lady Catherine and her daughter!" (p. 158). A longer example from *Northanger Abbey* shows her deploying Johnsonian antithetical structures, again for ironic or parodic purposes:

> Of the Alps and Pyrenees, with their pine forests and their vices, [Mrs. Radcliffe's works] might give a faithful delineation. . . . But in the central part of England there was surely some security for the existence even of a wife not beloved, in the laws of the land, and the manners of the age. Murder was not tolerated, servants were not slaves, and neither poison nor sleeping potions to be procured, like rhubarb, from every druggist. Among the Alps and Pyrenees, perhaps, there were no mixed characters. There, such as were not as spotless as an angel, might have the dispositions of a fiend. But in England it was not so. (p. 200)

Here the stern voice of the Age of Reason, speaking through its characteristic syntactical structures, seems to rebuke the folly of Catherine Morland's wild imaginings.

Elsewhere Jane Austen can reject this highly patterned prose, with its relentless symmetries, in favor of a more flexible, open-ended syntax that traces the fluctuations of thought and feeling—a prose that stands much closer to direct experience. While looking back to Sterne, and especially the experimental style of *A Sentimental Journey* (1768), this is a prose that also looks forward to a much later period. Thus, in *Sense and Sensibility*, she traces the shifts of Elinor's anxious feelings:

> About noon, however, she began—but with a caution—a dread of disappointment, which for some time kept her silent, even to her friend—to fancy, to hope she could perceive a slight amendment in her sister's pulse;—she waited, watched, and examined it again and again;—and at last, with an agitation more difficult to bury under exterior calmness, than all her foregoing distress, ventured to communicate her hopes. (p. 314)

The very punctuation here is dramatic, and it is notable that the only really strong and confident phrase occurs at the very end of this long sentence, as a verbal embodiment of Elinor's own greater confidence. This prose of sensibility is "truly mimetic of emotion," to use a phrase applied by Laurence Lerner (p. 169) to the following passage from *Persuasion*:

> And it was soon over. In two minutes after Charles's preparation, the others appeared; they were in the drawing-room. Her eye half met Captain Wentworth's; a bow, a curtsey passed; she heard his voice

—he talked to Mary, said all that was right; said something to the Miss Musgroves, enough to mark an easy footing: the room seemed full—full of persons and voices—but a few minutes ended it. Charles shewed himself at the window, all was ready, their visitor had bowed and was gone; the Miss Musgroves were gone too, suddenly resolving to walk to the end of the village with the sportsmen: the room was cleared, and Anne might finish her breakfast as she could. (pp. 59–60)

The abrupt phrases and the absence of coordination make this as far from the Johnsonian model as it could well be: it is in fact much closer to *Mrs. Dalloway* than to *The Rambler* in style and sensibility. Partly because so much of the heroine's emotional life is lived secretly, Jane Austen's last novel is especially rich in what amounted to an experimental prose.

Persuasion also furnishes an instance of descriptive writing that reminds us that although she was born in the age of Johnson, Jane Austen not only lived into the age of Wordsworth but responded to the new modes of feeling and writing. Of the "immediate environs" of Lyme Regis in Dorset she writes:

The scenes in its neighbourhood, Charmouth, with its high grounds and extensive sweeps of country, and still more its sweet retired bay, backed by dark cliffs, where fragments of low rock among the sands make it the happiest spot for watching the flow of the tide, for sitting in unwearied contemplation;—the woody varieties of the cheerful village of Up Lyme, and, above all, Pinny, with its green chasms between romantic rocks, where the scattered forest trees and orchards of luxuriant growth declare that many a generation must have passed away since the first partial falling of the cliff prepared the ground for such a state, where a scene so wonderful and so lovely is exhibited, as may more than equal any of the resembling scenes of the far-famed Isle of Wight: these places must be visited, and visited again, to make the worth of Lyme understood. (pp. 95–96)

Jane Austen here displays her mastery of the long sentence structured on a principle quite different from the Johnsonian—on feeling rather than argument, self-expression rather than didacticism. If she begins her career as an Augustan, she ends as a romantic, and some of the phrases here might have come straight from "Tintern Abbey" ("unwearied contemplation") or "Kubla Khan" ("green chasms between romantic rocks").

As this handful of scattered quotations suggests, the range of stylistic features and effects is wide, and wider than she has often been credited with; and each of the novels uses its own distinctive modes of style. From the early beginnings of her career as an author, Jane Austen showed a keen awareness of the medium of language. This awareness is most obviously manifested by the impulse to imitation and parody: in the *juvenilia*, as later in *Northanger Abbey*, there is abundant evidence of a sharp analytical and critical response to the writers she had read and of the playful or mischievous urge to expose stylistic pretentiousness and incompetence. In a sense language, and the misuse and abuse of language, is the subject of much of her early work. The same attitude persists throughout her career. The banalities and affectations of fashionable or would-be fashionable talk, for instance, are castigated by Henry Tilney in *Northanger Abbey* when he chides Catherine for her thoughtless use of such modish catchwords as "nice," "amazingly," and "faithfully" (see chaps. 1.XIV, 2.IX); later, Emma Woodhouse shares Jane Austen's impatience with the smart vulgarisms of Mrs. Elton. More profoundly, language often serves as a moral index: to be indifferent to linguistic decorum can betoken a fundamental unsoundness of judgment and principles; and when John Thorpe in *Northanger Abbey* rattles on in a style compounded of exaggerations and insincerities or when Mary Crawford in *Mansfield Park* ventures on a somewhat daring pun about "vices" and "rears," the reader ought to be prepared for the worst in their subsequent behavior and is not disappointed. Jane Austen's characters (and in this respect she is truly Shakespearean) continually betray their own follies and frailties through their speech. In the work of few novelists does dialogue carry such a significant burden, and the dialogue is often parodic and linguistically self-aware, as in the fulsome periods of Mr. Collins and the trivial obsessions of Mr. Woodhouse. Henry Tilney's sister's complaint of him that he is "for ever finding fault with me, for some incorrectness of language" (*NA*, p. 107) might be echoed by many of Jane Austen's characters with reference to their creator.

"Incorrectness of language" implies, of course, confidence in some positive standard of correctness, and Jane Austen inherited the eighteenth-century doctrine of prescriptivism and the conviction that the language was in need of being defended against the inroads of change and novelty. This conservatism applies especially to her vocabulary and is the other side of the coin from the remarkable innovations in syntax that have already been noted.

Her debt to the eighteenth century can be clearly seen through an examination of what may be termed her moral vocabulary, those recurring terms or key words with which she describes and analyzes character and conduct, bestowing approval or finding them wanting in accordance with a well-defined set of moral standards related to human strengths and shortcomings to which these staple items of her vocabulary correspond. As C. S. Lewis has said in his "Note on Jane Austen," "The great abstract nouns of the classical English moralists are unblushingly and uncompromisingly used. . . . These are the concepts by which Jane Austen grasps the world. In her we still breathe the air of the *Rambler* and *Idler*. All is hard, clear, definable" (p. 363). Again, a few examples will illustrate this point. Emma Woodhouse judges Jane Fairfax "very elegant"; but though the neighborhood speaks of Mrs. Elton as "handsome, elegant, highly accomplished, and perfectly amiable" (p. 181), Emma's verdict is that "there was no elegance;—ease, but not elegance" (*E*, p. 270). Elizabeth Bennet tells her sister Jane, "Affectation of candour is common enough;—one meets it every where. But to be candid without ostentation or design—to take the good of every body's character and make it still better, and say nothing of the bad—belongs to you alone" (*PP*, pp. 14–15). Marianne Dashwood, we learn, is "generous, amiable, interesting: she was every thing but prudent" (*SS*, p. 6), while she herself decides that Colonel Brandon has "neither genius, taste, nor spirit" (p. 51), and her sister Elinor tells Willoughby that it is her wish "to be candid in my judgment of every body" (p. 79). These words—nouns such as elegance, ease, candor, prudence, genius, and taste, and their related adjectives and adverbs—are samples of a fairly extensive vocabulary of terms that recur frequently and derive their precision partly from traditional usage and partly from their appearance in Jane Austen's writings in many different contexts. (It will be noted that at times she offers a definition of a word, as in Elizabeth Bennet's remarks on "candour" quoted above, or discriminates between two different senses of a word, as when Mr. Knightley lectures Emma on the varying connotations of "amiable," an epithet she has applied to Frank Churchill.)

Other characteristic keywords include openness and its opposite reserve, judgment, folly, firmness, principle, rapture, and benevolence; and the adjectives civil, polite, artless, respectable, worthy, and rational. Nor was this, for Jane Austen, an exclusively literary or public mode of discourse: in a letter of September 14, 1804, for instance, she says of a certain Miss Armstrong whom she has recently met, "I do not perceive wit or genius, but she has sense and some degree of taste, and her manners are very engaging." One has a sense of an individual personality analyzed and classified, her characteristics held against a moral yardstick: evidently, such judgments, and the conveying of them in carefully discriminated terms, were second nature to her.

An important point about many of these words is that they were much weightier in Jane Austen's time than they have since become: by a familiar process of semantic deterioration, a word such as "elegance" has lost much of its force in modern discourse, and if we are not to miss much of what Jane Austen intends to say, the conscious effort to recover the original meaning needs to be made. "Elegance," which now refers mainly to superficial appearances, could refer much more broadly to outlook and cast of mind, with something of the meaning of "sensitivity," as when Emma finds Frank Churchill guilty of "inelegance of mind." "Prudence," again, was a bolder and more substantial concept, denoting a quality more positive than the timid playing safe that the word nowadays often suggests; and when the author tells us that "Mr. Collins was not a sensible man" (p. 70) the notion of sense, as in the title of *Sense and Sensibility*, is a solid one. Genius, on the other hand, which Jane Austen found lacking in Miss Armstrong (and Mrs. Norris in Fanny Price), was a less remarkable quality than it later became, with the romantic exaltation of the exceptional individual, and for Jane Austen usually means little more than ability or aptitude (not far from the modern shibboleth of "intelligence").

Some words have not only undergone a loss of moral intensity but display a more radical shift that, if not properly appreciated, may lead to a distortion of Jane Austen's meaning. As in one of the above quotations, to be candid was in Johnson's definition to be "free from malice, not desirous to find fault," which is not far from being the opposite of the modern sense of frank, blunt, or unsparing in giving an opinion. Jane Austen's was the eighteenth-century usage of Pope's line "Laugh where we must, be candid where we can" (cf. *Vol. 2*, p. 153); its continued currency in her generation is illustrated by Byron's "Affect a candour which thou can'st not feel" ("English Bards and Scotch Reviewers," 1809).

But she was also aware of living in an age of transition and sensed the process of linguistic change that was soon to be greatly accelerated by the social and political upheavals of the new century. Henry Tilney's objections to the undiscriminating use of the epithet "nice" as a term of approval—"it does for every thing. . . . every commendation on every subject is comprised in that one word" (*NA*, p. 108)—enable Jane Austen to give the topic an airing. Her own views are clearly those of her mentor-heroes, such as Tilney and Knightley, and in general her position is of resistance to linguistic change, not on the grounds of an entrenched conservatism but because she felt that the changes she observed were working in the direction of an enfeebling of the language, especially as an instrument of moral and ethical discourse. In an age of revolution and widespread uncertainty, she helped to defend the language against what she saw as corruption and betrayal and to maintain linguistic authority based on precedent and prescription. From *Northanger Abbey* to *Emma* the romantic temperament and its undisciplined flights of feeling come under attack, and she sees extravagance of language as one of the symptoms of the malaise. When, in *Emma*, Mrs. Elton's proposal of "a sort of gipsy party" at Donwell Abbey (p. 355) is firmly squashed by Mr. Knightley, that very perfect eighteenth-century gentleman, we feel that a blow has been struck for rational behavior and rational conversation against a shallow enthusiasm (another word that has undergone a significant shift of meaning) and an irresponsible use of words.

As already noted, the development of Jane Austen's syntax is from a

Johnsonian balance and symmetry toward a much freer form that, rather than bringing experience and feeling fully under control, is capable of recording, as if seismographically, the shocks and tremors of emotion. When Elinor in *Sense and Sensibility* tells Willoughby, "If their praise is censure, your censure may be praise, for they are not more undiscerning, than you are prejudiced and unjust" (p. 50), her speech is patterned to a striking degree (not inappropriately, in one who sets her face against romantic spontaneity). The first half of her sentence is a chiasmus (*A B B A*), the second half a parallelism (*A B A B*). In the following quotation from the same novel, Edward Ferrars is less formal than Elinor, partly because his diction is concrete, whereas hers is abstract; but the underlying structure is still a pair of firm Johnsonian antitheses: "I have more pleasure in a snug farm-house than a watch-tower—and a troop of tidy, happy villagers please me better than the finest banditti in the world" (p. 98). Sometimes the formal sentence can be made to lend itself to comic purposes, the comedy arising from the incongruity between structure and content. Thus, the early "Love and Freindship" includes the not-so-solemn warning "Beware of the unmeaning Luxuries of Bath & of the Stinking fish of Southampton" (*Vol. 2*, p. 79).

This syntactical traditionalism is, however, only part of the story. Jane Austen, writing at the turn of the century, looks forward as well as backward and develops, as we have seen, a more dramatic syntax that, especially at the climaxes of feeling, decisively rejects the Johnsonian architectonics. Her reading of Richardson and Sterne must have taught her something about the possibilities of a syntax that seeks to trace the flow of experience, and it is not too much to say that she sometimes anticipates the stream-of-consciousness fiction of a hundred years later.

In its simplest form, what we may call her dramatic or mimetic syntax may be found in the kind of short sentence that conveys a rapid succession of events, as in this sentence from *Emma*: "They arrived, the carriage turned, the step was let down, and Mr. Elton, spruce, black, and smiling, was with them instantly" (p. 114), and again in the account of the departure from Mansfield Park of Fanny's brother William: "The ball was over—and the breakfast was soon over too; the last kiss was given, and William was gone" (p. 282). While the first of these sentences conveys the point of view of the narrator, the second seems to afford an insight into the feelings of the heroine, for whom the parting is a painful wrench; and a more extended example of this latter type, in which syntax mirrors a character's thoughts and feelings from moment to moment, is to be found in *Sense and Sensibility*:

> the figure of a man on horseback drew her eyes to the window. He stopt at their gate. It was a gentleman, it was Colonel Brandon himself. Now she should hear more; and she trembled in expectation of it.

But—it was *not* Colonel Brandon—neither his air—nor his height. Were it possible, she should say it must be Edward. She looked again. He had just dismounted;—she could not be mistaken;—it *was* Edward.... (p. 358)

The short sentences, nervous repetitions, and absence of the sense of order conveyed by coordination and subordination, even typographical devices such as punctuation and italics, all correspond to Elinor's confusion and her gradual realization of the truth. There is no sense here of feelings under control: as in Virginia Woolf's prose, the feelings develop and are modified as the sentences themselves unroll (or, at times, emerge jerkily in a manner that suggests the pressure of feelings).

The opening chapter of *Pride and Prejudice* is one of the most familiar instances of Jane Austen's use of dialogue as an important means of conducting the business of the novel, and her dialogue is of a kind that, while not often strongly idiosyncratic, is delicately differentiated. The realism and vitality of the speech she puts into the mouths of her characters were praised by some of her earliest critics; yet it is realism of a kind that is transmuted by art, so that characters such as Mr. Woodhouse and Miss Bates are bores who contrive never to be boring. (As Mary Lascelles has pointed out, Miss Bates's apparently inconsequential ramblings actually convey a good deal of pertinent information.) Not many of her characters are permitted to hold forth at length (Colonel Brandon's monologue in chapter 2.IX of *SS* is an exception to this rule). Much more characteristic is the quick-fire exchange such as that between Elizabeth and Lady Catherine in chapter 3.XIV of *Pride and Prejudice*.

In its different forms—different in fictional purpose as well as in technique of presentation—dialogue is of great importance in her novels: as F. W. Bradbrook says, "the importance of conversation in the novels makes them naturally dramatic" (1966, p. 48). Although she eschews the grotesque eccentricity to be found in the dialogue of Dickens or Smollett, and although the narrow social world of her novels excludes the wide range of regional, social, and occupational varieties of speech to be found in Scott or Hardy, her dialogue is subtly individualized, and each of her major characters, as well as many of her minor ones, have their own unmistakable modes of speech, from the stately periods of Sir Thomas in *Mansfield Park* and the prosy sermonizing of Mr. Collins in *Pride and Prejudice* to the smart and vulgar colloquialisms of Lucy Steele in *Sense and Sensibility* and the domestic banalities of Mrs. Price in *Mansfield Park*. Even within a single family, as with the Bennets of *Pride and Prejudice* and the Bertrams of *Mansfield Park*, the styles of the different members are clearly differentiated to reflect contrasts of character and temperament.

Direct speech, however—the presentation of words supposed to have been actually spoken—is only one of the ways of rendering dialogue open to the novelist; and Jane Austen's readiness to experiment and innovate is shown by her exploration of the alternative ways of rendering speech. The most obvious alternative is indirect or reported speech, as in the opening exchange of *Pride and Prejudice*—"'My dear Mr. Bennet, . . . have you heard that Netherfield Park is let at last?' Mr. Bennet replied that he had not"—where the oblique form hints at Mr. Bennet's detachment and taciturnity: it is his voluble wife's voice that the reader "hears," and we are free to surmise that his reply is confined to a single monosyllable. Less familiar than these is the intermediate form of free indirect speech, which combines something of the vividness and immediacy of direct speech with the ability of reported speech to merge readily with narrative style. Jane Austen would have encountered isolated examples of this form in Fielding and Fanny Burney, but her own use of it, particularly in her later novels, is much more extensive and ambitious than any earlier author's. Its characteristics will be clear from a couple of brief examples. One is from *Mansfield Park*: "He was after her immediately. 'She must not go, she must allow him five minutes longer,' and he took her hand and led her back to her seat" (p. 301). The other is from *Persuasion*: "she found herself accosted by Captain Wentworth, in a reserved yet hurried sort of farewell. 'He must wish her good night. He was going—he should get home as fast as he could'" (p. 190). In these passages, one effect of the free indirect form is to retain the narrative focus on the heroine: the reader is less aware of the character uttering the words—the character remains distanced by the third-person pronouns —than of the listener's reactions to him and his utterance. (It is not strictly necessary for the quotation marks to be retained in free indirect speech, and the practice of Jane Austen varies.)

Yet another variety of dialogue is the telescoping of a long speech or exchange into a few telegraphic phrases, as in the ruthless truncating of Mrs. Elton's gushing monologues. Frank Churchill's small talk to Emma receives the same treatment: "Was she a horse-woman?—Pleasant rides?—Pleasant walks?—Had they a large neighbourhood?—Highbury, perhaps, afforded society enough?" (p. 191) where the free indirect form is also employed.

When she judges it best, Jane Austen is capable of going even further and eschewing dialogue altogether, even at the price of disappointing the reader's expectations. Thus, she leads us to the point at which Emma is called on to reply to Mr. Knightley's proposal, and then, teasingly: "What did she say?—Just what she ought, of course. A lady always does" (p. 431).

Not all speech is spoken aloud: there is also the inner speech of the mind communing with itself; and some of my earlier quotations, such as that from *Persuasion* presenting Anne Elliot's reactions to seeing Captain Wentworth again after a long interval, are examples of Jane Austen's ability to represent a kind of interior monologue.

Mary Lascelles's excellent short chapter on "Style" in *Jane Austen and Her Art* suggests that Jane Austen "appears like one who inherits a prosperous and well-ordered estate" (p. 107), the legacy of the century in which she spent the greater part of her life. But she also extended that estate to incorporate new kinds of stylistic landscape: as Mary Lascelles also says, her style exhibits "a curiously chameleon-like faculty" (p. 102), adapting itself readily to character and situation. As a stylist, she both drew on the strengths of a disinctive tradition and, when necessary, was prepared to strike out as an innovator unparalleled in the fiction of her age.

Bibliography

BABB, HOWARD S. *Jane Austen's Novels: The Fabric of Dialogue* (Columbus, Ohio, 1962).

BRADBROOK, F. W. "Style and Judgment in Jane Austen's Novels," *Cambridge Journal*, 4 (1950–51), 515–37.

———. *Jane Austen and Her Predecessors* (Cambridge, England, 1966).

HOUGH, GRAHAM. "Narrative and Dialogue in Jane Austen," *Critical Quarterly*, 12 (1970), pp. 201–29.

LASCELLES, MARY. *Jane Austen and Her Art* (Oxford, 1939).

LERNER, LAURENCE. *The Truth-tellers* (London, New York, and Toronto, 1967).

LEWIS, C. S. "A Note on Jane Austen," *Essays in Criticism*, 4 (1954), 359–71.

———. *Studies in Words* (Cambridge, England, 1960).

LODGE, DAVID. "The Vocabulary of *Mansfield Park*," in his *Language of Fiction* (London and New York, 1966).

PAGE, NORMAN. *The Language of Jane Austen* (Oxford, 1972).

———. "The English Language: Tradition and Innovation," in *The New Pelican Guide to English Literature*, vol. 5, *From Blake to Byron* (Harmondsworth, 1982), 139–53.

PHILLIPPS, K. C. *Jane Austen's English* (London, 1970).

SOUTHAM, B. C., ed. *Jane Austen: The Critical Heritage* (London and New York, 1968).

TAVE, STUART M. *Some Words of Jane Austen* (Chicago and London, 1973).

TUCKER, SUSIE I. *Protean Shape: A Study in Eighteenth-century Vocabulary and Usage* (London, 1967).

WILLIAMS, RAYMOND. *Keywords* (London, 1976).

LETTERS/ CORRESPONDENCE

Jo Modert

In 1784, when Jane Austen was nine years old, revolutionary improvements in the British postal system led to a cult of letter writing among the country gentry (see "Post/Mail"). By January 1796, when Jane Austen had just turned twenty and her first known letter (original missing) appears, we find her writing on a regular, day-to-day schedule to absent family members, friends, and distant relatives, all in coordination with others around her to avoid repetition. Until 1814, practically all the known letters (original manuscripts, copies, fragments, or published excerpts of now missing originals) are to her sister Cassandra; but these letters show clearly that Cassandra was only one of many with whom she was corresponding.

These letters also show how the daily letter-writing time was planned. For example, whenever Cassandra is away, Jane Austen begins a new letter as soon as she has posted one, adding to it over the next few days. In the meantime, a letter arrives from Cassandra, so that Jane has first had a chance to give her own latest news and then to comment on or to answer the questions in Cassandra's.

"I assure you," she writes in 1808, "I am as tired of writing long letters as you can be. What a pity that one should still be so fond of receiving them!—Fanny Austen's Match is quite news, & I am sorry she has behaved so ill. There is some comfort to *us* in her misconduct, that we have not a congratulatory Letter to write" (*Letters*, June 30, 1808). Another time, she writes from London, "We are now all four of us young Ladies sitting round the Circular Table in the inner room writing our Letters, while the two Brothers are having a comfortable coze in the room adjoining" (*Letters*, September 16, 1813).

As Jane Austen's name was virtually unknown until after her death in 1817, her letters and the scanty correspondence of others are about the only primary source materials we have related to her life and works. Unfortunately, there are many gaps in the correspondence. There are no letters for 1797. From the end of May 1801 until 1805, there is only one letter, in September 1804. There are no letters for 1806, only three for 1807, none from July 1809 to April 1811, and only one (November 1812) from June 1811 to January 1813. Thus, there are many shadowy areas in any Austen biography, filled mostly by speculation.

On the other hand, the letters that have survived are so rich in the minutiae of everyday life that they provide a fascinating picture of the life of the country gentry during the late eighteenth and early nineteenth centuries as well as the truest picture we have of Jane Austen from the time she was twenty until she died some twenty-one years later.

Jane Austen had just turned twenty-five when she paused during a long letter to Cassandra to remark: "I have now attained the true art of letter-writing, which we are always told, is to express on paper exactly what one would say to the same person by word of mouth; I have been talking to you almost as fast as I could the whole of this letter" (*Letters*, January 3, 1801). This semblance to tête-à-tête conversation characterizes Jane Austen's letters, but no one else has ventured to call them works of art. In fact, it is amazing how much controversy these completely uncontroversial letters have stirred up and how little they have been appreciated by even Jane Austen's most devout followers. Part of the problem lies in the fifty-three-year gap between Jane Austen's death and the first publication of her letters.

The history of how the letters slowly became public can easily be charted:

1817 "Biographical Notice" (Chapman, *Novels*, vol. 5, pp. 3–9), unsigned but written by Henry Austen, published excerpts from two or more letters written shortly before Jane Austen's death. The first excerpt reworded the now-famous "bit of Ivory" section from the December 16, 1816 letter to Edward Austen (see *Letters* for comparison). Three other excerpts are from a missing letter or letters and are republished as they appeared in the "Notice" as Letter 147 by Dr. Chapman, who called them "Jane Austen's last known letter, and the first to be published" (*Letters*, Notes).

1867 *My Aunt Jane Austen: A Memoir* by Caroline Austen was not actually published until 1952 by the Jane Austen Society. However, it had a great influence on Austen-Leigh's *Memoir* (below) and is the primary source of many beliefs about Jane Austen's letters that are either false or cannot be proved true.

1870 *A Memoir of Jane Austen* by her nephew James Edward Austen-Leigh; all references here are to the expanded 1871 second edition. Austen-Leigh silently corrected the first excerpt in the "Biographical Notice" and treated the other excerpts as from two letters (see *Memoir*, pp. 153, 150, and 164). He relied heavily on advice and written accounts by his half sister Anna Lefroy (née Austen) and his younger sister Caroline plus papers and letters, mostly from the Charles Austen branch, including ten letters to Cassandra of the twelve published in part. Other letters (mostly excerpts) included eight to Anna Lefroy, three to Austen-Leigh, three to the Royal Librarian J. S. Clarke, four to publisher John Murray, and one each to Caroline, Martha Lloyd, Charles Austen, the countess of Morley, and Alethea Bigg, for a total of thirty-six letters (actually thirty-seven, if Austen-Leigh's treatment of the notice excerpts as from two letters was correct).

1884 *The Letters of Jane Austen*, 2 volumes, edited by Lord Brabourne (Edward Knatchbull-Huggessen), son of Lady Knatchbull née Fanny Knight, eldest daughter of the third brother Edward (who changed his name to Knight in 1812). Lord Brabourne published for the first time seventy-nine letters (with some parts silently deleted or changed) to Cassandra, found in packets inscribed to Fanny by Cassandra, together with five letters to Fanny and with two letters from Cassandra to Fanny describing Jane Austen's death and funeral, all apparently stored by Lady Knatchbull in 1853. Brabourne also published nine letters to Anna, four not in the *Memoir*, and one letter to Charles's daughter, "Little Cassey," for a total of eighty-nine more Jane Austen letters.

1906 *Jane Austen's Sailor Brothers* by John Hubback and Edith Hubback published five letters to the fifth brother, Francis.

1913 *Jane Austen: Her Life and Letters* by William Austen-Leigh and Richard A. Austen-Leigh added three more letters to Cassandra (two from the Charles Austen branch, one from Caroline), six more letters to Caroline, and one to publisher Crosby & Co. for a total of ten additions.

1932, *Jane Austen's Letters to Her Sister Cassandra and Others*, edited by
52, 79 R. W. Chapman, was a landmark in Austen scholarship, providing for the first time the complete texts of all letters Dr. Chapman could trace, plus additional information in a series of indexes, a list of location/ownership of the manuscript letters when known, and more. Dr. Chapman followed Lord Brabourne's system of cataloging the letters chronologically, a tremendous help when it came to cross-references but not as flexible when new letters unexpectedly appeared. Reissues of the *Letters*, over more than fifty years, have added two more letters to Anna Lefroy, three to Caroline Austen, three to Martha Lloyd, one each to Francis Austen, John Murray, Philadelphia Walters (?), Anne Sharp, C. Prowting, and Charles Haden, plus several undated, unsigned fragments, for a total of fifteen additions. (For later corrections and additions, see David Gilson's *Bibliography of Jane Austen*, especially "Letters," pp. 395–402, and his report in the *1983 Jane Austen Society Report*, pp. 13–15, on my corrections of Dr.

Chapman's list of location/ownership (*Letters*, pp. xviii–xxxiii up to October 1983; and my *St. Louis Post-Dispatch* article on an unrecorded fragment at Harvard).

Altogether, Dr. Chapman's *Letters* publishes 155 letters, around 130 of which exist in their original form, though sometimes mutilated by censorship, missing signatures, or even pages. The rest are known only by copies or fragments or published versions.

More difficult than following the publishing history of Jane Austen's known letters is the problem of distinguishing between actual facts about them as presented in secondary source material, such as the memoirs of relatives who had known Jane Austen, and the family myths that have grown up around them. Obviously, this affects not only how we read the letters but also how Jane Austen is perceived by her biographers and critics. (For two recent conflicting views, see Joan Austen-Leigh's "Austen Leighs and Jane Austen" and Margaret Kirkham's "Austen Portraits and the Received Biography.")

Henry Austen's overenthusiastic praise in the "Biographical Notice" for his sister's correspondence certainly did not prepare his Victorian nieces, nephews, and their offspring for their first look at some of Jane Austen's letters, especially those written in her earlier years. "The style of her correspondence," Henry wrote in late 1817, "was in all respects the same as that of her novels. Every thing came finished from her pen; for on all subjects she had ideas as clear as her expressions were well chosen. It is not hazarding too much to say that she never dispatched a note or letter unworthy of publication" (Chapman, *Novels*, vol. 5, p. 8). Henry could not know that his sister's more "refined" grand-nephew, Lord Brabourne, would silently change "Bowel" to "Stomach" and omit other accounts of physical complaints completely.

Fifty years after the "Biographical Notice," Caroline Austen—only twelve when her aunt died—noted that

> [Jane Austen's] handwriting remains to bear testimony to its own excellence; and every note and letter of hers, was finished off handsomely—There was an art *then* in folding and sealing—no adhesive envelopes made all easy—some people's letters looked always loose and untidy—but *her* paper was sure to take the right folds, and *her* sealing wax to drop in the proper place—(*My Aunt Jane Austen*, p. 7; *Memoir*, pp. 92–93; often quoted later)

Jane Austen's letters do indeed bear out Caroline's praise as to the fineness of her copperplate script, closely spaced lines with few if any corrections or ink blotches, and neat folds (see "Post/Mail"). But then Caroline's imagination takes over, because the letters were sealed with thin colored wafers, not hot wax, as both extant letters and some interior comments show (*Letters*, pp. 51, 70, and 347).

No one, to my knowledge, has questioned Caroline's accuracy till now, but she merits closer attention because of some crucial statements that have had a far greater influence than she probably intended:

> [My Aunt] wrote very fully to her Brothers when they were at sea, and she corresponded with many others of her family—
>
> There is nothing in those letters which *I* have seen that would be acceptable to the public—They were very well expressed, and they must have been very interesting to those who received them—but they detailed chiefly home and family events; and she seldom committed herself *even* to an opinion—so that to strangers they would be *no* transcript to her mind—they would not feel that they knew her the better for having read them—
>
> They were rather over-cautious, for excellence—Her letters to Aunt Cassandra (for they were sometimes separated) were, I dare say, open and confidential—My Aunt looked them over and burnt the greater part, (as she told me), 2 or 3 years before her own death—She left, or gave some as legacies to the Nieces—but of those *I* have seen, several had portions cut out— (ibid., pp. 9–10)

Significantly, Austen-Leigh did not mention Caroline's version of the destruction of Jane Austen's letters, though it became a smokescreen for the more massive destruction that he did describe. "The grave closed over my aunt fifty-two years ago," he wrote, "and during that long period no idea of writing her life had been entertained by any of the family. Her nearest relatives, far from making provisions for such a purpose, had actually destroyed many of the letters and papers by which it might have been facilitated" (*Memoir*, p. 195). To bear him out, there are no known letters to either Austen parent, James, Edward, Henry, or their wives; and there are only six letters to Francis and one to Charles, the sailor brothers, to whom Jane Austen probably wrote the most of all. It should also be noted that other letters or portions of them had been given to friends, other family members, or autograph seekers. This surely accounted for more mutilations than any censorship by Cassandra or others.

Austen-Leigh—who considered Walter Scott a "greater genius than my aunt" (p. 128, Footnote 1)—did agree with Caroline that Jane Austen's letters were of little interest outside the family:

> the reader must be warned not to expect too much from them. . . . The style is always clear, and generally animated, while a vein of humour continually gleams through the whole; but the materials may be thought inferior to the execution, for they treat only of the

details of domestic life. There is in them no notice of politics or public events; scarcely any discussions on literature, or other subjects of general interest. (ibid., p. 7)

Lord Brabourne, unaware of Caroline's comment about Cassandra's destroying most of her letters, merely noted that "it would seem that at Cassandra's death, in 1845, the correspondence must have been divided, and whilst the bulk of it came to my mother, a number of letters passed into the possession of Mr Austen Leigh's sisters, from whom he obtained them" (Brabourne, vol. 1, pp. xiii–xiv). Actually, although this remained the general impression until Dr. Chapman's report in the 1926 (London) *Times Literary Supplement*, Caroline seems to have received only three letters from Cassandra, Anna none. Twelve had gone to Charles Austen's daughters, with none to any nieces of the Francis Austen or Edward Knight branches with the exception of Fanny. Or did Cassandra bequeath more letters that were later lost or destroyed? Caroline merely says, "Nieces," not how many or which ones. We may never know.

Whatever actually happened to Cassandra's letters, they have dominated attention and have been used to excuse either the blandness of the preserved letters, the lack of any emotional or romantic disclosures, or the sometimes ribald fun that is closer to Jane Austen's *juvenilia* than to the published novels.

It was Fanny Caroline Lefroy, one of Anna's daughters, I suspect, who first claimed that Jane Austen had written mostly to Cassandra, that (repeating Caroline) she had only confided in her (which seems unlikely now that we have seen more letters to Martha Lloyd and one to Anne Sharp), and that Cassandra had destroyed every letter that might possibly be of interest. (As proud as Cassandra was of Jane, she more likely destroyed letters she considered not up to par.)

Constance Hill in *Jane Austen: Her Homes & Her Friends* called Fanny Caroline's interpretations to international attention:

> In an article by Miss Lefroy that appeared in "Temple Bar" some years ago the writer tells us that a large number of Miss Austen's letters, dealing with matters of a private nature, were burnt after her death. She goes on to say: "With all the playful frankness of her manner, her sweet sunny temper and enthusiastic nature, Jane Austen was a woman most reticent as to her own deepest and holiest feelings; and her sister Cassandra would have thought she was sinning against that delicacy and reserve had she left behind her any record of them." (p. 234)

By 1913, when William and Richard Austen Leigh published *Life and Letters* with the aim of being of use in "removing misconceptions, in laying some new facts before the reader, and in placing others in a fresh light" (p.

viii), Caroline's statement was now stretched to read that "Cassandra purposely destroyed many of the letters likely to prove the most interesting, from a distaste of publicity" (ibid., p. v) and to "the rule acted upon by Cassandra, destruction of her sister's letters, was proof of their emotional interest" (ibid., p. 156; see also pp. 81–83; Mary Augusta Austen-Leigh's *Personal Aspects of Jane Austen*, pp. 7 and 48–49; Dr. Chapman's introduction to *My Aunt Jane Austen*, pp. viii–ix; Lord David Cecil's *Portrait of Jane Austen*, pp. 72–73; Verlyn Klinkenborg's comments on Jane Austen's letters, *British Literary Manuscripts*, ser. II, p. 17).

What one perceives in most of the apologies for Jane Austen's letters is a tone of genuine distress, felt as when one overhears a private conversation that does not bear out one's own expectations. The Jane Austen of the letters, especially during the earlier years, has been ignored by devoted scholars like Dr. Chapman and by her biographers, who have surely felt in their troubled reflections that she sounds at times more like Lydia Bennet than Elizabeth. There is a lot of bucolic humor in the letters—jokes about someone wanting to kiss or propose to Cassandra, threats of being "hanged," and graveyard humor—that has always been ignored or rationalized or excused. In other words, there is a Jane Austen in the letters infinitely more interesting than any we have been shown thus far.

"You are very amiable & very clever to write such long Letters;" Jane Austen writes to Cassandra in 1808, "every page of yours has more lines than this, & every line more words than the average of mine. I am quite ashamed—but you have certainly more little events than we have" (*Letters*, June 20, 1808). For years and years now, Jane Austen has been trying to tell us in the novels that the little events of everyday life—what Austen-Leigh condescendingly called "only the 'details of domestic life'"—are the things that shape character and often spell the difference between happiness and sorrow, comfort and pain. When we begin to comprehend how fully Jane Austen uses the little events of her own life, as illustrated in the letters, we may understand more fully the ripening of her genius.

Bibliography

AUSTEN, CAROLINE MARY CRAVEN. *My Aunt Jane Austen: A Memoir* (Alton, 1952).
AUSTEN-LEIGH, JOAN. "The Austen Leighs and Jane Austen, or 'I have always maintained the importance of Aunts,'" in Janet Todd, ed., *Jane Austen: New Perspectives* (New York, 1983).
AUSTEN-LEIGH, MARY AUGUSTA. *Personal Aspects of Jane Austen* (London, 1920).
BRABOURNE, LORD EDWARD. *Letters of Jane Austen*, 2 vols. (London, 1884).

Jane Austen

British Literary Manuscripts, ser. II, *From 1800 to 1914*, Verlyn Klinkenborg, Herbert Cahoon, and Charles Ryskamp, eds. (New York, 1981).

CHAPMAN, ROBERT WILLIAM. "A Jane Austen Collection," in *Times Literary Supplement* (January 14, 1926), p. 27.

———. *Jane Austen: A Critical Bibliography* (Oxford, 1953, 2nd ed. 1955).

GILSON, DAVID. *A Bibliography of Jane Austen* (Oxford, 1982).

HILL, CONSTANCE. *Jane Austen: Her Homes & Her Friends* (London and New York, 1902).

HUBBACK, JOHN HENRY, AND EDITH CHARLOTTE HUBBACK. *Jane Austen's Sailor Brothers* (London and New York, 1906).

KIRKHAM, MARGARET. "The Austen Portraits and the Received Biography," in Janet Todd, ed., *Jane Austen: New Perspectives* (New York, 1983).

MODERT, JO. "Here for the First Time, a Jane Austen Letter," *St. Louis Post-Dispatch*, December 18, 1983.

MUNBY, ALAN N. L. *The Cult of the Autograph Letter in England* (London, 1962).

LIFE OF JANE AUSTEN

J. David Grey

Jane Austen was born on December 16, 1775 at the parsonage in the small Hampshire village of Steventon where her father, the Reverend George Austen, was rector. Her mother, Cassandra Austen (née Leigh), was a lively and witty woman, the niece of a famous master of Balliol College, Oxford. Jane Austen was the seventh child in a family of eight. Her closest friend and lifelong companion was her only sister, Cassandra, nearly three years older. Jane was especially devoted to her brother Henry, who—like the eldest brother, James—was educated at home and at Oxford. Two other brothers, Francis and Charles, entered the navy and rose to the rank of admiral. The Austen home, with its five-hundred-volume library, was distinctly bookish. Cassandra and Jane learned more from their fathers and brothers than from their formal years of schooling. About 1792, the Austen daughters went away from home for tutoring to Mrs. Cawley at Oxford and Southampton and later (1783 or 1784) to the Abbey School at Reading, where they remained for several years. Afterward, Jane Austen continued her education at home, reading voraciously in Shakespeare, English history, contemporary fiction, and the poets and moralists of the eighteenth century. The Austen household was an ideal environment for her development as a novelist of manners. Books were always under discussion: the novels of Samuel Richardson and Henry Fielding were family favorites, and the works of Sterne, Smollett, and Goldsmith were at hand. Amateur theatricals were a family passion. A Steventon dramatic company was recruited from the Austens and their neighbors, and the rectory barn was converted into a little theater for productions in the summer holidays, while at Christmas plays were performed in the house. The repertoire was not restricted and included the broader type of eighteenth-century comedy. During 1789–90 Jane Austen may have helped her brothers Henry and James in the production of an Oxford literary periodical, *The Loiterer*. The Steventon household included young men whom Mr. Austen was preparing for entry to Oxford and Cambridge, and there was a wide circle of relatives, particularly on Mrs. Austen's side, and friends to visit (sometimes for months at a stretch) and to be visited by.

Jane Austen began writing in the late 1780s, and between 1788 and 1793 she produced over twenty juvenile pieces (most of them satirical parody) that were collected in three manuscript volumes for the family's amusement. Even in these early works can be traced the outline of her later achievement: her gift for caricature, her good-humored realism, and her desire to correct the false emotions of gothic and sentimental fiction. Among the *juvenilia*, "Love and Freindship" (finished in 1790) stands out as a sustained burlesque of all the absurd conventions of "the land of fiction." Around 1794, Jane Austen attempted a more ambitious and serious work, a novel in letters called *Lady Susan*. This, the portrait of a woman bent on the exercise of her own powerful mind to the point of social self-destruction, is a study of woman's fate in a society that has no use for woman's stronger, more "masculine," talents. A year later, when she was only nineteen years old, Jane Austen wrote *Elinor and Marianne*, an early epistolary version of *Sense and Sensibility* that has not survived. It was followed in 1796–97 by *First Impressions*, the lost original of *Pride and Prejudice*, again presented through letters. Cadell, the London publisher, rejected the manuscript when it was offered by Jane's father in 1797. Undaunted, and since she was writing purely for her own satisfaction and for her family's pleasure, Jane Austen continued with *Elinor and Marianne* in 1797 and *Susan* (later revised as *Northanger Abbey*) that year and the next. From 1799 until 1809, with the exception of an unfinished novel of manners, *The Watsons* (1803–1804), she did little writing destined for an audience beyond her immediate circle.

The reason for her silence can be only a matter of conjecture. Up to the age of twenty-five, Jane Austen's life appears to have been happy and secure. From January 1796 onward, the surviving letters tell of her enjoyment of local parties and dances in Hampshire, of visits to London, Bath, Southampton, Kent, and seaside resorts in Devon and Dorset. (A gossipy recollection by Mary Mitford's mother, who had left the Steventon neighborhood when Jane Austen was seven, describes her as the "prettiest, silliest, most affected husband-hunting butterfly [she] ever remembers.") Only a remnant of "prettiness" can be glimpsed in the one authentic portrait, Cassandra's sketch of about 1810: here the dark eyes, dark ringlets, and round cheeks attend an expression of slightly soured resignation. Although she and her sister never married, courtship and marriage—the major subjects of Jane Austen's later fiction—were their natural concerns. Cassandra was engaged in 1795 to a young man who died soon afterward in the West Indies before they could marry. Jane's first recorded romantic association was a flirtation early in 1796 with Tom Lefroy, a handsome young Irishman, nephew of the rector of a village near Steventon. In 1798 or 1799 there was possibly a flirtation with one Samuel Blackall, a fellow of Emmanuel College, Cambridge, who was then staying with the Lefroys. In November 1802 it seems likely that she agreed to marry Harris Bigg-Wither, the twenty-one-year-old heir of a Hampshire family, but the next morning she changed her mind. There are also a number of mutually contradictory stories connecting her with someone (sometimes a naval officer, sometimes an army officer, sometimes a clergyman) with whom she fell in love while on a holiday at the seaside but who died very soon after. Unfortunately, the evidence is unsatisfactory and incomplete. Cassandra was a jealous guardian of her sister's private life, and after Jane's death she (and other members of the family) censored the surviving letters, destroying many and cutting up others.

In any event, the years after 1801 were not happy ones for Jane Austen. In 1801 her father suddenly retired to Bath, resigning his duties in Steventon to his eldest son, James, and Jane Austen was uprooted from the comforts of Steventon and subjected to a succession of rented residences in Bath, a place she little cared for. Her mother was gravely ill in 1804, and her father died in 1805, leaving Jane and Cassandra alone with Mrs. Austen. After visits to Clifton and Warwickshire, the Austens settled in Southampton from 1806 to 1809. In these difficult years Jane Austen must have come to terms with the limitations of spinsterhood so often portrayed in her novels. Her depressed mood at this time may be reflected in the bleak treatments of Bath and Portsmouth in the later works and was surely one reason for her lack of artistic energy.

George Austen's third son, Edward, had been adopted when very young by a kinsman, Thomas Knight of Godmersham, Kent, and later became his heir. When Edward's wife died in 1808, he felt that his mother and sisters should settle on one of his properties, and offered them a sizable cottage in the village of Chawton, Hampshire (a few miles from Winchester and not far from Jane Austen's beloved Steventon). The move to Chawton, where some measure of family stability could be regained, seems to have acted as a catalyst upon Jane Austen's imagination. She made inquiries about the manuscript of *Susan*, which had been sold for £10 to the publisher Richard Crosby in 1803 but was never issued. She began to rewrite *Elinor and Marianne* almost immediately, and in 1811 it appeared, anonymously, as *Sense and Sensibility*. She then undertook a radical recasting of *First Impressions* (now called *Pride and Prejudice*), but even before it was published, she had completed a new work, the first product of her mature artistic vision: *Mansfield Park*. This novel, begun in February 1811 and finished in the summer of 1813, tempers the youthful energy of *Pride and Prejudice* by emphasizing the difficult virtues of patience, restraint, and stoicism. The first edition of *Mansfield Park* was published anonymously in May 1814. (No novel appeared in Jane Austen's lifetime with her name on the title page, and the only recognition that she received was an invitation to tour the prince regent's library and permission to dedicate *Emma* to him.)

Emma (1815) received a highly favorable notice from Walter Scott in the

Quarterly Review (March 1816). In *Emma*, Jane Austen recovered the wit and energy of *Pride and Prejudice* while maintaining the complex narrative effects of *Mansfield Park*. The years 1815–16 were clouded by the illness and financial difficulties of her favorite brother, Henry (now a banker), but Jane Austen continued to write with unusual vigor. The lighthearted "Plan of a Novel" (1815–16), in which the "helpful" suggestions of various friends and family are woven into a burlesque of fictional conventions, reflects her confidence at this time. In February 1816 there was a second edition of *Mansfield Park*, published, like *Emma*, by Byron's publisher, John Murray ("a rogue, of course, but a civil one," Jane Austen commented). Although she remained at pains to preserve her anonymity, avoiding literary circles, Jane Austen was nonetheless concerned about the reception of the novels, not the least because they earned money as well as praise. At Chawton she remained a housekeeper and dutiful attendant on her mother. To an ever-growing band of nieces and nephews she was the favorite "Aunt Jane," a prized confidante and adviser on literature and affairs of the heart.

Persuasion (1817) was written between August 1815 and August 1816, but even as the novel was completed, Jane Austen's health began to fail. She prepared *Catherine* (originally *Susan*, later *Northanger Abbey*) for publication and wrote a brief advertisement, or preface, which may reflect her growing sense of mortality in its stress on the changes time brings to manners and customs. In January 1817 she began the satirical fragment later known as *Sanditon*, a critique of contemporary social fashions that returns in many ways to the spirit of her earliest works. The burlesque form of *Sanditon* marks a sharp break with the elegiac, "autumnal" mood of *Persuasion* and may be seen as Jane Austen's brave defiance against the depression of illness. *Sanditon* was abandoned on March 18, 1817 after twelve chapters had been drafted, presumably because of failing health. The symptoms (reported wryly and un-self-pityingly in her letters) make possible a modern clinical assessment that she was probably suffering from Addison's disease. Her condition fluctuated, and in April 1817 she made her will. The following month she moved to College Street, Winchester, to be near a surgeon; on the morning of July 18, at four-thirty, she died in the arms of her sister and was buried six days later in Winchester Cathedral. In December 1817 her brother Henry published *Northanger Abbey* and *Persuasion*, adding a "Biographical Notice." It was only in these posthumous volumes that Jane Austen's name became known to the world at large.

JANE AUSTEN IN LONDON

Anne-Marie Edwards

Jane Austen was very far from being a country mouse; she knew London well. The first letter she writes to Cassandra from London is dated August 1796 and headed Cork Street. Aged twenty, she is on her way to visit Kent, where her brother Edward had been adopted by wealthy relatives. She knows the anxiety her family at Steventon will be feeling for her, although she is accompanied by her brothers Edward and Frank. London was generally reputed to be a city of sin. Impishly, Jane writes: "I begin already to find my morals corrupted." In "Catharine," an unfinished novel Jane began when she was sixteen, she makes fun of straitlaced Mrs. Percival, who is unshakable in her belief that London is a "Hot house of vice." With her delight in people Jane Austen could not help enjoying the variety of London society, the excitement of its busy streets and shops, and the pleasures of its theaters, concerts, and galleries.

She enjoyed shopping, too, and noted the elegant shopping areas of the rich like Sackville Street, where, in *Sense and Sensibility*, she depicts Elinor and Marianne waiting in Thomas Gray's jewelry shop while the foppish Robert Ferrars dithers over his choice of toothpicks. But she was fully aware that while a few of the city's inhabitants lived comfortably in elegant surroundings the majority competed for the means to live in conditions of appalling squalor. In the same novel there is a vivid account of the sufferings and death of Colonel Brandon's childhood friend, Eliza, left destitute and friendless in London. There was no safety net for those without means, so money was all-important. What Jane saw clearly was the corruption of society, when the need to make money took precedence over everything else. The old-fashioned values—consideration for others, order, balanced opinions, even simple kindness—were being challenged and undermined. Yet if the new money-makers were heartless, they were awake and open to fresh ideas. The old standards were in danger of stagnating. These are the two sets of values that confront each other in her mature novel *Mansfield Park*. The old house, with its rigid values, cannot survive against modern pressures unless some compromise beneficial to both sides can be reached. London society is personified in Henry and Mary Crawford. Superficial but charming, they win the hearts of the simpler Mansfield gentlefolk. But having been brought up in London, in contact with all that was most corrupt in that society, they are finally seen for what they are; worldly, immoral, and self-seeking. Only Fanny Price, adopted into gentle society from a harsher background, has the balanced judgment and strength of character to save Mansfield Park.

As always, Jane is writing from close observation. Her favorite brother, Henry (like his namesake in *MP*, lively, witty, and charming) had married Eliza de Feuillide, the widow of a count guillotined in the French Revolution. She was as lively and charming as he was, and they rented a house in Sloane Square. (The house, no. 64, has been replaced by a Victorian building, but there is a plaque marking the site.) In Jane's time, the West End, as Miss Mitford writes, was "bordered by Hyde Park Corner on the one side and the Green Park on the other." Sloane Street was an isolated development across an area of marsh. Jane Austen stayed with them in 1811 while she corrected the proofs of *Sense and Sensibility*.

After Eliza died in 1813, Henry moved into the city to live at 10 Henrietta Street, over the bank in which he was a partner. The small town house stands today. The ground floor has been altered and the front stuccoed, but there is a typically eighteenth-century neat line of windows beneath a row of small balusters that run the length of the roof. Jane Austen arrived to comfort Henry and writes to Cassandra from the much more crowded and noisy conditions of "the breakfast, dining, sitting-room" (*Letters*, September 15, 1813). As ever, she finds amusement. Writing to Cassandra about the latest fashions, she comments, "I learnt from Mrs. Tickars's young lady, to my high amusement, that the stays now are not made to force the bosom up" (ibid.). And, as a devoted aunt, she made herself useful, accompanying Edward's children on painful visits to the dentist.

For a last glimpse of Jane Austen in London, we must visit Hans Square. After a few months in Henrietta Street, Henry came to live at number 23, which had a pretty garden to delight Jane and was almost entirely surrounded by fields. The house has been rebuilt, but it does have a plaque recalling Jane Austen's visits. Only one of the eighteenth-century houses remains, with rounded windows and a delicate wrought-iron balcony. Henry's house must have been just as charming, as Jane called it "a delightful place." Here, in 1814, Jane prepared *Mansfield Park* for its second edition, corrected the proofs of *Emma*, and continued her new novel, *Persuasion*. Henry fell ill, and she nursed him devotedly, to the detriment of her own health. When Henry was better—and *Emma* safely published—she returned to Chawton. Shortly afterward, Henry's business failed, and he decided to move to Chawton to take Holy Orders.

Today, enough remains of Jane Austen's London to help us recapture the atmosphere of the scenes and characters she depicts. Although she is primarily concerned with domestic life in country villages, her knowledge and understanding of London enriches her work and gives greater depth and contrast to her characters. She was deeply concerned about the decay of moral standards in city life, and this concern is at the heart of *Mansfield Park*. But there is always a subtle balance both in Jane Austen herself and in her novels. Her sympathies may lie with the old order of the countryside, but which of us among her readers has not responded with pleasure to the lively charm of Henry and Mary Crawford, reflecting as they do their creator's delight in the variety and excitement of London life?

Bibliography

EDWARDS, ANNE-MARIE. *In the Steps of Jane Austen* (London, 1979).

LOVE AND MARRIAGE

Juliet McMaster

Love, courtship, and the final happy marriage of the heroine to the right partner form the staple of the plots of all Jane Austen's novels. Yet as a novelist who has been famous for staying within the limits of her own experience, she has sometimes been taken to task for being a spinster and thus ignorant of married life and inexperienced in sexual matters.

But she did have some love life of her own, although, as the authors of the *Life* pointed out, "the emotional and romantic side of her nature—a very real one—has not been dwelt upon" (p. vii). At twenty she carried on an amusing flirtation with Tom Lefroy and joked about her expectations that he would propose. He did not, and subsequently married a lady of fortune in Ireland. Although she was clearly attracted, Jane Austen said she did not "care sixpence" for him (*Letters*, January 14, 1796); but in later life he admitted that he had been in love with her, though with a boy's love.

Two years later she was admired and courted by Samuel Blackall, a Cambridge don, but he prudently awaited preferment before committing himself to a proposal. "This is rational enough," wrote Jane; "there is less love and more sense in it than sometimes appeared before, and I am very well satisfied.... our indifference will soon be mutual" (*Letters*, November 17, 1798). Some years later, when she heard of his marriage to another lady, she wrote calmly, "He was a piece of Perfection, noisy Perfection himself which I always recollect with regard." And she added of his bride, "I would wish Miss Lewis to be of a silent turn & rather ignorant, but naturally intelligent & wishing to learn;—fond of cold veal pies, green tea in the afternoon, & a green window blind at night" (*Letters*, July 3, 1813). Clearly her heart had not been much touched.

About the most important romance in Jane Austen's life we have fewest reliable facts, and the exact date and place and the young man's identity are unknown. Her sister Cassandra revealed some years after Jane's death that while the family was on holiday in the west of England, they met an exceptionally charming gentleman and that he and Jane Austen were mutually attracted. He engaged to seek them out again after their travels, and it was Cassandra's expectation that he would propose and that Jane would accept. But the next news of him was of his sudden death. Cassandra did not commit this sad little story to paper, but there are several versions that have been handed down from different family sources. In one the gentleman was a clergyman, with a brother who was a doctor, and in another he was a naval officer. One probable conjecture is that the romance was set in Sidmouth, which the Austens visited in 1801, when Jane was twenty-five. It has been suggested that this crisis in her emotional life could have been the reason for the long hiatus in her creative activity in the first decade of the nineteenth century.

We know of only one more episode in her love life. When she was nearly twenty-seven (Anne Elliot's age in *Persuasion*), she received a proposal from Harris Bigg-Wither of Manydown, the brother of intimate friends near Steventon and some years younger than herself. The writer of the *Memoir* described him as "a gentleman who had the recommendations of good character, and connections, and position in life, of everything, in fact, except the subtle power of touching her heart" (p. 28). But in spite of the temptation of marriage for a single woman of slender means, she decided not to marry him without love.

Beyond her own individual experience she had an extended field for observation in the loves and marriages of her numerous family and acquaintance. Her letters show that she knew a larger section of the world than the three or four families in a country village that she considered the appropriate personnel for a novel. She maintained a high ideal of a marriage based on mutual love and esteem, but she also knew that marriage was not always a blessed state and could write with asperity of married couples she knew, like the Halls: "Mrs. Hall, of Sherborne, was brought to bed yesterday of a dead child, some weeks before she expected, owing to a fright. I suppose she happened unawares to look at her husband" (*Letters*, October 27, 1798). She had occasion to wonder, like Elinor in *Sense and Sensibility*, "at the strange unsuitableness which often existed between husband and wife" (p. 118).

In her novels Jane Austen presents courtship and love as practiced by ladies and gentlemen in the drawing room. She does not follow her lovers into the bedroom, and she shows them as under certain social restraints in both the verbal and the physical expression of their love. Hence, she has often been accused of lacking passion. Anthony Trollope, who wrote many tender proposal scenes himself, was disappointed that at the climax of *Emma*, when Mr. Knightley proposes, all we hear of Emma's answer is the teasing "What did she say?—Just what she ought, of course" (*E*, p. 431). The evasion of passionate utterance, wrote Trollope in the flyleaf of his copy of *Emma*, "robs the reader of much of the charm which he has promised himself." "The Passions are perfectly unknown to her," complained Charlotte Brontë, adding that Jane Austen made it her business to delineate only "the surface of the lives of genteel English people," without inquiring into their stormy hearts (letter of April 12, 1850). Jane Austen's great-niece Fanny Lefroy, writing in 1883, noted, "It is becoming the fashion to accuse her of being shallow and cold-hearted." "You are talking of Jane Austen and sex, gentlemen?" a man is reported to have inquired at a soiree at Gertrude Stein's home in Paris. "The subjects are mutually exclusive. That dried-up lady snob lived behind lace curtains all her life" (Glassco, p. 96). But there have been arguments on both sides. According to a recent critic, "The courtship plots she creates allow her to explore the relations between sex and moral judgement, sex and friendship, sex and knowledge—that is, between sex and character. In this sense, there is no escaping sexuality in Austen's novels" (Fergus, p. 66).

The dramatization of love is restrained but has its own intensity. The closest that Jane Austen comes to showing the kind of passionate physical embrace that Charlotte Brontë allowed to Rochester in *Jane Eyre* is the moment at which Mr. Knightley almost kisses Emma's hand:

> He looked at her with a glow of regard. She was warmly gratified — and in another moment still more so, by a little movement of more than common friendliness on his part.—He took her hand;—whether she had not herself made the first motion, she could not say—she might, perhaps, have rather offered it—but he took her hand, pressed it, and certainly was on the point of carrying it to his lips—when, from some fancy or other, he suddenly let it go.—Why he should feel such a scruple, why he should change his mind when it was all but done, she could not perceive.—He would have judged better, she thought, if he had not stopped.... She could not but recall the attempt with great satisfaction. (*E*, pp. 385–86)

As a rendering of a sexual advance this is perhaps very mild compared with, say, D. H. Lawrence. But for Jane Austen the interest of the incident resides in the state of mind of the protagonists. Emma's tense mental operations, while she registers Mr. Knightley's impulse to kiss, and her own regret that the kiss was not completed make the passage a stimulating one for the close reader. It is typical of Jane Austen's love scenes that however deeply the heroine's heart is touched, her head (except perhaps in the case of Marianne) is simultaneously active.

It is the message of *Sense and Sensibility*, perhaps not quite successfully articulated, that still waters run deep. Elinor's controlled love for Edward, we are to believe, is as strong as Marianne's for Willoughby, even though Elinor does not talk about it and makes successful efforts to conceal it. Later heroines, like Fanny Price and Anne Elliot, must also suffer in silence as they see the men they love respond to the wiles of other, inferior women. Restraint is essential to the strong loves in the novels, and the same applies to the author's presentation of them. The reader is treated to few grand passionate scenes and no histrionic rhetoric but must be watchful for small signs. Love is often suggested by indirection. In a crucial scene in

Sense and Sensibility, when Elinor meets Edward again, believing him recently married to someone else, she tells herself, "I *will* be calm; I *will* be mistress of myself" (p. 358). Presently, she can so command herself that "she sat down again and talked of the weather" (p. 359). Edward's own agitation in the tense interview is again conveyed indirectly, as he nervously toys with a pair of scissors, "spoiling both them and their sheath by cutting the latter to pieces as he spoke" (p. 360). Jane Austen became adept at conveying strong emotion by light suggestion. It takes an attentive reader of *Emma* to be aware that in the banter and badinage at Box Hill, Frank Churchill and Jane Fairfax, who are secretly engaged, are actually having a lovers' quarrel and breaking off their engagement. He speaks in general terms, but with a secret meaning that only she and the reader can comprehend, of the dangers of engagements (like theirs) formed on the basis only of acquaintance at a public place.

> "It is all guess and luck—and will generally be ill-luck. How many a man has committed himself on a short acquaintance, and rued it all the rest of his life!"
> Miss Fairfax, who had seldom spoken before, . . . spoke now.
> "Such things do occur, undoubtedly."—She was stopped by a cough. Frank Churchill turned towards her to listen.
> "You were speaking," said he, gravely. She recovered her voice.
> "I was only going to observe, that though such unfortunate circumstances do sometimes occur both to men and women, I cannot imagine them to be very frequent. A hasty and imprudent attachment may arise—but . . . it can be only weak, irresolute characters . . . who will suffer an unfortunate acquaintance to be an inconvenience, an oppression for ever." (*E*, pp. 372–73)

The hasty reader may pass over the passage as mere pointless moralizing. But the reader who knows of the engagement can recognize the strong and particular meaning that underlies the comments and may deduce that the hesitation in Jane's speech is caused by repressed tears. Beneath the apparently serene surface we glimpse the individual's agonies.

It is not only the heroine but many of the young people around her who are engaged in finding suitable mates in the novels. There are two marriages at the end of *Northanger Abbey*, four each in the course of *Sense and Sensibility*, *Pride and Prejudice*, and *Emma*, and three in *Mansfield Park* and *Persuasion*. So many couplings, of so many kinds, supply plot interest and give ample space for commentary on courtship and marriage and speculation on love. The question of who loves whom and how much is always to the fore, and the reader must be alert to such symptoms of love as sighs, blushes, pallor, sleeplessness, and signs of jealousy or confusion. From such symptoms Elizabeth and Darcy deduce the extent of Jane's and

Bingley's attachment, Mr. Knightley can discover a secret understanding between Jane Fairfax and Frank Churchill, and Emma leaps to conclusions about the state of heart of Mr. Elton, Frank Churchill, Harriet, and Mr. Knightley. Emma and Elizabeth, though they are both unaware for a large part of their novels of the state of their own hearts, set up as experts on the loves of others. Elizabeth sees it as a symptom of love in Bingley that he should look in her face for the trace of a resemblance to Jane's; but she herself had done the same thing in examining Lady Catherine's face for a likeness to Darcy, long before she recognizes her own attraction to him (*PP*, pp. 162 and 262). Emma, believing herself to be in love with Frank Churchill, says in soliloquy, "Oh! what would Frank Churchill say . . . ? Ah! there I am—thinking of him directly. Always the first person to be thought of! How I catch myself out!" But the first person she had thought of in the soliloquy was actually Mr. Knightley (*E*, p. 279). The placing of such small clues makes of the attentive reader a detective and diagnostician of love.

Although Jane Austen lived in an age in which marriages of convenience were frequent and matrimony was often almost the only means of support for a woman, she insisted that love was necessary for a happy marriage. Comprehended in her idea of love was esteem, moral approval; and the attraction that is merely stimulated by beauty rather than based on respect for a sound character, like Marianne's for Willoughby or Mr. Bennet's for his bride, is likely to go sour. The heroines sometimes feel such an attraction—for Mr. Wickham, Henry Crawford, Frank Churchill, or Mr. Elliot —and may briefly mistake it for love, but they learn to fasten their real love on men of more steady principles. In a letter to her niece Fanny Knight, who was courted by a man she was not sure she loved, Jane Austen made clear the love ethic that pertains in her novels: "His situation in life, family, friends, & above all his character—his uncommonly amiable mind, strict principles, just notions, good habits. . . . *All* that is really of the first importance—everything of this nature pleads his cause most strongly." Such qualities create the necessary esteem, but esteem alone is not enough. Fanny is advised of "the desirableness of your growing in love with him" if she can but is cautioned, if she cannot, that "anything is to be preferred or endured rather than marrying without Affection" (*Letters*, November 18, 1814).

If love for Jane Austen is a sine qua non in marriage, so is money. In the same letter of advice, she urged her niece to consider that her suitor was "the eldest son of a Man of Fortune, the Brother of your particular friend, & belonging to your own County.—Think of all this Fanny." Jane Austen had no admiration for people who are careless about money and often suggested that such an attitude was a disguised mercenariness. In "Love and Freindship" those who scorn "the false glare of Fortune" have presently "gracefully purloined" other people's money (*Vol. 2*, pp. 81 and 88).

However, although she shows that a due attention to income is necessary in a couple considering matrimony, Jane Austen disapproves of those who marry for money alone. The marriage of Charlotte Lucas in *Pride and Prejudice* becomes a test case. Charlotte is one of a large family. If she does not marry, she can look forward only to a life of dependence as the spinster aunt in the home of her brother. She knows Mr. Collins does not love her, for he has just proposed to another girl and been refused. And she can hardly love Mr. Collins, who is a pompous bore. Nevertheless, he is a young man in possession of a good living, with expectations of inheriting a handsome property; so she encourages his advances and accepts his proposal. "I am not romantic you know," she justifies herself to Elizabeth. "I never was. I ask only a comfortable home; and considering Mr. Collins's character, connections, and situation in life, I am convinced that my chance of happiness with him is as fair, as most people can boast on entering the marriage state" (*PP*, p. 125). It is a grim picture, but perhaps statistically not a wildly inaccurate one, for such married couples as the Allens, Middletons, Bennets, Prices, and Musgroves hardly suggest that perfect domestic felicity is the rule. Elizabeth is shocked: "she could not have supposed it possible that . . . [Charlotte] would have sacrificed every better feeling to worldly advantage" (ibid). But Charlotte is not severely punished and manages to be reasonably happy in her home at Hunsford, particularly when her husband is not at hand. Elizabeth, however, though her family circumstances are similar to Charlotte's, is true to her principles and wins her place as heroine and her happy marriage by rejecting not only Mr. Collins and his parsonage but Mr. Darcy and his £10,000 a year until she is sure she can love him, too. The issue of the delicate balance between love and worldly wisdom is explored in some detail in this novel in particular in the context of Mrs. Bennet's desperate mission to get her five daughters married and off her hands. Elizabeth asks, "what is the difference in matrimonial affairs, between the mercenary and the prudent motive? Where does discretion end, and avarice begin?" (p. 153). And though we are convinced that by the time she accepts Darcy she does love him, she herself jokingly suggests that her love began when she first saw "his beautiful grounds at Pemberley" (p. 373).

The advice of Tennyson's Northern Farmer "Doänt thou marry for munny, but goä wheer munny is" seems largely to pertain in the novels. The incomes of lovers are always relevant along with the state of their affections. Those who marry, or try to marry, for money alone come to grief in the same way as those who marry for looks alone. The Thorpes, brother and sister, in *Northanger Abbey* are fortune hunters, though both pay lip service to pure and disinterested love. "Where people are really attached, poverty itself is wealth," declares Isabella (p. 119). But her vision of marriage includes "a carriage at her command, a new name on her tickets, and a brilliant exhibition of hoop rings on her finger" (p. 122); and when she finds her fiancé's funds will not reach to such amenities, she sets her cap at a richer man, Captain Tilney, and so eventually loses both. Jane Austen is closer to agreeing with the ingenuous Catherine in the same novel, who neither hunts for money nor pretends to be indifferent to it: "If there is a good fortune on one side, there can be no occasion for any on the other. No matter which has it, so that there is enough. I hate the idea of one great fortune looking out for another. And to marry for money I think the wickedest thing in existence" (p. 124). The shrewd and calculating Lucy Steele in *Sense and Sensibility*, by underhanded maneuvers, catches a rich husband and prospers to this extent; but to do so she has to jilt an honorable man for an empty-headed coxcomb. Mary Crawford in *Mansfield Park*, a more complex character than the shallow Isabella or the heartless Lucy, is torn between love and prudence. When she comes to Mansfield, she intends to captivate Tom Bertram, the eldest son and heir to a baronetcy; but her moral taste leads her to fall in love, in spite of herself, with Edmund, the younger son, who has intelligence and sound principles instead of money.

The dynastic motive for marriage is less prominent than the mercenary one, but it receives some attention in the novels. Lady Catherine de Bourgh, who considers blood and birth of primary importance, had arranged a match for her daughter and her sister's son while they were still in their cradles and regards the engagement as binding Darcy when he is an adult. But Miss de Bourgh is sickly and insipid, and Jane Austen suggests that Pemberley will be the better for an infusion of such new blood as Elizabeth's. In *Persuasion*, Elizabeth Elliot is eager to marry her cousin William Elliot, who is the heir to her father's title, and even Anne is briefly tempted by the thought of following in her mother's footsteps in becoming Lady Elliot of Kellynch Hall. But Jane Austen chooses to match her to the self-made man, Captain Wentworth, rather than to the dynastically suitable Mr. Elliot, with all his "horrible eligibilities" (p. 244).

Class as well as money is undoubtedly relevant in the selection of a mate, though Jane Austen was no snob. When Lady Catherine accuses Elizabeth, "a young woman without family, connections, or fortune," of having "upstart pretensions" in aspiring to marry Mr. Darcy of Pemberley, Elizabeth counters with the proud statement "He is a gentleman; I am a gentleman's daughter; so far we are equal" (*PP*, p. 356). But there are other cases in which class differences are considered to render marriage unsuitable. Lucy Steele, with her bad grammar and her vulgar manners, is not good enough for Edward Ferrars; Emma is mistaken in trying to furbish up Harriet Smith, the illegitimate daughter of a merchant, as a wife for Mr. Elton or Frank Churchill; and Mrs. Clay, the widowed daughter of a country attorney, is not considered a suitable match for Sir Walter Elliot of Kellynch Hall. In general, Jane Austen advocates a similarity of class and education for the partners in a successful marriage.

In temperament, however, the partners may often be contrasted. Mr. Knightley, who tends toward moral seriousness himself, delights in Emma, "faults and all" (*E*, p. 462), for her vivacity and her "open temper" (p. 288). Elizabeth, who carries on a running battle with Mr. Darcy for most of *Pride and Prejudice*, views the difference between them as mutually beneficial: "By her ease and liveliness, his mind might have been softened, his manners improved, and from his judgment, information, and knowledge of the world, she must have received benefit of greater importance" (p. 312). Couples who match too closely, like the John Dashwoods and the Eltons, tend to double their bad qualities.

The legitimate courtships in Jane Austen's novels are carried on according to certain rather strict social conventions. Frequently, the couple will scarcely have been alone together before they become engaged. Marianne's visit with Willoughby to his home is considered rather improper and reason enough for assuming the two are secretly engaged; and Catherine Morland, invited to go on a drive alone with Mr. Thorpe in his curricle, is told by Mr. Allen, "These schemes are not at all the thing. Young men and women driving about the country in open carriages! . . . It is not right" (*NA*, p. 104). Such private conversation as a courting couple can snatch must often be conducted in low voices in large company, like Bingley's with Jane before the fire at Netherfield, or during a dance. Hence the importance of dances in the courtship ritual. The actual proposal must be made in private, and there is often a good deal of maneuvering to arrange for it. Mrs. Bennet makes an elaborate bustle about leaving Jane alone with Bingley so that he will have the chance to propose. Emma, another matchmaker, contrives to break her shoelace so that Mr. Elton may be alone with Harriet (though he does not avail himself of the opportunity she provides). Mr. Collins makes a parade of requesting a private interview with Elizabeth.

The proposal once made and accepted, the fortunate suitor must still apply for parental approval; and for Jane Austen this part of the transaction is no empty formality. Anne Elliot at nineteen gives up the man she loves because her surrogate mother, Lady Russell, thinks him unsuitable, though she later acknowledges that she would not do the same at twenty-seven.

But not all couples adhere to these rather exacting rules. There is a good deal of illicit sexual activity in Jane Austen's novels, and immoral liaisons, like Willoughby's with Miss Williams, Wickham's with Lydia, and Henry Crawford's with Mrs. Rushworth, are frequently prominent in the plot. Although consummation of these liaisons, like that of the marriage, takes place offstage, we are shown a good deal of the tactics of flirts and seducers.

Isabella Thorpe, when she is engaged to James Morland but angling for Captain Tilney, is able to carry on a flirtatious exchange with the captain, although they are in the middle of the Pump Room at Bath, and her friend is listening.

> "I wish your heart were independent. That would be enough for me" [he tells her].
> "My heart, indeed! What can you have to do with hearts? You men have none of you any hearts."
> "If we have not hearts, we have eyes; and they give us torment enough."
> "Do they? I am sorry for it; I am sorry they find any thing so disagreeable in me. I will look another way. I hope this pleases you, (turning her back on him,) I hope your eyes are not tormented now.
> "Never more so; for the edge of a blooming cheek is still in view—at once too much and too little." (*NA*, p. 147)

As subsequent events make clear, the lady is seeking to entangle the gentleman in marriage, while the gentleman would be ready only for a less permanent liaison. But this kind of sexual maneuvering in public, calling often for skillful use of innuendo, is frequent in the novels.

Henry Crawford in *Mansfield Park* is the most accomplished seducer and specializes in making holes in women's hearts. By his calculated tactics of lively gallantry and covert suggestion, he manages to make two sisters in love with him at once even though one of them is engaged to someone else. During the visit to Sotherton, when Maria Bertram is standing in the chapel with her fiancé in such a way as to suggest the future ceremony, Crawford intervenes, as he is subsequently to intervene in their marriage:

> Mr. Crawford . . . stepping forward to Maria, said, in a voice which she only could hear, "I do not like to see Miss Bertram so near the altar."
> Starting, the lady instinctively moved a step or two, . . . affected to laugh, and asked him, in a tone not much louder, "if he would give her away?"
> "I am afraid I should do it very awkwardly," was his reply, with a look of meaning. (p. 88)

His lowered voice and looks of meaning, and his implied but never declared devotion, are his effective armory in subduing women and making them in love with him. It is Jane Austen's technique to show us by such small scenes how Henry Crawford will eventually induce Maria to abandon her husband and live in adultery with him.

Perhaps the most abandoned and unscrupulous character in Jane Austen's fiction is a woman, Lady Susan, who specializes in a show of virtue while carrying on an affair with a married man and several separate courtships. *Lady Susan* is written in the broad style of eighteenth-century fiction, and the central character is reminiscent of Fielding's hypocrites. Here Jane Austen chooses to be more explicit than usual about sexual immorality and to show the lady's wiles and machinations in some detail.

While the young people in the novels are finding their mates, by legitimate and illegitimate means, they are surrounded by an older generation that is already married, like the parents of Catherine, Elizabeth, and Fanny; widowed, like those of the Dashwood girls and Anne; or conspicuously single, like Miss Bates. Marriage and its deprivation, then, is in one way or another the context for the courtship of the major characters. But however marriage may be presented as the consummation most devoutly to be wished for the young people, the examples of couples around them are often far from encouraging. Although Jane Austen writes romantic comedies, she is also a sharp satirist, and the sharpness predominates in her depiction of the Palmers, the Dashwoods, the Middletons, the Eltons, and the Bennets. "My child," says Mr. Bennet to his favorite daughter, with a rare touch of feeling, "let me not have the grief of seeing *you* unable to respect your partner in life" (*PP*, p. 376). The Bennet girls might well wonder that their mother should be so eager to push them into the married state. In the last novel, however, there are two couples, the Crofts and the Harvilles, whose mutual devotion and happiness are warmly and convincingly depicted. This may be another of the signs that if Jane Austen, like Anne Elliot, "had been forced into prudence in her youth, she learned romance as she grew older" (*P*, p. 30). *Persuasion* is certainly the novel most eloquent in the praise of "domestic virtues" (p. 252).

Although some have thought that Jane Austen "had more Acuteness, Penetration & Taste, than Love" (*Letters*, November 18, 1814), most readers who have come to know her novels well have found that she memorably and successfully dramatizes the perennially interesting topic of the proper choice of a mate.

Bibliography

BRONTË, CHARLOTTE. *The Brontës: Their Lives, Friendships and Correspondence*, Thomas J. Wise, ed. (Oxford, 1932).
CHAPMAN, R. W. *Jane Austen: Facts and Problems* (Oxford, 1948).
FERGUS, JAN S. "Sex and Social Life in Jane Austen's Novels," in David Monaghan, ed., *Jane Austen in a Social Context* (London, 1981), 66–85.
GLASSCO, JOHN. *Memoirs of Montparnasse* (Toronto and New York, 1970).

LEFROY, FANNY CAROLINE. "Is it Just?" *Temple Bar*, 67 (1883), 270–84.
MCMASTER, JULIET. *Jane Austen on Love* (Victoria, B.C., 1978).
SOUTHAM, B. C. "Jane Austen: A Broken Romance?" *Notes and Queries*, 206 (1961), 464–65.

MANNERS AND SOCIETY

Rachel Trickett

So effective is Jane Austen's realism that it persuades modern readers of their familiarity with her world and leads inevitably to misinterpretations. We think we understand her society because it seems so vivid to us, and translating it into our own terms, we inevitably distort it in the process. The manners of her time were conventional, formal, precise, and clearly defined, but she was writing without a thought for posterity, and it did not occur to her to explain or interpret the habits of her creatures. Whatever approach we take to her novels, then, whether historical or purely critical, we need information about the nature and customs of her time to avoid those simple mistakes that must distort historical perspective or invalidate critical interpretations.

Jane Austen records accurately the social distinctions and the status of her characters—the amount of their estate or the extent of their lack of it, their family background, their rise or fall in fortune. She does this not for the reader's enlightenment but for her own satisfaction in "placing" each element in her carefully contrived model of that branch of society to which she herself belonged and of which she preferred to write. This was a section extending from the landed gentry down to professional families in the church or the law or the armed forces and including the respectable mercantile rich who had made their fortunes in trade. She expresses no contempt or disparagement of any one of these sections of society. From her moral standpoint none is better or worse than another. Outside this range, however, her characters' attitudes are less predictably secure.

Jane Austen leaves us in no doubt of her distaste, on the one hand, for the sycophancy of Mr. Collins to his patron Lady Catherine de Bourgh or for Emma's wrongheaded dismissal of Robert Martin as a husband for Harriet Smith, on the other. Emma somewhat complacently explains to Harriet, "The yeomanry are precisely the order of people with whom I feel I can have nothing to do. A degree or two lower, and a creditable appearance might interest me; I might hope to be useful to their families in some way or other. But a farmer can need none of my help" (*E*, p. 29). In other words, Emma cannot patronize the independent yeoman farmer whose prosperity and property have secured his future, although not in "genteel" society. Harriet, the illegitimate child of unknown parents, belongs precisely to the order "a degree or two lower" to which Emma feels she may hope to be useful, although in Mr. Knightley's sensible view Harriet would be distinctly lucky to find as sound a husband as Robert Martin. For all his lack of "manner," the young farmer reads aloud from *Elegant Extracts* to his family, and Harriet boasts that he is familiar with *The Vicar of Wakefield*. Jane Austen's choice of books here is significant. Both were popular literary works she herself enjoyed—*Elegant Extracts* as a repository or anthology of the most popular pieces of prose and verse of the previous century and *The Vicar of Wakefield* as Goldsmith's influential and immensely popular idyllic tale of the 1760s. Emma's contempt for Robert Martin is as ill founded in her author's eyes as the Misses Bingley's in *Pride and Prejudice* for Mr. Gardiner, Elizabeth Bennet's uncle "in trade." In each case Jane Austen singles out the snobbery and limitation to censure it. She is the enemy of every sort of class distinction that fails to take into account personal merit, worth, and intelligence. Her own sense of these class distinctions is now often falsely interpreted as a limitation of snobbery on her part when it is, in fact, merely the effect of her art and observation and her grasp of the structure of social as well as of personal relationships.

In *Pride and Prejudice* Jane Austen locates every character of importance according to his or her status, social and financial. This is necessary information both for our understanding of the comedy of the marriage market and for the serious Johnsonian business of clearing the readers'— and the characters'—minds of cant. Are titles a guarantee of sense or merit? The titled characters in this novel, Lady Catherine de Bourgh and Sir William and Lady Lucas, could not be further apart in social status, but of them Sir William and his family are infinitely the superior in good nature and simple kindness, though he had only "risen to the honour of knighthood by an address to the King, during his mayoralty" (*PP*, p. 18). Both he and Lady Catherine are comic figures, but Sir William is affectionately portrayed.

Mr. Darcy, Lady Catherine's nephew, of "a noble mien" and possessing "a clear £10,000 a year," with his cousin Colonel Fitzwilliam, the younger son of an earl (about which rank Elizabeth teases him gently), are the highest in status of the male characters in the novel. They are distinguished from each other—Darcy by his patrician aloofness, Fitzwilliam by his gentle and unassuming good manners. In his own sphere at Pemberley, however, Darcy is revealed as a responsible, honorable, and generous landlord, whose life bears little resemblance to the vulgar idea of a nobleman's existence. One of the young Lucases observes that if he were as rich as Mr. Darcy, he would "keep a pack of foxhounds, and drink a bottle of wine every day" (p. 20), but such easygoing ostentation is rather more like Mr. Bingley's search for a country estate and a wife than like Darcy's real way of life. And Mr. Bingley, for all his charm and ease, is less secure than his friend Mr. Darcy, as his appallingly snobbish sisters betray their lack of breeding in their desperate efforts to assert it. Mr. Bingley, "good-looking and gentleman-like," has inherited "property to the amount of nearly an hundred thousand pounds from his father" (p. 15) and is trying to establish himself as a country landowner like his friend Darcy, but he lacks not only the inherited estate and the family consequence of the latter but the confidence attendant on them. Mr. Bingley in his less established position has some advantages: he is able to avoid Darcy's faults of pride and rigidity; he is not put off by Mrs. Bennet's folly and vulgarity, but at the same time he is more easily deflected from his purpose than his friend, more open to influence, and in the last resort, less capable of Darcy's honorable magnanimity. Jane Austen is not guilty of the vulgar error that assumes an aristocrat is necessarily a better man or woman than those without his advantages, as Lady Catherine de Bourgh, with her ridiculous pride in family, shows. But the author sees that once pride and prejudice are overcome, the patrician tradition of responsibility and honor may well reinforce natural virtue and magnanimity.

The position of the Bennet family is of crucial importance in the plot of *Pride and Prejudice*. They live on their father's estate (with an income of £2,000 a year), which is entailed to Mr. Collins in default of a male heir. None of the Bennet sisters has any hope of an inheritance—their mother having brought to her marriage a fortune of £4,000. The search for good connections for her daughters that so obsesses Mrs. Bennet has some justification, then, and Mr. Bennet's total indifference in the matter, though the source of much sympathetic wit, is not entirely approved of by the author. He merrily supports Elizabeth's refusal to marry the absurd Mr. Collins (whose intention to choose one of the Bennet sisters shows some sense of family propriety on his part), but he is relieved to see his frivolous daughter Lydia finally honorably united to Wickham, the adventurer with whom she has eloped. Elizabeth exclaims against the necessity of their marrying, reflecting what a dreadful man Wickham is—to whose charms she herself had already almost fallen a victim. By the mores of her own society Lydia must, and it turns out to be no great embarrassment or humiliation to either party. Their fate is that they deserve each other and are completely unabashed by their mutual unworthiness (a very different conclusion from the conventional fate of the ruined girl in the late-eighteenth-century novel and a comic reversal of the expected entirely typical of Jane Austen's realism).

In *Pride and Prejudice* Jane Austen goes out of her way to delineate Mr. and Mrs. Gardiner, Elizabeth's aunt and uncle who live in London in Gracechurch Street, next to the warehouse from which Mr. Gardiner makes his money. Like Henry James, she does not specify the actual articles Mr. Gardiner deals in, but he is described as "a sensible, gentlemanlike man, greatly superior to his sister as well by nature as education. The Netherfield ladies would have had difficulty in believing that a man who lived by trade, and within view of his own warehouses, could have been so well bred and so agreeable" (p. 139). He and his wife find no difficulty in conversing with Mr. Darcy at Pemberley, and the two standards of "nature and education," which Jane Austen uses to single him out from his sister Mrs. Bennet, are those she employs in all her novels to show us, in varying circumstances, the moral education of her heroines. Catherine Morland in *Northanger Abbey* possesses a sweet nature but must be educated into sense by a mixture of experience and Henry Tilney. Fanny in *Mansfield Park* benefits by her own observation of her cousins' neglected education and by her cousin Edmund's more careful "nurture." Even meek Anne Elliot in *Persuasion* must learn from the worldly vanity and stupidity of her father and sister not to submit too easily to the standards of those elders who are not necessarily her betters. Such lessons were acceptable to the society of Jane Austen's time, and her success and popularity suggest a greater freedom of decision and action on the part of its young women than has always been assumed.

Jane Austen's own upbringing indicates that in spite of what might seem to us rigid codes of manners in the conduct of everyday life, the education and the sphere of action of a young woman of the time was considerably less restricted than we might at first think. Jane and Cassandra, her elder sister, were sent away, first to Oxford and Southampton, to be educated by the widow of a principal of Brasenose College, and later to the Abbey School at Reading, a boarding establishment for young women, whose name has been adopted by a subsequent independent school which exists there today. Their education was completed at home by their father and brothers, their father himself, the Reverend George Austen, having been a teacher at Tonbridge School and later a fellow of St. John's College, Oxford. The large, affectionate, and talented Austen family was well connected—especially on Mrs. Austen's side—with the Leighs of Stoneleigh Abbey and the Leigh Perrots of Bath. Jane Austen stayed with both these branches of the family and from their lives became familiar with fashionable society, as well as being herself accustomed to civilized and educated company—that of her brothers and her cousins.

James Edward Austen-Leigh in his *Memoir of Jane Austen* (edited by R. W. Chapman, 1926), originally published in 1870, gives us the fullest account of her family background and provides a sharp-sighted comparison of the life of Jane Austen's time with that of the mid-Victorian age in which he was writing. Of her immediate relations, he singles out Eliza Hancock (p. 26), a cousin on her mother's side, married to the French comte de Feuillide, who was guillotined during the Revolution. This lady probably improved Jane and Cassandra's French and Italian; she certainly enlivened their family life by her gaiety and her love of amateur theatricals, in which the whole family frequently took part. From Jane Austen's correspondence and from family records, this lively young woman, an embryonic Mary Crawford, perhaps, exemplifies the adventuresomeness, the high spirits and enterprise, that eventually won her, as her second husband, Jane Austen's favorite brother, Henry. Jane Austen's closeness to her brother increased after their father's death, when the two unmarried daughters and their mother were supported by the Austen sons and in particular by Edward, who had early been adopted by the family of the local squire, the Knights, and who offered his mother and sisters a house either in Kent (where his principal seat was) or in Chawton, Hampshire. They accepted the latter as being more familiar and nearer to family and friends.

James Edward Austen-Leigh outlines the history of the landed families of the Kentish Weald, to which the Austens belonged: "The clothing business was exercised by persons who possessed most of the landed property in the Weald, insomuch that almost all the ancient families of these parts, now of large estates and genteel rank in life, and some of them ennobled by titles, are sprung from ancestors who have used this great staple manufacture, now almost unknown here" (quoted from Hasted's *History of Kent* in *Memoir*, p. 3). His insistence on this background is emphasized by a quotation from a letter of the late seventeenth century in which an ancestress of the Austens', Mary Brydges, is reminded of the straitened circumstances of her immediate family in contrast to the wealth of her grandmother, "widow of a Turkey merchant." "Then as now," Austen-Leigh writes, "it would seem rank had the power of attracting and absorbing wealth." He is at pains to draw attention to the respectability of the manufacturing and the mercantile backgrounds of the family and the way in which they were easily absorbed into the families of higher-ranking ancestors. The Austen background was itself—as he saw—entirely typical of the "upward mobility" of the landed gentry of the seventeenth and eighteenth centuries in England.

Everyday life in Jane Austen's time can be carefully and precisely followed from the accounts in her novels. This has already been done so well and thoroughly by R. W. Chapman in his essay "The Manners of the Age," printed as a supplement to volume 4 (*Emma*) of the standard edition of the works that any further catalog would be superfluous. Chapman's essay covers the details of conventions and customs of address, visits, balls, card games, dressing, eating, courting, and marrying. It needs only to be supplemented by some of the information in the *Memoir*, because of the latter's useful comparison between life in the early and the middle years of the nineteenth century. Modern readers of Victorian fiction can easily confuse the conventions of the two periods: it is all costume drama to them. But Jane Austen's nephew saw the subtle changes that had taken place between his aunt's world and his own, and some of them are worth recalling.

Austen-Leigh remembers that there was much more dancing in his aunt's day than in his own—a form of entertainment that people made for themselves and that reached back to their country ancestry. "Much less," he writes, "was left to the discretion and charge of servants" (p. 36), and "a young man who expected to have his things packed or unpacked for him by a servant when he travelled, would have been thought exceptionally fine, or exceptionally lazy" (p. 38). The impression given is one of a much more self-sufficient world, less dependent on servants, more active and independent than the Victorian. "Some gentlemen took pleasure in being their own gardeners, performing all the scientific, and some of the manual work themselves" (p. 39). Food was simpler and produced and dressed at home; hunt breakfasts were eaten in the kitchen, not the dining room, and beers and homemade wines rather than imported wines were drunk. Domestic furnishing was at once less ornate and less comfortable than that of a later period. Austen-Leigh notes fewer carpets, ornaments, or musical instruments and hardly any sofas or chairs for lounging: "to lie down or even to lean back" was "a luxury permitted only to old people or invalids" (p. 32).

To Jane Austen's nieces and nephews, according to their temperament and the way of life to which they were accustomed, her world—the one she inhabited and the one she wrote about—looked less well bred, less refined, less accomplished, than theirs. To us, with our own preconceptions about the Victorian age, Jane Austen's world appears more robust, outspoken (the characters, men and women, of her novels speak their minds very freely in spite of verbal conventions), independent, and down-to-earth. The illusion that she had no knowledge of current events has long since been shattered. It has been well pointed out that for most of her adult life England was at war and that with two brothers serving in the navy Jane Austen knew the deep anxiety and suspense of waiting for news of their welfare. She knew, as well, the insecurity attendant on unmarried women and widows. Mrs. Bates, widow of the vicar of Highbury in *Emma*, and her spinster daughter are a source of pathos and uneasy comedy. Their situation is too near what her own might well have been had it not been for the devotion of her brothers. Like Mr. Bennet, her father kept a carriage, the horses for which worked on the local squire's land. No doubt, like Mrs. Bennet, the Austens boasted a cook, for we don't hear of the sisters acquiring any competence in cookery, though their mother clearly possessed it. Needlework was Jane Austen's other skill along with writing.

This conventional country world, precise and formal, yet easy and independent, has too often been viewed as a limitation in Jane Austen's work. In fact, like most great comic novelists, she flourished in precisely the sort of restrictions that might hamper the genius of a less highly structured artist. The firm moral and intellectual standards by which she judged character and merit are displayed with greater subtlety and depth against the established customs and manners of a developing but inherently traditional society.

MEDICINE

David Waldron Smithers

Jane Austen handled doctors and medicine in her novels the same way she made use of many other social and personal features of her time, to advance the revelation of human nature within the confines of the middle-class world she so beautifully portrayed. She needed no more than an occasional sore throat, to which Harriet Smith was prone, or a small accident, such as the Musgrove boy's dislocated collarbone, to influence the course of her story, for it was the small affairs of everyday life together with the subtle influences of social position that best served her purpose. It seldom required the drama of personal affliction for her to persuade us into the detection of human foibles. There were exceptions, as when Marianne's fever with its putrid tendency was alarming enough to bring Willoughby to Cleveland in a mad rush, providing us with an excuse to admit some small redeeming feature to his character. Then there was Louisa's fall at Lyme, from which she suffered a severe contusion of the head, where Anne Elliot's instant, practical competence and understanding of Captain Wentworth's predicament helped to move the story toward its happy conclusion.

By 1815 Jane Austen had become acquainted with a number of doctors, most notably Dr. Charles Haden (1786–1824) in London, one of the early users of a stethoscope, who had studied in Paris under Laennec. She wrote to her sister Cassandra, who had referred to him as an apothecary, "he is no Apothecary . . . he is a Haden, nothing but a Haden, a sort of wonderful nondescript Creature on two legs, something between a Man & an Angel —but without the least spice of an Apothecary" (*Letters*, December 2, 1815).

We have to remember that though Jane was a contemporary of Dr. Edward Jenner's (1749–1823), she lived eighty years before anesthetics or X rays, at a time when serious illness was a desperate business. Nothing was done to diminish mortality from pneumonia until more than a century after her death. Patients were fortunate if they escaped much of the therapeutics of the day, with its drastic debilitating maneuvers of bleeding, purging, and vomiting and some of its more silly nostrums.

A true professional middle class was just emerging, and the clergy was divided between the sons of good families with livings at their disposal, like Henry Tilney or Edmund Bertram, and the acceptable but socially inferior, such as the dependent, obsequious Mr. Collins. The doctors, however, had no established position in society. Poor Sam Watson, who, though expected, never appears in the fragment *The Watsons*, is thought to have little chance with Mary Edwards, who will have a dowry of at least ten thousand pounds, as he "is only a Surgeon you know" (p. 321). Mr. Perry, the most famous of Jane's doctors, is an apothecary and, though an intelligent, gentlemanlike man whose frequent visits are one of the comforts of Mr. Woodhouse's life, is far from being his social equal. When Emma makes up a card table for her father in the evenings, Mrs. Perry is not invited.

Other doctors in the novels are mostly shadowy figures. Mr. Jones is called to Netherfield, where Jane Bennet has been conveniently retained with a sore throat and headache. Mr. Harris attends Marianne Dashwood in her more serious illness and is persistently encouraging even when his medicines fail and the fever continues unabated. Mr. Donovan, of Harley Street, is called to Charlotte Palmer's child, who is suffering from "the red-gum." *Persuasion* has the accident; after the famous fall from the Cobb, Louisa "was taken up lifeless!" (p. 109). The surgeon says, "The head had received a severe contusion, but he had seen greater injuries recovered from" (p. 112).

Jane's own health seems to have been excellent until the onset of her terminal illness. Her letters speak of medicine in much the same lighthearted vein as her novels with the exception of Mrs. Smith in *Persuasion*, the "poor, infirm, helpless widow," who, nevertheless, has the spirit to rise above serious debilitating illness. They contain references to many doctors, eight in Bath alone, and some seventeen others, with several sharp comments.

Jane died in July 1817. In March she wrote a long letter to Fanny Knight at Godmersham in which she said she had not been well for many weeks with fever and indifferent nights and was feeling languid and dull and in need of air and exercise. She added that she was "recovering my Looks a little, which have been bad enough, black & white & every wrong colour. I must not depend upon being ever very blooming again" (*Letters*, March 23, 1817). She wrote of weeks of indisposition, recovering enough strength to sit up in bed and write, scarcely any pain, head always clear, her chief sufferings feverish nights, weakness and languor (*Letters*, May 22, 1817).

It is unlikely that we will now obtain further evidence about Jane's terminal illness. The well-known surgeon Sir Zachary Cope attributed it to Addison's disease, a failure of the adrenal glands, making a likely guess on slender evidence. Responding in a letter, Dr. F. A. Bevan suggested that she might have had Hodgkin's disease, and the increasing fatigue, bouts of fever, and remissions during the course of a steady decline over a few months would fit his speculation well enough, though we hear nothing of lymph-node swelling. Zachary Cope relied heavily on Jane's "black and white and every wrong colour" as evidence for the brown pigmentation of Addison's disease, which occurs on the hands, face, axillae, nipples, and pressure points and in patches inside the mouth. This disease does have an insidious onset, usually between the ages of thirty and fifty, and is associated with severe fluctuating weakness. Fever does occur in sudden exacerbations but is seldom a marked feature; in fact, a subnormal temperature is usual. Whatever the cause of death, it cannot alter our sense of deprivation, for Jane was not yet forty-two years old, in the midst of her second spell of writing, and getting better and better.

Bibliography

BEVAN, F. A. Letter in response to Cope, below, *British Medical Journal* (August, 1964), 384.

COPE, SIR ZACHARY. "Jane Austen's Last Illness," *British Medical Journal* (July, 1964), 182–83.

MILITARY
(ARMY AND NAVY)

J. David Grey

Jane Austen was born the year of Bunker Hill and died two years after Waterloo. Her mature life paralleled the years that witnessed the rise and fall of Napoleon, and her sailor brothers were intimately involved in the naval campaigns waged during those wars. In the early years of the conflict with France, England's navy bore the brunt of the most strategic battles, most of which were fought far from home. Later, the constant fear of an invasion from the Continent called for a military establishment at home—the militia—which roamed the British countryside, camping at hospitable sites for relatively short durations and then moving on. Another brother, Henry, was a member of the militia, the first of his three careers. The second branch of the army, the regulars, occupied fixed camps throughout the kingdom.

Colonel Brandon "has seen a great deal of the world; [he] has been abroad" (*SS*, p. 51). His regiment was stationed in the East Indies when word came of his brother's marriage to the woman he also loved, and he purposely stayed away from England until after receiving news of their divorce. By the Treaty of Paris in 1783 the East Indies colonies had been returned to the Dutch. The British retained trading privileges and finally retook Sumatra in 1798. Colonel Brandon could easily, therefore, have "detained" himself amidst all the diversionary activity of those fifteen years. Edward Ferrars had "always preferred the church" (p. 102), had no inclination for the law, considered the army "a great deal too smart" and the navy, although fashionable, an impossible choice at his then-advanced age of eighteen. The idleness of Oxford was the only option left to him, for these were, indeed, the only occupations open to a gentleman's son in the late eighteenth century.

Two military encampments are situated at "Meryton" and Brighton, and their influence on the plot of *Pride and Prejudice* is crucial. Rowland Grey writes, "It would hardly be an exaggeration to call 'Pride and Prejudice' . . . the story of a militia regiment" (pp. 174–75). Talk of Mr. Bingley's fortune at the very outset of the novel is soon eclipsed when the "news and happiness [of] the recent arrival of a militia regiment in the neighborhood" (p. 28) reaches the ears, three pairs especially, of Longbourn. Mrs. Bennet reminisces about the time when she "liked a red coat" (p. 29) herself; later in the book she confesses to having "cried for two days together when Colonel Millar's regiment went away" (p. 229). She conjectures about the prospect of "a smart young colonel, with five or six thousand a year" (p. 29) for any of her five daughters' hands. This income, naturally exaggerated by her, indicates why military companionship might have been too smart for the retiring Edward Ferrars. When one considers the primary occupations of the officers in *Pride and Prejudice*—wining, dining, dancing, and general merrymaking—it is clear why the extrovert Mr. Wickham condescends to accept a commission in the corps: "It was the prospect of constant society, and good society . . . which was my chief inducement . . . and my friend Denny tempted me farther by his account of their present quarters, and the very great attentions and excellent acquaintance Meryton had procured them" (p. 79). No mention is made of military exercises, even of a parade; perhaps there is no time for such regularities. When the Gardiners visit Longbourn, between the Lucases and the officers "there was not a day without its engagement" (p. 142), and it can safely be assumed that the officers helped compose the Lucas company, as well.

The appointed stay is accomplished, the winter over, and it is time for Colonel Forster to remove his regiment to larger quarters at Brighton, certainly a felicitous and fashionable choice at a time when the prince regent was reigning there. Both Kitty and Lydia are inconsolable over the loss of such diversion, and the latter succeeds in getting permission to accept an invitation from the colonel and his wife to accompany them there. In her imagination, "she saw all the glories of the camp; its tents stretched forth in beauteous uniformity of lines, crowded with the young and the gay, and dazzling with scarlet; and to complete the view, she saw herself seated beneath a tent, tenderly flirting with at least six officers at once" (p. 232).

The possibility of entering and leaving the militia casually is evident when Wickham, despite his nefarious romantic and monetary activities (the word "that he had gone wild" had even reached Pemberley), is able to resign his commission and become an ensign in the regulars somewhere in the north. Mr. Darcy's influence and financial assistance must have been substantial, indeed.

Differing insights into the navy are given in *Mansfield Park* through revelations concerning Admiral Crawford's residence in Hill Street, London, communications about the fortunes and advancement of William Price's career, and details surrounding the Price household in that quintessential naval town, Portsmouth. Jane Austen underscores the contrast in the worlds of London and Mansfield Park through the words of the novel's "other heroine" Mary Crawford, who has been exposed to the society of her naval uncle: "with an air of grandeur," she claims to know "a great deal" about admirals, "the gradation of their pay, and their bickerings and jealousies.... Of *Rears*, and *Vices*, I saw enough. Now do not be suspecting me of a pun, I entreat" (p. 60). It is thanks to the connections of the well-tempered but profligate admiral, his friend Sir Charles, and Sir Charles's friend the secretary to the first lord (of the Admiralty), that William Price's second lieutenancy is secured. Such recourse to influence was a common necessity for the advancement of so young a sailor as Midshipman Price.

Because of his father's rank in the marines, William possibly attended the Royal Naval Academy at Portsmouth, the same school at which Jane Austen's own brothers, Francis and Charles, received their training. Boys entered between the ages of twelve and fifteen, the younger the better, for a three-year course. According to G. E. Mitton, sons of gentlemen, like some of the naval characters in the novels, might be taken on board ship at that age. This procedure, however, entailed serving six years before being allowed to take an officer's examination. The training aboard ship was meager, the art of navigation still complicated at that time, and "the wonder is that such boys . . . picked up enough seamanship to pass any but the most practical examination" (pp. 201–2). When the major action of *Mansfield Park* begins, William has been in the service six or seven years, aboard the *Antwerp* "in the Mediterranean—in the West Indies—in the Mediterranean again" (p. 236) for the past four years. His brother, Sam, is also a midshipman on board an Indiaman. The only elation that Fanny experiences in Portsmouth is provided by William's preparations for sailing off in his new ship, the sloop *Thrush*, and the thrill of finally seeing him in full dress. Jane Austen, in these scenes, alludes to three ships on which her brothers served—the *Endymion*, the *Cleopatra*, and the *Elephant*. Her brother Frank must have been responsible for the rare emendations she made, between the first and second editions, in the nautical terms that "only a sailor could have found necessary" (*MP*, p. 549).

In *Mansfield Park* we learn that Frances Ward married Lieutenant Price of the marines "to disoblige her family. . . . She could hardly have made a more untoward choice" (p. 3). Disabled "but not the less equal to company and good liquor" (p. 4), he is unable to provide adequately for his large family. His remorse is little and the distractions of the active port so great that Fanny is relegated to the position of a war orphan at Mansfield. Returning to her family after an absence of several years, she finds a slovenly home that increasingly disgusts her, then reawakens her to a preference for the orderliness of Mansfield Park and almost sends her into the arms of Henry Crawford.

The military enters the plotting of *Emma* only peripherally. Mr. Weston, formerly Captain Weston, had entered his country's militia to satisfy his "active cheerful mind and social temper" (p. 15). His marriage to a Miss Churchill, of a prominent Yorkshire family, proved unlucky, and when she died after three years, he left the militia and worked in trade with his brothers in London until his retirement to Highbury twenty years later. Lieutenant Fairfax of the infantry was happily married to Jane Bates, and their union had "its day of fame and pleasure, hope and interest" (p. 163). Unfortunately, he was killed in action abroad, his wife died of consumption three years later, and the upbringing of his daughter Jane was left to Colonel Campbell, whose relief from a bout with camp fever had been successfully accomplished by the ministrations of Lieutenant Fairfax. The colonel's income, "by pay and appointments, was handsome" (p. 164) but not sufficient to provide for any except his own daughter. Jane Fairfax, more distraught than Fanny Price and literally a war orphan, is returned to her aunt and grandmother at Highbury to restore her health in preparation for her career as a governess.

There is no account of the military exploits of General Tilney in *Northanger Abbey*, but the reader may well imagine what it would be like to serve under such a mercurial commander. Like Admiral Crawford, he enjoys a very large and consequential acquaintance. His son, Captain Frederick Tilney of the Twelfth Light Dragoons, stationed in Northampton, makes the expected good use of his leave in Bath to turn the heads of the girls there: "The mess-room will drink Isabella Thorpe for a fortnight" (p. 153). "There is no mention of a sailor [in *NA*] except William Thorpe, vaguely described as 'at sea'; but thinly veiled half-disdain for the Army, not unnatural in an essentially naval family, resulted in that creation of the heaviest of heavy fathers, General Tilney" (Grey, pp. 172–73).

Later Grey states, "There is not one group of sailors in 'Persuasion' that is not absolute flesh and blood" (p. 180). The story begins a month after the First Treaty of Paris was signed, May 30, 1814. It ends, presumably, in February 1815, less than a month before Napoleon landed at Cannes and about four months before the Battle of Waterloo, June 18, 1815. Sir Walter Elliot, well advised that the "peace will be turning all our rich Navy Officers ashore" (p. 17), reluctantly leases Kellynch Hall to Admiral and Mrs. Croft. Anne Elliot, arguing in their favor and for obvious reasons an ardent supporter of that branch of the military, claims on their behalf "all the comforts and all the privileges which any home can give" its members. Sir Walter objects on two counts: "First, as being the means of bringing persons of obscure birth into undue distinction, and raising men to honours which their fathers and grandfathers never dreamt of; and secondly, as it cuts up a man's youth and vigour most horribly" (p. 19).

Admiral Croft, rear admiral of the White (there were also a Red and a

Blue), served at Trafalgar in 1805 and, since that time, in the East Indies. This was the period (1811–16) when Stamford Raffles was extending European control and retaining native administration in Java. Mrs. Croft has been his almost constant companion aboard ship, proof of which was her "reddened and weather-beaten complexion" (p. 48). In the fifteen years of their marriage she had crossed the Atlantic four times (but not to "the West Indies. We do not call Bermuda or Bahama, you know, the West Indies" [p. 70]) and spent a long sojourn in the East. Captain Frederick Wentworth, her brother, attained that rank after the action off St. Domingo in February 1806. (One of Jane Austen's brothers was there.) "He had been lucky in his profession; but spending freely, what had come freely, had realized nothing" (p. 27). During his subsequent leave spent with his brother, he met and wooed Anne Elliot, unsuccessfully.

The Musgrove girls, themselves enraptured with Captain Wentworth, procure a navy list ("the first that had ever been at Uppercross" [p. 64]) and look for his first command, the *Asp*:

> You will not find her there.... I was the last man who commanded her.... The admiralty... entertain themselves now and then, with sending a few hundred men to sea, in a ship not fit to be employed. But they have a great many to provide for; and among the thousands that may just as well go to the bottom as not, it is impossible for them to distinguish the very set who may be least missed. (pp. 64–65)

The *Asp*, a sloop, was wrecked by a four-day gale in Plymouth Sound just after Captain Wentworth had brought in a French frigate. This coup, a few thousand pounds in 1808, supplied the beginnings of his prize money, which by 1814 had mounted to £20,000. Prize money was won by subduing foreign privateers. The bounty was divided proportionately among the officers and, infrequently, the crew of the victorious vessel. In 1793, for instance, each captain in Admiral Gell's squadron received almost £14,000 as his share in the capture of the St. Jago (Mitton, p. 208). Jane Austen, in a letter to her sister Cassandra (May 26, 1801), gives their brother "Charles great credit.... He has received 30£ for his share of the privateer & expects 10£ more.... He has been buying gold chains and Topaze crosses for us;—he must be well scolded." There can be no doubt that Charles Austen and William Price have something in common, as do Francis Austen and Captain Harville.

Wentworth's next assignment was aboard a frigate, the *Laconia*. The "troublesome, hopeless" Dick Musgrove, whom the Musgroves had "the good fortune to lose... before he reached his twentieth year" (p. 50), had been aboard the *Laconia* for six months. He had literally been sent to sea—the victim of his own domestic press gang—was forgotten, then was lost at sea and scarcely mourned. Mitton says, "On board [ships] there was bad food, bad water, wretched accommodations and often rank brutality.... The officers fared a little better than the men in regard to comfort" (p. 201).

The poetically inclined Captain James Benwick had served on the *Asp* as first lieutenant. While commanding the *Grappler*, Captain Wentworth had had the sad task of delivering him the news of his intended wife's death. She was the sister of another mutual friend, Captain Harville. A conversation between Anne Elliot and Captain Harville at the White Hart in Bath provides the climax of the novel. Anne displays her partiality for the navy: "You are always labouring and toiling, exposed to every risk and hardship. Your home, country, friends, all quitted. Neither time, nor health, nor life, to be called your own. It would be too hard indeed ... if woman's feelings were to be added to all this" (p. 233). Captain Harville politely disagrees and poignantly expresses the emotion felt by all sailors every time they sail away from their families:

> If I could but make you comprehend what a man suffers when he takes a last look at his wife and children, and watches the boat that he has sent them off in, as long as it is in sight, and then turns away and says, "God knows whether we ever meet again!" And then, if I could convey to you the glow of his soul when he does see them again; when, coming back after a twelvemonth's absence perhaps, and obliged to put into another port, he calculates how soon it be possible to get them there, pretending to deceive himself, and saying, "They cannot be here till such a day," but all the while hoping for them twelve hours sooner, and seeing them arrive at last, as if Heaven had given them wings, by many hours sooner still! (p. 235)

Captain Wentworth overhears, the lovers are reunited, and Jane Austen concludes with what is probably the most acclaimed ending to any of her novels. There can be no question that the military provided her with some of her most inspired moments. In *Mansfield Park* she gives an indication of why some of her most prominent characters are drawn from that profession: "Soldiers and sailors are always acceptable in society. Nobody can wonder that men are soldiers and sailors" (p. 109).

Bibliography

HUBBACK, JOHN H. AND EDITH C. HUBBACK. *Jane Austen's Sailor Brothers* (London and New York, 1906).

MITTON, GERALDINE EDITH. *Jane Austen and Her Times: 1775–1817* (London, 1905).

ROWLAND-BROWN, LILIAN ["ROWLAND GREY"]. "The Navy, the Army and Jane Austen," *Nineteenth Century and After*, 82 (1917), 169–84.

MUSIC

Patrick Piggott

Jane Austen's references to music in her letters suggest that her feeling for the art was somewhat ambivalent. That she was not always a willing listener is clear enough from her mention of an open-air concert in Bath to which she went in a family party and of which she wrote in a letter dated June 2, 1799, "the gardens are large enough for me to get pretty well beyond the reach of its sound." In more than one letter she admitted to an inability to enjoy singing, even that of the delightful Catherine Stephens in Arne's opera *Artaxerxes*; and in a letter of May 21, 1801, we find a jocular reference to a certain Miss Holder, whom Bath society deemed "very detestable" but who proved to be better than report, "especially as Miss Holder owns that she has no taste for music."

It is difficult to equate these rather philistine remarks and the scornful portrait of Mary Bennet, whose long hours of pianoforte practice and study of thorough bass are, it appears, to be regarded as attempts to compensate for a lack of personal beauty rather than as evidence of a genuine love of music, with the fact that Jane Austen herself was a competent amateur musician. She received part of her musical education from Mr. (later Dr.) George Chard, an excellent musician who in subsequent years officiated as organist and choirmaster at Winchester Cathedral. Throughout her life she practiced the pianoforte, probably as regularly, if not for such long hours, as Mary Bennet, sang the popular airs of the day in "a small but sweet voice," and added to her collection of printed music many pieces copied out in her clear and elegant music script. Her niece Caroline remembered that Aunt Jane liked to practice in the early morning so that she might not disturb her family, whose members, according to Caroline, did not care for music. She was always ready to oblige her younger friends and relations by playing dance music whenever they wanted to get up an impromptu ball, but she could never be prevailed upon to "exhibit" on more formal occasions, for music making, to her, was essentially a private activity. In this, as in other ways, she was like Anne Elliot, the heroine of her last completed novel, who, when she played, knew that "she was giving pleasure only to herself" (p. 47). But by the time she came to write Anne's love story, Jane Austen had published several novels in which her practical knowledge of amateur music making had been put to good use in the construction of plots and in the delineation of character.

Marianne Dashwood without her ability to play "a very magnificent concerto" (p. 149) and her enthusiastic singing (eventually to be choked into silence by grief) would be a different and a much less passionate young lady; Mary Crawford's fascination, which held the stolid Edmund Bertram in thrall, would be less potent without the aid of her harp "as elegant as herself" (p. 65) and without the mysterious Broadwood pianoforte, whose arrival in Highbury so greatly embarrassed Jane Fairfax and promoted so much gossip, the plot of *Emma* would be less complex and less entertaining. Catherine Morland, it is true, is not musical, and one remembers that Elinor Dashwood listens with less than half an ear to Marianne's brilliant playing. Fanny Price, too, though an excellent listener, could neither play nor sing; but *Mansfield Park*, with its family glee singing, the duet-playing Bertram sisters, and above all, Mary Crawford's harp, has nearly as much musical activity in it as have *Emma* and the earlier novels.

Most of Jane Austen's musical girls play the pianoforte (in early editions the word is spelled in diverse ways as pianoforté, piano-forté, and Piano Forte, as well as pianoforte), and some of them also sing. Elizabeth Bennet, Caroline Bingley, and Emma Woodhouse all play and sing well enough to give pleasure to uncritical ears, though their performances are obviously unpolished compared to those of Jane Fairfax and perhaps Anne Elliot. Jane Fairfax's singing is also said to be very good, though the fact that her voice "grew thick" after only two songs suggests otherwise. As for the harp, Mary Crawford's is by no means the only one mentioned in the novels. The Musgrove girls play the harp (probably as indifferently as they play the pianoforte), and Georgiana Darcy excels on both instruments. A harp is mentioned once in *Sense and Sensibility* and more than once in *Sanditon*. Jane Austen lived at a time when the harp had become a near rival to the pianoforte as the most popular domestic instrument, and though she could not play it herself, she had many opportunities of hearing harpists at close quarters: her lively cousin, Eliza Hancock, played it, as did her niece Fanny Knight; and on at least one occasion, at a musical party in London, she heard Johann Weippart, a celebrated harp virtuoso of the day.

We know very little about the music favored by the charcters in the Austen novels. Only one composer is named in them—J. B. Cramer, some of whose music was sent to Jane Fairfax as a thoughtful addition to Frank Churchill's gift of the Broadwood pianoforte. A collection of Irish airs was also among the music Frank selected. There were many such collections available then, but it is likely that Jane Austen had in mind the third volume of Moore's *Irish Melodies*, published in 1813.

The only other composer mentioned in Jane Austen's writings is James Hook, whose *Lessons for Beginners* is referred to in a letter to Cassandra of September 16, 1813. Although Marianne Dashwood and Mary Bennet both display their "execution" in concertos and Marianne on one occasion dashes off a "lesson" (today we should call it a study), we are not told whose music they played. There is the same lack of information about vocal music: "Italian airs" were sung by Caroline Bingley and her sister; Jane Fairfax, too, sang in Italian, and one of the most important scenes in *Persuasion* takes place at a public concert (the only such event in the novels) in Bath's Upper Rooms, an entertainment at which some Italian vocal music was performed before the interval. According to Dr. Chapman's reckoning, this concert would have taken place on February 22, 1814. Jane Austen was not in Bath at that time, but she could have obtained a copy of the "concert bill" (program) from one of her family connections then wintering in Bath. It would have told her that the first "act" of the concert ended with an Italian vocal *quartetto*, which may well have suggested the idea of Mr. Elliot's application to Anne for a translation of its words. It was this exchange between the cousins—the seeming intimacy between them—that appeared to confirm to Frederick Wentworth the rumors he had heard of their engagement, rumors that spurred his growing jealousy and helped to bring about a clarification of his feelings for her and, ultimately, of hers for him.

If one cannot discover from their texts much about the music performed in Jane Austen's novels, it is easy to learn about the type of music she played and sang herself by looking into the contents of her several music books. The first thing that strikes one about them is the poor general quality of the music, both vocal and instrumental, that they contain. Certainly there are pieces by a few great composers: Corelli, Handel, Gluck, and Haydn are all represented, though mostly by undemanding trifles. But there are only two works of real importance: a sonata in C by Haydn and a concerto in B flat by Handel. Jane Austen must have known the names of Mozart and Beethoven (their music was played in Bath during the years she lived there), but she possessed none of their keyboard works. Although her collection does include sonatas and variations by such respectable minor composers as Pleyel, Cramer, and J. C. Bach, the major part of it consists of trivia that can at best be described as merely pretty. One is forced to conclude, therefore, that though she practiced regularly, Jane Austen was not critical of the artistic value of the music she played—was perhaps unaware that it might be open to criticism. But if it is true, as has been suggested (by Jane Aiken Hodge in *The Double Life of Jane Austen*, pp. 113 and 133), that, like Anne Elliot, she developed an ability to think of other things "while her fingers were mechanically at work, proceeding for half an hour together, equally without error, and without consciousness" (*P*, p. 72), and that she was thus able to plan much of her writing during her solitary hours at the keyboard, then we who love her work care very little about her lack of that musical "taste" with which she so often credited her heroines: that the mere act of playing was in itself a stimulus to her literary imagination is a matter of infinitely greater importance.

NATURE

Alistair M. Duckworth

When Mrs. Elton proposes to "manage" the strawberry party in the grounds of Donwell Abbey, she claims that everything will be "as natural and simple as possible" (*E*, p. 355). Knightley's brusque reply defines an important meaning of "nature" in Jane Austen's novels: "My idea of the simple and the natural will be to have the table spread in the dining-room. The nature and the simplicity of gentlemen and ladies, with their servants and furniture, I think is best observed by meals within doors. When you are tired of eating strawberries in the garden, there shall be cold meat in the house" (ibid.). To be natural, that is, is to behave socially, to act in accordance with accustomed usages. Nature and culture are not, for Knightley, opposed but complementary terms. He would doubtless agree with Edmund Burke, who argues, in *An Appeal from the New Whigs to the Old Whigs* (1791), that rights are more natural in society than in the so-called state of nature. "Art," Burke concludes, "is man's nature."

In her early fiction particularly, Jane Austen gives expression to a view of nature that is both conservative and neoclassic. Disillusioned by Bingley's treatment of her sister Jane, Elizabeth Bennet exclaims: "What are men to rocks and mountains?" (*PP*, p. 154). Her tour to the Lake District is canceled, however, and she is "excessively disappointed," for like Jane Austen herself, she seems enamored of Gilpin's Tours, one of which—that to Cumberland and Westmorland—probably provides the itinerary of her aunt's projected trip. Despite her disappointment, however, Elizabeth finds more than adequate consolation in viewing the beautifully improved grounds of Pemberley: "She had never seen a place for which nature had done more" (p. 245). Darcy, it is evident, has not imposed his will on nature but, in a way that Pope would approve (and for which Aristotle could provide the rationale), has helped nature reach the ideal form toward which she was already aspiring.

Hampshire born and bred, Jane Austen loved the countryside of her native county, as well as of Surrey and Kent, through which she traveled on visits to her brothers Henry and Edward. Nature in these counties is nature improved, humanized, put to use, and Jane Austen took as much pleasure in viewing tastefully improved estates like Painshill and Esher (*Letters*, May 20, 1813) as she did in observing that "the wheat looked very well all the way" (*Letters*, August ?, 1814). Like the "fine country" Edward admires in his debate with Marianne over the picturesque (*SS*, pp. 96–98), the country she admired "unites beauty with utility," thus fulfilling an ideal as old as Horace's *utile dulci*. Rich in timber and pasture, such country is not picturesque if by picturesque is meant a preference for crooked overflourishing trees or for ruined cottages over comfortable farmhouses. When Fanny Price travels to Sotherton Court, she observes "the appearance of the country, the bearings of the roads, the difference of soil, the state of the harvest, the cottages, the cattle" (*MP*, p. 80), and we may be sure she has her author's approval. Just as surely Mary Crawford has her disapproval: Mary "saw nature, inanimate nature, with little observation; her attention was all for men and women" (p. 81).

Throughout her novels Jane Austen can show the absurdity of characters who discover sublimity—whether of a Burkean or Byronic kind—in nature. Sir Edward Denham's description of "the terrific Grandeur of the Ocean in a Storm" (*S*, p. 396) is a cliché of the cult of sensibility. And even Fanny Price is open to some criticism for the "enthusiasm" of her apostrophe to the "sublimity of Nature" at night (*MP*, p. 113) and for her ingenuous "rhapsodizing" over the wonderful growth of evergreens (p. 209). Yet as A. Walton Litz has argued, in her later novels Jane Austen reveals a less classical, more romantic attitude toward nature; her natural descriptions begin to express states of consciousness as her heroines respond feelingly to atmospheric moods and seasonal rhythms. Fanny's response to the rural spring, "that season which cannot, in spite of its capriciousness, be unlovely" (*MP*, p. 432), is quite different from Marianne's ridiculed "passion for dead leaves" (*SS*, p. 88), and Fanny's delight in the beautiful view from the ramparts at Portsmouth (a view that comprises sky, sea, ships, and the Isle of Wight; a view that is animated by the effects of lights, shadows, colors, and sounds) is a sign of her aesthetic, not to say synaesthetic, sensibility at an important juncture of the novel (p. 409). Emma, too, responds to nature with feeling, as when, at the low point of her life, she is invigorated by a change in the weather: "in the afternoon it cleared; the wind changed into a softer quarter; the clouds were carried off; the sun appeared; it was summer again. . . . Emma resolved to be out of doors as soon as possible. Never had the exquisite sight, smell, sensation of nature, tranquil, warm, and brilliant after a storm, been more attractive to her" (*E*, p. 424). At this moment, Knightley appears in the garden and proposes.

Jane Austen's "romantic" uses of natural setting are most evident in *Persuasion*, where Anne Elliot's sense of loss and separation is reflected by the external "autumnal" scene. During the walk to Winthrop, for example, Anne's consolation derives from "the view of the last smiles of the year upon the tawny leaves and withered hedges" or from the memory of "some tender sonnet, fraught with the apt analogy of the declining year, with declining happiness, and the images of youth and hope, and spring, all gone together" (pp. 84–85). This is romantic in the manner of Charlotte Smith's elegiac sonnets of 1784 or those of William Lisle Bowles in 1789, which continually deduce moral feelings from the natural scene. Bowles, however, also inspired Coleridge, and later in *Persuasion*, Coleridge's "Kubla Khan" may be echoed in the description of the village near Lyme: "Pinny, with its green chasms between romantic rocks" (p. 95).

Jane Austen's romantic interest in nature is further evidenced in her last fragment *Sanditon*, where—as E. M. Forster noted in his 1925 review— "topography comes to the front" in a new way. Yet we should not overstress Jane Austen's commitment to romantic attitudes. Captain Benwick's self-indulgent love of Scott and Byron (*P*, p. 100) is viewed critically by the more tough-minded Anne Elliot, and Anne's own movement from autumn to "a second spring of youth and beauty" (p. 124), though it is accompanied by images of nature and the seasons, depends also on qualities of self-reliance. During the walk to Winthrop, Anne does not indulge her grief but rouses herself to an awareness of her environment. It is, significantly, a "useful" agricultural scene: "large enclosures, where the ploughs at work, and the fresh-made path spoke the farmer, counteracting the sweets of poetical despondence, and meaning to have spring again" (p. 85).

Bibliography

FORSTER, E. M. *"Sanditon,"* *The Nation* (March 21, 1925), reprinted in *Abinger Harvest* (New York and London, 1936), 152–55.

LITZ, A. WALTON. "New Landscapes: *Persuasion* and *Sanditon*," in his *Jane Austen: A Study of Her Artistic Development* (London and New York, 1965), 150–69.

LOVEJOY, ARTHUR O. "'Nature' as Aesthetic Norm," *Modern Language Notes*, 42 (1927), 444–50; reprinted in his *Essays in the History of Ideas* (Baltimore, Md., 1948), 69–77.

OBITUARIES

David Gilson

Eleven published newspaper and periodical obituary notices of Jane Austen are known. The first, in the *Hampshire Chronicle and Courier* (vol. 44, no. 2254, July 21, 1817, p. 4), dated "Winchester, Saturday July 19th," reads: "Died, yesterday, in College-street, Miss Jane Austen, youngest daughter of the late Rev. George Austen, formerly Rector of Steventon, in this county." On the same day the *Hampshire Telegraph and Sussex Chronicle* (vol. 18, no. 928, p. 4) printed a brief announcement similarly dated but reading only: "On Friday last died, Miss Austen, late of Chawton, in this County."

The third notice, published in the *Courier* (July 22, 1817, no. 7744, p. 4), makes the first published admission of Jane Austen's authorship of the four novels then published: "On the 18th inst. at Winchester, Miss Jane Austen, youngest daughter of the late Rev. George Austen, Rector of Steventon, in Hampshire, and the Authoress of Emma, Mansfield Park, Pride and Prejudice, and Sense and Sensibility. Her manners were most gentle; her affections ardent; her candor was not to be surpassed, and she lived and died as became a humble Christian." A manuscript version of this notice exists, described by B. C. Southam, *Times Literary Supplement* (November 30, 1962, p. 944), believed to be a fair copy by Cassandra Austen of the notice actually sent to the newspaper office, with wording probably drafted by Henry or James Austen.

The *Hampshire Telegraph and Sussex Chronicle* made up for the brevity of its obituary notice of July 21, 1817 by printing in its next issue (July 28, 1817, p. 4), a longer notice, substantially that of the *Courier* but omitting the mentions of Jane Austen's manners, affections, and candor. On the same day the *Salisbury and Winchester Journal* (vol. 82, no. 4191, p. 4) published a virtual reprint of the *Courier* notice.

The sixth notice appeared in the *Kentish Gazette* (no. 5127, August 5, 1817, p. 4) a brief announcement mentioning only Jane Austen's parentage and her authorship of *Emma* and *Mansfield Park*, while the seventh, in the *Star* (no. 9498, August 8, p. 4), like that in the *Kentish Gazette*, omits the date of death, and also omits any mention of authorship—as does the eighth notice, in the *London Chronicle* (vol. 122, no. 9150, August 9–11, 1817, p. 143; identical with that in the *Star*).

The ninth obituary notice appeared in the August 1817 issue of the *Gentleman's Magazine* (vol. 86, part 2, p. 184; date of death, parentage, and titles of all four novels then published).

OBITUARIES

The Monthly Magazine (vol. 44, part 2, no. 302, September 1, 1817, p. 191) lists Jane Austen's death under "Provincial occurrences" omitting the date of death but giving parentage and titles of the four novels; while the last notice to appear, in the *New Monthly Magazine* (vol. 8, no. 44, September 1, 1817, p. 173), wrongly gives the novelist's father's name as "Jas." (= James) but describes her as "the ingenious authoress" of the four novels.

PERSUASION: THE CANCELED CHAPTERS

Brian Southam

The manuscript of the canceled chapters of *Persuasion*, printed at the end of Chapman's Oxford edition of the novel (*P*, pp. 253–63), is unique as being the only pages to have survived from the manuscripts of any of the published novels. It is also invaluable to students for illuminating Jane Austen's methods of composition and revision and the need that she faced, even as an experienced writer, to recast the novel's crucial scene.

Overall, *Persuasion* was written quickly, in almost exactly twelve months, between August 8, 1815 and August 6, 1816. On July 8, 1816, she began the penultimate chapter, chapter 10 of the second volume. Eight days later, this and chapter 11, a draft of thirty-two pages, was completed. On the last page, Jane Austen wrote, "Finis July 16 1816." At once, she had second thoughts, erasing these words and writing an additional paragraph, followed by "Finis July 18 1816." At this time, she also wrote a passage of five hundred words to be inserted in chapter 10.

According to the *Memoir*, Jane Austen was unhappy with this ending: "She thought it tame and flat, and was desirous of producing something better" (p. 166). The problem seems to have weighed upon her until one morning, some days later, "she awoke to more cheerful views and brighter inspiration: the sense of power revived; and imagination resumed its course." The outcome was a new chapter 11, incorporating more than a quarter of the original chapter 10; and so the original chapter 11, with some small verbal changes, became the final chapter 12.

The author's dissatisfaction was with the way in which she had effected the reunion of Anne and Wentworth. In the original chapter 10, it was a comedy scene, with the Crofts cast as sly matchmakers and the lovers' feelings for one another brought to light through a series of blunders and upsets. In itself, the scene is amusing and well written. However, it clouds a major issue in the novel—Anne's fitness of mind and feeling to judge and override Lady Russell's objection to the marriage, the "persuasion" that formerly kept her apart from Wentworth. The original version also fails to draw the intensity and depth of their love, nor do they come together with a full understanding of the past; whereas the new version shows their powers of self-determination, their control over their destinies, and

Wentworth's fitness for Anne. In contrast to the confusion and excitement of events that threw them together in the admiral's lodgings, at the White Hart there is an air of outward calm and spaciousness. The five people are carefully arranged about the room. The scene is highly pictured, and through the observation of movement, speech, and reaction, we are kept fully aware of the separate identities.

Henry James found the novels of Jane Austen "instinctive and charming." He advised readers to look elsewhere "for signal examples of what composition, distribution, arrangement can do, of how they intensify the life of a work of art" (p. 207). Yet, as the *Persuasion* manuscript reveals in the greatest detail, the inevitable rightness of the novel's conclusion was not, in the act of creation, a swift and effortless performance but a triumph of rethinking won through trial and error. Here, if anywhere, is the evidence of that conscious art that James was seeking.

Bibliography

CHAPMAN, R. W., ed. *Two Chapters of Persuasion* (Oxford, 1926).
JAMES, HENRY. "Gustave Flaubert," in Leon Edel, ed. *The House of Fiction* (New York, 1957), 207.
SOUTHAM, B. C., ed. *Jane Austen's Literary Manuscripts* (London, 1964), chap. 6.

PETS AND ANIMALS

J. David Grey

Considering the importance of animals in an agricultural economy and the fact that the countryside provides the major settings for her novels, Jane Austen pays little attention to pets and animals. Horses are, of course, an exception. They occupy the primary place in the catalog of her animal world and are mentioned close to two hundred times. Hunters, field horses, racers, and road and carriage horses appear in the novels, all of them in fact in *Mansfield Park*. Her characters travel frequently and employ post-horses when either private conveyances are unavailable or the distances to be traversed are too great. On occasion, the horses are minimally involved in the plotting. The farm horse that carries Jane Bennet, in the rain, toward Netherfield and the desired cold transports her to Mr. Bingley and, eventually, Elizabeth Bennet to Pemberley. Marianne Dashwood's proffered Queen Mab (the only horse that is granted a name) is emblematic of Willoughby's bad intentions. Fanny Price's mare, so essential to her health, provides the means whereby Jane Austen initially portrays the power that Mary Crawford has begun to wield over the unsuspecting Edmund Bertram. John Thorpe's handling and mishandling of his creatures is part and parcel of his characterization. The horse haggling he pretends to be involved with may well have taken place between Sir Walter and Mr. Elliot at Tattersall's (*P*, p. 8). There are mules in *Mansfield Park* (albeit foreign ones) and *Emma* and ponies in *Pride and Prejudice* and *Mansfield Park*. The pony that is predecessor to Fanny's mare is her "valued friend." Dr. Grant uses his to fetch the post. A reference occurs to the purchase of a donkey in *Emma*, just the rural transaction with which Jane Austen (who made use of a donkey cart when her health began to fail) was most familiar.

Household pets are few. It is fitting to find some terriers on hand, and a Newfoundland puppy, to welcome Catherine Morland to Henry Tilney's rustic Woodston abode. It causes wonder, however, that Lady Bertram's dog not only remains nameless (unless she has been so indolent as to have actually dubbed it Pug) but that it is inconsiderate enough to change its sex midstream. The "him" on page 74 of *Mansfield Park* is capable of producing a litter on page 333 (see *The Jane Austen Society Report for the Year 1974*, pp. 10–12). As a bona fide member of the family, room is made to accommodate him/her on the sofa.

Pets and Animals

John Willoughby's first appearance, a deceptive one, is in the company of his cavorting pointers. One, probably a black bitch, is awarded the only other name in the books—Folly. Henry Crawford's hunters are in Norfolk, Mr. Rushworth boasts of his dogs, Charles Musgrove maintains a pack at Uppercross, and Lord Osborne's hounds are mentioned twice in *The Watsons*. Lowly curs are encountered in *Emma* "quarrelling over a dirty bone" (p. 233) on the Highbury High Street.

Cows are raised at Delaford to supply Colonel Brandon with his double cream. Sotherton, also, has a herd. The Martins in *Emma* are proud of their "eight cows, two of them Alderneys, and one a little Welch cow" (p. 27), and there is talk of cattle shows. There must be pigs at Hunsford parsonage, since Elizabeth Bennet confuses their presence in the garden with the arrival of Lady Catherine and her daughter, but it is the Woodhouse stock that produces the inimitable pork of Hartfield. Mr. Knightley and Admiral and Mrs. Croft dote on their sheep. Delaford has poultry (*SS*), and a poultry house is an appropriate adjunct to Mrs. Weston's establishment. Unfortunately, however, her turkeys "disappear." Game is rarely alluded to, perhaps even scarce, since the Musgroves "guard" theirs. "Birds" have their coveys at Longbourn, and six brace of pheasants are pried from the copse beyond Mansfield Wood. The richest of the characters, Mr. Rushworth, sports domesticated pheasants at Sotherton Court, befitting his character and the outmoded fashion of the place.

In all the novels only two wild animals creep into the scenario: a hen-hunting fox (*SS*) and an elusive weasel (*P*). Charles Blake is anxious to show Emma Watson the stuffed fox and badger at Osborne Castle. A visit by the Dashwood family, for "poor" "dear" little Henry's sake, to "the wild beasts of Exeter Exchange" (p. 221) takes precedence, by a day, over a visit to John Dashwood's sisters, who have just arrived in London. Jane Austen's innuendos are most illuminating.

Cats deserve only one mention, and even that is metaphorical: "and how forlorn we shall be, when I come back!—Lord! we shall sit and gape at one another as dull as two cats" (*SS*, p. 280). Thus, Mrs. Jennings expresses her apprehension to Colonel Brandon at losing the company of the Misses Dashwood. As might be suspected, the preponderance of mentions is allotted to useful animals rather than household pets. The latter did not become a widespread vogue until urbanization occurred later in the nineteenth century.

THE PICTURESQUE

John Dixon Hunt

Jane Austen could not but help take notice of the picturesque, since the period of its elaboration and popularization coincided with her writing career (ca. 1790–1817). According to her brother Henry's "Biographical Notice," included in the posthumous first edition of *Persuasion* (1818), she had been "at a very early age . . . enamoured of Gilpin on the Picturesque; and she seldom changed her opinions either on books or men" (p. 7). Certainly she invokes Gilpin in the early burlesque, "Love and Freindship": Augusta tells Laura that she has been led to undertake a tour of Scotland as a result of reading Gilpin's *Observations on . . . Particularly the High-lands of Scotland* of 1789 (p. 105). Other less direct allusions to Gilpin and perhaps to other popularizers of the picturesque taste in Austen's mature fiction suggest that whether or not she was always "enamoured" of him, Gilpin's picturesque taste continued to serve her fictional purposes.

The picturesque was a romantic outgrowth of older, Renaissance ways of viewing art and nature. Whereas in landscape paintings of the sixteenth and seventeenth centuries scenery usually took second place to, but nevertheless supported, some central historical or mythological event, by the mid-eighteenth century English landscapists like Richard Wilson or Thomas Gainsborough emphasized scenery rather than emblematic or iconographic subjects. The former translation of visual into verbal (*ut pictura poesis*) ceased to be easy or popular and surrendered to more expressive, more personal, responses. This change coincided with and was fueled by a shifting of interest almost exclusively to the merely formal aspects of painting: chiaroscuro, variety of texture or what Gainsborough termed "business for the eye," composition, and an emphasis on subjects not for their own meaning but for their formal opportunities; the "character" or mood of a scene became the extent of its importance, and that character depended heavily on how it was represented or "expressed."

Gilpin's *Essay Upon Prints*, which preceded his picturesque tours, elaborated these formal criteria specifically in relation to engravings, but the implications for viewing and sketching actual scenery were clear: in a picture the landscape must be composed so that parts contribute to the whole, and if "design" and "distribution of light" are the key to the latter, the former will be enhanced by "expression," "grace," and accomplished "drawing." Gilpin followed his 1768 essay with three *Observations*, in

The Picturesque

which selected parts of Great Britain were visited with a view to their "Picturesque Beauty"; some further principles were formulated in his *Three Essays* of 1792, followed by more volumes of tours in which the English countryside was explored for its picturesque qualities and its opportunities for the amateur artist. By Austen's time the original emphases of *picturesque*—graphic or what "would look well in a picture" (*Three Essays*, pp. 18–19)—had acquired a sophisticated jargon, applicable to actual as well as painted landscapes and to parks and gardens.

Austen seems fully aware of these developments. In *Northanger Abbey* Catherine is instructed by the Tilneys, who view scenery "with the eyes of persons accustomed to drawing" and to judging "its capability of being formed into pictures" (p. 110). Tilney, with some irony, responds to views in terms not of their extent or clearness but "of fore-grounds, distances, and second distances—side-screens and perspectives—lights and shades," and Catherine is "so hopeful a scholar, that when they gained the top of Beechen Cliff, she voluntarily rejected the whole city of Bath, as unworthy to make part of a landscape" (p. 111).

Other references to the picturesque are less extensive but no less telling. In *Sense and Sensibility* Marianne's enthusiasm for the vogue encounters in the prosaic Edward Ferrars somebody who proclaims "no knowledge in the picturesque," refuses to employ its jargon ("I shall call . . . surfaces strange and uncouth, which ought to be irregular and rugged"), and prefers a landscape that proclaims its utility rather than picturesque beauty (pp. 96–97). Gilpin and other commentators admired groupings of three cattle for their irregular *ensemble* (see *Observations* on the Lake District, II.259), a pedantic absurdity to which Elizabeth Bennet alludes when she says to Miss Bingley and Mrs. Hurst, walking arm in arm with Darcy, "You are charmingly group'd, and appear to uncommon advantage. The picturesque would be spoilt by admitting a fourth" (p. 53). Picturesque taste cultivated ruins for their "irregular and rugged" aspect, for achieving which effect by his dissolution of the monasteries Austen satirically praises Henry VIII in "The History of England" (p. 142). Fanny Price's sitting room at Mansfield Park is decorated with transparencies made in schoolroom days (p. 152), which Bradbrook has shown signals her affection for three quintessentially picturesque subjects—Tintern Abbey, an Italian cave, and a moonlit lake in Cumberland. Bradbrook has also indicated other possible allusions or uses of picturesque writings: her choice of Box Hill, where Emma admires "the beautiful views" just before her rebuke by Knightley (p. 374) may be influenced by Gilpin's praise of it in *Observations on the Western Parts* (II.11–12), the account of Portsmouth in *Observations on the Coasts of Hampshire* . . . (II.15) may have suggested the walks that Fanny enjoys there in *Mansfield Park* (p. 409), while the suggestions of the Peak District and the setting of Pemberley in *Pride and Prejudice* and the picturesque prospects along Northamptonshire roads invoked in *Mansfield Park* may both derive from references in Gilpin's *Observations on . . . Cumberland*. George Mason's encomiums on Surrey—"*a school of landscape*" (*Essay on Design in Gardening* [2nd ed. 1795], p. 143)—have also been suggested as the occasion for similar conversations in *Emma* (p. 273). And to these may be added the writings of James Thomson, Oliver Goldsmith, and William Cowper, who all influenced picturesque taste and were among Austen's favorite and quoted authors.

Austen's allusions to the picturesque become more interesting as well as more problematic where they concern landscape gardening. The heroines of both *Pride and Prejudice* and *Emma* experience crucial recognitions when they are brought face-to-face with Pemberley Woods and Donwell Abbey, respectively, each of which is presented in subtly modified picturesque terms. Emma is made to recognize, first, how Donwell Abbey's situation is "characteristic," expressive of its best *genius loci* ("It was just what it ought to be, and it looked what it was," p. 358) and then is led to appreciate the place that Martin's farm has in a landscape dedicated to tradition and use rather than to modish picturesque fashion (p. 360). Pemberley pleases Elizabeth for its "variety," and she is quick to register "every remarkable spot and point of view" (which suggests an aptitude for recognizing picturesque "stations"). But she also recognizes that picturesque ideas have been accommodated tactfully. ("Natural beauty had been so little counteracted by an awkward taste.") The park delights her with "scenes" that conceal their art and provide various prospects from different rooms in the house (pp. 245ff.). If earlier she had asked, "What are men to rocks and mountains?" (p. 154), she now learns the human dimensions of landscape.

As various critics (Rosemarie Bodenheimer, Ann Banfield, Charles Murrah, among others) have pointed out, Austen uses such matters as landscape taste to signal judgments about her characters. In *Sense and Sensibility* the sensible Elinor sketches, but her sister enthuses over the picturesque and even admits its "mere jargon" (p. 97). The proposed expedition to Blaise Castle in *Northanger Abbey* (p. 85) mocks Catherine's romantic propensities by invoking what is held out to be a veritable picturesque dream of an old ruin but was in fact (did Austen expect her readers to know?) a folly of 1766 in the grounds of a neoclassic house. The education of Fanny Price in *Mansfield Park* is in part charted by her reactions to landscape. At first she is allowed both some sentimental moments of picturesque appreciation (notably pp. 113 and 209) and some sensible reactions to the removal of avenues of trees in the interests of avoiding straight lines (p. 56). In this instance she is aligned against those characters who would call in fashionable "improvers," landscape gardeners with picturesque ideas: Humphry Repton is singled out as the most fashionable contemporary example (p. 53), not entirely accurately (see the essay "Architecture and Buildings," above). By the end of the novel her maturity of social, moral, and aesthetic nature is indicated by her appreciation of the townscape at Portsmouth (p. 409) and, more importantly, by her delight in the landscape of Mansfield Park upon her return to it (p. 446).

Austen's ridicule was reserved for the excesses of the picturesque, amusingly satirized in such an early piece as "A Tour through Wales—in a Letter from a young Lady" (*Vol. 2*, p. 176). By itself it was too limited a perspective, too simply aesthetic. (Witness the wry description in *Sanditon* [p. 377] of "a tasteful little Cottage Ornèe, on a strip of Waste Ground.") She had no patience with picturesque jargon, which perhaps explains her apparent neglect of Uvedale Price and Richard Payne Knight, two prominent and wordy exponents of its aesthetic. To look solely with picturesque eyes also predetermined too much about social and historical factors, as the satire of Catherine Morland indicates and as Henry Crawford's animadversions on the old-fashioned style of Sotherton's gardens suggest (*MP*, pp. 85ff.). Picturesque taste, exemplified by Henry Crawford's proposal to revamp Edmund's parsonage (pp. 241ff.), fails to attend adequately to the useful or the socially apt; amusingly, Dr. Grant's "improvements" in the same novel (p. 54) are to make a "plantation to shut out the churchyard." The hints that Austen drops about good gardens suggest that their serviceableness was as crucial as their beauty: shrubberies, yew arbors, or rose gardens are outdoor extensions of social space not necessarily valued for their picturesque beauties. In *Sanditon*, Austen seems to approve of the old Parker house—"well fenced & planted, & rich in the Garden, Orchard & Meadows which are the best embellishments of such a Dwelling" (p. 379). Yet as her last novel shows, Austen could respond to nature without such "embellishments": Anne Elliot's country walk in *Persuasion* (pp. 84ff.) has nothing either of the picturesque taint that earlier novels have criticized, though in its personal responsiveness to scenery and the association of poetry with visible nature, which the sight of a farmer plowing the autumn land for spring crops "counteract[ed]," Austen is still in touch with traditions of the picturesque renewed and revalued in the interests of a new heroine and a new fiction.

Bibliography

William Gilpin's theoretical works are *Essay Upon Prints* (1768) and *Three Essays: On Picturesque Beauty; on Picturesque Travel; and on Sketching Landscape* (1792), but theoretical considerations are canvassed in the six books of *Observations* on various parts of Great Britain (1782–1809) and in *Remarks on Forest Scenery* (1791). Uvedale Price, *An Essay on the Picturesque* (1794) was expanded into *Three Essays on the Picturesque* (1810). See also Richard Payne Knight, *The Landscape, a Didactic Poem* (1794) and *An Analytical Inquiry into the Principles of Taste* (1805). Two studies of Gilpin are useful: William D. Templeman, *The Life and Work of William Gilpin* (Urbana, Ill., 1939) and Carl P. Barbier, *William Gilpin: His Drawings, Teaching and Theory of the Picturesque* (Oxford, 1963). Other studies of the topic are more general: Christopher Hussey, *The Picturesque: Studies in a Point of View* (London and New York, 1927); Elizabeth W. Manwaring, *Italian Landscape in Eighteenth-century England* (New York, 1925); David Watkin, *The English Vision: The Picturesque in Architecture, Landscape and Garden Design* (London, 1982). Some essays are: Martin Price, "The Picturesque Moment," in F. W. Hilles and Harold Bloom, eds., *From Sensibility to Romanticism* (New York, 1965), 259–92; John Dixon Hunt, "Sense and Sensibility in the Landscape Designs of Humphry Repton," *Studies in Burke and His Time*, 19 (1978), 3–28, and "Picturesque Mirrors and the Ruins of the Past," *Art History*, 4 (1981), 254–70.

On Jane Austen and the picturesque see Ann Banfield, "The Moral Landscape of *Mansfield Park*," *Nineteenth-century Fiction*, 26 (1971–72), 1–24, and "The Influence of Place: Jane Austen and the Novel of Social Consciousness," in David Monaghan, ed., *Jane Austen in a Social Context* (London, 1981), 28–48; Rosemarie Bodenheimer, "Looking at the Landscape in Jane Austen," *Studies in English Literature*, 21 (1981), pp. 605–23; Frank W. Bradbrook, *Jane Austen and Her Predecessors* (Cambridge, 1966), chap. 3; Alistair M. Duckworth, *The Improvement of the Estate* (Baltimore and London, 1971); Charles C. Murrah, "The Background of *Mansfield Park*," in R. C. Rathburn and Martin Steinmann, Jr., eds., *From Jane Austen to Joseph Conrad* (Minneapolis, Minn., 1958), 23–34.

"PLAN OF A NOVEL," "OPINIONS OF *MANSFIELD PARK*," AND "OPINIONS OF *EMMA*"

Mary Gaither Marshall

The correspondence between Rev. James Stanier Clarke and Jane Austen to arrange the dedication of *Emma* to the prince regent (*Letters*, November 15 and 16, December 11 and 21, 1815; March 27, April 1, 1816) provided the inspiration for "Plan of a Novel, according to hints from various quarters" (ca. 1815). Clarke suggested that Austen use his life as a clergyman or the history of the House of Coburg as the basis for her next work and further urged that she "continue to write, & make all your friends send Sketches to help you" (*Letters*, December 21, 1815).

Austen, although amused, politely replied that her talents were unequal to his topics; but two of his suggestions prompted her to write the burlesque "Plan," which satirized the romantic novel.

Austen naturally chose the burlesque as an appropriate framework for the "Plan," a private composition. She had previously used the form in her *juvenilia* and for family entertainment (Lefroy, pp. 162–64). As Clarke proposed, she solicited advice from her family and friends. If Austen used a suggestion, she noted its source in the margin of the manuscript.

Her niece Fanny Knight and second cousin Mary Cooke suggested the heroine's character and countenance: "faultless... very highly accomplished... quite beautiful" (p. 428). Clarke's clergyman appeared virtually unchanged as the Heroine's father: "Chaplain to a distinguished Naval Character about the Court... his having buried his own Mother... of a very literary turn... nobody's Enemy but his own" (p. 429). William Gifford, Joseph Sherer, Mrs. Pearse, Henry Sanford, and Mrs. Craven provided additional hints.

The "Plan's" story began in Austen's typical country neighborhood, but heroine and father were soon fleeing across Europe to escape the daughter's unprincipled would-be lovers. The father died after delivering a rambling deathbed speech; the heroine, still dodging "Anti-Heroes," "crawled back" home for a tender reunion with the hero.

Austen collected comments about her novels from many sources, including some individuals who had contributed to the "Plan." She recorded these impressions, which often compared *Mansfield Park* and *Emma* unfavorably to *Pride and Prejudice*, in "Opinions of *Mansfield Park*" and "Opinions of *Emma*" (ca. 1816). Some comments were amusing; others were serious and came from important sources. Austen's recording of these opinions reflected her own inimitable style. The publisher Mr. Egerton "praised [*MP*] for it's Morality, & for being so equal a Composition.—No weak Parts" (p. 433) and Mr. Jeffery of the *Edinburgh Review* "was kept up by [*E*] three nights" (p. 439). Mr. Fowle "read only the first & last Chapters, because he had heard [*E*] was not interesting" (ibid.). Mrs. Augusta Bramstone "owned that she thought S & S.—and P. & P. downright nonsense, but expected to like MP. better, & having finished the 1st vol.—flattered herself she had got through the worst" (p. 433).

Extracts of "Opinions of *Mansfield Park*" and "Opinions of *Emma*" and an inaccurate and incomplete text of "Plan" originally were published in the *Memoir*. The latter two first appeared in their entirety in the *Life*. R. W. Chapman's *Plan of a Novel* (1926) included the first complete publication of "Opinions of *Mansfield Park*," as well as complete texts of "Opinions of *Emma*" and "Plan," and manuscript facsimiles of all three works.

Bibliography

AUSTEN, JANE. *Plan of a Novel According to Hints from various Quarters With Opinions on "Mansfield Park" and "Emma" Collected and Transcribed by her and Other Documents*, R. W. Chapman, ed. (Oxford, 1926).
GILSON, DAVID. *A Bibliography of Jane Austen* (Oxford, 1982).
JENKINS, ELIZABETH. *Jane Austen: A Biography* (London, 1938).
LASCELLES, MARY. *Jane Austen and Her Art* (Oxford, 1939).
LEFROY, ANNA AUSTEN. *Jane Austen's "Sanditon": A Continuation by Her Niece Together with "Reminiscences of Aunt Jane,"* Mary Gaither Marshall, ed. (Chicago, 1983).
LITZ, A. WALTON. *Jane Austen: A Study of Her Artistic Development* (London and New York, 1965).
SOUTHAM, B. C. *Jane Austen's Literary Manuscripts* (Oxford, 1964).
TEN HARMSEL, HENRIETTA. *Jane Austen: A Study in Fictional Conventions* (The Hague, 1964).

PLOT SUMMARIES

A. Walton Litz

Sense and Sensibility

Sense and Sensibility was first composed in the late 1790s but revised prior to publication in 1811. Before Henry Dashwood died, he urged his son John to look after the interests of his stepmother, Mrs. Henry Dashwood, and his three half sisters, Elinor, Marianne, and Margaret. But John Dashwood fails to carry out his father's wish. Influenced by his selfish wife, Fanny, who fears that Elinor and her brother Edward Ferrars are attracted to each other, he makes life so uncomfortable for the Dashwood sisters and their mother that they retire to a cottage in Devonshire owned by a relation, Sir John Middleton. There Marianne, a lively believer in "sensibility," rejects the suit of a sensible thirty-five-year-old admirer, Colonel Brandon, and falls in love with John Willoughby, an attractive but untrustworthy young man. Willoughby appears to return her affection but then suddenly departs for London, leaving Marianne in great distress. Elinor and Marianne eventually journey to London, where they find Willoughby cold and indifferent, engaged to be married to an heiress. Marianne continues to defend Willoughby, but Colonel Brandon privately tells Elinor that his young ward was seduced and abandoned by Willoughby. Elinor has also learned from the selfish and ill-bred Lucy Steele that Edward Ferrars has been secretly engaged to Lucy for some time. When Edward's mother is told of the engagement, she is furious and settles the property intended for Edward on his feckless younger brother, Robert. Colonel Brandon arranges for Edward to become a curate on his estate, thus opening the way for marriage to Lucy. With characteristic good sense, Elinor conceals her grief, while Marianne displays her emotions.

On the way back to Devonshire, Marianne falls ill. Willoughby hears of her illness and attempts to visit her, hoping that a full account of his behavior will make her think better of him; but he is intercepted by Elinor. After Marianne has regained her health, Elinor tells her Willoughby's story, and gradually Marianne's love for him begins to fade. Meanwhile, Elinor learns from Edward Ferrars that the scheming Lucy Steele has married his brother Robert instead. Edward is free to ask Elinor to marry him, and she gladly accepts. Marianne, recovering from her infatuation with Willoughby, is won over by the kindness of Colonel Brandon and agrees to marry him.

Sense and Sensibility was less heavily revised than *Pride and Prejudice* and bears more of the hallmarks of Jane Austen's early style. The schematic title is reflected in the schematic characterizations, where Elinor's "sense" is balanced against Marianne's "sensibility," and many of the figures are modeled on the types of eighteenth-century drama and fiction. The language of the novel is replete with the abstract terms of the eighteenth-century essayists; but in its strong feeling for nature and its dramatic structure, *Sense and Sensibility* points forward to the triumphs of Jane Austen's later fiction.

Pride and Prejudice

An early version of *Pride and Prejudice* was written in 1796–97 under the title *First Impressions*, but it was heavily revised before publication in 1813. Mr. and Mrs. Bennet and their five daughters live in the village of Longbourn in Hertfordshire. When the wealthy Charles Bingley leases the house of Netherfield near Longbourn and comes to stay there accompanied by his sisters and his friend Fitzwilliam Darcy, Mrs. Bennet has high hopes that some of her daughters will be married. Mr. Bingley and Jane, the Bennets' sensible oldest daughter, are attracted to each other when they meet at the Meryton assembly ball, but Darcy's cold and proud behavior offends Jane's younger sister Elizabeth, a witty and intelligent young woman who is her father's favorite. Elizabeth's prejudice against Mr. Darcy is confirmed when Mr. Wickham, an attractive young officer, claims that Darcy cheated him out of an inheritance left by his godfather, Darcy's father. Darcy and the Bingley sisters, disgusted by the vulgarity of Mrs. Bennet, persuade Bingley to abandon his interest in Jane and return to London.

Mr. Collins, a foolish clergyman who will inherit the Bennet property by entail, arrives at Longbourn and proposes to Elizabeth, but she rejects him with her father's approval. Mr. Collins, who is a favorite of Mr. Darcy's aunt, Lady Catherine de Bourgh, next proposes to Elizabeth's friend Charlotte Lucas, who accepts him. Visiting Charlotte and her husband on Lady Catherine's estate, Elizabeth meets Darcy again and is surprised when he proposes to her. She refuses him, only to be shocked and mortified when Darcy writes a letter which convinces her that Wickham is a deceitful adventurer who tried to elope with Darcy's younger sister.

Elizabeth makes a trip to Derbyshire with her worthy uncle and aunt from London, Mr. and Mrs. Gardiner, and while they are in Derbyshire, they decide to visit Darcy's country estate, Pemberley, believing that he is absent. Darcy appears unexpectedly on the scene, insists on introducing

Elizabeth to his younger sister, and is in every way a changed man, perfectly agreeable. Elizabeth learns that her wayward sister Lydia has eloped with Wickham, and without her knowledge Darcy tracks down the couple and sees that they are properly established. Bingley and Jane renew their love, and after Elizabeth learns of Darcy's generosity she realizes her love for him and they are reconciled, in spite of the opposition of the proud Lady Catherine. At the end of the novel Elizabeth and Darcy are settled in Pemberley, where they are visited regularly by Mr. and Mrs. Gardiner and Elizabeth's father.

Pride and Prejudice has always been the most popular of Jane Austen's novels because it satisfies our natural longing for the probable and the possible. The social world of Darcy and Elizabeth is scrupulously described, but within these limitations the hero and heroine are allowed to achieve freedom and self-expression. Like all truly classical artists, Jane Austen welcomed the opportunity to demonstrate her freedom within restrictions, to prove—in André Gide's words—her "exquisite mastery of what can be mastered." In marrying Darcy, Elizabeth Bennet is satisfying our sense of social rightness *and* our sense of personal style. *Pride and Prejudice* has often been compared to the music of Mozart, because it gives us a sense of liberation while obeying the strictest laws of form and structure.

Mansfield Park

Mansfield Park was written in 1811–13 and published in 1814. Sir Thomas Bertram, the owner of Mansfield Park in Northamptonshire, has two sons, Tom and Edmund, and two daughters, Maria and Julia. His wife, Lady Bertram, a good-natured but indolent woman, has two sisters: Mrs. Norris, a selfish widow who lives nearby; and Mrs. Price, the wife of a naval lieutenant, who resides in Portsmouth with a family of nine children. To assist Mrs. Price, one of her children, Fanny, is brought to Mansfield Park at the age of ten. A quiet and sensitive girl, Fanny is neglected by all the family except Edmund.

When the action begins, Fanny is fifteen. Sir Thomas is on a business trip to the West Indies, and the glamorous Mary and Henry Crawford have arrived as guests of their brother-in-law, Mr. Grant, the local vicar. During her father's absence the elder daughter, Maria, has become engaged to Mr. Rushworth, a young man "with not more than common sense," and the fashionable Mr. Yates has arrived as a guest of the older brother, Tom. Mr. Yates is fresh from amateur theatricals at a country house, and he suggests that the young people of Mansfield Park put on *Lovers' Vows*, a popular melodrama translated from the German of August F. F. von Kotzebue.

Edmund, who wishes to be a clergyman, is sensitive to the impropriety of performing such a sensational play in an intimate setting and without his father's permission, but he finally yields to the desires of the others; only Fanny, who in her sincerity fears "acting" and role playing, will have nothing to do with the play. *Lovers' Vows* is cast and rehearsed, with each person playing a role that foreshadows his "real-life" fate, but the rehearsals are cut short by the return of Sir Thomas.

Henry Crawford has been flirting with Maria, but when she discovers his lack of feeling for her, she hides her love and marries Mr. Rushworth. Henry then begins a flirtation with Fanny and finds to his surprise that he is falling in love with her. He proposes but Fanny refuses him, thus incurring the displeasure of Sir Thomas, who regards her as ungrateful. Fanny's affections are all for Edmund, who is fascinated by the insincere Mary Crawford.

Fanny pays a visit to Portsmouth to escape the tensions at Mansfield Park, but she is depressed to find all of her family except her brother William noisy and ill-bred. While Fanny is at Portsmouth, several disasters occur at Mansfield: Tom falls seriously ill, Maria (now Mrs. Rushworth) runs away with Henry Crawford, and Julia elopes with Mr. Yates. Faced with the misbehavior of his own children, Sir Thomas comes to value Fanny's character. Edmund, in turn, is shocked by Mary Crawford's worldly response to these disasters and begins to understand her true nature. The novel ends happily. Tom recovers, Mr. Yates turns out to be more suitable than Sir Thomas had thought, and Edmund declares his love for Fanny. They are married and eventually settle in the parsonage at Mansfield Park.

Mansfield Park is a retreat from Jane Austen's characteristic wit and irony. It is as if the virtues of *Pride and Prejudice*—all that is "light, and bright, and sparkling" (*Letters*, February 4, 1813)—had become the sins of *Mansfield Park*. The novel is overtly moralistic, and Fanny lacks the energy and self-possession typical of the Jane Austen heroine. One explanation may be that *Mansfield Park* was the first product of Jane Austen's maturity, *Pride and Prejudice* having been begun in youth and revised many years later. In its rejection of so many comic conventions *Mansfield Park* may have been, as Lionel Trilling has speculated, the result of "an unusual state of the author's mind" (p. 218). But it is best to view the novel as another facet of Jane Austen's complex sensibility, a countertruth to *Emma* or *Pride and Prejudice*. Those who accuse Jane Austen of giving in to social conventions and betraying her own generous nature have too simple a view of her artistic intentions.

Emma

Emma was written between January 1814 and March 1815 and published later in 1815. Emma Woodhouse, "handsome, clever, and rich" (p. 5), is given free rein as mistress of the house by her hypochondriacal father. Her former companion and governess, Miss Taylor, has recently married a worthy neighbor, Mr. Weston. Mrs. Weston and Mr. Knightley, the owner of Donwell Abbey, "a sensible man about seven or eight-and-thirty" (p. 9), are loyal admirers of Emma, but they recognize her restless imagination and penchant for arranging the lives of others. As a substitute for Mrs. Weston, Emma befriends Harriet Smith, "the natural daughter of somebody" (p. 22), a boarder at the school in the nearby village of Highbury. Harriet, a foolish but good-natured young girl of seventeen, is engaged to an honest farmer, Robert Martin, whom Mr. Knightley greatly admires; but Emma feels that the match is beneath Harriet and persuades her to break it off. She then tries to arrange a match between Harriet and Mr. Elton, the local vicar, only to discover that Elton cares nothing for Harriet and instead wishes to marry her.

Somewhat embarrassed but undaunted, Emma next turns her attention to Frank Churchill, the son of Mr. Weston by his first marriage, who is visiting Highbury. She imagines that he may be in love with her and even visualizes him as a husband for Harriet, not realizing that he is secretly engaged to Jane Fairfax, the niece of the kindly but garrulous Miss Bates, the daughter of a former vicar of Highbury. When Frank Churchill ends his visit, he is on the verge of telling Emma the true story, but she does not encourage him because she fears he will propose to her.

Mr. Elton returns to Highbury with a new bride. His rudeness to Harriet helps her recover from her former infatuation, and she is encouraged by Mr. Knightley's kindness to hope that he may love her. When Emma discovers the secret engagement between Jane Fairfax and Frank Churchill and then learns that it is Mr. Knightley, not Frank Churchill, whom Harriet admires, she recognizes her own self-deceptions and suddenly understands her deepest wish, "that Mr. Knightley must marry no one but herself!" (p. 408). Humiliated and temporarily cured of her penchant for arranging other lives, Emma gladly accepts a proposal from Mr. Knightley, and Harriet is finally united with Robert Martin.

Emma is probably Jane Austen's most finely constructed novel. Emma Woodhouse is constantly at the center of the narrative; her lively personality gives the work its energy and charm. Yet Jane Austen never loses sight of Emma's defects, and through a masterful control of irony and aesthetic distance she keeps her heroine in critical perspective. With her self-deceptions and her love for fictions, Emma Woodhouse foreshadows Emma Bovary and all those other nineteenth-century heroines whose illusions lead to tragedy. But Jane Austen's aim is comedy, not tragedy, and through a painful process of moral education Emma is brought to a moment of self-recognition that allows her to remain a free spirit while accepting Mr. Knightley's role as guardian of her restless imagination.

Northanger Abbey

Northanger Abbey was written in the late 1790s but not published until 1817. Begun as a satire on the improbable plots and characters of the typical gothic novel, such as Mrs. Radcliffe's *Mysteries of Udolpho* (1794), *Northanger Abbey* developed into a treatment of Jane Austen's favorite theme, the initiation of a young woman into the complexities of adult social life. Catherine Morland, who comes from the comfortable family of a village clergyman, is invited to Bath for the season by her wealthy friends, Mr. and Mrs. Allen. In Bath she meets Isabella Thorpe, a sophisticated young woman whose brother John is a friend of Catherine's brother, James Morland. Isabella encourages Catherine's interest in romantic fantasies and "horrid" fictions. After Isabella becomes engaged to James Morland, she tries to promote a romance between Catherine and her irresponsible brother, John Thorpe, but Catherine is more interested in a young clergyman she has met, Henry Tilney, the son of General Tilney of Northanger Abbey. Under the illusion (fostered by John Thorpe) that Catherine is wealthy, General Tilney invites her to stay at Northanger Abbey. There Catherine's imagination runs wild: she becomes convinced that Northanger Abbey is like the setting of a gothic novel and that General Tilney had murdered his late wife. She is humiliated when Henry Tilney disabuses her of these fantasies and further humiliated when General Tilney returns suddenly from London and orders her to leave the abbey. This action is based on another false report from John Thorpe, who claims that Catherine is totally without wealth and has deceived the general.

Meanwhile, Henry Tilney's worldly brother, Captain Tilney, has flirted with Isabella Thorpe and caused her to break off her engagement to James Morland. But Captain Tilney is too shrewd to be taken in by the scheming Isabella, and she is left without a husband. Eleanor Tilney's fortunate marriage to a viscount and the discovery that Catherine will have a substantial income allay the general's anger, and after Henry has explained the misunderstanding to Catherine's family, the marriage both have desired finally takes place.

Although *Northanger Abbey* was drafted in 1798–99, after the first versions of *Sense and Sensibility* and *Pride and Prejudice* had been written, it received less radical revision than those works and consequently represents an early phase of Jane Austen's art, when high-spirited social and literary satire was mixed with a growing sense of more mature themes. Jane Austen sold the manuscript to a publisher in 1803, but it was never printed, perhaps because the fashion for gothic fiction was already declining. When Jane Austen prepared an "Advertisement" for the novel in 1816, shortly before her death, she asked the public "to bear in mind that thirteen years have passed since it was finished, many more since it was begun, and that during that period, places, manners, books, and opinions have undergone considerable changes" (*NA*, p. 10). Time has proved this apology to be unnecessary. Although the books that she mocks and the manners she satirizes now seem remote and quaint, her basic themes—the constant desire to substitute illusion for reality, the interdependence of spiritual and material values—remain fresh and compelling. It is one of the deeper ironies of *Northanger Abbey* that the gothic violence that Catherine imagines is dispelled, only to be replaced by a more rational view of the world that is almost as dark.

Persuasion

Persuasion was published after Jane Austen's death in 1817. Sir Walter Elliot, a vain and improvident widower, has three daughters: Elizabeth, twenty-nine and unmarried, who has inherited her father's pride in family; Anne, twenty-seven, who is gentle and intelligent but slighted by her father and older sister; and Mary, the youngest daughter, married to Charles Musgrove, the son of a nearby landowner. Sir Walter's wasteful habits oblige him to lease his estate, Kellynch Hall, to Admiral and Mrs. Croft, while he pays a visit to Bath, accompanied by Elizabeth and her untrustworthy friend Mrs. Clay, who hopes to marry Sir Walter. Anne, who is reluctant to join them, divides her time between her sister Mary and Lady Russell, a trusted friend of the family.

While staying with the Musgroves, Anne again meets Captain Frederick Wentworth, whom she had loved over seven years before and hoped to marry, until she yielded to the disapproving "persuasion" of her father and Lady Russell. Wentworth, now successful and relatively wealthy, is at first cool to Anne, harboring a resentment of his earlier treatment when he was a penniless young naval officer, but gradually his old love for Anne revives. At first, Wentworth is attracted to Charles Musgrove's sister Louisa; and after she is injured at the seaside resort of Lyme Regis in a fall for which Wentworth feels partly responsible, Anne is sure that they will marry. During Louisa's convalescence, however, she becomes engaged to Wentworth's friend and fellow officer Captain Benwick. Wentworth hastens to Bath, where Anne is unhappily established with her father, Elizabeth, and the scheming Mrs. Clay.

At Bath, Wentworth finds that Anne's cousin William Elliot, the heir of Kellynch Hall, is paying court to her, but Anne soon learns of William Elliot's true nature from an old schoolmate whose husband was ruined by him. Sensing Anne's patient love, Wentworth writes her a letter, and all is quickly arranged between them. Mrs. Clay follows William Elliot to London, giving up her interest in Sir Walter, and Wentworth is gratefully accepted into the family by the "foolish, spendthrift baronet" (p. 248).

In a sense, *Persuasion* begins where Jane Austen's other novels end: the heroine knows her heart, and the drama of the story lies in her struggle to overcome the obstacles of chance and social conventions. Anne Elliot is the most sympathetic of all Jane Austen's heroines and, one suspects, the closest to her creator. The novel is pervaded by an "autumnal" mood that gives it a special poignancy, making it a fitting climax to Jane Austen's career. In its open structure and poetic use of landscape, *Persuasion* reflects the influence of the new romanticism and points to later developments in the English novel.

A rare example of Jane Austen's methods of composition is provided by a surviving manuscript chapter (originally 2.X, now 2.X and XI) of *Persuasion*, printed in R. W. Chapman's standard edition (pp. 253–63).

The Watsons

This unfinished work was probably written in 1803–1804 but not published until 1871. Emma Watson, a sensible young lady who has been reared in comfortable circumstances by her aunt, returns to her family in a Surrey village and confronts the difficulties of making her way in provincial society without wealth or influence. At a local ball she meets Lord Osborne, who is cold and awkward but interested in Emma; Tom Musgrave, an attractive flirt; and Mr. Howard, a clergyman who is "a little more than Thirty" (p. 330). The story breaks off before the plot is fully developed, but it has been traditionally assumed (based on claims by the author's family) that Emma marries Mr. Howard.

In its characters and the personality of the heroine, *The Watsons* looks forward to *Mansfield Park* and *Emma*; but it differs from these later masterpieces in its depressed tone and dark view of an impoverished young lady's place in society. The fragment may reflect a difficult passage in Jane Austen's life, when family misfortunes and disappointment in love led to a failure of her characteristic energy and humor.

PLOT SUMMARIES

Sanditon

Sanditon, an unfinished novel, was written between January and March 1817, the year of Jane Austen's death, but not published in full until 1925. In *Sanditon* Jane Austen returned to the light-hearted burlesque and parody of her earliest works, perhaps as a defense against illness and depression; the rough draft was presumably broken off at chapter 12 because of failing health. Unlike the traditional settings of her other works, Sanditon is a small fishing village that has been turned into a modern seaside health resort by local speculators, and part of Jane Austen's satire is directed at the latest fashions in English culture. The characters in *Sanditon*, such as the sensible observer Charlotte Heywood and the pretentious Lady Denham, are familiar types from the earlier novels, but they exist as mere sketches, and it is difficult to guess how the novel would have developed if Jane Austen had lived. Attempts to finish *Sanditon* have been notably unsuccessful. What does stand out in *Sanditon* is a deeper sense of "place" and a new awareness of social dislocation that prefigures the Victorian novel.

Bibliography

TRILLING, LIONEL. "Mansfield Park," in *The Opposing Self* (New York, 1955).

THE PORTRAITS

Helen Denman

While there are extant a number of portraits of Jane Austen, only two can claim authenticity, and of these only one is a record of her features. The earliest is a watercolor drawing, signed and dated "C.E.A. 1804," presumably the work of Jane's sister Cassandra. It represents the profile (indeed, almost a back view) of a lady in a summer dress and bonnet, sitting on a grassy bank. Identification rests on a letter of 1862 from Jane's niece Anna Lefroy to James Edward Austen-Leigh, referring to "a sketch which Aunt Cassandra made of her in one of their expeditions—sitting down out of doors on a hot day, with her bonnet strings untied." Unfortunately, the peak of the sunbonnet almost completely obscures the face, so that the picture is no representation of Jane Austen's features. This drawing is still in the possession of the Austen family.

The most familiar portrait is another sketch by Cassandra. It was bought by the present owner, the National Portrait Gallery in London, at Sotheby's in 1948, described as a "pencil sketch . . . the face and hair in water colors, of Jane Austen, in a blue paper inscribed 'Cassandra's sketch of Jane, from which a picture was drawn by Mr. Andrews of Maidenhead to be engraved for the Memoir.'" The original provenance of this drawing was the collection that once belonged to Charles Austen's granddaughters. It has been dated by the National Portrait Gallery at about 1810. This sketch is of great interest as the sole authentic record of Jane Austen's features. It shows a round face with a pointed chin; keen eyes that appear dark (although we are told they were hazel); a rather long nose; and an uncompromising mouth. The arms are folded. Slight and unfinished as it is, it gives the impression that here is a real, unflattering picture of a real person.

The Andrews drawing was made to be engraved for the frontispiece of James Edward Austen-Leigh's *Memoir of Jane Austen*, first published in 1870. It was based on Cassandra's 1810 sketch, with presumably some coaching from the author of the book. It is a charming watercolor, but it is Cassandra's impression beautified for Victorian eyes and Victorian sensibilities, a pious imaginary delineation of "dear Aunt Jane." The arms are no longer severely folded; the expression is placid; even the chair has been improved. We are told that the surviving nieces gave it only "very guarded and qualified approval" (Chapman, p. 212). This drawing is in the possession of a descendant.

The 1870 engraving is yet further removed from the 1810 drawing.

Reproductions vary in quality, but in the original *Memoir* frontispiece the mouth has been made more generous, and the eyes have a gentle look very unlike the penetrating gaze of Cassandra's portrait.

In 1944 an English bookseller acquired volumes 1 and 2 of the second edition (1816) of *Mansfield Park*. In one of these volumes is pasted a hollow-cut silhouette of a woman's head (right profile) with a handwritten inscription "L'aimable Jane." The books were acquired by the National Portrait Gallery, which lists the silhouette as "identity uncertain." They bear a modern signature of "A. E. Oakley"; the third volume, which might provide a clue to previous ownership, has not been found. It is presumed that this "Jane" is Jane Austen. To quote Dr. Chapman, "Who would insert, in a copy of *Mansfield Park*, a portrait of any other Jane than its author?" (p. 214).

Another interesting silhouette was given in 1936 to the dean and chapter of Winchester Cathedral by Miss Jessie Lefroy, a great-grandniece of Jane Austen's. It is a left profile, endorsed on the back "Done by herself in 1815." The family connection may be significant. The profile is not dissimilar to the "L'aimable Jane" silhouette but shows a longer nose, which accords with Cassandra's sketch.

The Zoffany portrait, alleged to be of Jane Austen, has been the subject of much controversy. This full-length painting shows a girl in her early teens wearing a dress that has been dated by costume historians to about 1805, the year Jane Austen turned thirty. In 1973 the British Jane Austen Society appointed a committee to investigate the claims made for this portrait. It was the committee's conclusion (published in the Society's *Report* for 1973) that on the evidence of the dress and the apparent age of the sitter, the Zoffany picture could not be accepted as a portrait of the novelist. The evidence of costume experts was designated "overwhelming."

An imaginary portrait, which probably deserves to be mentioned because it is so often reproduced, is the so-called wedding-ring drawing, a three-quarter-length engraving notable for the ring on the third finger of the left hand—an anomaly, as Jane Austen was never married. The pose of the head and shoulders resembles the various developments of Cassandra's drawing of about 1810.

In June 1983 Christie's sold the house at Godmersham Park in Kent — once the home of Jane Austen's brother Edward Austen-Knight—and its contents. Included in the sale were two drawings cataloged as portraits of the novelist:

> *Lot 1130*: English school 19th century, portrait of Jane Austen, full length, in a white dress, seated writing at a table. Pencil and watercolor, 11½ by 7 inches. (Private collection.)

Lot 1131: English school 19th century, portrait of Jane Austen, full length, in white dress, watercolor, 12 by 9½ inches. (Private collection.)

It is unknown whether these drawings had been at Godmersham since regency times. If they had, there is a chance that they may be authentic records of Jane Austen's appearance, but they should perhaps be approached with caution. In the opinion of more than one expert, they may well have been painted substantially later in the nineteenth century. They are judged to be amateur work, and apparently no documentation that might authenticate them has been found.

If we want to know what Jane Austen looked like, we must go back to the only real record we have, her sister's unfinished sketch in the National Portrait Gallery.

Bibliography

CHAPMAN, R. W. *Jane Austen: Facts and Problems*, rev. ed. (Oxford, 1949).
CHRISTIE, MANSON & WOODS LTD. *Godmersham Park, Canterbury, Kent*, vol. 1 (London, 1983).
The Jane Austen Society Report for the Year 1973 (Alton, 1974).
KIRKHAM, MARGARET. "The Austen Portraits and the Received Biography," in Janet Todd, ed., *Jane Austen: New Perspectives*, Women and Literature, n.s. 3 (New York, 1983).

POST/MAIL

Jo Modert

"The post-office is a wonderful establishment!" exclaims Jane Fairfax in *Emma*. "The regularity and dispatch of it! . . . it is really astonishing!" (p. 296). Jane Austen thus paid tribute in 1814 to the remarkable advances in postal services during her lifetime, and one often glimpses their effect on the lives of the country gentry in her novels and letters.

London's efficient postal system dated from the late seventeenth century. For one penny (till 1801), letters were picked up and delivered four to eight times daily with ten to twelve deliveries in business centers. Outside London, however, service was slow and undependable through most of the eighteenth century.

One improvement came when Ralph Allen, proprietor of the Bath Theater and the model for Fielding's Squire Allworthy, established cross-stations between larger towns (before, all mail was routed through London). Then, in 1784, when Jane Austen was nine, another Bath resident, John Palmer, replaced post boys on horses with mail coaches, which were exempted from toll charges, operated on strict time schedules, and were protected by armed guards.

Mail volume increased dramatically. In 1792, sixteen mail coaches left London every day, and as many returned, with fifteen more serving cross-country stations. By 1811, around 220 coaches covered over eleven thousand miles daily.

As volume rose, so did postal charges in 1784, 1796, 1801 (when the famous London penny post became twopenny), 1805, and 1812, the "high-water mark of postal charges" (Marshall, p. 15). By then, a "single" letter (one sheet of paper folded and sealed) cost fourpence for 15 miles or less, rising to seventeen pence for 700 miles. Charges, based on mileage and number of sheets of paper (not weight), were paid by recipients, except for "free" letters franked by members of Parliament (*see Letters*, October 14, 1813, and note).

Jane Austen lived, of course, before adhesive postage stamps and manufactured envelopes came into being. The "single" letter, mentioned above, is typical of most she wrote and can be envisioned as a sheet of legal-sized paper, folded to make four pages about eight-by-eleven inches. Increasingly, as charges rose, the lines became more closely spaced and finely written; sometimes additional lines were written at a right angle directly over the filled page. Jane Fairfax, for example, generally "fills the whole paper and crosses half" (*E*, p. 157).

The center third of page 4, when the letter was folded from top and bottom, became the front of the "envelope" for the address and hand-stamped postmarks, while the folded-over sides were sealed with a wax wafer. To allow for damage when the seal was removed, an indentation about an inch square was left blank on the right-hand side of page 3.

Out of the several thousand letters Jane Austen must have written, less than 160 are known today—some only fragments or copies of now missing originals. For those which have survived, we are indebted to Jane Austen's family, friends, and devoted collectors—and also to that wonderful establishment, the British post office of her day.

Bibliography

HEMMEON, JOSEPH C. *The History of the British Post Office* (Cambridge, Mass., 1912).

MARSHALL, C. F. DENDY. *The British Post Office from Its Beginnings to the End of 1925* (London, 1926).

JANE AUSTEN'S READING

Margaret Anne Doody

The record of what any individual has read is almost always incomplete. In Jane Austen's case, we must content ourselves with the allusions and references in her works and in the available letters as the only sure means of telling not only what she read but *how* she read.

It seems suitable first to examine Austen's knowledge of the literature of the public world, of judgment and opinion. One might refer to "serious reading" save that the phrase, in Austen's day, referred to a special category of the literature of judgment and tradition, that is, to religious and devotional literature. The two big public texts that would have affected Jane Austen almost from birth are the Bible and the Book of Common Prayer. Even had she done no private Bible reading, she would have heard the Bible read aloud every week of her life. The Bible is primary text, but in an Anglican life the Book of Common Prayer is (or has been) intimately linked with every stage of religious development and every passage of life. The prayers composed by Jane Austen (*Minor Works*, pp. 453–57) exhibit a devotion nurtured on the language and rhythms of the prayer-book petitions, often closely echoing the litany.

The Book of Common Prayer is, to speak profanely, a good influence on style. Its sentiments are emphatic without crudity, and its cadences have the grace of strength rather than of decoration. It is also a language meant to be spoken aloud. Its common petitions have entered English language and thoughts; regular churchgoers knew by heart such passages as these:

> We have followed too much the devices and desires of our own hearts. We have offended against thy holy laws. We have left undone those things which we ought to have done; And we have done those things which we ought not to have done; And there is no health in us. (*General Confession*)
> O God who knowest us to be set in the midst of so many and great dangers, that by reason of the frailty of our nature we cannot always stand upright; Grant to us such strength and protection, as may support us in all dangers, and carry us through all temptations. (*Collect for the fourth Sunday after the Epiphany*)

It is here, I believe, that we must look for the origin of Austen's balanced and coordinated sentences rather than to the later and more partial influence of Johnson. Perhaps these rhythms, though noticeable everywhere, are most to be felt in *Mansfield Park*:

> She was invested, indeed, with the office of judge and critic, and earnestly desired to exercise it and tell them all their faults; but from doing so every feeling within her shrank, she could not, would not, dared not attempt it; had she been otherwise qualified for criticism, her conscience must have restrained her from venturing at disapprobation. She believed herself to feel too much of it in the aggregate for honesty or safety in particulars. To prompt them must be enough for her; and it was sometimes *more* than enough.... At last the scene was over ... and when again alone and able to recall the whole, she was inclined to believe their performance would, indeed, have such nature and feeling in it, as must ensure their credit, and make it a very suffering exhibition to herself. Whatever might be its effect, however, she must stand the brunt of it again that very day. (*MP*, p. 170)

The liturgy itself is a topic of conversation in this novel, when Henry Crawford gives Edmund his opinions about reading the services (*MP*, p. 340). We may take it that Henry's opinion is not worth too much and that the "redundancies and repetitions" to which he objects are elements of the prayers that insist on the petitioner's not glossing over reality. Such redundancies and repetitions are matched in the texture of the novel by Fanny's language of memory and the repetition of her "No."

The reference to the liturgy of the Book of Common Prayer in *Mansfield Park* is of great importance, but it remains general. We are reminded of no particular passages, given no quotations. Austen seems to have made it a rule to herself as a writer of fiction not to allude closely to sacred texts. She is singular among novelists of her age in her refusal to admit references to the Bible, or to biblical characters, scenes, or stories. Her characters' names (e.g. Mary) are never felt as references to sacred history. There was never a novelist less inclined to biblical typology. She appears to have broken her rule as to biblical reference only once. Miss Bates misquotes a line of Scripture: "We may well say that 'our lot is cast in a goodly heritage'" (*E*, p. 174). The reference (Ps. 16:7) brings in a verse often used by rising gentry as a secular gratulation on flourishing estates. Miss Bates's simple use of it points to a misappropriation; she has no heritage—that is her problem. She is referring to charity, the only heritage the minister's daughter may expect. Austen's own relation to this truth may have tempted her in this instance to forsake her own custom. Otherwise, the great serious texts do not enter at all into her novels.

In "Catharine or the Bower," Kitty's irate aunt says:

I had hoped to see you respectable and good; to see you able & willing to give an example of Modesty and Virtue to the Young people here abouts. I bought you Blair's Sermons, and Cœlebs in Search of a Wife, I gave you the key to my own Library, and borrowed a great many good books of my Neighbours for you, all to this purpose. (*Vol. 3*, p. 232)

Hannah More's *Cœlebs* (which Austen much disliked) is a substitution; the manuscript originally read "Seccar's explanation of the Catechism." Presumably Austen deleted the reference to Thomas Secker's *Explanation of the Catechism* as uncomfortably close to a sacred text. Blair's *Sermons* are referred to again, in *Mansfield Park*, where Mary thinks sermons have little effect, "even supposing them worth hearing, supposing the preacher to have the sense to prefer Blair's to his own" (*MP*, p. 92). Austen may have had her own doubts about the value of Blair's sermons.

That both of the Crawfords are able to refer to sermons is one of the many indications that Austen did not believe written material, whether read or heard, has much power to convert or rectify the individual. The activity of Kitty's aunt, trying to produce a model niece with "a great many good books," is seen as absurd. Similarly, in *Northanger Abbey*, Mrs. Morland's endeavor to attack what she sees as her daughter's repining through the application of "a very clever Essay in one of the books up stairs" (*NA*, p. 241) is ridiculous. Elsewhere in the novel the Thorpes show the inefficacy of any kind of reading to alter the basic nature of the reader. John Thorpe, for instance, has learned nothing from *Tom Jones*, and his classing it with *The Monk* shows that he reads both only for sexual stimulus. In Austen's last novel, Sir Edward Denham, another bad reader, has learned from Richardson and his successors only to admire rakes. And nonfiction has a similar perverse effect:

He read all the Essays, Letters, Tours & Criticisms of the day—& with the same ill-luck which made him derive only false Principles from Lessons of Morality, & incentives to Vice from the History of it's Overthrow, he gathered only hard words & involved sentences from the style of our most approved Writers. (*S*, pp. 404–5)

It would seem that the good heart may indeed make good use of literature, but good books of any kind cannot give wisdom to a fool or create a right heart in a perverse reader.

Austen seems to have enjoyed a number of moral essays and periodical pieces while remaining tranquilly and fundamentally skeptical as to their instructional value. There is no reason to doubt Austen's genuine appreciation of Johnson's works. She also knew the *Letters*, published by Mrs. Piozzi, and Boswell's *Life* and the *Journal of a Tour to the Hebrides*.

Admiration never precluded parody; a passage in "Love and Freindship" plays with a famous passage in Johnson's *Journey to the Western Islands*. Austen treats her own letter writing jestingly as Johnsonian (February 8, 1807). To Fanny Price, her reading heroine, Austen gave the *Idler* for amusement; Fanny also mentally refers to *Rasselas*.

Austen did not, however, follow Johnson's advice and give her days and nights to the study of Addison. There is only one reference to the *Spectator*, and that reference is an onslaught:

> the substance of its papers so often consisting in the statement of improbable circumstances, unnatural characters, and topics of conversation, which no longer concern any one living; and their language, too, frequently so coarse as to give no very favourable idea of the age that could endure it. (*NA*, p. 38)

Austen heretically challenges the position of Addison's papers as models. No doubt Addison's condescending references to "the fair sex" roused her spirit; she takes revenge by declaring him unfit to be read by a "young lady," "a young person of taste." The *Spectator* papers are accused of the very defects for which modern fiction is often faulted—improbability, unnatural characters, coarse language. In addition, Addison's work is outdated, not relevant "to any one living"—a very serious charge from Austen, who is much more concerned with the living than the dead.

A knowledge of the past had, however, become required of ladies as well as gentlemen. History was a schoolroom subject for children of both sexes. Like Fanny and Susan Price, Jane Austen began with Goldsmith's *History of England*, and it is this one-date history that she parodies in her own mock-"History," written at age sixteen. The work "By a partial, prejudiced, & ignorant Historian" (*Vol. 2*, p. 138), ornamented by Cassandra's caricature portraits of monarchs, is a revenge by two schoolgirls on the history they have been taught and an Augustan satire on history. Like Swift, Austen doubts whether the history we are given to read is ever anything much more than a convenient fiction—a doubt expressed through the naive expressions of Catherine Morland:

> I can read poetry and plays, and things of that sort, and do not dislike travels. But history, real solemn history, I cannot be interested in. . . . I read it a little as a duty, but it tells me nothing that does not either vex or weary me. The quarrels of popes and kings, with wars or pestilences, in every page; the men all so good for nothing, and hardly any women at all—it is very tiresome: and yet I often think it odd that it should be so dull, for a great deal of it must be invention. (*NA*, p. 108)

Catherine Morland's tastes appear to be a true caricature of her author's own, reflecting them as the reading habits of young Waverley mirror those of the young Walter Scott. Catherine is not witty like Jane Austen, but they have similar positions. Writing her mock-"History," Jane Austen, vexed and wearied by the absence of women from most pages of histories, defiantly turned the history of England into a quarrel between two women, Elizabeth (a villain) and Mary Stuart (a heroine). The men *are* very largely good for nothing save for Richard III, whose reputation is rehabilitated in a manner suggesting the author's acquaintance with Horace Walpole's *Historic Doubts on the Life and Reign of King Richard the Third*. (The joke about Richard's being "respectable" recurs on the first page of *Northanger Abbey*.)

The few references we have by the mature Jane Austen to the reading of history suggest that in later life she sought what the more obtuse Catherine Morland also sought—entertainment and a glimpse of what we now call social history, something connected with the habits of daily life. In 1800 Austen tells Martha Lloyd,

> I am now laying in a stock of intelligence to pour out on you as *my* share of Conversation.—I am reading Henry's History of England, which I will repeat to you in any manner you may prefer, either in a loose, disultary, unconnected strain, or dividing my recital as the Historian divides it himself, into seven parts, The Civil & Military—Religion—Constitution—Learning & Learned Men—Arts & Sciences—Commerce Coins & Shipping—& Manners;—so that for every evening of the week there will be a different subject; The friday's lot, Commerce, Coin & Shipping, You will find the least entertaining; but the next Eveng:'s portion will make amends. (November 12, 1800)

She may have been amused by the Scottish historian's pride in his seven divisions, as elaborated in his "General Preface." The history does promise to give a picture of "our ancestors . . . both in private life," if along binary lines: "the virtues with which they were adorned, and the vices with which they were infected; the pleasures and amusements in which they delighted, and the distresses and miseries to which they were exposed" (I.x). Henry claims he is unlike previous historians:

> not one of them hath given . . . any thing like a history of learning, arts, commerce, and manners. . . . Are these subjects then unworthy of a place in history? . . . Can we form just ideas of the characters and circumstances of our ancestors, by viewing them only in the flames of civil and religious discord, or in the fields of blood and slaughter; without ever attending to their conduct and condition, in the more permanent and peaceful scenes of social life? (I.xiv–xv)

Phrases such as these in the preface may have attracted Austen at the outset. Henry's multivolume history (which does not reach the Renaissance) is disappointing after his promises. He is a partial and prejudiced historian who can see nothing but evil and superstition in the Catholic church and hence in much of the life of the Middle Ages. But there are glimpses of other ways of life, and some curious facts, such as that the tenth-century laws of Hywel Dda "allow of a divorce for so trifling a cause as an unsavoury or disagreeable breath" (I.320). In Henry's pages, Austen could have read some fragments of Anglo-Saxon and of medieval poets including Chaucer, as well as learning about habits, fashions in clothing (largely judged "indecent"), and mealtimes of the past. But we have no idea whether she did complete her task and read all the volumes. Despite her suggestion that Henry's seventh portion of each section might "make amends," Austen does not register unlimited enthusiasm: "With such a provision on my part, if you will do your's by repeating the French Grammar, & Mrs Stent will now & then ejaculate some wonder about the Cocks & Hens, what can we want?" (November 12, 1800). What one could want is some real entertainment—Robert Henry's *History* is certainly not acquitted of the charge of dullness.

Like Catherine Morland, Jane Austen did not dislike travels. Some of the references in the letters are too cryptic for us to be absolutely certain as to the book meant, though hazarded guesses are probably correct, as with Sir George Steuart Mackenzie's *Travels in Iceland*. The references in the letters to "Macartney" allude, like the similar reference in *Mansfield Park*, to John Barrow's edition of Lord Macartney's "Journal of the Embassy to China" (1807). Macartney's "Journal" is an appropriate piece for Fanny to read; not only does its presence illustrate her extensive view of mankind, but it is indirectly an object lesson. One of the most striking aspects of Macartney's embassy to Peking (1792–94) was his refusal to agree to make the customary humiliating prostrations before the emperor; Macartney is an example of someone who successfully said, "No."

Austen read a more controversial travel book, which made England the object of scrutiny: "We have got the 2^d vol. of Espriella's Letters, & I read it aloud by candlelight. The Man describes well, but is horribly antienglish. He deserves to be the foreigner he assumes" (October 1, 1808). This work, *Letters from England, by Don Manuel Alvarez Espriella* (1807), was at first taken to be the genuine work of a Catholic Spaniard and "Translated from the Spanish." The real author, Robert Southey, enjoyed the first mystification; he used the device of his imaginary foreign traveler as a way of challenging the English to face their own defects. Austen's indignant patriotic reaction is shared by many of the reviewers. Yet she continued to read *Letters from England* aloud. Someone who had enjoyed (and parodied) William Gilpin's *Three Essays* on the picturesque and his

Observations Relative Chiefly to Picturesque Beauty, Made . . . on Several Parts of Great Britain would have found much to enjoy in Southey's Spaniard's description of walking through parts of the Lake District. It is interesting that the future author of *Sanditon* read Southey's views of the new seaside watering places:

> Now the Nereids have as many votaries as the Naiads, and the tribes of wealth and fashion swarm down to the sea coast as punctually as the land crabs in the West Indies march the same way. . . . The price they pay for . . . lodgings is exorbitant. . . . In their haunts, however, these visitors are capricious; they frequent a coast some seasons in succession, like herrings, and then desert it for some other, with as little apparent motive as the fish have for varying their track. (Southey, Letter xxx)

One can imagine Austen enjoying this. It is harder to gauge her reaction to the more excoriating passages of social criticism such as this on Birmingham:

> I am still giddy, dizzied with the hammering of presses, the clatter of engines, and the whirling of wheels; my head aches with the multiplicity of infernal noises, and my eyes with the light of infernal fires,—I may add, my heart also at the sight of so many human beings employed in infernal occupations, and looking as if they were never destined for any thing better. . . . Not that the labourers repine at their lot; it is not the least evil of the system, that they are perfectly well satisfied to be poisoned soul and body. (Letter xxxvi)

Jane Austen's own voice read such passages, though we cannot know precisely what she thought of them.

She has left on record a more favorable response to another controversial work:

> *I* am reading a Society octavo, an Essay on the Military Police & Institutions of the British Empire by Capt Pasley of the Engineers, a book which I protested against at first, but which upon trial I find delightfully written & highly entertaining. I am as much in love with the author as ever I was with Clarkson or Buchanan, or even the two Mr Smiths of the city—the first soldier I ever sighed for—but he does write with extraordinary force & spirit. (January 24, 1813)

Capt. Charles William Pasley's *Essay on the Military Policy and Institutions of the British Empire* (1810), a work written during the height of Napoleon's imperial success, is a spirited attack on Britain's entire foreign policy in peace and war. In contrast to Southey's liberal criticism, this is an attack from the right, and even more cutting. The English, Pasley believes, are conditioning themselves to lose land battles; they will lose Spain if they go on as they are doing. The British are fighting an empire without seeing to their own empire and its possibilities. The British have been overfond of conquering small islands, more expensive to keep up than their political or military value justifies. They are also too fond of giving conquered lands back to previous governments without inquiring as to the nature and habits of these. Thus, the British army inspires despondency in potential allies, and governmental policy creates nervous fear among those who might otherwise be disposed to friendship.

> Is it reasonable to suppose, that men, in any part of the world, will unite with us, and expose their lives and property to certain destruction, from a principle alone of hatred to the French, or of attachment to some former government, which they know cannot possibly stand of itself, even if they should succeed in a re-establishment of it? . . . How can they be expected to join a British army, which they foresee may, if threatened by a superior force, fly to its transports, leaving them on the beach, to be slaughtered, or pardoned, at the pleasure of an exasperated conqueror. It is true, that we may give those who have joined us, the permission of embarking with us, if there is room in our ships . . . but can this reasonably be considered sufficient encouragement? May not the foreign soldier, who eats our bread in the West Indies . . . be sometimes filled with secret indignation, when he recollects that the appearance of a British army first tempted him to take up the musket, in order to drive out a body of hateful oppressors from his country; that that army afterwards abandoned the cause, for which alone he became a soldier; and that he now finds himself degraded from a patriot into a mercenary, and an exile from his own country? the only country in the world, probably, in which he takes the smallest interest. (pp. 217–18)

Pasley is capable of moral imagination, and real passion; he also speaks from living experience. One can see why Austen, to her own surprise, was "in love with" a soldier—rating his book as "entertaining" as the Smiths' new volume of comic parodic verse, the *Rejected Addresses*. Pasley's "force & spirit" entail a strong command of the common phrase: "It is no economy, either of money or of lives, to make war by driblets" (p. 188). He is a vigorous attacker of clichés and received ideas, whether those of Gibbon on the delicacy of the modern soldier or of the English newspapers on the Spanish guerrillas, whose real sufferings Pasley describes. Here is history with war on every page—yet it is not the "real solemn history" deplored by Catherine Morland but living history, current affairs, real life vividly conveyed. Austen jokingly but decisively draws the difference:

> I have been applied to for information as to the oath taken in former times of Bell, Book, & Candle but have none to give. Perhaps you may be able to learn something of its origin & meaning at Manydown. Ladies who read those enormous great stupid thick quarto volumes which one always sees in the Breakfast parlour there, must be acquainted with everything in the world. I detest a quarto. Capt Pasley's book is too good for their Society. They will not understand a man who condenses his thoughts into an octavo. (February 9, 1813)

Austen knew nothing, when applied to, of a medieval curse and had little interest in pursuing the matter herself. "Great stupid thick quarto volumes" genuinely did not attract her. She would rather encounter play of mind than store of information for its own sake. Undeniably, too, her interest in the past was severely limited. Current affairs attracted her much more than times past. The past could seem to her dead material, supplying now-lifeless topics, like those of the *Spectator*, "which no longer concern any one living." Jane Austen responded primarily to living concerns.

Jane Austen is, almost disconcertingly, very much a Modern. There is nothing of the Ancient discernible in her composition. Those who insist on the classical nature of her writing are of course right. Austen's writing is indeed "classical" in its perfection, its harmony of form and matter. But we must not confuse her own classical nature with any interest on her part in antiquity or in classical literature in the stricter sense. Austen herself puns on the two senses of the word: "I am sorry my verses did not bring any return from Edward.... It might be partiality, but they seemed to me purely classical—just like Homer and Virgil, Ovid and Propria que Maribus" (January 24, 1809). "Classical" finally means the Eton Grammar, which Austen was not expected to know. There is no indication of any interest in the authors whose names are here cited as synonymous with the classical. We do not know whether she had ever read any part of any of them; we do not even know that she ever read Pope's translations of the *Iliad* and the *Odyssey*. There are a couple of Latin phrases in her writing; Frank Churchill reveals his status as a gentleman (and his falsity) in his assertion of a dubious "*amor patriæ*" (*E*, p. 200). But in all Jane Austen's fictional works there is no classical allusion save in the Bertram girls' absurd general catalog which includes "the Roman emperors as low as Severus; besides a great deal of the Heathen Mythology" (*MP*, pp. 18–19). There is not one other reference to any classical myth, story, or character. There is no other novelist, male or female, of her time of whom this is true. Other women writers as various as Burney and Edgeworth, West and Wollstonecraft, exhibit a respect for the ancient public tradition of letters—a respect apparently absent in Austen. At least she makes no sign of claiming that heritage as her own.

On turning to the modern literature produced primarily rather to delight than to instruct, we find Shakespeare is the one great English "classic" that Austen freely admits into her pattern of references. She presumably agreed with Henry Crawford that Shakespeare "is a part of an Englishman's constitution" (*MP*, p. 338). The hero's name in that novel can be seen as a Shakespearean joke; Austen's man (a noninheriting brother) is named Edmund as a counterpart to Burney's Edgar in *Camilla* (an heir to large estates). Part of Austen's education in Shakespeare came from family readings and family theatricals. The list of plays canvassed by the young Bertrams and their friends offers a fair specimen of the plays the Austens knew; we know, for instance, that they put on Sheridan's comedies. From drama Austen received invaluable training for a novelist interested in scenes and dialogue. Her allusions show her acquainted (often through acting) with such farces as Colman's *Heir at Law* or such new comedies as Hannah Cowley's *Which Is the Man?*—works not usually known to the general reader in the twentieth century. Jane Austen's admiration of Shakespeare does not extend at all to other old plays; she offers no indication of any reading in Jacobean or indeed in Restoration drama.

Similarly, Austen's liking for Shakespeare did not apparently lead her to investigate other sixteenth- or seventeenth-century poets. We can doubt if she ever read Spenser. Rather more surprisingly, there is no hint that this last of the Augustans had ever read Dryden. She did know Pope, though evidently, like Marianne Dashwood, admiring him "no more than is proper" (*SS*, p. 47). We cannot ignore the fact that Austen had a "low" taste for verse riddles and conundrums. As the compiler of *A New Collection of Enigmas, Charades, Transpositions, &c.* (1791) says in her preface, "true genius is not apprehensive of incurring suspicion by condescending to trifle occasionally; 'tis where a pretension is formed, and the pretender doubts his own claim, that he affects to contemn what is not great and sublime" (p. vi). Austen did not affect to contemn; she made up charades, and the word games in *Emma* provide the modern critic with happy instances of semiotics and a deconstructive sense of language.

Jane Austen was well-read in the poetry of her contemporaries. She evidently knew Byron, Scott, and Burns quite well. Disappointingly, she has left us no record of any opinion on Wordsworth or Coleridge, though as an admirer of the Smiths' *Rejected Addresses* she would have known parodies of them as of all the new poets. She loved Cowper and gave the same taste to Marianne Dashwood and Fanny Price. Fanny also enjoys Crabbe. Edmund, commenting on her reading Macartney, adds, "And here are Crabbe's Tales, and the Idler, at hand to relieve you, if you tire of your great book" (*MP*, p. 156). This sentence is of some importance, showing us how Austen felt reading should be done. A real reader has several books on the hob at once, preferably a "great" or heavy book, a light one, and something in between. Crabbe's *Tales* of 1812 is here the most light and bright and sparkling of the three. Austen is up-to-date in her allusion to Crabbe, as she was in taking to Southey's *Poet's Pilgrimage to Waterloo* (1816), which the Austens were reading in January 1817.

No foreign poets figure in Austen's letters or her works. She has no interest in Ariosto, Tasso, or Metastasio; although Anne Elliot could translate an Italian song, there is no evidence that her author could have done the same. Jane Austen could read French, but we expect in vain any reference to French poetry, even the La Fontaine from whom she might have gathered hints for the use of *style indirect libre*.

A similar national taste prevails in her reading of prose fiction—and here indeed we come to the heart of the matter. In 1798 Jane Austen commented on the opening of a subscription library: "As an inducement to subscribe Mrs. Martin tells us that her Collection is not to consist only of Novels, but of every kind of Literature, &c. &c.—She might have spared this pretention to *our* family, who are great Novel-readers & not ashamed of being so" (December 18, 1798). Austen *is* a great novel reader and not ashamed of being so. Her letters move easily into allusions to novels, often to matters so minute as to prove an extraordinary knowledge of the works in question. She can remember Tom Jones's white coat, evidently as a sartorial error (January 9, 1796). She picks up *Tristram Shandy* in a reference to "an uncle Toby's annuity" (September 14, 1804); Maria Bertram quotes from *A Sentimental Journey* (*MP*, p. 99). A phrase in French reminds Austen as she writes it of Mme. Duval, a character in *Evelina* whom she goes on to quote (February 8, 1807). Her nephew's contention about Jane Austen's intimate knowledge of *Sir Charles Grandison* is borne out by the reference to James Selby (a very minor character in Richardson's novel) and his "thirst for travelling," which was "so much reprobated" (September 14, 1804).

Sometimes we catch Austen in the process of reading a novel, as we do with *Camilla* in August and September 1796, when references to it abound in the letters. She also read the work of Frances Burney's younger sister, Sarah Harriet Burney: "We are reading Clarentine, & are surprised to find how foolish it is. I remember liking it much less on a 2^d reading than at the 1st & it does not bear a 3^d at all" (February 8, 1807). "We" indicates a reading aloud. Much more of Austen's reading was reading aloud than is likely to be the case with most writers and readers today. *Clarentine* (1798) may perhaps have appealed at first because of the sailor-guardian. The book did not wear well. But the striking fact of this passage is that Austen read and reread novels, even minor or mediocre novels. For her a whole judgment does not get made on a first reading; novels are allowed a second trial and are supposed to bear the weight of reperusal. Charlotte Lennox's *Female Quixote* stood up to the test: "the 'Female Quixotte' ... now makes our evening amusement; to me a very high one, as I find the work quite equal to what I remembered it" (January 7, 1807).

It is to novel reading that Austen brings her energies, her discrimination, her really serious judgment. Read aloud, then reread, novels formed her mind so that she could re-form the novel. Her reading within the genre is disconcertingly persistent and at once sufficiently catholic (she has tolerance for the mediocre) and sufficiently narrow (she likes domestic fiction by women writers) to puzzle or offend some critics. Scholarly admirers of Jane Austen have often tended to insist that she saw in works we regard as "inferior" only matter for parody. But no woman is a hypocrite in her pleasures. We don't undertake several readings of something simply detested. The *juvenilia* are the joyful result of intense formal study of well-loved material. After all, she could parody Johnson in the Highlands, but that does not mean she despised Dr. Johnson. Austen's parody is creative, not dismissive. It is her means of finding her own voice. Richardson's *Sir Charles Grandison*, for instance, which is parodied and drawn upon from "Jack and Alice" onward, is an almost-constant presence in Austen's fiction. Jocelyn Harris has illustrated, for example, how intimately it is related to *Mansfield Park* in themes and in responsive or allusive detail. Beyond the joyous crudity of burlesque, Austen is always reworking other novels. She answers, recasts them, carries on a creative argument with them. *Northanger Abbey* is obviously a fabric of novelistic allusion. But Austen's later novels are more subtly novelistic fictions, with a complex and hidden texture of novel reference.

Pride and Prejudice, for instance, very openly takes its title from Burney's *Cecilia*. And Mr. Darcy's disdainful first proposal is closely related to Mortimer Delville's insultingly careful description of his own internal struggle and the reasons he cannot ask Cecilia to marry him. His explanation arouses anger in the heroine, who judges in him "the powerful instigation of hereditary arrogance" (III.341). But *Pride and Prejudice* has for one of its initial complications the story George Wickham tells Elizabeth. Wickham's story is a kind of reworking of *Tom Jones*, with the late Mr. Darcy playing the part of Allworthy, "one of the best men that ever breathed" (*PP*, p. 78). Wickham figures as Tom and Darcy as Blifil, "inmates of the same house, sharing the same amusements, objects of the same parental care" (*PP*, p. 81). Elizabeth (who must be a novel reader) is readily moved by the story of the proud and mean-spirited heir who wrests an inheritance away from his more lowly childhood companion. Miss Bingley's sneer at Wickham's low origin only fuels Elizabeth's ardent desire to champion him, while Jane's intimation (from Bingley) that Wickham "has been very imprudent" (*PP*, p. 96) only increases Wickham's resemblance (according to his own story) to Tom. Eventually, the truth is known. Darcy is certainly no Blifil, and Wickham is not a Tom Jones—or perhaps in some ways he is too much like Tom, and a young man's amiability and imprudence can damage a woman. If Austen is answering Fielding, she also rewrites Richardson, creating in Darcy a Grandisonian figure far from universally popular and truly faulty even to being disagreeable. The descent of Lady Catherine upon Elizabeth is a new modern version of the descent of the arrogant and vulgar Lady Davers upon Pamela. But we need not and should not look always to the highest examples of eighteenth-century novels for Austen's inspiration or references. The name of Charles Bingley seems stolen from Sir Charles Bingley, a secondary admirer of the heroine in *The Children of the Abbey* by Regina Maria Roche.

That *The Children of the Abbey* was to the taste of Harriet Smith (who recommended it to Robert Martin) need not cause us to assume that Austen had never enjoyed it. This story would seem to have had its effect on *Sense and Sensibility*; there is a vulgar Mrs. Jennings who militates against the heroine's happiness, while forsaken love, abandonment, and laments make up much of the tale. The heroine apostrophizes her childhood home much in the spirit of Marianne Dashwood. But *The Children of the Abbey* is also perhaps a suggestive presence in a later novel. Roche's dark-haired heroine, Amanda Fitzalan, romantically penniless, is treated unfeelingly by vain ladies in company. But she quells them with her playing and singing:

> Amanda . . . turned over the leaves of the book to a lesson much more difficult than that Lady Euphrasia had played. Her touch at first was tremulous and weak, but she was too susceptible of the powers of harmony, not soon to be inspired by it; and gradually her style became so masterly and elegant, as to excite universal admiration, except in the bosoms of those who had hoped to place her in a ludicrous situation; their invidious scheme, instead of depressing, had only served to render excellence conspicuous. . . . When the lesson was concluded, some gentlemen . . . entreated her to sing. She chose a plaintive Italian air, and the exquisite taste and sweetness with which she sung, equally astonished and delighted. . . .
> "I declare, I never knew anything so monstrously absurd," exclaimed Lady Euphrasia, "as to let a girl in her situation learn such things, except indeed, it was to qualify her for a governess, or an opera singer" (I.243–44).

This situation is replayed in *Emma* when another dark-haired lady of fiction, Jane Fairfax, delights the company by her playing and singing. Her individious enemy, the rich girl, is forced (like Lady Euphrasia) to regret "the inferiority of her own playing and singing" (*E*, p. 231). This jealous rival is likewise careful to point out what a humble fate the beautiful musician is destined for. Of course, *Emma* reverses its originals. Jane, who has all the qualifications of a conventional heroine—including the secret attachment to the *jeune premier* whom she at last is able to marry—is not the center of the revisionary novel, which demotes her to an inferior place in the reader's interest, inferior not only to the wealthy snob Emma but even to the silly Harriet Smith.

The relation of Emma to Harriet is based on a relationship within another novel. In Burney's *Cecilia*, the heroine befriends an affectionate girl of a lower class. Henrietta Belfield, the shopkeeper's daughter, feels warm admiration for Cecilia, but proves an innocent source of complication when she falls in love with Cecilia's lover, Mortimer Delville, the hero. When he calls and asks to see her, Henrietta convinces herself that he must be going to ask her to marry him and goes downstairs "with expectations of happiness almost too potent for her reason" (V.153). Austen takes the hint from Henrietta's folly in creating as Emma's protégée a "simple" girl in good earnest, and she elaborates on the idea by subjecting to an unflattering examination the motives that cause the benefactress to choose her companion.

Certain allusions, such as that to *Cecilia* in the title of *Pride and Prejudice* or to *Camilla* in *Sanditon*, are open and thematic; the reader is expected to comprehend an allusion. Perhaps the reference to *The Children of the Abbey* in *Emma* is of this kind. But often the reader is not expected to recognize even specific allusions, and indeed there seem to be a number of unnamed novels present, novels largely unknown to twentieth-century readers.

One such source of unrecognized reference is probably Frances Sheridan's *Memoirs of Miss Sidney Bidulph*, especially its second part or sequel, the *Conclusion*, dealing with the younger generation. The charming and worldly Sir Edward Audley and his sister (who become the villains of the piece) are possible models for the Crawfords. If only Mrs. Norris had been a novel reader, she would have been disabused of the notion that having children "brought up . . . always together like brothers and sisters" is "the only sure way" of providing against their falling in love: "It is morally impossible. I never knew an instance of it" (*MP*, p. 6). Had she read *Sidney Bidulph*, she would have known an instance, for hers is precisely the mistake made by Sidney, when she brings orphaned Orlando Faulkland up with her own daughters, believing that "it seldom happens that persons brought up together from childhood, conceive a passion for each other" (IV.20).

Another of these unnamed presences in Austen's fiction is surely Agnes Maria Bennett's *Agnes De-Courci* (1789), which seems (with many other works) to be first picked up in "Love and Freindship." In this novel, hero and heroine marry, only to discover, just after the ceremony, that they are brother and sister. The hero rushes off distracted and is not seen again until someone notices "something coming down with the stream, so very brilliant it dazzles my sight" (IV.187). This is the body of Edward, still sparklingly attired in his wedding clothes, "embroidered in the first taste, with foil and spangles" (IV.193). The heroine is greatly distressed:

> Her hair torn and dishevelled, hanging in loose ringlets;—her headclothes and neck covering, lying in tatters on the ground; her beautiful arms bare; and all the symptoms of wild distraction glaring round the lovely ruin.
> She was just then changing from a fit of raving, to melancholy madness; and was sitting on the ground by the dead body of our lost Edward; his head, swollen and disfigured, was on her lap ;—with one hand she held a smelling bottle to his nose. (IV.192)

Doubtless this is one of the fictional episodes behind "Love and Freindship's" description of the deaths of Edward and Augustus (of the memorable waistcoat) and Laura's raving for *her* Edward.

We need not, however, assume that such a work supplied Austen with material only for burlesque. We can perhaps find a touch of *Agnes DeCourci* seriously assimilated in *Emma*, that great treasury of fictional moments revitalized. In Mrs. Bennett's novel, the hero Edward Harley, when he first meets Agnes, believes (wrongly) that she is Colonel Moncrass's mistress. He listens as she plays the organ

> and sung from Handel's Music
>   "Love's sweet poison."
> It was involuntary, Caroline, I could not help it, I leaned over her chair, and repeated
>   "Sweet Harmonist, and beautiful as sweet,
>   And young as beautiful, and gay as young."
> And oh, sister! the pity of it, the pity of it that I could not add
>   "And *Innocent* as gay." (III.241)

Emma, from different motives, harbors a similar false opinion, inwardly accusing Jane of something akin to sexual misconduct and then alternatively pitying her helplessness:

> Emma was very willing now to acquit her of having seduced Mr. Dixon's affections from his wife, or of any thing mischievous which her imagination had suggested at first. If it were love, it might be simple, single, successless love on her side alone. She might have been unconsciously sucking in the sad poison. (*E*, p. 168)

The alliterations mock the gloating vanity of Emma's mean fancies. The tones of her attempt to sink her rival seem related to the serious tones of Harley's pity—and the quotation of "Love's sweet poison" in Bennett may well have suggested to Austen the wording of Emma's inner suspicions.

The more novels of the late eighteenth century one reads, the more visible becomes Austen's complex relation to them. It is tempting to paraphrase Dryden on Ben Jonson's relation to the Ancients: "You may track her everywhere in their snow." Novels were her most important reading; we may never know all she read or find all the reworkings, momentary parodies, rethinkings, that crowd her work. Neither the great works of the Western past nor contemporary nonfiction meant a great deal to her save as they came through novels. She has claims to be considered as a historian and a philosopher, but she did not spend her time studying history or philosophy. English domestic novels were the classics of her own reading, but she had a thirst for the contemporary and did not think in terms of the great tradition or "classics" but of living fiction.

Bibliography

Contemporary Writings

BENNETT, AGNES (ANNA?) MARIA. *Agnes De-Courci: A Domestic Tale*, 2nd ed., 4 vols. (London, 1797).

BURNEY, FRANCES. *Cecilia, or Memoirs of an Heiress*, 5 vols. (London, 1782).

HENRY, ROBERT. *The History of Great Britain, from the First Invasion of It by the Romans Under Julius Caesar*, 2nd ed., 10 vols. (London, 1788).

A New Collection of Enigmas, Charades, Transpositions, &c., 2 vols. (London, 1791): the charade "Court-ship" is found at II.15; "Wo-man" at I.31; and "Kitty, a fair but frozen maid" at I.42.

PASLEY, C. W. *Essay on the Military Policy and Institutions of the British Empire*, 2nd ed. (London, 1811; original ed., 1810).

ROCHE, REGINA MARIA. *The Children of the Abbey: A Tale*, 2nd American ed., 2 vols. (New York, 1805; orig. 1798).

SHERIDAN, FRANCES. *Conclusion of the Memoirs of Miss Sidney Bidulph* (London, 1772), printed as vols. 4 and 5 of *Memoirs of Miss Sidney Bidulph*.

[SOUTHEY, ROBERT.] *Letters from England, by Dom Manuel Alvarez Espriella*, Jack Simmons, ed. (London, 1951; original ed., 1807), letter 30, p. 164; letter 36, pp. 196–97.

Studies

BRADBROOK, FRANK W. *Jane Austen and Her Predecessors* (Cambridge, England, 1966).

HARRIS, JOCELYN. "'As If They Had Been Living Friends': *Sir Charles Grandison* Into *Mansfield Park*," *Bulletin of Research in the Humanities*, 83 (1980), 360–405.

Johnson, Claudia L. *Using the Mind Well: The Moral Life in Jane Austen's Novels and the Heritage of Johnson and Locke* (unpublished dissertation, Princeton University, 1981).
Lascelles, Mary. *Jane Austen and Her Art* (Oxford, 1939).
Litz, A. Walton. *Jane Austen: A Study of Her Artistic Development* (New York and London, 1965).
Moler, Kenneth L. *Jane Austen's Art of Allusion* (Lincoln, Neb., 1968).

JANE AUSTEN AND ROMANTICISM

Susan Morgan

The difficulty with discussing Jane Austen in relation to romanticism is initially one of critical method. There is serious disagreement about the lineaments of romanticism and agreement that, whatever romanticism is, it is more varied than all the elements its sophisticated critics have so far named. Even if we could agree on the characteristics of romanticism or, specifically, of English romantic literature, do we really want to engage Austen's fiction by approaching it with our checklist of qualities declared to be romantic and rummaging around in the novels to see if we can find some of them there? And having found some, as we will if we make the appropriate list, the worst difficulty remains. What do we learn, what do we change, by declaring Austen's work to be to that extent romantic?

Why, then, even begin the enterprise? For over 150 years, readers did not. There was the romantic period, from 1798 to 1832, and somewhere else—usually in a backward but socially formal rural village, still reading Dr. Johnson's essays, too proper to thrill to Rousseau, too conservative to understand the French Revolution, too genteel to roam the rapturous woods of Wordsworth—there was Jane Austen. Intrusive facts and new readings of the novels have begun to challenge this familiar portrait. Austen was born in 1775, five years after Wordsworth and three years after Coleridge. Her first published novel came out in 1811, and her intensive writing time was from around 1809 until her death in 1817. That "somewhere else" where her readers located her is actually the familiar countryside of England, not so remote from the Lake district. In time and in place, Austen belongs in the romantic age.

We can still declare her an exception or remind ourselves that any age is not culturally or spiritually or emotionally homogenous, that the notion of a romantic period is simplistic, a mere critical convenience. We can still decide that the romantic poets were advanced thinkers and Austen a conservative thinker, in spite of writing at the same historical moment. But the point is that we do have to decide. We cannot pretend that Austen did not write when and where she did or presume without examination that she is a throwback to an earlier age.

And we cannot partly because we have come to realize the injustice, the sexual discrimination, in that presumption, invoking an image of a sharp-eyed spinster watching life dance by, her delicate talents employed as often with her needlework as her pen. Women artists always have trouble being seen as equal to male contemporaries, particularly in terms of their influence on the culture. If women are not believed to originate ideas, they can never be understood as innovative but only as conservative, because they must get their ideas from male predecessors, apparently without experiencing the anxiety of influence. This traditional bias is exacerbated for an age whose art is characterized as both politically and philosophically radical. Romantic art is seen as a kind of frontier literature, aesthetically and socially and politically aggressive, challenging and transforming the old, daring to invent or explore the new: the English form of the French Revolution. All this is man's work, like those journeys to France and Germany and Italy that seem somehow indispensable for an English romantic thinker. Women, especially unmarried women, stayed home.

Moreover, writing poetry was understood as a higher art form than writing "only a novel" (*NA*, p. 38). Many critics still assume that the truly seminal and influential work of the early nineteenth century was done in the medium of poetry and not of fiction. The literature of the romantic period means romantic poetry. And romantic poetry, in its practitioners and many of its perceived characteristics, is male. We have come back to the dilemma with which this essay began: the limitations of connecting Austen's work at points to that of the romantic poets and thus of rescuing her from the charge of backwardness by declaring her an occasional romantic herself, a member of the reigning group, one of the boys.

The dilemma is not only a matter of gender but also one of genre, of the constant difficulty in finding points of connection between poetry and fiction. Scott's novels read in the light of their age have fared only slightly better than Austen's. Literary history has not really known what to do with either of them. Once 1798–1832 was declared the romantic period, with "romantic" effectively meaning romantic poetry, a whole period of British fiction was displaced. We have leaped from eighteenth-century fiction, ending around 1770 with Sterne or Smollett, to Dickens and the Victorian novel. Between lies a dark abyss of sixty years of minor domestic and gothic novelists, brightened randomly by Austen and Scott. Writing the literary history of Austen and romanticism means rescuing romantic fiction from that temporal abyss and thereby rewriting the literary history of the novel.

The ways we might want to call Austen's work romantic depend on a sense of her relations to her genre, which we do not have because we have established so little about the novel of her age. Many well-known novelists of the decades following 1770 were women, their heroes often were heroines, and their plots were generated by issues of love and/or marriage. Austen's work, as well as Scott's and that of other novelists in the beginning years of the century, emerges from and replies to this tradition.

Maria Edgeworth's preface to *Castle Rackrent*, a novel that strongly influenced Scott, was published the same year as *Lyrical Ballads* and declared new ideas of what fiction should be and do. Austen began what was probably her first completed novel, *Northanger Abbey*, with a comic attack on the conventions of gothic and sentimental fiction. In his 1816 review of *Emma*, Scott reminded readers that "a style of novel has arisen, within the last fifteen or twenty years, differing from the former" (Southam, p. 63). Austen's novels are iconoclastic in response to the formal conventions of her genre much as Wordsworth's poetry is innovative in response to the conventions of his. But we are familiar with his tradition and contemporary literary context, not with hers. Without that familiarity, we lose a major area of evidence for showing how she is, indeed, revolutionary, and perhaps romantic.

Before that new history of the romantic age and of British fiction is written, I can only suggest some of the qualities of Austen's fiction that I find particularly powerful and influential. Perhaps they will shape a new definition of romanticism, one that accepts Austen's originality without making her imaginatively obsolete in her own time. Such a definition would be based on our sense that what the poets and novelists of the period share is not the solutions but rather the problems, both formal and philosophical, their art explored.

The opening of *Northanger Abbey*—"No one who had ever seen Catherine Morland in her infancy, would have supposed her born to be an heroine"—directs us to a primary aspect of Austen's originality, her idea of character. This idea firmly allies her with her romantic contemporaries rather than with their eighteenth-century fathers. Unlike the work of Fielding or Dr. Johnson, Austen's fiction does not define human nature as either fixed or universal. Her parodies of gothic and sentimental fiction attack literary conventions of character as typical and therefore predictable. Instead, characters, and thus the truths of our human natures, are a matter of particulars. They are shaped by where and among whom they live, by the past and their memory of it, and by the present interaction of self and event, character and plot, that defines their future by shaping what they become.

We see Austen's insistence on the active relation between character and context not only in Catherine Morland's spontaneity but also in Fanny Price's slow growth into confidence or in Elizabeth Bennet's combination of laughter with efforts to understand others and herself. The second half of *Pride and Prejudice* sparkles less than the first because the satisfactions of its heroine have come to require more involved relations between her neighborhood and herself than simply "to make sport for our neighbours, and laugh at them in our turn" (*PP*, p. 364). And *Persuasion*, that beautiful final novel about the retelling of a tale, takes up as its explicit subject an openness to life and the power of time and circumstance to transform our stories and ourselves. The value of persuasion is the value of change. And it is surely appropriate to ask how distant these concerns are from the senses of place and of memory that infuse Wordsworth's "Tintern Abbey" or from Keats's description of life as a vale of soul making.

The fluid but not random sense of human nature links to a suspicion of absolutes that try to contain or judge the richness of experience. Understanding each other requires a sense of time and place. We need the fictions with which we structure our lives in order to give them comprehensible and communicable form. But we also need to recognize these fictions as fictions and not to mistake them as natural or inevitable truths. Character is character in process, and Austen characters like Mary Crawford in *Mansfield Park* or Marianne Dashwood for much of *Sense and Sensibility*, who reject change, whose "opinions are tolerably fixed" (*SS*, p. 93), have given up their futures. These two characters, seemingly so different—one the rational realist, the other the emotional idealist—share an attitude that Austen's work consistently attacks. Both rely on preconceptions, on the convenience of "a truth universally acknowledged," which they apply dogmatically to experience. Lucy Steele and Mr. Bennet, Mr. Woodhouse and Edmund Bertram, and Catherine Morland or Elizabeth Bennet or Emma Woodhouse for most of their stories, prefer abstract structures to the more demanding and less certain process of consulting their own sense of what is passing around them. As Henry Tilney reminds Catherine, "if it is to be guess-work, let us all guess for ourselves" (*NA*, pp. 151–52).

Guessing for ourselves requires "giving oneself time" (*SS*, p. 93) to develop judgment. It also requires a commitment to imagination and emotion as well as to reason. Elinor is the most feeling as well as the most reasonable of the Dashwood sisters; Emma Woodhouse learns not to repress imagination but to use it to understand her world; while Fanny Price and Anne Elliot, in many ways so different, combine a delicacy of heart with the power to think about what they see around them. In Austen's novels, for the first time, problems of perception within a temporal frame assume a central place as a subject of fiction. Reaching past our structures, both social and epistemological, past the boundaries of our immediate experience, and using all our faculties instead of just one, we can learn to perceive and create the meanings of our lives.

Is all this romantic? Certainly there are similarities between Austen's exploration, through novels of education, of the elements that make up understanding and establish our human connectedness and Wordsworth's fascination with our growth into separateness and sympathy. Surely there are links between the issues explored in Austen's fiction and Scott's historical sense of the centrality of circumstance to shape character, or Blake's commitment to throw off abstraction, to cleanse the doors of perception. And surely most British writers of the early nineteenth century share a sense of the temporal quality of truth, of the value of change along with the need to remember what is past.

But it remains of dubious value to declare Austen, even in particular points, a romantic. What is of value and, I think, crucially important is to read Austen's work afresh, freed from the preconceptions, often gender based, of critics who decided that since Austen wasn't a romantic, she was a daughter of the enlightenment. That oppressive either/or labeled Austen's novels bright reflections of someone else's thought and kept us from exploring her philosophical as well as her formal achievement. It is time to recognize that while Austen need not be termed a romantic in the tradition of Wordsworth or Coleridge, her work is firmly a part of the romantic revolution in British literature. And because our vision of the romantic period emphasizes so delightedly its revolutionary quality, its inventiveness and its high seriousness, we may also be directed to a vision of Austen's work that takes seriously its attempts to use fictions to create meanings that would change the future of British fiction.

Bibliography

MORGAN, SUSAN. *In the Meantime: Character and Perception in Jane Austen's Fiction* (Chicago, Ill., 1980).

[RUOFF, GENE W., ed.] *The Wordsworth Circle*, 7, no. 4 (1976), a special issue on Jane Austen and British Romanticism.

[RUOFF, GENE W. AND L. J. SWINGLE, eds.] *The Wordsworth Circle*, 10 (1979), special issue on British Romantic Fiction.

SOUTHAM, B. C., ed. *Jane Austen: The Critical Heritage* (London and New York, 1968).

TAVE, STUART M. "Jane Austen and One of Her Contemporaries," in John Halperin, ed., *Jane Austen: Bicentenary Essays* (Cambridge, England, 1975).

SANDITON

Brian Southam

From the dates on the manuscript we know that Jane Austen began work on this untitled and unfinished fragment on January 27, 1817. By mid-March she was well into the twelfth chapter, having written and corrected about twenty-four thousand words. By this time her last illness was far advanced. Unable to continue further, she entered the date "18 March" below the last line. Four months later to the day, on July 18, she died. And so we are left with this substantial but tantalizing opening to a seventh novel—tantalizing, because it takes a new and wholly unexpected direction in subject matter and style and marks the opening of an entirely fresh phase in Jane Austen's art. Its outcome we can only guess at, although there have been several attempts to complete the story and there is a single clue in a family tradition that Jane Austen's own title for the book was *The Brothers*.

Nonetheless, we have no need to engage in speculation; nor do we need to explain anything away on the grounds of Jane Austen's illness; for *Sanditon* is energetic, with no trace of fatigue in its style, invention, or design. It reveals the author responding as never before to the landscape, the sea and the sun, answering the spirit of the age, the current of romantic sensibility, and catching its buoyancy and zest. At the same time she holds an amused stance toward both romanticism and the raffishness, restlessness, and the shallowness of regency society. The follies of literary enthusiasm, business speculation, and hypochondria are treated with scathing and caustic comedy. Yet there is in *Sanditon* no lack of tenderness and compassion, a remarkable intermingling of feeling and wit. And with this widened subject matter and a fuller response to the beauty and energy of nature, there comes an enrichment of her descriptive and narrative prose. The neatness and formality of her accustomed style, a personal adjustment of the Augustan tradition, is relaxed and varied with a new rhythmical freedom and a fresh use of language, particularly in figurative and symbolic devices that are notably poetic, developments for which there is little hint in the earlier novels.

That Jane Austen is embarking on something wholly new is apparent in the first few lines. We are pitched unceremoniously into events in motion, without any trace of the formal opening or elegant framing that Jane Austen had hitherto provided, as a matter of convention. Immediately, we are taken away from the event of the accident to the behavior of the driver:

> He had grumbled & shaken his shoulders so much indeed, and pitied & cut his Horses so sharply, that he might have been open to the suspicion of overturning them on purpose (especially as the Carriage was not his Masters own) if the road had not indisputably become considerably worse than before, as soon as the premises of the said House were left behind—expressing with a most intelligent portentous countenance that beyond it no wheels but cart wheels could safely proceed. (p. 364)

The awkwardness of this sentence is not, as one might expect, the clumsiness of an uncorrected trial, the difficulty of expression that an author may have to overcome before he warms to his story; nor is it due to a failure in the writer's critical censor. These lines are heavily corrected and revised. The roughness is a contrived effect, to enforce our sense of the driver's recalcitrance, the difficulty of the road, and the foundering of the coach. Never before had Jane Austen directed her style to such an end. Equally remarkable are the material being described and its treatment. Our attention is drawn to details scarcely related to the accident or its consequences. The account of the driver's behavior is prominent. We might well expect to meet him again or to be shown a significant interplay of character and action. But he has no place in the story. His character is irrelevant to the action, although of course it may be relevant to some other aspect of the work as yet unrevealed. Whatever intention we attribute to Jane Austen's design here, it is apparent that her technique and purpose of description and narration differ radically from the method of the earlier novels.

We are to understand this as the author's announcement to her readers that they are to forget about the previous novels and abandon any lingering preconceptions about the style of fiction now forthcoming from "the Author of *Northanger Abbey, Persuasion,* &.c."—as would have been the wording of *Sanditon*'s title page. The message of these opening lines is to read on with an open mind and a sensitive ear. Accordingly, we find much more that is new. Sanditon itself is given a distinctive *genius loci* in its topography, its atmosphere of wind and sun, its social climate, and its ways of life. It possesses a palpable presence such as Bath, in *Northanger Abbey* and *Persuasion*, never had. It is, moreover, a working neighborhood. We hear about the servants and local tradesmen, the day-to-day concerns of people outside Jane Austen's conventional middle-class family groups.

Its central figures are eccentrics, dominated by some wild, leading passion. These are the idiosyncratic types usually found at the edge of Jane Austen's scene—the Palmers, Miss Bates, Mr. Collins, Mr. Yates—now drawn with Dickensian intensity and expanded to take the center of the stage. And what of the heroine? Charlotte Heywood seems cast for the role. But she is cool and detached, largely a narrative device, a "Jamesian" point of view from which to observe, question, and begin to penetrate the other persons and events. Charlotte is daringly uncharacterized, and Jane Austen makes little attempt to win our sympathy for her. Nor is there any hint at the future course of events. Other than in *Emma*, suspense and guesswork have little part to play in the early novels. The stories wind their inevitable course to marriage, delayed and complicated as they may be by the interference of rivals crossing the paths of the hero and heroine. But there is no evidence of this structure in *Sanditon*. The threads of the action and plot are not united in any single or converging pattern, and we are left to guess at the possible lines of development—the extent, for example, that the success or failure of Sanditon itself will occupy the book. What we can say is that it looks like a regency South Sea bubble and that the accidents and frustrations of the opening—the foundering of Mr. Parker's coach up an impassable lane; the collapse of his ankle; and his wild-goose chase for the Willingden surgeon—foreshadow its collapse. Then what of the characters? Is Clara Brereton to be Charlotte's rival? Is Sidney Parker to be a Frank Churchill, a Henry Crawford, or a Bingley/Darcy? What is to be the importance of the eccentrics to the outcome? And what is to be the role of Lady Denham, the most complex figure in the story? Overall, we read in *Sanditon* a shift in emphasis from the individual in society to society itself.

At the same time, there is abundant evidence of Jane Austen's close engagement with contemporary literature and thought; and as much as *Sanditon* is a comedy of manners, it is also a burlesque on a new kind of fiction, the discussion novel and novel of ideas. The beginning of *Sanditon* is a playful version of Thomas Love Peacock's *Headlong Hall*, published in 1816, which opens with the four "illuminati" in a coach heatedly discussing "improvements." Soon there is the comedy of a twisted ankle and an intrusive coachman. Jane Austen echoes these events, and the "improvements" debate soon follows in the exchange of views between the improver, the enthusiastic Mr. Parker, and Mr. Heywood, the skeptical gentleman farmer, a spokesman for the sober stability of traditional country life. Peacock assembles his characters at Headlong Hall; Jane Austen gathers hers at Sanditon, where we hear the spirited monologues of Mr. Parker, his sister Diana, and Sir Edward Denham, a ventriloquial mouthpiece for a Peacockian succession of topics: sentimentalism, romanticism, potted science, theories of digestion, and so on. Jane Austen also conducts a further burlesque comedy based on *The Magic of Wealth*, a "Vehicle of Opinions." This propaganda novel by Thomas Skinner Surr, published in 1815, tells the story of Mr. Flim-Flam, a tradesman turned banker, who transforms the fishing village of Thiselton into the resort of Flimflampton.

Sanditon is an elegant and allusive joke upon these and other contemporary novels and tracts, upon modern digests of knowedge designed to equip ladies and gentlemen with lines of conversation with which to impress and edify their friends, upon the theories of the political economists, upon the "Charitable hearts" and "Benevolence" of the Parker sisters epitomizing the rise of organized charity under the name of philanthropy. In all this, Jane Austen is reflecting the serious concern of contemporary commentators at the changes they discerned in the nature of postwar society and the marked decline in social relationships. A specific case was land speculation—the very activity to which Mr. Parker and Lady Denham are so eagerly and optimistically committed. By its critics, this was seen as a prime instance of the cash nexus. Here was exemplified the triumph of profit over tradition, in this instance the tradition of family stewardship that preserved estates intact from generation to generation and preserved with them the care and concern for their dependent servants and workers. An ancient social fabric was being torn apart, and with its destruction went the human values that sustained it. Emblematic of the new age and its new values was the coastal resort, the rootless town, the place of visitors, of cash transaction, of change labeled as "improvement."

Jane Austen's concern with this subject is, of course, that of the creative artist. She has no causes to argue in the manner of Cobbett or Surr; nor does she convey anything of Coleridge's grave indignation. Her engagement is with the hilarious comedy of eccentricity, extravagance, and the collisions of character and opinion and with the subtler tensions of uncertainty and change. There is no question that her personal sympathies lie other than with Mr. Heywood, with his "very quiet, settled, careful course of Life" in the country, "rendered pleasant by Habit." But part of Jane Austen's continuing success as a writer, at this point in her life, was her openness to fresh experience and her readiness to explore fresh means for its expression. In *Sanditon*, she is nostalgic about the past. But it is a nostalgia that she admits to, just as she admits to the attraction of improvement, the very thing that threatens the past, just as she also admits to her own insecurity in the pull of these forces. In *The Statesman's Manual* (1816), Samuel Taylor Coleridge speaks of "that restless craving for the wonders of the day." This is a craving to which Jane Austen's imagination was not immune and which in *Sanditon* she explored and submitted to, accepting the beguiling power of the new "wonders" of the regency-romantic age.

Describing his sense of the novelist's task, Henry James declared, "Catching the very note and trick, the strange irregular rhythm of life, that is the attempt whose strenuous force keeps Fiction upon her feet" (p. 38). These words might well stand as an epigraph to *Sanditon*, fragment though it is. Here Jane Austen strove as never before to catch "the very note and trick, the strange irregular rhythm" in the new life of the nineteenth century. In this attempt, prematurely ended as it was, she won artistic liberation, a new feedom, the ends of which we are left to imagine.

Bibliography

AUSTEN, JANE. *Sanditon*, B. C. Southam, ed. (Oxford and London, 1975), introduction to the facsimile edition.

JAMES, HENRY. "The Art of Fiction," in Leon Edel, ed., *The House of Fiction* (New York, 1958), 38.

SOUTHAM, B. C. "*Sanditon*: The Seventh Novel," in Juliet McMaster, ed., *Jane Austen's Achievement* (London, 1976), 1–26.

———, ed. *Jane Austen's Literary Manuscripts* (London, 1964), chap. 7.

THE SEQUELS TO JANE AUSTEN'S NOVELS

Marilyn Sachs

According to her nephew, Jane Austen "would, if asked, tell us many little particulars about the subsequent career of some of her people" (*Memoir*, p. 376). We learn that Miss Steele never did catch the doctor; that Mr. Woodhouse lived only two years after Emma's marriage to Mr. Knightley; and that Jane Fairfax was too good for Frank Churchill and would die young.

Followers of Jane Austen have an incurable addiction to the fate of her characters and greedily, if disdainfully, gobble up sequels to her novels. Only *Northanger Abbey* has not had a sequel; Andrew Lang's little spoof in the form of a letter—"From Miss Catherine Morland to Miss Eleanor Tilney" in his book *Old Friends* (1890)—doesn't count. In it Catherine Morland visits Thornfield, the estate of Mr. Rochester in *Jane Eyre*, and discovers that the laughing, gurgling sounds so terrifying to readers of that book can be traced to a hysterical Jane Eyre herself filling the boots of all the guests with water.

The novel with the greatest number of sequels is the popular favorite *Pride and Prejudice*. *Old Friends and New Fancies* by Sybil G. Brinton (1913) contains the longest opening sentence of all the sequels, with a paragraph consisting of ninety-nine words. It also ties with another sequel, *Gambles and Gambols* by Memoir (1983), for the largest number of characters from the other novels. Elizabeth and Darcy are happily married. She calls him dear Darcy. They have a boy and a girl and live at Pemberley with Georgiana, who has just broken her engagement to Colonel Fitzwilliam. Kitty Bennet is in love with William Price, who falls in love with Georgiana, who is proposed to by Tom Bertram. By the end of this dizzying story, Mary Crawford marries Colonel Fitzwilliam; Georgiana marries William Price; Kitty Bennet ends up with James Morland, the new vicar at Pemberley; and poor Tom Bertram gets Isabella Thorpe.

A better-known and much more orderly sequel is *Pemberley Shades* by D. A. Bonavia Hunt (1949), which contains only the characters found in *Pride and Prejudice*. Elizabeth and Darcy are happily married, and she calls him Fitz. They live at Pemberley with Georgiana, and their guests speak at some length of Napoleon. Elizabeth reads the newer poets, and Darcy at one point quickly glances at one of her books, called *The Ancient Mariner*. By the end of the book, Kitty Bennet continues to fulfill Jane Austen's prophecy by marrying a neighbor of Darcy's, who happens to be a part-time clergyman; Miss de Bourgh marries an actor-con man; Georgiana ends up with the new vicar at Pemberley; and Elizabeth gives birth to her second son.

"The Darcys of Rosings," in *The Ladies*! by E. Barrington (1922)—a chapter in one of those sprightly books, happily not often written nowadays—picks up the trail of the Darcys after they have inherited Rosings upon the deaths of Lady Catherine and her daughter. In it, the Darcys have two daughters, one of whom is abducted by Willoughby's illegitimate son and rescued by Wickham, who is thus restored to favor with the Darcys.

In *Teverton Hall* by Jane Gillespie (1984), Mr. Collins' son and daughter (both of whom take after their poor mother) manage to find happiness in spite of their father.

Surprisingly, the most controversial of all Jane Austen's novels, *Mansfield Park*, has had the second greatest number of sequels. *Susan Price, or Resolution* by Mrs. Francis Brown (1930), a great-grandniece of Jane Austen's, plugs along loyally in a story that brings Edmund and Fanny back to the vicarage at Mansfield Park with their three children. Susan Price, now resident at Mansfield Park and attendant on her Aunt Bertram, is loved by her cousin Tom Bertram; but he thinks he wants to marry Mary Crawford, who has reappeared. A sense of déjà vu hangs over this story particularly when Mrs. Norris returns, after Maria's marriage to an apothecary, and specializes in tormenting Susan. At the end, the two cousins marry, and Mary Crawford, who incidentally gets a good press here, as she does in all the sequels she appears in, finds another worthy spouse.

The second sequel, a more recent and much livelier entry, is *Gambles and Gambols*. The faithful will enjoy the exchange between Fanny and Edmund over their respective mothers' health and should be happy to know that Edmund, grown even stuffier than he was in *Mansfield Park*, is the author of various books of sermons, including one called "Man as an Excretion of the Rotting Rock."

Ladysmead, by Jane Gillespie (1982), also a recent work, is only partially a sequel to *Mansfield Park*. The story concerns the second daughter of a rural clergyman who appears to be headed for spinsterhood. Along come Mrs. Norris and Maria Bertram to rent a small, empty house called Ladysmead and to muddy the waters. When last seen, the two of them, with Maria's new husband, have emigrated to America.

A sequel to *Sense and Sensibility* and a companion volume to *Susan Price* is *Margaret Dashwood or Interference* by Mrs. Francis Brown (1929). Shadowy reincarnations of Elinor, Marianne, Mrs. Jennings, and the rest flit through the book as Margaret meets a stranger while walking on the downs and enjoys a romance remarkably similar to her older sister's but with a happier ending.

Not so much a sequel as another view of *Emma* is *Jane Fairfax* by Naomi Royde Smith (1940), a leisurely, well-researched book containing more details of contemporary life than any of the other sequels. Mrs. Campbell struggles gallantly to bring up her daughter Euphrasia and her foster daughter Jane Fairfax and to control her philandering husband, Colonel Campbell. We learn what Jane thinks of Emma and her piano playing and what really happened at Weymouth. Characters not only from Jane Austen's novels but from other nineteenth-century books as well troop through this story. A letter from Mrs. Elton to Mrs. Suckling provides a fitting ending to the book.

The most remarkable of all the sequels is *Virtues and Vices* by Grania Beckford (1981), a bawdy retelling of *Persuasion*. Readers will note that the period has been changed, as have the names of some of the characters, no doubt to protect the innocent. Sir Wilfred Elliot has three daughters, Edwina, Angela, and Marigold. Captain Wentworth is a con man who sleeps with Lady Russell, whose attachment to her beloved Angela is far from motherly. Benwick and Harville are two crooked pimps, and every other page graphically presents an endless variety of sexual encounters from incest to child molesting (and molesting by a child). Jane Austen would certainly not approve, but it appears unlikely that devoted admirers will ever stop luring her characters into sequels.

Bibliography

BARRINGTON, E. (PSEUD. OF LILY ADAMS BECK). "The Darcys of Rosings," in her *The Ladies!* (Boston, 1922), 235–68.
BECKFORD, GRANIA. *Virtues and Vices* (New York, 1981).
BONAVIA-HUNT, D. A. *Pemberley Shades* (London, 1949).
BRINTON, SYBIL G. *Old Friends and New Fancies* (London, 1913; reprinted 1939).
BROWN, MRS. FRANCIS. *Margaret Dashwood, or Interference* (London, 1929).
———. *Susan Price, or Resolution* (London, 1930).
GILLESPIE, JANE. *Ladysmead* (London, 1982).
———. *Teverton Hall* (London, 1984).
LANG, ANDREW. "From Miss Catherine Morland to Miss Eleanor Tilney," in his *Old Friends* (London and New York, 1890), 97–101.
MEMOIR. *Gambles and Gambols* (Shelter Cove, 1983).
SMITH, NAOMI ROYDE. *Jane Fairfax* (London, 1940).

SERVANTS

Janet Todd

Servants are ubiquitous in Jane Austen's world. In her letters they enter discreetly under the titles of cook, nanny, coachman, and maid or under a few common names like Eliza, Hannah, and Sally. Although she occasionally noted drunkenness and negligence, Austen indulged little in the contemporary habit of complaining about servants, seeing such complaint as signifying a discontented character. Instead, she approved where she could, declaring one servant "quick and quiet," another civil and well-meaning, and praising all the servants in Lyme faced with dirty and inconvenient lodgings. Only a few servants are followed through many years: Browning in Chawton, for example, or Eliza in Southampton. One or two function almost as friends, such as the asthmatic Mme. Bigeon at Henry Austen's, who wished to make up the deficiencies of her master's pantry from her own stock.

In 1801, just before their removal to Bath, Jane Austen and her mother comforted themselves with a servant fantasy: they would have "a steady Cook, & a young giddy Housemaid, with a sedate, middle aged Man, who is to undertake the double office of Husband to the former & sweetheart to the latter" with no children on either side (*Letters*, January 3, 1801). There are no such interesting complications among the hundred or so of Jane Austen's fictional servants. Their feelings go unrecorded and their relationships unacknowledged except where they occasionally impinge on their masters. In this lack of interest, Austen contrasts with the sentimental novelists she so unsparingly mocked who treat servants as loyal retainers and receptive confidantes. In the parodic *juvenilia*, a cook might aspire to the exemplary hero, while an exemplary governess elopes with the butler; in "Edgar & Emma" (*Vol. 1*) the heroine tries to take a footman as confidant, but he excuses himself from the duty. In the novels, however, servants are not candidates for social elevation, and the inelegant Nanny shouting from the doorway in *The Watsons*, the slatternly Rebecca of *Mansfield Park*, and the unappreciated Harry of *Emma* are unlikely to change their station.

In the early long fiction, servants enter according to their ordinary functions, except for the ominous Dorothy, the "ancient housekeeper" of Henry Tilney's gothic plot, and the treacherous or foolish servant of Colonel Brandon's cousin in the colonel's equally gothic history. Henry Tilney's real housekeeper is as ancient as his pretended one, but she is mentioned only for her need of four days' notice to prepare for the general's visit. The numerous attendants at the abbey, the "inferiors" whose labor has been softened by the general's modernization, exist to proclaim the dignity of their master, while the amiability of the Dashwood ladies is confirmed by the joy their few servants show at their arrival in their new small house. In *Pride and Prejudice* servants continue muted, and the composition of even the Bennet household is not entirely clear, although there is certainly Mrs. Hill, two housemaids, a butler, and a footman. Little is known of any of them, but the reader lightly feels the gaze of Mrs. Hill on the follies of her employers. Other characters in the novel have appropriate servants; the Bingley sisters employ "two elegant ladies," and Mrs. Reynolds, the housekeeper of Pemberley, is fitting custodian of Darcy's family and character.

Of the later novels, *Emma* and *Mansfield Park* display the most servants, since both are concerned with communities. Both avoid any ideology of service and instead use servants merely to thicken the texture of society. For example, William Larkins, Mr. Knightley's bailiff, is connected with the Bateses when he mentions their cooking apples, given by his master, and with Mr. Elton, to whom he reports Mr. Knightley's absence of mind and taciturnity. The taciturnity is emphasized by Mr. Knightley himself when he admits that, preoccupied with love, he has avoided Larkins. Another unprobed connecting agent is Mr. Woodhouse's coachman, whose daughter Hannah, on Mr. Woodhouse's recommendation, goes to Randalls as housemaid. Emma uses the relationship to join the two houses when her father feels their distance. The conversation provokes one of the longest speeches on a servant in the Austen canon, when the self-centered Mr. Woodhouse praises Hannah as "a very good servant" (p. 9) who curtsies nicely and never bangs doors.

In *Mansfield Park* servants function to suggest the hierarchical nature of country life and the populated context of the major characters, and perhaps to comment subtly on their betters. At Sotherton a lack of control is implied by the power of the housekeeper and an inappropriate moral standard by the fact that family prayers are discontinued but housemaids are dismissed for wearing white gowns and wine is prohibited from the second table. At Mansfield, where the head of the house acts partly as he ought, servants display proper attitudes and are solemn-looking after the family disaster. In Sir Thomas's absence, however, five of the under-servants are made idle by the scene painter. Servants help to display Mrs. Norris's officious character. She subjects the old rheumatic coachman to her persuasion against an especially dirty trip, and on the morning of the ball she grows angry with the housekeeper who will have her way with the supper. To Mrs. Norris, servants are always encroaching, and she sees most encounters in terms of power struggles. In the poultry yard she spies a boy coming to his father and assumes he has a motive for arriving at the servants' dinnertime; she sends him packing as a marauder. A similar struggle occurs with the butler Baddeley, who manages to best her twice, suggesting a male intimacy with his master to which she herself aspires. When Mrs. Norris insists that she, not Fanny, is wanted by Sir Thomas, Baddeley is "stout" in his refusal, and his "half smile" indicates that he, unlike Mrs. Norris, knows his master's business (p. 325). In one other instance Baddeley seems to convey triumph in terms of class and gender: in Sir Thomas's absence Mrs. Norris is concerned to appropriate his power and to stage-manage his arrival dead or alive; yet when Sir Thomas does return, he seeks "no confidant but the butler" (p. 180).

TOPOGRAPHY

J. David Grey

Jane Austen approached topography as carefully as she did the chronology within the novels. She rarely strayed outside the English terrain with which she was familiar from her travelings and shifts of residence, and when she did (as in the case of the Northamptonshire hedgerows), she sought the advice of others. Other women writers of her time roamed the map of Europe, indeed the entire world, in search of eccentric locales and presented them cloaked in fantastic imaginings. Jane Austen makes only passing references to places outside England, "Swisserland" and Venice among them.

Sense and Sensibility

"The family of Dashwood had been long settled in Sussex" (p. 3), at Norland Park, but Jane Austen gives no further evidence of its specific location. Sir Frank MacKinnon deduces that it is probably near the coast, since the Dashwoods' furnishings are conveyed to their new home in Devonshire by sea (p. 87). This choice of transport leads John Frye-Bourne, in his unpublished "Sidbury and Barton," to conclude that "Exeter", should be read as "Sidmouth" and that Barton Valley is actually the valley of the Sid with Sidbury, four miles to the north, disguised as Barton in the novel. Jane Austen, however, situates Barton that distance north of Exeter, and the Earl of Iddesleigh states: "I fully believe that Pynes [his home at Upton Pyne] was Barton Park and that I am writing these lines in the room in which Sir John Middleton ate his dinner" (p. 818). "H. F. P." places the venue at Stoke Canon, "a small village near Exeter" and "*M*" opts for "Barton Place in the parish of St. David, Exeter, near Cowley Bridge" (p. 285).

Allenham is a mile and a half from Barton, and Whitwell, with its "noble piece of water" (p. 62), about twelve miles away. Real or imagined, the neighborhood's setting is idyllic: high hills, open downs, woods, pastures, and winding valleys proliferate. Delaford is relatively near and must, therefore, be in the westernmost part of Dorset. Trips to London (over 170 miles) are made via Honiton, and Mrs. Jennings and the Dashwood girls arrive at her home in Berkeley Street, Portman Square, at three o'clock in the afternoon of their third day of traveling. Cleveland, the Palmers' house in Somersetshire, is 80 miles from Barton (a 160-mile round trip, therefore, for Colonel Brandon in less than a day) and 120 from London. Willoughby makes the latter journey in ten hours, stopping only for a ten-minute "nuncheon" at Marlborough. His home, Combe Magna, is thirty miles southeast of Cleveland. The Steele girls' uncle lives at "Longstaple," near Plymouth, and Lucy and Robert Ferrars honeymoon in fashionable Dawlish.

Pride and Prejudice

Longbourn, in Hertfordshire, and its village are a mile from Meryton, as is Lucas Lodge. Netherfield is three miles away. Meryton lies ten miles off the Great North Road, and MacKinnon speculates that, if to the west, it and "———" are Hemel Hempstead and Watford; if to the east, Ware and Hertford. In an unpublished essay "Longbourn, Hunsford, Meryton and Netherfield," the author concurs that Meryton is Hertford but poses a good case for the posting town being Barnet. Longbourn is twenty-four miles from the Gardiners' home in Gracechurch Street, London, and Hunsford Parsonage, in Kent, the same distance (four hours by coach) farther south. The normal posting stop for Elizabeth Bennet's journey south from London would have been at Bromley at "The Bell," as Lady Catherine later suggests for her return trip. "Hunsford" is a mile from Westerham, "a pleasant walk of about a half a mile across the park" (p. 161) from Rosings. Sir David Waldron Smithers claims: "In the long history of Chevening there surely was a time between 1792 and 1812 when Jane Austen paid a visit [to her distant relations there] and made it a model for a house which was, through her, to become known around the world even better as Rosings than as Chevening" (p. 56).

Jane Austen specifies that the road north from Longbourn that is traveled by Elizabeth and her aunt and uncle on their holiday to Derbyshire passes through Oxford, Blenheim, Warwick, "Kenelworth," and Birmingham. Their final destination is "Lambton," only five miles from Pemberley. Much contention and confusion surround Jane Austen's topography here. Some claim that Lambton is Bakewell, but then, she mentions both by name. The same problem persists for those who claim Chatsworth as the original for Pemberley: both names appear. In "Persuasion No. 1," 1979 (the publication of the Jane Austen Society of North America), Donald Greene writes about "the astonishingly close correspondence of the topography of Pemberley to that of Chatsworth" (p. 14). This was more than a decade after Elizabeth Jenkins's attempt to debunk that myth in the "Jane Austen Society [England] Report for the Year 1965" (pp. 9–14). Marjorie Blount theorizes that Pemberley is Chatsworth as described to Jane Austen by her brother Henry: he was fond of hunting and had visited Matlock and its neighborhood, possibly more than once (p. 71). The discussion verges on the absurd when one reads in Ward Lock's Red Guide, "The Peak District," that in Bakewell's square "is the Rutland Arms hotel where Jane Austen stayed whilst revising her 'First Impressions,' later to become 'Pride and Prejudice'" (p. 82). In flattening this rumor, Miss Jenkins quotes Dr. Chapman's famous comment: "No evidence she was ever north of the Trent." Five years later, however, an unsigned article about the Rutland Arms boasts: "In 1811 Jane Austen is said to have stayed at [the hotel] and her room is still in use as one of the hotel bedrooms. The desk on which she is reputed to have revised part of her novel 'Pride and Prejudice' is still in the room" (p. 63)! By 1978 a reporter, Tamie Watters, simply takes it for granted that Pemberley and Chatsworth are synonymous (*B*16).

"The dreadful news from Jane [Bennet] caused [the Gardiner party] to hurry back to Longbourn; the whole distance would be 140 or 150 miles" (MacKinnon, p. 94). This was an extremely long trip to be accomplished in two days. The reason for such haste is, of course, the escapade of Lydia Bennet and Wickham, a pair of the greatest travelers in the novels. Since they never make it to her destination of Gretna Green, their assignation is made at Brighton (Sussex); his new military assignment will take them to Newcastle for the ensuing winter. Wickham has already compromised Georgiana Darcy at Ramsgate, and at the conclusion of the novel that young lady is vacationing at Scarborough, where she will undoubtedly get the news of the impending weddings.

Mansfield Park

Although there should be no question in placing Mansfield Park in Northamptonshire, about four miles north of Northampton, more absurd theories have arisen as to the identification of possible prototypes of the house. "My friend the Master of Downing has shown . . . Mansfield Park to coincide roughly with Easton, near Huntingdon" (Darwin, 1917, p. 75). Easton is thirty miles east of Northampton! "My own conviction is that Mansfield Park is Easton Neston House, rebuilt in 1702" (Lady Vaux of Harrowden, p. 188), but this is southeast of Northampton, and any approach to it would not be made through that city. R. W. Chapman puts forth some sound reasons for accepting Cottesbrooke Hall as the original (although it is nine miles north of Northampton), citing the fact that its owner at that time, Sir James Langham, had personal, perhaps even business, connections with Henry Austen (p. 1006) and was familiar with Jane Austen's works (*Opinions*, pp. 434 and 439). Harleston Park, demolished in 1940, has the best claim according to Ellinor Hughes (1932, p. 22) and

Wendy Craik (p. 66). Dr. Chapman uses Humphry Repton's colored overlay of Harleston as the frontispiece for his definitive 1923 edition of the novels and in his "Notes on Illustrations" quotes Repton, who, as Jane Austen was writing *Mansfield Park*, had just finished "improving" Harleston: "few places have undergone so much alteration, both in the House and Grounds" (*MP*, p. 552).

Mrs. Norris's White House is "not much above a quarter of a mile" from the Park, and she claims, "often do I pace it three times a-day" (p. 73). The park and the parsonage "were not within sight of each other; but by walking fifty yards from the hall door, [Fanny] could look down the park, and command a view of the parsonage and all its demesnes, gently rising beyond the village road" (p. 67). This will be her future residence, but at present Edmund and she will live at Thornton Lacey, eight miles away. In preparation for his ordination at Peterborough, Edmund visits with friends at "Lessingby." His sister and brother-in-law, the Rushworths, live at Sotherton Court, "ten miles of indifferent road" from Mansfield.

Fanny and William Price pass through Oxford and stop at Newbury for the night on their way to Portsmouth, a trip of 120 miles. On her return with her sister Susan, they stay at Oxford. Her first journey was made with "Nanny" through London and was therefore a longer route: over 140 miles. The Rushworths take Julia Bertram with them on their honeymoon (a common custom) to Brighton. Later, there is little wonder that Henry Crawford chooses to spend a few days at Richmond at the same time that Mrs. Rushworth is "with the Aylmers at Twickenham" (p. 434), just across the Thames. Mr. Crawford's estate is at Everingham, in Norfolk.

Emma

Highbury, in "Surry," is a "large and populous village almost amounting to a town" (p. 7). The Woodhouses' Hartfield was the only property in Highbury that did not belong to Mr. Knightley's Donwell estate, the seat of which was Donwell Abbey, a mile from the village and in another parish. Adjoining the estate was Abbey Mill Farm, occupied by the Martins. Randalls, the Westons' home, was a safe half-mile walk from Hartfield. Jane Austen outlines a very detailed plan of Highbury and even names five of its thoroughfares. Highbury is sixteen miles from London (p. 7), nine from Richmond (p. 317), and seven from Box Hill (p. 367). (Emma had never been to the last-named place!) No one place in Surrey fits that location, but claims as to the original have been made, those for Leatherhead much more convincingly so than the ones for Esher or Cobham. Mary Trebeck gives a very strong argument in favor of Leatherhead, if we accept her theory that the picnicking party takes a roundabout approach to the top of Box Hill (p. 276). Moreover, Jane Austen had made visits to her cousin and godfather, the Reverend Samuel Cooke, in the Bookhams (which are a few miles from Leatherhead), the last visit being made at the time she was starting to write *Emma*. R. F. Pechey suggests Highbury is in actuality Alton in linguistic disguise: "altus+burgh" (p. 513). Finally, Mrs. Craik's original for Hartfield, Polesden Lacey (p. 157), is hardly credible, since the house was not built until 1824.

As elsewhere, Jane Austen is meticulous about the distances between places. The mileages from London to Cromer and Southend, real seaside resorts, are almost exact. The Churchills reside at Enscombe, 190 miles north of London in Yorkshire, and Maple Grove is 125 miles west of that city, therefore past Bristol. Mr. Suckling's two round trips to London within a week must have been quite an ordeal. Miss Hawkins and the Sucklings, who are "extremely fond of exploring" in their barouche-landau, have made two visits to King's Weston (Weston-super-Mare?) the previous summer.

Northanger Abbey

There actually is a Fullerton near Salisbury, but it is twice the nine-mile distance given in *Northanger Abbey*. This village and Mottisfont Abbey, a few miles south, are in Hampshire, so that both Catherine Morland and Jane Austen may have known them.

Catherine's brother James and John Thorpe pass through Tetbury on their trip from Oxford to Bath. The importance of even the slightest mention from Jane Austen is found in a 1978 "History of Tetbury": "The principal coaching house was the Three Cups Inn in Church Street.... This inn is thought to have been in Jane Austen's mind when in writing 'Northanger Abbey' she referred to a (fictional) journey from Tetbury to Bath" (Hodgson, p. 83). She uses the correct distance again, that is, twenty-three miles. The abbey was situated in Gloucestershire, thirty miles from Bath. The trip north with General Tilney was broken midway at "Petty France," where Catherine felt "the tediousness of a two hours' bait, ... in which there was nothing to be done but to eat without being hungry, and loiter about without any thing to see" (p. 156). Henry Tilney's Woodston, "a large and populous village, in a situation not unpleasant" (p. 212), was twenty miles away, nearly a three-hour drive. This was probably southeast of the Abbey, since Catherine retraces the first fourteen miles of her trip to Woodston when the general peremptorily banishes her from his home. This seventy-mile return to her home at Fullerton was accomplished via postmasters, in stages, and took eleven hours.

Persuasion

Kellynch Hall was in Somerset (near "Crewkherne"). Lady Russell, the Elliots' friend, occupied its lodge half a mile away. Kellynch has been equated with Racedown Lodge even though the latter is in Dorset. It is, however, just over the Somerset line, fifty miles from Bath (the distance furnished by Jane Austen) and on one of the roads from Bath to Lyme Regis with which she would have been familiar. (It is curious that the attribution should be made to a house that was inhabited by William and Dorothy Wordsworth, 1795–97.) Sir Francis Darwin prefers Buckland-St.-Mary, which is in Somerset (1917, p. 75), but its inhabitants would frequent Chard or Ilminster, which are both much closer than Crewkerne. "Uppercross was a moderate-sized village, which a few years back had been completely in the old English style" (p. 36). The cottage belonging to the Musgroves was three miles from Kellynch. Winthrop, the Hayters' farm, required an uphill walk of half a mile from Uppercross to command a view of its buildings.

It was seventeen miles from Uppercross to Lyme Regis. The "long hill into Lyme" and "the still steeper street of the town itself" (p. 95) continue to surprise the pleasure seekers who descend on this stretch of the Dorset coast. Jane Austen's beautiful description of the town and its environs deserves to be quoted in its entirety:

> the remarkable situation of the town, the principal street almost hurrying into the water, the walk to the Cobb, skirting round the pleasant little bay, which in the season is animated with bathing machines and company, the Cobb itself, its old wonders and new improvements, with the very beautiful line of cliffs stretching out to the east of the town, are what the stranger's eye will seek; and a very strange stranger it must be, who does not see charms in the immediate environs of Lyme, to make him wish to know it better. The scenes in its neighbourhood, Charmouth, with its high grounds and extensive sweeps of country, and still more its sweet retired bay, backed by dark cliffs, where fragments of low rock among the sands make it the happiest spot for watching the flow of the tide, for sitting in unwearied contemplation;—the woody varieties of the cheerful village of Up Lyme, and, above all, Pinny, with its green chasms between romantic rocks, where the scattered forest trees and orchards of luxuriant growth declare that many a generation must have passed away since the first partial falling of the cliff prepared the ground for such a state, where a scene so wonderful and lovely is exhibited, as may more than equal any of the resembling scenes of the far-famed Isle of Wight: these places must be visited, and visited again, to make the worth of Lyme understood. (pp. 95–96)

The street that hurries down into town is Broad Street. The assembly rooms, where Jane Austen danced, were located at the foot of it, on the sea. They were demolished in 1929. Farther up the hill was the Cups, the inn where, according to John Vaughan, the Musgrove party stayed (p. 230). It was burned in the disastrous fire of 1844. Cyril Wanklyn, the chronicler of Lyme, claims that "Wings" was the cottage where Jane Austen herself stayed in 1804. It was torn down in 1945. "The houses opposite were a good deal knocked about by the gale of 1824 [which also destroyed much of the Cobb], but in one of them, say Bay Cottage [No. 29, Marine Parade], Jane Austen put the Harville family" (p. 223).

Genius will never be limited by lack of geographical knowledge, but neither will it allow guesswork in its productions. Jane Austen was scrupulous about topography because she realized the importance of the function it served in providing the background for the action of her works. By employing her personal observations of the places he had lived and traveled to and researching other reliable sources of information, Jane Austen laid the basis for the strictures that control the realistic novel.

Bibliography

ADAMS, OSCAR FAY. "In the Footsteps of Jane Austen," *New England Magazine*, n.s. 8 (1893), 594–608.

ATKINSON, EDMUND. "Jane Austen and Sussex," *Jane Austen Society, Report for the Year 1977* (Alton, 1978), 7–12.

AUSTEN-LEIGH, EMMA. *Jane Austen and Steventon* (London, 1937).

———. *Jane Austen and Bath* (London, 1939).

AUSTEN-LEIGH, RICHARD ARTHUR. *Jane Austen and Lyme Regis* (London, 1941).

———. *Jane Austen and Southampton* (London, 1949).

BLOUNT, MARJORIE. "Pemberley," *The Derbyshire Countryside*, 20 (1954), 69–71.

CHAPMAN, R. W. "Mansfield Park," *Times Literary Supplement* (December 10, 1931), 1006.

CRAIK, WENDY ANN. *Jane Austen in Her Time* (London, 1969).

DARWIN, SIR FRANCIS. *Rustic Sounds, and Other Studies in Literature and Natural History* (London, 1917).

———. "Mansfield Park," *Times Literary Supplement* (March 25, 1920), 201.

EAGLE, DOROTHY AND HILARY CARNELL, eds. *The Oxford Literary Guide to the British Isles* (Oxford, 1977).

EDWARDS, ANNE-MARIE. *In the Steps of Jane Austen* (London, 1979).

FREEMAN, JEAN. *Jane Austen in Bath* (Alton, 1969).

HODGSON, ERIC. *A History of Tetbury* (Dursley, 1976).

HOLYOAKE, GREGORY. "Jane Austen in Kent: Part I: Goodnestone and Rowling," *Bygone Kent*, 3 (1982), 301–8.

———. "Jane Austen in Kent: Part II: Godmersham," *Bygone Kent*, 3 (1982), 349–56.

TOPOGRAPHY

HUGHES, ELLINOR W. "Jane Austen and Northamptonshire," *Library List: Journal of the Northampton County Library*, 2 (May 1932), 22–23.

———. "The Last of Mansfield Park," *Times Literary Supplement* (November 9, 1940), 572.

IDDESLEIGH, WALTER STAFFORD, 2ND EARL OF. "A Chat About Jane Austen's Novels," *Nineteenth Century*, 47 (1900), 811–20.

LOCK, F. P. "Jane Austen and the Seaside," *Country Life Annual* (1972), 114–16.

"M." "Jane Austen," *Notes & Queries*, 163 (1932), 285.

MACKINNON, SIR FRANK D. "Topography and Travel in Jane Austen's Novels," *Cornhill Magazine*, n.s. 59 (1925), 184–99.

NABOKOV, VLADIMIR. *Lectures on Literature: British, French and German Writers* (New York, 1980).

"P., H. F." "Jane Austen," *Notes & Queries*, 163 (1932), 285.

PALGRAVE, FRANCIS T. "Miss Austen and Lyme," *The Grove: A Monthly Miscellany* (June–July 1971), 58–63, 141–46.

PEACH, ROBERT E. *Historic Houses in Bath, and Their Associations* (London, 1883).

PECHEY, R. F. "Emma and Alton," *Times Literary Supplement* (September 11, 1948), 513.

PINION, FRANCIS B. *A Jane Austen Companion* (London, 1973).

RAGG, LAURA M. *Jane Austen in Bath* (London, 1938).

SMITHERS, SIR DAVID WALDRON. *Jane Austen in Kent* (Westerham, Kent, 1982).

TREBECK, MARY. "Was Highbury Leatherhead?" *Times Literary Supplement* (June 13, 1918), 276.

VAUGHAN, JOHN. "Jane Austen at Lyme," *Monthly Packet*, 86, n.s. 6 (1893), 271–79.

VAUX, LADY MARGARET, OF HARROWDEN. "Mansfield Park," *Times Literary Supplement* (March 18, 1920), 188 and (April 1, 1920), 213.

WALKLEY, ARTHUR BINGHAM. *Pastiche and Prejudice* (London, 1921).

WANKLYN, CYRIL. *Lyme Regis: A Retrospect* (London, 1922).

WATSON, WINIFRED. *Jane Austen in London* (Alton, 1960).

WATTERS, TAMIE. "Deep into Derbyshire with Jane Austen," *Christian Science Monitor*, 70 (April 3, 1978), B16.

WELLESLEY, LORD GERALD [LATER 7TH DUKE OF WELLINGTON]. "Houses in Jane Austen's Novels," repr. in *Collected Reports of the Jane Austen Society, 1949–1965* (London, 1967), 185–88.

TRAVEL AND TRANSPORTATION

Lorraine Hanaway

Travel episodes abound in Jane Austen's novels. Characters elope, move house, go to London or Bath for the season, take trips on business or for pleasure, pay lengthy visits to friends and family, and amuse themselves with excursions. They ride horseback, walk, and travel by chair, especially in Bath. Families of naval officers sail from one port to another. Mrs. Croft, "a great traveller" (*P*, p. 70), has crossed the Atlantic four times and has sailed to the East Indies and back and to Cork, Lisbon, and Gibraltar. The principal means of transportation, however, is the horse-drawn carriage, of which nearly a dozen types appear in the novels, carriage being the generic term for all.

The traveling times and "distances between places, real or fictitious, are always consistent," according to Sir Frank MacKinnon, who had little doubt that "Jane Austen used Paterson's or Carey's road-books for the travels of her heroes and heroines" (p. 86). James Morland "pleaded the authority of road-books, innkeepers, and milestones" to calculate distances in *Northanger Abbey* (p. 45).

"Although lights were used . . . the state of the roads made traveling in darkness unpleasant and dangerous. Even in daylight carriage accidents were frequent," notes R. W. Chapman in an appendix to *Mansfield Park* (p. 565). In the opening passage of *Sanditon*, "A Gentleman & Lady travelling . . . towards . . . the Sussex Coast" (p. 363) overturn in their carriage, consequently meeting the novel's heroine. Sunday traveling is condemned as one of William Elliot's former "bad habits" (*P*, p. 161), so General Tilney's dismissal of seventeen-year-old Catherine Morland on a Sunday is especially egregious; she faces a seventy-mile journey home "alone, unattended" (*NA*, p. 226). Luckily, Eleanor Tilney lends Catherine ample money, and "her youth, civil manners and liberal pay, procured her all the attention that a traveller like herself could require; and stopping only to change horses, she travelled on for about eleven hours without accident or alarm" (*NA*, p. 232). Catherine travels "post," that is, from one post, or station, to the next, where she changes horses. Traveling post usually means changing chaises and transferring luggage at each post unless the traveler owns the chaise. Earlier, Catherine admires the Tilneys' style of traveling: "fashionable chaise-and-four—postilions handsomely liveried . . . numerous out-riders properly mounted" (*NA*, p. 156).

"Travelling post in a hack carriage is not considered desirable" according to Chapman, and using public transportation (stagecoaches) "is hardly mentioned" (*MP*, p. 564). Ladies do not travel in public conveyances; gentlemen seldom do. Miss Steele emphasizes that it was "not in the stage" that she had come to London (*SS*, p. 218). Edmund Bertram arrives in Portsmouth "by the mail" (*MP*, p. 443), but he, Fanny, and Susan Price return to Mansfield in a chaise, with Susan "sitting forward" (*MP*, p. 445). Mrs. Jennings, however, sends her maid to London by the coach, and Robert Martin returns in it to Highbury. "People of consequence used their own carriages. They did not as a rule use their own horses, except for the first stage," writes Chapman (*MP*, p. 564). Mrs. Bennet supposes that Darcy did not converse with Mrs. Long because she "does not keep a carriage, and had come to the ball in a hack chaise" (*PP*, p. 19). Mr. Knightley does "not use his carriage so often as became the owner of Donwell Abbey," Emma thinks, so when he arrives in it at the Coles's party, she declares, "This is coming as you should . . . like a gentleman" (*E*, p. 213).

It is imperative that a lady travel with an attendant. Lady Catherine lectures Elizabeth Bennet on this point before her departure from Hunsford. When she arrives at Longbourn in a chaise-and-four ("the horses were post," *PP*, p. 351), her waiting woman and a liveried servant accompany her. Mrs. Rushworth "removed herself, her maid, her footman, and her chariot, with true dowager propriety, to Bath" (*MP*, pp. 202–3).

For short trips two horses are generally felt necessary, and for longer journeys four are required. Traveling with four horses has a certain cachet. Anne Elliot thinks "that the sacrifice of one pair of horses would be hardly less painful than of both" for Elizabeth and Sir Walter (*P*, p. 13); he "wanted to know whether the Crofts travelled with four horses" coming to Bath (*P*, p. 165). Lady Bertram journeys with four horses over ten miles of indifferent roads to call on Mrs. Rushworth, promoting Maria's engagement. The carriage must have been a coach, because Wilcox is on the box and Charles on the leaders (foremost pair of horses). Other romantic errands take Edward Ferrars by the nearest road from Oxford to Barton, Henry Tilney from Woodston to Fullerton, Captain Wentworth from Monkford to Bath, Henry Crawford to Portsmouth, and Frank Churchill to Highbury. Willoughby covers 120 miles in twelve hours in a chaise-and-four when he races to Cleveland to seek Marianne's forgiveness; "the flaring lamps" announce his carriage (*SS*, p. 316).

Excursions to Sotherton Court, Box Hill, and Lyme are some of the most famous episodes in the novels. Henry Crawford, in common with other barouche owners, prefers to drive himself. Going to Sotherton, Julia sits beside him on the box, "generally thought the favourite seat" (*MP*, p. 78); Julia had protested at riding "box'd up three in a post-chaise in this weather, when we may have seats in a barouche" (*MP*, p. 77). "Seven miles were travelled in expectation of enjoyment" at Box Hill, the five ladies in two carriages, "the gentlemen on horseback" (*E*, p. 367). Although they set off after an early breakfast, it is past noon when "Mr. Musgrove's coach containing the four ladies, and Charles's curricle, in which he drove Captain Wentworth" descend into Lyme (*P*, p. 95), seventeen miles away. Wentworth hires a chaise-and-four from the inn to expedite his flight back to Uppercross after Louisa's accident; he stays only to deliver the news and see the horses fed before reversing his route. Colonel Brandon performs a similar mission in *Sense and Sensibility*.

After a Christmas visit to Longbourn, Mr. and Mrs. Gardiner take Jane Bennet with them to London, where she stays for more than three months; meanwhile, Elizabeth visits the Collinses in Kent. Mr. Gardiner's servant fetches Elizabeth to London. She joins Jane for their return home, Mr. Bennet's carriage, with Kitty and Lydia, meeting them in —— for the journey's last stage. "After some contrivance, the whole party, with all their boxes, workbags, and parcels" set off (*PP*, p. 221). Elinor and Marianne Dashwood travel to London and later to Cleveland with Mrs. Jennings in her chaise; Elinor accepts the Cleveland invitation because it is within eighty miles of Barton, where their mother's servant can collect them. (John Dashwood congratulates Elinor on traveling so far without any expense.)

Business takes Mr. and Mrs. Thomas Parker to Willingden and General Tilney and Messrs. Bennet, Darcy, Knightley, Weston, and Robert Martin to London. Colonel Brandon travels to Delaford, Willoughby to Combe Magna, and Henry Crawford to Everingham, evidence that they do look in on their estates.

Mr. Bennet, Mr. Musgrove, Lady Catherine de Bourgh, the Richardsons, and the Edwardses own coaches, large, four-wheeled, closed vehicles with two facing seats for six persons, sometimes a side seat, and a driver's box. Other four-wheeled, closed carriages are the chaise, "the regular family-carriage" (*MP*, p. 561), post-chaise, and the chariot (a chaise with driver's box added), having one seat for two facing the horses and a jump seat. The chaise is driven by a postboy, or postilion, riding the "near," or left, horse of a team. Mrs. Jennings, Robert Ferrars, Lady Catherine, Lady Bertram, Sir William Lucas, and Messrs. Bingley, Gardiner, and Heywood keep chaises; Mrs. Jennings, John Dashwood, and Mrs. Rushworth own chariots. The barouche, barouche-landau, and landaulette are convertibles with various styles of collapsible tops. Henry Crawford, the Palmers, and Lady Dalrymple own barouches, Mr. Suckling a barouche-landau, and Mrs. Frederick Wentworth, a landaulette. The phaeton is the sports car of the day, an open carriage with elevated seat for the driver and one passenger; Miss de Bourgh has a low phaeton; Mrs.

Gardiner wants "a low phaeton, with a nice little pair of ponies" (*PP*, p. 325) to tour Pemberley park. Open carriages with two wheels are the curricle, gig, and tandem, each having a seat for the driver and one passenger and sometimes a groom's seat behind. Messrs. Willoughby, Darcy, Bingley, William Goulding, Henry Tilney, and Charles Musgrove drive curricles; Mr. Collins, Admiral Croft, John Thorpe, and Sir Edward Denham drive gigs (Thorpe describes his at *NA*, p. 46); Sidney Parker drives a tandem.

Mrs. Dashwood's "furniture was all sent round by water" (*SS*, p. 26) when she moves house from Sussex to Devonshire. Mary Crawford's harp has to be fetched from Northampton in Henry's barouche; it is not conveyed "by a waggon or cart . . . I might as well have asked for porters and a hand-barrow" (*MP*, p. 58). Mr. Elton's trunk is "lifted into the butcher's cart, which was to convey it to where the coaches past" (*E*, p. 186), there being no "run on the road" or regular coach stop at Highbury. Wagons are used for bulky goods; Anne Elliot has to repack on leaving Kellynch because she has not "understood in time what was intended as to the waggons" (*P*, p. 39). When Elizabeth leaves Hunsford, the "trunks were fastened on, the parcels placed within" (*PP*, p. 216), one of the few times we learn how the luggage travels.

Bibliography

FELTON, WILLIAM. *A Treatise on Carriages*, 2 vols. (London, 1794–95), printed for the author.

MACKINNON, SIR FRANK D. "Topography and Travel in Jane Austen's Novels," *Cornhill Magazine*, n.s. 59 (1925), 184–99; reprinted in his *The Murder in the Temple and Other Holiday Tasks* (London, 1935), 86–109.

MCCAUSLAND, HUGH. *The English Carriage* (London, 1948).

STRATTON, EZRA. *The World on Wheels; or, Carriages* (New York, 1878), published by the author.

VERSES

David Gilson

George Henry Lewes wrote to Charlotte Brontë in January 1848: "Miss Austen is not a poetess... has... none of the ravishing enthusiasm of poetry," to which Charlotte Brontë retorted on January 18, 1848: "Can there be a great artist without poetry?" (Southam, p. 127). Richard Simpson suggested in 1870 (ibid., p. 243) that Jane Austen deserves the title of "a prose Shakespeare.... Within her range her characterization is truly Shakespearian; but she has scarcely a spark of poetry," while George Whalley's article "Jane Austen: Poet" sees the novelist as a poet primarily "in her craftsmanship in language." James Edward Austen-Leigh's *Memoir* of his aunt notes: "Among her favourite writers, Johnson in prose, Crabbe in verse, and Cowper in both, stood high" (p. 89), and the prosaic nature of the verses of the last two writers is reflected in Jane Austen's own few surviving writings in verse form.

Jane Austen wrote in verse at all periods of her life, largely for amusement or entertainment; occasional verses appear in the *juvenilia*, composed 1787–1793 (*Minor Works*, pp. 5, 9, 10, 34, 50, 74–75, and 174), but the majority of surviving verse pieces must be dated between 1800 and 1817, and of most of them autograph manuscripts are extant (see my article "Jane Austen's Verses," *The Book Collector*, 33 (1984), 25–37, which describes these manuscripts and gives their whereabouts, with textual variants). Apart from one letter in verse (to Francis Austen from Chawton, July 26, 1809) the texts of the verses are given in *Minor Works* (pp. 440–52).

The longest verse piece is also the most serious, thirteen quatrains written in 1808 in memory of the novelist's friend Mrs. Anne Lefroy, beginning, "The day returns again, my natal day," a passionless tribute in the eighteenth-century manner.

Other pieces were written for friends: "Verses Given with a Needlework Bag" to Mary Lloyd in 1792, two quatrains; "Lines to Martha Lloyd," Mary's sister, 1806, three quatrains printed in *Minor Works* (the full text has eleven); and "To Miss Bigg with some Pockethandkerchiefs" 1808, four lines (and an alternative version, eight lines).

The remaining pieces seem to have been written for amusement only, some focusing on events or persons of national or local importance: "Mock Panegyric on a Young Friend," seven quatrains; "Mr. Gell and Miss Gill," 1811, two quatrains; "A Middle-aged Flirt," 1812, four lines; "Verses to Rhyme with 'Rose'," after 1802, twelve lines; "On Sir Home Popham's Sentence," 1807, eight lines; "On a Headache," 1811, five six-line stanzas;

VERSES

"Lines on Maria Beckford," 1811, four quatrains; "I am in a Dilemma" and "On the Weald of Kent Canal Bill," 1811, a couplet and six lines; "Charades," three quatrains; and "Venta" (or "Winchester Verses"), 1817, six quatrains.

Bibliography

SOUTHAM, B. C., ed. *Jane Austen: The Critical Heritage* (London and New York, 1968).
WHALLEY, GEORGE. "Jane Austen: Poet," in Juliet McMaster, ed., *Jane Austen's Achievement* (London, 1976), 106–33.

THE WATSONS

David Hopkinson

Among Jane Austen's unsuccessful attempts to create a novel acceptable to a publisher was a work probably begun late in 1804, when she was living at Bath. She wrote about seventeen thousand words and then broke off forever. Her manuscript, though much corrected, clearly stands in need of further revision. The same little town, for instance, around which the action centers is first described as D and later as R. Her heroine was called Emma Watson, and within a short space of time she has won our sympathy and respect, if not our affection. But then few readers can have fallen in love with Anne Elliot at first sight. Other characters in the fragment make their mark immediately as we are introduced to them at home in the evenings or at a ball in the Surrey town of D. We look forward to an extension of this first acquaintance. Indeed, this projected novel seems as much capable of being molded into a product satisfactory to Jane Austen herself as was *First Impressions, Susan,* or *Elinor and Marianne.*

The manuscript was given no title, and yet it must frequently have been referred to in conversation between the Austen sisters. Perhaps it was known to them as *Emma* until that title was appropriated for another story, or perhaps as *The Younger Sister,* a title that Cassandra is supposed to have passed on to their niece Catherine, who was later to use it for her own novel about the Watson family. Later still, the fragment itself received its first publication, appended to the second edition of Austen-Leigh's *Memoir* under a title perhaps chosen because *Persuasion* had first been known to the family as *The Elliots.*

Critics and close readers have often commented on a progressive development in Jane Austen's work from frivolous irony and satirical burlesque through lighthearted comedy of morals and manners to more penetrating studies of human nature, where not just selfishness and vanity but malevolence and rapacity are displayed and where distinctions of sex, class, wealth, and education exert deeper and more complex influences on human behavior and interaction than in the earlier novels. *The Watsons* comes at a nodal point in its author's development. It is the one extant fresh product of otherwise barren years. From the period in which it was written only one of Jane Austen's letters has survived. But we know that she worked in 1803 on the preparation of *Susan* (later *Northanger Abbey*) for submission to a publisher and that *Elinor and Marianne* (converted into *Sense and Sensibility*), her first published novel, appeared late in 1811.

From then on she worked steadily at Chawton on a sequence of successful new creations. But this leaves a gap of about nine years in which there is no novel writing in evidence except this one abortive fragment, which starts with such a tingling burst of creative energy. When *Pride and Prejudice* was published some fifteen years after its conception, she referred to it as "my own darling child" (*Letters*, January 29, 1813). Of *Sense and Sensibility* she wrote, "No indeed, ... I can no more forget it, than a mother can forget her sucking child" (April 25, 1811). It seems extraordinary, therefore, that any work of her imagination should have suffered the fate of *The Watsons*, turned adrift to become a foundling. But abandoned it was and abandoned forever, though not by Cassandra or by their dear friend Martha Lloyd, another enthusiastic reader of Jane Austen's early work. Cassandra, and eventually Cassandra's nieces, became as familiar with this story, due to end with the marriage of Emma Watson and Mr. Howard, as they were with the story of Fanny Price or of Catherine Morland.

The manuscript is not divided into chapters. It contains conversations between two sisters, short scenes of preparation for coming events, and two set pieces in which the principal characters are grouped together, first at a ball and somewhat later at an informal evening party in the modest home of the Watson family. The pace is notably brisk, and the characters are drawn with broad strokes. The heroine, as in other Jane Austen novels, is in some degree alienated from her large and initially scattered family, which includes a cold, calculating lawyer brother with a very unamiable wife.

Here, as in *Emma* and *Pride and Prejudice*, encounters in the ballroom are clearly to have a significant impact on several lives. Fuses are lit, and we perceive anxieties and events of moment to come. Swiftly and with precision the world of the Watson family is mapped, and we find Emma, the youngest sister, at odds with it. But she behaves with spirit. Of her own deportment at a ball Jane Austen once wrote, "I am almost afraid to tell you how my Irish friend and I behaved.... I *can* expose myself, however, only *once more*, because he leaves the country soon after next Friday, on which day we *are* to have a dance at Ashe after all" (*Letters*, January 9, 1796). Emma Watson's background, temperament, character, and outlook are exposed for our admiration in one of those ballroom scenes in which Jane Austen delighted.

The ball at D also affords the opportunity for other principal characters to expose themselves: Tom Musgrave, a squireen out to cut a dash on a fortune of eight or nine hundred per annum; Lord Osborne, whose social position entitles him to submit young girls he fancies to a continuous, unsmiling stare; his stately handsome mother, insensitive sister, and their clergyman companion immediately recognizable to anyone familiar with Henry Tilney.

But it is not Lord Osborne with whom Emma dances, although he is quick to demand an introduction to her from his toady, Tom Musgrave. By then Emma has found occasion to act with confidence and courage. The decisive incident of *The Watsons* has taken place before she has been in the room for more than a few minutes. We are told that Miss Osborne has promised the first two dances to the clergyman's young nephew, uncommonly fond of dancing for a boy of his age and confident that they will dance down every couple on the floor. This engagement is cruelly broken, and it is Emma who steps in, perceiving the boy's change of expression from a happiness that had caught her interest to a mortification that does more than that; it brings her sympathy to the point of action.

There is no small boy in Jane Austen's works as important as Charles Blake, and nowhere does she get a fleeting moment more precisely right. She converts his and Emma's isolation into "a Partnership which c^d not be noticed without surprise. It gained her a broad stare from Miss Osborne.... 'Upon my word Charles you are in luck,' [she said], 'you have got a better partner than me'—to which the happy Charles answered 'Yes'" (p. 331). The plain truth of the matter has been stated in a single syllable.

Emma's mettle has been tested and found sterling stuff. She has now to face confusing and exacting new conditions due to a sudden translation from surroundings of wealth, affection, and good taste to an impoverished household where ill-educated, husband-hunting sisters live with a querulous invalid father and only two servants. Such a metamorphosis might well lead her into resentment and self-pity. A fine display of the novelist's art is required if our sympathy and affection for a heroine so placed is to grow; for she is a Fanny Price in reverse, a girl who proceeds from riches to rags instead of rags to riches. Fanny's timid, nearly tepid, goodness forfeits some of our regard, and Emma's firm, perhaps censorious, good sense runs a similar risk. Emma is sensitive and fastidious; her sister Elizabeth seems on occasion more practical and more realistic. Was Emma Watson, we wonder, to run into the same problems as Emma Woodhouse through discriminating too much in favor of wealth and refinement against simple homely values?

On the contrary, there are clear differences between Jane Austen's two Emmas, not only of situation—for one is rich and secure, the other poor and vulnerable—but of character. Emma Watson has a mind of her own and the intelligence to speak it, but she is without vanity. She is honest with herself. We guess that her judgments are to be relied on. Her sister impatiently demands, "'I should like to know the Man you *do* think agreable.' 'His name is Howard.' 'Howard! Dear me. I cannot think of *him*, but as playing cards with Ly Osborne, & looking proud'" (p. 343). Emma knows differently.

Howard himself has not a single line of direct speech. Introduced to Emma at the ball, he engages her for two dances. The only unpleasant part of that engagement lay in Lord Osborne's insistence on being continually at his elbow during the dances. "The two dances seemed very short, & she had her partner's authority for considering them so" (p. 335). Three days later ("Here's an unaccountable Honour" cries Elizabeth, p. 347) Musgrove and Lord Osborne call, but not Mr. Howard. Perhaps, Emma hopefully reflects, he had wanted no part in an action "which carried quite as much Impertinence in it's form as Goodbreeding" (p. 348).

Mr. Watson is an invalid more seriously affected by ill health than Mr. Woodhouse. When Tom Musgrove pays his next visit, he introduces the fashionable game of speculation and chatters away about the Osborne circle and the attention that Emma has attracted there. "Says Howard to Ld Osborne . . ." he begins, developing this theme, but is cut off to settle a disputed point in the new card game, to Emma's sad disappointment (p. 359). She is a modest, sensible girl but not without curiosity. More light is thrown on Mr. Howard's character when Mr. Watson describes the fine delivery of his excellent sermon, his reading of the service "without any Theatrical grimace," and his care for a gouty invalid over negotiating a flight of steps (p. 343).

The reader is now eagerly awaiting the first conversation to be recorded between Emma and the man in whom her interest has been aroused. Under what circumstances will it arise? Not, we learn, from an invitation to the Castle, for Mr. Watson was indignant at such a suggestion after the fourteen years of Emma's absence in which the Osbornes had not noticed any of his family. But that is all we do learn.

As the manuscript ends, Emma's cheerful disposition is severely tested. She is out of tune with the rest of the family to the same degree as Fanny Price at Mansfield Park, but for reasons similar to those that at first made Fanny's return to the paternal home at Portsmouth so trying. To avoid the rest of the family by sitting out every evening in silence, or in gentle conversation with her bedridden father, has become the most satisfying element in her day.

In a situation as incongruous as that of Fanny Price, with a brother and two of her three sisters every bit as incompatible as the younger sisters of Elizabeth Bennet, Emma Watson remains, like Emma Woodhouse, a devoted daughter, but unlike Mr. Woodhouse, there can be no question of his consent to her marriage, for according to Cassandra, Mr. Watson will be dead before that happy event is even contemplated. Humiliation is inflicted on Emma Woodhouse eventually, but Emma Watson, we realize, must meet continuous humiliation throughout her story until that transcendent moment when Mr. Howard declares his love. She has nothing but her own resources with which to counter the crude selfishness of her sister

Margaret, the mercenary patronage of her brother and his vulgar wife, the jealous contempt of Lady Osborne and her daughter, and the unacceptable attentions of the boorish lordling. She is to be scarred in her struggle, as was Fanny Price. Like Jane Fairfax, she may face the disagreeable prospect of going out to work as a governess and remaining unmarried. "It is very bad to grow old & be poor & laughed at," as her sister Elizabeth remarks (p. 317). Clearly, *The Watsons* was not intended to be a light comedy but a novel about honest simplicity and pretentious grandeur, respectable poverty and corrupting wealth, above all about the employment in any society of intelligence and good taste.

And so why cannot we read on to a conclusion so easily foreseen? To answer this question, it is first necessary to reach a more precise conclusion about the date of the fragment's composition. From the watermark we know that this cannot have been before 1803, but in the early part of that year Jane Austen was working on *Northanger Abbey*. It is likely therefore that *The Watsons* was begun in 1804, and perhaps later in that year because in September Jane wrote to Cassandra about a ball she had attended while staying at Lyme Regis. She described the strange behavior of a young man who was the son of an Irish viscount. I believe she drew on this experience for the ballroom behavior of the Osbornes. She may also have based the character of Emma Watson's friend Mary Edwards on that of a new friend she herself had made at Lyme.

In December her twenty-ninth birthday came around, and it was marked by a bitter blow, the sudden tragic death of her greatest friend, Mrs. Lefroy. This was soon followed by the death of her father. She now faced a future uncertain and insecure. It rested with the Austen brothers to provide a home for their mother and unmarried sisters. Her own situation had become too sadly similar to that in which the further development of her novel was to place the Watson family.

It was suggested by James Edward Austen-Leigh that Jane Austen gave up because she had no wish to continue with a family that, presumably like the Bennets, was insufficiently refined. It may be, as Margaret Drabble has suggested, that she felt herself to be writing a book too much like *Pride and Prejudice*. But it is surely more interesting and more profitable to look toward the future rather than to the past. And in the future came her masterpieces, *Mansfield Park* and *Emma*. So Emma Watson, though cut off in her prime, seems not to have been created in vain; the predicaments of her life are those of others to come after her; her modest loyalty, her flashing wit, and her beauty are subsumed into the characters of the great Austen heroines whose completed life cycles lie ahead.

A DICTIONARY OF JANE AUSTEN'S LIFE AND WORKS

H. Abigail Bok

The following comprehensive list, with identifications and citations, is drawn from the complete canon of Jane Austen's works and letters as they are available in print today. Included from her literary oeuvre—comprising the novels, the minor works, and the play *Sir Charles Grandison*—are (1) all the characters, (2) every place mentioned, real or imaginary, and (3) all known literary allusions. In addition, (4) all known literary allusions in her letters, (5) the members of her family and important friends, and (6) many of the places she lived in or visited are cited and defined. Finally: (7) some of Jane Austen's more famous quotations appear.

The purpose of this dictionary is to provide a handy reference tool for making identifications and finding items in the works. Much of the information included herein is drawn from the appendixes to R. W. Chapman's standard editions, and assistance was also provided by G. L. Apperson's *Jane Austen Dictionary* (1932). The quotations are drawn from the standard Oxford editions of her literary works and letters, abbreviated as follows:

from *Minor Works*, ed. R. W. Chapman, rev. ed. by B. C. Southham (rev. ed. London, 1969), by page number:

Vol. 1	Volume the First
Vol. 2	Volume the Second
Vol. 3	Volume the Third
LS	Lady Susan
W	The Watsons
S	Sanditon
Verses	collected poems
SS	*Sense and Sensibility*, ed. R. W. Chapman, 3rd ed. (Oxford, 1933); by volume number (arabic) and chapter number (roman)
PP	*Pride and Prejudice*, ed. R. W. Chapman, 3rd ed. (Oxford, 1932); by volume number (arabic) and chapter number (roman)
MP	*Mansfield Park*, ed. R. W. Chapman, 3rd ed. (Oxford, 1934); by volume number (arabic) and chapter number (roman)

E	*Emma*, ed. R. W. Chapman, 3rd ed. (Oxford, 1933); by volume number (arabic) and chapter number (roman)

from *Northanger Abbey and Persuasion*, ed. R. W. Chapman, 3rd ed. (Oxford, 1933); by volume number (arabic) and chapter number (roman):

NA	*Northanger Abbey*
P	*Persuasion*
CG	*Sir Charles Grandison*, ed. Brian Southam (Oxford, 1981); by act number (capital roman) and scene number (lowercase roman)
Letters	*Jane Austen's Letters*, ed. R. W. Chapman, 2nd ed. (London, 1952); by page number

A. F., initials of an unnamed correspondent in the first of "A Collection of Letters" (*Vol. 2*, p. 152).

ABBEY SCHOOL, Reading, where Jane Austen studied for a short time, around 1784; she had also briefly attended schools in Oxford and Southampton in 1783. Afterward, she was educated at home.

ABBEYLAND, THE, near Barton, where one of Sir John Middleton's plantations is located (*SS*, 3.X).

ABBEY-MILL FARM, home of the Martins, in Donwell parish, with a "broad, neat gravel-walk, which led between espalier apple-trees to the front door" (*E*, 2.V).

ABBOTT, Misses, two pupils at Mrs. Goddard's school in Highbury (*E*, 1.IX).

ABDY, JOHN, a poor, bedridden old man who had been clerk for twenty-seven years to Mrs. Bates's deceased husband, the Reverend Dr. Bates; his son John, the head man and ostler at the Crown, is also mentioned (*E*, 3.VIII).

ABERDEEN, mentioned several times in "Lesley Castle": Mr. Lesley owns an estate nearby (*Vol. 2*, p. 118).

ACCOMPLISHMENTS: Lady Susan believes that it is important to have grace and manner; but she doesn't advocate "the prevailing fashion of acquiring a perfect knowledge in all the Languages Arts & Sciences; it is throwing time away; to be Mistress of French, Italian, German, Music, Singing, Drawing &c. will gain a Woman some applause, but will not add one Lover to her list" (*LS*, p. 253).

ADAMS, CHARLES, "an amiable, accomplished & bewitching young Man; of so dazzling a Beauty that none but Eagles could look him in the Face"—"Jack & Alice" (*Vol. 1*, p. 13).

ADDRESS TO TOBACCO. See Browne, Isaac Hawkins.

ADELAIDE AND THEODORE. See Genlis, Mme. de.

ADLESTROP, Glos., where Jane Austen's great-grandfather Leigh and some of his descendants lived; Thomas Leigh (d. 1813) was rector there.

ADMIRALTY, THE (offices from which the business of the navy is conducted, situated in Whitehall, next to the Horse Guards): according to Captain Wentworth, they "'entertain themselves now and then, with sending a few hundred men to sea, in a ship not fit to be employed'" (*P*, 3.VIII).

"ADVENTURES OF MR. HARLEY, THE," a "short, but interesting Tale" dedicated to Jane Austen's brother Francis William (*Vol. 1*, p. 40).

AGATHA (1), youngest daughter of Lord St. Clair and mother of the disreputable Gustavus—"Love and Freindship" (*Vol. 2*, p. 92).

AGATHA (2), a character in Mrs. Inchbald's *Lovers' Vows*, to be played at Mansfield by Maria Bertram (*MP*, 1.XIV).

AGINCOURT, BATTLE OF (October 25, 1415): "His Majesty [Henry V] then turned his thoughts to France, where he went & fought the famous Battle of Agincourt"—"The History of England" (*Vol. 2*, p. 139).

AGRICOLA (Cneius Julius Agricola, A.D. ca. 40–93), Roman general who conquered Britain, mentioned by Eleanor Tilney (*NA*, 1. XIV).

AGRICULTURAL REPORTS (short title of *General Reviews of the Agriculture of the County of Surrey*, by William Stevenson, 1809–13), the favorite reading matter of Robert Martin (*E*, 1.IV).

ALBION PLACE, Ramsgate, the address of the Sneyds, friends of Tom Bertram (*MP*, 1.V).

ALFRED THE GREAT (849–901), king of the West Saxons, mentioned by Eleanor Tilney (*NA*, 1.XIV).

ALICE: Eleanor Tilney asks Catherine Morland to write her telling of her safe journey, "'under cover to Alice,'" who must be either Eleanor's maidservant or a daughter of Lord Longtown (*NA*, 2.XIII).

ALICIA, LADY, an acquaintance of Lady Russell in Bath; she particularly admires the curtains in a window in Pulteney St. (*P*, 4.VII).

ALICIA DE LACY. See **West, (Mrs.) Jane.**

ALLEN, MR., "a sensible, intelligent man," the principal landowner around Fullerton, who had to go to Bath for his gout (*NA*, 1.II).

ALLEN, MRS., who invites Catherine Morland to accompany her and her husband to Bath: "She had neither beauty, genius, accomplishment, nor manner. The air of a gentlewoman, a great deal of quiet, inactive good temper, and a trifling turn of mind, were all that could account for her being the choice of . . . Mr. Allen" (*NA*, 1.II).

ALLENHAM, Devon., a hamlet in the valley adjacent to Barton, where Mrs. Smith (1) lives (*SS*, 1.IX).

ALLENHAM COURT (also called Allenham House), Mrs. Smith (1)'s house, "an ancient respectable looking mansion" (*SS*, 1.IX).

ALMANE, LA BARONNE D', a character in Mme. de Genlis's *Adelaide and Theodore*, mentioned by Emma Woodhouse (*E*, 3.XVII).

ALPHONSINE: OR MATERNAL AFFECTION. See **Genlis, Mme. de.**

ALPS, THE: of "the Alps and Pyrenees, with their pine forests and their vices, [Mrs. Radcliffe's works] might give a faithful delineation" (*NA*, 2.X).

ALTON, Hants., neighboring village to Chawton; Jane Austen often walked there to do errands and to visit friends.

AMELIA, a character in Mrs. Inchbald's *Lovers' Vows*, to be played at Mansfield by Mary Crawford (*MP*, 1.XIV).

"AMELIA WEBSTER," a short epistolary tale dedicated to Jane Austen's mother (*Vol. 1*, p. 47).

AMERICA: Tom Bertram alludes to "a strange business" in America—possibly referring to the War of 1812 (*MP*, 1.XII).

AMYATT, LORD AND LADY, exalted relatives of the Reverend Dudley of Chetwynde—"Catharine or the Bower" (*Vol. 3*, p. 204).

ANDERSON, MISS, a sister of Charles Anderson whom Tom Bertram first met when she was not out (*MP*, 1.V).

ANDERSON, CHARLES, of Baker St., a crony of Tom Bertram (*MP*, 1.V).

ANDREW, a purveyor of vegetables and fruits in Sanditon, possibly employed by Lady Denham (*S*, p. 382).

ANDREWS, MISS, a young lady from the neighborhood of Putney, devoted to horrid novels: "'a sweet girl, one of the sweetest creatures in the world,'" but "'amazingly insipid,'" according to Isabella Thorpe (*NA*, 1.VI).

ANHALT, the character of a clergyman in Mrs. Inchbald's *Lovers Vows*, to be played at Mansfield by Edmund Bertram (*MP*, 1.XIV).

ANNA (1) "is always recurring to the pleasures we once enjoyed when Melissa was well"—"A Fragment written to inculate the practice of Virtue" (*Vol. 1*, p. 72).

ANNA (2), subject of a "Mock Panegyric": "her mind is unconfined / Like any vast savannah" (*Verses*, p. 442); this is probably Jane Elizabeth Austen.

ANNE, the addressee of a letter from Georgiana Stanhope in the epistolary tale "The Three Sisters" (*Vol. 1*, p. 60).

ANNE (NANNY), a servant in the Percivals' house at Chetwynde—"Catharine or the Bower" (*Vol. 3*, p. 213).

ANNE OF DENMARK (1574–1619), James I's queen consort—"The History of England" (*Vol. 2*, p. 147).

ANNESLEY, ADMIRAL, deceased, father of "Miss Jane," in the second of "A Collection of Letters" (*Vol. 2*, p. 154).

ANNESLEY, MRS., Miss Darcy's companion, "a genteel, agreeable-looking woman, whose endeavor to introduce some kind of discourse, proved her to be more truly well bred" than either Miss Bingley or Mrs. Hurst (*PP*, 3.III).

ANNESLEY, MISS JANE: "'She is now about 35, & in spite of sickness, Sorrow and Time is more blooming than I ever saw a Girl of 17'"—the second of "A Collection of Letters" (*Vol. 2*, p. 152).

ANTIGUA, where Sir Thomas Bertram has an estate; he had to spend two years there to get it running profitably (*MP*, 1.III).

ANTIQUARY, THE. See **Scott, Sir Walter**.

ANTWERP, the ship on which William Price was a midshipman (*MP*, 1.XI).

ARABELLA, one of the party entertained by Wilhelminus under tents near the cottage he leased in Pembrokeshire—"Scraps" (*Vol. 2*, p. 177).

ARABIAN NIGHTS ENTERTAINMENTS, translated from the French of M. Galland, 12 vols. in 6 (1728–38), many subsequent editions: (*a*) fourth volume mentioned by Mary Stanhope (erased in the manuscript)—"The Three Sisters" (*Vol. 1*, p. 65); (*b*) "the Sultaness Scheherazade" is mentioned (*P*, 4.XI).

ARBLAY, MME. D'. See **Burney, Frances**.

ARGYLE BUILDINGS, Bath, just below Laura Place, is mentioned (*NA*, 1.XI).

ARNE, THOMAS A. (1710–78), composer: *Artaxerxes* (first produced in London, 1762), a three-act opera, the libretto being a translation of Metastasio's *Arteserse*: Jane Austen saw it in London on March 5, 1814 (*Letters*, p. 384).

ARTAXERXES. See **Arne, Thomas A.**

ARTHUR FITZ-ALBINI. See **Brydges, Sir Egerton.**

ARUNDEL, MISS. See **Mountague, Lady (1).**

ASHBURNHAM, MR., a gentleman who gave a private ball attended by "a young Lady in distress'd Circumstances" (Maria Williams)—"A Collection of Letters" (*Vol. 2*, p. 155).

ASHBURNHAM, the seat of Mr. Ashburnham—"A Collection of Letters" (*Vol. 2*, p. 157).

ASHE, Hants., a village adjacent to Steventon where Isaac Peter George Lefroy was rector.

ASHWORTH, one of the houses Mrs. Bennet considers for Mr. Wickham and Lydia; she rejects it because it is too far from Longbourn (*PP*, 3.VIII).

ASIA MINOR: the ten-year-old Fanny Price is ridiculed by her female cousins for never having heard of it (*MP*, 1.II).

ASP, a sloop, Captain Wentworth's first command: "'Quite worn out and broken up'" (*P*, 3.VIII).

ASTLEY'S (Astley's Royal Amphitheatre, Lambeth), an early circus in London, founded by Philip Astley (1742–1814), with equestrian exhibitions; it was attended by the John Knightleys, their children, Harriet Smith, and Robert Martin (*E*, 3.XVIII).

ATKINSON, MISS, an acquaintance of the Wallises who admires Mr. Elliot (*P*, 4.VII).

ATLANTIC OCEAN: (*a*) Henry Crawford wishes that "a steady wind, or a calm" on the Atlantic might have delayed Sir Thomas Bertram's passage from Antigua (*MP*, 2.V); (*b*) Mrs. Croft has crossed it four times (*P*, 3.VIII).

AUGUSTA, a young lady about to make her "appearance in the World"—"A Collection of Letters" (*Vol. 2*, p. 150).

AUGUSTA. See also **Barlow, Augusta; Lindsay, Augusta.**

AUGUSTUS, a friend of Edward Lindsay's living at M—— who extends hospitality to Laura and Edward after their elopement—"Love and Freindship" (*Vol. 2*, p. 86).

AUSTEN, ANNA. See **Austen, Jane Anna Elizabeth.**

AUSTEN, ANNE (née Mathew, d. 1795): first wife of Jane Austen's eldest brother, James; she was the daughter of General and Lady Jane Mathew and the mother of Jane Anna Elizabeth Austen.

AUSTEN, CAROLINE MARY CRAVEN (1805–80), daughter of James Austen and his second wife, Mary Lloyd; she helped her brother James Edward Austen-Leigh with the *Memoir*.

AUSTEN, CASSANDRA (1) (née Leigh, 1739–1827), daughter of the Reverend Thomas Leigh of Harpsden, married to the Reverend George Austen in 1764; the mother of Jane Austen. "Amelia Webster" (*Vol. 1*, p. 47) is dedicated to her.

AUSTEN, CASSANDRA (2) ELIZABETH (1773–1845), Jane Austen's sister. In 1797 she was engaged to a clergyman, Thomas Fowle, who died of yellow fever in the West Indies that same year. Of the *juvenilia*, "The Beautifull Cassandra"

(*Vol. 1*, p. 44), "Ode to Pity" (*Vol. 1*, p. 74), "The History of England" (*Vol. 2*, p. 138), and "Catharine or the Bower" (*Vol. 3*, p. 192) are dedicated to her.

AUSTEN, CHARLES JOHN (1779–1852), later admiral, Jane Austen's youngest brother. He married Frances Fitzwilliam Palmer in 1807 (three daughters) and her sister Harriet in 1820 (three sons and one daughter). "Sir William Mountague" (*Vol. 1*, p. 40) and "Memoirs of Mr. Clifford" (*Vol. 1*, p. 42) are dedicated to him.

AUSTEN (KNIGHT), EDWARD (1767–1852), Jane Austen's third brother: he was adopted by Thomas and Catherine (Knatchbull) Knight of Godmersham etc., and married Elizabeth Bridges in 1791 (six sons and five daughters). "The Three Sisters" (*Vol. 1*, p. 57) is dedicated to him.

AUSTEN, ELEANOR (née Jackson), second wife of the Reverend Henry Thomas Austen.

AUSTEN, ELIZA (née Hancock, 1761–1813), cousin of the Austens and first wife of Henry Thomas, Jane Austen's fourth brother. Her first husband had been Jean Capotte, comte de Feuillide, who was guillotined during the French Revolution. "Love and Freindship" (*Vol. 2*, p. 76) is dedicated to her.

AUSTEN (KNIGHT), ELIZABETH (née Bridges, 1773–1808), wife of Edward Austen Knight and daughter of Sir Brook Bridges of Goodnestone, Kent.

AUSTEN (KNIGHT), FANNY CATHERINE (1793–1882), daughter of Edward Austen Knight; in 1820 she married Sir Edward Knatchbull. "Scraps" (*Vol. 2*, p. 170) is dedicated to her.

AUSTEN, FRANCES FITZWILLIAM (née Palmer, 1790–1814), first wife of Charles John Austen.

AUSTEN, FRANCIS, Jane Austen's great-uncle. He cared for her father when the latter was orphaned at the age of nine; his wife, Jane, was Jane Austen's godmother.

AUSTEN, FRANCIS WILLIAM (1774–1865), later Admiral Sir, Jane Austen's fifth brother. He married Mary Gibson in 1806 (six sons and five daughters) and Martha Lloyd in 1828. "Jack & Alice" (*Vol. 1*, p. 12) and "The Adventures of Mr. Harley" (*Vol. 1*, p. 40) are dedicated to him.

AUSTEN, GEORGE (1) (1731–1805), Jane Austen's father, a clergyman, rector of Steventon (1761–1801) and of Deane (1773–1801). In 1764 he married Cassandra Leigh (six sons and two daughters). "The Mystery" (*Vol. 1*, p. 55) is dedicated to him.

AUSTEN, GEORGE (2) (1766–1838), Jane Austen's second brother, apparently retarded or severely handicapped, since he never joined the family circle.

AUSTEN, HARRIET (née Palmer), second wife of Charles John Austen.

AUSTEN, HENRY THOMAS (1771–1850), Jane Austen's fourth and favorite brother. He held various professions, eventually taking orders in 1816. In 1797 he married Eliza (Hancock) de Feuillide, and in 1820, Eleanor Jackson. "Lesley Castle" (*Vol. 2*, p. 109) is dedicated to him.

AUSTEN, JAMES (1765–1819), Jane Austen's eldest brother, a clergyman. He married Anne Mathew in 1792 (one daughter) and Mary Lloyd in 1797 (one son and one daughter). "The Visit" (*Vol. 1*, p. 49) is dedicated to him.

AUSTEN, JANE. See p. 279.

AUSTEN, JANE ANNA ELIZABETH (1793–1872), daughter of James Austen and his first wife, Anne (Mathew); she married Ben Lefroy in 1814. "A Fragment written to inculcate the practise of Virtue" (*Vol. 1*, p. 71) is dedicated to her.

AUSTEN, MARTHA (née Lloyd, d. 1843), daughter of the Reverend Nowes Lloyd and second wife of Francis William Austen. One of Jane Austen's poems is directed to her (*Verses*, p. 445).

AUSTEN, MARY (1) (née Gibson, d. 1823), eldest daughter of John Gibson and first wife of Francis William Austen.

AUSTEN, MARY (2) (née Lloyd, d. 1843), daughter of the Reverend Nowes Lloyd and second wife of James Austen. She is the object of the "Verses given with a Needlework bag to Mrs. James Austen" (*Verses*, p. 444).

AUSTEN, PHILADELPHIA (d. 1791/2), Jane Austen's aunt, the sister of George Austen. She married a surgeon, Mr. Hancock (d. 1775); her daughter was Eliza (Hancock de Feuillide) Austen.

AUSTEN(-LEIGH), JAMES EDWARD (1798–1874), clergyman, son of James and Mary Austen, and author of the *Memoir*. In 1837 he changed his name to Austen-Leigh, after he became the heir of the Leigh Perrots.

AVIGNON, where Colonel Brandon's sister is staying for her health (*SS*, 1.XIII).

AWBERRY, MRS., Sir Hargrave Pollexfen's accomplice in the abduction of Harriet Byron (*CG*, II i).

AWBERRY, DEBORAH and **SALLY**, Mrs. Awberry's daughters (*CG*, II i).

AYLMERS, "a family of lively, agreeable manners, and probably of morals and discretion to suit," whom Maria Rushworth visits in Twickenham (*MP*, 3.XVI).

BADDELEY (also Baddly), the butler at Mansfield Park (*MP*, 2.I).

BAHAMA, which sailing people do not call the West Indies, according to Mrs. Croft (*P*, 3.VIII).

BAKER ST., London, where the Andersons live (*MP*, 1.V).

BAKEWELL, Derbys., not far from Pemberley, is one of the stages of the Gardiners' journey (*PP*, 3.I).

BALDWIN, ADMIRAL, according to Sir Walter Elliot "'the most deplorable looking personage you can imagine, his face the colour of mahogany, rough and rugged to the last degree, all lines and wrinkles, nine grey hairs of a side, and nothing but a dab of powder at top'" (*P*, 3.III).

BALYCRAIG (also Baly-craig), the Dixons' seat in Ireland (*E*, 2.I).

BANBURY, Oxon., a stage in Henry Crawford's journey from Mansfield to Bath (*MP*, 2.II).

BANK (the Bank of England, Threadneedle St., London), built by Sir John Soane starting in 1788: it is mentioned by Henry Tilney (*NA*, 1.XIV).

BAR, BENJAMIN, the clandestine correspondent of Miss Sally Hervey —"Amelia Webster" (*Vol. 1*, p. 48).

BARETTI, JOSEPH (1719–89), travel writer: Jane Austen mentions *An Account of the Manners and Customs of Italy* (1768), in which Baretti is "dreadfully abusive of poor Mr. Sharpe" (*Letters*, p. 185). See also **Sharp, Samuel**.

BARKER. See **Barlow**.

BARLOW, AUGUSTA (also called Barker), an acquaintance of Camilla Stanley, she is described as a sweet girl, although her hair is too dark—"Catharine or the Bower" (*Vol. 3*, p. 204).

BARLOW, SIR PETER, an acquaintance of Camilla Stanley, he "is *always* laid up with the Gout, which is exceedingly disagreeable to the Family"—"Catharine or the Bower" (*Vol. 3*, p. 204).

BARNET, suburb of London where Colonel Forster made inquiries, without success, for the fugitives Wickham and Lydia (*PP*, 3.IV).

"BARONETAGE," Sir Walter Elliot's Bible (*P*, 3.I): the book Jane Austen had in mind may have been J. Debrett, *Baronetage of England*, 2 vols. (London, 1808).

BARRETT, EATON STANNARD (1786–1820), novelist: Jane Austen read *The Heroine, or Adventures of a Fair Romance Reader* (1813) in March 1814 "and was very much amused by it" (*Letters*, p. 376).

BARROW, SIR JOHN (1764–1848), editor of Lord Macartney's *Journal of the Embassy to China* (1807), is mentioned (*Letters*, p. 294).

BARTLETT'S BUILDINGS, Holborn, where the two Misses Steele stay with their cousins in London; an unfashionable part of town (*SS*, 2.X).

BARTON, Devon, a village four miles north of Exeter, "a pleasant fertile spot, well wooded, and rich in pasture" (*SS*, 1.VI).

BARTON COTTAGE, "though small, was comfortable and compact; but as a cottage it was defective, for the building was regular, the roof was tiled, the window shutters were not painted green, nor were the walls covered with honeysuckles": in these unromantic surroundings Mrs. Dashwood and her daughters are forced to live after the death of Mr. Henry Dashwood (*SS*, 1.VI).

BARTON CROSS, Devon, near Barton, where one of Sir John Middleton's plantations is located (*SS*, 3.X).

BARTON PARK, Devon, the seat of Sir John and Lady Middleton; "the house was large and handsome" (*SS*, 1.VII).

BASINGSTOKE, Hants., (*a*) where Jane and Cassandra Austen often danced at the monthly assemblies; (*b*) one of the stages in Mr. Clifford's journey from Overton to "Mr. Robins's"—"Memoirs of Mr. Clifford" (*Vol. 1*, p. 44).

BATES, MRS., "the widow of a former vicar of Highbury, was a very old lady, almost past every thing but tea and quadrille" (*E*, 1.III).

BATES, (MISS) HETTY, Mrs. Bates's garrulous daughter, who "enjoyed a most uncommon degree of popularity for a woman neither young, handsome, rich, nor married.... she had no intellectual superiority to make atonement to herself, or frighten those who might hate her, into outward respect.... And yet she was a happy woman" (*E*, 1.III).

BATES, JANE. See **Fairfax, Jane (1)**.

BATH, Som.: (*a*) where Mr. Clifford lived—"Memoirs of Mr. Clifford" (*Vol. 1*, p. 43); (*b*) Isabel warns Laura to "beware of the unmeaning Luxuries of Bath & of the Stinking fish of Southampton"—"Love and Freindship" (*Vol. 2*, p. 79); (*c*) Mr. Millar was traveling thither when he stopped to visit the female philosopher— "Scraps" (*Vol. 2*, p. 170); (*d*) Mr. Johnson failed to go to visit his aunts there (*LS*, p. 295); (*e*) Eliza Williams was seduced by Willoughby (*SS*, 2.IX) there, and the Palmers go to stay with relatives near Bath (*SS*, 3.VII); (*f*) Lieutenant Wickham occasionally went off to enjoy himself alone there after his marriage (*PP*, 3.XIX); (*g*) Henry Crawford goes there to visit his uncle; also, Mrs. Rushworth retires there after her son's marriage (*MP*, 2.II); (*h*) Mr. Elton becomes engaged to Miss Hawkins there during the course of a visit of four weeks (*E*, 1.XVII); (*i*) half of the action of *Northanger Abbey* takes place there; its "fine and striking environs" are mentioned (*NA*, 1.II); (*j*) the Elliots remove there after they are forced to retrench and to rent Kellynch Hall (*P*, 3.II); also mentioned (*Vol. 1*, pp. 48 and 49; *S*, p. 374). See also **Argyle Buildings; Bath St; Beechen Cliff; Belmont; Bond St.; Broad St.; Brock St.; Camden Place; Cheap St.; Claverton Down; Crescent; Edgar's Buildings; Gay St.; Green Park Buildings; Lansdown Crescent; Lansdown Hill; Lansdown Rd.; Laura Place; Lower Rooms; Market Place; Marlborough Buildings; Milsom St.; Octagon Room; Old Bridge; Pulteney St.; Pump Room; Pump Yard; Queen's Square; Rivers St.; Sydney Place; Sydney Terrace; Union Passage; Union St.; Upper Rooms; Westgate Buildings; White Hart Inn; Wick Rocks.**

BATH ST., Bath, (*a*) where Isabella Thorpe last encountered Captain Tilney (*NA*, 2.XII); (*b*) where the clandestine rendezvous of William Elliot and Mrs. Clay is seen by Mary Musgrove (*P*, 4.X).

BATTEL (Battle Abbey, Sussex), not very far from where the Heywoods live (*S*, p. 366).

BATTLERIDGE. See **Cooke, Cassandra**.

BEACHEY HEAD (Beachy Head, Sussex), mentioned by William Price (*MP*, 2.VII).

BEARD, MR., a solicitor in Gray's Inn, visiting Sanditon (*S*, p. 389).

BEATTIE, JAMES (1735–1803), poet: "The Hermit" is quoted (*Letters*, p. 331).

BEAUFORT, MISS and **LETITIA**, students at Mrs. Griffiths' seminary, "very accomplished & very Ignorant, their time being divided between such pursuits as might attract admiration, & those Labours & Expedients of dexterous Ingenuity, by which they could dress in a stile much beyond what they *ought* to have afforded" (*S*, p. 421).

BEAULIEU ABBEY, Hants., where Perkin Warbeck took shelter—"The History of England" (*Vol. 2*, p. 141).

BEAUMONT, FRANCIS and **JOHN FLETCHER** (1584–1616 and 1579–1625), collaborating playwrights: *The Chances* (altered by the duke of Buckingham) was performed at Steventon in January 1788.

"BEAUTIFULL CASSANDRA, THE," "a novel in twelve chapters" dedicated to Jane Austen's sister Cassandra (*Vol. 1*, p. 44).

BEAZLEY, SAMUEL (1786–1851), architect and playwright: Jane Austen saw part of *The Boarding House; or, Five Hours at Brighton* (1811), a musical farce, in 1813 (*Letters*, p. 321).

BECKFORD, MARIA (cousin of the author of *Vathek*), a sister-in-law of one John Middleton of Chawton, with whom she lived from 1808 to 1812: a lady suffering from a headache, according to a poem by Jane Austen (*Verses*, pp. 448–49).

BEDFORD, a coffeehouse in Covent Garden frequented by Tom Musgrave (*W*, p. 356) and by John Thorpe (*NA*, 1.XII), both of whom mention it in order to prove themselves to be men-about-town.

BEDFORD SQUARE, London, where some cousins of the Bertrams live; Julia Bertram elopes from their house with Mr. Yates (*MP*, 3.XIV).

BEDFORDSHIRE, the county in which the Lindsay family lives—"Love and Freindship" (*Vol. 2*, p. 81).

BEECHEN CLIFF, on the outskirts of Bath, "that noble hill, whose beautiful verdure and hanging coppice render it so striking an object" (*NA*, 1.XIV); it is the object of Catherine Morland's walk with the young Tilneys—an ambitious undertaking, since her lodgings were toward the northeastern end of the town and the cliff lies to the southwest.

BEEHIVE, THE. See **Millingen, John Gideon**.

"BEGGAR'S PETITION, THE." See **Moss, Thomas**.

BELINDA. See **Edgeworth, Maria**.

BELL, the: an inn at Bromley patronized by Lady Catherine de Bourgh (*PP*, 2.XIV).

BELLE, the unknown lady to whom "a Young lady crossed in Love" is writing—"A Collection of Letters" (*Vol. 2*, p. 152).

BELLEVUE COTTAGE, one of the newly built houses in Sanditon, intended for rental (*S*, p. 384).

BELMONT, an outlying region of Bath, quieter than the center of the town (*P*, 4.VI).

BENGAL, where Miss Wynne was sent to find a husband—"Catharine or the Bower" (*Vol. 3*, p. 194).

BENNET, MR., a gentleman with an income of £2,000 per annum and five daughters, living at Longbourn; he "was so odd a mixture of quick parts, sarcastic humour, reserve, and caprice, that the experience of three and twenty years had been insufficient to make his wife understand his character" (*PP*, 1.I).

BENNET, MRS. (née Gardiner), Elizabeth's mother, the daughter of a Meryton attorney: "She was a woman of mean understanding, little information, and uncertain temper. When she was discontented she fancied herself nervous. The business of her life was to get her daughters married; its solace was visiting and news" (*PP*, 1.I).

BENNET, CATHARINE (KITTY), the fourth Bennet daughter, was "weak-spirited, irritable, and completely under Lydia's guidance . . . ignorant, idle, and vain" (*PP*, 2.XIV).

BENNET, ELIZABETH, the heroine of *Pride and Prejudice*, twenty years old; "she had a lively, playful disposition, which delighted in any thing ridiculous" (*PP*, 1.III); Mr. Darcy finds that her face "was rendered uncommonly intelligent by the beautiful expression of her dark eyes" (*PP*, 1.VI).

BENNET, JANE, the eldest and most beautiful Bennet daughter, at twenty-three; her father says of her and her fiancé, Mr. Bingley, "'You are each of you so complying, that nothing will ever be resolved on; so easy, that every servant will cheat you; and so generous, that you will always exceed your income'" (*PP*, 3.XIII).

BENNET, LYDIA, the youngest daughter, was "a stout, well-grown girl of fifteen, with a fine complexion and good-humoured countenance; a favourite with her mother, whose affection had brought her into public at an early age" (*PP*, 1.IX).

BENNET, MARY, the third Bennet daughter, "who piqued herself upon the solidity of her reflections" (*PP*, 1.V); she "had neither genius nor taste; and though vanity had given her application, it had given her likewise a pedantic air and conceited manner, which would have injured a higher degree of excellence than she had reached" (*PP*, 1.VI).

BENTLEY, Hants., not far from Chawton, where Henry Austen had his first curacy, in 1816.

BENWICK, (CAPT.) JAMES, "an excellent young man and an officer... uniting very strong feelings with quiet, serious, and retiring manners, and a decided taste for reading, and sedentary pursuits" (*P*, 3.XI).

BERESFORD, COLONEL, with whom Miss Osborne dances, breaking her promise to Charles Blake (*W*, p. 330).

BERKELEY ST., London, where Mrs. Jennings lives (*SS*, 2.V).

BERKSHIRE, where Lady Williams's father lived—"Jack & Alice" (*Vol. 1*, p. 16).

BERMUDA, which sailing people do not call the West Indies, according to Mrs. Croft (*P*, 3.VIII).

BERNARD, MR., with whom Maria Williams dances at Ashburnham, "the most agreable partner in the room"—"A Collection of Letters" (*Vol. 2*, p. 157).

BERQUIN, ARNAUD (1747–91), miscellaneous writer: a copy of *L'Ami de l'adolescence* (1785) with Jane Austen's name inscribed in volume 1 is in the library of the Swansea Training College.

BERTHA: "the amiable Bertha" was Lord St. Clair's third daughter and Philander's mother—"Love and Freindship" (*Vol. 2*, p. 92).

BERTRAM, EDMUND, younger son of Sir Thomas, destined for the church: "he was not pleasant by any common rule, he talked no nonsense, he paid no compliments, his opinions were unbending, his attentions tranquil and simple. There was a charm, perhaps, in his sincerity, his steadiness, his integrity" (*MP*, 1.VII).

BERTRAM, JULIA. See **Yates, Julia**.

BERTRAM, LADY MARIA (née Ward), Sir Thomas's wife, "a woman of very tranquil feelings, and a temper remarkably easy and indolent," she remains throughout a caricature of laziness (*MP*, 1.I).

BERTRAM, MARIA. See **Rushworth, Maria**.

BERTRAM, SIR THOMAS, BART., M.P., of Mansfield Park, Fanny Price's uncle, a very respectable and rather stiff gentleman (*MP*, 1.I).

BERTRAM, THOMAS (TOM), Sir Thomas's elder son and heir: "he was the sort of young man to be generally liked, his agreeableness was of the kind to be oftener found agreeable than some endowments of a higher stamp, for he had easy manners, excellent spirits, a large acquaintance, and a great deal to say" (*MP*, 1.V).

BEST, MR., an unknown gentleman who did not escort Martha Lloyd to Harrogate (*Verses*, p. 445).

BETTY (1), the Watsons' kitchen maid (*W*, p. 346).

BETTY (2), Mrs. Jennings's maid (*SS*, 2.III); she has a sister who needs work whom Mrs. Jennings would like to have employed by Lucy Steele after the latter marries Edward Ferrars (*SS*, 3.I).

BEVERLEY, HENRY, a friend of George Hervey who marries Miss (Maud) Hervey—"Amelia Webster" (*Vol. 1*, p. 47).

BICKERSTAFFE, ISAAC (ca. 1735–ca. 1812), playwright, producing mostly musical farces: (1) Jane Austen was "well entertained" by *The Hypocrite* (1768), adapted from Colley Cibber's version of *Tartuffe*, which she saw in London in 1811 (*Letters*, p. 275); and (2) *The Sultan, or A Peep Into the Seraglio* (1775) was performed at Steventon in 1790.

BICKERTON, MISS, a "parlour boarder at Mrs. Goddard's" school in Highbury who runs afoul of some gypsies (*E*, 3.III).

BIGG, CATHERINE (b. 1773), fifth daughter of Lovelace Bigg Wither of Manydown, six miles from Steventon. (The Biggs were close friends of the Austens.) Jane Austen sent her some cambric handkerchiefs, along with a few lines of poetry, before her marriage to Herbert Hill in 1808 (*Verses*, p. 446).

BIGLAND, JOHN (1750–1832), scholar, schoolmaster, and author: it may be his *Letters on the Modern History and Political Aspect of Europe* (1804), his *History of Spain* (1810), or his *System of Geography and History* (1812) that Jane Austen mentions reading with her niece Fanny Austen Knight in 1813 (*Letters*, p. 333); Bigland is also mentioned elsewhere (*Letters*, p. 294).

BINGLEY, (MISS) CAROLINE: she and her sister "were in fact very fine ladies; not deficient in good humour when they were pleased . . . but proud and conceited. They were rather handsome, had been educated in one of the first private seminaries in town, had a fortune of twenty thousand pounds, were in the habit of . . . associating with people of rank. . . . They were of a respectable family in the north of England; a circumstance more deeply impressed on their memories than that their brother's fortune and their own had been acquired by trade" (*PP*, 1.IV).

BINGLEY, CHARLES, a young man of twenty-three with four or five thousand pounds a year, "was good looking and gentlemanlike; he had a pleasant countenance, and easy, unaffected manners" (*PP*, 1.III).

BINGLEY, LOUISA. Seee **Hurst, Louisa.**

BIRD, MRS. (née Milman), an acquaintance of Mrs. Elton, she gave up music after marrying (*E*, 2.XIV).

BIRMINGHAM, (*a*) through which Elizabeth Bennet passed on her journey with the Gardiners to Derbyshire (*PP*, 2.XIX); (*b*) from which the upstart Tupmans came; according to Mrs. Elton, "'One has not great hopes from Birmingham'" (*E*, 2.XVIII).

BLAIR, HUGH (1718–1800), minister and noted preacher: (1) his *Sermons* (1777–1801) (*a*) are provided by Mrs. Percival for her niece Catharine to help "breed [her] up virtuously"—"Catharine or the Bower" (*Vol. 3*, p. 232), (*b*) are mentioned by Mary Crawford (*MP*, 1.IX); (2) his *Lectures on Rhetoric and Belles Lettres* (1883) is probably the work referred to by Eleanor Tilney (*NA*, 1.XIV).

BLAIZE CASTLE (Blaise Castle House, near Henbury, Som.), built 1795, is the object of a projected exploring tour by the Thorpes and the Morlands (*NA*, 1.XI).

BLAKE, MRS., "a lively pleasant-looking little Woman of 5 or 6 & 30," the widowed sister of Mr. Howard (*W*, p. 330).

BLAKE, CHARLES, age ten, Mrs. Blake's eldest child; Emma Watson "was immediately struck with the fine Countenance & animated gestures of the little boy" (*W*, p. 330).

BLENHEIM, Oxon., which Elizabeth Bennet visited on her journey with the Gardiners to Derbyshire (*PP*, 2.XIX).

BLOOMER, LADY BELL, a character in Hannah Cowley's *Which Is the Man?*—"The Three Sisters" (*Vol. 1*, p. 65).

BLOOMSBURY SQUARE, London, where Cassandra encountered Maria—"The Beautifull Cassandra" (*Vol. 1*, p. 46).

BOARDING HOUSE, THE. See **Beazley, Samuel.**

"BOARDING SCHOOL, THE," mentioned by Jane Austen (*Letters*, p. 115): R. W. Chapman suggests, following M. H. Dodds, that it might be the anonymous *The Governess; or Evening Amusements at a Boarding-school* (1800).

BOLEYN, ANNE. See **Bullen, Anna**.

BON TON. See **Garrick, David**.

BOND ST., Bath, (*a*) where Catherine Morland encounters Anne Thorpe on the day of the expedition to Clifton (*NA*, 1.XIV); (*b*) where Sir Walter Elliot stood in a shop and "'had counted eighty-seven women go by, one after another, without there being a tolerable face among them'" (*P*, 4.III).

BOND ST., London, (*a*) where Cassandra's mother had a millinery shop—"The Beautifull Cassandra" (*Vol. 1*, p. 44); (*b*) where Mr. Willoughby had lodgings (*SS*, 3.VIII); (*c*) where Mr. Elton had Emma Woodhouse's portrait of Harriet Smith framed (*E*, 1.VII).

BONOMI, JOSEPH (1739–1808), architect: Robert Ferrars mentions that a friend of his, Lord Courtland, has had three plans done by Bonomi for cottages; but Bonomi would have been dead at the time (*SS*, 2.XIV).

BOOKHAM, Surrey. See **Great Bookham**.

BOSSI, CESARE (1773–1802), composer born in Ferrara: some piece from the music he did for *Laura and Lenza* (1800), a "Grand Fairy Ballet" in two acts, is doubtless what Jane Austen refers to (*CG*, III i)—information courtesy of Brian Southam's introduction to *Sir Charles Grandison*.

BOSWELL, JAMES (1740–95), biographer and paparazzo: (1) there is a paraphrase of *Life of Johnson* (1791), Dec. 20, 1784, in a poem by Jane Austen (*Verses*, p. 442); also mentioned (*Letters*, p. 33); (2) *Journal of a Tour to the Hebrides* (1785) is mentioned (*Letters*, p. 32).

BOSWORTH, BATTLE OF (Aug. 22, 1485), where Richard III was killed—"The History of England" (*Vol. 2*, p. 141).

BOURGH, (MISS) ANNE DE, Lady Catherine's only child: Maria Lucas exclaims, "'She is quite a little creature. Who would have thought she could be so thin and small!'" and Eliza Bennet adds that she "'looks sickly and cross'" (*PP*, 2.V).

BOURGH, THE RIGHT HONORABLE LADY CATHERINE DE, Fitzwilliam Darcy's aunt, "a tall, large woman, with strongly-marked features, which might once have been handsome. Her air was not conciliating, nor was her manner of receiving [Sir William Lucas and Eliza Bennet], such as to make her visitors forget their inferior rank" (*PP*, 2.VI).

BOURGH, SIR LEWIS DE (deceased), Lady Catherine's husband (*PP*, 1.XIII).

BOX HILL, near Dorking, to which Highbury society takes an exploring tour; it is the highest elevation of that part of the county, with extensive views (*E*, 3.VI).

BRABOURNE, LORD, great-nephew of Jane Austen and the first editor of her letters.

BRAGGE, MR., a cousin-in-law of Mr. Suckling's living near Maple Grove (*E*, 2.XVIII).

BRAGGE, MRS., a cousin of Mr. Suckling's alleged by Mrs. Elton to move in the first circles (*E*, 2.XVII).

BRAITHWAITE FAMILY, old friends of the Churchill family who are occasionally invited to Enscombe but always put off before the visit takes place (*E*, 1.XIV).

BRAMPTON, Cumberland, where Edward Stanley's favorite hunter died—"Catharine or the Bower" (*Vol. 3*, p. 222).

BRAND, ADMIRAL, and his brother, acquaintances of Admiral Croft, who thinks the former a "shabby fellow" for depriving him of some of his best men (*P*, 4.VI).

BRANDON, COLONEL, a former army man with an income of £2,000 per annum, over thirty-five, who marries Marianne Dashwood: "His manners, though serious, were mild; and his reserve appeared rather the result of some oppression of spirits, than of any natural gloominess of temper" (*SS*, 1.X).

BRANDON, ELIZA, Colonel Brandon's adoptive sister; she was forced to marry his brother, then ran off with a lover, and ended her life in ruin. Her daughter is Eliza Williams (*SS*, 2.IX).

BRANXHOLM HALL, LADY OF, a character in Sir Walter Scott's *Lay of the Last Minstrel*, mentioned in passing (*MP*, 2.X).

BRERETON, MISS (1). See **Denham, Lady**.

BRERETON, MISS (2) CLARA, Lady Denham's poor-relation companion: "Elegantly tall, regularly handsome, with great delicacy of complexion & soft Blue eyes, a sweetly modest & yet naturally graceful Address," she seems to Charlotte Heywood to be the very model of a fictional heroine (*S*, p. 391).

"BRIDE OF ABYDOS, THE." See **Byron, George Gordon, Lord**.

BRIDGES, ELIZABETH. See **Knight, Elizabeth**.

BRIDGET (1), the unprepossessing daughter of a widow who shelters Laura and Sophia: "she was very plain & her name was Bridget. . . . Nothing therefore could be expected from her"—"Love and Freindship" (*Vol. 2*, p. 100).

BRIDGET (2), a maidservant at the house of Mr. and Mrs. Reeves, cousins of Harriet Byron (*CG*, I ii).

BRIGDEN, CAPTAIN, a friend of Admiral Croft seen on the street in Bath (*P*, 4.VI).

BRIGHTHELMSTONE. See **Brighton**.

BRIGHTON, Sussex, a seaside resort made fashionable by the prince regent: (*a*) according to Mr. Parker, it was one of "your large, overgrown Places, like . . . Worthing" (*S*, p. 368); (*b*) Colonel Forster's regiment is quartered there after leaving Meryton; Lydia Bennet follows them as Mrs. Forster's guest (*PP*, 2.XVI); (*c*) James and Maria Rushworth, accompanied by Julia Bertram, go there for their honeymoon (*MP*, 2.III); also mentioned (*Vol. 2*, p. 138).

BRINSHORE, Sussex, the principal local rival to Sanditon; Mr. Parker calls it "that paltry Hamlet, lying, as it does between a stagnant marsh, a bleak Moor & the constant effluvia of a ridge of putrifying sea weed" (*S*, p. 369).

BRISTOL, Som., (*a*) from which Miss Lutterell writes to Miss (Margaret) Lesley—"Lesley Castle" (*Vol. 2*, p. 119); (*b*) the Palmers' seat, Cleveland, is within a few miles of it (*SS*, 3.III); (*c*) Mrs. Elton's father was in some line of trade there: "but, as the whole of the profits of his mercantile life appeared so very moderate, it was not unfair to guess the dignity of his line of trade had been moderate also" (*E*, 2.IV); (*d*) it was the object of the Morlands' and Thorpes' abortive expedition (*NA*, 1.XI).

BROAD ST., Bath, mentioned by John Thorpe (*NA*, 1.XI).

BROADWAY LANE, Highbury, where Emma Woodhouse, walking with Miss Taylor, first had the notion of a match between the latter and Mr. Weston (*E*, 1.I).

BROADWOOD'S (Great Pulteney St., London), the shop and manufactory of John Broadwood (1732–1812) and his descendants, makers of very fine pianofortes; Frank Churchill bought one for Jane Fairfax there (*E*, 2.VIII).

BROCK ST., Bath, on the Tilneys' way to their lodgings at the upper end of Milsom St. from the Pump Room (*NA*, 1.XIII).

BROCKHAM, Glos., near Northanger; it is where General Tilney's surveyor lives or works (*NA*, 2.XI).

BROMLEY, Kent, where Eliza Bennet and Maria Lucas are to change their post-horses on their journey from Hunsford to London (*PP*, 2.XIV).

BROMPTON, suburb of London where Jane Austen's brother Henry lived for a while, with his first wife, around 1805.

BROOK ST., London, where the Halifaxes live—"Catharine or the Bower" (*Vol. 3*, p. 202).

BROWN, DR. and **MRS. (1)**, visitors to Sanditon (*S*, p. 389).

BROWN, MRS. (2), probably the wife of an officer stationed at Gibraltar; her hairstyle makes William Price suspect her sanity (*MP*, 2.VI).

BROWN, MRS. (3), an imaginary prototype (*E*, 2.IV).

BROWN, MARY, an imaginary prototype: Robert Ferrars imagines his brother "reading prayers in a white surplice, and publishing the banns of marriage between John Smith and Mary Brown" (*SS*, 2.V).

BROWNE, ISAAC HAWKINS (the elder, 1705–60), poet: "A Pipe of Tobacco" (called in *MP* "Address to Tobacco") was included in Robert Dodsley's *Collection of Poems by Several Hands* (*MP*, 1.XVII).

BRUDENELL, MR. (1), a friend of Sir William's—"Sir William Mountague" (*Vol. 1*, p. 41).

BRUDENELL, MR. (2), "'the handsomest Man I ever saw in my Life,'" according to Georgiana Stanhope—"The Three Sisters" (*Vol. 1*, p. 68).

BRUDENELL, SIR HENRY, of Leicestershire, the father of Mr. Brudenell (2)—"The Three Sisters" (*Vol. 1*, p. 68).

BRUNSWICK SQUARE, London, where the John Knightleys live (*E*, 1.I).

BRUNTON, MARY (1778–1818), novelist: *Self-control: A Novel* (1810) is mentioned (*Letters*, pp. 278 and 423); and in 1813 Jane Austen is "looking over Self Control again, & my opinion is confirmed of its being an excellently-meant, elegantly-written Work, without anything of Nature or Probability in it" (*Letters*, p. 344).

BRYDGES, SIR SAMUEL EGERTON (1762–1837), genealogist, poet, and M.P., brother-in-law of the Austens' neighbor the Reverend Isaac Lefroy: he wrote *Arthur Fitz-Albini: A Novel* (1798), of which Jane Austen says, "it does not quite satisfy my feelings that we should purchase the only one of Egerton's works of which his family are ashamed" (*Letters*, p. 32; also mentioned p. 67).

BUCHANAN, CLAUDIUS (ca. 1766–1815), chaplain in India, active in establishing the church in India and author of sermons and miscellaneous writings on ecclesiastical affairs: he is mentioned in passing (*Letters*, p. 292).

BUCKINGHAM, a character in *Henry VIII*, parts of which are read by Henry Crawford to the Bertrams (*MP*, 3.III).

BUCKINGHAM, DUKE OF. See **Villiers, George.**

BUCKINGHAMSHIRE is mentioned (*Vol. 1*, p. 6).

BULLEN, ANNA (Anne Boleyn, 1507–36), Henry VIII's second queen: "this amiable Woman was entirely innocent of the Crimes with which she was accused"—"The History of England" (*Vol. 2*, p. 142).

BURGESS, MRS., a friend of the Steeles living in Exeter; Miss Steele goes to stay with her after Lucy elopes (*SS*, 3.XIII).

BURLEIGH, LORD (William Cecil, Lord Burghley, 1520–98), minister of state and Queen Elizabeth I's favorite adviser, mentioned—"The History of England" (*Vol. 2*, p. 145).

BURNABY, MRS., one of the attendants at Melissa's sickbed—"A Fragment written to inculcate the practise of Virtue" (*Vol. 1*, p. 72).

BURNEY, FRANCES (1752–1840), novelist: (1) *Evelina, or a Young Lady's Entrance Into the World* (1778), which a Mr. Gould of Jane Austen's acquaintance thinks was written by Dr. Johnson (*Letters*, p. 64; it is also quoted on pp. 180 and 438 and mentioned on p. 388); (2) *Cecilia, or Memoirs of an Heiress* (1782), (*a*) is one of the works "in which the greatest powers of the mind are displayed, in which the most thorough knowledge of human nature, the happiest delineation of its varieties, the liveliest effusions of wit and humour are conveyed to the world in the best chosen language" (*NA*, 1.V); (*b*) Anne Elliot compares herself to Miss Larolles (*P*, 4.VIII); (*c*) Miss Beverley is mentioned (*Letters*, p. 254); (3) *Camilla, or a Picture of Youth* (1796), (*a*) since Charlotte Heywood "had not *Camilla's* Youth, & had no intention of having her Distress," she does not buy this book (*S*, p. 390); (*b*) according to John Thorpe, "'it is the horridest nonsense you can imagine; there is nothing in the world in it but an old man's playing at see-saw and learning Latin'" (*NA*, 1.VII); (*c*) "The advantages of natural folly in a beautiful girl have been already set forth by the capital pen of a sister author" (*NA*, 1.XIV) refers to Indiana in this book; (*d*) also mentioned (*Letters*, pp. 9, 13, and 14); (4) *The Wanderer, or Female Difficulties* (1814) is referred to (*Letters*, p. 334).

BURNEY, SARAH HARRIET (ca. 1770–1844), novelist: in 1807, Jane Austen is reading *Clarentine; a Novel* (1798) and is "surprised to find how foolish it is" (*Letters*, p. 180).

BURNS, ROBERT (1759–96), Scots poet: Charlotte Heywood finds that "'poor Burns's known Irregularities, greatly interrupt my enjoyment of his Lines'" (*S*, p. 398).

BURTON, MISS. See **Lesley, Louisa (1).**

BURTON ON TRENT, Staffs., where a "Charitable Repository" has been established to which, Diana Parker hopes, Lady Denham will give money (*S*, p. 424).

BUTLER, THE RHYMING, a character in Mrs. Inchbald's *Lovers' Vows*, to be played by Tom Bertram at Mansfield (*MP*, 1.XIV).

BYRON, GEORGE GORDON, LORD (1788–1824), poet: (1) "The Giaour" (1813) and "The Bride of Abydos" (1813) are the subject of conversation between Anne Elliot and Captain Benwick; they are "trying to ascertain . . . how ranked the *Giaour* and *The Bride of Abydos*; and moreover, how the *Giaour* was to be pronounced" (*P*, 3.XI); (2) "The Corsair" (1814) (*a*) is quoted briefly by Captain Benwick (*P*, 2.XII); (*b*) Jane Austen mentions reading it, March 5, 1814 (*Letters*, p. 379).

BYRON, HARRIET, heroine of *Sir Charles Grandison*; according to Sir

Charles, "'She is the happy medium between gravity and over-liveliness. She is lively or grave as the occasion requires'" (*CG*, IV i).

CADELL, MR., a London publisher who declined to publish *First Impressions*, the early version of *Pride and Prejudice*, in 1797.

CALSHOT, Hants., near Southampton: Frederic Gower was drowned in the nearby ocean—"Evelyn" (*Vol. 3*, p. 185).

CAMBERWELL, a suburb of London where Mrs. Griffiths's school is located (*S*, p. 387).

CAMBRIDGE (*a*) is mentioned in a stanza "On the Universities" (*Verses*, p. 447); (*b*) is where Wickham was educated at the senior Mr. Darcy's expense (*PP*, 2.XII); (*c*) is where Henry Crawford was educated (*MP*, 1.VI).

CAMDEN PLACE, Bath (in the Belmont area), where the Elliots are living while Kellynch Hall is let (*P*, 4.I).

CAMILLA. See **Burney, Frances**.

CAMPBELL, COLONEL, the friend of Jane Fairfax's father who informally adopts Jane (*E*, 1.XII).

CAMPBELL, MISS. See **Dixon, Mrs**.

CAMPBELL, MR., surgeon on the *Thrush*, the ship to which William Price is assigned as a second lieutenant (*MP*, 3.VII).

CAMPBELL, MRS., the wife of Colonel Campbell (*E*, 1.XII).

CAMPBELL, THOMAS (1777–1844), Scots poet: Sir Edward Denham says that in the "Pleasures of Hope" (1799) Campbell "'has touched the extreme of our Sensations'" (*S*, p. 397).

CANOPUS, a ship anchored at the Spithead, Portsmouth harbor (*MP*, 3.VII).

CAPE (probably the Cape of Good Hope, South Africa), where the miniature of Captain Benwick was painted (*P*, 4.XI).

CAPPER, MISS, the friend of a friend of Diana Parker (*S*, p. 408).

CAR (Robert Carr [Ker], created Earl of Somerset; d. 1645), a favorite of James I—"The History of England" (*Vol. 2*, p. 148).

CARACTACUS (fl. A.D. 50), king of some of the British tribes, who resisted the Roman invaders: mentioned by Eleanor Tilney (*NA*, 1.XIV).

CAREY, the two Misses, young ladies living in Newton, near Barton; when Marianne is ill, Margaret Dashwood goes to stay with them (*SS*, 1.XIII).

CARLISLE, Cumb., is mentioned in passing—"Evelyn" (*Vol. 3*, p. 185).

CARLTON HOUSE, London, built in 1709, demolished in 1829. It formerly stood on the site of Waterloo Place and the York Column; the palace of the prince regent, it was visited by Jane Austen in 1815, on which occasion the prince regent's chaplain suggested that she might dedicate one of her novels to the prince (*Letters*, p. 429; also mentioned p. 442).

CARMARTHEN, where Fanny and Elizabeth Johnson had their shoes capped and heelpieced after their walking tour through Wales—"Scraps" (*Vol. 2*, p. 176).

CARR, (MISS) FANNY: according to Tom Musgrave, she is "'a most interesting little creature. You can imagine nothing more *naive* or *piquante*'" (*W*, p. 340).

CARR, SIR JOHN (1772–1832), a writer of travel books: his *Descriptive Travels in the Southern and Eastern Parts of Spain and the Balearic Isles*, in the

Year 1809 (1811) informed Jane Austen that she must change "Government House" at *MP*, 2.VI, to "the Commissioner's" (*Letters*, p. 292).

CARTER, CAPTAIN, an officer admired by Lydia Bennet before the arrival of Lieutenant Wickham (*PP*, 1.VI).

CARTERET, THE HONORABLE MISS, a cousin of the Elliots from Ireland, daughter of the Viscountess Dalrymple; she "was so plain and so awkward, that she would never have been tolerated in Camden-place but for her birth" (*P*, 4.IV).

CARTWRIGHT, probably Mrs. Jennings's man of business (*SS*, 2.IV).

CASSANDRA: heroine of a short tale, she is the "Daughter of a celebrated Millener in Bond Street"—"The Beautifull Cassandra" (*Vol. 1*, p. 44).

CASSEL, COUNT, a character in Mrs. Inchbald's *Lovers' Vows*, to be played at Mansfield by Mr. Rushworth (*MP*, 1.XIII).

CASTLE OF WOLFENBACH. See **Parsons, Mrs. Eliza**.

CATHARINE. See **Percival, Catharine**.

"CATHARINE OR THE BOWER," Jane Austen's longest teenage story, dedicated to her sister Cassandra (*Vol. 3*, p. 192).

CATHERINE [WOODHOUSE?], mentioned as the name of Isabella and Emma Woodhouse's grandmother (*E*, 1.IX).

CATHERINE OF FRANCE ([of Valois], 1401–37), youngest daughter of Charles VI of France and Isabel of Bavaria, "a very agreeable Woman by Shakespear's account"—"The History of England" (*Vol. 2*, p. 139).

CECELIA, one of Wilhelminus's guests in his Pembrokeshire cottage—"Scraps" (*Vol. 2*, p. 177).

CECIL, HENRY, Lady Harriet's lover, who deserts her to marry Eliza Harcourt—"Henry and Eliza" (*Vol. 1*, p. 35).

CECILIA. See **Burney, Frances**.

CHAMBERLAYNE, one of the junior officers in Colonel Forster's regiment; in a party at the Forsters', he is dressed up as a woman (*PP*, 2.XVI).

CHANCES, THE. See **Beaumont, Francis** and **John Fletcher**.

CHAPMAN, MRS., Lady Bertram's personal maid; the lady considers her responsible for Fanny Price's beauty on the evening of Fanny's first ball (*MP*, 2.IX).

CHARLES I (1600–49), king of England: "This amiable Monarch seems born to have suffered Misfortunes.... Never certainly was there before so many detestable Characters at one time in England as in this period of its History; Never were amiable Men so scarce"—"The History of England" (*Vol. 2*, p. 148).

CHARLES II (1630–85), king of England, during whose reign an Elliot ancestor distinguished himself and was made a baronet (*P*, 3.I).

CHARLES (1): one of the watchers at Melissa's sickbed is "the melancholy Charles"—"A Fragment written to inculcate the practise of Virtue" (*Vol. 1*, p. 72).

CHARLES (2), an employee at an inn—"Scraps" (*Vol. 2*, p. 172).

CHARLES (3), a groom at Mansfield Park who doubles as a postilion when members of the household travel (*MP*, 2.II).

CHARLES, SIR, a friend of Admiral Crawford who arranges William Price's promotion (*MP*, 2.XIII).

CHARMOUTH, Dorset, near Lyme, "with its high grounds and extensive sweeps of country" (*P*, 3.XI).

CHATSWORTH, Derbys.: the Gardiners and Eliza Bennet must forgo its "celebrated beauties" when their vacation time is cut short (*PP*, 2.XIX).

CHAWTON, Hants., where the Knights had property; Edward Austen Knight offered his mother and sisters a house there in 1809, and Jane Austen lived most of the remainder of her life there.

CHAWTON HOUSE, Hants., owned by Thomas Knight and later by Edward Austen Knight.

CHEAP ST., Bath: "Every body acquainted with Bath may remember the difficulties of crossing Cheap-street" opposite Union Passage, from the archway that leads out of the Pump Yard (*NA*, 1.VII).

CHEAPSIDE, part of the City of London, near which the Gardiners are alleged to live; in fact, they are a good way to the east of Cheapside, near Cornhill (*PP*, 1.VIII).

CHELTENHAM, Glos., mentioned in passing (*Vol. 3*, p. 203, and *MP*, 2.III).

CHESHIRE, where the Elliot family was first settled, before the reign of Charles II (*P*, 3.I).

CHETWYNDE, Glos., where Catharine and Mrs. Percival live—"Catharine or the Bower" (*Vol. 3*, p. 195); later in the story, though, Chetwynde is described as being near Exeter, Devon.

CHICHESTER, Sussex, (*a*) where Penelope Watson is visiting friends (*W*, p. 317); (*b*) a stage in the younger Parkers' journey to Sanditon (*S*, p. 407).

CHILDREN OF THE ABBEY. See **Roche, Regina Maria**.

CHINA: Fanny Price reads, at Edmund Bertram's suggestion, Lord Macartney's *Journal of the Embassy to China* (*MP*, 1.XVI).

CHLOE, a lady on her way to London to marry Strephon—"Scraps" (*Vol. 2*, p. 172).

CHRISTCHURCH (COLLEGE), Oxford, attended by Freeman, a friend of John Thorpe's (*NA*, 1.VII).

CHURCHILL, MISS. See **Weston, Mrs. (1)**.

CHURCHILL, MR., the brother of the first Mrs. Weston; he adopted her son Frank (*E*, 1.II).

CHURCHILL, MRS., sister-in-law of the first Mrs. Weston; even according to the generous Mr. Weston, "'she has no more heart than a stone to people in general; and the devil of a temper'" (*E*, 1.XIV).

CHURCHILL, FRANK C. WESTON, Mr. Weston's son, brought up by his uncle Mr. Churchill; "he was a *very* good looking young man; height, air, address, all were unexceptionable, and his countenance had a great deal of the spirit and liveliness of his father's; he looked quick and sensible" (*E*, 2.V).

CHURCHILL, Sussex, where Charles Vernon and his family live, the site of the principal action of *Lady Susan* (p. 243).

CLANDESTINE MARRIAGE, THE. See **Colman, George (the elder)**.

CLAPHAM, Surrey, in the outskirts of London: (*a*) Colonel Forster traced Lydia Bennet and Lieutenant Wickham this far in their flight from Brighton and then lost the trail (*PP*, 3.IV); (*b*) it is one of the places Harriet Byron was sought after her abduction by Sir Hargrave Pollexfen (*CG*, I ii); also mentioned (*S*, p. 412).

CLARA, to whom Elizabeth Johnson sent the account of her walking tour through Wales—"Scraps" (*Vol. 2*, p. 176).

CLARENTINE. See **Burney, Sarah Harriet.**

CLARKE, a family living in Staffordshire, near Vernon Castle; Frederica Vernon's only friends (*LS*, p. 268).

CLARKE, MRS., an acquaintance of Mrs. Jennings encountered in Kensington Gardens (*SS*, 3.II).

CLARKE, (REV.) JAMES STANIER (ca. 1765–1834), author and chaplain to the prince regent: he conveyed to Jane Austen the recommendation that she dedicate one of her novels to the prince; they met at Carlton House and corresponded briefly over the business (*Letters*, pp. 429–30, 442–45, and 451–53).

CLARKE, LOUISA: according to Arabella Smythe, "'Louisa Clarke . . . is in general a very pleasant Girl, yet sometimes her good humour is clouded by Peevishness, Envy & Spite'"—"Scraps" (*Vol. 2*, p. 172).

CLARKE'S, the lending library in Meryton (*PP*, 1.VII).

CLARKSON, THOMAS (1760–1846), abolitionist: *History of the Abolition of the African Slave Trade* (1808) is perhaps what Jane Austen has in mind when she says, "I am as much in love with [Captain Pasley] as ever I was with Clarkson or Buchanan" (*Letters*, p. 292).

CLAUDIA, Laura's mother—"Love and Freindship" (*Vol. 2*, p. 81).

CLAVERTON DOWN, Bath, where John Thorpe takes Catherine Morland for a drive (*NA*, 1.IX).

CLAY, (MRS.) PENELOPE, a daughter of Mr. Shepherd, Sir Walter Elliot's man of business, "who had returned, after an unprosperous marriage, to her father's house, with the additional burthen of two children. She was a clever young woman, who understood the art of pleasing" (*P*, 3.II).

CLAYTON PARK, near Highbury, is mentioned, but its occupants are not named (*E*, 1.VIII).

CLEOPATRA, a ship anchored at the Spithead, Portsmouth harbor (*MP*, 3.VII); Jane Austen's brother Charles commanded it in 1811.

CLERGYMAN (unnamed), a character in *Sir Charles Grandison*; he is foiled in his attempt to marry Harriet Byron to Sir Hargrave Pollexfen by Harriet's throwing his prayer book into the fire (*CG*, II i).

CLERMONT, LORD and **LADY**, expected for dinner at Lady Greville's—"A Collection of Letters" (*Vol. 2*, p. 159).

CLERMONT. See **Roche, Regina Maria.**

CLEVELAND, MR., Mrs. Marlowe's brother, with "a very good estate" —"Lesley Castle" (*Vol. 2*, p. 121).

CLEVELAND, Som., the Palmers' place, "a spacious, modern-built house, situated on a sloping lawn. It had no park, but the pleasure-grounds were tolerably extensive" (*SS*, 3.VI).

CLIFFORD, MR., a very rich young man of delicate health—"Memoirs of Mr. Clifford" (*Vol. 1*, p. 43).

CLIFTON, the Misses, three young ladies of Kilhoobery Park with whom the susceptible Sir William was in love—"Sir William Mountague" (*Vol. 1*, p. 41).

CLIFTON, Glos., near Bristol, a watering place (*a*) recommended by Mrs. Elton for Mrs. Churchill's health (*E*, 2.XVIII); (*b*) it was the object of one of John Thorpe's proposed exploring parties (*NA*, 1.XI); (*c*) it is where the Elliots spent a holiday in 1806 (*P*, 3.VI).

COBB, the, a two-leveled seawall bounding the harbor in Lyme Regis; Louisa Musgrove fell from the upper level, about eight feet above the lower, where the rest of the party was walking (*P*, 3.XI).

COBHAM, LORD (Sir John Oldcastle, Baron Cobham, d. 1417): during the reign of Henry V, he "was burnt alive, but I forget what for"—"The History of England" (*Vol. 2*, p. 139).

COBHAM, Surrey, where the John Knightleys took their children for a holiday, after Mr. Weston assured them that there was no scarlet fever there (*E*, 1.XI).

CŒLEBS IN SEARCH OF A WIFE. See **More, Hannah**.

COFFEY, CHARLES (d. 1745), Irish dramatist: he collaborated with John Mottley on *The Devil to Pay* (1731), a three-act opera adapted from Thomas Jevon's *Devil of a Wife* (1686); Jane Austen intended to see the former on March 5, 1814 (*Letters*, p. 384).

COLE, MR., a resident of Highbury: he and his wife were "very good sort of people—friendly, liberal, and unpretending; but, on the other hand, they were of low origin, in trade, and only moderately genteel" (*E*, 2.VII).

COLE, MRS., wife of Mr. Cole, a good-natured lady; some little children of hers are also mentioned (*E*, 2.I).

"COLLECTION OF LETTERS, A": according to the dedication, "this Clever Collection of Curious Comments, which have been Carefully Culled, Collected & Classed by [Miss Cooper's] Comical Cousin" (*Vol. 2*, p. 149).

COLLINS, (MRS.) CHARLOTTE (née Lucas), the eldest Lucas child, "a sensible, intelligent young woman, about twenty-seven" (*PP*, 1.V); to the horror of her best friend, Eliza Bennet, she marries Mr. Collins.

COLLINS, WILLIAM, a clergyman and nephew of Mr. Bennet: "He was a tall, heavy looking young man of five and twenty. His air was grave and stately, and his manners were very formal" (*PP*, 1.XIII); he "was not a sensible man, and the deficiency of nature had been but little assisted by education or society" (*PP*, 1.XV).

COLMAN, GEORGE (THE ELDER, 1732–94), dramatist: he collaborated with David Garrick on *The Clandestine Marriage* (1766), which Jane Austen saw on Sept. 15, 1813; she called it "the most respectable of the performances" she saw during that visit to London (*Letters*, pp. 321 and 338).

COLMAN, GEORGE (THE YOUNGER, 1762–1836), dramatist and theater manager: Tom Bertram would like to stage *The Heir at Law* (1797) at Mansfield and is willing to play either Lord Duberley or Dr. Pangloss (*MP*, 1.XIV).

COLNEBROOK, west of London, the estate of Lord and Lady L. (*CG*, III i).

COLUMELLA. See **Graves, Richard**.

COMBE, WILLIAM (1741–1823), soldier of fortune and miscellaneous writer: he wrote "Tour of Doctor Syntax in search of the Picturesque" (1812), to which Jane Austen refers, saying "I have seen nobody in London yet with such a long chin as Dr. Syntax, nor anybody quite so large as Gogmagoglicus" (*Letters*, p. 378).

COMBE or **COMBE MAGNA**, Som., Mr. Willoughby's estate (*SS*, 1.XIV).

COMPTON, the estate of a friend of Mr. Rushworth, the grounds of which were improved by Humphry Repton: "'The approach *now* is one of the finest things in the country'" (*MP*, 1.VI).

CONDUIT ST., London, where Sir John and Lady Middleton are lodging during the winter (*SS*, 2.V).

COOKE, CASSANDRA (née Leigh, 1744–1826), daughter of Theophilus Leigh (and thus first cousin to Jane Austen's mother), she married the Reverend Samuel Cooke (1741–1820), vicar of Great Bookham, Surrey. Jane Austen was close to their three children, Theophilus, George, and Mary, and visited Great Bookham. Mrs. Cooke wrote *Battleridge, an Historical Tale Founded on Facts* (1799), mentioned in passing (*Letters*, p. 24).

COOPER, (DR.) EDWARD (1) (1728–92), rector of Whaddon, near Bath, and Sonning, Berks. In 1768 he married Cassandra Austen (1)'s elder sister, Jane Leigh (one son and one daughter).

COOPER, EDWARD (2) (1770–1835), rector of Hamstall, Staffs., a cousin of Jane Austen; his family and the Austens were not close. He wrote *Practical and Familiar Sermons Designed for Parochial and Domestic Instruction* (1809) (*Letters*, pp. 252 and 255) and *Two Sermons Preached at Wolverhampton* (1816) (*Letters*, p. 467).

COOPER, MRS. JAMES (née Milman), an acquaintance of Mrs. Elton, she gave up music after marriage (E, 2.XIV).

COOPER, JANE (1) (née Leigh, d. 1783), elder sister of Jane Austen's mother; in 1768 she married the Reverend Dr. Edward Cooper (1).

COOPER, JANE (2) (d. 1798), cousin of Jane Austen to whom was dedicated "A Collection of Letters" (*Vol. 2*, p. 149) and "Henry and Eliza" (*Vol. 1*, p. 33). Later she became Lady Williams, the wife of Adm. Sir Thomas Williams.

COPE, MRS., and her daughter: they drink tea with A. F. and her daughters, who are making their "entrée into life"—"A Collection of Letters" (*Vol. 2*, p. 150).

CORINNA. See **Staël, Mme. de:** *Corinne.*

CORK, Ireland, one of the places Mrs. Croft lived while following her husband in the course of his career (*P*, 3.VIII).

CORNWALL is mentioned (*MP*, 1.XIII).

"CORSAIR, THE." See **Byron, George Gordon, Lord.**

CORYDON, a cameo part in "The Mystery" (*Vol. 1*, p. 55).

COTTAGER and **COTTAGER'S WIFE**, characters in Mrs. Inchbald's *Lovers' Vows*; the latter part was to be played by Mrs. Grant (*MP*, 1.XIV).

COURIER (daily newspaper published 1792–1842 in London; the official title was the *Courier and Evening Gazette*), in which the marriage of Lydia and Lieutenant Wickham receives notice (*PP*, 3.XI).

COURTENEY, GENERAL, a friend of General Tilney; his failure to appear in Bath makes the latter eager to return home (*NA*, 2.II).

COURTLAND, LORD, a crony of Robert Ferrars, he is supposedly planning to build a cottage (*SS*, 2.XIV).

COVENT GARDEN (THEATRE), London, where Philander and Gustavus act, under the names of Lewis and Quick—"Love and Freindship" (*Vol. 2*, p. 109). This would have been the second of three theaters so named, that is, the one built by Sir Robert Smirke.

COWLEY, HANNAH (1743–1809), dramatist and poet: *Which Is the Man?* (1782) (*a*) was acted at Steventon in 1787; (*b*) is to be acted in the theater in the house Mr. Watts is to buy for Miss Stanhope—"The Three Sisters" (*Vol. 1*, p. 65); (*c*) "tell him what you will" is a quotation of IV i (*Letters*, p. 469).

COWPER, WILLIAM (1731–1800), poet: (*a*) Jane Austen mentions her father's reading his poetry aloud (*Letters*, p. 39); (*b*) Marianne Dashwood refers to his "'beautiful lines which have frequently almost driven me wild'" (*SS*, 1.III); (1) "Truth" (from *Poems*, 1782) is paraphrased by Mr. Parker (*S*, p. 370); (2) *Tirocinium* (1785): when Fanny Price is homesick in Portsmouth, its lines are in her mind (*MP*, 3.XIV); (3) *The Task* (1785): (*a*) the words "Syringa, iv'ry pure" are referred to (*Letters*, p. 178); (*b*) "The Sofa," line 338, is quoted by Fanny Price (*MP*, 1.VI); (*c*) "The Winter Evening," line 290, is quoted (*E*, 3.V); (4) "Verses on Alexander Selkirk" (1782) is paraphrased (*Letters*, p. 335); Cowper is also mentioned (*SS*, 1.X, 1.XVII; *Letters*, pp. 33 and 368).

COX, MISS, sister of William Cox: one of the young ladies attending the Westons' ball at the Crown Inn, Highbury (*E*, 2.XI).

COX, ANNE, another sister of William Cox; she and her sister are described by Emma Woodhouse as "without exception, the most vulgar girls in Highbury" (*E*, 2.IX).

COX, WILLIAM (also Coxe), "a pert young lawyer" living in Highbury (*E*, 1.XVI); his father is also an attorney, and another young male Cox is also mentioned (*E*, 2.XI).

CRABBE, GEORGE (1754–1832), poet, mentioned in passing (*Letters*, pp. 319, 323, 358, and 370): his *Tales* (1812) is one of the books on Fanny Price's table in the East Room (*MP*, 1.XVI).

CRAMER, JOHANN BAPTIST (1771–1858), pianist, composer, and publisher: Frank Churchill sends a composition of his with the pianoforte he gives to Jane Fairfax (*E*, 2.X).

CRANKHUMDUNBERRY, where Charlotte Drummond's father was rector —"Frederic & Elfrida" (*Vol. 1*, p. 5).

CRAWFORD, ADMIRAL, uncle and guardian of Henry and Mary Crawford, "a man of vicious conduct, who chose, instead of retaining his niece [on his wife's death], to bring his mistress under his own roof" (*MP*, 1.IV).

CRAWFORD, MRS. (deceased), the admiral's ill-used wife (*MP*, 1.IV).

CRAWFORD, HENRY, a young man with a great deal of town polish, an estate in Norfolk, and £4,000 a year; of libertine propensities, when disappointed in his hopes of marrying Fanny Price, he ruins Maria Rushworth; "though not handsome, [he] had air and countenance" (*MP*, 1.IV).

CRAWFORD, MARY, Henry's sister, loved for a time by Edmund Bertram; she "was remarkably pretty.... Matrimony was her object, provided she could marry well" (*MP*, 1.IV).

CRAWFORDS, two young men with whom the susceptible Sophia was temporarily in love—"A Collection of Letters" (*Vol. 2*, p. 152).

CRESCENT (the Royal Crescent, Bath), an eighteenth-century residential development of great architectural merit, where most of Bath society walks on a Sunday afternoon "to breathe the fresh air of better company" (*NA*, 1.V).

CREWKHERNE (Crewkerne, Som.), on Mr. Elliot's way from Sidmouth to London (*P*, 3.XII).

CRITIC, THE. See **Sheridan, Richard Brinsley**.

CROFT, ADMIRAL: according to Mr. Shepherd "a very hale, hearty, well-looking man, a little weather-beaten, to be sure, but not much" (*P*, 3.III).

CROFT, SOPHIA (née Wentworth), Frederick Wentworth's elder sister, who "though neither tall nor fat, had a squareness, uprightness, and vigour of form, which gave importance to her person.... Her manners were open, easy, and decided, like one who had no distrust of herself, and no doubts of what to do; without any approach to coarseness, however, or any want of good humour" (*P*, 3.VI).

CROMER, Norfolk, according to Mr. Perry, "the best of all the sea-bathing places. A fine open sea, ... and very pure air" (*E*, 1.XII).

CROMWELL, the character in *Henry VIII*, parts of which are read by Henry Crawford to the Bertrams (*MP*, 3.III).

CROMWELL, OLIVER (1599–1658), one of the leaders of the antiroyalist forces in the English civil war, later made lord protector of the Commonwealth: he is vilified in "The History of England" (*Vol. 2*, p. 148).

CROSBY & SON, MESSRS., London, publishers who bought the manuscript of *Northanger Abbey*, under the title *Susan*, in 1803. Since they did not publish it, one of Jane Austen's brothers bought it back in about 1815.

CROWN, the inn in Portsmouth at which Henry Crawford stays while visiting Fanny Price there (*MP*, 3.X).

CROWN INN, Highbury, where the weekly whist parties are held and where the Westons host a ball for the neighborhood: "an inconsiderable house, though the principal one of the sort, where a couple of pair of post-horses were kept" (*E*, 2.VI).

CROYDON, Surrey, where the Robert Watsons live (*W*, p. 319).

CUMBERLAND, RICHARD (1732–1811), playwright: *The Wheel of Fortune* (1795) is one of the plays that Tom Bertram would like to see enacted at Mansfield (*MP*, 1.XIV).

CUMBERLAND, (*a*) where Colonel Drummond lives—"Lesley Castle" (*Vol. 2*, p. 117); (*b*) Fanny Price has a transparency of "a moonlight lake in Cumberland" on a window in the East Room, left over from schoolroom days (*MP*, 1.XVI).

CURTIS, MR., the surgeon to whom Sam Watson is apprenticed at Guildford (*W*, p. 321).

D. See **Dorking**.

DALRYMPLE, DOWAGER VISCOUNTESS: she "had acquired the name of 'a charming woman,' because she had a smile and a civil answer for every body" (*P*, 4.IV).

DALRYMPLE, VISCOUNT (deceased), the dowager's husband, a cousin of the Elliots, from Ireland. The Elliots' failure to send a letter of condolence at his death causes a breach between the two families (*P*, 4.IV).

DANVERS: Louisa Lesley left her husband, "her Child & reputation ... in company with Danvers & dishonour"—"Lesley Castle" (*Vol. 2*, p. 110).

DAPHNE, a character in "The Mystery" (*Vol. 1*, p. 55).

DARCY, MR. (deceased), Fitzwilliam Darcy's father; according to Lieutenant Wickham, he "was one of the best men that ever lived" (*PP*, 1.XVI).

DARCY, LADY ANNE (née Fitzwilliam, deceased), Fitzwilliam Darcy's mother and Lady Catherine de Bourgh's sister; she was the daughter of an earl (*PP*, 1.XVI).

DARCY, FITZWILLIAM, a young man of family and fortune, with an income of £10,000 a year; on his first appearance in the neighborhood of Meryton, he "drew the attention of the room by his fine, tall person, handsome features, noble mien; and the report which was in general circulation within five minutes after his entrance, of his having ten thousand a year" (*PP*, 1.III).

DARCY, GEORGIANA, Fitzwilliam Darcy's younger sister: she "was tall . . . and, though little more than sixteen, her figure was formed, and her appearance womanly and graceful. She was less handsome than her brother, but there was sense and good humour in her face, and her manners were perfectly unassuming and gentle" (*PP*, 3.II).

DARKWOOD, LADY BRIDGET. See **Dashwood, Lady Bridget**.

DARLING, MRS., a friend of Miss Capper and correspondent of Mrs. Griffiths (*S*, p. 408).

DARTFORD, Kent, near which Robert Ferrars's friends, (Sir or Lord) Elliott and Lady Elliott, live (*SS*, 2.XIV).

DASHWOOD, MR., uncle of Henry Dashwood; the former was "a single man, who lived to a very advanced age," the owner of Norland Park. His unmarried sister, Miss Dashwood, is also mentioned (*SS*, 1.I).

DASHWOOD, MRS., age forty, widow of Henry Dashwood (his second wife) and mother of Elinor, Marianne, and Margaret Dashwood: she possessed an "eagerness of mind . . . which must generally have led to imprudence" (*SS*, 1.I).

DASHWOOD, LADY BRIDGET, Miss Jane's sister, with whom she visits the "Young lady crossed in Love"—"A Collection of Letters" (*Vol. 2*, p. 152).

DASHWOOD, ELINOR, the eldest Dashwood daughter, she "possessed a strength of understanding, and coolness of judgment, which qualified her, though only nineteen, to be the counsellor of her mother" (*SS*, 1.I).

DASHWOOD, (MRS.) FANNY (née Ferrars): she was "a strong caricature of [her husband, John Dashwood];—more narrow-minded and selfish" (*SS*, 1.I).

DASHWOOD, HARRY, one of John Dashwood's sons (*SS*, 1.II).

DASHWOOD, HENRY (1) (deceased), the father of Elinor, Marianne, and Margaret, whose death necessitates their move to Barton (*SS*, 1.I).

DASHWOOD CAPTAIN HENRY (2) (deceased), Miss Jane's husband, who died "fighting for his Country in America"—"A Collection of Letters" (*Vol. 2*, p. 154).

DASHWOOD, MRS. HENRY. See **Annesley, Miss Jane**.

DASHWOOD, JOHN, only son of Henry Dashwood and half brother of Elinor, Marianne, and Margaret: "He was not an ill-disposed young man, unless to be rather cold hearted, and rather selfish, is to be ill-disposed: but he was, in general, well respected; for he conducted himself with propriety in the discharge of his ordinary duties" (*SS*, 1.I).

DASHWOOD, MARGARET, the youngest daughter of Mrs. (Henry) Dashwood: she "was a good-humoured well-disposed girl; but as she had already imbibed a good deal of Marianne's romance, without having much of her sense, she did not, at thirteen, bid fair to equal her sisters at a more advanced period of life" (*SS*, 1.I).

DASHWOOD, MARIANNE, at seventeen, "was sensible and clever; but eager in every thing; her sorrows, her joys, could have no moderation. She was generous, amiable, interesting: she was every thing but prudent" (*SS*, 1.I); "her face was so lovely, that when in the common cant of praise she was called a beautiful girl, truth was less violently outraged than usually happens" (*SS*, 1.X).

DAVENPORT, MR., the man Rosa Gower married—"Evelyn" (*Vol. 3*, p. 190).

DAVIES, DR., a divine, fond of the color pink; Anne Steele wishes he were in love with her (*SS*, 2.X).

DAVIS, MRS., a visitor to Sanditon (*S*, p. 389).

DAVIS, CHARLOTTE, a young lady in Bath to whom Captain Tilney pays marked attentions (*NA*, 2.XII).

DAVISON, T., of Lombard St., London, the printer of *Persuasion* in 1818.

DAWLISH, Devon, where Robert and Lucy Ferrars took their honeymoon (*SS*, 3.XII).

DAWSON, a servant of Lady Catherine de Bourgh, probably her dresser (*PP*, 2.XIV).

DAWSON, MISS, a lady who is coming to visit A. F. and her daughters on Saturday—"A Collection of Letters" (*Vol. 2*, p. 150).

DEAL, Kent, where Mrs. Croft spent a winter not long after her marriage (*P*, 3.VIII).

DEANE, Hants., near Steventon, George Austen's second parish; James, his eldest son, was later curate there.

DE BOURGH. See **Bourgh.**

DE COURCY, LADY (probably Catherine), Catherine Vernon's mother (*LS*, p. 246).

DE COURCY, CATHERINE. See **Vernon, Catherine (1).**

DE COURCY, REGINALD (1), Catherine Vernon's brother, temporarily enamored of Lady Susan, who says of him, "He is lively & seems clever, & when I have inspired him with greater respect for me than his sister's kind offices have implanted, he may be an agreable Flirt" (*LS*, p. 254).

DE COURCY, SIR REGINALD (2), Reginald (1)'s father: Alicia Johnson tells Lady Susan that he "'is very infirm, & not likely to stand in your way very long'" (*LS*, p. 256).

DEFOE, DANIEL (ca. 1661–1731), journalist and novelist: *Robinson Crusoe* (1719) is mentioned (*Letters*, p. 143).

DELAFORD, Dorset, parish of Colonel Brandon's estate (*SS*, 1.XIV).

DELAFORD HOUSE, Colonel Brandon's estate (*SS*, 3.XIV).

DELAMERE, FREDERIC, hero of *Emmeline*. See **Smith, Charlotte.**

DEMAND, MESSRS., & CO., imaginary bankers supposed to pay Jane Austen one hundred guineas for "Lesley Castle" (*Vol. 2*, p. 110).

DENHAM, LADY (née Brereton), "of middle height, stout, upright & alert in her motions, with a shrewd eye, & self-satisfied air—but not an unagreable Countenance" (*S*, p. 391).

DENHAM, SIR EDWARD, BART.: his "great object in life was to be seductive.—With such personal advantages as he knew himself to possess, & such Talents as he did also give himself credit for, he regarded it as his Duty.—He felt that he was formed to be a dangerous Man—quite in the line of the Lovelaces" (*S*, p. 405).

DENHAM, (MISS) ESTHER, "a fine young woman, but cold & reserved, giving the idea of one who felt her consequence with Pride & her Poverty with Discontent" (*S*, p. 394).

DENHAM, SIR HARRY, BART. (deceased), Lady Denham's second husband, whom she married for his title (*S*, p. 375).

DENHAM PARK, seat of Sir Edward Denham; his sister speaks of its dampness (*S*, pp. 375 and 402).

DENHAM PLACE, a new street in Sanditon (*S*, p. 384).

DENNISON, MRS., the hostess of the musical evening at which Elinor Dashwood meets Robert Ferrars (*SS*, 2.XIV).

DENNY, MR., an officer in Colonel Forster's regiment, and friend of George Wickham (*PP*, 1.XIV).

DERBYSHIRE, where Pemberley is situated; according to Caroline Bingley, "'There is not a finer county in England than Derbyshire'" (*PP*, 1.VIII); also mentioned (*Vol. 2*, p. 160; *Vol. 3*, p. 200).

DEVEREUX, SIR HENRY, who is supposed to accompany Camilla Stanley and her family to the Lake District—"Catharine or the Bower" (*Vol. 3*, p. 199).

DEVEREUX, ROBERT (second earl of Essex, 1566–1601), traitor to Queen Elizabeth: "It is sufficient to say that he was beheaded on the 25th of Febry, after having been Lord Leuitenant of Ireland, after having clapped his hand on his sword, and after performing many other services to his Country"—"The History of England" (*Vol. 2*, p. 146).

DEVIL TO PAY, THE. See **Coffey, Charles**.

DEVIZES, Wilts., (*a*) where Mr. Clifford regaled himself with a boiled egg on his journey from Bath to London—"Memoirs of Mr. Clifford" (*Vol. 1*, p. 43); (*b*) a stage in John Thorpe's journey from Bath to London (*NA*, 1.XV).

DEVONSHIRE, (*a*) the county in which Catharine and her aunt live—"Catharine or the Bower" (*Vol. 3*, p. 215); (*b*) the county in which Barton is located (*SS*, 1.IV).

DIBDIN, CHARLES (1745–1814), dramatist and songwriter: Jane Austen saw, at Covent Garden, *The Farmer's Wife* (1814), "a Musical thing in 3 Acts" (*Letters*, p. 315).

DICKINS, MISS, Lady Williams's governess, who eloped with the butler—"Jack & Alice" (*Vol. 1*, p. 17).

DISHONOUR, RAKEHELLY, ESQRE.: "the Worthless Louisa left [her husband], her Child & reputation a few weeks ago in company with Danvers & dishonour*" ("dishonour" is identified in a footnote)—"Lesley Castle" (*Vol. 2*, p. 110).

DIXON, MR., according to Miss Bates, "'an amiable, charming young man,'" with an estate in Ireland named Balycraig; he marries Miss Campbell but is suspected by Emma Woodhouse of an attachment to Miss Fairfax (*E*, 2.I).

DIXON, MRS. (née Campbell), Jane Fairfax's adoptive sister; according to Miss Bates, she "'always was absolutely plain—but extremely elegant and amiable'" (*E*, 2.I).

DODSLEY, ROBERT (1703–64), poet, dramatist, and bookseller: Jane Austen owned a copy of his *Collection of Poems by Several Hands* (1748–49 and 1758), which a Mr. Bent valued at ten shillings (*Letters*, p. 133); volume 2 contains Browne's "Pipe of Tobacco" and Whitehead's "Je ne scai Quoi": Mary Crawford parodies what she calls the "'Address to Tobacco'" (*MP*, 1.XVII), and there is an indirect quotation from "Je ne scai Quoi" (*MP*, 2.XII).

DOGE, THE FAMOUS, at the court of Louis XIV, referred to by Mary Crawford. When he was asked what he found most remarkable at Versailles, he replied, "C'est de m'y voir" (*MP*, 2.IV).

DON JUAN, OR THE LIBERTINE DESTROYED (1792) is a pantomime based on Thomas Shadwell's *Libertine* (1676), which Jane Austen saw with a sister-in-law and two nieces on Sept. 14, 1813 (*Letters*, p. 321); later she described it as "singsong & trumpery" (*Letters*, p. 338).

DONAVAN, MR., the physician who attends Mrs. Palmer after the birth of her child (*SS*, 3.I).

DONWELL, Surrey, the parish in which Donwell Abbey is situated; the land is largely owned by Mr. Knightley (*E*, 1.III).

DONWELL ABBEY, near Highbury, George Knightley (1)'s home; Emma Woodhouse admires "the respectable size and style of the building, its suitable, becoming, characteristic situation, low and sheltered—its ample gardens stretching down to meadows washed by a stream . . . and its abundance of timber in rows and avenues, which neither fashion nor extravagance had rooted up" (*E*, 3.VI).

DONWELL LANE, which runs between Highbury and Donwell, "'is never dusty,'" according to Mr. Knightley (*E*, 3.VI).

DORKING, Surrey, (*a*) is where the action of *The Watsons* is thought to take place: it is referred to as "D." throughout the fragment (*W*, p. 314); (*b*) it is a few miles from Highbury: Frank Churchill mentions it during the exploring party to Box Hill (*E*, 3.VII).

DOROTHEA, LADY: she was "lovely and Engaging," but Edward Lindsay refused to marry her because he did not wish it to be said that he had ever obliged his father—"Love and Freindship" (*Vol. 2*, p. 81).

DOROTHY, an imaginary housekeeper created by Henry Tilney (*NA*, 2.V).

DORSETSHIRE, (*a*) is where Eliza Williams was sent to live, at age fourteen, "under the care of a very respectable woman" (*SS*, 2.IX), and also the county in which Delaford is located (*SS*, 2.XI); (*b*) it is where Charles Hayter obtains his first living, on a temporary basis (*P*, 4.X).

DOUGLAS. See **Home, John.**

DOVEDALE, Derbys.: the Gardiners and Eliza Bennet must forgo its "celebrated beauties" when their vacation time is cut short (*PP*, 2.XIX).

DOVER, Kent, (*a*) where Eliza Cecil is seized by officers of the "Dutchess of F."—"Henry and Eliza" (*Vol. 1*, p. 36); (*b*) Sir William retires to a nearby village "in the hope of finding a shelter from the Pangs of Love"—"Sir William Mountague" (*Vol. 1*, p. 41).

DOWKINS, DR., the punning physician who attends Melissa's sickbed—"A Fragment written to inculcate the practise of Virtue" (*Vol. 1*, p. 72).

DRAKE, SIR FRANCIS (ca. 1540–96), admiral and global explorer: "the ornament of his Country & his profession"—"The History of England" (*Vol. 2*, p. 146).

DRAYTON, DR., who dined with Mr. Evelyn and fell asleep during the course of the evening—"A Collection of Letters" (*Vol. 2*, p. 160).

DRESDEN (china), mentioned by General Tilney (*NA*, 2.VII).

DREW, SIR ARCHIBALD, a crony of Admiral Croft, sighted in Bath accompanied by his grandson. He mistakes Anne Elliot for Mrs. Croft (*P*, 4.VI).

DRUMMOND, COLONEL and **MRS.,** the Lesleys' cousin and his wife, living in Cumberland—"Lesley Castle" (*Vol. 2*, p. 117).

DRUMMOND, MISS. See **Tilney, Mrs.**

DRUMMOND, REVEREND, Charlotte Drummond's father, the rector of Crankhumdunberry—"Frederic & Elfrida" (*Vol. 1*, p. 5).

DRUMMOND, CHARLOTTE, "whose character was a willingness to oblige every one"; on realizing that she had agreed to become engaged to two different men, "the reflection of her past folly, operated so strongly on her mind, that she resolved to be guilty of a greater, & to that end threw herself into a deep stream which ran thro' her Aunt's pleasure Grounds in Portland Place"—"Frederic & Elfrida" (*Vol. 1*, pp. 4 and 9).

DRURY LANE (THEATRE), London: Willoughby meets Sir John Middleton there and discovers that Marianne Dashwood is dangerously ill (*SS*, 3.VIII).

DUBERLY, LORD, a character in George Colman the younger's *Heir at Law* (*MP*, 1.XIV).

DUBLIN, where the Dixons are meeting Colonel and Mrs. Campbell on the latters' visit to Ireland (*E*, 2.I).

DUDLEY, MISS: Camilla Stanley met her at Ranelagh, "'and she had such a frightful Cap on, that I have never been able to bear any [of the Dudley family] since'"—"Catharine or the Bower" (*Vol. 3*, p. 204).

DUDLEY, REVEREND, who replaced Mr. Wynne in the living of Chetwynde—"Catharine or the Bower" (*Vol. 3*, p. 195).

DUGDALE, SIR WILLIAM (1605-86), Garter king of arms: his *Antient usage in bearing of such ensigns of honour as are commonly call'd arms; to which is added a catalogue of the present nobility and baronets of England* (1682) is mentioned as containing an early reference to the Elliot family (*P*, 3.I).

DUNBEATH, Caithness, where Mr. Lesley had an estate on which he lived after his marriage to "the Worthless Louisa"—"Lesley Castle" (*Vol. 2*, p. 118).

DUPUIS, MRS. CHARLES, a friend of Diana Parker who is acquainted with Mrs. Griffiths (*S*, p. 411).

DURANDS, the little: a well-known Bath family attending the concert in Bath, "'with their mouths open to catch the music,'" according to Mrs. Smith (*P*, 4.IX).

DUTTON, KITTY and **JEMIMA**, over whom Miss Stanhope will triumph by virtue of the offer she received from Mr. Watts; their brother John is also mentioned—"The Three Sisters" (*Vol. 1*, p. 57).

EAST BOURNE, Sussex: (*a*) Sanditon was supposed to be situated on "that part of the Sussex Coast which lies between Hastings & E. Bourne" (*S*, p. 363); (*b*) Mr. Gell and Miss Gill lived there (*Verses*, p. 444); also mentioned (*PP*, 3.VI).

EAST INDIES: (*a*) the elder Miss Wynne "had been obliged to accept the offer of one of her cousins to equip her for the East Indies . . . to embrace the only possibility that was offered to her, of a Maintenance"—"Catharine or the Bower" (*Vol. 3*, p. 194; later it is said that she went to Bengal instead); (*b*) Colonel Brandon's regiment had been stationed there at the time of his father's death (*SS*, 2.IX); (*c*) Mrs. Norris hopes William Price will buy her a shawl there (*MP*, 2.XIII); (*d*) Admiral Croft was stationed there after Trafalgar; Mrs. Croft accompanied him (*P*, 3.III, 3.VIII); also mentioned (*SS*, 1.X).

EAST KINGHAM FARM, "where old Gibson used to live," adjacent to Norland Park in Sussex; John Dashwood claims that its purchase put a severe strain on his purse (*SS*, 2.XI).

EAST ROOM, at Mansfield Park: formerly the schoolroom, it later became Fanny Price's sitting room (*MP*, 1.XVI).

EASTON, Northants., a village near Mansfield (*MP*, 2.I).

ECCLESFORD, Cornwall, the seat of the Right Honorable Lord Ravenshaw, whose private theatricals inspired Mansfield to emulation (*MP*, 1.XIII).

"EDGAR & EMMA," a tale of failures in communication (*Vol. 1*, p. 29).

EDGAR'S BUILDINGS, Bath (at the top of Milsom St.), where the Thorpes had lodgings (*NA*, 1.VI); it was evidently a pretty fashionable (though noisy) location and very close to where the Tilneys stayed.

EDGECUMBE, MRS., and her daughters: Kitty suggests cattily to her sister Mary that she should chaperone the six Misses Edgecumbe to the first ball she attends as a married lady in order to make her "Entrée very respectable"—"The Three Sisters" (*Vol. 1*, p. 69).

EDGEWORTH, MARIA (1767–1849), novelist: in 1814, Jane Austen tells her niece Anna, "I have made up my mind to like no Novels really, but Miss Edgeworth's, Yours & my own" (*Letters*, p. 405); (1) *Belinda* (1801) is one of the works "in which the greatest powers of the mind are displayed, in which the most thorough knowledge of human nature, the happiest delineation of its varieties, the liveliest effusions of wit and humour are conveyed to the world in the best chosen language" (*NA*, 1.V); (2) *Tales from Fashionable Life* (second series, 1812) is probably what Jane Austen refers to (*Letters*, p. 305); (3) *Patronage* (1814) is mentioned (*Letters*, p. 398).

EDINBURGH, Scotland, (*a*) is where Laura goes after Sophia's death on a stagecoach driven by Philippa and her husband—"Love and Freindship" (*Vol. 2*, p. 102); (*b*) Sir George Lesley writes to his daughter Matilda from there—"Lesley Castle" (*Vol. 2*, p. 122).

EDWARD IV (1442–83), king of England, "famous only for his Beauty & his Courage . . . & his undaunted Behaviour in marrying one Woman while he was engaged to another"—"The History of England" (*Vol. 2*, p. 140).

EDWARD V (1470–83), king of England: "This unfortunate Prince lived so little a while that no body had time to draw his picture"—"The History of England" (*Vol. 2*, p. 140).

EDWARD VI (1537–53), king of England, mentioned in passing—"The History of England" (*Vol. 2*, p. 143).

EDWARD ST., London, (*a*) is where the Johnsons live (*LS*, p. 252), and (*b*) where Lieutenant Wickham's accomplice, Mrs. Younge, had a house for lodgers (*PP*, 3.X).

EDWARDS, MR., a gentleman living in D. who "had lived long enough in the Idleness of a Town to become a little of a gossip" (*W*, p. 325).

EDWARDS, MRS., his wife, who, "tho' a very freindly woman, had a reserved air, & a great deal of formal Civility" (*W*, p. 322).

EDWARDS, MARY, who has "the shew of good sense, a modest unpretending mind, & a great wish of obliging" (*W*, p. 323).

EGERTON, THOMAS (Military Library, Whitehall, London), the original publisher of *Sense and Sensibility*, *Pride and Prejudice*, and *Mansfield Park*.

ELEGANT EXTRACTS. See **Knox, Vicesimus**.

"ELEGY WRITTEN IN A COUNTRY CHURCHYARD." See **Gray, Thomas**.

A DICTIONARY OF JANE AUSTEN'S LIFE AND WORKS

ELEPHANT, a ship in Portsmouth harbor (*MP*, 3.VII).

ELINOR AND MARIANNE, the title assigned to an early epistolary version of *Sense and Sensibility*; no longer extant.

ELIZA. See **Brandon, Eliza; Williams, Eliza.**

ELIZABETH, QUEEN (1533–1603) of England: (*a*) "It was the peculiar Misfortune of this Woman to have bad Ministers—Since wicked as she herself was, she could not have committed such extensive mischief, had not these vile & abandoned men connived at, & encouraged her in her crimes"—"The History of England" (*Vol. 2*, p. 144); (*b*) Mrs. Stanley believes that she "lived to a good old age, and was a very Clever Woman"—"Catharine or the Bower" (*Vol. 3*, p. 201); (*c*) Sotherton Court was built during her reign (*MP*, 1.VI).

ELIZABETH OF YORK (1465–1503), Henry VII's queen—"The History of England" (*Vol. 2*, p. 141).

ELIZABETHS, prototypical wives of Elliots (*P*, 3.I).

ELLINOR, Anna Parker's correspondent—"Scraps" (*Vol. 2*, p. 174).

ELLIOT, MRS. (deceased), the wife of William Elliot: "She was certainly not a woman of family, but well educated, accomplished, rich, and excessively in love" with Mr. Elliot (*P*, 4.III).

ELLIOT, ANNE, heroine of *Persuasion*, aged twenty-seven, "with an elegance of mind and sweetness of character, which must have placed her high with any people of real understanding" (*P*, 3.I).

ELLIOT, LADY ELIZABETH (1) (deceased, née Stevenson): she "had been an excellent woman, sensible and amiable; whose judgment and conduct, if they might be pardoned the youthful infatuation which made her Lady Elliot, had never required indulgence afterwards" (*P*, 3.I).

ELLIOT, ELIZABETH (2), age twenty-nine, Sir Walter (2)'s eldest daughter and a junior replica of him; "still the same handsome Miss Elliot that she had begun to be thirteen years ago" (*P*, 3.I).

ELLIOT, MARY. See **Musgrove, Mary.**

ELLIOT, SIR WALTER, BART. (1), grandfather of the current Sir Walter (*P*, 3.I).

ELLIOT, SIR WALTER, BART. (2), of Kellynch Hall: "Vanity was the beginning and the end of Sir Walter Elliot's character; vanity of person and of situation. He had been remarkably handsome in his youth; and, at fifty-four, was still a very fine man" (*P*, 3.I).

ELLIOT, WILLIAM WALTER, by education a lawyer, heir to the baronetcy; Sir Walter (2) "did justice to his very gentlemanlike appearance, his air of elegance and fashion, his good shaped face, his sensible eye, but, at the same time, 'must lament his being very much under-hung, a defect which time seemed to have increased'" (*P*, 4.III).

ELLIOTT, ——, and **LADY ELLIOTT**, friends of Robert Ferrars living in a cottage near Dartford (*SS*, 2.XIV).

ELLIOTT, COLONEL and **FANNY**, characters in "The Mystery" (*Vol. 1*, p. 55).

ELLIS, the personal maid of the Misses Bertram (*MP*, 1.I).

ELLISON, MR. and **MRS.**, the guardians of Miss Grey (later Mrs. Willoughby; *SS*, 2.VIII).

ELTON, (MRS.) AUGUSTA (née Hawkins), the second daughter of a Bristol merchant: "Her person was rather good; her face not unpretty; but neither feature, nor air, nor voice, nor manner, were elegant.... a vain woman, extremely well satisfied with herself, and thinking much of her own importance; ... she meant to shine and be very superior, but with manners which had been formed in a bad school, pert and familiar" (*E*, 2.XIV).

ELTON, PHILIP, the vicar of Highbury, about twenty-six or twenty-seven; according to Emma Woodhouse, "He was reckoned very handsome; his person much admired in general, though not by her, there being a want of elegance of feature which she could not dispense with" (*E*, 1.IV).

EMILY (1), a character in Mrs. Radcliffe's *Mysteries of Udolpho*; she and her father are mentioned by Catherine Morland (*NA*, 1.XIV), and she and her aunt by Henry Tilney (*NA*, 1.XIV).

EMILY (2), with her sister (?) Sophia, "two of the sweetest girls in the world, who had been [Anne Thorpe's] dear friends all the morning" (*NA*, 1.XIV).

EMMA (1), a character in Matthew Prior's "Henry and Emma," mentioned in negative analogy to Anne Elliot (*P*, 3.XII).

EMMA (2): Henry Gipps is "'in a Dilemma, for want of an Emma'" (*Verses*, p. 449): this probably refers to Emma Maria Plumtre, whom he married about 1812.

EMMELINE. See **Smith, Charlotte**.

ENDYMION, a ship anchored at the Spithead, Portsmouth harbor (*MP*, 3.VII).

ENSCOMBE, Yorks., the estate of the Churchills (*E*, 1.II).

EPSOM, Surrey: when Lieutenant Wickham and Lydia Bennet elope, they hire a chaise to take them from Epsom to Clapham (*PP*, 3.IV).

ESPRIELLA. See **Southey, Robert**: *Letters from England, by Dom Manuel Alvarez Espriella*.

ESSAY ON MAN. See **Pope, Alexander**.

ESSEX, where the "young Lady rather impertinent" lives—"A Collection of Letters" (*Vol. 2*, p. 160).

ESSEX, ROBERT, EARL OF: Jane Austen praises "those first of Men Robert Earl of Essex, Delamere, or Gilpin"—"The History of England" (*Vol. 2*, p. 143): see **Devereux, Robert**.

ETHELINDE. See **Smith, Charlotte**.

ETON, Bucks., the school attended by Tom and Edmund Bertram; for several centuries it has been the preeminent school for scions of the English aristocracy (*MP*, 1.II).

EVELINA. See **Burney, Frances**.

EVELYN, MR. and **MRS.**, a couple with whom the "young Lady rather impertinent" dines—"A Collection of Letters" (*Vol. 2*, p. 160).

"**EVELYN**," a romantic tale (*Vol. 3*, p. 180).

EVELYN, Sussex, "perhaps one of the most beautiful Spots in the south of England"—"Evelyn" (*Vol. 3*, p. 180).

EVERINGHAM, Norfolk, Henry Crawford's estate (*MP*, 1.VI).

EXETER, Devon, (*a*) about five miles from Chetwynde—"Catharine or the Bower" (*Vol. 3*, p. 240); (*b*) Barton is situated about four miles north of Exeter, which is mentioned passim (*SS*, 1.V); (*c*) it is where Henrietta and Louisa Musgrove went to school (*P*, 3.V).

EXETER EXCHANGE, London, where was housed a collection of wild animals that young Harry Dashwood was very eager to see (*SS*, 2.XI).

F., DUTCHESS OF: "Her passions were strong, her freindships firm & her Enmities, unconquerable"—"Henry and Eliza" (*Vol. 1*, p. 35).

F., LADY HARRIET, the duchess's daughter, "on the point of marriage with a young Man of considerable fortune"—"Henry and Eliza" (*Vol. 1*, p. 35).

FAINTING: Sophia's deathbed advice to Laura is "'Beware of swoons.... A frenzy fit is not one quarter so pernicious; it is an exercise to the Body & if not too violent, is I dare say conducive to Health in its consequences—Run mad as often as you chuse; but do not faint"—"Love and Freindship" (*Vol. 2*, p. 102).

FAIRFAX, LIEUTENANT, an infantryman who married Miss Jane Bates and died, not long after, "in action abroad ... an excellent officer and most deserving young man" (*E*, 2.II).

FAIRFAX, JANE (1) (née Bates), younger sister of Miss Hetty Bates, she died of "consumption and grief" when her daughter, Jane Fairfax (2), was a baby (*E*, 2.II).

FAIRFAX, JANE (2), orphaned daughter of Lieutenant and Mrs. Fairfax, brought up by the Bateses and the Campbells and destined to be a governess, until she captivates Frank Churchill; according to Emma Woodhouse, she "was very elegant, remarkably elegant; ... her face, her features—there was more beauty in them all together than [Emma] had remembered; it was not regular, but it was very pleasing beauty" (*E*, 2.II).

FAIRFAX, THOMAS (third baron Fairfax, 1612–71), a general under Cromwell, among the list of "original Causers of all the disturbances Distresses & Civil Wars in which England for many years was embroiled"—"The History of England" (*Vol. 2*, p. 148).

FALKNOR, ELFRIDA, and her cousin Frederic "were exceedingly handsome and so much alike, that it was not every one who knew them apart"—"Frederic & Elfrida" (*Vol. 1*, p. 4).

FALKNOR, FREDERIC: "in any threatening Danger to his Life or Liberty, Frederic was as bold as brass yet in other respects his heart was as soft as cotton"—"Frederic & Elfrida" (*Vol. 1*, p. 11).

FANNY (1), Mary Stanhope's correspondent—"The Three Sisters" (*Vol. 1*, p. 57).

FANNY (2), a cousin of Colonel Brandon (*SS*, 1.XIII).

FARMER'S WIFE, THE. See **Dibdin, Charles**.

FATHER'S INSTRUCTIONS, A. see **Percival, Thomas**.

FAULKLAND, VISCOUNT (Lucius Cary, second viscount Falkland, ca. 1610–43), according to Jane Austen, one of Charles I's five loyal supporters—"The History of England" (*Vol. 2*, p. 148).

FEMALE QUIXOTE, THE. See **Lennox, Charlotte**.

FERRARS, MRS., the mother of Edward and Robert: she "was a little, thin woman, upright, even to formality, in her figure, and serious, even to sourness, in her aspect. Her complexion was sallow; and her features small, without beauty, and naturally without expression; but a lucky contraction of the brow had rescued her countenance from the disgrace of insipidity, by giving it the strong characters of pride and ill nature" (*SS*, 2.XII).

FERRARS, EDWARD, who marries Elinor Dashwood: "He was not handsome, and his manners required intimacy to make them pleasing. He was too diffident to do justice to himself; but when his natural shyness was overcome, his behaviour gave every indication of an open affectionate heart. His understanding was good, and his education had given it solid improvement" (*SS*, 1.III).

FERRARS, FANNY. See **Dashwood, Fanny.**

FERRARS, LUCY (née Steele), age twenty-three; after being engaged for several years to Edward Ferrars, she marries his brother clandestinely; she had "considerable beauty; her features were pretty, and she had a sharp quick eye, and a smartness of air, which though it did not give actual elegance or grace, gave distinction to her person" (*SS*, 1.XXI).

FERRARS, ROBERT, Edward's younger brother and the favorite of his mother; he had "a person and face, of strong, natural, sterling insignificance, though adorned in the first style of fashion" (*SS*, 2.XI).

[FERRARS], SIR ROBERT, the uncle of Edward and Robert (assumed to be a Ferrars, though he might be on their mother's side; *SS*, 2.XIV).

FEUILLIDE, ELIZA, COMTESSE DE. See **Austen, Eliza.**

FIELDING, HENRY (1707–54), novelist: *Tom Jones* (1749) is (*a*) one of the few novels that appeals to John Thorpe's taste (*NA*, 1.VII); (*b*) mentioned (*Letters*, p. 3).

FIRST IMPRESSIONS: title given to an early, probably epistolary version of *Pride and Prejudice*; it has not survived.

FISHER, MISS, and **MRS. JANE,** visitors to Sanditon (*S*, p. 389).

FITZGERALD, LORD and **MISS,** the host and his daughter—"The Visit" (*Vol. 1*, p. 50).

FITZGERALD, SUSAN. See **Lesley, Lady Susan.**

FITZGERALD, WILLIAM, "certainly one of the most pleasing young Men [Margaret Lesley] ever beheld," the brother of Lady Susan Lesley, Margaret's stepmother—"Lesley Castle" (*Vol. 2*, p. 122).

FITZGIBBON, SIR GEORGE, a cousin who arranged that the elder Miss Wynne should go to India—"Catharine or the Bower" (*Vol. 3*, p. 203).

FITZOWEN, one of a fickle young lady's passing attachments—"A Collection of Letters" (*Vol. 2*, p. 152).

FITZROY, MRS., a lady who moves into the neighborhood where Frederic and Elfrida live—"Frederic & Elfrida" (*Vol. 1*, p. 6).

FITZROY, JEZALINDA, daughter of Mrs. Fitzroy, a young lady with an "engaging Exterior & beautifull outside—"Frederic & Elfrida" (*Vol. 1*, p. 6).

FITZROY, REBECCA, daughter of Mrs. Fitzroy: Frederic, Elfrida, and Charlotte praise her thus: "'Lovely & too charming Fair one, notwithstanding your forbidding Squint, your greazy tresses & your swelling Back, which are more frightful than imagination can paint or pen describe, I cannot refrain from expressing my raptures, at the engaging Qualities of your Mind, which so amply atone for the Horror, with which your first appearance must ever inspire the unwary visitor'"—"Frederic & Elfrida" (*Vol. 1*, p. 6).

FITZWILLIAM, COLONEL, a younger son of an earl and Fitzwilliam Darcy's cousin, "about thirty, not handsome, but in person and address most truly the gentleman" (*PP*, 2.VII).

FIVE HOURS AT BRIGHTON. See **Beazley, Samuel.**

FLAMBEAU, LADY, with whom the Lesleys dine in London—"Lesley Castle" (*Vol. 2*, p. 137).

FLETCHER, SAM, a friend of John Thorpe, with a horse to sell (*NA*, 1.X).

FOLLY, a pointer bitch belonging to Sir John Middleton (*SS*, 2.X).

FOOTE, (CAPT.) EDWARD JAMES (1767–1833) and **MARY FOOTE** (née Patton), his second wife: among Jane Austen's minor works is a stanza (*Verses*, p. 452) in honor of their marriage in 1803; the *Memoir* ascribes it to Mrs. Leigh Perrot.

FORD, MRS., a shopkeeper in Highbury (*E*, 2.IX).

FORD'S in Highbury, "the principal woollen-draper, linen-draper, and haberdasher's shop united" (*E*, 2.III).

FORDYCE, JAMES (1720–96), Presbyterian minister and poet: Mr. Collins reads three pages from his *Sermons to Young Women* (1766) to the Bennets (*PP*, 1.XIV).

FORSTER, COLONEL, commander of the regiment stationed in Meryton (*PP*, 1.VI).

FORSTER, HARRIET, Colonel Forster's new wife, who invites Lydia Bennet to visit in Brighton (*PP*, 2.XVI).

FORTHERINGAY CASTLE (Fotheringay, Northants.), where Mary Queen of Scots was executed—"The History of England" (*Vol. 2*, p. 145).

FOWLE, THOMAS, fiancé of Cassandra Austen (2), when he was rector at Allington, Wilts. He died in the West Indies of yellow fever in 1797.

"A FRAGMENT WRITTEN TO INCULCATE THE PRACTISE OF VIRTUE," "Miscellaneous Morsels" dedicated to Jane Anna Elizabeth Austen (*Vol. 1*, p. 71).

FRANCE, SOUTH OF: Catherine Morland extols its beautiful weather (*NA*, 1.XI); "Italy, Switzerland, and the South of France, might be as fruitful in horrors as they were represented" by Mrs. Radcliffe (*NA*, 2.X).

FRANKLAND, MRS., an acquaintance of Lady Russell in Bath, she particularly admires the curtains in a window in Pulteney St. (*P*, 4.VII).

FRASER, the Ladies, neighbors of General Tilney in Gloucestershire (*NA*, 2.XI).

FRASER, MR., a gentleman living in London; Mary Crawford describes him as "'ill-tempered, and *exigeant*'" (*MP*, 3.V).

FRASER, MRS. JANET (née Ross), an old and despised friend of Mary Crawford and Mr. Fraser's second wife (*MP*, 3.V).

FRASER, MARGARET, a daughter of Mr. Fraser by his first wife; she tries to ensnare Henry Crawford (*MP*, 3.V).

FREDERIC, a servant at Lord and Lady L.'s house at Colnebrook (*CG*, IV i).

"FREDERIC & ELFRIDA," a romance of two cousins (*Vol. 1*, p. 4).

FREDERICK, a character in Mrs. Inchbald's *Lovers' Vows*, to be played at Mansfield by Henry Crawford (*MP*, 1.XIV).

FREEMAN, the Christchurch man who sold John Thorpe his curricle-hung gig (*NA*, 1.VII).

FULLERTON, Wilts., where the Morland family lives, about nine miles from Salisbury (*NA*, 1.I).

G., LORD, the suitor of Charlotte Grandison (*CG*, IV i).
GAMESTER, THE. See **Moore, Edward.**
GARDINER, EDWARD, Mrs. Bennet's businessman brother, "a sensible, gentlemanlike man, greatly superior to his sister as well by nature as education" (*PP*, 2.II).
GARDINER, MRS. M., Mrs. Bennet's sister-in-law, with two daughters and two sons: she "was an amiable, intelligent, elegant woman, and a great favourite with all her Longbourn nieces" (*PP*, 2.II).
GARRICK, DAVID (1717–79), actor and playwright: (1) *Isabella, or The Fatal Marriage: A Tragedy* (1757), adapted from Thomas Southerner's *Fatal Marriage*, is mentioned (*Letters*, pp. 415 and 417); (2) *Bon Ton, or High Life Above Stairs* (1775) was acted at Steventon in 1787; (3) "Kitty, a Fair but Frozen Maid," a riddle published in various sources (though not, as claimed, in Vicesimus Knox's *Elegant Extracts*), is misquoted by Mr. Woodhouse (*E*, 1.IX). See also **Colman, George (the elder):** *The Clandestine Marriage;* **High Life Below Stairs; Moore, Edward:** *The Gamester.*
GARRISON CHAPEL, Portsmouth, attended by the Prices (*MP*, 3.XI): built in 1212 as a hospice, the Domus Dei; after the dissolution of the monasteries, became the residence of the military governor, and its chapel was used by the naval personnel stationed there.
GASCOIGNE, SIR WILLIAM (ca. 1350–1419), chief justice of the king's bench: according to Jane Austen, he was beaten by Henry V. This apocryphal claim is based on Sir Thomas Elyot's *Gouvernour* (1531)—"The History of England" (Vol. 2, p. 139).
GAY, JOHN (1685–1732), poet and dramatist: from his *Fables* (1727), (*a*) "The Hare and Many Friends" is quoted by Mrs. Elton (*E*, 3.XVI); (*b*) Catherine Morland learned "The Hare and Many Friends" "as quickly as any girl in England" (*NA*, 1.I).
GAY ST., Bath, a respectable address where the Crofts "had placed themselves in lodgings . . . perfectly to Sir Walter's satisfaction" (*P*, 4.VI).
GELL, MR. See **"Mr. Gell and Miss Gill."**
"GENEROUS CURATE, THE," a "moral Tale, setting forth the Advantages of being Generous and a Curate" (*Vol. 1*, p. 73).
GENLIS, MME. DE (Stéphanie Félicité du Crest de St.-Aubin, 1746–1830), French novelist: (1) *Adelaide and Theodore* (1782, trans. 1783) is mentioned by Emma Woodhouse (*E*, 3.XVII); (2) *Les veillées du château* (1784): (*a*) Jane Austen mentions reading the first volume in 1800 (*Letters*, p. 82); (*b*) of *Olympe et Théophile*, which is one part of *Les veillées*, Jane Austen says, "I do not think I could even now, at my sedate time of life, read *Olimpe et Theophile* without being in a rage" (*Letters*, p. 450); (3) of *Alphonsine: or Maternal Affection* (1806, trans. 1807), Jane Austen says, "'Alphonsine' did not do. We were disgusted in twenty pages, as, independent of a bad translation, it has indelicacies which disgrace a pen hitherto so pure" (*Letters*, p. 173).
GEORGE, the, an inn at Meryton (*PP*, 2.XVI).
"GIAOUR, THE." See **Byron, George Gordon, Lord.**
GIBRALTAR: (*a*) William Price visited there while he was a midshipman on the *Antwerp* (*MP*, 2.VI); (*b*) Captain Wentworth met the Musgroves' son Richard

there; it is also one of the places Mrs. Croft visited while following her husband in the course of his career (*P*, 3.VIII).

GIBSON, a farmer who had owned land adjacent to Norland Park, presumably until his death (*SS*, 2.XI).

GIBSON, MARY. See **Austen, Mary**.

GILBERT, the name of a family living near Barton; they owe the Middletons an invitation (*SS*, 1.XX).

GILBERT, MISS, the sister-in-law of Mrs. Gilbert, expected to visit Highbury: there are also apparently at least two Mr. Gilberts (*E*, 2.XI).

GILBERT, MRS., a lady attending the ball given by the Westons at the Crown Inn, Highbury (*E*, 3.II).

GILL, MISS. See "**Mr. Gell and Miss Gill.**"

GILPIN, WILLIAM (1724–1804), miscellaneous writer and arbiter of the picturesque, described by Jane Austen as one of the "first of Men"—"The History of England" (*Vol. 2*, p. 143); *Observations on . . . Particularly the High-lands of Scotland* (1789) inspires Augusta Lindsay with a desire to undertake a tour of Scotland—"Love and Freindship" (*Vol. 2*, p. 105).

GIPPS, REVEREND HENRY, an acquaintance of the Austens, and the subject of two lines of verse by Jane Austen (*Verses*, p. 449).

GISBORNE, THOMAS (the elder, 1758–1846), clergyman and miscellaneous writer: *An Enquiry Into the Duties of the Female Sex* (1797) may be the reference when Jane Austen says to her sister, "I am glad you recommended 'Gisborne,' for having begun, I am pleased with it" (*Letters*, p. 169).

GLENFORD, Sussex, from which Charlotte Lutterell writes to Margaret Lesley—"Lesley Castle" (*Vol. 2*, p. 112).

GLOUCESTERSHIRE, (*a*) the county in which Northanger Abbey is situated (*NA*, 1.III); (*b*) where South Park, the childhood home of Lady Elliot, is located (*P*, 3.I).

GODBY, MISS, a London gossip mentioned in passing by Miss Steele (*SS*, 3.II).

GODDARD, MRS., mistress of a boarding school in Highbury, "a plain, motherly kind of woman, who had worked hard in her youth, and now thought herself entitled to the occasional holiday of a tea-visit" (*E*, 1.III).

GODMERSHAM PARK, Kent, near Canterbury, the principal seat of the Knights. After they had made Jane Austen's elder brother Edward their heir, she often visited there.

GODWIN, WILLIAM (the elder, 1756–1836), dissenting minister and political writer: "*He* [Mr. Pickford] is as raffish in his appearance as I would wish every Disciple of Godwin to be" (*Letters*, p. 133).

GOETHE, JOHANN WOLFGANG VON (1749–1832), German poet, dramatist, novelist, and scientist: *The Sorrows of Young Werther* (1774, various English translations before 1790) is a book the prosaic Graham is supposed never to have read—"Love and Freindship" (*Vol. 2*, p. 93).

GOLDSMITH, OLIVER (1728–74), poet, novelist, playwright, and miscellaneous belletrist: (1) *The Vicar of Wakefield* (1766) (*a*) is one of the few novels Robert Martin has read (*E*, 1.IV); (*b*) "When lovely woman stoops to folly" is a song appearing in chapter 29 of *The Vicar*; of Mrs. Churchill, Jane Austen says, "Goldsmith tells us, that when lovely woman stoops to folly, she has nothing to do but to die; and when she stoops to be disagreeable, it is equally to be recommended as a clearer of ill-fame" (*E*, 3.IX); (2) *History of England* (1771) is probably the work of Goldsmith that Fanny Price read to her sister Susan (*MP*, 3.XII).

GOSSIP: Mr. Bennet asks, "For what do we live, but to make sport for our neighbours, and laugh at them in our turn?'" (*PP*, 3.XV).

GOULDING, WILLIAM, the son in a gentleman's family that lives at Haye Park, in the neighborhood of Meryton (*PP*, 3.IX).

GOWER, FREDERIC, the sensitive and forgetful hero of "Evelyn" (*Vol. 3*, p. 180).

GOWER, SIR JAMES, one of Margaret Lesley's "too numerous Admirers"—"Lesley Castle" (*Vol. 2*, p. 136).

GOWER, MARIA (née Webb), the wife of Frederic Gower—"Evelyn" (*Vol. 3*, p. 183).

GOWER, ROSE, the thirteenth child of the Gower family: "From the clearness of her skin & the Brilliancy of her Eyes, she was fully entitled to all their partial affection. Another circumstance contributed to the general Love they bore her, and that was one of the finest heads of hair in the world"—"Evelyn" (*Vol. 3*, p. 184).

GOWLAND, a lotion used by Mrs. Clay for removing her freckles (*P*, 4.IV): R. W. Chapman found a Mrs. Vincent Gowland's lotion advertised in the Bath *Chronicle*, Jan. 6, 1814.

GRACECHURCH ST., London, a street unfashionably located in the City, where the Gardiners live (*PP*, 2.II).

GRAHAM, MR. (1), fiancé of Janetta Macdonald: "he was sensible, well-informed, and Agreable; . . . but [Sophia and Laura] were convinced he had no soul, that he had never read the Sorrows of Werter, & that his Hair bore not the slightest resemblance to Auburn"—"Love and Freindship" (*Vol. 2*, p. 93).

GRAHAM, MR. (2), a friend of John Knightley, he plans to have a Scottish bailiff to look after his estate (*E*, 1.XII).

GRANDISON, SIR CHARLES, hero of the playlet that Jane Austen adapted freely from Richardson's novel (*CG*, III ii).

GRANDISON, SIR CHARLES. See **Richardson, Samuel.**

GRANDISON, CHARLOTTE, Sir Charles's younger sister, a lady much addicted to raillery (*CG*, III i); according to Mr. Selby, "'a fine girl, only she is too nice about an husband'" (*CG*, V i).

GRANT, REVEREND DR., the incumbent of Mansfield Parsonage after the death of Mr. Norris, "a hearty man of forty-five," who, in Tom Bertram's view, "'was a short-neck'd, apoplectic sort of fellow, and, plied well with good things, would soon pop off'" (*MP*, 1.III); instead, he obtains preferment at Westminster Abbey, leaving the parish open to Edmund Bertram.

GRANT, MRS., a very good-natured lady of thirty-one, who invites her half sister Mary Crawford to live with her at Mansfield after Mrs. Crawford's death (*MP*, 1.III).

GRANT, (MRS.) ANNE (1755–1838), miscellaneous Scottish writer: (1) *Letters from the Mountains, Being the Real Correspondence of a Lady, Between the Years 1773 and 1807* (1807) is mentioned (*Letters*, pp. 184, 292, 294, and 305); (2) likewise *Memoirs of an American Lady* (1808) (*Letters*, p. 248).

GRANTLEY, MISS, an acquaintance of Miss Bingley, she makes designs for tables (*PP*, 1.X).

GRAPPLER, a ship commanded by Captain Benwick (*P*, 3.XII).

GRASMERE, Westmorland, as described in Charlotte Smith's *Ethelinde*, is mentioned by Camilla Stanley—"Catharine or the Bower" (*Vol. 3*, p. 199).

GRAVES, RICHARD (the younger, 1715–1804), poet and novelist: Mrs. Dashwood refers to *Columella; or, The Distressed Anchoret* (1779), in saying to Edward Ferrars, "'your sons will be brought up to as many pursuits, employments, professions, and trades as Columella's'" (*SS*, 1.XIX).

GRAY, MR., proprietor of Gray's Jewelers, is mentioned (*SS*, 2.XI).

GRAY, THOMAS (1716–71), poet: "Elegy Written in a Country Churchyard" (1750) is misquoted by Mrs. Elton (*E*, 2.XV) and by Jane Austen herself (*NA*, 1.I): the error is probably based on Cowper.

GRAY'S (JEWELERS), Sackville St., London, "where Elinor was carrying on a negociation for the exchange of a few old-fashioned jewels of her mother" (*SS*, 2.XI).

GRAY'S INN (one of the four Inns of Court, the centers of the legal profession in London where the law is taught and practiced and where many attorneys live): Mr. Beard, a visitor in Sanditon, is a solicitor there (*S*, p. 389).

GREAT BOOKHAM, Surrey, where Jane Austen's godfather, Samuel Cooke, was vicar; she often visited there and was close to his children, her second cousins. Sometimes it is claimed that the Cookes lived in Little Bookham, the neighboring parish.

GREAT WILLINGDEN. See **Willingden Abbots, Sussex.**

GREEN, MR. (1), probably the steward at Mansfield Park (*MP*, 1.VII).

GREEN, MR. (2), an imaginary prototype (*E*, 2.IV).

GREEN PARK BUILDINGS, Bath, where the Austens lived during part of their four-year stay in Bath.

GREGORY, LUCY, and an older sister, friends of the young Prices at Portsmouth, "'grown up amazing fine girls'" according to William Price (*MP*, 2.VII).

GRENVILLE, MISS, a relation of Mrs. Evelyn, "a very agreable looking Girl," who is interrogated by "a young Lady rather impertinent"—"A Collection of Letters" (*Vol. 2*, p. 160).

GRETNA GREEN, Scotland, (*a*) where Janetta Macdonald eloped with Captain M'Kenzie, "which they chose for the celebration of their Nuptials, in preference to any other place although it was at a considerable distance from Macdonald-Hall"—"Love and Freindship" (*Vol. 2*, p. 95); (*b*) to which Lieutenant Wickham and Lydia Bennet were supposed to have eloped (*PP*, 3.IV). People eloped to Gretna Green because it was just over the border in Scotland, where a minor could be married without his or her parents' consent.

GREVILLE, LADY, probably a model for Lady Catherine de Bourgh; she uses her condescending kindness to Maria Williams as an excuse to offer her insults about her character, circumstances, and family—"A Collection of Letters" (*Vol. 2*, p. 156).

GREVILLE, MR., is mentioned (*CG* I ii).

GREVILLE, ELLEN and **MISS**, daughters of the obnoxious Lady Greville, who patronizes a "young Lady in distress'd Circumstances"—A Collection of Letters" (*Vol. 2*, p. 156).

GREY, LADY JANE (Lady Jane Dudley, 1537–54), a cousin of Edward VI, "an amiable young woman and famous for reading Greek while other people were hunting," later described as being remarkable for an excess of vanity—"The History of England" (*Vol. 2*, pp. 141 and 144).

GREY, SOPHIA. See **Willoughby, (Mrs.) Sophia.**

GRIERSON, LADY MARY, and her daughters, ladies whom Captain Wentworth narrowly avoided having to transport on his ship (*P*, 3.VIII).

GRIFFITHS, MRS., a schoolmistress from Camberwell who brings some pupils to Sanditon (*S*, p. 408).

GROSVENOR ST., London, (*a*) from which Mrs. Marlowe writes to Eloisa Lutterell—"Lesley Castle" (*Vol. 2*, p. 133); (*b*) where Mr. Hurst had a house (*PP*, 1.XXI); (*c*) where Mr. and Mrs. Reeves, cousins of Harriet Byron, live (*CG*, I i).

GROVE, THE, name of Mrs. Percival's house, where Catharine lived—"Catharine or the Bower" (*Vol. 3*, p. 240).

GUILFORD (Guildford, Surrey), where Sam Watson is a surgeon (*W*, p. 321).

GUSTAVUS, one of the grandsons of Lord St. Clair, the son of Agatha, "a Gracefull Youth"—"Love and Freindship" (*Vol. 2*, p. 92).

HAGGERSTON, Mr. Gardiner's attorney, who takes care of the legal arrangements for Lydia Bennet's marriage to Lieutenant Wickham (*PP*, 3.VII).

HAILSHAM, Sussex, on the route from Willingden to Sanditon (*S*, p. 367).

HALIFAX, DOWAGER LADY, MISS CAROLINE, MISS MARIA, etc.: Mary Wynne went to live with this family when her father died—"Catharine or the Bower" (*Vol. 3*, p. 195).

HALTON, HENRIETTA, a "Young Lady very much in love" with Thomas Musgrove—"A Collection of Letters" (*Vol. 2*, p. 162).

HAMILTON, a family of friends of Alicia Johnson who visited the Lake District (*LS*, p. 298).

HAMILTON (Rt. Hon. William Gerard Hamilton, 1729–96), known as "Single-speech Hamilton": he is mentioned as paying tribute to Samuel Johnson at the latter's death (*Verses*, p. 442).

HAMILTON, MISS. See **Smith, Mrs. (2).**

HAMILTON, ELIZABETH (1758–1816), miscellaneous writer: Jane Austen refers to her as "a respectable Writer" (*Letters*, p. 372).

HAMLET. See **Shakespeare, William.**

HAMPDEN, JOHN (ca. 1594–1643), member of Parliament during the reign of Charles I: one of the "original Causers of all the disturbances Distresses & Civil Wars in which England for many years was embroiled"—"The History of England" (*Vol. 2*, p. 148).

HAMPSHIRE, the county in which Diana, Susan, and Arthur Parker live (*S*, p. 420).

HAMPSTEAD, a suburb of London: (*a*) the Beautifull Cassandra travels there in a hackney coach—"The Beautifull Cassandra" (*Vol. 1*, p. 45); (*b*) it is one of the places Harriet Byron is sought after her abduction by Sir Hargrave Pollexfen (*CG*, I ii).

HAMPTON, LADY, SIR ARTHUR, and **SOPHY**, characters in "The Visit" (*Vol. 1*, p. 50).

HANCOCK, ELIZA. See **Austen, Eliza.**

HANKING, REVEREND MR., a visitor to Sanditon (*S*, p. 389).

HANNAH, a housemaid at Randalls, daughter of the coachman at Hartfield (*E*, 1.I).

HANOVER SQUARE, London, (*a*) where the Palmers have a house (*SS*, 1.XX); (*b*) where St. George's Church is located (*MP*, 3.XII).

HANS PLACE, London, where Jane Austen's brother Henry lived from 1814 until he went bankrupt in 1816.

HARCOURT, ELIZA, the unreliable heroine of "Henry and Eliza" (*Vol. 1*, p. 34).

HARCOURT, SIR GEORGE and **LADY POLLY**, the adoptive parents of Eliza; at the beginning of the tale they are discovered "superintending the Labours of their Haymakers, rewarding the industry of some by smiles of approbation, & punishing the idleness of others, by a cudgel"—"Henry and Eliza" (*Vol. 1*, p. 33).

HARDING, DR., a rich old clergyman whom Penelope Watson is supposed to be pursuing with matrimonial ambitions (*W*, p. 317).

HARDING, MR., a friend of Sir Thomas Bertram, living in London, who alerts the family to Maria's flight with Henry Crawford (*MP*, 3.XVI).

HARE AND MANY FRIENDS, THE. See **Gay, John.**

HARLEY, MR., the hero of "a short, but interesting Tale"—"The Adventures of Mr. Harley" (*Vol. 1*, p. 40).

HARLEY, EMMA, "about 17 with fine dark Eyes & an elegant Shape," whom Mr. Harley married before he went to sea—"The Adventures of Mr. Harley" (*Vol. 1*, p. 40).

HARLEY ST., London, where the John Dashwoods are lodging (*SS*, 2.XII): it is a smart address, but is not in the most fashionable or expensive part of town.

HARRINGTON, HARRIET and **PEN**, young ladies living in the neighborhood of Meryton and friends of Mrs. Forster (*PP*, 2.XVI).

HARRIS, MR., the apothecary who treats Marianne Dashwood when she is ill in Somerset (*SS*, 3.VII).

HARRISON, COLONEL, a gentleman living in the neighborhood of Mansfield Park who attends the ball given there in Fanny Price's honor (*MP*, 2.XI).

HARROGATE, Yorks., where Martha Lloyd was not taken by Mr. Best (*Verses*, p. 445).

HARRY, a footman at Donwell Abbey who is criticized by Mrs. Elton (*E*, 3.XVI).

HARTFIELD, the Woodhouses' house on the outskirts of Highbury (*E*, 1.I).

HARVILLE, CAPTAIN, a friend of Captain Wentworth living in Lyme Regis: "a tall, dark man, with a sensible, benevolent countenance; a little lame" (*P*, 3.XI).

HARVILLE, MRS., "a degree less polished than her husband" (*P*, 3.XI); she has three children; and a female cousin of hers is mentioned (*P*, 3.VIII).

HARVILLE, FANNY (deceased), the sister of Captain Harville, engaged to Captain Benwick at the time of her death (*P*, 3.XI).

HASTINGS, Sussex: Sanditon was supposed to lie in "that part of the Sussex Coast which lies between Hastings & E. Bourne" (*S*, p. 363).

HATFIELD, Herts., where Colonel Forster made inquiries in vain after Lieutenant Wickham and Lydia Bennet on their elopement (*PP*, 3.IV).

HATTON, SIR CHRISTOPHER (1540–91), lord chancellor of England during Queen Elizabeth's reign: according to Jane Austen, he was Sir Walter Ralegh's friend, and there are anecdotes about him in Sheridan's *Critic*—"The History of England" (*Vol. 2*, p. 147).

HAWKINS, AUGUSTA. See **Elton, (Mrs.) Augusta.**

HAWKINS, SIR JOHN (1719–89), miscellaneous author: his *Life of Johnson* (1787), page 9, refers to "a master named Winkworth, but who, affecting to be thought allied to the Strafford family, assumed the name of Wentworth": this is apparently the basis for Sir Walter Elliot's remark about Mr. Edward Wentworth (*P*, 3.III).

HAWKINS, LAETITIA MATILDA (1760–1835), novelist: *Rosanne; or a Father's Labour Lost* (1814) is described as "very good and clever, but tedious. . . . There are a thousand improbabilities in the story" (*Letters*, p. 422).

HAWKINS, SELINA. See **Suckling, (Mrs.) Selina.**

HAYE-PARK, where the Gouldings live, in the neighborhood of Meryton (*PP*, 3.VIII).

HAYTER, the Misses, cousins of the Musgroves; they "would, from their parents' inferior, retired, and unpolished way of living, and their own defective education, have been hardly in any class at all, but for their connexion with Uppercross" (*P*, 3.IX).

HAYTER, MR., a brother-in-law of Mrs. Musgrove, living at Winthrop (*P*, 3.IX).

HAYTER, MRS., a sister of Mrs. Musgrove, but she made an inferior match (*P*, 3.IX).

HAYTER, CHARLES, the eldest son, a clergyman, "a very amiable, pleasing young man, between whom and Henrietta [Musgrove] there had been a considerable appearance of attachment previous to Captain Wentworth's introduction" (*P*, 3.IX).

HEELEY, WILLIAM, a shoemaker in Sanditon (*S*, p. 383).

HEIR AT LAW, THE. See **Colman, George (the younger).**

HEMMINGS, MR., an acquaintance of the Robert Watsons in Croydon (*W*, p. 353).

HENRIETTA ST., London, where Jane Austen's brother Henry lived in 1813–14.

HENRY (1), a character in Matthew Prior's "Henry and Emma," mentioned in analogy to Captain Wentworth (*P*, 3.XII).

HENRY (2) ———, son of Lord and Lady ——— and suitor of Rose Gower, he died in a shipwreck—"Evelyn" (*Vol. 3*, p. 188).

HENRY (3), SIR, one of the guests at Lord Ravenshaw's while the private theatricals were going on (*MP*, 1.XIII).

HENRY IV (1367–1413), king of England: "he did not live for ever, but falling ill, his son the Prince of Wales came and took away the crown; whereupon the King made a long speech, for which I must refer the Reader to Shakespear's Plays, & the Prince made a still longer"—"The History of England" (*Vol. 2*, p. 139).

HENRY V (1387–1422), king of England: "after he succeeded to the throne [he] grew quite reformed & Amiable, forsaking all his dissipated Companions, & never thrashing Sir William [Gascoigne] again"—"The History of England" (*Vol. 2*, p. 139).

HENRY VI (1421–71), king of England: "I cannot say much for this Monarch's Sense"—"The History of England" (*Vol. 2*, p. 139).

HENRY VII (1457–1509), king of England: "This Monarch soon after his accession married the Princess Elizabeth of York, by which alliance he plainly proved that he thought his own right inferior to hers"—"The History of England" (*Vol. 2*, p. 141).

HENRY VIII (1491–1547), king of England, "whose only merit was his not being *quite* so bad as his daughter Elizabeth"—"The History of England" (*Vol. 2*, p. 142).

HENRY, PRINCE (Henry Frederick, Prince of Wales, 1594–1612), eldest son of James I—"The History of England" (*Vol. 2*, p. 147).

HENRY IV. See **Shakespeare, William.**

HENRY VIII. See **Shakespeare, William.**

HENRY, ROBERT (1718–90), historian and Presbyterian minister: Jane Austen reads *The History of Great Britain* (1771–93) in 1800 (*Letters*, p. 89).

"**HENRY AND ELIZA**," a tale of an opportunistic girl and her adventures, dedicated to Miss Jane Cooper (*Vol. 1*, p. 33).

"**HENRY AND EMMA**." See **Prior, Matthew.**

HENSHAWE, BIDDY, the aunt of Miss Grey, who is mentioned by Mrs. Jennings as having married a very wealthy man (*SS*, 2.VIII).

HEREFORD, (*a*) from which Clara and Fanny hopped home after their walking tour through Wales—"Scraps" (*Vol. 2*, p. 176); (*b*) Lord Longtown's seat is nearby (*NA*, 2.XIII); Herefordshire is mentioned in the same context.

HERMITAGE WALK, where Henry Tilney went to finish by himself *The Mysteries of Udolpho*, which he was supposed to be reading to his sister (*NA*, 1.XIV): Apperson claims that this walk is in Bath, but I think it more likely to be a walk on the grounds of Northanger Abbey.

HEROINE, THE, OR ADVENTURES OF A FAIR ROMANCE READER. See **Barrett, Eaton Stannard.**

HERTFORDSHIRE, the county in which Meryton is situated (*PP*, 1.III).

HERVEY, (MRS.) DIANA, aunt of Henry Hervey; she settled in the neighborhood of the Lutterells in Sussex about a year before the action of "Lesley Castle" takes place (*Vol. 2*, p. 129).

HERVEY, GEORGE, the man who marries the eponymous heroine of "Amelia Webster" (*Vol. 1*, p. 48).

HERVEY, HENRY, Eloisa Lutterell's fiancé; he dies of a fall from his horse, causing Charlotte Lutterell much annoyance on account of all the trouble she had gone through to prepare food for the wedding festivities—"Lesley Castle" (*Vol. 2*, p. 113).

HERVEY, MATILDA, a young lady who corresponds with Amelia Webster in the story of that name; this may be an error for *Maud* Hervey (*Vol. 1*, p. 47).

HERVEY, MAUD, Amelia Webster's correspondent; she marries Henry Beverley (*Vol. 1*, p. 48).

HERVEY, SALLY (SARAH), a young lady engaged in a clandestine correspondence with Benjamin Bar, whom she subsequently marries—"Amelia Webster" (*Vol. 1*, p. 48).

HEYWOOD, MR., "a well-looking Hale, Gentlemanlike Man, of middle age," residing in Willingden, Sussex (*S*, p. 365).

HEYWOOD, MRS.: "older in Habits than in Age," she has fourteen children (*S*, p. 373).

HEYWOOD, CHARLOTTE, "a very pleasing young woman of two and twenty," the protagonist of *Sanditon* (*S*, p. 374).

HIGH LIFE BELOW STAIRS (1759), a farce attributed to David Garrick, but more likely by James Townley (1714–78), acted at Steventon, January 1790.

HIGH ST., Portsmouth, where Mrs. Price takes a walk on Sunday afternoons with her daughters (*MP*, 3.X).

HIGHBURY, Surrey, the scene of the action in *Emma*, a "large and populous village almost amounting to a town" (*E*, 1.I).

HIGH-CHURCH DOWN, a hill above Barton Cottage where Marianne Dashwood first meets Willoughby (*SS*, 1.XII).

HILL, MRS., the Bennets' housekeeper at Longbourn (*PP*, 1.XIII).

HILL ST., London, where Admiral Crawford had a house (*MP*, 1.V).

HILLIER, MR. and **MRS.,** the tenants of the Parkers' old house outside Sanditon (*S*, pp. 380 and 381).

"**HISTORY OF ENGLAND, THE,**" dedicated to Jane Austen's sister Cassandra "by a partial, prejudiced, & ignorant Historian" (*Vol. 2*, p. 138).

HISTORY OF ENGLAND. See **Goldsmith, Oliver.**

HISTORY OF GREAT BRITAIN, THE. See **Henry, Robert.**

HOARE, PRINCE (1755–1834), dramatist and artist: *My Grandmother* (1793), a musical farce, is mentioned in connection with Lord and Lady Ravenshaw (*MP*, 1.XIII).

HODGES, MRS., Mr. Knightley's housekeeper (*E*, 2.IX).

HODGES, CHARLES, an admirer of Isabella Thorpe in Bath (*NA*, 2.I); later she attends the play with his family (2.XII).

HOGSWORTH GREEN, where Emma Harley lives—"The Adventures of Mr. Harley" (*Vol. 1*, p. 40).

HOLBORN, London, (*a*) where Laura makes inquiries regarding her husband, Edward Lindsay—"Love and Freindship" (*Vol. 2*, p. 89); (*b*) the unfashionable quarter of town where some cousins of the Steeles live (*SS*, 2.X).

HOLFORD, MRS., a lady of Tom Bertram's acquaintance in London; it is at her house that he is embarrassed by Miss Anderson's behavior (*MP*, 1.V).

HOLLIS, MR., Lady Denham's first husband, "a man of considerable Property in the Country" (*S*, p. 375).

HOLYHEAD, an island off Anglesey, Wales, from which the Campbells are to embark on their journey to Ireland (*E*, 2.I).

HOME, JOHN (1722–1808), dramatist: *Douglas, a Tragedy* (1756) is proposed for enactment at Mansfield; Tom Bertram was made to recite a passage from it during a Christmas holiday when he was a schoolboy (*MP*, 1.XIII).

HOMER: Jane Austen says that her verses are "purely classical—just like Homer and Virgil, Ovid and Propria que Maribus" (*Letters*, p. 256).

HONITON, Devon, not far from Barton, where travelers to London may hire post-horses (*SS*, 1.XIII, 3.VIII).

HOOK'S *LESSONS FOR BEGINNERS*: this phrase (*Letters*, p. 328) possibly refers to James Hook (1746–1827), *Guida di Musica, Being a Complete Book of Instructions for the Harpsichord or Pianoforte* (1790, new ed. 1810).

HORRID MYSTERIES. See **Will, Peter.**

HOUNSLOW, Middlesex, where sits the inn in which the action of "The first Act of a Comedy" takes place—"Scraps" (*Vol. 2*, p. 173).

HOUSE OF COMMONS: (*a*) Thomas Musgrove wishes he were a member so he could pass a law requiring aunts and uncles to give up their estates to their nieces and nephews—"A Collection of Letters" (*Vol. 2*, p. 169); (*b*) one of the symptoms of universal degeneration, in Mrs. Percival's view, is that the House "'did not break up sometimes till five in the Morning, and Depravity never was so general before'"—"Catharine or the Bower" (*Vol. 3*, p. 200); (*c*) Mr. Stanley is an M.P. —"Catharine or the Bower" (*Vol. 3*, p. 204); (*d*) Mr. Palmer is a candidate for the House of Commons (*SS*, 1.XX); (*e*) Sir Thomas Bertram is an M.P. (*MP*, 1.II); (*f*) an early ancestor of Sir William Elliot, the first baronet, served in "three successive parliaments" (*P*, 3.I).

HOWARD, MR., the vicar of Wickstead, formerly tutor of Lord Osborne, intended to be the hero of *The Watsons*: "there was a quietly-chearful, gentlemanlike air in Mr. H. which suited [Emma]" (*W*, p. 333).

HUGHES, DR., MRS., and **RICHARD** (their son), a family attending the Westons' ball at the Crown Inn, Highbury (*E*, 3.II).

HUGHES, MRS., an acquaintance of both the Thorpes and the Tilneys (*NA*, 1.VIII).

HUMBUG, OLD, YOUNG, and **MRS.**, characters in "The Mystery" (*Vol. 1*, p. 55).

HUME, DAVID (1711–76), philosopher and historian, mentioned by Eleanor Tilney (*NA*, 1.XIV).

HUNSFORD, Kent, near Westerham, the parish in which Lady Catherine de Bourgh's estate, Rosings, is located (*PP*, 1.XIII).

HUNSFORD LANE, where Mr. Collins walked all one morning in order to see when Mr. Darcy arrived at Rosings (*PP*, 2.VII).

HUNSFORD PARSONAGE, where the Collinses live: "It was rather small, but well built and convenient; and every thing was fitted up and arranged with a neatness and consistency of which Elizabeth gave Charlotte all the credit" (*PP*, 2.V).

HUNT, CAPTAIN, an acquaintance of the Thorpes who attends the winter assemblies at Putney (*NA*, 1.VI).

HUNTER, CAPTAIN, a young man possibly attached to Miss Edwards (*W*, p. 320).

HUNTER, MRS. RACHEL (1754–1813), novelist: (*a*) there is a sarcastic reference to this lady's works (*Letters*, p. 406); (*b*) when Jane Austen's niece Fanny says, "'Tell Mama that I am quite Palmerstone!'" (*Letters*, p. 161), it may be a reference to *Letters from Mrs. Palmerstone to Her Daughters, Inculcating Morality by Entertaining Narratives* (1803).

HUNTINGDON, Cambridges., where lived the Wards: the three daughters of the family became Mrs. Norris, Lady Bertram, and Mrs. Price (*MP*, 1.I).

HURST, MR., the husband of one of Mr. Bingley's sisters, with a house in Grosvenor St.: "he was an indolent man, who lived only to eat, drink, and play at cards, who when he found [Elizabeth to] prefer a plain dish to a ragout, had nothing to say to her" (*PP*, 1.VIII).

HURST, (MRS.) LOUISA: she and her sister "were fine women, with an air of decided fashion" (*PP*, 1.III). See also **Bingley, (Miss) Caroline.**

HURST AND WILFORD: reference unclear; Reginald De Courcy dined with Mr. Smith there (*LS*, p. 248).

HUTCHINSON, SARAH, a friend of Mrs. Percival who died in consequence of staying out too late and getting wet—"Catharine or the Bower" (*Vol. 3*, p. 233).

HYPOCRITE, THE. See **Bickerstaffe, Isaac**.

IBBOTSON, a family attending the concert in Bath, according to Mrs. Smith (2) (*P*, 4.IX).

IDLER. See **Johnson, (Dr.) Samuel**.

IGNORANCE: according to Jane Austen, "Where people wish to attach, they should always be ignorant. To come with a well-informed mind, is to come with an inability of administering to the vanity of others, which a sensible person would always wish to avoid. A woman especially, if she have the misfortune of knowing any thing, should conceal it as well as she can" (*NA*, 1.XIV).

ILLUSION, OR THE TRANCES OF NOURJAHAD (1813), a melodrama seen by Jane Austen in March 1814; she found "a great deal of finery & dancing in it, but I think little merit" (*Letters*, p. 380).

INCHBALD, (MRS.) ELIZABETH (1753–1821), novelist, dramatist, and actress: *Lovers' Vows* (1798), the play to be enacted at Mansfield (*MP*, 1.XIII) is her translation of August F. F. von Kotzebue's *Das Kind der Liebe* (1790).

IRELAND (*a*) is where Laura's father came from—"Love and Freindship" (*Vol. 2*, p. 77); (*b*) is where Isabel moved after her marriage—"Love and Freindship" (*Vol. 2*, p. 90); (*c*) is where Emma Watson's aunt moved after her second marriage, to Captain O'Brien (*W*, p. 326); (*d*) taunting Fanny Price's ignorance, her cousins say, "We asked her . . . which way she would go to get to Ireland; and she said, she would cross to the Isle of Wight" (*MP*, 1.II); (*e*) Mr. Dixon has an estate there (*E*, 2.I); (*f*) the Viscount Dalrymple's estate is located there (*P*, 4.IV).

ISABEL, Laura's "most intimate freind"; most of the chronicle is addressed to her daughter Marianne—"Love and Freindship" (*Vol. 2*, p. 76).

ISABELLA. See **Garrick, David**.

ISLE OF WIGHT, (*a*) is where Rose Gower's suitor was sent for a fortnight, "with the hope of overcoming his Constancy by Time and Absence in a foreign Country"—"Evelyn" (*Vol. 3*, p. 185); (*b*) Sidney Parker had a plan to go there (*S*, p. 387); (*c*) Fanny Price, at age ten, thinks it is on the way from Northamptonshire to Ireland (*MP*, 1.II); (*d*) its beauty is compared to that of the countryside around Lyme Regis (*P*, 3.XI).

ITALIAN, THE. See **Radcliffe, Mrs. Ann**.

ITALY: (*a*) there is a transparency of "a cave in Italy" in the window of the East Room (formerly the schoolroom) at Mansfield Park (*MP*, 1.XVI); (*b*) "Italy, Switzerland, and the South of France, might be as fruitful in horrors" as they are represented in Mrs. Radcliffe's novels (*NA*, 2.X); (*c*) Lady Clementina della Porretta lives there (*CG*, V i).

"**JACK & ALICE**," a tale of a young lady with a drinking problem, dedicated to Francis William Austen (*Vol. 1*, p. 12).

JACKSON, an acquaintance of John Thorpe, attending Oriel College, Oxford (*NA*, 1.VII).

JACKSON, CHRISTOPHER, the handyman at Mansfield Park (*MP*, 1.XIII).

JACKSON, DICK, the ten-year-old son of Christopher Jackson; Mrs. Norris accuses him of hanging around Mansfield at the servants' dinner hour in order to get a free meal (*MP*, 1.XV).

JACKSON, ELEANOR. See **Austen, Eleanor**.

JAMES I (1566–1625), king of England, the son of Mary Queen of Scots: "His Majesty was of that amiable disposition which inclines to Freindships, & in such points was possessed of a keener penetration in Discovering Merit than many other people"—"The History of England" (*Vol. 2*, p. 147).

JAMES II (1633–1701), king of England: the chapel at Sotherton was remodeled during his reign (*MP*, 1.IX).

JAMES (1), Reginald De Courcy's groom (*LS*, p. 283).

JAMES (2), the Watsons' groom (*W*, p. 319).

JAMES (3), the Woodhouses' coachman (*E*, 1.I).

JANE, MISS. See **Annesley, Miss Jane**.

JANE SHORE. See **Rowe, Nicholas**.

JEBB'S, a store, apparently a milliner's establishment, in Sanditon (*S*, p. 381).

JEFFEREYS, MRS., "Clara Partridge that was," an acquaintance of Mrs. Elton who gave up music after marriage (*E*, 2.XIV).

JEFFERIES, MRS., an acquaintance of Mrs. Norris who is to write a letter to her about the son of a groom at Mansfield (presumably recommending him as a stable hand) (*MP*, 1.VII).

JEFFERSON, REVEREND T. (no biographical data), of Tunbridge: Jane Austen wishes to subscribe to his *Two Sermons* (1808) (*Letters*, p. 199; also mentioned p. 191).

JEMIMA, the nurserymaid at Uppercross Cottage, "'the trustiest, steadiest creature in the world,'" according to Mary Musgrove (*P*, 3.VI).

JENKINSON, MRS., "in whose appearance there was nothing remarkable," is the former governess and now companion of Miss de Bourgh (*PP*, 2.VI).

JENNER, EDWARD (1749–1823), who discovered the benefits of vaccination, published various pamphlets on cowpox between 1798 and 1800, which are referred to (*Letters*, p. 93).

JENNINGS, MR. (deceased): before his death he "had traded with success in a less elegant part of town" than Berkeley St., where his widow now lives (*SS*, 2.III).

JENNINGS, MRS., the mother of Lady Middleton, who invites Elinor and Marianne Dashwood to London, "a good-humoured, merry, fat, elderly woman, who talked a great deal, seemed very happy, and rather vulgar" (*SS*, 1.VII).

JENNY, a servant in Lord and Lady L.'s house at Colnebrook (*CG*, III ii).

JERVOIS, EMILY, a ward of Sir Charles Grandison (*CG*, IV i).

JOAN OF ARC (Jeanne d'Arc, ca. 1412–31), French visionary and martyr: she "made such a *row* among the English. They should not have burnt her—but they did"—"The History of England" (*Vol. 2*, p. 140).

JOHN (1), an outdoor servant at the Grove—"Catharine or the Bower" (*Vol. 3*, p. 210).

JOHN (2), the Collinses' manservant (*PP*, 2.XIV).

JOHN (3), the Gardiners' manservant (*PP*, 3.IV).

JOHN (4), a groom at Mansfield Park; a son of his is also mentioned (*MP*, 1.VII).

JOHN (5), footman in the Reeves's household in Grosvenor St. (*CG*, I ii).

JOHN, KING. See **Shakespeare, William.**

JOHNSON, MR. (1), father of the hero and heroine of "Jack & Alice"; the story opens with the celebration of his fifty-fifth birthday (*Vol. 1*, p. 12).

JOHNSON, MR. (2), Alicia's husband, "just old enough to be formal, ungovernable & to have the Gout—too old to be agreable, & too young to die" (*LS*, p. 298).

JOHNSON, ALICE, eponymous heroine of "Jack & Alice": hers is "a family of Love, & though a little addicted to the Bottle & the Dice, had many good Qualities" (*Vol. 1*, p. 13).

JOHNSON, ALICIA, Lady Susan's best friend and confidante, to whom much of the story is addressed (*LS*, p. 244).

JOHNSON, ELIZABETH and **FANNY**, sisters who wore out two pairs of shoes apiece on a walking tour through Wales—"Scraps" (*Vol. 2*, p. 176).

JOHNSON, JACK, the hero of "Jack & Alice": "oweing to his unfortunate propensity to Liquor, which so compleatly deprived him of the use of those faculties Nature had endowed him with, ... he never did anything worth mentioning" (*Vol. 1*, p. 25).

JOHNSON, (DR.) SAMUEL (1709–84), lexicographer and polymath: (*a*) mentioned by Eleanor Tilney (*NA*, 1.XIV); (*b*) two stanzas by Jane Austen are adapted from words of Boswell, commemorating Johnson's death (*Verses*, p. 442); (*c*) Jane Austen refers to "my dear Dr. Johnson" (*Letters*, p. 181); (*d*) in 1813 she refers to a servant, William, who is leaving Henry Austen's employ voluntarily, as having "more of Cowper than of Johnson in him, fonder of Tame Hares & Blank verse than of the full tide of human Existence at Charing Cross" (*Letters*, p. 368); also mentioned (*Letters*, pp. 64 and 362); (1) *The Rambler* (essays published biweekly, March 20, 1750–March 14, 1752): (*a*) no. 107, "The world is not their friend, nor the world's law," is misquoted by Emma Woodhouse (*E.* 3.X); (*b*) no. 97 is paraphrased thus: "no young lady can be justified in falling in love before the gentleman's love is declared" (*NA*, 1.III); (2) *The Idler* (essays published Apr. 15, 1758–Apr. 5, 1760; collected ed. 1761) is among the reading material on Fanny Price's table in the East Room at Mansfield (*MP*, 1.XVI); (3) *Rasselas* (1759): the phrase "Marriage has many pains, but celibacy has no pleasures" is paraphrased (*MP*, 3.VIII).

JONES, MR., apothecary at Meryton (*PP*, 1.VII); his shop boy is also mentioned (*PP*, 1.XV).

JONES, MR. and **MRS.**, guests at Mr. Johnson's birthday party: they were both "rather tall & very passionate, but were in other respects, good tempered, wellbehaved People"—"Jack & Alice" (*Vol. 1*, p. 12).

JONES, PHILIP, a bricklayer, Philander's reputed father—"Love and Freindship" (*Vol. 2*, p. 106).

JOURNAL OF A TOUR TO THE HEBRIDES. See **Boswell, James.**

JULIA, "ever lamenting the situation of her friend," Melissa, who is ill—"A Fragment written to inculcate the practise of Virtue" (*Vol. 1*, p. 72).

JULIAS, prototypical heroines of gothic novels, mentioned by Henry Tilney (*NA*, 1.XIV).

JULIUS CAESAR (Caius Julius Caesar, ca. 102 B.C.–44 B.C.), Roman general and ruler: mentioned (*MP*, 1.XIII) as the eponymous hero of Shakespeare's play.

KAMSCHATKA, to which the heroine of "Plan of a Novel" and her father are compelled to flee (p. 430).

KELLYNCH, Som., where the Elliots lived until forced to retrench (*P*, 3.I).

KELLYNCH HALL, the Elliots' estate, rented to Admiral Croft (*P*, 3.I).

KELLYNCH LODGE, the house belonging to Lady Russell in Kellynch (*P*, 3.II).

KENELWORTH (Kenilworth, Warwicks.), which Elizabeth Bennet visited on her journey with the Gardiners to Derbyshire (*PP*, 2.XIX).

KENSINGTON GARDENS, London, where Elinor Dashwood and Mrs. Jennings go walking (*SS*, 3.II).

KENT, (*a*) where Parklands, the De Courcy estate, is situated (*LS*, p. 254); (*b*) where Rosings, the de Bourgh estate, is situated (*PP*, 1.XIII).

KENTISH GAZETTE (from 1768), a newspaper in which Mr. Parker found an advertisement by a surgeon in Willingden Abbots (*S*, p. 366).

KEYNSHAM, Som.: the Thorpes' and Morlands' ill-fated expedition to Blaize Castle only got about seven miles out of Bath, not even as far as Keynsham (*NA*, 1.XI).

KICKABOUT, THE HONORABLE MRS., a lady who held a rout attended by Margaret and Matilda Lesley, escorted by their stepmother—"Lesley Castle" (*Vol. 2*, p. 136).

KILHOOBERY PARK, home of the three Miss Cliftons, with whom the susceptible Sir William falls in love—"Sir William Mountague" (*Vol. 1*, p. 41).

KING, MR. JAMES, master of ceremonies of the Lower Rooms in Bath from 1785, and of the Upper Rooms from 1805: he is mentioned as presenting Henry Tilney to Catherine Morland in the Lower Rooms (*NA*, 1.III).

KING, (MISS) MARY, a young lady in the Meryton neighborhood who enjoys Lieutenant Wickham's attentions after coming into some money; Lydia Bennet refers to her as "'a nasty little freckled thing'" (*PP*, 2.XVI).

KING JOHN. See **Shakespeare, William.**

KING'S BENCH, the criminal court in England: Lady Greville asks Maria Williams if her grandfather was not tried there as part of her campaign to discredit Miss Williams's respectability—"A Collection of Letters" (*Vol. 2*, p. 158).

KINGSTON, Surrey, the nearest market town to Highbury (*E*, 1.IV).

KING'S-WESTON, Glos., near Bristol, (*a*) where the Sucklings led exploring parties (*E*, 2.XIV); (*b*) one of the proposed goals of the Thorpes' and Morlands' exploring party (*NA*, 1.XI).

KITTY. See **Percival, Catharine.**

"**KITTY, A FAIR BUT FROZEN MAID.**" See **Garrick, David.**

"**KITTY, OR THE BOWER.**" See "**Catharine or the Bower.**"

KNATCHBULL, CATHERINE. See **Knight, Catherine.**

KNATCHBULL, LADY FANNY CATHERINE. See **Austen (Knight), Fanny Catherine.**

KNIGHT, CATHERINE (née Knatchbull, 1753–1812), wife of Thomas Knight of Godmersham and Chawton, who adopted Jane Austen's brother Edward. She is named as one of the advocates of Mary Queen of Scots—"The History of England" (*Vol. 2*, p. 145).

KNIGHT, EDWARD. See **Austen, (Knight), Edward.**

KNIGHT, ELIZABETH. See **Austen, Elizabeth.**

KNIGHT, THOMAS (d. 1794), of Godmersham Park and Chawton, married to Catherine Knatchbull: he adopted Jane Austen's brother Edward, who took the name of Knight in 1812.

KNIGHTLEY, BELLA, the second child of the John Knightleys (*E*, 1.XII).

KNIGHTLEY, EMMA, "a nice little girl about eight months old," the youngest child of the John Knightleys (*E*, 1.XII).

KNIGHTLEY, GEORGE (1), owner of Donwell Abbey and most of the parish of Highbury. He eventually marries Emma Woodhouse; "a sensible man about seven or eight-and-thirty" (*E*, 1.I).

KNIGHTLEY, GEORGE (2), the third son of the John Knightleys (*E*, 1.VI).

KNIGHTLEY, HENRY, the eldest child of the John Knightleys, "a fine boy" (*E*, 1.IX).

KNIGHTLEY, ISABELLA (née Woodhouse), Emma's elder sister, with five children; "a pretty, elegant little woman, of gentle, quiet manners, and a disposition remarkably amiable and affectionate; wrapt up in her family.... She was not a woman of strong understanding or any quickness" (*E*, 1.XI).

KNIGHTLEY, JOHN (1), George Knightley's younger brother, a lawyer in London, "a tall, gentleman-like, and very clever man; rising in his profession, domestic, and respectable in his private character; but with reserved manners which prevented his being generally pleasing; and capable of being sometimes out of humour" (*E*. 1.XI).

KNIGHTLEY, JOHN (2), the second son of the John Knightleys, "'very like his mamma,'" according to Mr. Woodhouse (*E*, 1.IX).

KNOX, VICESIMUS (1752–1821), essayist and miscellaneous writer: *Elegant Extracts, or Useful and Entertaining Pieces of Poetry* (1789) is favorite reading material of Harriet Smith (*E*, 1.IX) and supposedly her source for the riddle about "Kitty, a fair but frozen maid"; but the latter does not appear in this book.

KYMPTON, Derbys., the parish near Pemberley of which Mr. Wickham was to have had the living (*PP*, 3.X).

L., LORD, in whose household Harriet Byron comes to stay after her ordeal in Paddington (*CG*, III i).

L., LADY CAROLINE, the elder sister of Sir Charles Grandison (*CG*, III i).

LACONIA, a frigate captained by Frederick Wentworth (*P*, 3.VI).

LADY OF BRANXHOLM HALL. See **Scott, Sir Walter:** *Lay of the Last Minstrel.*

LADY OF THE LAKE. See **Scott, Sir Walter.**

LAKE DISTRICT, THE, (*a*) where the Stanleys plan to travel in autumn, making Camilla "quite Mad with Joy"—"Catharine or the Bower" (*Vol. 3*, p. 199); (*b*) where Alicia Johnson wanted to travel with the Hamiltons (*LS*, p. 298); (*c*) where Eliza Bennet was to go with the Gardiners before their vacation time was cut short (*PP*, 2.IV).

LAKE OF KILLARNEY. See **Porter, Anna Maria.**

LAMBE, MISS, one of Mrs. Griffiths's charges, "about 17, half Mulatto, chilly & tender," rich and in delicate health (*S*, p. 421).

LAMBTON, Derbys., a small town within five miles of Pemberley where Mrs. Gardiner once lived; on their visit to Derbyshire, Eliza Bennet and both Gardiners stay at an inn there (*PP*, 2.XIX).

LAND'S END, Cornwall, is mentioned (*S*, p. 380).

LANGFORD, where the Manwarings live; Lady Susan's behavior there nearly proves her undoing (*LS*, p. 243).
LANGHAM, Surrey, a village near Highbury (*E*, 1.XII).
LANSDOWN CRESCENT, Bath, where Mr. Elliot was to dine (*P*, 4.III).
LANSDOWN HILL: John Thorpe offers to drive Catherine Morland there the first time he meets her (*NA*, 1.VII); in fact, he takes her to Claverton Down.
LANSDOWN RD., Bath, where John Thorpe claimed to see Henry Tilney and his sister in a carriage the morning Catherine Morland was to have a walk with them (*NA*, 1.XI).
LARKINS, WILLIAM, the bailiff of Mr. Knightley's estates (*E*, 2.IX).
LAROLLES, MISS, a character in Frances Burney's *Cecilia* to whom Anne Elliot compares herself (*P*, 4.VIII).
LASCELLES, LADY, the previous tenant of the Rushworths' house in Wimpole St. (*MP*, 3.IX).
LASCELLES, MR., the man whom Cecilia Wynne married in Bengal, "double her own age, whose disposition was not amiable, and whose Manners were unpleasing, though his Character was respectable"—"Catharine or the Bower" (*Vol. 3*, pp. 194 and 239).
LASCELLES, MRS. See **Wynne, Cecilia**.
LATHOM, FRANCIS (1777–1823), novelist: *Midnight Bell* (1798) (*a*) is one of the books on the reading list provided by Isabella Thorpe for Catherine Morland's education (*NA*, 1.VI); (*b*) Jane Austen's father reads it in October 1798 (*Letters*, p. 21).
LATOURNELLE, MRS., proprietress of the Abbey School, which Jane and Cassandra Austen attended briefly.
LAUD, ARCHBISHOP (William Laud, 1573–1645), archbishop of Canterbury, one of Charles I's loyal followers—"The History of England" (*Vol. 2*, p. 148).
LAURA. See **Lindsay, Laura**.
LAURA PLACE, Bath, (*a*) on the way from the Allens' lodgings in Pulteney St. to the center of town (*NA*, 1.XI); (*b*) where Lady Dalrymple has lodgings (*P*, 4.IV).
"LAURE AND LENZE." See **Bossi, Cesare**.
LAURENTINA, a character in Mrs. Radcliffe's *Mysteries of Udolpho*; Catherine Morland believes her skeleton to be behind the black veil (*NA*, 1.VI).
LAURINA. See **St. Clair, Lady Laurina**.
LAY OF THE LAST MINSTREL. See **Scott, Sir Walter**.
LEE, MISS, the governess at Mansfield (*MP*, 1.I).
LEFROY, ANNE (née Brydges, 1749–1804), wife of the Reverend George Lefroy of Ashe and sister of Sir Samuel Egerton Brydges: (*a*) she is named as one of the advocates of Mary Queen of Scots—"The History of England" (*Vol. 2*, p. 145); and (*b*) Jane Austen composed a poem to her memory (*Verses*, p. 440).
LEFROY, REV. ISAAC PETER GEORGE (1745–1806), rector of Ashe, a neighboring parish to Steventon: he married Anne Brydges (three sons and one daughter: John Henry George, Christopher Edward, Benjamin, and Jemima Lucy).
LEFROY, JANE ANNA ELIZABETH. See **Austen, Jane Anna Elizabeth**.
LEICESTER ABBEY: Cardinal Wolsey told its abbot that "'he was come to lay his bones among them'"—"The History of England" (*Vol. 2*, p. 142).

LEICESTERSHIRE, where John Thorpe thinks of taking a house with his friend Fletcher for the hunting season (*NA*, 1.X).

LEIGH, CASSANDRA (1). See **Austen, Cassandra (1).**

LEIGH, CASSANDRA (2). See **Cooke, Cassandra.**

LEIGH, JANE. See **Cooper, Jane.**

LEIGH, THEOPHILUS (1) (d. 1724) of Adlestrop, Glos., Jane Austen's great-grandfather.

LEIGH, THEOPHILUS (2), the son of Theophilus Leigh (1); he was a master of Balliol College: his daughter was the Cassandra Leigh who married Samuel Cooke.

LEIGH, THOMAS (d. 1763), rector of Harpsden, Jane Austen's grandfather.

LEIGH (PERROT), JAMES (d. 1817), brother of Cassandra Austen, Jane's mother. He and his wife, née Jane Cholmeley, made James Austen's son, James Edward, their heir.

LENNOX, CHARLOTTE (1720–1804), writer: on reading *The Female Quixote; or, The Adventures of Arabella* (1752) for the second time, in 1807, Jane Austen finds its amusement "quite equal to what I remembered it" (*Letters*, p. 173).

LESLEY, MR., Margaret and Matilda's brother, who has "given himself up to melancholy and Despair" after his wife, "the Worthless Louisa," runs off with another man—"Lesley Castle" (*Vol. 2*, p. 110).

LESLEY, SIR GEORGE, an aging baronet "fluttering about the streets of London, gay, dissipated, and Thoughtless"; he precipitates much of the action of "Lesley Castle" by marrying a much younger second wife (*Vol. 2*, p. 111).

LESLEY, LOUISA (1) (née Burton): "naturally ill-tempered and Cunning," she married Mr. Lesley, but after a few years runs off "in company with Danvers & dishonour" (*Vol. 2*, pp. 110 and 119).

LESLEY, LOUISA (2), her daughter, a little child (*Vol. 2*, p. 111).

LESLEY, MARGARET, younger daughter of Sir George, one of the principal correspondents in "Lesley Castle"; her stepmother calls her and Matilda "two great, tall, out of the way, over-grown Girls, just of a proper size to inhabit a Castle almost as Large in comparison as themselves" (*Vol. 2*, p. 123).

LESLEY, (MISS) MATILDA, Margaret's elder sister, to whom William Fitzgerald becomes attached (*Vol. 2*, p. 122).

LESLEY, LADY SUSAN (née Fitzgerald), Sir George's second wife: "'She is short, and extremely well-made; is naturally pale, but rouges a good deal; has fine eyes, and fine teeth, as she will take care to let you know as soon as she sees you'"—"Lesley Castle" (*Vol. 2*, p. 119).

LESLEY CASTLE, the seat of the Lesley family, "situated two miles from Perth on a bold projecting Rock"—"Lesley Castle" (*Vol. 2*, p. 111).

"LESLEY CASTLE," an unfinished epistolary novel dedicated to Jane Austen's brother Henry (*Vol. 2*, p. 109).

LESSINGBY, near Peterborough, Hunts., the estate of the Owens, friends of Edmund Bertram (*MP*, 3.IV).

LEWIS XIV (1638–1715), king of France; mentioned in passing by Mary Crawford (*MP*, 2.IV).

LEWIS: stage name of Philander (q.v.). There was a real-life actor named Lewis at the Drury Lane Theatre in Jane Austen's day.

LEWIS, MATTHEW GREGORY (1775–1818), miscellaneous writer and man-about-town: *Ambrosio, or The Monk* (1795) was one of the few novels enjoyed by John Thorpe (*NA*, 1.VII).

LIFE OF NELSON. See **Southey, Robert.**

LIMEHOUSE, London, where Captain Little is from (*S*, p. 389).

LINDSAY, AUGUSTA, the sister of Edward Lindsay: Laura Lindsay, her sister-in-law, "found her exactly what her Brother had described her to be—of the middle size"—"Love and Freindship" (*Vol. 2*, p. 82).

LINDSAY, SIR EDWARD (1), "seduced by the false glare of Fortune and the Deluding Pomp of Title," he tried to force his son Edward to marry Lady Dorothea—"Love and Freindship" (*Vol. 2*, p. 81).

LINDSAY, EDWARD (2), "the most beauteous and amiable Youth" Laura has ever beheld; his real name is Lindsay, but "for particular reasons" she conceals it under that of Talbot—"Love and Freindship" (*Vol. 2*, p. 80).

LINDSAY, LAURA, wife of Edward Lindsay and principal narrator of "Love and Freindship"; she tells her correspondent, Marianne, "In my Mind, every Virtue that could adorn it was centered; it was the Rendezvous of every good Quality & of every noble sentiment" (*Vol. 2*, p. 78).

LION, the name of the room in which Strephon stays, in the inn that is the site of "The first Act of a Comedy"—"Scraps" (*Vol. 2*, p. 172).

LISBON, Portugal, one of the places Mrs. Croft visited while following her husband in the course of his career (*P*, 3.VIII).

LITTLE, CAPTAIN, of Limehouse, a visitor to Sanditon (*S*, p. 389).

LITTLE BOOKHAM. See **Great Bookham.**

LITTLE THEATRE, London, formerly on the site of the present Haymarket Theatre, it was torn down in 1821: although "London was rather thin" in August, according to Lydia Wickham, "the little Theatre was open" (*PP*, 3.IX).

LIVERPOOL, Lancs., (*a*) where Mary King was sent to stay with her uncle, to get her out of the clutches of the fortune-hunting Lieutenant Wickham (*PP*, 2.XVI); (*b*) where Sir Thomas Bertram landed at the end of his journey from Antigua (*MP*, 2.I).

LLOYD, MARTHA. See **Austen, Martha.**

LLOYD, MARY. See **Austen, Mary (2).**

LOITERER, THE, a periodical founded and heavily contributed to by Jane Austen's eldest brother, James, while he was an undergraduate at St. John's College, Oxford (around 1779).

LONDON: (*a*) Isabel advises Laura, "Beware of the insipid Vanities and idle Dissipations of the Metropolis of England"—"Love and Freindship" (*Vol. 2*, p. 78); (*b*) Chloe is bound thither in "The first Act of a Comedy"—"Scraps" (*Vol. 2*, p. 173); (*c*) Tom Musgrave visits the Watsons on his way home from it (*W*, p. 355); (*d*) most of the principal characters of *Sense and Sensibility* spend the winter there; (*e*) various characters in *Pride and Prejudice* live there, and others visit; (*f*) mentioned passim in *Mansfield Park*; some characters spend considerable time there, but it is always offstage; (*g*) the John Knightleys and the Campbells live there, mentioned passim in *Emma*; (*h*) visited by John Thorpe after his stay in Bath (*NA*, 1.XV), and mentioned in passing elsewhere; (*i*) Sir Walter and Elizabeth Elliot spent every spring there until they were forced to retrench (*P*, 3.II); also mentioned passim in

"Lesley Castle," *Lady Susan*, and *Sanditon*. See also **Baker St.; Bank; Bartlett's Buildings; Bedford Square; Berkeley St.; Bloomsbury Square; Bond St.; Brook St.; Brunswick Square; Camberwell; Carlton House; Cheapside; Conduit St.; Covent Garden; Drury Lane (Theatre); Edward St.; Exeter Exchange; Gracechurch St.; Gray's Inn; Grosvenor St.; Hampstead; Hanover Square; Hans Place; Harley St.; Henrietta St.; Hill St.; Holborn; Kensington Gardens; Limehouse; Manchester St.; Newgate (Prison); Pall Mall; Park St.; Portland Place; Portland Square; Putney; Ranelagh (Gardens); Sackville St.; St. Clement's (Church); St. George's (Church); St. George's Fields; St. James's (Palace); St. James's Square; St. James's St.; St. Paul's; Sloane St.; Temple; Thames (River); Tower of London; Upper Berkeley St.; Upper Seymour St.; Westminster (Abbey); Westminster (School); Wigmore St.; Wimpole St.**

LONG, MRS., a neighbor of the Bennets in Hertfordshire, with two nieces of marrying age (*PP*, 1.I).

LONGBOURN, Herts., the name of the village and possibly of the house where the Bennets live (*PP*, 1.III).

LONGSTAPLE, near Plymouth, where Mr. Pratt lives: he was the Steeles' uncle and Edward Ferrars's tutor (*SS*, 1.XXII).

LONGTOWN, MARQUIS OF, a crony of General Tilney; he invites the Tilneys to his seat in Herefordshire on short notice, giving the general an excuse to turn Catherine Morland from the house without ceremony (*NA*, 2.II).

LORD ———, an earl, is Colonel Fitzwilliam's father (*PP*, 2.VII).

LORD CHANCELLOR: Camilla Stanley believes that if she were Mr. Pitt or the lord chancellor, her father would take care that she should not be insulted — "Catharine or the Bower" (*Vol. 3*, p. 224).

LORDS AND BARONETS, of whom "Mrs. Morland knew so little . . . that she entertained no notion of their general mischievousness, and was wholly unsuspicious of danger to her daughter from their machinations" (*NA*, 1.II).

LOUISAS, prototypical heroines of gothic novels, mentioned by Henry Tilney (*NA*, 1.XIV).

"LOVE AND FREINDSHIP," an epistolary story dedicated to Mme. La Comtesse de Feuillide (see **Austen, Eliza**); its epigraph is "Deceived in Freindship & Betrayed in Love" (*Vol. 2*, p. 76).

LOVELACE. See **Richardson, Samuel**: *Clarissa*.

LOVERS' VOWS. See **Inchbald, (Mrs.) Elizabeth**.

LOWER ROOMS, Bath, the older assembly rooms, where balls were held on Tuesdays and Fridays: (*a*) Mr. Edwards danced with Emma Watson's Aunt Turner there about thirty years before the story takes place (*W*, p. 325); (*b*) Catherine Morland and Henry Tilney meet there (*NA*, 1.III).

LUCAS, LADY, "a very good kind of woman, not too clever to be a valuable neighbour to Mrs. Bennet"; she has a number of children (*PP*, 1.V).

LUCAS, CHARLOTTE. See **Collins, (Mrs.) Charlotte**.

LUCAS, MARIA, a younger daughter of Sir William Lucas: "a good humoured girl, but as empty-headed as himself, [she] had nothing to say that could be worth hearing" (*PP*, 2.IV); a further "young Lucas" is also mentioned (*PP*, 1.V), as well as "the younger Miss Lucases" (*PP*, 2.XVI).

LUCAS, SIR WILLIAM, the nearest neighbor of the Bennets: he "had been formerly in trade in Meryton, where he had made a tolerable fortune and risen to the honour of knighthood by an address to the King, during his mayoralty" (*PP*, 1.V).

LUCAS LODGE, where the Lucas family lives, about a mile from Meryton (*PP*, 1.V).

LUCY, a beautiful young lady physically and emotionally abused by Charles Adams—"Jack & Alice" (*Vol. 1*, p. 23).

LUTTERELL, CHARLOTTE, one of the principal correspondents in "Lesley Castle"; she tells Margaret Lesley, "I never wish to act a more principal part at a Wedding than the superintending and directing the Dinner" (*Vol. 2*, p. 121).

LUTTERELL, ELOISA, Charlotte's sister; her fiancé is killed shortly before their marriage by a fall from his horse—"Lesley Castle" (*Vol. 2*, p. 113).

LYME (REGIS), Dorset, visited by the younger Musgroves, Captain Wentworth, and Anne Elliot: "the remarkable situation of the town, the principal street almost hurrying into the water, . . . with the very beautiful line of cliffs stretching out to the east of the town, are what the stranger's eye will seek" (*P*, 3.XI).

LYONS, France, where Edward Stanley was sojourning when he heard of the illness of his favorite hunter—"Catharine or the Bower" (*Vol. 3*, p. 218).

MACARTNEY, LORD (George Macartney, Earl, 1737–1806), diplomat and colonial governor, mentioned in passing (*Letters*, p. 294); his "Journal of the Embassy to China," in Sir John Barrow's *Some Account of the Public Life, and a Selection from the Unpublished Writings of the Earl of Macartney* (1807) is found among the reading materials on Fanny Price's table in the East Room at Mansfield (*MP*, 1.XVI).

MACBETH. See **Shakespeare, William.**

MACDONALD, Sophia's cousin, who shelters her and Laura after they are abandoned by Lord St. Clair—"Love and Freindship" (*Vol. 2*, p. 92).

MACDONALD, JANETTA, Macdonald's daughter, aged fifteen, "naturally well disposed, endowed with a susceptible Heart, and a simpathetic Disposition"—"Love and Freindship" (*Vol. 2*, p. 93).

MACDONALD-HALL, Macdonald's house—"Love and Freindship" (*Vol. 2*, p. 93).

M'KENRIE. See **M'Kenzie, Captain.**

MACKENZIE, the gardener at Kellynch Hall (*P*, 3.V).

M'KENZIE, CAPTAIN, "whose modesty . . . had been the only reason of his having so long concealed the violence of his affection for Janetta"; on being encouraged by Laura and Sophia he elopes with Janetta to Gretna Green—"Love and Freindship" (*Vol. 2*, p. 94).

MACKENZIE, SIR GEORGE STEUART (1780–1848), mineralogist and author of travel literature such as *Travels in Iceland* (1811): he is mentioned (*Letters*, p. 294).

MACKENZIE, HENRY. See *Mirror*.

MACLEAN, LADY MARY, an elderly resident of Bath, addicted to concertgoing (*P*, 4.IX).

M'LEODS, M'KENZIES, M'PHERSONS, M'CARTNEYS, M'DONALDS, M'KINNONS, M'LELLANS, M'KAYS, MACBETHS AND MACDUFFS, families visited by the Lesleys in Perthshire—"Lesley Castle" (*Vol. 2*, p. 111).

MADDISON, most likely Henry Crawford's agent at Everingham (*MP*, 3.XI).

MADDOX, the Misses, sisters of Charles Maddox, they attend the ball given at Mansfield in Fanny Price's honor (*MP*, 2.XI).

MADDOX, CHARLES, a neighbor of the Bertrams, moving in a different social circle but "as gentlemanlike a man as you will see anywhere" (*MP*, 1.XV).

MAGDALEN BRIDGE, Oxford, mentioned by John Thorpe in his chatter about carriages and horseflesh (*NA*, 1.VII).

"MALBROOK," according to Charlotte Lutterell "the only tune I ever really like"—"Lesley Castle" (*Vol. 2*, p. 130).

MANCHESTER ST., London, where the Churchills stayed during their brief visit to the Metropolis before Mrs. Churchill's death; they may have owned a house there (*E*, 3.I).

MANSFIELD, the parish in which Mansfield Park is located (*MP*, 1.I).

MANSFIELD COMMON, where Mary Crawford wants to ride (*MP*, 1.VII).

MANSFIELD PARK, Northants., the Bertrams' estate, to which Fanny Price is brought to live at the age of ten (*MP*, 1.I).

MANSFIELD PARSONAGE, occupied first by the Norrises, then by the Grants, and last by Edmund and Fanny Bertram (*MP*, 1.I).

MANSFIELD WOOD, on the Bertram lands; they hunt pheasant there in October (*MP*, 2.I).

MANWARING, MR., Lady Susan's lover, a man "uncommonly pleasing" (*LS*, p. 244).

MANWARING, MRS., former ward of Mr. Johnson (2), Manwaring's wife: "'Silly Woman, to expect constancy from so charming a Man!'" (*LS*, p. 296).

MANWARING, MARIA, Manwaring's sister, disappointed in her conquest of Sir James Martin (*LS*, p. 245).

MAPLE GROVE, near Bristol, the seat of Mr. Suckling and the source of all of Mrs. Elton's notions of elegance (*E*, 2.XIV).

MARGARET, one of A. F.'s daughters, she is "all Life & Rapture" at the prospect of her entrée into the world—"A Collection of Letters" (*Vol. 2*, p. 151).

MARGARET OF ANJOU (1430–82), queen consort of Henry VI, "a woman whose distresses & Misfortunes were so great, as almost to make me who hate her, pity her"—"The History of England" (*Vol. 2*, p. 140).

MARGIANA. See **Sykes, Mrs. S.**

MARIA (1), whom Cassandra encounters in Bloomsbury Square—"The Beautifull Cassandra" (*Vol. 1*, p. 46).

MARIA (2), one of the watchers at Melissa's bedside, "more mild in her greif talks of going to Town next week"—"A Fragment written to inculcate the practise of Virtue" (*Vol. 1*, p. 72).

MARIA (3), a maid in the inn where "The first Act of a Comedy" is set—"Scraps" (*Vol. 2*, p. 172).

MARIA (4), "a middle-aged Flirt," the subject of a stanza by Jane Austen, quoted in the *Memoir* (*Verses*, p. 444).

MARIANNE, daughter of Isabel; Laura addresses the account of her adventures to her—"Love and Freindship" (*Vol. 2*, p. 77).

MARINA, a lady to whom Wilhelminus is "tenderly attached" and one of his guests at his cottage in Pembrokeshire—"Scraps" (*Vol. 2*, p. 178).

MARKET PLACE, Bath, below Laura Place, near the river; it is mentioned at the beginning of the expedition undertaken by the Morlands and the Thorpes, which gets no farther than seven miles on the road to Clifton (*NA*, 1.XI).

MARLBOROUGH, Wilts., where Willoughby paused to refresh himself on his journey from London to Cleveland (*SS*, 3.VIII).

MARLBOROUGH BUILDINGS, Bath, where Colonel and Mrs. Wallis live "in very good style" (*P*, 4.III).

MARLHURST, Sussex, the seat of Sir Godfrey and Lady Marlow—"Edgar & Emma" (*Vol. 1*, p. 30).

MARLOW, SIR GODFREY and **LADY**: they "were indeed very sensible people & tho' . . . like many other sensible People, they sometimes did a foolish thing, yet in general their actions were guided by Prudence & regulated by discretion"—"Edgar & Emma" (*Vol. 1*, p. 30).

MARLOWE, MR., MRS., EMMA, and a son, "very agreable people" staying in Bristol when the Lutterells are there—"Lesley Castle" (*Vol. 2*, p. 121).

MARMION. See **Scott, Sir Walter**.

MARSHALL, CAPTAIN, commander of the *Antwerp* while William Price is a midshipman on board (*MP*, 1.VI).

MARSHALL, MR., an acquaintance of the Robert Watsons in Croydon (*W*, p. 353).

MARTIN, COLONEL, the second son of Sir John, who is engaged to Anna Parker—"Scraps" (*Vol. 2*, p. 175).

MARTIN, MRS., Robert Martin's mother, who has "'*two* parlours, two very good parlours indeed . . . [and] a little Welch cow, a very pretty little Welch cow, indeed,'" according to Harriet Smith's account (*E*, 1.IV).

MARTIN, ELIZABETH, a sister of Robert Martin and one of Harriet Smith's best friends at school; another Miss Martin is also mentioned (*E*, 1.IV).

MARTIN, SIR JAMES, a rich man, but "contemptibly weak," whom Lady Susan tries to unite with her daughter; eventually, he is caught by Lady Susan herself (*LS*, p. 245).

MARTIN, SIR JOHN, "who died immensely rich"; the temptation of his fortune is too much for the principles of Anna Parker—"Scraps" (*Vol. 2*, p. 175).

MARTIN, ROBERT, aged twenty-four, the farmer of Abbey-Mill Farm in Donwell parish who marries Harriet Smith; according to Emma Woodhouse, "His appearance was very neat, and he looked like a sensible young man, but his person had no other advantage" (*E*, 1.IV); but Mr. Knightley finds him "'open, straight forward, and very well judging'" (*E*, 1.VIII).

MARTIN, SIR THOMAS, Sir John's elder son and principal heir—"Scraps" (*Vol. 2*, p. 175).

MARY (1) (1496–1533), youngest daughter of Henry VII: she "married first the King of France & secondly the D. of Suffolk"—"The History of England" (*Vol. 2*, p. 141).

MARY (2) (1516–58), queen of England, daughter of Henry VIII and Catherine of Aragon—"The History of England" (*Vol. 2*, p. 144).

MARY (3), probably a housemaid of the landlady in the Westgate Buildings who waits on Mrs. Smith (*P*, 4.IX).

MARY (STUART), QUEEN OF SCOTS (1542–87), daughter of James V of

Scotland and Mary of Guise: "this bewitching Princess" is the subject of Jane Austen's juvenile adulation—"The History of England" (*Vol. 2*, p. 145).
MARYS, prototypical wives of Elliots (*P*, 3.I).
MASON, MISS: Lady Greville uses this lady as a stick to beat Maria Williams with—"A Collection of Letters" (*Vol. 2*, p. 158).
MATHEW, ANNE. See **Austen, Anne**.
MATHEWS, MRS., MISS, MISS E., and **MISS H.**, visitors to Sanditon (*S*, p. 389).
MATILDA (1), Lord St. Clair's eldest daughter and Sophia's mother—"Love and Freindship" (*Vol. 2*, p. 91).
MATILDA (2), Henrietta Halton's correspondent—"A Collection of Letters" (*Vol. 2*, p. 163).
MATILDA (3), imaginary heroine in Henry Tilney's tale of terror (*NA*, 2.V).
MATLOCK, Derbys., (*a*) which Camilla Stanley might chance to visit in the course of her journey to the Lake District—"Catharine or the Bower" (*Vol. 3*, p. 199); (*b*) Eliza Bennet and the Gardiners must miss its "celebrated beauties" when their vacation time is cut short (*PP*, 2.XIX).
MAXWELL, "MRS. ADMIRAL," godmother of Fanny Price's little sister Mary, who died in childhood (*MP*, 3.VII).
MEDITERRANEAN, (*a*) where William Price had various tours of duty (*MP*, 1.XVI); (*b*) one of Captain Wentworth's tours of duty (*P*, 3.VIII).
MELISSA, the ailing lady whose illness tests the sensibilities of her various friends and relatives—"A Fragment written to inculcate the practise of Virtue" (*Vol. 1*, p. 72).
"MEMOIRS OF MR. CLIFFORD," a brief tale of the travels of a man in delicate health (*Vol. 1*, p. 43).
MERCHANT OF VENICE, THE. See **Shakespeare, William**.
MERCHANT-TAYLORS' (SCHOOL), London, founded in 1561 in Suffolk Lane, Upper Thames St., where the second Thorpe boy, Edward, is a student (*NA*, 1.IV).
MERRYWEATHER, MISS, a visitor to Sanditon (*S*, p. 389).
MERYTON, Herts., the town at the center of the neighborhood in which most of the action of *Pride and Prejudice* takes place (1.IV).
METCALFE, LADY, an acquaintance of Lady Catherine de Bourgh living in Kent (*PP*, 2.VI).
MICKLEHAM, Surrey, not far from Highbury: it is mentioned by Frank Churchill on the exploring party to Box Hill (*E*, 3.VII).
MIDAS. See **O'Hara, Kane**.
MIDDLESEX, where lives the aunt whom Edward Stanley tried to visit after breaking with his father—"Love and Freindship" (*Vol. 2*, p. 81).
MIDDLETON, ANNAMARIA, the three-year-old daughter of Sir John (*SS*, 1.XXI).
MIDDLETON, SIR JOHN (1), a cousin of Mrs. (Henry) Dashwood, "a good looking man about forty," very sociable and hospitable, who owns Barton Park in Devonshire (*SS*, 1.VI).
MIDDLETON, JOHN (2), a six-year-old son of Sir John (*SS*, 1.XXI).
MIDDLETON, LADY MARY (née Jennings), "not more than six or seven and

twenty ... though perfectly well-bred, she was reserved, cold, and had nothing to say for herself beyond the most common-place inquiry or remark" (*SS*, 1.VI).

MIDDLETON, WILLIAM, another of Sir John's sons (*SS*, 1.XXI).

MIDNIGHT BELL. See **Lathom, Francis**.

MIDSUMMER NIGHT'S DREAM, A. See **Shakespeare, William**.

MILLAR, COLONEL, commander of the regiment in Mrs. Bennet's neighborhood twenty-five years before the story begins, when she was a young lady (*PP*, 2.XVIII).

MILLAR, MR., a gentleman on his way to Bath for his health—"Scraps" (*Vol. 2*, p. 170).

MILLAR, CHARLOTTE and JULIA: the former "appears to have infinite wit and a good humour unalterable; her conversation during the half hour they set with us, was replete with humorous Sallies, Bonmots & repartees; while the sensible, the amiable Julia uttered Sentiments of Morality worthy of a heart like her own"—"Scraps" (*Vol. 2*, p. 171).

MILLINER, a bit part in *Sir Charles Grandison* (I i): usually, a milliner is a maker of ladies' hats, bonnets, and caps, but in this case she appears to be a dressmaker's assistant.

MILLINGEN, JOHN GIDEON (1782–1862), physician and writer: the libretto of *The Bee-hive* (1811), a musical farce, is attributed to him by the *DNB*; Jane Austen says that it is "rather less flat and trumpery" than *Five Hours at Brighton* (*Letters*, p. 321).

MILMAN, the two Misses. See **Bird, Mrs.; Cooper, Mrs. James**.

MILSOM ST., Bath, (*a*) where the Tilneys lodged—at the upper end, near Edgar's Buildings—and a street of fashionable shops (*NA*, 1.VI); (*b*) mentioned passim in *Persuasion*.

MILTON, JOHN (1608–74), poet, mentioned in passing (*NA*, 1.V; *Letters*, p. 402).

MINEHEAD, Som., visited by the Crofts (*P*, 4.VI).

MIRROR, THE (published January 23, 1779–May 27, 1780), edited by Harry Mackenzie: Mrs. Morland inappropriately recommends an essay from it to Catherine, "'about young girls that have been spoilt for home by great acquaintance'"—according to R. W. Chapman, probably essay no. XII, of March 6, 1779 (*NA*, 2.XV).

"MR. CLIFFORD." See **"Memoirs of Mr. Clifford."**

"MR. GELL AND MISS GILL," a poem, reproduced in the *Memoir*, that Jane Austen wrote, "On reading in the Newspaper, the Marriage of 'Mr. Gell of Eastbourne to Miss Gill'" (*Verses*, p. 444).

"MR. HARLEY." See **"Adventures of Mr. Harley, The."**

MITCHELL (1), a farmer whose house is near Broadway Lane, Highbury (*E*, 1.I).

MITCHELL (2), a family acquainted with the Thorpes in Bath (*NA*, 1.XI).

MITCHELL, ANNE, a rival of Isabella Thorpe in Bath (*NA*, 2.XII).

MOLIÈRE, JEAN BAPTISTE POQUELIN (1622–73), playwright: *The Hypocrite* (see **Bickerstaffe, Isaac**) is based on his *Tartuffe, ou l'Imposteur* (1664) (*Letters*, p. 275).

MOLLAND'S, Milsom St., Bath, a shop in which Anne Elliot encounters Frederick Wentworth on his first arriving in Bath (*P*, 4.VII).

MONK, THE. See **Lewis, Matthew Gregory.**

MONKFORD, Som., a parish not far from Kellynch where Edward Wentworth was curate in 1806 (*P*, 3.III).

MONTGOMERY, JAMES (1771–1854), poet: Sir Edward Denham says, "'Montgomery has all the Fire of Poetry'" (*S*, p. 397).

MONTONI, the villain of *The Mysteries of Udolpho*: Catherine Morland compares General Tilney to him (*NA*, 2.VIII).

MOON, the name of a room in an unnamed inn that is occupied by Popgun and Pistoletta in "the first Act of a Comedy"—"Scraps" (*Vol. 2*, p. 172).

MOORE, EDWARD (1712–57), dramatist: *The Gamester* (1753), written in collaboration with Garrick, was one of the plays proposed for enactment at Mansfield (*MP*, 1.XIV).

MORE, HANNAH (1745–1833), author of religious writings: (1) *Cœlebs in Search of a Wife* (1809) (*a*) is one of the improving works Mrs. Percival gave Catharine in order to "breed [her] up virtuously"—"Catharine or the Bower" (*Vol. 3*, p. 232); (*b*) Jane Austen is reluctant to read this because "I do not like the Evangelicals" (*Letters*, p. 256), and she finds the name *Cœlebs* "pedantry & affectation" (p. 259); (2) in 1811 Jane Austen refers to "Mrs. H. More's recent publication," probably *Practical Piety* (1811) (*Letters*, p. 287).

MORGAN, the Parkers' butler (*S*, p. 389).

MORGAN, LADY. See **Owenson, Sydney.**

MORLAND, MRS., the mother of ten children, "a woman of useful plain sense, with a good temper, and, what is more remarkable, with a good constitution. She had three sons before Catherine was born; and instead of dying in bringing the latter into the world, as any body might expect, she still lived on" (*NA*, 1.I).

MORLAND, CATHERINE, the heroine of *Northanger Abbey*: "her heart was affectionate, her disposition cheerful and open, without conceit or affectation of any kind—her manners just removed from the awkwardness and shyness of a girl; her person pleasing, and, when in good looks, pretty—and her mind about as ignorant and uninformed as the female mind at seventeen usually is" (*NA*, 1.II).

MORLAND, GEORGE, age six, the next-to-youngest Morland (*NA*, 2. XIV).

MORLAND, HARRIET, age four, the youngest Morland (*NA*, 2.XIV).

MORLAND, JAMES, Catherine's eldest brother, a student at Oxford; he suffers a brief romance with Isabella Thorpe (*NA*, 1.IV).

MORLAND, RICHARD (1), Catherine's father, was "a clergyman, without being neglected, or poor, and a very respectable man, though his name was Richard—and he had never been handsome" (*NA*, 1.I).

MORLAND, RICHARD (2), one of Catherine's elder brothers, for whom she is sewing cravats (*NA*, 2.XV): or perhaps this is only a reference to her father.

MORLAND, SARAH (SALLY), the next daughter after Catherine (*NA*, 1.I).

MORLEY, SIR BASIL, a friend of Sir Walter Elliot (*P*, 3.III).

MORNING POST, a fashionable London newspaper in which Mr. Parker found an advertisement for a surgeon in Willingden Abbots (*S*, p. 366).

MORRIS, MR., the man who leased Netherfield Park to Mr. Bingley (*PP*, 1.I).

MORTON, HONORABLE MISS, an heiress whom Mrs. Ferrars hopes will marry one of her sons (*SS*, 2.XI).

MORTON, LORD (deceased), who died leaving his only daughter thirty thousand pounds (*SS*, 2.XI).

MOSS, REV. THOMAS (d. 1808), clergyman and poet: his *Poems on Several Occasions* (1769) contains "Beggar's Petition," a poem that took Catherine Morland three months to learn (*NA*, 1.I).

MOTHERBANK, a stretch of shallow water to the west of the Isle of Wight used as an anchorage for the fleet; it is one of the few subjects of Lieutenant Price's conversation (*MP*, 3.VIII).

MOUNTAGUE, LADY (née Arundel), who marries Sir William after he shoots Mr. Stanhope, her preferred suitor—"Sir William Mountague" (*Vol. 1*, p. 42).

MOUNTAGUE, (LADY) EMMA (née Stanhope), the sister of the murdered Mr. Stanhope, she demands 14s. in recompense for her brother's death, then marries his killer—"Sir William Mountague" (*Vol. 1*, p. 42).

MOUNTAGUE, SIR WILLIAM, a wealthy young man very susceptible to the charms of the opposite sex—"Sir William Mountague" (*Vol. 1*, p. 40).

MOUNTEAGLE, LORD (William Parker, fourth Baron Monteagle, 1575–1622), to whom Sir Henry Percy [sic]'s "Attentions were entirely confined"—"The History of England" (*Vol. 2*, p. 147): he informed against the "gunpowder plot" of 1604, of which Thomas Percy was an organizer and Henry Percy, ninth earl of Northumberland, was suspected of being a conspirator.

MOYES, J., of Greville St., Hatton Garden, London: the printer of volume 3 of *Emma*'s first edition, in 1816.

MULLINS, the name of a family in distressed circumstances in Sanditon (*S*, p. 423).

MURRAY, JOHN, of Albemarle St., London, the publisher of the first editions of *Emma, Northanger Abbey*, and *Persuasion*.

MUSGRAVE, MRS., one of Jane Austen's godparents.

MUSGRAVE, TOM: Emma Watson says of him, "I allow his person & air to be good—& that his manners to a certain point—his address rather—is pleasing.—But I see nothing else to admire in him" (*W*, p. 342).

MUSGROVE, MRS., "was of a comfortable substantial size, infinitely more fitted by nature to express good cheer and good humour, than tenderness and sentiment" (*P*, 3.VIII).

MUSGROVE, CHARLES (1), of Uppercross Great House, and his wife "were a very good sort of people; friendly and hospitable, not much educated, and not at all elegant" (*P*, 3.V).

MUSGROVE, CHARLES (2), Mary's husband, "was civil and agreeable; in sense and temper he was undoubtedly superior to his wife" (*P*, 3.VI).

MUSGROVE, CHARLES (3), Charles (2) and Mary's elder son, who injured his spine in a fall (*P*, 3.V).

MUSGROVE, HARRY, the youngest child of Charles (1) and Mrs. Musgrove, "the very last, lingering and long-petted master Harry" (*P*, 4.I).

MUSGROVE, HENRIETTA, Charles (1) and Mrs. Musgrove's second daughter, age nineteen; she and Louisa "had brought from a school at Exeter all the usual stock of accomplishments, and were now, like thousands of other young ladies, living to be fashionable, happy, and merry" (*P*, 3.V).

MUSGROVE, LOUISA, the eldest daughter of Charles (1) and Mrs. Musgrove, age twenty, "'a very amiable, sweet-tempered girl, and not deficient in understanding,'" according to Captain Wentworth (*P*, 4.VIII).

MUSGROVE, MARY (née Elliot), Anne's younger sister, did not have her "understanding or temper. While well, and happy, and properly attended to, she had great good humour and excellent spirits; but any indisposition sunk her completely; she had no resources for solitude; and inheriting a considerable share of the Elliot self-importance, was very prone to add to every other distress that of fancying herself neglected and ill-used" (*P*, 3.V).

MUSGROVE, RICHARD, "a very troublesome, hopeless son" of Charles (1) and Mrs. Musgrove who "had been sent to sea, because he was stupid and unmanageable on shore" (*P*, 3.VI).

MUSGROVE, THOMAS, the object of Henrietta Halton's affection: according to his cousin, Lady Scudamore, he is "'a charming young fellow, has seen a great deal of the World, and writes the best Love-letters I have ever read'"—"A Collection of Letters" (*Vol. 2*, p. 165).

MUSGROVE, WALTER, Charles (2) and Mary's younger son, "a remarkable stout, forward child, of two years old" (*P*, 3.IX).

MY GRANDMOTHER. See **Hoare, Prince**.

MYSTERIES OF UDOLPHO, THE. See **Radcliffe, Mrs. Ann**.

MYSTERIOUS WARNINGS. See **Parsons, Mrs. Eliza**: *The Mysterious Warning*.

"MYSTERY, THE," a comic play dedicated to Jane Austen's father, the Reverend George Austen, "which tho' an unfinished one, is I flatter myself as *complete* a *Mystery* as any of its kind" (*Vol. 1*, p. 55).

NANNY (1), the Watsons' upper housemaid (*W*, p. 341).

NANNY (2), Mrs. Norris's housekeeper at the White House (*MP*, 1.I).

NANNY. See also **Anne (Nanny)**.

NAPLES, from which Mr. Lesley writes to say that he "has turned Romancatholic, obtained one of the Pope's Bulls for annulling his 1st Marriage and has since actually married a Neapolitan Lady of great Rank & Fortune"—"Lesley Castle" (*Vol. 2*, p. 137).

NASH, MISS, the head teacher at Mrs. Goddard's school, much enamored of Mr. Elton (*E*, 1.IV).

NAVY-LIST (*Steel's Original and Correct List of the Royal Navy*, semiannual 1782–1816, giving ships and officers, their assignments, and seniority), (*a*) reading matter of Lieutenant Price, Fanny's father (*MP*, 3.VIII); (*b*) a copy was purchased by the Miss Musgroves, the better to converse with Captain Wentworth (*P*, 3.VIII).

NECROMANCER OF THE BLACK FOREST. See **Teuthold, Peter**.

NEIGHBORHOOD: Laura Lindsay explains to Marianne, "Our neighborhood was small, for it consisted only of your mother"—"Love and Freindship" (*Vol. 2*, p. 78).

NETHERFIELD PARK (also called Netherfield House), the place rented by Mr. Bingley in the neighborhood of Meryton, in Hertfordshire (*PP*, 1.I).

NEVILLE, one of the objects of the fickle Sophia's affection—"A Collection of Letters" (*Vol. 2*, p. 152).

NEW LONDON INN, Exeter, where the Dashwoods' manservant encounters Lucy Ferrars and her husband, whom he mistakes for Edward Ferrars (*SS*, 3.XI).

NEWBURY, Berks., where William and Fanny Price break their journey on their way to Portsmouth (*MP*, 3.VII).

NEWCASTLE (-ON-TYNE), Northumb., where Lieutenant Wickham's new regiment is stationed (*PP*, 3.IX).

NEWFOUNDLAND, where Mr. Williams's eldest son lives, "from whence he regularly sent home a large Newfoundland Dog every Month to his family"—"The Generous Curate" (*Vol. 1*, p. 73).

NEWGATE (PRISON), London, where Sophia's husband Augustus is incarcerated—"Love and Freindship" (*Vol. 2*, p. 89).

NEWMARKET, Suffolk, where Tom Bertram developed a serious fever while attending the races (*MP*, 3.XIII).

NEWNHAM, DR., a physician living in Alton, Hants., mentioned in a poem by Jane Austen (*Verses*, p. 449).

NEWTON, Devon, near Barton, where the Careys live (*SS*, 1.XIII).

NIAGARA: in "Mock Panegyric on a Young Friend," Jane Austen says, "Her wit descends on foes and friends / Like famed Niagara's Fall" (*Verses*, p. 443).

NICHOLLS, MRS., the cook and/or housekeeper at Netherfield Park (*PP*, 1.XI).

NORFOLK, DUKE OF (Thomas Howard, fourth Duke, 1536–72), named as the only friend of Mary Queen of Scots at the time of her imprisonment by Elizabeth—"The History of England" (*Vol. 2*, p. 145).

NORFOLK, (*a*) where Mrs. Ferrars has an estate, which she settles on her son Robert (*SS*, 3.I); (*b*) where Henry Crawford's estate, Everingham, is situated (*MP*, 1.IV).

NORLAND COMMON, which John Dashwood has enclosed (*SS*, 2.XI): the reference is probably intended to imply that he is a rather harsh landlord, profiting by taking advantage of the poor tenants of his land.

NORLAND PARK, Sussex, a large estate where the Dashwoods had lived for many generations (*SS*, 1.I).

NORRIS, REVEREND MR., "a friend of [Sir Thomas Bertram], with scarcely any private fortune"; he held the living of Mansfield until his death (*MP*, 1.I).

NORRIS, MRS. (née Ward), widowed sister of Lady Maria Bertram and Frances Price: "As far as walking, talking, and contriving reached, she was thoroughly benevolent, and nobody knew better how to dictate liberality to others: but her love of money was equal to her love of directing, and she knew quite as well how to save her own as to spend that of her friends" (*MP*, 1.I).

NORTH SEAS, one of Admiral Croft's tours of duty when he was a captain (*P*, 3.VIII).

NORTH YARMOUTH, Norfolk, where the Crofts first lived after their marriage (*P*, 3.X).

NORTHAMPTON, Northants., (*a*) a few miles from Mansfield (*MP*, 1.II); (*b*) where Captain Tilney's regiment, the Twelfth Light Dragoons, is stationed (*NA*, 1.XIV).

NORTHAMPTONSHIRE, (*a*) where Mansfield Park is situated (*MP*, 1.I); (*b*) where Harriet Byron's uncle and aunt, the Selbys, live (*CG*, V i).

NORTHANGER ABBEY, Glos., the Tilneys' estate (*NA*, 2.II).

NORTHLEIGH, Oxon., the principal seat of Jane Austen's uncle, James Leigh Perrot. (The Leigh Perrots also lived in Bath.)

NORTHUMBERLAND, DUKE OF (John Dudley, ca. 1502–53), one of the regents under Edward VI—"The History of England" (*Vol. 2*, p. 143).

NORTON, MR., a cousin of Captain Hunter and one of Mary Edwards' dancing partners (*W*, p. 337).

NORVAL, a character in John Home's *Douglas* (*MP*, 1.XIII).

NOVELS: Sir Edward demands of his defiant son, "'Where Edward in the name of wonder... did you pick up this unmeaning Gibberish? You have been studying Novels I suspect'"—"Love and Freindship" (*Vol. 2*, p. 81).

NOYCE, FANNY, a "very particular friend" of Diana Parker (*S*, p. 408).

OAKHAM MOUNT, a hill near Longbourn from which a good view may be obtained (*PP*, 3.XVII).

O'BRIEN, CAPTAIN, the second husband of Emma Watson's aunt; he sent Emma home to her family rather than let her live with them in Ireland (*W*, p. 326).

O'BRIEN, MRS., Emma Watson's aunt, who remarried after Mr. Turner's death and moved to Ireland; Mr. Edwards says of her: "'When an old Lady plays the fool, it is not in the course of nature that she should suffer from it many years'" (*W*, p. 326).

OCTAGON ROOM, one of the Upper (New) Assembly Rooms, Bath, where balls were held Mondays and Thursdays: the Elliots, Mrs. Clay, Lady Dalrymple, and Miss Carteret gather there before the concert (*P*, 4.VIII); also mentioned (*NA*, 1.VII).

"ODE TO PITY," a poem dedicated to Jane Austen's sister Cassandra "from a thorough knowledge of her pitiful Nature" (*Vol. 1*, p. 74).

O'HARA, KANE (ca. 1714–82), author of burlesques: *Midas: An English Burletta* (1764), a travesty of Italian burlettas as introduced in Ireland by the D'Amici family, was one of the shows seen by Jane Austen with her sister-in-law and two of her nieces in 1813 (*Letters*, p. 321).

OLD BRIDGE, Bath, by which Lady Russell and Anne Elliot enter Bath (*P*, 4.II).

OLD MAIDS: Emma Woodhouse claims, "'A single woman, with a very narrow income, must be a ridiculous, disagreeable, old maid! the proper sport of boys and girls; but a single woman, of good fortune, is always respectable, and may be as sensible and pleasant as anybody else'" (*E*, 1.X).

OLD ROOMS, Bath. See **Lower Rooms, Bath**.

OLIVER, TOM, a neighbor of the Bertrams who moves in a different circle—"a very clever fellow"; his brother is also mentioned indirectly (*MP*, 1.XV).

OLYMPE ET THÉOPHILE. See **Genlis, Mme. de:** *Les veillées du château*.

ONTARIO: in "Mock Panegyric on a Young Friend," Jane Austen says that "Ontario's lake may fitly speak / Her fancy's ample bound" (*Verses*, p. 443).

ORIEL COLLEGE, Oxford, attended by John Thorpe's friend Jackson (*NA*, 1.VII).

ORMOND, DUKE OF (James Butler, first duke of Ormonde, 1610–88), one of Charles I's few supporters—"The History of England" (*Vol. 2*, p. 148).

ORPHAN OF THE RHINE. See **Sleath, Eleanor**.

OSBORNE, LADY: "Of the females, Ly. Osborne had by much the finest person;—tho' nearly 50, she was very handsome, & had all the Dignity of Rank" (*W*, p. 329).

OSBORNE, LORD, "was a very fine young man; but there was an air of

Coldness, of Carelessness, even of Awkwardness about him, which seemed to speak him out of his Element in a Ball room" (*W*, p. 329).

OSBORNE, MISS: Tom Musgrave says of her, "'Perhaps she is not critically handsome, but her Manners are delightful'" (*W*, p. 340).

OSBORNE CASTLE, the seat of Lord Osborne in Wickstead parish: according to Charles Blake, "'There is a monstrous curious stuff'd Fox there, & a Badger" (*W*, p. 333).

OSTALIS, COMTESSE D', a character in Mme. de Genlis's *Adelaide and Theodore*, mentioned by Emma Woodhouse (*E*, 3.XVII).

OTHELLO. See **Shakespeare, William**.

OTWAY, MR. and **MRS., MISS, CAROLINE, GEORGE**, and **ARTHUR** all attend the ball given by the Westons at the Crown Inn (*E*, 3.II).

OVERTON, Hants., near Steventon, (*a*) the first place Jane Austen's eldest brother James held a curacy; (*b*) one of the stages of Mr. Clifford's journey from Bath to London—"Memoirs of Mr. Clifford" (*Vol. 1*, p. 43).

OVID (Publius Ovidius Naso, 43 B.C.–A.D. 18), poet: Jane Austen says that her verses are "purely classical—just like Homer and Virgil, Ovid and Propria que Maribus" (*Letters*, p. 256).

OWEN, MR., a friend of Edmund Bertram living near Peterborough; he has three grown-up sisters. He and Edmund are ordained together (*MP*, 2.XI).

OWENSON, (MISS) SYDNEY (Sydney, Lady Morgan, ca. 1783–1859), novelist and traveler: Jane Austen mentions *The Wild Irish Girl* (1806) and *Woman, or Ida of Athens* (1809) and remarks, "If the warmth of her Language could affect the Body it might be worth reading in this weather" (*Letters*, p. 251).

OXFORD: (*a*) its inhabitants were "always loyal to [Charles I] & faithful to his interests"—"The History of England" (*Vol. 2*, p. 148); (*b*) it is mentioned in a verse "On the Universities" (*Verses*, p. 447); (*c*) Edward Ferrars matriculated there; he returns there to be prepared for ordination (*SS*, 1.XIX); (*d*) Elizabeth Bennet visited it on her journey with the Gardiners to Derbyshire (*PP*, 2.XIX); (*e*) Edmund Bertram attended university there; also Fanny Price passed through it on her way to and from Portsmouth (*MP*, 1.II); (*f*) Frank Churchill made his final stop there on his first journey from Enscombe to Randalls (*E*, 2.V); (*g*) James Morland and John Thorpe are students there (*NA*, 1.IV).

PADDINGTON, London, where live the Awberrys, in whose house Sir Hargrave Pollexfen attempts to marry Harriet Byron by force (*CG*, II i).

PALL MALL, a thoroughfare running from St. James's Palace to the Haymarket, lined with clubs and fashionable shops, where, in a stationer's shop, Colonel Brandon hears of Willoughby's engagement (*SS*, 2.VIII); later, Edward Ferrars lodges in Pall Mall after being cast off by his mother (*SS*, 3.II).

PALMER, CHARLOTTE (née Jennings), Lady Middleton's sister, who was "totally unlike her in every respect. She was short and plump, had a very pretty face, and the finest expression of good humour in it that could possibly be.... She came in with a smile, smiled all the time of her visit, except when she laughed, and smiled when she went away" (*SS*, 1.XIX).

PALMER, FANNY. See **Austen, Frances**.

PALMER, HARRIET. See **Austen, Harriet**.

PALMER, THOMAS, "a grave looking young man of five or six and twenty, with an air of more fashion and sense than his wife, but of less willingness to please or be pleased" (*SS*, 1.XIX).

PAMMYDIDDLE, the parish in which the Johnson family and other principal characters of "Jack & Alice" live (*Vol. 1*, p. 12).

PANGLOSS, DR., a character in George Colman the younger's *The Heir at Law* (*MP*, 1.XIV).

PARIS, one of the stages in Mr. Lesley's travels, from which he writes that "he thinks it very good fun to be single again"—"Lesley Castle" (*Vol. 2*, p. 116).

PARK ST., Grosvenor Square, London, the very elegant address of Mrs. Ferrars (*SS*, 1.XXII).

PARKER, ANNA, "a Young Lady, whose feelings being too Strong for her Judgement led her into the commission of Errors which her heart disapproved": after assisting her fiancé to rob his brother of his inheritance, she announces her intention to murder her sister—"Scraps" (*Vol. 2*, p. 174).

PARKER, ARTHUR, "quite as tall as his Brother [Thomas] & a great deal Stouter—Broad made & Lusty—and with no other look of an Invalide, than a sodden complexion" (*S*, pp. 413–14).

PARKER, DIANA, "about 4 & 30, of middling height & slender;—delicate looking rather than sickly; with an agreable face, & a very animated eye"; she proves to be an unconscionable busybody (*S*, p. 407).

PARKER, (MRS.) MARY (1), "evidently a gentle, amiable, sweet tempered Woman," Thomas Parker's wife (*S*, p. 372).

PARKER, MARY (2), one of the elder Parkers' children (*S*, p. 381).

PARKER, SIDNEY, one of Thomas's younger brothers, "a very clever Young Man,—and with great powers of pleasing" (*S*, p. 382).

PARKER, SUSAN, Diana Parker's younger sister, "more thin & worn by Illness & Medecine, more relaxed in air, & more subdued in voice" (*S*, p. 413).

PARKER, THOMAS, "generally kind-hearted;—Liberal, gentlemanlike, easy to please;—of a sanguine turn of mind, with more Imagination than Judgement" (*S*, p. 372).

PARKLANDS, Kent, the De Courcy estate (*LS*, p. 248).

PARLIAMENT. See **House of Commons**.

PARRY (1) family, friends of Mrs. Jennings (*SS*, 2.VIII).

PARRY (2) family, acquaintances of Mrs. Allen (*NA*, 1.II).

PARRY, GEORGE, with whom Catherine Morland might have danced if his family had come to Bath (*NA*, 1.II).

PARSONS, MRS. ELIZA (d. 1811), novelist and dramatist: *The Castle of Wolfenbach* (1793) and *The Mysterious Warning* (1796) are two of the books on the reading list provided by Isabella Thorpe for Catherine Morland's education (*NA*, 1.VI).

PARTRIDGE, MRS., a lady living in Bath with whom Mrs. Elton stayed when visiting there; the latter claims her as "'my particular friend,'" but it is more likely that her daughter Clara was the friend and Mrs. Partridge only the hostess (*E*, 2.XIV).

PARTRIDGE, CLARA. See **Jeffereys, Mrs. Clara**.

PASLEY, SIR CHARLES WILLIAM (1780–1861), a captain in the corps of engineers: Jane Austen finds his *Essay on the Military Policy and Institutions of the*

British Empire (1810) "delightfully written & highly entertaining" (*Letters*, p. 292; also mentioned on pp. 294 and 304).

PATRONAGE. See **Edgeworth, Maria**.

PATTON, MARY. See **Foote, (Capt.) Edward James** and **Mary Foote**.

PATTY, the Bateses' only servant (*E*, 2.III).

PEAK, THE, Derbys.: Eliza Bennet and the Gardiners must miss its "celebrated beauties" when their vacation time is cut short (*PP*, 2.XIX).

PEMBERLEY HOUSE, Derbys., "a large, handsome, stone building, standing well on rising ground, and backed by a ridge of high woody hills;—and in front, a stream of some natural importance was swelled into greater, but without any artificial appearance. . . . [Eliza Bennet] had never seen a place for which nature had done more, or where natural beauty had been so little counteracted by an awkward taste" (*PP*, 3.I).

PEMBROKESHIRE, where the cottage let by the gullible Wilhelminus is situated—"Scraps" (*Vol. 2*, p. 176).

PERCIVAL, LADY, "a young Widow of Quality, . . . accomplished & lovely": Sir William falls in love with her and almost marries her, but is saved by her naming the first day of the hunting season as their nuptial day—"Sir William Mountague" (*Vol. 1*, p. 41).

PERCIVAL (or **PETERSON**), **MRS.** (called "Mrs." even though she is described as a "Maiden Aunt"), "who while she tenderly loved [Catharine], watched over her conduct with so scrutinizing a severity, as to make it very doubtful to many people . . . whether she loved her or not"—"Catharine or the Bower" (*Vol. 3*, p. 192).

PERCIVAL, CATHARINE (KITTY): "her Spirits were naturally good, and not easily depressed, and she possessed such a fund of vivacity and good humour as could only be damped by some serious vexation"—"Catharine or the Bower" (*Vol. 3*, p. 193).

PERCIVAL, THOMAS (1740–1804), physician: *A Father's Instructions; consisting of Moral Tales, Fables, and Reflections* . . . (1768) is mentioned (*Letters*, p. 219).

PERCY, SIR HENRY (Jane Austen means either Thomas Percy, 1560–1605, organizer of the "gunpowder plot," or his kinsman Henry Percy, ninth Earl of Northumberland, 1564–1632, also suspected of complicity), who, "tho' certainly the best bred Man of the [Roman Catholics], had none of that general politeness which is so universally pleasing, as his Attentions were entirely confined to Lord Mounteagle"—"The History of England" (*Vol. 2*, p. 147).

PERROT. See **Leigh (Perrot), James**.

PERRY, MR., the apothecary in Highbury and Donwell, "an intelligent, gentlemanlike man" (*E*, 1.II).

PERRY, MRS., wife of the apothecary and mother of a numerous family: "all the little Perrys" are mentioned occasionally (*E*, 1.II).

PERSEVERANCE, the ship on which Francis William Austen was midshipman in 1793 (*Vol. 1*, p. 12).

PERTH, two miles from which Lesley Castle is situated—"Lesley Castle" (*Vol. 2*, p. 111).

PETER, SIR. See **Barlow, Sir Peter**.

PETERBOROUGH, Hunts.: the Owens' estate, Lessingby, is not far away; Edmund Bertram is ordained there (*MP*, 2.VIII).

PETERSON. See **Percival, Mrs.**

PETTY-FRANCE, a posting stage about fifteen miles north of Bath, where Catherine Morland and the Tilneys stopped for two hours to eat and rest the horses during the journey to Northanger Abbey (*NA*, 2.V).

PHILANDER, "a most beautifull Young Man" and grandson of Lord St. Clair; his stage pseudonym was Lewis—"Love and Freindship" (*Vol. 2*, pp. 91 and 109).

PHILIP, KING OF SPAIN (Philip II, 1527–98): he married the English queen Mary (1), and "in her Sister's reign was famous for building Armadas"—"The History of England" (*Vol. 2*, p. 144).

PHILIPPA, Edward Stanley's aunt, living in Middlesex—"Love and Freindship" (*Vol. 2*, p. 82).

PHILIPS, MR., Mrs. Bennet's brother-in-law, an attorney in Meryton, formerly clerk to her father Mr. Gardiner; he is seen by Eliza Bennet as her "broad-faced stuffy uncle Philips, breathing port wine" (*PP*, 1.XVI).

PHILIPS, MRS. (née Gardiner), Mrs. Bennet's sister living in Meryton, a foolish, inelegant lady (*PP*, 1.VII).

PHILLIPS, the Misses, who might come to tea with A. F. and her daughters—"A Collection of Letters" (*Vol. 2*, p. 150).

PINNY, near Lyme Regis, "with its green chasms between romantic rocks" (*P*, 3.XI) is mentioned by Jane Austen in her panegyric on the beauties of Lyme.

PIOZZI, MRS. (Hester Lynch Thrale Piozzi, 1741–1821), occasional author and friend of Dr. Johnson and Fanny Burney: Jane Austen apes the style of her *Letters to and from the Late Samuel Johnson LL.D.* (1788) (*Letters*, p. 66); and she quotes volume 1, p. 270 of the same (*Letters*, p. 235).

PISTOLETTA, the daughter of Popgun, in "The first Act of a Comedy" —"Scraps" (*Vol. 2*, p. 172).

PITT, MR. (William Pitt, 1759–1806), statesman, the second son of William Pitt, first earl of Chatham: Camilla Stanley claims that if she were Mr. Pitt or the lord chancellor, her father would be more concerned to protect her from insult —"Catharine or the Bower" (*Vol. 3*, p. 224).

PLEASURES OF HOPE. See **Campbell, Thomas.**

PLOUGHBOYS, CHORUS OF, who sing a particularly footling refrain to Chloe's song in "The first Act of a Comedy"—"Scraps" (*Vol. 2*, p. 173).

PLYMOUTH, Devon (*a*) Mr. Pratt's place, Longstaple, is nearby (*SS*, 1.XVI); (*b*) where Captain Wentworth landed after his successful tour of duty in the *Asp* (*P*, 3.VIII).

POET'S PILGRIMAGE TO WATERLOO, THE. See **Southey, Robert.**

POLLEXFEN, SIR HARGRAVE, the villain who abducts Harriet Byron and tries to force her into marriage (*CG*, II i).

POLYDORE, Laura's father—"Love and Freindship" (*Vol. 2*, p. 81).

POMFRET CASTLE, where Richard II retired after being deposed by Henry IV and "where he happened to be murdered"—"The History of England" (*Vol. 2*, p. 139).

POOLE, the name of a family living near Uppercross, friends of the Musgroves (*P*, 3.V).

POPE, MISS, a young Lady for whom Lady Catherine de Bourgh found a position as governess in Lady Metcalfe's household (*PP*, 2.VI).

POPE, ALEXANDER (1688–1744), poet: in their second meeting, Marianne Dashwood receives from Willoughby "every assurance of his admiring Pope no more than is proper" (*SS*, 1.X); (1) *Essay on Man* (1733): (*a*) Miss Jane's remark "'Ride where you may, Be Candid where You can'" is a parody of epistle I, line 15: "Laugh where we must, be candid where we can"—"A Collection of Letters" (*Vol. 2*, p. 153); (*b*) the line "Whatever is, is best" is quoted (*Letters*, p. 362); (2) "Elegy to the Memory of an Unfortunate Lady" (ca. 1712) is quoted (*NA*, 1.I).

POPGUN, father of Pistoletta, who is to marry Strephon, in "The first Act of a Comedy"—"Scraps" (*Vol. 2*, p. 172).

POPHAM, SIR HOME RIGGS (1762–1820), a naval commander who was court-martialed for withdrawing his squadron from the Cape of Good Hope without receiving orders to do so, is the subject of a short poem by Jane Austen, who is sympathetic to the defendant (*Verses*, p. 446).

PORRETTA, LADY CLEMENTINA DELLA, is mentioned (*CG*, V i); Sir Charles Grandison did not consider himself free to marry Harriet Byron until Lady Clementina married, because he was previously engaged to her.

PORTER, ANNA MARIA (1780–1832), novelist: *Lake of Killarney* (1804) is mentioned (*Letters*, p. 228).

PORTLAND PLACE, London, where Charlotte Drummond's aunt Mrs. Williamson lives—"Frederic & Elfrida" (*Vol. 1*, p. 8).

PORTMAN SQUARE, London, (*a*) where Sir George and Lady Lesley have their town house—"Lesley Castle" (*Vol. 2*, p. 123); (*b*) Mrs. Jennings lives "in one of the streets near Portman-square," that is, in Berkeley St. (*SS*, 2.III).

PORTSMOUTH, Hants., (*a*) the Prices live there (*MP*, 1.I); (*b*) Captain Wentworth transported Mrs. Harville, her sister, her cousin, and her three children from there to Plymouth (*P*, 3.VIII).

PRATT, MR. (1), the Steeles' uncle and Edward Ferrars's tutor, living at Longstaple, near Plymouth (*SS*, 1.XXII).

PRATT, MR. (2), one of the officers in Colonel Forster's regiment (*PP*, 2.XVI).

PRATT, MR. RICHARD, a visitor to Sanditon (*S*, p. 389).

PRESCOTT, LADY, one of the guests at the ball given at Mansfield in Fanny Price's honor (*MP*, 2.XI).

PRICE, LIEUTENANT, Fanny Price's father; on meeting him as a young woman, she finds that "his habits were worse, and his manners coarser, than she had been prepared for. He did not want abilities; but he had no curiosity, and no information beyond his profession . . . he swore and he drank, he was dirty and gross" (*MP*, 3.VIII).

PRICE, BETSEY, a spoiled little girl of five, the youngest child in the Price family (*MP*, 3.VI).

PRICE, CHARLES, the Prices' sixth son, age eight; he and Tom Price are "two rosy-faced boys, ragged and dirty" (*MP*, 3.VII).

PRICE, (MRS.) FRANCES (1) (née Ward), Fanny's mother: when Fanny visits Portsmouth as a young woman, she finds her mother to be "a partial, ill-judging parent, a dawdle, a slattern, who neither taught nor restrained her children, whose house was the scene of mismanagement and discomfort from beginning to end, and who had no talent, no conversation, no affection towards herself" (*MP*, 3.VIII).

PRICE, FRANCES (2) (FANNY): Edmund Bertram, after talking to her as a ten-year-old, "was convinced of her having an affectionate heart, and a strong desire of doing right; and he could perceive her to be farther entitled to attention, by great sensibility of her situation, and great timidity" (*MP*, 1.II).

PRICE, JOHN and **RICHARD**, the Prices' second and third sons; one is a clerk in a public office in London, and the other is a midshipman on a merchant vessel (*MP*, 3.VII).

PRICE, MARY (deceased), a younger sister of Fanny Price who died in childhood (*P*, 3.VIII).

PRICE, SAM, the Prices' fourth son, about to embark on a naval career, "a fine tall boy of eleven years old" (*MP*, 3.VII).

PRICE, SUSAN, the Prices' second daughter, "a well-grown fine girl of fourteen" with whom Fanny becomes quite close; she takes Fanny's place at Mansfield when Fanny marries Edmund Bertram (*MP*, 3.VII).

PRICE, TOM, the Prices' fifth son, age nine (*MP*, 3.VII).

PRICE, WILLIAM, the eldest Price child, in the navy, "a young man of an open, pleasant countenance, and frank, unstudied, but feeling and respectful manners" (*MP*, 2.VI).

PRINCE, MISS, a teacher at Mrs. Goddard's school in Highbury (*E*, 1.IV).

PRIOR, MATTHEW (1664–1721), poet and diplomat, mentioned (*NA*, 1.V); the feelings of the heroine for the hero of "Henry and Emma" (paraphrase of the ballad "The Nut-brown Maid") are negatively compared to those of Anne Elliot for Captain Wentworth (*P*, 3.XII).

PROSPECT HOUSE, one of the newly built houses in Sanditon, intended for rental (*S*, p. 384).

PUG, Lady Maria Bertram's dog and constant companion (*MP*, 1.II).

PULTENEY ST., Bath, (*a*) where the Allens took lodgings (*NA*, 1.II); (*b*) where Anne Elliot sees Captain Wentworth while she is driving with Lady Russell (*P*, 4.VII).

PUMP ROOM, Bath, the fashionable morning lounge in Bath, named for the pump that draws up the mineral water that is supposed to be drunk for one's health: the scene of many meetings between Isabella Thorpe and Catherine Morland (*NA*, 1.III). The Pump Room at Clifton is also mentioned (*NA*, 1.XV).

PUMP YARD, Bath, the entrance to the Pump Room, opening onto Cheap St.: (*a*) mentioned (*NA*, 1.VII); (*b*) Mrs. Clay and Mr. Elliot are seen there in a clandestine rendezvous (*P*, 4.X).

PURVIS, MR., a young man to whom Elizabeth Watson was formerly attached (*W*, p. 316).

PURVIS LODGE, near Longbourn, one of the houses Mrs. Bennet considers for the Wickhams' occupation; she rejects it because "the attics are dreadful" (*PP*, 3.VIII).

PUTNEY, a suburb of London where the Thorpes live (*NA*, 1.XV).

PYM (John Pym, 1584–1643), statesman of the parliamentary period in England: according to Jane Austen, he was one of "the original Causers of all the disturbances Distresses & Civil Wars in which England for many years was embroiled"—"The History of England" (*Vol. 2*, p. 148).

PYRENEES: of "the Alps and Pyrenees, with their pine forests and their vices, [Mrs. Radcliffe's novels] might give a faithful delineation" (*NA*, 2.X).

"QUARTERLY REVIEW" (begun February 1809), (*a*) copies of which are in the drawing room at Sotherton, for the entertainment of guests (*MP*, 1.X); (*b*) in 1816 John Murray, Jane Austen's publisher, sends her the copy containing a review of *Emma* by Sir Walter Scott (*Letters*, p. 453).

QUEEN MAB, the name of a horse Willoughby wanted to give to Marianne Dashwood (*SS*, 1.XII).

QUEEN SQUARE, Bath, in an unfashionable area; it is mentioned with disdain by the Misses Musgrove (*P*, 3.VI).

QUICK, the stage name of Gustavus (q.v.). There was a real-life actor named Quick working in London in Jane Austen's day.

R. See **Reigate**.

RADCLIFFE, MRS. ANN (1764–1823), novelist: John Thorpe admits that "'her novels are amusing enough; they are worth reading; some fun and nature in them'" (*NA*, 1.VII); she is also mentioned in passing (*Letters*, p. 377); (1) *The Romance of the Forest* (1791) is mentioned by Harriet Smith as among the books Robert Martin has not read (*E*, 1.IV); (2) *The Mysteries of Udolpho* (1794) is read by Catherine Morland with terror and delight (*NA*, 1.VII); (3) Isabella Thorpe and Catherine Morland plan to read *The Italian* (1797) together (*NA*, 1.VI).

RALEIGH, SIR WALTER (Ralegh, ca. 1552–1618), military and naval commander: the reader of "The History of England" is referred for details of his life to Sheridan's *Critic* (*Vol. 2*, p. 147).

RAMBLER. See **Johnson, (Dr.) Samuel**.

RAMSGATE, Kent, (*a*) where Miss Darcy went to spend the summer; Lieutenant Wickham attempted to elope with her from there (*PP*, 2.XII); (*b*) Tom Bertram's friends, the Sneyds, live there (*MP*, 1.V).

RANDALLS, a small house near Highbury bought by Mr. Weston shortly before his marriage (*E*, 1.I).

RANELAGH (GARDENS), Chelsea, a popular pleasure ground during the late eighteenth century, similar to Vauxhall Gardens: it is where Camilla Stanley claims to have met Miss Dudley and Lady Amyatt—"Catharine or the Bower" (*Vol. 3*, p. 204).

RASSELAS. See **Johnson, (Dr.) Samuel**.

RAVENSHAW, LORD, a friend of Mr. Yates who organized private theatricals at one of his house parties at Ecclesford; according to Yates, he is "'A little man, with a weak voice.'" His wife, Lady Ravenshaw, is also mentioned (*MP*, 1.XIII).

READING, Berks., on the way from London to Cleveland (*SS*, 3.VI).

REBECCA, the upper servant at the Prices' in Portsmouth; she is described as "trollopy-looking" (*MP*, 3.VII).

REEVES, MR., with whom Harriet Byron was staying when she was abducted; Miss Grandison calls him "a very nice man. . . . He disputes charmingly" (*CG*, III i).

REEVES, MRS., a cousin of Harriet Byron, with whom she stayed in London (*CG*, I i).

REIGATE, Surrey: the action of *The Watsons* is generally thought to take place around Dorking; but in one place (*W*, p. 338) Jane Austen mentions "R." for "Reigate" instead.

REJECTED ADDRESSES. See **Smith, James and Horace (Horatio) Smith.**

REPTON, HUMPHRY (1752–1818), landscape designer, mentioned as having improved Compton, the estate of a Mr. Smith, a crony of Mr. Rushworth (*MP*, 1.VI).

REYNOLDS, MRS., the housekeeper at Pemberley: "a respectable-looking, elderly woman, much less fine, and more civil, than [Eliza Bennet] had any notion of finding her" (*PP*, 3.I).

RICHARD (1), one of the Steeles' Holborn cousins (*SS*, 3.II).

RICHARD (2), a manservant in the Philipses' household (*PP*, 1.XIV).

RICHARD II (1367–1400), king of England, was deposed by Henry IV and later murdered in Pomfret Castle—"The History of England" (*Vol. 2*, p. 139).

RICHARD III (1452–85), king of England: (*a*) Jane Austen says, "The Character of this Prince has been in general very severely treated by Historians, but as he was *York*, I am rather inclined to suppose him a very respectable Man"—"The History of England" (*Vol. 2*, p. 141); (*b*) Catharine and Edward Stanley discuss his character—"Catharine or the Bower" (*Vol. 3*, p. 231); (*c*) as eponymous protagonist of Shakespeare's play, he is mentioned by Henry Crawford (*MP*, 1.XIII).

RICHARD III. See **Shakespeare, William.**

RICHARDS, DR., a Surrey clergyman who showed Mr. Watson particular consideration at a visitation (*W*, p. 344).

RICHARDSON, MISS, a teacher at Mrs. Goddard's school in Highbury (*E*, 1.IV).

RICHARDSON, MRS., a friend of the Steeles' cousins who takes Miss Steele to Kensington Gardens (*SS*, 3.II).

RICHARDSON, SAMUEL (1689–1761), novelist: Sir Edward Denham's "fancy had been early caught by all the impassioned, & most exceptionable parts" of Richardson's novels (*S*, p. 404): (1) *Sir Charles Grandison* (1753), (*a*) Maria Gower is afforded an opportunity "of shining in that favourite character of Sir Charles Grandison's, a nurse"—"Evelyn" (*Vol. 3*, p. 186); (*b*) Isabella Thorpe, who has never read it, thinks it is "'an amazing horrid book'" (*NA*, 1.VI); (*c*) its heroine, Harriet Byron, is mentioned (*Letters*, pp. 322 and 344); (2) a letter by Richardson, no. 97 in the *Rambler*, is paraphrased (*NA*, 1.III).

RICHMOND, Surrey, (*a*) where Maria Rushworth stayed over Easter with the Aylmers, who gave Henry Crawford access to their house, thus promoting his affair with Maria (*MP*, 3.XIV); (*b*) where the Churchills go after London disagrees with Mrs. Churchill and where the latter dies (*E*, 3.I); (*c*) where Isabella Thorpe imagines settling with James Morland (*NA*, 1.XV).

RIVALS, THE. See **Sheridan, Richard Brinsley.**

RIVERS ST., Bath, where Lady Russell has lodgings (*P*, 4.II).

ROBERT, the gardener at Mansfield Parsonage (*MP*, 2.IV).

ROBERTSON, (DR.) WILLIAM (1721–93), historian, is mentioned by Eleanor Tilney (*NA*, 1.XIV).

ROBERTUS, the brother of Wilhelminus and one of the visitors to his cottage in Pembrokeshire—"Scraps" (*Vol. 2*, p. 177).

"ROBIN ADAIR," a common name for an Irish air actually titled "Eileen Aroon," to be found in Thomas Moore's popular collection *Moore's Irish Melodies*, volume 1 (1807; information from Patrick Piggott's *Innocent Diversion*, 1979): Jane Fairfax plays this tune, Frank Churchill's favorite, on the pianoforte he has given her (*E*, 2.X).

ROBINSON, probably the gardener or outdoors man at Woodston Parsonage; possibly a tenant of Henry Tilney (*NA*, 2.XI).

ROBINSON, MR. (1), a gentleman living in the neighborhood of Meryton (*PP*, 1.V).

ROBINSON, MR. (2), the apothecary in the area of Uppercross (*P*, 3.VII).

ROBINSON CRUSOE. See **Defoe, Daniel.**

ROCHE, REGINA MARIA (ca. 1764–1845), novelist: (1) *Children of the Abbey* (1798), which Robert Martin has never read, is mentioned by Harriet Smith (*E*, 1.IV); (2) *Clermont* (1798) is one of the novels on the reading list provided by Isabella Thorpe for Catherine Morland's education (*NA*, 1.VI).

ROGER, CAPTAIN, who marries Rebecca Fitzroy; he is "little more than 63"—"Frederic & Elfrida" (*Vol. 1*, p. 7).

ROGER, ELEANOR, the daughter of Captain and Mrs. Roger; Frederic develops an attachment to her—"Frederic and Elfrida" (*Vol. 1*, p. 11).

ROMANCE OF THE FOREST, THE. See **Radcliffe, Mrs. Ann.**

ROOKE, MRS., a nurse in Bath who attended Mrs. Wallis, during her lying-in (*P*, 4.V), and also cared for Mrs. Smith.

ROSANNE; OR A FATHER'S LABOUR LOST. See **Hawkins, Laetitia Matilda.**

ROSE, MR., a clerk in Exeter, "a prodigious smart young man, quite a beau" (*SS*, 1.XXI).

ROSINGS, Kent, Lady Catherine de Bourgh's estate (*PP*, 1.XIV).

ROSS, FLORA. See **Stornoway, Lady Flora.**

ROSS, JANET. See **Fraser, Mrs. Janet.**

ROWE, NICHOLAS (1674–1718), dramatist and poet laureate: a play, *Jane Shore* (1714), is mentioned in "The History of England" (*Vol. 2*, p. 140).

ROWLING, Kent, where Jane Austen's brother Edward lived before he inherited Godmersham.

RODWORTH, C., of Bell Yard, Temple Bar: the printer of the first edition of *Sense and Sensibility* (1811) and certain volumes of other novels.

RUMFORD (Sir Benjamin Thompson, Count von Rumford, 1753–1814), invented, among other things, the modern open fireplace: the sitting room at Northanger Abbey boasts a Rumford fireplace (*NA*, 2.V).

RUSHWORTH, MRS., James Rushworth's mother, "a well-meaning, civil, prosing, pompous woman, who thought nothing of consequence, but as it related to her own and her son's concerns" (*MP*, 1.VIII).

RUSHWORTH, JAMES, with £12,000 a year, "who had recently succeeded to one of the largest estates and finest places in the country.... a heavy young man, with not more than common sense" (*MP*, 1.IV); he is cuckolded by Maria Bertram, whom he divorces.

RUSHWORTH, MARIA (née Bertram), the elder daughter of Sir Thomas Bertram: of her and her sister it is said that "it is not very wonderful that with all their promising talents and early information, they should be entirely deficient in the less common acquirements of self-knowledge, generosity, and humility" (*MP*, 1.II). She is ruined by Henry Crawford and divorced by her husband.

RUSSELL, LADY, a friend of Lady Elliot, settled in Kellynch; she is Anne Elliot's mother-substitute, "a woman rather of sound than of quick abilities. . . . She was a benevolent, charitable, good woman, and capable of strong attachments; most correct in her conduct, strict in her notions of decorum, and with manners that were held a standard of good-breeding" (*P*, 3.II).

RUSSELL, SIR HENRY (deceased), knight, Lady Russell's husband (*P*, 4.V).

RUSSIA: at ten Fanny Price cannot list the principal rivers there, to the disgust of her older and better-educated cousins (*MP*, 1.II).

SACKVILLE ST., London, (*a*) whence Thomas Musgrove wrote his love letter to Henrietta Halton—"A Collection of Letters" (*Vol. 2*, p. 162); (*b*) Gray's Jewelers was located there (*SS*, 2.XI).

ST. ANTHONY, CHAPEL OF, an imaginary shrine near the fictional Northanger Abbey created by Henry Tilney (*NA*, 2.V).

ST. AUBIN, a character in Mrs. Radcliffe's *Mysteries of Udolpho* who died on a night of beautiful weather (*NA*, 1.XI).

ST. CLAIR, LORD, the grandfather of the four principals of "Love and Freindship" (*Vol. 2*, p. 91).

ST. CLAIR, LADY LAURINA, wife of Lord St. Clair—"Love and Freindship" (*Vol. 2*, p. 91).

ST. CLEMENT'S (CHURCH), London, where Lieutenant Wickham and Lydia Bennet were married (*PP*, 3.IX).

ST. DOMINGO: Frederick Wentworth was made a captain as a result of his performance in a battle there in 1806 (*P*, 3.IV).

ST. GEORGE'S (CHURCH), Hanover Square, London: Mary Crawford suggests to Fanny Price in a letter that she would enjoy "seeing the inside" of this church on her way through London—probably a hint about her possible marriage to Henry Crawford (*MP*, 3.XII).

ST. GEORGE'S FIELDS, London, where Henry Tilney envisages mobs assembling in order to tease Catherine Morland and his sister (*NA*, 1.XIV).

ST. IVES, LORD, whom Sir Walter Elliot dismisses because his "father we all know to have been a country curate, without bread to eat" (*P*, 3.III).

ST. JAMES'S (PALACE), London, where subjects were presented to the British monarch and where they received titles: Sir William Lucas is fond of telling anecdotes of his presentation (*PP*, 1.V).

ST. JAMES'S SQUARE, London, where Sir Charles Grandison is presumed to be at the beginning of *Sir Charles Grandison* III i.

ST. JAMES'S ST., London, where Colonel Brandon lodges (*SS*, 3.IV).

ST. JOHN'S COLLEGE, Oxford, of which Jane Austen's father was a fellow in 1751; later attended by his sons James and Henry.

ST. MARK'S PLACE (Piazza San Marco, Venice): among the books collected in the sitting room at Donwell Abbey for Mr. Woodhouse's entertainment is one containing engravings of "views of St. Mark's Place" (*E*, 3.VI).

ST. PAUL'S, London, is mentioned in passing (*MP*, 2.IV).

SALISBURY, Wilts., the nearest major town to Fullerton (*NA*, 1.III).

SALLY (1), a maidservant at Barton Park (*SS*, 3.XI).

SALLY (2), the Forsters' maidservant in Brighton (*PP*, 3.V).

SALLY (3), the lower servant in the Prices' household in Portsmouth (*MP*, 3.VII).

SALLY (4), servant in the Reeveses' household in London, possibly Harriet Byron's maid (*CG*, I i).

SAM, an elderly porter in the hotel at Sanditon (*S*, p. 407).

SANDCROFT HILL, on the way from Mansfield to Sotherton (*MP*, 2.II).

SANDERSON, a family of friends of Mr. Jennings (*SS*, 2.VIII).

SANDITON, Sussex, a village that Mr. Parker and Lady Denham hope to transform into a "small, fashionable Bathing Place" (*S*, p. 371).

SANDITON HOUSE, Lady Denham's place, inherited from Mr. Hollis: its grounds, "though not extensive had all the Beauty & Respectability which an abundance of very fine Timber could give" (*S*, p. 426).

SARAH (1), a personal maid at Longbourn (*PP*, 3.XII).

SARAH (2), the former nurserymaid of the Musgroves' children, brought back to care for Louisa after her fall at Lyme (*P*, 4.I).

SAUNDERS, JOHN, possibly a handyman or pharmacist in Highbury; he is thought of as the person to fix Mrs. Bates's spectacles (*E*, 2.IX).

SCARBOROUGH, Yorks., (*a*) which Camilla Stanley and her family might visit on their way to the Lake District—"Catharine or the Bower" (*Vol. 3*, p. 199); (*b*) where the Hursts and Miss Bingley went to spend part of the summer (*PP*, 3.XI).

SCARLETS, Berks., one of the estates of Jane Austen's uncle James Leigh Perrot.

SCHEHEREZADE, THE SULTANESS, mentioned in *Persuasion*: "Mr. Elliot's character, like the Sultaness Scheherazade's head, must live another day" (4.XI).

SCHOLEY, an old man living in Portsmouth (*MP*, 3.VII).

SCHOOL FOR SCANDAL, THE. See **Sheridan, Richard Brinsley**.

SCOTLAND, THE QUEEN OF. See **Mary Queen of Scots**.

SCOTLAND: (*a*) visited by Laura and Sophia in hopes of obtaining the protection of Sophia's cousin Macdonald—"Love and Freindship" (*Vol. 2*, p. 90); (*b*) Mary Wynne removed there after her father's death, going as a companion to the Dowager Lady Halifax's daughters—"Catharine or the Bower" (*Vol. 3*, p. 195); (*c*) Colonel Brandon planned to elope there with his adoptive sister, Eliza (*SS*, 2.IX); (*d*) Lydia Bennet was originally supposed to have gone there with Lieutenant Wickham (*PP*, 3.IV); (*e*) Julia Bertram eloped there with Mr. Yates (*MP*, 3.XV); also mentioned (*E*, 1.XII). See also **Gretna Green**.

SCOTT, SIR WALTER (1771–1832), novelist and poet: Sir Edward Denham tells Charlotte Heywood that the "'Man who can read [Scott's lines on the sea] unmoved must have the nerves of an Assassin'" (*S*, pp. 396–97); also mentioned (*SS*, 1.X, 1.XVII; *Letters*, pp. 300 and 404): (1) *Lay of the Last Minstrel* (1805), (*a*)

Fanny Price misquotes ii.10 (*MP*, 1.IX); (*b*) i.20 is quoted in narrative (*MP*, 2.X); (*c*) of the glees mentioned by Jane Austen (*Letters*, p. 274), "'In Peace Love tunes'" is adapted by J. Attwood from iii.2, and "'Rosabelle'" by John W. Call from vi.23; (2) *Marmion* (1808), (*a*) vi.30 is quoted by Sir Edward Denham (*S*, p. 397); (*b*) this work is argued over by Anne Elliot and Captain Benwick (*P*, 3.XI); (*c*) Jane Austen is not very pleased by it in the early going (*Letters*, p. 197), and she parodies vi.38 (*Letters*, p. 298; also mentioned on p. 248); (3) *Lady of the Lake* (1810), (*a*) ii.22 is quoted by Sir Edward Denham (*S*, p. 397); (*b*) this work is argued over by Anne Elliot and Captain Benwick (*P*, 3.XI); also mentioned (*Letters*, p. 290); (4) *The Field of Waterloo* (1815) was lent to Henry Austen by John Murray, publisher of *Emma* (*Letters*, pp. 431 and 432); (5) *Paul's Letters to His Kinsfolk* (1815) are what Jane Austen intends when she asks John Murray to lend her "Scott's account of Paris" (*Letters*, pp. 432 and 433); (6) *The Antiquary* (1816) is referred to (*Letters*, p. 468); (7) his review of *Emma* in the *Quarterly Review* is mentioned (*Letters*, p. 453).

"SCRAPS," miscellaneous pieces dedicated to her niece Fanny Catherine Austen (Knight), purportedly to offer her "Admonitions on the conduct of Young Women" (*Vol. 2*, p. 170).

SCROGGS, MISS, a visitor to Sanditon (*S*, p. 389).

SCUDAMORE, LADY, at whose house Thomas Musgrove met and fell in love with Henrietta Halton—"A Collection of Letters" (*Vol. 2*, p. 163).

SEATON, COLONEL: his family is expected to visit Sophia, "a Young lady crossed in Love—"A Collection of Letters" (*Vol. 2*, p. 152).

SECCAR'S EXPLANATION OF THE CATECHISM. See **Secker, Thomas**.

SECKER, THOMAS (1693–1768), archbishop of Canterbury: *Lectures on the Catechism of the Church of England* (1769) was originally one of the works provided by Mrs. Percival to her niece Catharine to help "breed [her] up virtuously"; Jane Austen later substituted Hannah More's *Cœlebs in Search of a Wife* —"Catharine or the Bower" (*Vol. 3*, p. 232).

SELBY, MR., a countrified uncle of Harriet Byron, living in Northamptonshire (*CG*, III i).

SELBY, MRS., wife of Mr. Selby (*CG*, III i).

SELBY, LUCY and NANCY, cousins of Harriet Byron (*CG*, III i). One wonders if the similarity in names of the Misses Steele in *Sense and Sensibility* is in any way significant.

SELF-CONTROL. See **Brunton, Mary**.

SERLE, the cook at Hartfield, who "'understands boiling an egg better than any body'" (*E*, 1.III).

SERMONS TO YOUNG WOMEN. See **Fordyce, James**.

SÊVE (SÈVRES CHINA), mentioned by General Tilney (*NA*, 2.VII).

SEVERUS (Lucius Septimius Severus, A.D. 146–211), Roman emperor, is mentioned (*MP*, 1.II).

SÉVIGNÉ, MME. DE (Marie de Rabutin-Chantal, Marquise de Sévigné, 1626–96), French belletrist: "la Mere Beauté" (*Letters*, p. 371) is a reference to her *Lettres* (1726; English trans. 1758).

SEWELL'S FARM, located not far from Mansfield (*MP*, 2.VII).

SHAKESPEARE, WILLIAM (1564–1616), playwright and poet: Henry

Crawford says, "'Shakespeare one gets acquainted with without knowing how. It is part of an Englishman's constitution'" (*MP*, 3.III): (1) *King John* (ca. 1595) is mentioned (*Letters*, pp. 271 and 275); (2) *Richard III* (1597) (*a*) is mentioned (*Letters*, p. 386), (*b*) and also its protagonist (*MP*, 1.XIII); (3) *1 Henry IV* (1598), "the Shrewsbury Clock" (*Letters*, p. 95) is a reference to V iv; (4) there is an elliptical reference to *Julius Caesar* (ca. 1599) (*MP*, 1.XIII); (5) *2 Henry IV* (1600) is referred to in "The History of England" (*Vol.* 2, p. 139); (6) *The Merchant of Venice* (1600): (*a*) Shylock is mentioned (*MP*, 1.XIII); (*b*) the play is referred to (*Letters*, p. 290); (*c*) Jane Austen saw Kean as Shylock in 1814 (*Letters*, pp. 377 and 381); (7) *A Midsummer Night's Dream* (1600), I i line 132 is quoted (*E*, 1.IX); (8) *Twelfth-night* (ca. 1601), II iv line 116 is quoted (*NA*, 1.I); (9) *Hamlet* (1603) (*a*) is read by Willoughby to the Dashwoods (*SS*, 1.XVI); (*b*) it is one of the plays proposed for enactment at Mansfield (*MP*, 1.XIV); (*c*) it is mentioned (*Letters*, p. 271); (10) *Othello* (1604) (*a*) is one of the plays proposed for enactment at Mansfield (*MP*, 1.XIV); (*b*) III iii line 323 is misquoted (*NA*, 1.I); (11) *Measure for Measure* (ca. 1604), III i line 79 is misquoted (*NA*, 1.I); (12) *Macbeth* (ca. 1605) (*a*) is played by the traveling theatrical company that Gustavus and Philander join after spending the remainder of their mothers' combined fortunes—"Love and Freindship" (*Vol.* 2, p. 108); (*b*) it is one of the plays proposed for enactment at Mansfield (*MP*, 1.XIV); (*c*) it is mentioned (*Letters*, p. 271).

SHARP, SAMUEL (ca. 1700–78), surgeon: he is the "poor Mr. Sharpe" of whom Baretti is "dreadfully abusive" (*Letters*, p. 185). The second edition (1769) of Baretti's *Account of the Manners and Customs of Italy* contains an appendix directed at rebutting Sharp's *Letters from Italy* (1766).

SHARPE, MARTHA, a confidante of Miss Steele (*SS*, 3.II).

SHAW, MRS., Penelope Watson's friend in Chichester (*W*, p. 317).

SHELDON, MRS., an acquaintance of Diana Parker in Hampshire (*S*, p. 386).

SHEPHERD, JOHN, "a civil, cautious lawyer," Sir Walter Elliot's agent (*P*, 3.II).

SHERIDAN, RICHARD BRINSLEY (1751–1816), politician and dramatist: (1) readers are referred for details of Sir Walter Ralegh's life to *The Critic* (1779), "where they will find many interesting Anecdotes as well of him as of his friend Sir Christopher Hatton"—"The History of England" (*Vol.* 2, p. 147); (2) *The School for Scandal* (1783) and *The Rivals* (1775) are two of the plays proposed for enactment at Mansfield (*MP*, 1.XIV).

SHERLOCK, THOMAS (1678–1761), bishop of London: in 1814 Jane Austen says, "I am very fond of Sherlock's Sermons, prefer them to almost any" (*Letters*, p. 406), referring to *Several Discourses Preached at the Temple Church* (1754–97, 2nd ed. 1812).

SHIRLEY, MRS. (1), wife of the rector of Uppercross (*P*, 3.XII).

SHIRLEY, (MRS.?) (2), a grandmother of Harriet Byron (*CG*, III i).

SHIRLEY, REVEREND DR., the rector of Uppercross "who for more than forty years had been zealously discharging all the duties of his office, but was now growing too infirm for many of them" (*P*, 3.IX).

SHORE, JANE (d. ca. 1527), one of Edward IV's mistresses—"The History of England" (*Vol.* 2, p. 140). See also **Rowe, Nicholas**.

SHROPSHIRE, (*a*) where Emma Watson grew up with her aunt and uncle, the Turners (*W*, p. 320); (*b*) where Edward Wentworth has a living (*P*, 3.IX).

SHYLOCK, the character in Shakespeare's *Merchant of Venice,* is mentioned by Henry Crawford (*MP,* 1.XIII). See also **Shakespeare, William:** *The Merchant of Venice.*

SICILY, from which William Price brought his sister Fanny an amber cross (*MP,* 2.VIII).

SIDMOUTH, Devon, from which Mr. Elliot had traveled to Lyme (*P,* 3.XII).

SIDNEY, G., Northumberland St., the Strand: the printer of volumes 2 and 3 of *Pride and Prejudice*'s first edition, and volumes 1 and 3 of *Mansfield Park*'s first edition.

SIMNEL, LAMBERT (ca. 1475–1525), impersonator of Edward, earl of Warwick: "for if Perkin Warbeck was really the Duke of York, why might not Lambert Simnel be the Widow of Richard"—"The History of England" (*Vol. 2,* p. 141).

SIMPSON, MR., of Exeter; he has a clerk, Mr. Rose, who is "quite a beau" (*SS,* 1.XXI).

SIMPSON, (MISS) CAROLINE, SUKEY, and **CECILIA,** neighbors of Mr. Johnson: "Miss Simpson was pleasing in her person, in her Manners & in her Disposition; an unbounded ambition was her only fault. Her second sister Sukey was Envious, Spitefull & Malicious. Her person was short, fat & disagreable. Cecilia (the youngest) was perfectly handsome but too affected to be pleasing"—"Jack & Alice" (*Vol. 1,* p. 13).

SIR CHARLES GRANDISON. See *Grandison, Sir Charles;* Richardson, Samuel.

"SIR WILLIAM MOUNTAGUE," a brief tale of a fickle baronet, dedicated to Jane Austen's brother Charles (*Vol. 1,* p. 40).

SKINNER, DR., and his family, an acquaintance of the Allens who came to Bath for his gout the year before the story begins (*NA,* 1.II).

SLEATH, ELEANOR (no biographical data), novelist, possibly the wife of a John Sleath (1767–1847), schoolmaster: her *Orphan of the Rhine* (1798) is one of the books on the reading list Isabella Thorpe gave Catherine Morland for her education (*NA,* 1.VI).

SLOANE ST., London, where Jane Austen's brother Henry lived for a short time (at no. 64); she visited there in 1811 and 1813.

SMALLRIDGE, MRS., a friend of the Sucklings, living near Maple Grove; she has three daughters, to whom Jane Fairfax is briefly engaged to go as governess (*E,* 3.VIII).

SMITH, LIEUTENANT, of the navy, a visitor to Sanditon (*S,* p. 389).

SMITH, MISS, a young lady with whom Henry Tilney danced in the Upper Rooms (*NA,* 1.X).

SMITH, MR. (1), a friend of James Rushworth with an estate named Compton that was improved by Humphry Repton (*MP,* 1.VI).

SMITH, MR. (2), mentioned (*CG,* I ii), is possibly an apothecary.

SMITH, MRS. (1), Willoughby's elderly cousin, an invalid, who owns Allenham Court (*SS,* 1.XIII).

SMITH, MRS. (2) (née Hamilton), a former schoolfellow of Anne Elliot: "She was a widow, and poor. Her husband had been extravagant; and at his death, about two years before, had left his affairs dreadfully involved. She had had difficulties of every sort to contend with, and in addition to these distresses, had been afflicted with a severe rheumatic fever, which finally settling in her legs, had made her for the present a cripple" (*P*, 4.V).

SMITH, CHARLES (1), a friend of Reginald de Courcy, he tries to warn the latter of Lady Susan's iniquity (*LS*, p. 248).

SMITH, CHARLES (2) (deceased), husband of Mrs. Smith (2), he "had the finest, most generous spirit in the world," according to his widow (*P*, 4.IX).

SMITH, (MRS.) CHARLOTTE (1749–1800), novelist: (1) *Emmeline, or the Orphan of the Castle* (1788): (*a*) its unfortunate hero, Frederic Delamere, is mentioned—"The History of England" (*Vol. 2*, pp. 143 and 146); (*b*) according to Camilla Stanley, "'Emmeline is *so much* better than any of the others'"—"Catharine or the Bower" (*Vol. 3*, p. 199); (2) according to Camilla Stanley, *Ethelinde, or the Recluse of the Lake* (1789) "'is so long'"—"Catharine or the Bower" (*Vol. 3*, p. 199).

SMITH, HARRIET, a very pretty young lady of illegitimate birth who is a parlor boarder at Mrs. Goddard's school; she "certainly was not clever, but she had a sweet, docile, grateful disposition; was totally free from conceit; and only desiring to be guided by any one she looked up to" (*E*, 1.IV).

SMITH, JAMES (1775–1839), author and humorist, and his younger brother **HORACE (HORATIO) SMITH** (1779–1849), poet and miscellaneous author: in 1813 Jane Austen refers to "the two Mr. Smiths of the city" and their *Rejected Addresses: Or the New Theatrum Poetarum* (1812) (*Letters*, pp. 292–94).

SMITH, JOHN, an imaginary prototype: Robert Ferrars imagines his brother "'reading prayers in a white surplice, and publishing the banns of marriage between John Smith and Mary Brown'" (*SS*, 3.V).

SMYTHE, ARABELLA, "the female philosopher": author of a letter in "Scraps" (*Vol. 2*, p. 172).

SNEYD, MR. and MRS., with three children, one boy and two girls (the younger of whom is named Augusta), a family living in Ramsgate: the son is a crony of Tom Bertram (*MP*, 1.V).

"SOFA, THE." See **Cowper, William.**

SOMERSET, DUKE OF (Edward Seymour, first duke of the Seymour family, ca. 1506-52), maternal uncle of Edward VI, and protector of the realm during Edward's minority—"The History of England" (*Vol. 2*, p. 143).

SOMERSET, EARL OF (Robert Carr, d. 1645): in the reign of James I, "The principal favourites of his Majesty were Car, who was afterwards created Earl of Somerset . . . and George Villiers"—"The History of England" (*Vol. 2*, p. 148).

SOMERSETSHIRE, (*a*) where Cleveland and Combe Magna are located (*SS*, 1.IX); (*b*) where Kellynch and Uppercross are located (*P*, 3.I).

SOPHIA (1), the wife of Edward [Lindsay] Talbot's particular friend Augustus: "A soft Langour spread over her lovely features, but increased their Beauty. . . . She was all Sensibility and Feeling. We [Laura and Sophia] flew into each others arms & after having exchanged vows of mutual Friendship for the rest of our Lives, instantly unfolded to each other the most inward Secrets of our Hearts"—"Love and Freindship" (*Vol. 2*, p. 85).

SOPHIA (2), "a Young Lady crossed in love"—"A Collection of Letters" (*Vol 2*, p. 153).

SOPHIA (3), with her sister (?) Emily, "two of the sweetest girls in the world, who had been [Anne Thorpe's] dear friends all the morning" (*NA*, 1.XIV).

SORROWS OF WERTER, THE. See **Goethe, Johann Wolfgang von**: *The Sorrows of Young Werther*.

SOTHERTON COURT, the Rushworth estate in Northamptonshire: Edmund Bertram, describing it to Mary Crawford, says, "'The house was built in Elizabeth's time, and it is a large, regular, brick building—heavy, but respectable looking, and has many good rooms. It is ill placed. It stands in one of the lowest spots in the park'" (*MP*, 1.VI).

SOUTH END, Essex, where the John Knightleys spent their autumn holiday (*E*, 1.XII).

SOUTH PARK, Glos., the estate of the Stevensons: a Miss Stevenson became Lady Elliot (*P*, 3.I).

SOUTHEY, ROBERT (1774–1843), poet and historian: (1) of his *Letters from England, by Dom Manuel Alvarez Espriella* (1807) Jane Austen says, "The Man describes well, but is horribly anti-english" (*Letters*, p. 212); (2) his *Life of Nelson* (1813) is mentioned (*Letters*, p. 345); (3) in 1817 the Austens read *The Poet's Pilgrimage to Waterloo* (1816), "generally with much approbation" (*Letters*, p. 476).

SOUTHAMPTON, Hants., (*a*) where Jane Austen went to school in 1783; (*b*) where she lived with her mother, sister, and Martha Lloyd, in Castle Square, from 1806 to 1809; (*c*) Isabel warns Laura, "Beware of the unmeaning Luxuries of Bath & of the Stinking fish of Southampton"—"Love and Freindship" (*Vol. 2*, p. 79).

SPAIN, where Laura was born—"Love and Freindship" (*Vol. 2*, p. 77).

SPANGLE, SIR EDWARD, who is asleep "in an elegant Attitude on a Sofa" throughout I iii of "The Mystery" (*Vol. 1*, p. 55).

SPARKS, MISS, a London gossip mentioned in passing by Miss Steele (*SS*, 3.II).

SPECTATOR, THE (March 1, 1711–December 6, 1712), a set of essays published daily in periodical form, about half of which were composed by Joseph Addison; they were collected in book form in 1714, and this book is mentioned (*NA*, 1.V).

SPEED, MRS., the landlady of Westgate Buildings, where Mrs. Smith (2) lodges (*P*, 4.IX).

SPICER, the name of a family extending patronage to Charles Hayter (*P*, 3.IX).

SPITHEAD (Roadstead), a point at the outer end of Portsmouth harbor where ships anchor while waiting to put out to sea (*MP*, 2.VI).

STAËL, MME. DE (Anne Louise Germaine Necker, Baronne de Staël-Holstein, 1766–1817), French/Swiss belletrist: Jane Austen recommended *Corinne* (1807, English trans. the same year) to a Mr. Fitzhugh (*Letters*, p. 242).

STAFFORDSHIRE, where Vernon Castle is located (*LS*, p. 247).

STAFFORDSHIRE (CHINA), patronized by General Tilney (*NA*, 2.VII).

STAINES, from which Strephon was driven in the first act of a comedy —"Scraps" (*Vol. 2*, p. 174).

STANHILL, where the Henry Dashwoods lived before moving to Norland Park (*SS*, 1.II).

STANHOPE, MR., a gentleman who was preferred by Miss Arundel and was therefore shot by the hero of "Sir William Mountague" (*Vol. 1*, p. 42).

STANHOPE, EMMA. See **Mountague, Emma.**

STANHOPE, MARY, SOPHIA, and **GEORGIANA,** heroines of "The Three Sisters" (*Vol. 1*, p. 57.)

STANLEY, MR. and **MRS.**, were "people of Large Fortune & high Fashion"—"Catharine or the Bower" (*Vol. 3*, p. 197).

STANLEY, CAMILLA, their daughter, "had been attended by the most capital Masters from the time of her being six years old to the last Spring, which comprehending a period of twelve Years had been dedicated to the acquirement of Accomplishments which were now to be displayed and in a few Years entirely neglected.... And she now united to these Accomplishments, an Understanding unimproved by reading and a Mind totally devoid either of Taste or Judgement"—"Catharine or the Bower" (*Vol. 3*, pp. 197–98).

STANLEY, EDWARD, Camilla's brother, is "one of the hansomest young Men you would wish to see"—"Catharine or the Bower" (*Vol. 3*, p. 213).

STANLEY, SIR THOMAS, and his family are expected to dine with Lady Greville—"A Collection of Letters" (*Vol. 2*, p. 159).

STANLY, a character in "The Visit," enamored of Cloe Willoughby (*Vol. 1*, p. 50).

STANLY, MR., and his family are to drink tea with A. F. and her daughters in order to assist the latters' "entrée into life"—"A Collection of Letters" (*Vol. 2*, p. 150).

STANTON, Surrey, the village in which the Watsons live (*W*, p. 317).

STANTON WOOD, where Lord Osborne's hunt will commence on a Wednesday in late October (*W*, p. 347).

STANWIX LODGE, near Mansfield, which Henry Crawford contemplates renting after marrying Fanny Price (*MP*, 2.XII).

STAVES, GREGORY, an Edinburgh stay maker, the father of Gustavus —"Love and Freindship" (*Vol. 2*, p. 106).

STEELE, MR., either the Steeles' father or their uncle (*SS*, 3.II).

STEELE, (MISS) ANNE (NANCY), "was nearly thirty, with a very plain and not a sensible face, nothing to admire" (*SS*, 1.XXI).

STEELE, LUCY. See **Ferrars, (Mrs.) Lucy.**

STEPHEN, one of the grooms at Mansfield Park (*MP*, 2.II).

STERLING (Stirling, Scotland): Philippa and her husband drove a stagecoach between Stirling and Edinburgh every other day in consequence of the husband's having spent all of Philippa's fortune—"Love and Freindship" (*Vol. 2*, p. 105).

STERNE, LAURENCE (1713–68), humorist and sentimentalist (according to the *Dictionary of National Biography*), mentioned (*NA*, 1.V); "uncle Toby's annuity" (*Letters*, p. 140) is a reference to *Tristram Shandy* (1760–65).

STEVENSON, ELIZABETH. See **Elliot, Lady Elizabeth.**

STEVENSON, JAMES, of South Park, Glos., the father of Lady Elizabeth Elliot (*P*, 3.I).

STEVENTON, Hants., Jane Austen's birthplace. It was her father's first parish (presented by Thomas Knight, a connection by marriage); he held it until his retirement in 1801, when the family moved to Bath. His eldest son, James, then held the incumbency until his death in 1819.

STOKE (1), near Meryton: the "great house" there is one of the houses that Mrs.

Bennet contemplates for the Wickhams' use; she rejects it because the drawing room is too small (*PP*, 3.VIII).

STOKE (2), near Mansfield, is where the Olivers and Maddoxes live (*MP*, 1.XV).

STOKES, MRS., the innkeeper's wife at the Crown in Highbury. (It is not made explicit that there is actually a Mr. Stokes; *E*, 2.XI.)

STOKES, JACK, and his uncle are acquaintances of the Watsons who will deliver a letter from Elizabeth Watson to Sam in Guil[d]ford (*W*, p. 341).

STONE, MR., a business associate of Mr. Gardiner (*PP*, 3.IX).

STORNOWAY, LORD: "'that horrid Lord Stornoway, who has about as much sense . . . as Mr. Rushworth, but much worse looking, and with a blackguard character,'" according to Mary Crawford; he is the husband of her old friend Flora Ross (*MP*, 3.V).

STORNOWAY, LADY FLORA (née Ross), a long-standing friend of Mary Crawford (*MP*, 3.V).

STRAFFORD, EARL OF (Thomas Wentworth, first earl, 1593–1641), one of five men, according to the author, who remained loyal to King Charles I—"The History of England" (*Vol. 2*, p. 148).

STRAFFORD, where there is a family named Wentworth, not related to the hero of *Persuasion* (3.III).

STREPHON, a character in "the first Act of a Comedy" who wishes to marry Cloe—"Scraps" (Vol. 2, p. 172).

STRINGER, the elder and the younger, purveyors of vegetables and fruits in Sanditon (*S*, pp. 381 and 382).

STYLES, MR., a friend of Captain Hunter and one of Mary Edwards's dancing partners (*W*, p. 337).

SUCKLING, MR. (1), "old Mr. Suckling," the father of the present owner of Maple Grove, who may or may not have completed the purchase of this estate before his death (*E*, 2.XVIII).

SUCKLING, MR. (2), Mrs. Elton's brother-in-law, the owner of Maple Grove (*E*, 2.XIV).

SUCKLING, (MRS.) SELINA (née Hawkins), Mrs. Elton's elder sister, who married advantageously (*E*, 2.XIV).

SUFFOLK, DUKE OF (Charles Brandon, first duke of the Brandon family, d. 1545): he married the younger daughter of Henry VII—"The History of England" (*Vol. 2*, p. 141).

SUFFOLK, the county from which Miss Grenville has recently arrived—"A Collection of Letters" (*Vol. 2*, p. 160).

SULTAN OR A PEEP INTO THE SERAGLIO, THE. See **Bickerstaffe, Isaac**.

SUMMERS, MISS, the mistress of an academy in London (at 10 Wigmore St.) where Frederica Vernon is briefly a pupil (*LS*, p. 246).

SUN, the name of a room in an unnamed inn, which is occupied by Cloe in "the first Act of a Comedy"—"Scraps" (*Vol. 2*, p. 172).

SURRY (Surrey), (*a*) the county in which the action of *The Watsons* takes place (p. 314); (*b*) where Mrs. Griffiths' school is located (*S*, p. 387); (*c*) where all the action of *Emma* takes place; (*d*) also mentioned (*Vol. 1*, p. 41).

SUSAN, supposedly the title of an earlier version of *Northanger Abbey*, bought by a publisher in 1803 but never printed.

Flammenberg's [Karl Friedrich Kahlert, 1765–1813] *Der Geisterbanner* as *Necromancer of the Black Forest* (1794): this is one of the books on the reading list provided by Isabella Thorpe for Catherine Morland's education (*NA*, 1.VI).

TEXEL, THE: Lieutenant Price tells his son William that "'old Scholey was saying ... that he thought you would be sent first to the Texel.'" He is referring to the channel between the Dutch mainland and the island of Texel, through which ships can enter the Waddenzee from the North Sea; since Napoleon held the Netherlands at the time *Mansfield Park* was written, it seems likely that the British kept up a naval blockade at the mouth of this important channel (3.VII).

THAMES (RIVER) is mentioned (*P*, 3.V).

THOMAS (1), the Dashwoods' manservant (*SS*, 3.XI).

THOMAS (2), a footman in the Reeveses' household in London (*CG*, I ii).

THOMSON, JAMES (1700–48), poet: (*a*) he is mentioned (*SS*, 1.XVII); (*b*) the section "Spring" of "The Seasons," line 1149, is misquoted (*NA*, 1.I).

THORNBERRY PARK, seven miles from Bath, where live some friends of Mr. Elliot (*P*, 4.X).

THORNTON LACEY, a parish not far from Mansfield where Edmund Bertram receives his first living (*MP*, 2.VII).

THORPE, MRS., of Putney, a former schoolfellow of Mrs. Allen; "a widow, and not a very rich one; she was a good-humoured, well-meaning woman, and a very indulgent mother" (*NA*, 1.IV).

THORPE, ANNE, Mrs. Thorpe's second daughter (*NA*, 1.XIV).

THORPE, EDWARD, Mrs. Thorpe's second son, at Merchant-Taylors' (*NA*, 1.IV).

THORPE, ISABELLA, age twenty-one, Mrs. Thorpe's eldest daughter; she has "great personal beauty" (*NA*, 1.IV) and "decided pretension,... resolute stilishness" (1.VIII) and was "ungenerous and selfish, regardless of every thing but her own gratification" (1.XIII).

THORPE, JOHN, a crony of James Morland; he is "a stout young man of middling height, who, with a plain face and ungraceful form, seemed fearful of being too handsome unless he wore the dress of a groom, and too much like a gentleman unless he were easy where he ought to be civil, and impudent where he might be allowed to be easy" (*NA*, 1.VII).

THORPE, MARIA, Mrs. Thorpe's third daughter (*NA*, 1.XIV).

THORPE, WILLIAM, Mrs. Thorpe's third son, at sea (*NA*, 1.IV).

"THREE SISTERS, THE," a brief epistolary tale of an avaricious family, dedicated to Jane Austen's brother Edward (*Vol. 1*, p. 57).

THRUSH, the sloop on which William Price was second lieutenant (*MP*, 2.XIII).

TILNEY, GENERAL, the father of Henry, Frederick, and Elinor: "a handsome man, of a commanding aspect, past the bloom, but not past the vigour of life" (*NA*, 1.X) but very rigid in his notions and status-bound.

TILNEY, MRS. (deceased, née Drummond), a young lady of "very large fortune" (*NA*, 1.IX) who died of a recurrent bilious fever; the mother of Frederick, Henry, and Eleanor.

TILNEY, ELEANOR, sister of Henry and Frederick, with "a good figure, a pretty face, and a very agreeable countenance" (*NA*, 1.VIII); Jane Austen claims, "I

SUSAN, LADY (1), who gave Augusta Barlow a new regency walking dress—"Catharine or the Bower" (*Vol. 3*, p. 211).
SUSAN, LADY (2). See **Lady Susan**; **Vernon, Lady Susan**.
SUSAN, MRS., Charles Adams's cook—"Jack & Alice" (*Vol. 1*, p. 21).
SUSSEX, (*a*) where Churchill is situated, at which most of the action of *Lady Susan* takes place (p. 254); (*b*) where Sanditon is located (*S*, passim); (*c*) where Norland Park is located (*SS*, 1.I); also mentioned (*Vol. 1*, p. 30; *Vol. 2*, pp. 1 and 171; *Vol. 3*, p. 185).
SWIFT, JONATHAN (1667–1745), political satirist and dean of St. Patrick Dublin: an acquaintance of the Austens, Mr. Evelyn, is referred to as a Yal (*Letters*, p. 70), a reference to *Gulliver's Travels* (1726).
SWISSERLAND (Switzerland): one of the books of engravings placed in sitting room at Donwell Abbey for Mr. Woodhouse's entertainment con "views in Swisserland" (*E*, 3.VI). See also **Switzerland**.
SWITHIN, ST. (St. Swithun), on whose feast day, July 15, a few days b her death, Jane Austen wrote a poem entitled "Venta" (*Verses*, pp. 451–52
SWITZERLAND: "Italy, Switzerland, and the South of France, might fruitful in horrors" as they are represented in Mrs. Radcliffe's novels (*NA*,
SYDNEY PLACE, Bath (called Sydney Terrace in the *Memoir*), whe Austens first lived (at no. 4) after George Austen's retirement in 1801.
SYDNEY TERRACE. See **Sydney Place**.
SYKES, MRS. S. (no biographical data), novelist: Jane Austen read *M or Widdrington Fair* (1808) and liked it "very well indeed" (*Letters*, p.

TALBOT. See **Lindsay, Edward**.
TALES. See **Crabbe, George**.
TARTUFFE. See **Molière, Jean Baptiste Poquelin**.
"TASK, THE." See **Cowper, William**.
TATTERSAL'S (Tattersall's, Grosvenor Place, London): the most f horse dealer's of the regency period, where Mr. Elliot was once seen in with Sir Walter Elliot (*P*, 3.I).
TAUNTON, the county town of Somerset, where Mr. Shepherd Admiral Croft (*P*, 3.III).
TAYLOR, MISS. See **Weston, (Mrs.) Anne**.
TAYLOR, MRS., a crony of Mrs. Jennings (*SS*, 2.VIII).
TEMPÉ, VALLEY OF, Thessaly: the parsonage at Crankhumdur purling Stream, brought from the Valley of Tempé by a p ground"—"Frederic & Elfrida" (*Vol. 1*, p. 5).
TEMPLE (one of the four Inns of Court, the centers of the legal profess where the law is taught and practiced, and where many attorneys live): (*a* (*SS*, 1.XIX); (*b*) Charles Smith and William Elliot became friends there (*l*
TERRACE, THE, a fashionable lounge in Sanditon, poor Steyne in Brighton (*S*, p. 384).
TETBURY, Glos., twenty-three miles from Bath; this jour Thorpe three and one-half hours, not an impressive speed. (Fast h light carriages of the period could travel about fifteen miles an h
TEUTHOLD, PETER (no biographical data), translato

know no one more entitled, by unpretending merit, or better prepared by habitual suffering, to receive and enjoy felicity" (*NA*, 2.XVI).

TILNEY, CAPTAIN FREDERICK, General Tilney's elder son; compared to his brother, in Catherine Morland's prejudiced view, "his air was more assuming, and his countenance less prepossessing. His taste and manners were beyond a doubt decidedly inferior" (*NA*, 2.I).

TILNEY, HENRY, a clergyman, the hero of *Northanger Abbey*; the first time he was introduced to Catherine Morland, "He seemed to be about four or five and twenty, was rather tall, had a pleasing countenance, a very intelligent and lively eye, and, if not quite handsome, was very near it" (*NA*, 1.III). His sister's penetrating judgment of him is that he is "'more nice than wise'" (*NA*, 1.XIV).

TIMBUCTU. See **Tombuctoo**.

TIMES of London (founded in 1785 as *The Daily Universal Register*, the *Times* from 1788), in which the marriage of Lydia and George Wickham receives notice (*PP*, 3.XI).

TINTERN ABBEY, Monmouths., of which there is a transparency in a window of the East Room, formerly the schoolroom, at Mansfield Park (*MP*, 1.XVI).

"TIROCINIUM." See **Cowper, William**.

TOM (1), a servant at The Grove, possibly a footman, who "looks so awkward . . . now his hair is just done up"—"Catharine or the Bower" (*Vol. 3*, p. 213).

TOM (2), a servant, probably a groom, at Randalls (*E*, 3.VIII).

TOM JONES. See **Fielding, Henry**.

TOMBUCTOO: in Edward Denham's romantic scheme for Clara Brereton's ruin, "he felt a strong curiosity to ascertain whether the Neighbourhood of Tombuctoo might not afford some solitary House adapted for Clara's reception" (*S*, pp. 405–6).

TOMLINSON, MR., a banker who recently erected a house at the edge of D., with a "Shrubbery & sweep" (*W*, p. 322).

TOMLINSON, MRS., whose family always arrives first at the assemblies in D. so that she can sit by the fire (*W*, p. 336).

TOMLINSON, JAMES, one of the banker's sons, with whom Mary Edwards did not dance (*W*, p. 336).

"TOUR OF DOCTOR SYNTAX." See **Combe, William**.

TOUR TO THE HIGHLANDS. See **Gilpin, William**: *Observations on . . . Particularly the High-lands of Scotland*.

TOWER OF LONDON, mentioned by Henry Tilney (*NA*, 1.XIV).

TOWNLEY, JAMES. See *High Life Below Stairs*.

TRAFALGAR, BATTLE OF (October 21, 1805), a naval engagement in which the British fleet defeated the allied French and Spanish fleets: Admiral Croft participated in it (*P*, 3.III).

TRAFALGAR HOUSE, Mr. Parker's house in Sanditon, "a light elegant Building, standing in a small Lawn with a very young plantation round it" (*S*, p. 384).

TRENT, GOVERNOR, a former resident of Monkford, near Kellynch (*P*, 3.III).

"TRUTH." See **Cowper, William**.

TUNBRIDGE (Tunbridge Wells, Kent), (*a*) mentioned in "Lesley Castle" (*Vol. 2*, p. 112); (*b*) a stage in the Parkers' journey from London to Sanditon (*S*, p. 363; also mentioned, p. 374); (*c*) mentioned (*MP*, 2.III); (*d*) the more worldly-wise Isabella Thorpe has an advantage in conversation with Catherine Morland, from being familiar with the balls of Tunbridge (*NA*, 1.IV); (*e*) Charles and Mrs. Smith (2) lived there for a while (*P*, 4.IX).

TUPMAN, the name of a family near Maple Grove, "'very lately settled there, and encumbered with many low connections, but giving themselves immense airs, and expecting to be on a footing with the old established families'" (*E*, 2.XVIII).

TURNER, MR. (deceased), Emma Watson's uncle, "who had formed her mind with the care of a Parent" (*W*, p. 361).

TURNER, MRS. See **O'Brien, Mrs.**

TURNER'S, Portsmouth, a shop that outfitted sailors, at 85 High St. (*MP*, 3.VII).

TUSCANY: Catherine Morland extols the weather there (*NA*, 1.XI).

TWELFTH-NIGHT. See **Shakespeare, William.**

TWICKENHAM, a suburb of London where Admiral Crawford bought a summer cottage (*MP*, 1.VI).

UDOLPHO, THE MYSTERIES OF. See **Radcliffe, Mrs. Ann.**

UNION PASSAGE, Bath (formerly Cock Lane, according to R. W. Chapman), exiting from Cheap St. opposite the Pump Yard's archway (*NA*, 1.VII).

UNION ST., Bath, where Captain Wentworth catches up with Anne Elliot in order to propose to her (*P*, 4.XI; also mentioned 4.VII).

UP LYME, Dorset, a "cheerful village" above Lyme Regis (*P*, 3.XI).

UPPER BERKELEY ST., London, where Jane Austen's brother Henry lived for a number of years with his first wife, Eliza Hancock (de Feuillide).

UPPER ROOMS, Bath, opened in 1771, where balls (Mondays and Thursdays) and concerts (Wednesdays) were held during the Season (winter; *NA*, 1.II). See also **Octagon Room.**

UPPER SEYMOUR ST., London, where Alicia Johnson takes "a very nice Drawingroom-apartment" for Lady Susan (*LS*, p. 296).

UPPERCROSS, Som., "a moderate-sized village, which a few years back had been completely in the old English style; containing only two houses superior in appearance to those of the yeomen and labourers" (*P*, 3.V).

UPPERCROSS COTTAGE, a farmhouse transformed into a gentleman's residence, "with its viranda, French windows, and other prettinesses," occupied by Charles (2) and Mary Musgrove (*P*, 3.V).

UPPERCROSS GREAT HOUSE (also called the Mansion House or Uppercross Hall), the senior Musgroves' house, "with its high walls, great gates, and old trees, substantial and unmodernized" (*P*, 3.V).

USKE, VALE OF (Usk, Monmouths.): Laura believed that she was "doomed to waste [her] Days of Youth & Beauty in an humble Cottage" there—"Love and Freindship" (*Vol. 2*, p. 79).

VALANCOURT, a character in Mrs. Radcliffe's *Mysteries of Udolpho*, abandoned by Emily (*NA*, 1.XIV).

VEILLÉES DU CHÂTEAU, LES. See **Genlis, Mme. de.**
VENICE: "St. Mark's Place, Venice" is mentioned (*E*, 3.VI).
VENTA. See **Winchester.**
VERGIL (Publius Vergilius Maro, 70–19 B.C.), Roman poet: Jane Austen says that her verses are "purely classical—just like Homer and Virgil, Ovid and Propria que Maribus" (*Letters*, p. 256).
VERNON, CATHERINE (1) (née De Courcy), wife of Charles Vernon, Lady Susan's most determined enemy; Lady Susan says that she "dearly loves to be first, & to have all the sense & all the wit of the Conversation to herself" (*LS*, p. 274).
VERNON, CATHERINE (2), daughter of Catherine (1) and Charles Vernon (*LS*, p. 277).
VERNON, CHARLES, Lady Susan's brother-in-law, "amiable & mild" (*LS*, p. 247).
VERNON, (MR.) FREDERIC (1) (deceased), Lady Susan's husband, whom she apparently ruined and hounded to his grave (*LS*, p. 252).
VERNON, FREDERIC (2), one of Catherine (1) and Charles Vernon's numerous children (*LS*, p. 250).
VERNON, FREDERICA SUSANNA, Lady Susan's sixteen-year-old daughter; according to her mother, "She is a stupid girl, & has nothing to recommend her" (*LS*, p. 252).
VERNON, LADY SUSAN, eponymous protagonist of *Lady Susan*, "the most accomplished Coquette in England" (p. 248).
VERNON CASTLE, Staffs., Frederic Vernon's seat, which he was forced to sell because of Lady Susan's extravagance; she prevented her brother-in-law Charles from buying it (*LS*, p. 249).
"VERSES ON ALEXANDER SELKIRK." See **Cowper, William.**
VICAR OF WAKEFIELD, THE. See **Goldsmith, Oliver.**
VICARAGE, THE, Highbury, where Mr. Elton resides, is "an old and not very good house, almost as close to the road as it could be" (*E*, 1.X).
VICARAGE LANE, Highbury, at right angles to the main thoroughfare of the town (*E*, 1.X).
VILLIERS, GEORGE (first duke of Buckingham, 1592–1628), one of James I's favorites—"The History of England" (*Vol. 2*, p. 148).
VISCOUNT (unnamed), Eleanor Tilney's husband; he "was really deserving of her; independent of his peerage, his wealth, and his attachment, being to a precision the most charming young man in the world" (*NA*, 2.XVI).
"VISIT, THE," a "comedy in 2 acts" dedicated to Jane Austen's brother James; it contains an account of one of the most extraordinary meals in English literature (*Vol. 1*, p. 49).
VOLTAIRE, FRANÇOIS MARIE AROUET DE (1694–1778), French philosopher and miscellaneous author: he is mentioned in connection with Cowper's poem "Truth" (*S*, p. 370).

WAKE, MR., who was entrapped in matrimony by "a middle-aged Flirt" (*Verses*, p. 444).
WALCOT, a suburb of Bath: John Thorpe mentions passing its church on his way to Bath (*NA*, 1.VII).

WALES, (*a*) Lucy's father is "one of the most capital Taylors" there—"Jack & Alice" (*Vol. 1*, p. 20); (*b*) Laura grew up there—"Love and Freindship" (*Vol. 2*, p. 77); (*c*) Elizabeth and Fanny Johnson take a walking tour there with their mother—"Scraps" (*Vol. 2*, p. 176); (*d*) mentioned in passing (*MP*, 3.III).

WALKER, MISS, a London gossip, friend of a friend of Mrs. Jennings (*SS*, 2.VIII).

WALLIS, COLONEL, a friend of Mr. Elliot, "a highly respectable man, perfectly the gentleman, (and not an ill-looking man, Sir Walter added) who was living in very good style in Marlborough Buildings" (*P*, 4.III).

WALLIS, MRS. (1), the baker or the baker's wife in Highbury; a son is also mentioned (*E*, 2.IX).

WALLIS, MRS. (2), Colonel Wallis's wife, about to have a baby when Anne Elliot arrives in Bath (*P*, 4.III).

WALSH, CAPTAIN, a crony of Lieutenant Price (*MP*, 3.VII).

WALSINGHAM, SIR FRANCIS (ca. 1530–90), politician, one of the "vile & abandoned men" who were Queen Elizabeth's ministers of state—"The History of England" (*Vol. 2*, p. 145).

WANDERER, THE. See **Burney, Frances.**

WARBECK, PERKIN (1474–99, pretender to the throne, probably not, as he claimed to be, Richard, the second son of Edward IV: he was put in the stocks—"The History of England" (*Vol. 2*, p. 141).

WARD, MISS. See **Norris, Mrs.**

WARD, FRANCES. See **Price, (Mrs.) Frances.**

WARD, MARIA. See **Bertram, Lady Maria.**

WARLEIGH (Warley, Worcs.), where Mrs. Cope lives—"A Collection of Letters" (*Vol. 2*, p. 151).

WARWICK, EARL OF (Edward, 1475–99), son of George Plantagenet, duke of Clarence: he was beheaded—"The History of England" (*Vol. 2*, p. 142).

WARWICK, Warwicks., which Eliza Bennet visited on her journey with the Gardiners to Derbyshire (*PP*, 2.XIX).

WARWICKSHIRE, where Mr. Williams lived with his family "in a part little known"—"The Generous Curate" (*Vol. 1*, p. 73).

WATERLOO, BATTLE OF (June 18, 1815), the final defeat of Napoleon: Mr. Parker says of his house, "'I almost wish I had not named [it] Trafalgar—for Waterloo is more the thing now'" (*S*, p. 380).

WATERLOO CRESCENT, a new block of houses in Sanditon (*S*, p. 380).

WATKINS, MRS., a distant relation of Lady Williams's father; according to Lady Williams, "'She had too high a forehead, Her eyes were too small & she had too much colour'"—"Jack & Alice" (*Vol. 1*, p. 17).

WATSON, MISS, a young lady living in Meryton (*PP*, 1.VII).

WATSON, MR., Emma's invalid father: "if ill, [he] required little more than gentleness & silence; &, being a Man of Sense and Education, was if able to converse, a welcome companion" (*W*, p. 361).

WATSON, AUGUSTA, the young daughter of Mr. and Mrs. Robert Watson (*W*, p. 350).

WATSON, ELIZABETH, the eldest Miss Watson, "whose delight in a Ball was not lessened by a ten years Enjoyment, had some merit in chearfully undertaking to drive [Emma] & all her finery in the old chair to D." (*W*, p. 315).

WATSON, EMMA, the heroine of *The Watsons*: "It was well for her that she was naturally chearful;—for the Change [in her circumstances] had been such as might have plunged weak spirits in Despondence" (*W*, p. 362).

WATSON, JANE, Emma's sister-in-law, "pleased with herself for having had ... six thousand pounds, & for being now in possession of a very smart house in Croydon, where she gave genteel parties, & wore fine cloathes" (*W*, p. 349).

WATSON, MARGARET, the third Watson daughter: Elizabeth tells Emma that "'she is all gentleness & mildness when anybody is by.—But she is a little fretful & perverse among ourselves'" (*W*, p. 319).

WATSON, PENELOPE, the second Watson daughter: according to Elizabeth, "'she has her good qualities, but she has no Faith, no Honour, no Scruples, if she can promote her own advantage'" (*W*, p. 317).

WATSON, ROBERT, Mr. Watson's elder son, "an Attorney at Croydon, in a good way of Business; very well satisfied with himself for the same, & for having married the only daughter of the Attorney to whom he had been Clerk" (*W*, pp. 348–49).

WATSON, SAMUEL, Mr. Watson's younger son: Mr. Edwards says that he "'is a very good sort of young Man, & I dare say a very clever Surgeon, but his complexion has been rather too much exposed to all weathers'" (*W*, p. 324).

WATTS, MR., "quite an old Man, about two & thirty," who has proposed to Mary Stanhope at the outset of "The Three Sisters" (*Vol. 1*, p. 57).

WEALD, THE, a wooded upland area of Sussex and Kent, mentioned (*S*, p. 366).

WEALD OF KENT CANAL BILL, excoriated in verse by Jane Austen (*Verses*, p. 449; *Letters*, p. 279). Her brother Edward is mentioned as hating this bill; presumably, the proposed canal would have cut across his estates in Kent.

WEBB, THE MISSES (1), daughters of Mr. and Mrs. (Anne Augusta) Webb: the elder of the two, Maria, marries Mr. Gower—"Evelyn" (*Vol. 3*, p. 183).

WEBB, THE MISSES (2), a family known to Lady Catherine de Bourgh: there are at least three of them, and they all play an instrument (*PP*, 2.VI).

WEBB, MR. and **MRS. ANNE AUGUSTA**, a couple distinguished by excessive generosity who give up their house in Evelyn to Mr. Gower—"Evelyn" (*Vol. 3*, p. 181).

WEBSTER, AMELIA, a correspondent who marries George Hervey (*Vol. 1*, p. 49).

WENTWORTH, the name of a Strafford family not related to Frederick Wentworth (*P*, 3.III); see **Hawkins, Sir John.**

WENTWORTH, MISS, the sister of Lady Percival and one of the many objects of Sir William's errant affections—"Sir William Mountague" (*Vol. 1*, p. 42).

WENTWORTH, EDWARD, Frederick's brother, formerly a curate at Monkford, near Kellynch, now married and living in Shropshire (*P*, 3.III).

WENTWORTH, CAPT. FREDERICK, brother of Edward Wentworth and Mrs. Croft, "a remarkably fine young man, with a great deal of intelligence, spirit and brilliancy" (*P*, 3.IV).

WENTWORTH, SOPHIA. See **Croft, (Mrs.) Sophia.**

WEST, (MRS.) JANE (1758–1852), author, mentioned (*Letters*, p. 446); also, Jane Austen says, "I am quite determined however not to be pleased" with *Alicia de Lacy, an Historical Romance* (1814) (*Letters*, pp. 404–5).

WEST HALL, where the Tupmans live, near Maple Grove (*E*, 2.XVIII).

WEST INDIANS: Mr. Parker is pleased by the rumor that a family of West Indians will visit Sanditon, because "'No people spend more freely, I believe, than W. Indians'" (*S*, p. 392).

WEST INDIES, (*a*) where Sir Thomas Bertram had an interest in a plantation (*MP*, 1.I); (*b*) where Charles Smith had an estate; also one of the places where Captain Wentworth had a tour of duty (*P*, 4.IX, 3.VIII). See also **Antigua**.

WESTBROOK, where A. F. and her daughters are to dine on Wednesday—"A Collection of Letters" (*Vol. 2*, p. 150).

WESTERHAM, Kent, the town nearest to Hunsford, where Lady Catherine de Bourgh and Mr. and Mrs. Collins live (*PP*, 1.XIII).

WESTERN ISLANDS: that is, Bermuda and the Bahamas, mentioned by Mrs. Croft (*P*, 3.VIII).

WESTGATE BUILDINGS, Bath, a very unfashionable address (*a*) where the Webbs go to live after giving up their house to Mr. Gower—"Evelyn" (*Vol. 3*, p. 191); (*b*) where Mrs. Smith (2) has lodgings (*P*, 4.V).

WESTMINSTER (ABBEY), London: Mr. Grant receives an appointment as prebendary there (*MP*, 3.XVII).

WESTMINSTER (SCHOOL), London, where Robert Ferrars (*SS*, 2.XIV) and Henry Crawford (*MP*, 1.VI) went to school.

WESTON, the name of a family due to visit the Palmers after the latters' visit to Barton Park (*SS*, 1.XX).

WESTON, MR. (formerly Captain), the father of Frank Churchill living at Randalls, "a man of unexceptionable character, easy fortune, suitable age and pleasant manners" (*E*, 1.I).

WESTON, MRS. (1) (deceased, née Churchill), the mother of Frank Churchill, cast off by her family after she married Captain Weston: "She had resolution enough to pursue her own will in spite of her brother, but not enough to refrain from unreasonable regrets at that brother's unreasonable anger, nor from missing the luxuries of her former home" (*E*, 1.II).

WESTON, ANNA, Mrs. Weston (2)'s newborn daughter (*E*, 3.XVII).

WESTON, MRS. (2) ANNE (née Taylor), formerly Emma Woodhouse's governess and mother substitute; she "had been a friend and companion such as few possessed, intelligent, well-informed, useful, gentle, knowing all the ways of the family, interested in all its concerns" (*E*, 1.I). *Emma* opens with her marriage to Mr. Weston.

WESTON, FRANK. See **Churchill, Frank C. Weston**.

WEYMOUTH, Dorset, (*a*) where an uncle of Mrs. Palmer lives (*SS*, 1.XX); (*b*) where Tom Bertram amused himself during the second summer that his father spent in the West Indies (*MP*, 1.XII); (*c*) where Frank Churchill and Jane Fairfax fell in love (*E*, 1.XI).

WHEEL OF FORTUNE, THE. See **Cumberland, Richard**.

"WHEN LOVELY WOMAN." See **Goldsmith, Oliver**.

WHICH IS THE MAN? See **Cowley, Hannah**.

WHITAKER, the name of a family living near Barton Park (*SS*, 1.XVIII).

WHITAKER, MR., apparently an acquaintance of Jane Austen, mentioned as a supporter of the reputation of Mary Queen of Scots—"The History of England" (*Vol. 2*, p. 145).

WHITAKER, MRS., the housekeeper at Sotherton, "'that good old Mrs. Whitaker'" according to Mrs. Norris (*MP*, 1.X).

WHITBY, MISS: she is "hurried down from her Toilette, with all her glossy Curls & smart Trinkets" to wait on Charlotte Heywood in the lending library (*S*, p. 390).

WHITBY, MRS., proprietess of the lending library and bookstore in Sanditon (*S*, p. 389); another "young Whitby" is mentioned (*S*, p. 403).

WHITBY'S, originally a general store in Sanditon run by the Whitby family; Mrs. Whitby added a lending library to it (*S*, p. 381).

WHITE HART INN (1), D., where the monthly assemblies are held throughout the winter (*W*, p. 321).

WHITE HART INN (2), Bath, in Stall St.: (*a*) where Mr. Elton stays while courting Augusta Hawkins (*E*, 2.V); (*b*) where the Musgroves stay on first arriving in Bath (*P*, 4.X).

WHITE HORSE INN, an alehouse in the village of Evelyn—"Evelyn" (*Vol. 3*, p. 191).

WHITE HOUSE, Mansfield, the house Mrs. Norris occupies after the death of her husband (*MP*, 1.III).

WHITEHEAD, WILLIAM (1715–85), poet laureate: (*a*) "Yes I'm in love I feel it now / And Henrietta Halton has undone me" is a parody of lines in "The *Je ne scai quoi*"—"A Collection of Letters" (*Vol. 2*, p. 167); (*b*) there is an indirect quote of the lines "And yet I'll swear I can't tell how / The pleasing plague stole on me," also from "The *Je ne scai quoi*" (*MP*, 2.XII). See also **Dodsley, Robert**.

WHITWELL, an estate twelve miles from Barton to which Colonel Brandon was to lead an expedition; it had "a noble piece of water; a sail on which was to form a great part of the morning's amusement" (*SS*, 1.XII).

WICK ROCKS, on the northern boundary of Bath: John Thorpe claims that the Tilneys are going there (*NA*, 1.XI).

WICKHAM, MR. (deceased), steward to the elder Mr. Darcy at Pemberley (*PP*, 1.XVIII).

WICKHAM, (LT.) GEORGE, the unscrupulous son of the Darcys' late steward, who, after scheming to marry various heiresses, must content himself with Lydia Bennet: "His appearance was greatly in his favour; he had all the best part of beauty, a fine countenance, a good figure, and a very pleasing address" (*PP*, 1.XV).

WICKSTEAD, Surrey, Mr. Howard's parish, where Osborne Castle is situated (*W*, p. 331).

WIGHT, ISLE OF. See **Isle of Wight**.

WIGMORE ST., London: Miss Summers' academy for young ladies is located at no. 10 (*LS*, p. 245).

WILCOX, the Bertrams' coachman (*MP*, 1.VIII).

WILD IRISH GIRL, THE. See **Owenson, (Miss) Sydney**.

WILDENHAIM, BARON, a character in Mrs. Inchbald's *Lovers' Vows*, to be played at Mansfield by Mr. Yates (*MP*, 1.XIV).

WILHELMINUS, a gullible young man who rents a cottage in Pembrokeshire —"Scraps" (*Vol. 2*, p. 177).

WILL, PETER (1764–1839), translator of the Marquis of Pharmusa's [Carl F. A. Grosse] *Der Genius*, five volumes (1791–95), as *Horrid Mysteries* (1796): this is one of the books on the reading list Isabella Thorpe provides for Catherine Morland's education (*NA*, 1.VI).

WILLIAM (1), Edward Lindsay's manservant—"Love and Freindship" (*Vol. 2*, p. 81).

WILLIAM (2), a servant in the Lutterells' household—"Lesley Castle" (*Vol. 2*, p. 114).

WILLIAM (3), a servant in the Webbs' household—"Evelyn" (*Vol. 3*, p. 182).

WILLIAM (4), the Tilneys' footman (*NA*, 1.XIII).

WILLIAM (5), a footman in the Reeveses' household in London (*CG*, I ii).

WILLIAM, SIR, one of those keeping vigil at Melissa's sickbed—"A Fragment written to inculcate the practise of Virtue (*Vol. 1*, p. 72).

WILLIAM OF WYKHAM (William of Wykeham, bishop of Winchester 1367–1404): Jane Austen speculates that his "approval was faint" of the Winchester races (*Verses*, p. 451).

WILLIAMS, MRS., Maria's mother; Lady Greville supposes her to be "'too wise to be extravagant'"—"A Collection of Letters" (*Vol. 2*, p. 156).

WILLIAMS, REVEREND MR., a clergyman of limited means and large family—"The Generous Curate" (*Vol. 1*, p. 73).

WILLIAMS, ELIZA, the illegitimate daughter of Colonel Brandon's sister-in-law, Eliza Brandon; not, as rumored by Mrs. Jennings, Colonel Brandon's own natural daughter (*SS*, 1.XIII): she is seduced and abandoned by Willoughby (*SS*, 2.IX).

WILLIAMS, HELEN MARIA (1762–1827), poet and novelist: John Murray, publisher of *Emma*, lent Jane Austen *A Narrative of the Events Which Have Lately Taken Place in France* (1815) (*Letters*, p. 433).

WILLIAMS, LADY KITTY, in whom "every virtue met. She was a widow with a handsome Jointure & the remains of a very handsome face"—"Jack & Alice" (*Vol. 1*, p. 13).

WILLIAMS, MARIA, a "young Lady in distress'd Circumstances" who is much abused by Lady Greville—"A Collection of Letters" (*Vol. 2*, p. 156).

WILLIAMSON, MRS., Charlotte Drummond's aunt, living in Portland Place—"Frederic & Elfrida" (*Vol. 1*, p. 8).

WILLINGDEN, Sussex, where the Heywoods live (*S*, p. 366).

WILLINGDEN ABBOTS, Sussex (also called Great Willingden), a town lying seven miles from Willingden, "on the other side of Battel—quite down in the Weald" (*S*, p. 366).

WILLIS, MRS. SARAH, the original landlady of the White Horse Inn—"Evelyn" (*Vol. 3*, p. 181).

WILLMOT, MR.: he was "the representative of a very ancient Family & possessed besides his paternal Estate, a considerable share in a Lead mine & a ticket in the Lottery"—"Edgar & Emma" (*Vol. 1*, p. 31); his family "were too numerous to be particularly described; it is sufficient to say that in general they were virtuously inclined & not given to any wicked ways" (*Vol. 1*, p. 31).

WILLMOT, EDGAR, eponymous hero of "Edgar & Emma," a son of Mr. Willmot; he never appears in the tale, being at college while the action is taking place (*Vol. 1*, p. 33).

WILLMOT LODGE, "a beautifull Villa not far from Marlhurst"; it houses the large Willmot family—"Edgar & Emma" (*Vol. 1*, p. 31).

WILLOUGHBY, MR. and **CLOE**, minor characters in "The Visit" (*Vol. 1*, p. 50).

WILLOUGHBY, EDWARD: the fickle Sophia is much distressed by her frustrated romance with him—"A Collection of Letters" (*Vol. 2*, p. 152).

WILLOUGHBY, JOHN, of Combe Magna, age twenty-five, "a young man of good abilities, quick imagination, lively spirits, and open, affectionate manners" (*SS*, 1.X); but to Elinor Dashwood he personifies "the irreparable injury which too early an independence and its consequent habits of idleness, dissipation, and luxury, had made in the mind, the character, the happiness, of a man who, to every advantage of person and talents, united a disposition naturally open and honest, and a feeling, affectionate temper" (*SS*, 3.VIII).

WILLOUGHBY, (MRS.) SOPHIA (née Grey), John Willoughby's wife: according to Mrs. Jennings "'a smart, stilish girl they say, but not handsome,'" her only attraction is the possession of fifty thousand pounds (*SS*, 2.VIII).

WILLSON, (MRS.) SARAH, landlady of the Red Lion in M.—"Henry & Eliza" (*Vol. 1*, p. 34).

WILSON (1), a servant, possibly the butler or housekeeper, at Churchill (*LS*, p. 284).

WILSON (2), possibly the butler in the Reeveses' household in London (*CG*, I ii).

WILTSHIRE, where the Morlands' hometown of Fullerton is located (*NA*, 1.I).

WIMPOLE ST., London, where the Rushworths have taken a house for the Season (*MP*, 3.IX).

WINCHESTER, Hants., (*a*) where Jane Austen visited in 1814; in 1817 she moved there with her sister to consult a physician, lodged in College St., died there on July 18, and is buried in the cathedral; (*b*) "Venta" (the Romans' name for the town) is a poem she wrote about the Winchester races (*Verses*, p. 451).

WINDSOR, Berks., where Mr. Churchill and Frank go to stay with an old friend of the former after Mrs. Churchill's death (*E*, 3.IX).

WINGFIELD, MR., Isabella Knightley's doctor in London (*E*, 1.XI).

"WINTER EVENING, THE." See **Cowper, William**.

WINTHROP, Som., where the Hayter house is located (*P*, 3.IX).

WOLSEY, CARDINAL (Thomas Wolsey, ca. 1475–1530), politician: (*a*) Laura, at the overturning of a phaeton, exclaims, "'What an ample subject for reflection on the uncertain Enjoyments of this World, would not that Phaeton & the Life of Cardinal Wolsey afford a thinking Mind!'"—"Love and Freindship" (*Vol. 2*, p. 99); (*b*) he is mentioned in "The History of England" (*Vol. 2*, p. 142); (*c*) also mentioned as the character in Shakespeare's *Henry VIII* (*MP*, 3.III).

WOOLWICH, suburb of London, mentioned in passing (*MP*, 1.I).

WOMAN, OR IDA OF ATHENS. See **Owenson, (Mrs.) Sydney**.

WOODCOCK, MR., proprietor of the hotel in Sanditon (*S*, p. 407).

WOODHOUSE, EMMA, eponymous heroine of *Emma*, at age twenty, "handsome, clever, and rich, with a comfortable home and happy disposition, seemed to unite some of the best blessings of existence" (*E*, 1.I).

WOODHOUSE, (MR.) HENRY, of Hartfield, father of Isabella and Emma: "having been a valetudinarian all his life, without activity of mind or body, he was a much older man in ways than in years; and though everywhere beloved for the friendliness of his heart and his amiable temper, his talents could not have recommended him at any time" (*E*, 1.I).

WOODHOUSE, ISABELLA. See **Knightley, Isabella.**

WOODSTON, probably in Glos., where Henry Tilney holds the living, "a large and populous village, in a situation not unpleasant" (*NA*, 2.XI).

WOODSTON PARSONAGE, Henry Tilney's home, "a new-built substantial stone house, with its semi-circular sweep and green gates" (*NA*, 2.XI).

WOODVILLE (WYDEVILLE), ELIZABETH (ca. 1437–92), Edward IV's queen, "afterwards confined in a Convent by that Monster of Iniquity & Avarice Henry the 7th"—"The History of England" (*Vol. 2*, p. 140).

WORCESTERSHIRE is mentioned (*S*, p. 424).

WORDSWORTH, WILLIAM (1770–1850), poet: Sir Edward Denham proclaims that "'Wordsworth has the true soul of [poetry]'" (*S*, p. 397).

WORTHING, Sussex: according to Mr. Parker, it is one of "'your large, overgrown Places, like Brighton'" (*S*, p. 368).

WORTING, Hants., one of the stages in Mr. Clifford's journey from Bath to London—"Memoirs of Mr. Clifford" (*Vol. 1*, p. 44).

WRIGHT, Mrs. Elton's housekeeper at the vicarage in Highbury (*E*, 2.XV).

WYNNA, SIR JOHN. See **Wynne, Sir John.**

WYNNE, REV. MR. and **MRS.**, the clergyman of the parish in which Catharine and Mrs. Percival live, and his wife; they both died about two years before the story begins—"Catharine or the Bower" (*Vol. 3*, p. 194).

WYNNE, CECILIA and **MARY**, whose father, the Reverend Mr. Wynne, died, leaving them at the mercy of their relations' charity: Cecilia was shipped to Bengal to marry a colonial; Mary became a companion to the Dowager Lady Halifax's daughters—"Catharine or the Bower" (*Vol. 3*, p. 193). See also **Lascelles, Mr.**

WYNNE, CHARLES, the son of the Reverend Mr. Wynne, he was sent to sea instead of being sponsored into the church—"Catharine or the Bower" (*Vol. 3*, p. 206).

WYNNE, SIR JOHN, a gentleman who is holding a private concert on Friday, which is to be attended by A. F. and her daughters—"A Collection of Letters" (*Vol. 2*, p. 150).

YATES, THE HONORABLE JOHN, a friend of Tom Bertram; he "had not much to recommend him beyond habits of fashion and expense, and being the younger son of a lord with a tolerable independence" (*MP*, 1.XIII); he elopes with Julia Bertram.

YATES, JULIA, Sir Thomas Bertram's younger daughter, hard to separate from her sister, with "a warm temper and a high spirit"; she eventually elopes with Mr. Yates (*MP*, 1.XVII).

YORK, DUKE OF (Richard, 1411–60), son of Richard of Conisborough, earl of Cambridge: he fought with Henry VI in various campaigns in France; later in his life, however, he came to oppose the king and even claimed his own right to the throne; in this conflict Jane Austen feels that York "was of the right side"—"The History of England" (*Vol. 2*, p. 139).

YORK, Yorks., (*a*) is mentioned (*S*, p. 424); (*b*) Mrs. Bennet rather bewilderingly accuses her daughter Elizabeth of "caring no more for us than if we were at York" (*PP*, 1.XX); (*c*) is mentioned in passing (*MP*, 2.II), and (*d*) referred to by John Thorpe (*NA*, 1.IX).

YORK HOTEL, Clifton, where the exploring party of James Morland and John, Isabella, and Maria Thorpe dined (*NA*, 1.XV).

YORKSHIRE: (*a*) Camilla Stanley does not know where it is—"Catharine or the Bower" (*Vol. 3*, p. 200); (*b*) the Churchills' estate, Enscombe, is located there (*E*, 1.II).

YOUNGE, MRS., formerly Miss Darcy's companion, she was dismissed for conniving with Wickham to arrange his elopement with Miss Darcy and later appears keeping lodgings in Edward St. (*PP*, 2.XII).

Contributors

JOHN BAYLEY holds the Thomas Warton Chair of English Literature at Oxford. He has published studies of Tolstoy, Hardy, Shakespeare, and Henry James, as well as essays on Jane Austen, Dickens, and George Eliot.

H. ABIGAIL BOK wrote her undergraduate thesis at Princeton University on *The Watsons*. She is a free lance editor.

KATRIN RISTKOK BURLIN is assistant professor of English at Bryn Mawr College. She has published numerous articles and essays on Jane Austen.

MARILYN BUTLER'S books include *Jane Austen and the War of Ideas* and *Romantics, Rebels and Reactionaries*. She is a Fellow of St. Hugh's College, Oxford.

PENELOPE BYRDE is Keeper of the Museum of Costume and Fashion Research Centre, Bath, England, and author of several books on the history of dress.

MAGGIE HUNT COHN is regional coordinator and newsletter editor for the Jane Austen Society of North America in the Chicago area, and collects Jane Austen illustrations, having read Jane Austen unillustrated for 45 years.

EDWARD COPELAND is professor of English at Pomona College where he teaches the eighteenth-century novel. He has written on Richardson, Smollett, Cleland, Burney, and Austen.

HELEN DENMAN of Ottawa has lived in the United States and England besides her native Canada. She has been a student of Jane Austen since she was a teenager.

MARGARET ANNE DOODY, professor of English at Princeton, is the author of books on Samuel Richardson, Augustan poetry, and Fanny Burney, as well as two novels.

ALISTAIR M. DUCKWORTH is the author of *The Improvement of the Estate: A Study of Jane Austen's Novels*, and of other essays on Jane Austen and English fiction.

JOSEPH DUFFY is professor of English at the University of Notre Dame. He has published on twentieth-century Irish, English, and American fiction, and on Dickens and Jane Austen.

ANNE-MARIE EDWARDS, a writer and broadcaster, lectures on Jane Austen and Thomas Hardy. She is the author of *Discovering Hardy's Wessex* and *In the Steps of Jane Austen*.

DAVID GILSON is a librarian in the Taylor Institution Library at Oxford, and a committee member of the Jane Austen Society. He is the author of *A Bibliography of Jane Austen*.

J. DAVID GREY is a co-founder, past president, and permanent board member of

Contributors

the Jane Austen Society of North America. He is an assistant principal of a junior high school in East Harlem, and an editor of the present volume.

JOAN GRIGSBY is a British journalist, author, and broadcaster, and a member of the Jane Austen Society. She lives in Hampshire.

LORRAINE HANAWAY is president of the Jane Austen Society of North America. She edits the *Newsletter* of the Center for the Study of Aging at the University of Pennsylvania.

JOAN HASSALL studied at the Royal Academy Schools and at Bolt Court. She is the daughter of poster artist John Hassall and the sister of poet and biographer Christopher Hassall.

PEGGY HICKMAN lives in Sussex and is the author of *A Jane Austen Household Book*. Her article "Jane Austen's Family in Silhouette" appeared in *Country Life*.

PARK HONAN, professor of English and American Literature at Leeds University, has written articles on Jane Austen and is writing a full-scale biography of her.

DAVID HOPKINSON is a graduate of Oxford University and a former staff inspector for the Department of Education and Science. He has written on education, English history, and literature.

JOHN DIXON HUNT is professor of English Literature at the University of East Anglia, England. He is the author of many books and articles, and the editor of *The Journal of Garden History* and *Word and Image*.

MARGARET KIRKHAM is a part-time tutor in the Open University. She is the author of *Jane Austen, Feminism and Fiction*.

A. WALTON LITZ, Holmes Professor of English Literature at Princeton University, is the author of *Jane Austen: A Study of Her Artistic Development*. He has also published studies of James Joyce, Wallace Stevens, T. S. Eliot, and other modern writers.

DAVID LODGE is the author of seven novels and several works of literary criticism. He is professor of Modern English Literature at the University of Birmingham, England.

MARY GAITHER MARSHALL is a rare-book bibliographer and a board member of the Jane Austen Society of North America. She edited Anna Lefroy's *Sanditon: A Continuation* and has lectured on collecting Jane Austen.

JULIET MCMASTER is professor of English at the University of Alberta. She has published on Thackeray and Trollope, and has written and edited books on Jane Austen.

JO MODERT, a *St. Louis Post-Dispatch* book reviewer, is updating Chapman's list of owners and locations of extant Austen letters for a possible facsimile edition.

SUSAN MORGAN has taught at Cornell and Stanford, and now teaches at Vassar College. She has written a book on Austen, *In the Meantime*, and articles on Scott, Gaskell, Meredith, and Eliot.

Contributors

MARION MORRISON is a professional linguist, educated in Scotland. She has traveled widely in Europe and Africa, and is a fifteen-year resident of Bath.

NORMAN PAGE has published *The Language of Jane Austen* and numerous other books. He is professor of English at the University of Alberta and has held a Guggenheim Fellowship and other awards.

PATRICK PIGGOTT, a noted composer and a Fellow of the Royal Academy of Music, has published a number of books on musical subjects as well as a study of music in Jane Austen's life and writings.

ROBERT M. POLHEMUS is professor and chairman of the English Department at Stanford University. His latest book is *Erotic Faith: Being in Love from Austen to Joyce.*

RUTH APROBERTS is professor of English at the University of California, Riverside. She has written on Jane Austen and published books on Anthony Trollope and Matthew Arnold.

MARILYN SACHS has written twenty-four books for children and young adults. She is currently at work on a novel involving Jane Austen.

SIR DAVID WALDRON SMITHERS, M.D. is the author of *Jane Austen in Kent* and other books. He is the former director of the Radiotherapy Department at Royal Marsden Hospital in London.

BRIAN SOUTHAM has written widely on Jane Austen, T. S. Eliot, and Tennyson. Formerly a university teacher at Oxford and London, he has been a publisher for twenty years.

JANET TODD, Fellow of Sidney Sussex College, Cambridge, is the author of *Women's Friendship in Literature* and *The Dictionary of British and American Women Writers: 1660–1800.*

RACHEL TRICKETT has been a Commonwealth Fellow at Yale, a lecturer in English at the University of Hull, and a Fellow and tutor at St. Hugh's College, Oxford, where she is now principal.

GEORGE HOLBERT TUCKER is a retired journalist, columnist, and researcher with eighteenth-century interests. He is the author of *A Goodly Heritage: A History of Jane Austen's Family.*

ANDREW WRIGHT, professor of English at the University of California, San Diego, has written books on Fielding, Blake, Austen, Trollope, and Joyce Cary. He is a Fellow of the Royal Society of Literature.

Index

Abbey-Mill Farm 179, 383
Abbey School (Reading) 149, 279, 300
Adams, Samuel and Sarah Adams: *The Complete Servant* 80–82
adaptations. *See* dramatizations; sequels
Addison, Joseph 350; *The Spectator* 15, 146, 350, 355
Addison's disease 150, 282, 305–6
Adlestrop 145, 223
Age of Reason. *See* Enlightenment
agriculture 160, 161, 197, 201–2, 225, 319, 324, 371
Allenham 6, 225, 380
almanacs 53, 55
Alton 36, 148, 200, 202, 384
"Amelia Webster" 245
Angus, William: *The Seats of the Nobility and Gentry* 5, 6
animals 324–25. *See also* travel
Another: *The Watsons* 75–76
Another Lady: *Sanditon* 75–76
Antigua 1, 204, 206
antithesis 267
Antwerp 309
architecture 5–11, 16, 37, 209–14, 225, 328. *See also* improvements; *specific buildings*
Ariosto, Lodovico 15
Aristotle 317
army 307–12; militia 148, 307, 308, 309–10; regulars 307, 308. *See also* Waterloo, Battle of

Arne, Thomas A.: *Artaxerxes* 314
art for art's sake 98, 100
Asp 311, 312
assemblies. *See* balls
Astell, Mary 154, 155
auction sales 13–15
Augustan period. *See* Enlightenment
Austen, Anne [Mathew] 146
Austen, Caroline Mary Craven 36, 43, 48, 146, 273, 314; help with *Memoir* 18, 146, 272; inaccuracy 275–77; *My Aunt Jane Austen* 21, 38, 146, 272, 274
Austen, Cassandra [Leigh] 16, 35, 38, 144–45, 279
Austen, Cassandra Elizabeth 14, 16, 18–20 passim, 74, 149–50, 202–3, 279–80, 282, 320; at Chawton 35, 37, 38; confidante of JA 72–73, 281, 286, 394, 395; correspondence 147, 149, 160, 271–77; illustrations 219, 221, 350; Memorandum 49, 50, 51; portrait 15, 219, 342–43
Austen, Charles John 21, 36, 152–53, 198, 273, 275, 276, 279, 309, 311
Austen (Knight), Edward 35, 37, 38, 39, 147, 161, 197, 199, 200, 272, 275, 276, 281, 283, 284, 301, 317, 343
Austen, Eleanor [Jackson] 149
Austen, Eliza [Hastings de Feuillide] 1–5, 20, 143–44, 148, 256, 284, 300, 301, 315
Austen, Elizabeth [Bridges] 147

Index

Austen, Fanny Catherine. *See* Knatchbull, Lady Fanny Catherine [Austen Knight]

Austen, Frances Fitzwilliam [Palmer] 152

Austen, Francis William 21, 38, 150–52, 205, 246, 273, 275, 276, 283, 311, 392; career 151, 198, 200, 279, 309; piety 151, 204; in Southampton 35–36, 161, 199

Austen, George (brother) 146, 197

Austen, George (father) 16, 51, 72, 143, 144, 197, 203, 279, 281, 300, 320, 398

Austen, Harriet [Palmer] 152

Austen, Henry Thomas 147–49, 185, 198, 202, 248, 275, 279, 282, 307, 320, 377, 381–82; Biographical Notice 21, 136, 149, 244, 272, 274, 282, 326; and Eliza de Feuillide 1–4, 144, 148, 256, 301; JA's visits 135–36, 148, 161, 284, 317

Austen, James 1–4, 18, 20, 145, 149, 203–4, 275, 279, 320; *The Loiterer* 146, 248, 279; rector at Steventon 144, 145, 197, 281

Austen Jane Anna Elizabeth [Mrs. Benjamin Lefroy]. *See* Lefroy, Anna

Austen, Martha [Lloyd] 35, 72–73, 151, 161, 162, 164, 273, 276, 351, 392, 395

Austen, Mary [Gibson] 151

Austen, Mary [Lloyd] 20, 146, 392

Austen family history 19, 143–44, 197, 301

Austen-Leigh, James Edward 74, 146, 201; *Memoir* 18–19, 21, 73, 102, 110, 146, 238, 244, 245, 256, 272–73, 275, 300–302, 322, 342–43, 392, 394, 398

Austen-Leigh, Mary Augusta 21, 41, 277

Austen-Leigh, Richard A. 4, 20; *Life and Letters* 19, 106, 240, 244, 245, 273, 276–77

Austen-Leigh, William: *Life and Letters* 19, 106, 240, 244, 245, 273, 276–77

Bage, Robert: *Hermsprong* 15

balls 41, 45, 67, 118–19, 152, 161, 162, 164, 213, 216, 253, 280, 314, 340, 398; assemblies 118, 119, 152, 161, 199, 334, 395–97

Balzac, Honoré de 171, 229

banking 78; Henry Austen and 148, 199, 202, 282, 284

Barrington, E.: *The Ladies!* 375

Barrow, John, ed. of Lord Macartney's "Journal of the Embassy to China" 352, 356

Barthes, Roland 171

Barton: Cottage 6, 42, 209–10, 225, 333, 389, 390; Park 41, 118, 210, 380

Basingstoke 119, 199

Bath: JA there 5, 10, 16–17, 35, 47, 131, 144, 161, 199, 200, 280, 281, 300, 305, 316, 377, 385, 394; in the novels 9, 10, 16–17, 55, 58, 82, 118, 182, 214, 215, 258, 281, 294, 310, 312, 316, 323, 327, 338, 339, 340, 370, 384, 385, 388, 389

Beach, Joseph Warren 112

"The Beautifull Cassandra" 245

Beckford, Grania: *Virtues and Vices* 376

Bedford Coffee House (London) 10

Beechen Cliff 17, 327

Bennet, Arnold 240–41

Bennett, Agnes Maria: *Agnes De-Courci* 360–61

Berkeley St. (London) 380

Berquin, Arnaud: *L'Ami des enfans* 15

Bevan, Dr. F. A. 305

Bible 347–48

Bickerstaffe, Isaac: *The Sultan* 2, 3

Bigg-Wither, Harris 20, 280–81, 287

Bildungsroman 8

Biographical Notice. *See* Austen, Henry Thomas

biography 18–22, 116, 271–72, 274, 277, 279–82

Birrell, Augustine 239
Blackall, Samuel 280, 286
Blair, Hugh: *Sermons* 349
Blaise Castle 7, 328
Blake, William 367
bluestockings 154
Bonavia Hunt, D. A.: *Pemberley Shades* 374
Bonomi, Joseph 5
Book of Common Prayer 53, 347–48
Boswell, James 349
Bovary, Emma. *See* Flaubert, Gustave
Bowles, William Lisle 319
Box Hill 29, 57, 88, 289, 327, 383–84, 389, 390
Brabourne, Lord. *See* Knatchbull Huggessen, Edward
Bradbrook, Frank W. 9, 114, 268, 327
Bradley, A. C. 106, 108, 111, 240
Brighton 10, 16, 307, 308, 382, 383
Brinton, Sybil G.: *Old Friends and New Fancies* 374
Bristol 5, 384
British Critic review of *SS* 94
broadcloth trade 143, 197, 301
Brock, Charles E. and Henry M. Brock 138, 219–21 passim
Bromley 381
Brontë, Charlotte 95, 97, 288, 374; opinion of JA 98–99, 237, 261, 287, 392
Brontë, Emily 216, 229
The Brothers. See Sanditon
Brown, Barbara 221
Brown, Capability 224
Brown, Edith [Hubback] and Francis Brown 75, 375–76
Browning, Elizabeth Barrett 98
Burke, Edmund 156, 196, 224–25, 317, 318
Bulwer-Lytton, Edward 97
burlesque 62, 188, 262, 264, 282, 331, 341, 371, 394; *juvenilia* 48, 149, 245–54 passim, 263, 279–80, 326, 331

Burney, Fanny (Frances d'Arblay) 20, 93, 105, 166, 168, 169, 190, 235, 248, 253, 257, 269, 355; *Camilla* 79, 152, 172, 356, 357, 360; *Cecilia* 79, 358, 360; *Evelina* 26, 51, 154, 166, 357; *The Wanderer* 79, 93, 194
Burney, Sarah Harriet: *Clarentine* 357
Burns, Robert 356
Burrows, Abe: *First Impressions* 124, 126–27
Bush, Douglas 117
Butler, Joseph 155, 190
Butler, Marilyn 77, 191
Byron, George Gordon, Lord 74, 229, 266, 282, 318, 319, 356

Cadell, Mr. 51, 157, 280
calendar 53–58. *See also* time
Cambridge 279, 280, 286
Camden Place (Bath) 16, 214
Capotte, Jean Gabriel, comte de Feuilllide 144
card games. *See* games
Carey's road book 388
caricature 27–31, 280. *See also* burlesque; characterization; satire
Carlton House 136, 148
carriages 36, 80, 82, 87, 90, 293, 302, 324, 345, 370, 388–91
"Catharine or the Bower" 49, 245, 253–54, 283, 348–49
Catherine. See Northanger Abbey
causality. *See* realism
Cecil, Lord David 18, 20–21, 108, 234
Centlivre, Susannah: *The Wonder!* 1–2
Cervantes, Miguel de 169
Chapman, R. W. 13, 22, 51, 53–58, 116, 187, 241, 276, 277, 301, 316, 332, 382, 382,; standard editions 107, 111, 116, 138, 219, 273–74, 322, 340, 388, 389
Chapone, Hester 156
Chappell, Warren 220

characterization 24–34, 65–66, 229, 261, 314, 366–67, 371. *See also* individualism
Chard, George 314
Chatsworth 205, 381, 382
Chawton 18, 19, 35–39, 146, 148, 284; JA museum 39, 119; JA there 35–38, 150, 185, 201, 223, 281, 282, 320, 377, 394; Manor 35, 36, 38, 39, 147, 164, 199, 200, 202, 301
Cheltenham 150
Chesterton, G. K. 107, 254
chiasmus 267
children 41–46, 179, 396
chronology: of composition 47–52, 116; within the novels 53–58, 173–75
Cinderella 118
Cirlin, Edgar 221
Clarke, James Stanier 61, 148, 230, 273, 331
class, social 65, 77–78, 156, 191–202 passim, 297–303
Cleopatra 309
Cleveland 30, 54, 176, 210, 304, 380, 381, 389, 390
Clifton 5, 281
clothing. *See* dress
Coates, John: *The Watsons* 75
Cobbett, Alice: *Somehow Lengthened* 74
Cobbett, William 202, 372
Coleridge, Samuel Taylor 263, 319, 356, 364–68 passim, 372, 374
"A Collection of Letters" 49, 251
College St. (Winchester) 282, 320
Collins, Wilkie 97
Colman, George (the Younger): *The Heir at Law* 356
Combe Magna 381, 390
comedy 21, 25–33, 53, 60–69, 168–69, 188, 229, 235, 249, 252, 267, 295, 299, 302, 303, 322, 338, 372, 398; dramatic 169–70, 228, 247, 279, 356; of manners 165, 228, 253, 254, 298, 371

comic vision 26, 60–69 passim, 394
commerce. *See* trade
completions 72–76, 116
Condorcet, Antoine Caritat, Marquis de 155
Congreve, William 169, 228, 256
consumer revolution 77–90, 202. *See also* economy
continuations. *See* completions; sequels
Cooke, Mary 331
Cooke, Rev. Samuel 384
Cooke, William C. 219, 221
cooking 160–63, 184, 185
Cooper, Edward (cousin) 145
Cooper, Edward (uncle) 145
Cooper, Jane (Lady Williams) 2, 145
Cooper, Jane [Leigh] 145
Cope, Sir Zachary 305–6
Cork St. (London) 283
costume. *See* dress
Covent Garden (London) 10
Cowley, Hannah: *Which Is the Man?* 356
Cowper, William 190, 224, 328, 356, 392
Crabbe, George 356, 357, 392
Craik, Henry 105
Craik, Wendy Ann 383, 384
Cramer, J. B. 315, 316
Crewkerne 385
Critical Review review of *SS* 94
criticism 93–117, 190, 237–42
Crosby, Richard and Co. 47, 49, 51, 136–37, 273, 281
Cross, Wilbur L. 105, 240

dancing 18, 67, 118–19, 152, 302. *See also* balls
Dawlish 10, 381
Deane 18, 144, 197
deconstruction 117, 168, 356
Delaford 54, 80, 184, 209, 210, 224, 325, 380, 390
Derbyshire 42, 205, 334
Devonshire 209, 280, 333, 391

dialogue 228–35 passim, 251, 254, 264, 268, 269
Dickens, Charles 24, 28, 97, 229, 233, 237, 261, 268, 365, 370
diegesis 169, 175
discourse. *See* dialogue; monologue; speech
displacement 166–67
doctors. *See* medicine
Donoghue, Dennis 25
Donwell Abbey 7, 57, 58, 185, 212–13, 224, 266, 317, 328, 337, 383, 389
Dorsetshire 202, 210, 263, 280, 380, 385
drama. *See* theatricals, amateur; *specific playwrights*
dramatizations 116, 120–30, 169
dress 20, 131–34, 215–17, 219
Drury Lane Theatre (London) 10
Dryden, John 223, 224, 356, 362
Duckworth, Alistair M. 77, 114, 179, 182
dullness. *See* triviality

East Indies 132, 151, 153, 307, 311, 388
economy: consumer 77–90, 372; domestic 77, 86, 89; metaphor of 79, 85–90, 172
"Edgar & Emma" 245, 377
Edgar's Buildings (Bath) 16
Edgeworth, Maria 79, 99, 166, 167, 168, 169, 193–95, 198, 235, 355, 366
editions of the novels 14–15, 116, 135–39; Bentley Collected 97, 102, 137–38, 219; R. W. Chapman's 107, 111, 116, 138, 219, 273–74, 322, 340, 388, 389
education 140–42, 149, 194, 279, 293, 300, 314, 328, 356, 367; accomplishments 140–41, 314–16; governesses 140, 141, 310, 337, 398; moral 141–42, 154, 155, 300; schools 140, 141, 149; of women 140–41, 194. *See also* Cambridge; Oxford
Egerton, Thomas 135, 332

Eldon, Mark: *Pride and Prejudice* 127
Elegant Extracts 298
Elephant 309
Elinor and Marianne. See Sense and Sensibility
Eliot, George (Mary Ann Evans Cross) 24, 25, 95, 97, 99, 228, 229, 230–31, 232, 234, 235
Emma 19, 43, 48, 50, 52, 57–58, 85, 87–89, 90, 95, 98, 112, 118, 119, 129, 167, 181–82, 201, 202, 232, 287, 288–89, 309–10, 337–38, 376, 378, 383–84; architecture 6–10 passim, 212–13; editions 15, 136–38 passim, 148, 281–82; heroine 27, 28–30, 32–33, 64, 69, 106
Endymion 309
Enlightenment 63, 155–56, 158, 190, 193, 262–63, 368, 369
Enscombe 384
epic 169, 192, 229
epistolary form. *See* novels, epistolary
Esher 317
ethics. *See* moral vision
Evangelical movement 149, 156, 202, 204–7
"Evelyn" 49, 244, 245
Everingham 211, 383, 390
Exeter Exchange (London) 325

fabric. *See* dress
fabula 172–74
fallacy, pathetic 172
farming. *See* agriculture
Farr, Thomas 7
Farrer, Reginald 106–7, 108, 111, 112
fashion. *See* dress
feminism 60, 61, 106, 108, 117, 154–58, 192–95, 229, 280
Feuillide, comte de. *See* Capotte, Jean Gabriel, comte de Feuillide
Feuillide, Eliza de. *see* Austen, Eliza
Feuillide, Hastings de 144
fiction. *See* novels

INDEX

Fielding, Henry 2, 93, 95, 168, 169, 175, 237, 247, 249, 256, 269, 279, 295, 366; *Tom Jones* 99, 228, 345, 349, 357, 358–59
"The first Act of a Comedy" 2, 245
First Impressions. See Pride and Prejudice
Flaubert, Gustave 112
Fletcher, John: *The Chances* 2
food and drink 160–64, 302. *See also* agriculture; cooking
Fordyce, James: *Sermons to Young Women* 44, 155
form 165–78. *See also* novels
formalism 117, 171, 172
Forster, E. M. 107, 228, 229–30, 234–35, 241–42, 319
Fowle, Thomas 149–50, 280
Fox, Charles James 196
Francklin, Dr. Thomas: *Matilda* 1
"Frederic & Elfrida" 245, 246, 247
Fullerton 44, 384, 389
furniture 8, 209–14 passim, 216, 225, 302, 317, 391

Gainsborough, Thomas 326
Gambier, Admiral 204
games 57, 179–83; cards 119, 163, 179–82, 305, 397. *See also* word games, gardens 9, 38, 80, 184–86, 209–14 passim, 224–26, 284, 314, 318, 327–29; greenhouses 7, 9, 184, 225; kitchen 37, 185, 225, 226; lawns 10, 184, 185, 210, 212, 224; plantations 7, 10, 184, 210, 329; shrubbery 9, 184, 185, 210, 223, 329. *See also* cooking; improvements
Garrick, David, 2, 57, 248
Garrod, H. W. 107, 241
Gaskell, Mrs. Elizabeth 33, 97, 229, 230, 233–34, 235
Genette, Gérard 173–74
genius 18, 93, 156, 248
Genlis, Mme. de: *Adelaide and Theodore* 44
Gibraltar 388

Gide, André 335
Gifford, William 331
Gillespie, Jane 375
Gilpin, William 224, 317, 326–28, 352, 353. *See also* picturesque
Gilson, David 110, 116, 120, 128, 219, 273
Gisborne, Thomas 204
Gloucestershire 384
Godmersham Park 5, 20, 21, 35, 38, 39, 144, 147, 161–64 passim, 197, 200, 204, 223, 281, 305, 343–44
Godwin, William 157
Goethe, Johann Wolfgang von 257
Goldsmith, Oliver 15, 220, 224, 279, 298, 328; *History of England* (and its *Abridgement*) 187–88, 249–51, 350
Goodnestone 5, 147, 223
Gore, Mrs. Catherine 96
Gosse, Edmund 105
gothic 20, 168, 225, 339. *See also Northanger Abbey*; novels, gothic
Gouges, Olympe de 155
Gough, Philip 138
Gracechurch St. (London) 42, 299
Grandison. See Richardson, Samuel; *Sir Charles Grandison or the Happy Man*
Grappler 312
Gray, Thomas 283
Greatbatch, William 219
Gretna Green 382
Greywall 5

Hackwood 5
Haden, Dr. Charles 273, 304
Hammond, Chris 138
Hampshire 35, 38, 119, 147, 149, 150, 152, 164, 190, 197, 198, 200, 201, 202, 280, 281, 317, 320, 384
Hancock, Eliza. *See* Austen, Eliza
Hancock, Philadelphia [Austen] 19, 143–44, 254
Hancock, Tysoe Saul 19, 143
Handel, George Frederick 316, 361
Hans Square (London) 284

502

Hanway, Mary Ann: *Falconbridge Abbey* 78
Harding, D. W. 30, 32, 112
Hardy, Barbara 115–16
Hardy, Thomas 95, 229, 268
Harley St. (London) 305
Hartfield 6, 174, 184, 212, 213, 216, 325, 383–84
Hassall, Joan 138, 215–18, 220, 221
Hastings 74
Hastings, Warren 19, 143
Haydn, Franz Joseph 316
Hazlitt, William 93
Henrietta St. (London) 284
Henry, Robert: *History of England* 351–52
"Henry and Eliza" 245
heroines 26–33, 63–64, 79, 105–6, 107, 141, 156–58, 165–66, 192, 229–32 passim, 331, 395
Hertfordshire 334, 381
Highbury 8, 10, 88, 118, 162, 171, 174, 201, 235, 302, 310, 315, 325, 337, 383–84, 389, 391
Hill, Constance 21, 276
Hill St. (London) 308
history, literary 114, 116, 190, 256, 365. *See also* reading
"The History of England" 188, 196, 219, 245, 246, 248–51, 327, 350–51
Hobbes, Thomas: *Leviathan* 62
Hodgkin's disease 305
Homer 175, 355
Honiton 380
Hook, James: *Lessons for Beginners* 315
Horace 318
Horsmonden 143
horticulture 160, 161
houses. *See* architecture; furniture; specific buildings
Howells, William Dean 104–8 passim, 239
Hubback, Catherine 20, 21, 72, 74; *The Younger Sister* 72–73, 75, 76, 394
Hubback, John H. and Edith C.

Hubback: *Jane Austen's Sailor Brothers* 21, 75, 273. *See also* Brown, Edith
Huizinga, Johan 179–83 passim
Hume, David: *History of England* 15
humor. *See* burlesque; comedy; satire
Hunsford Parsonage 210, 291, 325, 381, 389, 391
Hurstbourne Park 5
Hutton, R. H. 102, 239
Huxley, Aldous and Jane Murfin: film script of *PP* 122, 125–26, 128, 221

illustrations 215–22. *See also* portraits of JA
improvements 9, 82, 114, 184, 211, 212, 223–26, 234, 329, 371, 372
Inchbald, Mrs.: *Lovers' Vows* 170, 192, 335–36
income 77–90, 194, 291
India 143
individualism 60, 63–65, 68, 193, 194, 371
irony 29, 33, 61, 64, 66–67, 69, 86, 111, 112–13, 167, 168, 172, 176, 228–30 passim, 235, 254, 257, 262, 336, 337, 394

"Jack & Alice" 245, 246, 247, 358
Jacobs, Joseph 105
Jakobson, Roman 171
James, G. P. R. 97
James, Henry 24, 25, 229–32 passim, 235, 261, 299, 370; essays 96, 102–8 passim, 111, 112, 177–78, 238, 240, 323, 372
Jane Austen Society 39, 272, 343, 381
Janeites 102–8, 111, 115, 232, 237–42
Jeffery, Mr. 332
Jenkins, Elizabeth 18, 19, 20, 116, 381–82
Jenner, Dr. Edward 304
Jerome, Helen: *Pride and Prejudice* 121, 122–23, 125, 126
Johnson, Dr. Samuel 1, 140, 192, 229, 262–63, 267, 298, 348, 349,

Index

Johnson, Dr. Samuel (*continued*) 350, 358, 364, 366, 392; *The Idler* 264, 350, 356; *The Rambler* 28, 60, 146, 263, 264
juvenilia 2–3, 13, 47, 48–49, 94, 244–54, 256, 276, 279–80, 331, 358, 377, 392. *See also specific works*

Kavanagh, Mrs. 107
Kaye-Smith, Sheila 242
Keats, John 190, 367
Kellynch Hall 8, 58, 89, 213, 214, 225, 310, 339, 340, 385, 391
Kemble, John 127
Kent 5, 35, 143, 147, 197–200 passim, 210, 223, 280, 281, 283, 301, 317, 381, 390. *See also* Godmersham Park
Kent, William 7
Kettle, Arnold 156, 170–71, 228–29
Keynes, Geoffrey 107
Kipling, Rudyard 232, 240
Knatchbull, Lady Fanny Catherine [Austen Knight] 21, 50, 90, 147, 199, 204, 273, 276, 290, 305, 315, 331
Knatchbull-Huggessen, Edward 138, 147, 273, 274, 276
Knight, Fanny. *See* Knatchbull, Lady Fanny Catherine
Knight, Richard Payne: *The Landscape* 224, 329
Knight, Thomas (I) 144, 197
Knight, Thomas (II) 147, 197, 198, 281, 301
Knight family history 35
Kotzebue, August F. F. von. *See* Inchbald, Mrs.: *Lovers' Vows*

Lady Susan 13, 18, 47, 49, 138, 147, 256–59, 280, 295
Lake District 224, 317, 327, 353, 364
Lang, Andrew 374
language 72, 115–16, 261–70, 334, 347–48, 369–70, 392; economic 85–90; moral 115, 264–66. *See also* speech; style

Lascelles, Mary 19, 49, 53, 102, 106, 108, 112, 254, 261, 268, 270
Laski, Marghanita 22, 116
laughter 61–62, 68–69
Lawrence, D.H. 107, 229, 240, 288
Lawrence, George 97
Leavis, F. R. and Q. D. Leavis 93, 107, 112, 113, 156, 177, 259
LeFanu, Sheridan 97
Lefroy, Anna 3, 19–20, 21, 37, 72, 146, 149, 187, 244, 276; help with *Memoir* 18, 146, 272, 342; *Sanditon* continuation 13, 73, 74, 146
Lefroy, Anne 13, 18, 392, 398
Lefroy, Fanny 20, 38, 271
Lefroy, Fanny Caroline 51, 276, 287–88
Lefroy, Jessie 343
Lefroy, Tom 280, 286
Leigh (Perrot), James 145, 161, 197, 199, 300
Leigh (Perrot), Jane [Cholmeley] 145, 300
Leigh, Theophilus 145, 279
Leigh family history 19, 143, 144–45, 196
Lennox, Charlotte: *The Female Quixote* 357–58
"Lesley Castle" 245, 251–52
letters 13–14, 60, 138, 147, 150, 160, 195, 204, 271–77, 346, 357; triviality 18, 131, 272, 277; physical appearance 274–75, 345–46. *See also* novels, epistolary; postal system, British
Lewes, George Henry 98–100, 110, 231, 237–38, 261, 392
Lewis, C. S. 24, 264
Lewis, Matthew Gregory: *The Monk* 349
limitations argument 33, 97, 100, 101, 103, 105, 111, 113, 157, 174, 228–29, 232, 302–3. *See also* triviality
Lisbon 388
Lister, Thomas H. 26, 96–97
Litz, A. Walton 33, 54, 56, 259, 318

504

Index

Lloyd, Martha. *See* Austen, Martha [Lloyd]
Lloyd, Mary. *See* Austen, Mary [Lloyd]
Locke, John 141
Lodge, David 111, 115
The Loiterer 146, 248, 279
London 10, 79–80, 131, 200, 201, 345; architecture 9, 10, 210, 212, 308, 325, 333; in the novels 42, 54, 57, 84, 212, 258, 283–85, 299, 305, 308, 310, 334, 338, 340, 380–84 passim, 388–90 passim; Henry Austen there 148–49, 161, 185, 202, 256, 284; J.A. there 135–36, 148, 271, 280, 283–85, 315
Longbourn 43, 55, 84, 121–26 passim, 184, 210, 307, 308, 325, 334, 381, 382, 389, 390
"Love and Freindship" 245, 246, 248–49, 251, 254, 267, 280, 290–91, 326, 350, 360–61
Lubbock, Percy 107, 111, 112
Luckcock, James: *Hints for Practical Economy* 80, 81
Lyme Regis 8, 10, 214, 215, 263, 304, 319, 339, 377, 385, 386, 389, 390, 398

Macaulay, Thomas Babington, Baron 237, 238
Macaulay, Zachary: *Christian Observer* 204, 261
MacKaye, Mary K. M.: *Pride and Prejudice* 120–21
Mackenzie, George Steuart: *Travels in Iceland* 352
MacKinnon, Sir Frank 51, 53–58, 380, 381, 382, 388
mail. *See* letters; postal system, British
Malden, Mrs. S. F. 104, 239
manners 41, 162–63, 300–303. *See also* class, social
Mansfield Park 8, 9, 31, 118, 162, 164, 211, 212, 309, 329, 335, 336, 378–79, 382, 397; East Room 8, 185, 327

Mansfield Park 19, 31, 43–44, 55–56, 64, 85–87, 90, 112–14, 118, 181, 198, 205–6, 234, 256, 283, 308–9, 335–36, 348–49, 378–79, 382–83; amateur theatricals 1–4, 7, 31, 170, 206, 211; architecture 7–11 passim, 211–12; composition 38, 48, 51, 259, 281; editions 135–38 passim; improvements 5, 224–25; sequels 375
Manydown 119, 287, 355
Maple Grove 212, 384
Marat, Jean-Paul 155
marriage 24, 64, 68, 85, 90, 119, 165, 167, 192, 194, 204, 232, 233, 235, 280, 286–95, 371; for money 78–79, 192, 197, 252–53, 290–91. *See also* sex
Marshall, Jane: *A Series of Letters* 79
Martineau, Harriet 26, 97
Mason, George: *An Essay on Design in Gardening* 328
medicine 282, 304–6. *See also* Addison's disease
Mediterranean Sea 152, 153, 309
Meeke, Mary: *Conscience* 78
"Memoir": *Gambles and Gambols* 374, 375
Meryton 10, 118, 125, 210, 307, 308, 334, 381
metaphors 79, 85–90, 171, 172
metonyms 7, 171–72, 182
military. *See* army; navy
Mills, A. Wallis 219
Milne, A. A.: *Miss Elizabeth Bennet* 123–25
Milsom St. (Bath) 10, 16
mimesis 169, 175, 262, 267
mind, lively 63–65, 68
"Mr. Clifford" 245
"Mr. Harley" 245, 246
Molière, Jean Baptiste Poquelin 99, 169
money. *See* income
monologue 66, 268, 269
monotony. *See* triviality
Moore, George 107, 254

Index

Moore's Irish Melodies 315
moral vision 11, 24, 25, 28, 33, 60, 63, 65, 86, 112–13, 156, 157–58, 229–35 passim, 259
moral vocabulary 115, 264–66
More, Hannah 154, 204; *Cœlebs in Search of a Wife* 49, 85, 86, 89, 349
Mozart, Wolfgang Amadeus 2, 316, 335
Mudrick, Marvin 107, 112, 259
Muir, Edwin 107
Murray, John 135–36, 273, 282
music 119, 140–41, 144, 163, 314–16
musical instruments: harp 87, 213, 315, 391; pianoforte 57, 85, 87, 88, 176, 177, 200, 209, 213, 302, 314, 315
mystery 167
"The Mystery" 2–3, 244, 245

Nabokov, Vladimir 56
Napoleonic Wars 67, 96, 148, 151, 152, 184, 193, 196–207 passim, 302, 307, 310, 353–54, 374
narrative method 115, 167, 169–70, 232, 259, 282, 370. See also speech; style
National Portrait Gallery 342, 343
naturalism. See realism
nature 317–19, 326, 328–29, 334, 369. See also improvements; picturesque navy 205–7, 307–12; JA's brothers 150– 53, 198, 279, 302. See also Portsmouth; Royal Naval Academy; Trafalgar, Battle of
needlework 18, 302, 365
Netherfield 118, 122, 124, 125, 210, 293, 300, 305, 324, 334, 381
Newcastle 382
New Criticism 111–12, 190
Newman, John Henry 96
New Monthly 98
New Town (Bath) 10
Nineteenth Century 106
Norfolk 211, 325, 383

Norland Park 209, 380
Northamptonshire 202, 310, 328, 335, 380, 382
Northanger Abbey 7, 55, 82, 213, 216, 225, 338, 384
Northanger Abbey 19, 26, 44, 48, 49–50, 82–83, 95, 167–68, 264, 291–92, 310, 338–39, 358, 366, 384; architecture 6, 7, 10, 213, 225; Bath 10, 16–17, 82, 118–19, 310, 327, 338, 384; *Catherine* 47, 48, 49–50, 136, 282; editions 15, 136–38 passim, 149, 282; *Susan* 47, 49–50, 94, 136, 157, 280, 394
novels: didactic 94, 96, 165, 168, 188, 194, 371; domestic 33, 98, 110, 192, 229, 230, 234, 358, 362; epistolary 47, 49, 50, 53, 94, 165, 175, 187, 249, 256–59; gothic 97, 107, 168, 193, 280, 338, 339, 366; historical 61, 96, 97, 193, 228, 230, 250; picaresque 169; propaganda 371; provincial 96, 230, 233–34; sentimental 93, 95, 96, 101, 110, 149, 165–69, 190, 237, 246–51 passim, 280, 331, 366, 377
novels of fashionable life 96
novels of manners. See realism

obituaries 320–21
"Ode to Pity" 245
O'Hara, Kane: *The Tragedy of Tom Thumb* 2
Oliphant, Mrs. Margaret 102, 103, 104, 107, 108, 238
"Opinions of *Emma*" 332, 382
"Opinions of *Mansfield Park*" 332, 382
Osborne Castle 325
Oulton, L.: *The Watsons* 74–75
Oxford 141, 146, 147, 248, 279, 307, 381, 383, 384, 389; Balliol 145, 279; Brasenose 300; JA there 140, 149, 279, 300; St. John's 144, 148, 197, 300
Oxford St. (London) 10
oxymoron 176

Page, Norman 115
Painshill 317
parody. *See* burlesque
Pasley, Capt. Charles William: *Essay on the Military Policy and Institutions of the British Empire* 205–6, 353–55
Paterson's road book 388
Peacock, Thomas Love 254, 371
Pellew, George 104
Pemberley 6, 121, 122, 185, 205, 210–11, 216, 223, 225, 291, 298, 300, 317, 324, 328, 334–35, 374, 375, 378, 381, 382, 390
peripeteia 167
Perseverance 246
Persuasion 31, 44–45, 48, 52, 85, 89–90, 95, 118, 151, 157, 202, 206–7, 225–26, 262–63, 310–12, 318–19, 339–40, 385–86; architecture 7–10 pas- sim, 213–14; Bath 16–17, 312, 339– 40, 385; canceled chapters 18, 52, 322–23; editions 15, 136–39 passim, 149, 282; sequel 376
Peterborough 383
pets. *See* animals
Petty, William 7
Petty France 384
philanthropy 38, 154, 201, 372
"Pickering" 219
picturesque 209, 318, 326–29, 352–53. *See also* nature
Piozzi, Mrs. (Thrale): *Letters* 349
Pitt, William (the Elder and the Younger) 145, 196
"Plan of a Novel" 48, 51, 282, 331
Plato 169
play. *See* games
plot 73, 84, 112, 166, 167, 172, 229, 246, 253, 286, 293, 314, 315, 333–41, 365, 366, 371
Plumptre, Anne: *The History of Myself and My Friend* 83
Plumtre, John Pemberton 204
Plymouth 311, 381

poetry 24, 191–93, 237, 261, 392. *See also* verses by JA
point of view 173–78, 267–69
politics 156, 190, 191–202, 205
Pollock, W. F. 100
Polwhele, Richard: *The Unsex'd Females* 157
Pope, Alexander 223, 224, 225, 266, 317, 355, 356
Portman Square (London) 70, 380
portraits of JA 15, 219, 280, 342–44
Portsmouth 9, 31, 36, 43, 56, 150, 151, 152, 201, 206, 212, 281, 308, 309, 318, 327, 329, 336, 383, 389, 397
postal system, British 271, 345–46
prayers by JA 204, 347
Price, Richard: *A Review of the Principal Questions in Morals* 155
Price, Uvedale 224, 329
Pride and Prejudice 19, 27, 30, 42–43, 45, 48, 51, 54–55, 64, 77, 82, 84– 85, 118, 120–29, 166–67, 181, 205, 298–300, 307–8, 332, 334–35, 381–82, 395; architecture 6–10, passim, 210– 11; editions 15, 38, 135–39 passim, 281; *First Impressions* 47, 50, 51, 53, 55, 94, 118, 157, 280, 281, 334, 394; sequels 374–75
Priestley, J. B. 107
primitivism 191, 193
prince regent 61, 136, 148, 281, 308, 331
Pump Room (Bath) 10, 294
punctuation 262
Pym, Barbara 33, 229–30, 235

Rabelais, François 169
Radcliffe, Mrs. Ann 168; *The Mysteries of Udolpho* 79, 167, 338
Raffles, Stamford 311
Raleigh, Sir Walter 105
Ramsgate 10, 151, 204, 382
Randalls 6, 119, 174, 213, 383
Read, Herbert 107
Reading 140, 149, 279, 300

Index

reading 38, 347–62
realism 26, 93–97, 100, 104, 110, 165, 168, 170–75, 193, 228–30 passim, 244, 248, 251, 268, 280, 297, 299, 386
Reeve, Clara: *Plans of Education* 78
regency period 20, 115, 116, 226, 258, 369–72 passim
religion 191, 202–7
Repplier, Agnes 104, 105, 239, 242
Repton, Humphry 5, 9, 184, 212, 223, 224, 329, 383
Retrospective Review (1823) 93
Revolution, French 77, 144, 152, 193, 196, 284, 300, 364, 365
Revolution, Industrial 77
Richardson, Samuel 25, 53, 93, 140, 167, 168–69, 175, 190, 249, 252, 253, 257, 267, 279, 349; *The History of Sir Charles Grandison* 3, 187–88, 223, 357, 358, 359; *Pamela* 154, 165–66, 168, 249
Richmond 57, 383
Rider's "British Merlin" 53, 55
Robespierre, Maximilien 155
Roche, Regina Maria: *The Children of the Abbey* 359, 360
romance 61, 165, 166, 167, 295, 338. *See also* novels: gothic; historical; sentimental
romanticism 33, 156, 229, 263, 318, 319, 326, 340, 364–72. *See also* individualism
Rosings Park 7, 84, 210, 211, 225, 381
Rousseau, Jean-Jacques 155, 156, 192, 193, 364; *Émile* 157, 158, 193; *Julie* 169, 192, 193
Royal Crescent (Bath) 10
The Royal Kalender 53, 55
Royal Naval Academy 151, 152, 309
"Rumford, Count." *See* Thompson, Sir Benjamin
Rundell, Maria Eliza: *New System of Domestic Cookery* 89

Sackville St. (London) 84, 283

Sadleir, Michael 107
Saintsbury, George 96, 105, 240
Sampson, George 107
Sanditon 9, 10, 11, 202, 226, 370, 371
Sanditon 10–11, 13, 18, 32, 48, 51, 202, 226, 282, 319, 341, 369–72; completions 72–76
satire 27, 28, 60, 62, 93, 157, 180–81, 187–88, 202, 203, 229, 249, 254, 282, 295, 338, 339, 341, 350
Scarborough 382
Schorer, Mark 172
Scotland 326
Scott, Sir Walter 50, 54, 96, 97, 99, 101, 170, 175, 190, 193, 195, 224, 228, 229, 237, 268, 275, 319, 351, 356, 365, 367; review of *Emma* 95, 105, 106, 110, 157, 238, 281–82, 366
"Scraps" 245
Secker, Thomas: *Lectures on the Catechism* 49, 349
Sense and Sensibility 14–15, 19, 26, 28, 32, 41–42, 48, 50, 54, 82, 83–84, 94, 105, 118, 225, 249, 283, 288–89, 333–34, 380–81, 395; architecture 6, 8–10 passim, 209–10; *Elinor and Marianne* 47, 49, 50, 53, 54, 118, 165, 256, 257, 280, 281, 394; first editions 14, 38, 135–38 passim, 148, 281; sequels 375–76
sensibility 20, 156–57, 191, 193, 194, 262–63, 318, 333, 334, 369. *See also* novels: sentimental
sequels 374–76
servants 80–82, 90, 302, 317, 370, 372, 377–79; bailiffs 160, 378; butlers 377, 378, 379; coachmen 377, 378; cooks 161, 162, 163, 164, 302, 377; footmen 377, 378; gardeners 186, 302; governesses and nannies 140, 141, 310, 337, 377, 398; housekeepers 211, 377, 378; housemaids 377, 378
Sevenoaks 144, 197

Index

sex: illicit 84, 165–66, 192, 193, 293–95, 361; in marriage 25, 32, 68, 166, 192, 288
Shaftesbury, A. A. C. (3d earl) 33, 62, 190
Shakespeare, William 29, 33, 127, 140, 169, 170, 190, 229, 248, 262, 279, 356; JA comparison 105, 111, 237, 241, 261, 392
Shaw, George Bernard 228
Shelley, Percy Bysshe 193
Sheridan, Frances: *The Memoirs of Miss Sidney Bidulph* 360
Sheridan, Richard Brinsley 1, 228, 248, 356
Sidmouth 287, 380
Simpson, Richard 24, 102, 103, 107, 108, 110–11, 254, 392
Sir Charles Grandison. See Richardson, Samuel
Sir Charles Grandison or the Happy Man 3, 13, 187–89
"Sir William Mountague" 245
sjuzet 172–75
slavery 204, 206
Sloane Square (London) 284
Smith, Charlotte 194, 318–19
Smith, Goldwin 104, 105
Smith, James and Horace Smith: *Rejected Addresses* 354
Smith, Naomi Royde: *Jane Fairfax* 376
Smollett, Tobias 28, 93, 169, 247, 257, 268, 279, 365
Somersetshire 210, 213, 380, 385
Sophocles 99
Sotherton Court 9, 11, 185, 212, 224, 225, 318, 325, 329, 378, 383, 389
Southam, B. C. 3, 21–22, 114, 115, 225, 259, 320
Southampton 18, 47, 119, 140, 149, 161, 200, 201; JA there 5, 35, 199, 223, 279, 280, 281, 300, 377
Southend 10, 384
Southey, Robert 58, 352–53, 357
The Spectator 15, 146, 350, 355

speech 65–66, 268–70; and character 65, 251, 253, 254, 264; free indirect 175–76, 269, 357; indirect 269. *See also* dialogue; monologue
Spenser, Edmund 356
Spurgeon, Caroline 241
Squire, Eileen and J. C. Squire: *Pride and Prejudice* 121–22
Staël, Germaine de 156–57
Stein, Gertrude 288
Stendhal, Marie Henri Beyle 229
Stephen, Leslie 103, 104, 239
Stephens, Catherine 314
Stern, G. B. 242
Sterne, Laurence 93, 169, 173, 247, 262, 267, 279, 357, 365
Steventon 16, 18, 21, 35, 44, 47, 144, 149, 152, 160, 161, 163, 197, 198, 199, 200, 201, 248, 279, 280, 287; amateur theatricals 1–4, 145, 187, 279; Henry rector there 148; James rector there 145, 203, 281
Stoneleigh Abbey 5, 161, 163, 197, 223, 300
Strachey, Ray 154
stream of consciousness 173, 174
structuralism 116, 117, 171
structure 165–66, 334, 371. *See also* plot
style 73, 115, 231, 250, 253–54, 261–70, 347, 355, 369–70. *See also* language
Summers, Montague 240
Surr, Thomas Skinner: *The Magic of Wealth* 371, 372
Surrey 73, 185, 201, 202, 317, 328, 340, 394
Susan. See Northanger Abbey
suspense 167
Sussex 74, 202, 209, 380, 382, 388, 391
Swift, Jonathan 350
Swinnerton, Frank 107
Switzerland 380

Tattersall's 324
Tave, Stuart M. 115

Tennyson, Alfred, Lord 291
Thackeray, Anne 238
Thackeray, William Makepeace 97, 257
theatricals, amateur: in *MP* 1–4, 7, 31, 170, 206, 211, 335–36; at Steventon 1–4, 145, 187, 248, 301, 356
Thompson, Sir Benjamin ("Count Rumford") 7, 213, 225
Thomson, Hugh 105, 138, 217, 219–21 passim, 223–34, 240
Thomson, James 15, 328
Thornton Lacey 86, 211, 224–25, 383
"The Three Sisters" 49, 245, 252–53
Thrush 309
Tilney, F. C. 219
time 173–75, 246. *See also* chronology: within the novels
Tolstoy, Leo 24, 229
Tonbridge 143, 144, 149; School 144, 197, 300
Townley, James: *High Life Below Stairs* 2, 3, 4, 248
trade 87, 143, 197, 299–300, 301, 310
Trafalgar, Battle of 151, 311
Trafalgar House 10, 11, 226
tragedy 68, 169, 192
transportation. *See* carriages; travel
travel 352–53, 388–91
Trilling, Lionel 25, 113, 158, 336
Trimmer, Mrs. Sarah 154
triviality 27–34, 63–64, 66
Trollope, Anthony 96, 97, 103, 228, 232–33, 235, 287
Trusler, John 78, 80, 81
Tucker, George Holbert 21, 116
Twain, Mark (Samuel L. Clemens) 240

Uppercross: Cottage 7, 10, 226, 325; Great House 10, 45, 118, 184, 202, 213, 225–26, 311, 385, 390
Upper Rooms (Bath) 316

values. *See* moral vision
Venice 380
verses by JA 13, 392–93

"The Visit" 2–3, 245
Volume the First 48, 244, 245
Volume the Second 13, 244, 245
Volume the Third 13, 48, 49, 244, 245
Vox, Maximilien 219

Wales 224
Walpole, Horace 351
Ward, John 195
Ward, Mrs. Humphry 103
Warwickshire 5, 197, 281
Waterloo, Battle of 148, 307, 310
Waterloo Crescent (Sanditon) 11
The Watsons 7, 13, 18, 27, 45, 54, 138, 195, 341, 394–98; completions 72–76; dates of composition 47, 50–51, 53, 280, 398
Watt, Ian 112–13, 228
Watts, William 5, 6, 223
Waugh, Evelyn: *Brideshead Revisited* 230
Weippart, Johann 315
West, Jane: *Letters to a Young Lady* 89, 355
West, Rebecca 106, 107, 108
West Indies 152, 170, 204, 280, 309, 311, 335
Weymouth 10
Whalley, George 392
Wharton, Edith 107
Whately, Richard 95–96, 105, 106, 110, 157, 195
White Hart (Bath) 10, 182, 312, 323
White House (Mansfield) 211, 383
Wilberforce, William 204, 205
Wilde, Oscar 228
Willoughby, Vera 221
Wilson, Angus 33
Wilson, Edmund 190
Wilson, Richard 326
Wimpole St. (London) 212
Winchester 36, 37, 150, 200, 281, 282, 320, 393; Cathedral 150, 282, 314, 343
Winthrop 318, 319, 385
Wollstonecraft, Mary 154, 155–57, 158, 193–94, 355

Woodston Parsonage 6, 324, 384, 389
Woolf, Virginia 6, 106, 107, 228, 235, 241, 261, 263, 268
word games 57, 181–82, 356
wordplay 182, 246

Wordsworth, William 190, 224, 263, 356, 364–68 passim, 385

Yonge, Charlotte 97
Yorkshire 310, 384